Canadian Federalism: Myth or Reality

second edition

I shall pass through this world but once. Any good therefore that I can do or any kindness that I can show to any human being, let me do it now. Let me not defer or neglect it for I shall not pass this way again.

EX LIBRIS

Canadian Federalism:
Myth or Reality
second edition

edited by

J. Peter Meekison

Methuen
Toronto   London   Sydney   Wellington

Canadian Federalism:
Myth or Reality
second edition

Library of Congress Catalog Card Number 68-8671

ISBN 0-458-90800-2   (hc)
ISBN 0-458-90810-X   (pb)

75   74   73   72   71   1   2   3   4   5

Printed and bound in Canada

Contents

Part Four
Intergovernmental Relations

Part Five
Regionalism and Canadian Federalism

Part Six
Quebec and Canadian Federalism

Preface

During the past few years, Canadian governments have been participating in the most comprehensive review of the constitution since it was drafted over 100 years ago. While the review has not been concluded, its future is uncertain given the rejection by Quebec of the Canadian Constitutional Charter drafted in Victoria in June. The existence of a continuing constitutional conference has meant that many people have had to give more thought to the problems of federalism than might otherwise have been the case. The public, with the advent of televised conferences, have had a rare opportunity to observe for themselves the bargaining which has become so much a part of our federal system. This collection was designed to present to students of Canadian government some idea of the complexity of the system and an appreciation of the difficulties facing those involved in the review process.

To accomplish this objective, the material has been arranged by content into six sections. It is hoped that the first part will provide students with some understanding of federalism as a form of government. The material in the other five sections has been selected to illustrate the intricacies, development, operation and dilemmas of Canadian federalism. An effort has been made to include as much current material as possible. The material has not been selected to give a particular point of view, but covers a cross-section of opinion on the subject matter. Where appropriate, material relating to constitutional review has been added. The sections on federal-provincial financial relations and co-operative federalism, which appeared in the first edition, have been merged into a section on intergovernmental relations and a new section on regionalism has been inserted.

This collection, like any other book of essays, does not exhaust the literature on the subject. Unfortunately, in revising the volume, a number of worthwhile essays had to be excluded to allow for the new material. Ideally, the essays will suggest areas for additional research or new approaches to the problem. The issues presented by the authors are both exciting and topical and hopefully, they will stimulate the interest of students in the subject. Many of the questions raised have been present since Confederation; their answers remain to be discovered.

I would like to thank the authors and publishers who gave me permission to reprint the material contained within this volume. I would especially like to thank Professor S. J. R. Noel of the University of Western Ontario and Mr. Howard Leeson of the University of Alberta for allowing me to print their material as original essays for this volume. I would also like to thank Gail Armstrong of the University of Alberta for assisting me in preparing the manuscript.

University of Alberta   J. Peter Meekison
Edmonton
June 28, 1971

Part One

What is Federalism?

1 Some Prerequisites of Federal Government*

K. C. Wheare

1

WALTER BAGEHOT, in discussing the prerequisites of Cabinet government in his *English Constitution,* uses words which we may appropriately adopt for federal government. Federal government 'is rare because its prerequisites are many. It requires the co-existence of several national characteristics which are not often found together in the world, and which should be perceived more distinctly than they often are'.

In what circumstances is it appropriate to adopt a system of federal government? This is probably the most difficult question we have to consider in this book.[1] But it must be attempted because it is in many respects the most important. The best way in which to approach it seems to be through a study of the definition we have already given of the term 'federal government' itself. Federal government exists, it was suggested, when the powers of government for a community are divided substantially according to the principle that there is a single independent authority for the whole area in respect of some matters and that there are independent regional authorities for other matters, each set of authorities being co-ordinate with and not subordinate to the others within its own prescribed sphere. From a consideration of this definition it is possible to infer the sort of conditions which should exist before the federal principle is adopted.

To begin with, the communities or states concerned must desire to be under a single independent government for some purposes at any rate. That is essential. Unless they are prepared to go as far as this, the question of federal government does not arise. If they are not prepared to submit themselves to an independent government, but desire rather to retain a control over the general authority, then they have not achieved the first prerequisite

---

[1] I have not been able to discover any thorough discussion of the problem. Some suggestive hints are found in Mill, *Representative Government,* Chapter XVII; in Dicey, *The Law of the Constitution,* 9th Ed., Chapter III and Appendix III, and, scattered here and there, in Freeman's *History of Federal Government in Greece and Italy.* A modern outline of the way in which the subject might profitably be treated is given by William P. Maddox in an article on "The Political Basis of Federation", in *American Political Science Review,* Vol. XXXV no. 6 (December, 1941).

---

* From K. C. Wheare, *Federal Government,* 4th Ed. (New York, Oxford University Press, 1963), pp. 35-52. Reprinted by permission of the author and Oxford University Press.

K. C. WHEARE – Professor of Political Science, Oxford University.

of federal government. A league, an alliance, a confederation may be appropriate for them, but not federal government. It is for this reason that the members of the British Commonwealth of Nations, for example, or the islands of the West Indies which joined the short-lived federation of 1957-62 are not ready for federal government. Indeed it was for this reason also that in Latin America, in the first half of the nineteenth century, the communities which composed, under Bolivar, the state of Great Columbia, soon disintegrated into the three states of Ecuador, Columbia and Venezuela, while the Confederation of the United Provinces of Central America, formed in 1823, had become by 1838 the five separate states of Central America— Guatemala, Salvador, Honduras, Costa Rica and Nicaragua.

But the desire to be under a single independent government is not enough. They must desire at the same time to retain or to establish independent regional governments in some matters at least. Without this desire to be separate in some things, the communities could form a unitary state with some appropriate degree of decentralization. There would be no reason why the federal principle should be invoked. The example of South Africa illustrates this position. The colonies desired to be united under a single independent government. But they did not desire to be under *independent* regional governments for some purposes. They were content with provincial authorities which, although powerful and distinct, were ultimately subordinate bodies.

So far, then, it would seem that federal government is appropriate for a group of states or communities if, at one and the same time, they desire to be united under a single independent general government for some purposes and to be organized under independent regional governments for others. Or, to put it shortly, they must desire to be united, but not to be unitary.

It seems necessary, however, to go further than this. It can be admitted that, if these two desires exist simultaneously, then there is good cause *prima facie* for saying that federal government is appropriate. But more is needed. To say that a thing is desired by a group of states is not to say that it is the right thing for them. They must not only desire it; they must also be able to operate it. They must have the capacities to work the system they desire. Federal government is not appropriate unless the communities concerned have the capacity as well as the desire to form an independent general government and to form independent regional governments. Some inquiry into the capacities of communities as well as into their desires or aspirations will be necessary before it can be decided whether federal government is the system which they ought to adopt.

2

The propositions so far stated are abstract and they do not appear to take us very far. If we pass now to more concrete matters, the answers become less concise, but they may be more helpful. The first inquiry which naturally comes to mind is this: What are the factors or circumstances which lead communities to desire union and at the same time to desire separation within the union? And, secondly, what produces in them the capacity to form an independent general government and, at the same time, independent regional governments? If we know the answers to these questions, we can begin to see what ingredients should be present before it can be asserted that federal government should be adopted for a given territory.

Communities have been led to desire union from a variety of reasons. But in the modern federation some factors seem always to have been present. A sense of military insecurity and of the consequent need for common defence,[2] a desire to be independent of foreign powers, and a realization that only through union could independence be secured; a hope of economic advantage from union; some political association of the communities concerned prior to their federal union either in a loose confederation, as with the American states and the Swiss cantons, or as parts of the same Empire, as with the Canadian and Australian colonies; geographical neighbourhood; and similarity of political institutions—these half-dozen factors all operated in the United States, Switzerland, Canada and Australia, to produce a desire for union among the communities concerned. They operated in varying degree in each case, but they were all present. Some of them were present also in other examples of voluntary unions where the federal principle was not adopted. Thus, the need for common defence, the desire to be independent, geographical contiguity, and the hope of economic advantage all helped to produce a desire for union which was a force in leading England and Scotland to form the United Kingdom of Great Britain in 1707,[3] the Italian states to form the Kingdom of Italy in the years from 1856 to 1864,[4] the German states to form, first the North German Confederation of 1867, and then the German Empire of 1871,[5] and the South African Colonies—Transvaal, Orange River, the Cape and Natal—to form the Union of South Africa in 1909[6]. And in all these cases, except the Italian states, there was some form of previous political association[7] and some substantial similarity of political institutions.

When we see that certain factors such as these have always been present in modern cases where the desire for union has been produced, we may feel tempted to conclude that this desire will not be produced unless all or most of these factors are present. That would be going further than is warranted. But it is justifiable to say, I think, that it is unlikely that states will desire

---

[2] It is significant that this factor was absent in the case of the West Indian territories in 1957 when they formed a federation. See on the whole question H. W. Springer, *Reflections on the Failure of the first West Indian Federation* (1962).

[3] See G. M. Trevelyan, *Ramillis and the Union with Scotland;* Dicey and Rait, *Thoughts on the Union of England and Scotland.*

[4] See Bolton King, *A History of Italian Unity* (2 vols.), and Bolton King and Thomas Okey, *Italy Today.*

[5] See C. Grant Robertson, *Bismarck,* and A. W. Ward, *Germany 1815-1890.*

[6] See Walker, *Lord de Villiers and his Times;* Walton, *The Inner History of the National Convention of South Africa; Cambridge History of the British Empire,* Vol. VIII, and L. M. Thompson, *The Unification of South Africa.*

[7] Even in the Italian States there had been associations of some or all the states in the past, although not immediately prior to union.

union unless these factors—or most of them—are present. To that extent they may be clased as prerequisites of federal government.

I have mentioned certain factors which seem always or usually to have been needed before the desire for union could be produced. It is interesting to notice that some factors are unexpectedly absent. Thus community of language, of race,[8] of religion or of nationality[9] have not been listed as likely essential prerequisites of the desire for union. This is surprising, but the facts support it. Undoubtedly common language and common race assisted to produce the desire for union in the United States, in Australia, in Germany and in Italy. Common nationality operated strongly in Germany and in Italy. In Australia the desire for union remained long dormant until in the 1890's a campaign was undertaken by the advocates of union to awaken in the people of the colonies a feeling that they were all Australians as well as Victorians or Queenslanders or the like. The campaign had a striking success and the sense of common nationality thus produced made the desire for union effective. But in the United States the union was formed before any such sense of common nationality had come into being. In the words of Professor Morison, 'most citizens of the United States in 1790, if asked their country or nation, would not have answered "American" but Carolinian, Virginian, Pennsylvanian, New Yorker or New Englander'. 'The United States of 1788 were not a nation by any modern standard.'[10]

More striking still are the examples of Canada and Switzerland where the desire to unite arose in spite of differences of language and race—French and English in Canada; German, French, Italian and Romansch in Switzerland—of religion as between Catholic and Protestant, and of nationality. And the Union of South Africa occurred in spite of similar differences between Dutch

---

[8] The notions of race and of racial differences have become so discredited in recent years as a result of a reaction against the theories of the German Nazis that it may seem necessary for me to justify my use of the term. But what is sufficient for my purpose is not whether differences of race exist in fact but the undoubted fact that the groups of people think that they differ from others in race. It is this belief which makes differences of race and community of race factors which must be included in any discussion on the prerequisites of federal government. For my part I may add that it seems to me that there are such things as differences of race. I would refer the reader to an interesting discussion of the subject by Dr. G. M. Morant in an article entitled "Racial Theories and International Relations", in *The Journal of the Royal Anthropological Institute,* Vol. LXIX, Part II, (1939).

[9] 'Nationality' is defined in many ways. I have in mind here that sense which people have that they are bound together and marked off from others by common sympathies, common sympathies which arise usually from the possession of a common language, common race or common religion. This sense of being a distinct people may lead a community to demand a distinct and independent state, the national state, but in my view this is not an essential element in the notion of nationality. For a discussion of the question see C. A. Macartney, *National States and National Minorities,* pp. 1-18, and the report of a study group of the Royal Institute of International Affairs entitled *Nationalism.*

[10] S. E. Morison, *History of the United States* Vol. 1, p. 10.

and English.[11] It is clear that, strong as these forces of language, race, religion and nationality are in producing a desire for union—as the whole history of national movements shows—it has proved possible none the less to produce a desire for union among peoples who differ in all these important particulars. Community in these matters cannot therefore be described as an essential prerequisite of federal government.

Much the same may be said of another factor which has produced a desire for union among communities, namely similarity of social institutions. Such similarity existed in the Australian colonies for example, but it was modified in the American states notably by the fact that some states favoured the institution of slavery and others did not. In Canada and Switzerland there were differences of custom and of private law between the uniting regions. In the case of the union between England and Scotland, to take a non-federal example, there were differences in the law touching marriage and inheritance; there were distinct systems of judicial procedure. Yet these differences of social institutions did not prevent the desire for union from growing. But the example of the United States shows the limits that must be imposed upon this statement. For, although the difference of opinion about slavery did not prevent the growth of a desire for union and the establishment of the union, yet seventy years later that divergence had become so acute that it created in the Southern States a desire to break the union, a desire that issued in civil war. There is a limit to the degree of divergence that is compatible with the existence of a desire to unite.

It is well to add, perhaps, that the mere presence of all these factors in a given territory will not necessarily produce of itself a desire to unite, a desire of sufficient strength to prevail over contrary forces. A great deal will depend, for example, on leadership or statesmanship at the right time. It needed not only resistance to a common enemy and geographical contiguity and community of language and race and religion, and similarity of political institutions, for example, to produce a desire in the American colonies to unite. These factors had been present for a long time and had failed to produce much more than a desire to be loosely associated in a confederation. What was needed also was leadership and that came from Washington, from Hamilton, Jay and Madison, from Benjamin Franklin and James Wilson. In the same way the desire for union in Canada was made effective by the leadership of such men as John A. Macdonald, Alexander Galt and George Etienne Cartier; in South Africa of Smuts, de Villiers, Merriman and Botha; in Australia of Parkes, Barton and Deakin; in Germany of Bismarck; in Italy of Victor Emmanuel, Garibaldi, Cavour and Ricasoli; in Great Britain of Godolphin on the English side and of Queensberry, Argyle and Seafield on the Scottish. This factor of leadership, of skill in negotiation and propaganda, can make all the difference between stagnation and an active desire for union.

---

[11] H. C. Calpin felt justified, even after thirty years of the union, in entitling this book *There are no South Africans*. After fifty years of the union, there is no reason for the title to be altered.

3

If these are the sort of factors which produce in communities the desire to be united for some purposes, what are the factors which, operating at the same time, produce the desire to be separate for other purposes? It is not so easy in this case to generalize. One factor which was present in all the modern federations was that the regions which desired to unite had all had a previous existence as distinct colonies or states, although it is to be noted that none of them had had a long history as a truly sovereign, independent state. But the American states, the Swiss cantons, the Canadian provinces and the Australian states, although associated together prior to union in some way, enjoyed each a distinct history and distinct government. Thus, although they came to desire union in some things, they still desired to remain separate in others.

Partly as a result of their previous history as independent states, these communities had developed a divergence of economic interests. Thus, although, as I have mentioned, the hope of economic advantage led them to desire union, divergence of economic interest made them anxious not to surrender more power over economic affairs than was absolutely necessary. For, though union might mean economic advantage for some, it meant economic loss, in the short run at least, for others. They desired therefore to remain independent for some economic purposes at any rate.

Geographical factors also assisted the desire to be separate. In the United States, Canada and Australia it was great distance which was most important. Distance isolated the communities and developed a regional consciousness which made them desire to keep to themselves. In Switzerland it was the barrier of mountains which divided up the country into isolated communities. In the West Indies there was the extreme example of each unit being separated by sea.

These seem to be the only factors for separation within union which are common to all modern federations. It is possible to detect their presence also—though in a modified form—in the process by which certain unitary states like Austria, Russia, Mexico, and some South American Republics—notably Brazil and Venezuela, for example—have adopted constitutions framed to some extent on federal lines. Here at first sight one would not expect to find these factors in operation. Since the countries concerned had been previously unitary states, the desire for separation could not come for example from a previous independent existence of their component parts. Yet it is to be noticed that in many cases where the federal principle was applied, the units chosen as regions of the federation had been the divisions of provincial or local administration under the previous system, which, though unitary, was often highly decentralized in practice. In Austria the provinces had had a previous history as divisions of the Empire and had had provincial diets of their own; in Russia, Mexico and South America the old lines of provincial administration were often followed. Moreover economic divergences had been there also, in spite of a unitary government. The federalism of Argentina,

Brazil and Austria owed something to this. And the great size of the country, producing a revolt against centralized administration, was important also in creating a desire for local independence in all these countries with the exception of Austria. Is it permissible to assert, then, that a previous existence as a distinct governmental unit, economic divergence and a sense of isolation through geographical factors, are essential prerequisites of that desire for separation within union which goes to produce federal government?

It does not seem possible to accept this conclusion. There is one factor, at least, which itself alone quite certainly could produce the desire for separation among communities otherwise prepared to unite. This factor is divergence of nationality. It is surely quite conceivable that communities which had had no previous existence as distinct governmental units, no divergence of economic interest and no isolation through geographical factors, but which none the less differed in nationality from each other, would desire separation within union. This factor of difference of nationality did co-operate, of course, with other factors for separation in three of the four cases mentioned—in a moderate degree in the United States, and much more strongly in Switzerland and in Canada. In the last two cases it was assisted by differences of language, race and religion. These in their turn are very strong forces for separation; any one of them might alone produce a desire for separation within union. Indeed it is usually a matter of surprise that union is possible at all among communities which differ in language, race, religion or nationality. In Switzerland and Canada the desire for union grew in spite of these differences, but the desire for separation within the union, the desire, that is, for *federal* union, was directly produced by these differences. And it seems most likely that communities which were ready to unite but which differed in some one or all of these four particulars, might desire the federal form of union.

Another factor which might produce the desire for separation is dissimilarity of social (including political) institutions. This undoubtedly operated in Canada when Quebec desired to be separate in order that it might safeguard its own peculiar system of civil law. It had its effect in the United States where slave-states and free-states were anxious to keep within their own control decisions about the future of the institution of slavery within their own borders.

These are the kind of factors which, given the existence of a desire for union, are likely to produce a desire for federal union. It is not possible to pick on any one of them or any one combination of them and say that unless this or these are present, the desire for federal union will not arise. That desire may be produced by any one of them.

And here again, as with the desire for union itself, a great deal will depend on leadership. The factors which could produce a desire for federal union may be there but they may not come to the surface; or, if they do, they may be overcome by more effective leadership in favour of the unitary form of union. Thus in South Africa, where there existed all the factors which had produced the desire for federal union in Canada—separate existence as distinct colonies, divergence of economic interest, geographical isolation, difference of language, race, religion and nationality,[12] difference of social institutions, and where in addition to all this there had recently been a bitter civil war between the two peoples, none the less the desire for federal union was overcome by the desire for a unitary — albeit highly decentralized — state. And this was done largely by the force of leadership exercised by certain men —Smuts, Merriman and de Villiers in particular.[13] They had decided that there must be a union but that federal union was unsuitable. It was too expensive, too legalistic, too weak at the centre and too strong at the circumference. They urged their case with great effectiveness. The whole issue of federal versus unitary union was debated in the press[14] and on the platforms of the colonies and the desire for federal union, which Natal in particular felt strongly, was overcome.

A similar example is that of the union of England and Scotland where many of the same forces which produced a desire for federal union in Canada had been present—a distinct government, a different religious system, a divergence of economic interests, a different system of civil law and a distinct literature, as well as a common literature. Here also leadership had its effect. The English delegates firmly overruled any plan for the continued existence of a Scottish parliament in which they saw a centre of Stuart and French intrigue against England. Nor did the Scottish delegates press the suggestion very hard.[15]

For there was another factor operative at that time. No example of federal government, as we understand it, was in existence when the plan for the union of England and Scotland was being discussed. There was no successful working model to which those who desired to be united but not unitary could point. There were and had been confederations. There was the United Netherlands. But the main lesson such associations taught was the weakness which beset general governments when they had to suffer the existence of regional governments.[16] The model of the United Netherlands could not commend itself to the English delegates and the Scottish delegates could not produce anything better. For this reason—and for other reasons of equal or greater importance —the desire to remain separate within union was overcome and Scotland accepted union with decentralization and autonomy, more particularly in matters of church government, private law and the judicial system.

The example of the union of England and Scotland thus illustrates one factor of importance which assists to produce the desire for federal union.

---

[12] But it is right to stress that the communities which differed in these respects were not territorially concentrated and organized in South Africa in a single province or provinces as were the French Canadians in Quebec.

[13] See L. M. Thompson, *op. cit.*

[14] An interesting example of the way in which federalism and unitarianism were discussed is Olive Schreiner's *Memorandum on the Mutual Relations of the South African Colonies.*

[15] See Trevelyan, *op. cit.*, Dicey and Rait, *op. cit.*

[16] See K. C. Wheare, *Federal Government,* 4th Ed., Chapter II.

England and Scotland had no model of federal government before them; they had nothing to imitate. Now, since the establishment of the United States, communities have had something to imitate. They can see a model of what they would like to do. This force of imitation can have great influence in producing the desire to form a federal union. There is no doubt that it influenced Switzerland, Canada and Australia.[17] They did not imitate the form of American government blindly, but they were influenced by it and led by its example to desire the federal form of union. The example of other federations clearly influenced also the constitution makers in India, Rhodesia and Nyasaland, Malaya, the West Indies and Nigeria in the years after the Second World War. In Central and South America the force of imitation is even more clearly seen.[18] For there, where many of the factors which might be expected to produce a desire for federal union were absent—difference of language, race, religion or nationality, and separate existence as independent states—a desire to introduce federalism did arise. And this was largely due to the imitation of the constitution of the United States. It was almost as if they said: 'We have attained our independence from European control just as did the American colonies. They adopted the federal form of government. So must we.'[19] And this imitation explains in some measure why federal government has not taken root in the Central and South American republics. The factors which might produce a desire for it were not rooted in the communities themselves. The force of imitation works well when it provides from outside a plan which fits the circumstances inside the country.

4

So far we have dealt only with the factors which produce the *desire* for union combined with the *desire* for independence within union which we stated to be one of the prerequisites of federal union. We have next to ask: Granted the existence of these desires, what conditions are necessary before it is possible to say that the communities which desire the federal form of union have also the *capacity* to work it? For unless they have this capacity, federal government is not appropriate for them.

It goes almost without saying that the desires themselves provide some guarantee of the capacity to form and work the system of government desired. If states really desire to form an independent general government for some purposes, then they have gone a long way towards being able to work such a government. And the same is true of the desire to remain as independent governments inside the union. A desire for federal union among communities

---

17 See W. Menzies Whitelaw on "American Influence on British Federal Systems", in *The Constitution Re-considered* (ed. Conyers Read).
18 The subject is treated by several writers in Conyers Read, *op. cit.*, Part III.
19 This appears to have been true of Mexico in 1824 particularly, although the Spanish Constitution of 1812 had a strong influence there also. See J. Lloyd Mecham in Conyers Read, *op. cit.* pp. 359-64.

is a first and obvious factor which produces in them the capacity to make and work a federal union.

And again the forces which produce the desire for federal union are in some cases—but by no means in all—forces which also produce a capacity to work federal union. Thus hostility to or fear of a common enemy and the need for common defence produces the desire to unite. It also provides cohesive forces which compel the communities concerned to stand together and accustom them to work together. They develop common external antagonisms which override internal antagonisms. John Stuart Mill says: 'The federation binds them always to fight on the same side; and if they have such feelings towards one another, or such diversity of feeling towards their neighbours, that they would generally prefer to fight on opposite sides, the federal tie is neither likely to be of long duration, nor to be well-observed while it subsists.'[20] Switzerland is the classic example of the way in which the need for common defence produced in communities which differed in language, race and nationality not only the desire but also the capacity to form a federal union.

It will be obvious also that community of race, language, religion and nationality would produce a capacity for union. With so much in common, states could inevitably work easily together. Although, as I have shown, such community has not always been present where federal union has been chosen, it is important to stress the value any such community of interest can give. The United States with its factors for separation—difference of nationality, difference on the cardinal issue of slavery, geographical isolation, previous independence of its component units, and the like—owed much of its capacity to form a union to the capacity for working together which community of race, religion and language helped to produce. And it is to be noted that even where differences in these points existed, as in Canada and Switzerland, there was community in some of the regions concerned. It is important to remember that Switzerland, for the first five hundred years of its existence as a confederation, was composed entirely of German cantons. It was only with the French invasion of 1798 followed by Napoleon's Act of Mediation in 1803 that French and Italian-speaking cantons were added. The Act of Mediation added six new cantons to the already existing thirteen, creating them chiefly out of territories which had been allied to or were considered subject to the German-speaking cantons. In 1815 three more French-speaking cantons were added. For centuries, therefore, the Swiss cantons were enabled to work together by the common race and language which distinguished them. It remains remarkable, nevertheless, that the Swiss cantons were able to form their closest union, the federal union of 1848, *after* the inclusion of the non-German cantons, when differences of language, race or nationality had come to play their part. In the initiation and working of this federal union it is clear, however, that community of language, race, religion and nationality helped the German-Swiss cantons to work together, and the French-Swiss similarly. In the same way this community brought the English-speaking provinces of Canada together.

---

[20] *Representative Government* (Everyman ed.), pp. 366-67.

But of all the factors which produce the desire for union, the one which at the same time produces best the capacity for union is similarity of social, and particularly political institutions. It has been remarked already that the desire for union has practically never been aroused unless similarity of political institutions was present either actually or potentially among those who envisaged the union. This factor is one of the strongest of the forces which help states to work together. So strongly is this felt that statesmen in framing federal constitutions have even insisted that all the units should adopt the same form of government. The Constitution of the United States and that of Switzerland requires that the state and cantonal governments respectively should be republican. In Canada and Australia the forms of constitutional monarchy are explicitly established in all the units. When the quasi-federal Weimar Constitution of Germany was drawn up in 1918 it was required that all the member states should be republican. It replaced a constitution in which all but three of the members were monarchies—a constitution which was confederate, not federal.

The example of Switzerland is most instructive. Before the federal form of union was established in 1848 there had been great divergence of political institutions in the cantons. There had been oligarchies, democracies, aristocracies and, in one case, Neuchâtel, a monarchy. Cantons with similar institutions had banded themselves together inside the Confederation from time to time and had damaged what unity it had. A condition of the closer union which federation required was similarity of political institutions and after a hard struggle the democratic and republican cantons prevailed and all were brought into line. There seems little doubt that just as the desire to form a federal union is unlikely to arise among states which differed in régime, the capacity to form and work such a union can hardly exist without substantial similarity.

It would not do to state absolutely that a union between states of different régimes is impossible to work. Much depends on the régime. American states and Canadian provinces differ in political institutions. The former have the non-parliamentary executive, the latter the parliamentary executive. Yet it is conceivable that the two systems could find a place in the same union. For they are fundamentally at one—they are founded on the democratic principles of free election, free criticism and representative institutions. What would be harder to combine are authoritarian or oligarchic institutions and democratic institutions. For this reason it would seem particuarly difficult to operate a union between the states and provinces of India, as envisaged in the Government of India Act, 1935. At the Round Table Conference of 1930 the Indian princes offered to join a federation with the provinces of British India, although the princes governed their states autocratically and the provinces were on the way to representative and responsible government. It is clear that this dissimilarity would have added one more difficulty to the working of Indian government in a system of federal union. It is significant that Indian leaders, before inaugurating the union established by the Constitution of 1950, took steps to promote homogeneity in the political institutions of the component states in the union. What is more, the form of government in the States—cabinet government— is prescribed in some detail in the Constitution itself.

But I think one may go further on this matter of similarity of political institutions. Not only is it desirable that there should be similarity of political institutions in the majority at any rate, of the federating units, but it is essential, I believe that these institutions should not be autocratic or dictatorial. For autocracy or dictatorship, either in the general governments or in the regional governments, seem certain, sooner or later, to destroy that equality of status and that independence which these governments must enjoy, each in its own sphere, if federal government is to exist at all. Thus, suppose all the regional governments or a majority of them were dictatorships, what machinery could exist to choose a general government which would be independent of the regional governments? No free election by the people of the autocratic regions is to be expected. The general government would be composed of nominees of the autocrats in the regions. In the Indian Constitution of 1935, for example, it was assumed that the representatives of the Indian states in the general legislature would be nominees of their rulers and not elected representatives of the people of the states. Or suppose that the general government is a dictatorship, can it be expected that it will refrain from extending its control into the regions and so ensuring that the regional governments are its agents or representatives. This has been the experience in South American countries with federal constitutions. Dictatorial presidents have brought the regional governments under their control by thrusting their own supporters into the regional governments. So also at the outset of the Nazi régime in Germany, what elements of independent jurisdiction were left to the regions under the quasi-federal Weimar Constitution were immediately brought under the control of the central government.[21]

It may be possible in theory to conceive a federal government in which general and regional governments are dictatorships and yet each remains strictly within its own sphere, but it is difficult to imagine such a federal government coming into existence in the realm of practical politics or continuing to exist for any length of time. Dictatorship, with its one-party government and its denial of free election, is incompatible with the working of the federal principle. Federalism demands forms of government which have the characteristics usually associated with democracy or free government. There is a wide variety in the forms which such government may take, but the main essentials are free election and a party system, with its guarantee of a responsible opposition.[22]

What is said of similarity in political institutions can be said of the wider issue—similarity of social institutions generally. Here, as I have said, the desire to unite can be created in spite of dissimilarity of social institutions, as the examples of the United States, Canada and Great Britain alone show. But such differences do make government more difficult, and there is a limit to the degree of dissimilarity which can be permitted. The capacity to work together

---

[21] See R. H. Wells, "The Liquidation of the German Lander", *American Political Science Review*, Vol. XXX (April, 1936).

[22] This point is well made by William P. Maddox, *loc. cit.*, *American Political Science Review*, Vol. XXXV at p. 1125, and in Freeman, *History of Federal Government in Greece and Italy*, pp. 73-75.

cannot survive an extreme divergence. That is the lesson of the slavery issue in the United States. For many years compromise had saved the union of the American people, but there came a point where the divergence became so acute that the capacity to work together could not live with it. That is one meaning of Abraham Lincoln's words of 1858: 'A house divided against itself cannot stand. I believe this government cannot endure permanently half slave and half free. . . . It will become all one thing or all the other.' And so it was that after the Civil War there were inserted in the Constitution of the United States amendments designed to remove all traces in law of this particular divergence of social institution as between one state and another in the American union.[23]

So also in Canada, though some divergence is allowed, some uniformity is also required. Quebec has her own civil law; but there is one criminal law only for Canada. So Scotland has her distinct judicial system and private law, but the House of Lords is her final court of appeal and there is a common statute law on many matters for England and Scotland. This is not to say that the differences of social institutions in these countries are unimportant. They are important and it is remarkable that they are contained within a single government. But it must be emphasized that the capacity of states to form and work a federal union depends upon some agreement to differ but not to differ too much.

5

If these are some of the factors which give communities or states a capacity to unite, what are the factors which give them the capacity to remain distinct and separate inside a union? First of all it appears that, here again, some of the factors which cause states to desire to remain independent in some matters inside a union, also create in them the capacity to do so. Most important of these seems to be their previous existence as distinct governments. This means that the states joining to form a new general government, have at their disposal in their own regions a well-established system of government which will enable them to carry out their functions and maintain their integrity in the new system. More than that, it relieves the strain imposed upon the new system, by guaranteeing the stability of regional administration and leaving energies free for the one formidable task of establishing the new general government. This is a great gain. It means that the communities will be required to establish one new government and not a collection of half a dozen or more governments.

The value of this factor can be illustrated from the history of Italian unity. There was a party which advocated federal union for the Italian states. But the makers of Italian unity rejected it. When first it was put forward they rejected it because they did not believe that the despotic and usually alien rulers of most of the states—and particularly Naples and Sicily—would be prepared to surrender their independence in certain matters to an Italian government. They did not believe, that is, that these states desired union—the first essential of federal union. They decided, therefore, that the defeat of these despotisms was

---

[23] Amendments XIII, XIV and XV.

the first essential to union. But when this defeat was accomplished, nothing was left. There were no governments with authority rooted in the society they governed. It would have been a gigantic task to establish new and stable governments in these states, while at the same time establishing the new government for united Italy. And wisely, therefore, if only for this reason, the makers of Italian unity rejected the federal form.

The same can be said to a great extent of federal experiments in Central and South America and in particular of Mexico, Brazil, Argentina and Venezuela. The regions for which independent governments were estabilshed in these Latin American constitutions had had in most cases no history as distinct and established governments. They had been merely administrative divisions of an Empire. They had no deep-rooted political institutions of their own which could stand up to the pressure of central administration. And for this reason, among others, federal government did not become a reality in these republics.[24]

Thus this factor of a past history as an individual and established government which does so much to produce the desire for the federal form of union as opposed to the unitary form, is one which also produces the capacity in states to work the federal form. It gives the regions strength to stand upon their own feet; it also allows the energies of statesmen to be concentrated upon one task, the making of the general government. It helps to produce both the capacity to be separate and independent in some things and to be under a general government for others.

It will be apparent that this factor needs to be nicely balanced in the sum of forces at work in the union. People must have an established government to which they can be attached, but that attachment must not be too strong. Therein lies always a possible source of weakness in a federal government—that state loyalty may prevail over general loyalty. More particularly is this likely to be true where state boundaries coincide with racial, linguistic or national boundaries. It is obviously an advantage that the units in a federation should be homogeneous; nothing strengthens a regional government so much. But the danger is that the region may inspire a loyalty greater than that of the union and that in time of conflict the union will fall apart. It is the continual problem of statesmanship in a federation to avoid this clash of rival loyalties. That the two loyalties must be there is the prerequisite of federal government, but that the one should not overpower the other is also a prerequisite. The Italian example already quoted illustrates both dangers. So long as the despots ruled their states, there could be no certain loyalty to a general Italian government. Once they were swept away, there could be no stable system of institutions round which regional loyalty could establish itself.

---

[24] The fact that a few of the regions, such as Sao Paulo and Mines Geraes in Brazil and Buenos Aires in Argentina, did enjoy the strength that came from an independent existence in the past, only made the subordination of the weaker regions like Pará and Ceará more noticeable and indeed more expedient in the eyes of the general government.

It follows from what has been said, also, that although it is possible for a state which differs in race, religion, language, nationality and the like to form a union and although such differences provide a good basis for a federal union, it is also desirable that some feeling of common attachment to the new general government should be developed. At the making of the United States, of Switzerland and of Canada there were differences of nationality, but as time went on a common nationality came to impose itself upon the differences. Citizens of these federal states came to feel a sense of double nationality. They are Swiss and German-Swiss; they are American and Virginian; they are Canadian and French-Canadian. Nationality in a federal state means something more complicated than it does in a unitary state. And one of the factors which produce in states the capacity to work a federal union is the growth of this sense of a new common nationality over and above but not instead of their sense of separate nationality.[25]

6

The capacity of states to work a federal union is also greatly influenced by their size. It is undesirable that one or two units should be so powerful that they can overrule the others and bend the will of the federal government to themselves. The example of Prussia in the German Empire shows how this factor can transform even a confederation into a unitary state. On the other hand, some divergence in size between the units is almost certain to be present before federal union is desired. It is this divergence which leads the poorer or less populous states to desire federal rather than unitary government for in it they see a safeguard for their independence. It is an important factor in making and maintenance of federal systems today. The agricultural states of Western America with their smaller populations find in the federal form of union their safeguard against the wealth and population of the East and especially New York; the Canadian maritime provinces and the prairie provinces seek protection from Ontario and Quebec; the Australian states of Western Australia, Tasmania and South Australia with their small, predominantly agricultural, population seek protection from the more populous industrialized states of New South Wales and Victoria. A problem in the working of federal government is found to be therefore the harmonizing of the conflicting interests of these differing units. But the essential is, as John Stuart Mill says, 'that there should not be any one State so much more powerful than the rest as to be capable of vying in strength many many of them combined. If there be such a one, and only one, it will insist on being master of the joint deliberations: if there be two, they will be irresistible when they agree; and whenever they differ everything will be decided by a struggle for ascendancy between the rivals.'[26] The size of

---

[25] James Wilson saw this clearly at the framing of the Constitution of the United States. He said: 'A Citizen of America may be considered in two points of view-as a citizen of the general government, and as a citizen of the particular state, in which he may reside. . . . I am both a citizen of Pennsylvania and of the United States.' Farrand, *Records of the Federal Convention* Vol. 1, p. 413.

[26] *Representative Government* (Everyman ed.) pp. 367-68.

the units concerned—in wealth, area and population—is therefore of prime importance. There must be some sort of reasonable balance which will insure that all the units can maintain their independence within the sphere allotted to them and that no one can dominate the others. It must be the task of those who frame and work a federal government to see that no unit shall be too large, and, equally important, none too small.

And size reflects itself in one further aspect. If a federal government is to work there must be available a supply of men with capacity to govern, a supply sufficient not for one government only but for many. Federal government makes a big demand on a community's human resources. As a rule a small population cannot be expected to supply so many trained and capable men as a large population. In this sense a state's size will affect its capacity to form part of a federal union.

7

A discussion of the relative resources of the units in a federation leads to the consideration of a final factor which ensures the capacity of states to form a federal union. They must possess sufficient economic resources to support both an independent general government and independent regional governments. It is not enough that the general government should be able to finance itself; it is essential also that the regional governments should be able to do likewise. At the very outset, therefore, in considering whether federal government is appropriate, the question of adequate economic resources arises. If a general government is to be established and supported—and that is the first assumption of any union, federal or non-federal—will there be sufficient resources also to support independent regional governments? If there are not, then no matter how much states desire a federal union and no matter whether a federal constitution is drawn up, in practice federal government will not be possible. Soon the regional governments will be unable to perform their functions or they will be able to perform them only at the price of financial dependence upon the general government, that is, at the price of financial unification.

It was on economic grounds, among others, that federal union was rejected by the leaders in South Africa. They thought that the financial resources of the country would be unduly taxed if they were required to support not only a general government but also independent regional governments. For federalism is expensive and it is always a question whether the independence it gives is worth the price that must be paid for it. It has been alleged in the case of Australia, too, that federal government has not been appropriate there because it imposes an undue financial burden on the people—the provision of a full paraphernalia of government in six states as well as for the Commonwealth as a whole.[27] It seems likely also that one of the main reasons why federalism has not survived in the Latin American republics has been the extreme poverty of so many of the regions which have for long remained undeveloped economi-

---

[27] This question is considered in Chapter VI. K. C. Wheare, *Federal Government*, 4th Ed.

lcally.[28] But the general principle here is clear. There must be sufficient economic resources available both to regions and to general governments to make it possible for them to be financially independent.

It is not, however, a question merely of what resources are available throughout the communities as a whole. A great deal will depend on how these resources are divided between the general and regional governments when the federal union is established. It may well be proper that a region which desires independence in a federal union but which lacks resources to make that independence real, after it has surrendered certain of its revenues for the maintenance of the general government, should be guaranteed certain incomes from the resources of its wealthier neighbours. There arise, therefore, questions of allocating resources as between regions and general government and as between one region and another. These allocations are most important in establishing a federal system. They raise questions not only of what total resources are available, but also what is the right way— granted or assuming that they are sufficient for the needs of all governments—to allocate them, so that each government will get what it needs.

We verge here on the problem not of when federal government is appropriate but of how federal government shall be organized. Once it is seen what conditions are necessary if states are to have not merely the desire but also and more particularly the capacity to form a federal union, it becomes necessary next to ask how it can be ensured that, if these desires and capacities are there, they may be entitled to express themselves effectively in a system of government. And it is to this question, therefore, that we must turn.

2   A Note on the Nature of Federalism*

W. S. Livingston

Federalism as a Juridical Concept

Almost every treatment of federal government and its problems has begun with the assumption that the problem here concerned is one of legal formalism and formal jurisprudence. Nearly all theorists have been at pains to point out that

---

[28] The point is made by R. A. Humphreys in his pamphlet *Latin American History* (Historical Association no. 127).

* From *Political Science Quarterly*, Vol. LXVII no. 1, March 1952 (Reprinted by permission of the author and The Academy of Political Science), pp. 81-95.

W. S. LIVINGSTON – Professor of Government, University of Texas.

a federal constitution is a device for associating a number of distinct political and constitutional entities in such a manner that a new body is produced which is above and different from those that have come together. But the component states still retain their identity, sacrificing to the collectivity only such powers and functions as are necessary for the implementation of the purpose for which the association is formed. Or, as it is described in some instances, the powers of the central government are devolved upon the subordinate bodies in such a way that both central and regional units are thenceforth endowed with certain powers and functions of which neither can be deprived by the other. This is to say that the central government's functions cannot be assumed by the local governments, or the local governments' by the central. Each is placed in relation to the other in a position of autonomy; neither is subordinate and each may exercise within its sphere the full extent of its powers. There is also substantial agreement among writers on federalism that the extent of these powers is strictly limited by the simultaneous existence of comparable, though never identical, powers in the other unit. The problem thus becomes that of the proper delineation of these spheres. Where is the boundary between the central and the component governments to be drawn? How much power does the central government have and how much power do the local units have? This attempt to quantify power seems to be characteristic of the juridical approach to the problems of federal government.

In order that this line of demarcation between the two governments may be precise and understood by all it is ordinarily considered necessary that the constitution of a federal state be written. Most writers have held it impossible for a distribution of this nature to be produced by the slow evolution of institutions such as is found in Great Britain. The experience of federal governments in the modern world is cited to show that in fact they all do have written constitutions. Only a written constitution, it is held, could precisely assign powers and functions in the necessary manner.

Once the distribution of powers is made, the accounts continue, it must be protected; and this requires that some kind of obstacle be put in the way of constitutional change. If the component units have entered the federation on the understanding that they are to possess certain rights and functions, then these must not be taken from them except in circumstances where some agreed-upon criterion demands such reassignment. Conversely the powers of the general government must not be alienated unless this is clearly necessary. In order to protect the allotment of powers to local and central units, the constitution must be *rigid*. By this is meant simply that to amend the constitution a procedure different from (that is, more difficult than) that of ordinary legislation is to be used. Indeed, since Lord Bryce published his *Studies in History and Jurisprudence* the definition of a rigid constitution has turned on this very point. A rigid constitution, as contrasted with a flexible one, has come to mean one that can be amended only by a procedure more difficult than that by which ordinary laws are made.

This procedure for constitutional amendment in a federal state, it is ordinarily said, must be designed to protect the federal allocation of governmental powers and functions. Since one of the purposes of employing a federal rather than a unitary constitution is to assure the different units of their proper and agreed-upon share in governmental activity, the power to amend the constitution cannot be lodged in either the general government exclusively or in the local governments exclusively, for this would permit the one to take from the other without its consent those functions that it desires to retain. Hence the federal system necessitates an amending procedure in which the consent of both the general and the local governments must be secured before any change can be made. But, the accounts continue, this does not mean that the consent of all the local governments is necessary, for this would effectively cripple the federation and prevent all important change; it would also, according to some, transform the federation into a confederation. But the procedure must consist of some form of consent on the local level as well as some form of consent on the national level. Usually the need for local concurrence takes the form of a requirement that a majority or more of the component units must consent to the amendment, though the means by which this consent is secured and measured vary greatly.

It requires little demonstration to show that the constant emphasis throughout this chain of thought is on the legal aspect of federal organization. The questions are always of a legal nature. How much power? What vote is required? Upon what right may this or that action be based? Does it violate the constitutional distribution of power? Does it violate the principles of federalism? The ordinary treatment of federalism is based upon a legalistic foundation and its problems are treated as problems of constitutional law.

The Operation of Federal Institutions

This is assuredly a convenient method of approaching the problem and in many instances it is the only possible one. But it is not the only one. If a question arises that requires a legal answer, it can be answered only in legal terms. But the validity of such an answer is limited to the frame of reference within which the question is posed. Legal answers are of value only in the solution of legal problems. And federalism is concerned with many other problems than those of a legal nature.

Above and beyond this legalism there is an aspect of federalism that has been largely ignored. The essential nature of federalism is to be sought for, not in the shadings of legal and constitutional terminology, but in the forces— economic, social, political, cultural — that have made the outward forms of federalism necessary. Federalism, like most institutional forms, is a solution of, or an attempt to solve a certain kind of problem of political organization. It is true, on the whole, that federal governments and federal constitutions never grow simply and purely by accident. They arise in response to a definite set of stimuli; a federal system is consciously adopted as a means of solving the problems represented by these stimuli.

Whether a constitutional structure may properly be called federal, however, depends not so much on the arrangement of the institutions within it as it does on the manner in which those institutions are employed. Institutions have a habit of serving purposes other than those for which they are designed. The passage of time produces changes in the purposes of any society and these new purposes are reflected in new modes of operating old institutions which frequently retain their original forms. Thus a society may possess institutions that are federal in appearance but it may operate them as though they were something else; and, what is more likely, it may possess a unitary set of institutions and employ them as though they were federal in nature. The institutions themselves do not provide an accurate index of the federal nature of the society that subtends them.

Federalism as a Sociological Phenomenon

This leads us another step forward in the analysis. We have said that institutions may not be suited to the actual needs of the society and this point will be explored in greater detail later. If one could know exactly how the institutions are operated, one would have a much more accurate picture of the nature of the society itself. But the picture would still be incomplete and unclear; for institutional devices, both in form and in function, are only the surface manifestations of the deeper federal quality of the society that lies beneath the surface. The essence of federalism lies not in the institutional or constitutional structure but in the society itself. Federal government is a device by which the federal qualities of the society are articulated and protected.

Every society, every nation if you will, is more or less closely integrated in accordance with its own peculiar historical, cultural, economic, political and other determinants. Each is composed of elements that feel themselves to be different from the other elements in varying degrees and that demand in varying degrees a means of self-expression. These diversities may turn on all sorts of questions—economic, religious, racial, historical; any of these can produce in a certain group within the population a demand for such self-expression. Furthermore, these diversities may be distributed among the members of a society in such a fashion that certain attitudes are found in particular territorial areas, or they may be scattered widely throughout the whole of the society. If they are grouped territorially, that is geographically, then the result may be a society that is federal. If they are not grouped territorially, then the society cannot be said to be federal. In either case coherence in the society may depend on the devolution upon these groups of the exercise of functions appropriate to the diversities that they represent. But in the first case only can this take the form of federalism or federal government. In the latter case it becomes functionalism, pluralism or some form of corporativism.

I realize that in using the term federal only in this restricted territorial sense I am taking from it some of the meaning attributed to it by writers who profess to see federal elements in the various forms of pluralism, such as feudalism or corporativism. But I suggest that these writers have added a meaning that was not there before and one that introduces an element of confusion into the term. No government has ever been called federal that has been organized on any but the territorial basis; when organized on any other it has gone by another name.

It is true that the geographical diversities may not always follow the boundary lines of the component units. In many countries, and particularly in the United States, the operation of the federal system has displayed patterns of diversity that are more nearly associated with regions or groups of states than with the individual states themselves. This is easily understood. Federalism embraces not merely a diversity of opinion on one issue but a whole pattern of diversities on a number of issues. It can scarcely be expected that state boundary lines will be adequate to mark off areas in which opinions differ on all possible questions. Indeed on many or even most, questions the state boundaries will be of little significance in thus eliminating the areas of diversity. Federal organization is not perfect in every case.

No one supposes that it is, however. Component states exist because of some great significant diversity of such importance that it is felt that only a federal organization can offer it sufficient protection. Day-to-day issues may easily and reasonably produce alignments that follow regional lines. Regionalism in this sense is a valid manifestation of the federal principle. It conforms to the criterion suggested above, namely, that the diversities in the society be grouped territorially. It should be noted, moreover, that regionalism in the politics of a federal country is made possible only by the federal allocation of functions to the states themselves. The fact that several states within a larger region are dominated by similar opinions and hence unite in an effort to transform these views into policy does not detract from the importance of the states as the basic units of the federal system.

On the other hand, federalism becomes nothing if it is held to embrace diversities that are not territorially grouped, for there are then no territorial units that can serve as components of the federal system. I readily agree that this is a question of the definition of federalism and that society can be organized in accordance with any principle upon which there is substantial agreement among the members of the society. But if the distribution of powers, which is the essential feature of the federal structure, is made between the nation as a whole and component units that are functional in character, such as industries, trade unions, churches, and so on, then the traditional and, I think, necessary quality of federalism is lost. We confuse two distinct principles when we apply the terminology of federalism to a society organized on a functional basis.

It may be objected that the federal division of powers among territorial areas is in reality functional, since these areas differ from one another on questions of a functional character. I agree. But the important point is that they are territorially organized. Such areas naturally differ in opinions, in composition, in interests, in function. This, however, only brings us back to the point that they differ. If there were no functional differences, there might be no need for federalism. But the point that must be emphasized is that these functional differences are territorially grouped; and thus they provide a reason for and a demand for a federal system of government.

Federal Institutions as a Reflection of Societal Diversities

The nature of a society is roughly reflected in the external forms of its political and constitutional arrangements; and it is true that the extent to which the society is federal can be more or less accurately measured by the extent to which these external forms are federal. The institutional patterns reflect the federal quality of the societies in varying degrees; they may be more or less "federal" in the way in which they manifest the degree to which the political society behind the institutional facade is integrated or diversified. But the institutional patterns and the constitutional structure are far from an adequate test of the federal qualities of the society; dependence upon them alone can lead to serious error in assessing the nature of the society itself.

If these did serve as an accurate measurement of the society, the problems of the constitution maker and of the political analyst would be much simpler and this essay would not have been written. But the weighing of the various forces that go into the making and maintaining of a political community is an extremely difficult task. Those who devise institutions can never be sure that the institutions they devise will accurately represent the nature of the society or will be adequate to the needs they are designed to fulfill. Moreover, social patterns are constantly changing. What may be good for today will very likely be outmoded and less adequate by tomorrow. Finally, institutions mean different things to different people; the same set of institutions may produce widely different results when adopted and operated in different communities. Hence there can be no assurance at any time that the institutional patterns fit the needs of the society below.

From this it follows that the real nature of the society cannot be divined merely by an analysis, however brilliant and profound, of the institutions only. No amount of reading of constitutions can properly inform the analyst about the societies served by those constitutions. The nature of the political society can be examined only by observing how the institutions work in the context of that society. It is the operation, not the form, that is important; and it is the forces that determine the manner of operation that are more important still.

The Spectrum of Federal Societies

This is no less true of federalism than it is of any other form of political organization. Federalism is a function not of constitutions but of societies. Viewed in this way, it will be seen that federalism is not an absolute but a relative term; there is no specific point at which a society ceases to be unified and becomes diversified. The differences are of degree rather than of kind. All countries fall somewhere in a spectrum which runs from what we may call a theoretically wholly integrated society at one extreme to a theoretically wholly diversified society at the other. Some are more unified than others; some are more diversified than others; and the differences between adjacent societies in this spectrum may be so slight or so incommensurable as to be incapable of assessment. But that there is a gradation is clear from observing societies that are widely separated in the spectrum.

As one moves from one end of this hypothetical spectrum to the other the societies encountered are more and more diversified. And the more diversified the society, the greater is the necessity of providing some means for articulating the diversities; for these diversities are nothing less than tensions and as tensions they demand and require means of self-expression. But there is no point at which it can be said that all societies on one side are unitary and all those on the other are federal or diversified. If a society contains territorial groups that are so different from the rest of the society that they require some instrumentality to protect and articulate their peculiar qualities, then the society is likely to provide some means for the creation of such an instrumentality. One such circumstance doubtless does not make a society or a constitution federal. But two or six or twenty may produce a result that may be properly so called.

It cannot be said that when a society is just so diversified, it requires a federal constitution. In the first place we are unable to quantify social and political forces to the degree necessary to warrant such a demarcation; and secondly the forces themselves are incommensurable. (Which is more diversified, a society rent by religious schisms or one in which the members are divided by differences of language?) Societies employ instrumentalities for the expression of diversities in accordance with what men in particular societies think is necessary; and this view of what is necessary and what is not will vary considerably from society to society. Thus some societies which would seem to be highly diversified are able to get along with a set of institutions that seem to be nearly unitary; and, conversely, some that seem quite unified adopt institutions that we call federal. It may be that one espcially strong unifying tendency in a society, such as a long historical tradition of unity, will overcome diversities of economic interest, language and the like which, in another society, with a weaker historical tradition, would necessitate federal institutions.

Types of Diversities

The social diversities that produce federalism may be of many kinds. Differences of economic interest, religion, race, nationality, language, variations in size, separation by great distances, differences in historical background, previous existence as separate colonies or states, dissimilarity of social and political institutions—all these may produce a situation in which the particular interests and qualities of the segments of the larger community must be given recognition. At the same time these differences must not be too great, else the community must break up into independent groups. Federalism cannot make coherent a society in which the diversities are so great that there can be no basis for integration.

There is no way to estimate the relative weights of these factors except in results; we have observed already that they are largely incommensurable. But it seems clear that some are more significant than others, at least within a single society. For example a society that enjoys a uniformity of social and political background can still hold together despite cleavages in other matters.

The point is that the diversities and similarities are of many different kinds and when taken together they produce a total picture of the extent to which the society is integrated or diversified.

The total pattern of these diversities produces a demand for some kind of federal recognition of the diversities. This demand must in most cases meet a counterdemand (or intertia, which is equally a force) for increased unity or integration. These two demands or forces—the one impelling toward autonomy and independence for the component units, the other impelling toward centralization and the suppression of diversity—meet each other head on; the result of their conflict is the federal system. The federal system is thus an institutionalization of the compromise between these two demands, and the federal constitution draws the lines of this compromise. The constitution will be more or less federal in accordance with the relative strength of the two demands. Thus societies in which the demand for integration is stronger than the demand for decentralization will produce a set of institutions that is more nearly unitary; and a contrary situation will produce a contrary result. It is in this sense that federalism is a matter of degree and not of kind. The varying degrees of federalism are produced by societies in which the patterns of diversity vary and in which the demands for the protection and articulation of diversities have been urged with more or less strength. But what determines the federal quality of the government is not only the constitution that draws the lines of the compromise but the whole pattern of instrumentalities that are employed as a result of the demands.

Types of Instrumentalities

The diversities within a society require certain instrumentalities for their expression and protection. Just as the diversities take many forms, so do the instrumentalities; the latter are designed to fit the needs of the former. But the relation and correspondence between the diversities and the instrumentalities that express them will vary from society to society. A diversity that requires one kind of instrumentality for its expression in one social complex will require another kind in another social complex. So also similar instrumentalities in different social complexes will serve different kinds of diversities. It is this fact that has been largely ignored by most analysts of federal institutions.

We are too prone to say that federal constitutions must contain a certain five or eight or ten characteristics and that all constitutions lacking any of these are not federal. Such a set of criteria ignores the fundamental fact that institutions are not the same things in different social and cultural contexts. Two societies equally diversified with respect to a particular matter may require very different instrumentalities for the implementation of that diversity. By the same token, similar institutions or instrumentalities in different social contexts may serve to implement dissimilar diversities.

The word "instrumentality" is a broad one and necessarily so; but we must be clear about what is meant. First of all, it does not mean merely a clause in the constitution, though such clauses may be examples of such instrumentalities and it may be said that the provisions of the constitution are a good rough guide to the pattern of instrumentalities, though they become less adequate with the passage of time. But the word includes not only the constitutional forms but also the manner in which the forms are employed; it includes the way in which the constitution and its institutions are operated. Beyond this, moreover, it includes many things that are far from constitutional in importance in the ordinary sense of the word. It includes such things as habits, attitudes, acceptances, concepts and even theories. It includes perhaps the rules of the American Senate, the make-up of the Canadian cabinet, the zeal of the Baptist Karens in Burma. All these may serve as instrumentalities for the expression of the diversities within a society, and whether a country is federal or not may best be determined by examining the pattern of these instrumentalities and not by checking its constitution against an *a priori* list of the characters of a federal constitution.

Federal Constitutions and Federal Instrumentalities

Indeed the documentary constitution may be a poor guide in attempting to discover whether or not the society itself is federal. Several South American countries have adopted federal constitutions and yet an examination of those countries reveals a rather high degree of integration. Are we to infer that Soviet Russia is more federal than, say, the United States because it provides in its constitution for a right of secession?

Other examples may better illustrate the point. It is meaningless to insist that the Union of South Africa is unitary and not federal because of certain characteristics of its constitution. I should be quite willing to agree that the component units may be overwhelmed by the central government, if the testimony of the constitution is to constitute the only evidence. But I should at the same time insist that what is significant is, not what the constitution says, but how the people of South Africa employ it. The fact is that in many instances South Africa operates its institutions as though its constitution were federal; it works federally despite the unitary character of its legal forms. If one examines the South African policy from a strictly legal or constitutional point of view, it is clearly unitary. But if one probes deeper into the processes of politics one quickly perceives that federalism is still an operative principle in that society.

A similar argument may be advanced in regard to Great Britain, a country whose constitution is most often cited as being typically unitary. Many elements of British public life are witness of the vitality of the federal principle on British society. Indeed there would seem to be an operative right to secede from that community, exemplified by the withdrawals from it in recent years of such elements as Burma and Ireland. If Northern Ireland or Scotland, or perhaps even other elements, were to seek actively for secession, it seems most unlikely that the right would be challenged. A right of secession as an operative idea in a society suggests diversities of a rather acute nature and places that society, as far as the particular point is concerned, well over toward the diversity side of the spectrum of federalism. Federal elements in Great Britain take other forms as well. Northern Ireland has its own parliament; Scotland has its own courts and legal system as well as its own church. Scotland, further-more, is especially protected in the House of Commons by a Scottish Committee which deals with questions pertaining to that area. If the central government were to attempt to abolish any of these institutions, the outraged complaints of injustice would bear adequate witness to the extent to which this society is diversified and to the necessity of providing these instrumentalities for the articulation and protection of the federal qualities.

Even France under the *ancien régime,* which is ordinarily considered to have been a very highly centralized executive state, manifested certain federal quali-ties. The laws and customs of the provinces were far from standardized. Each had its own legal code, its own body of customary law, its own historical tradition and a very considerable degree of local patriotism.

The Causal Relation Between Federalism and its Instrumentalities

The point has been made that the pattern of forces within the society changes with the passage of time. Society is never static but changes constantly in accordance with the interplay of the various dynamic forces within it. As a result the diversities within the society wax and wane in intensity so that the need for their articulation increases or decreases. A complex of psychological and so-ciological factors may require one type of instrumentality at one time and another type at some other time. As the nature of society changes, demands for new kinds of instrumentalities are created and these demands are met by changing or abolishing old instrumentalities and substituting new ones in their place. But it can scarcely be hoped that the instrumentalities will keep pace with the changing pattern of social relationships, and as a result the pattern of instrumentalities tends to lag behind the changes in society itself (though it may be observed that the functioning of the instrumentalities will not be so rigid in this respect as the constitutional forms).

This is complicated further by the fact that the instrumentalities, once put into operation, become rigidified and acquire a status of their own. They become substantive instead of merely adjectival; they become ends in themselves instead of merely means toward other ends. Their procedures become stan-dardized; they may take on an honorific quality; they become matters of pride to the diverse elements that they serve; and ultimately the instrumentalities enter into and become part of the psycho-sociological complex itself.

This is by no means an unusual occurrence; almost every society manifests this tendency in one form or another. The Scottish Committee of the British House of Commons, mentioned above, is an example. This Committee was at the outset a device, an instrumentality, to permit the organized expression of Scottish opinion on affairs that directly concerned Scotland; it is still that. But it is also much more, for it has become a thing of value in itself, a thing to be preserved because it is an essential part of the federal relation between England and Scotland.

Another example is the Supreme Court of the United States which began as a mere court of law. But as judicial supremacy developed in the United States the Supreme Court became more and more an institution that connoted the maintenance of justice in federal relations in this country. (It came to mean many other things as well, but it is the federal arrangement that concerns us here.) Few men now claim that the Court is a mere court of law; and few men would dare to disturb its position without serious consideration of the effects of such a change on the shifting balance of national power and state power. The Court has ceased to be a mere instrumentality and has entered into the psycho-sociological complex that determines the nature of the instrumentalities.

Another example is to be found in the United States themselves. America adopted a federal constitution at the outset because the elements that were to make up the new country were so diversified that they could be brought together in no other form. But since that time the Federal Constitution has continued in force and has collected around it all the aura of a highly revered institution. As other states have entered the union they have taken their places in the federal arrangement and have found that all the prerequisites and particularities of the established states have accrued to them. Although at the time of their entry these later states may not have been sufficiently diversified to justify such special treatment, they rapidly acquired such consciousness of individuality that they now would be unwilling to part with the instrumentalities that permit the expression of that individuality. It is doubtful that the two Dakotas warranted the dignity of separate statehood at the time of their entry into the union; but who can deny now that, having lived as states for a number of years, they would look with disfavor upon any proposal to deprive them of their individuality by merging them into one? The Constitution, which endows the states with the characteristics of diversity, treats them indiscriminately and thus tends to create diversity where none previously existed. The Constitution with its federal plan, though designed as an instrumentality, has become a part of the complex of sociological and psychological values that constitutes the pattern of diversities. It is no longer merely an instrumentality serving to protect and articulate the diversities; it has itself become a part of that complex of values which *is* the pattern of diversities and which determines the pattern of the instrumentalities.

Thus the problem of the student of federalism is made much more difficult, for he cannot clearly distinguish between society and the instrumentalities it employs. Similarly with the problems of the statesman; he cannot devise means to accomplish new ends without disturbing the old relationship, for the old means have themselves become ends and the old techniques have become values.

The effort to draw the distinction must be made, however; for otherwise we end by confusing cause with effect and by attributing to the instrumentalities values that belong properly to the anterior diversities. The student of federalism must probe deeper than the institutional patterns, for these are but the products of the diversities in the society; it is to the pattern of these diversities that we must go if we would assess the federal qualities of the society.

3   Federal Political Systems and Federal Societies*

Michael Stein

In the past few years a number of studies have been published which offer different approaches and interpretations to the subject of federalism. Until these recent studies appeared, the theory of federalism was embodied largely in the work of K. C. Wheare. Wheare published the first truly path-breaking book in the comparative study of federalism shortly after World War II.[1] He defined federalism as that system of government in which the federal and regional governments are both coordinate and independent. In applying this definition, he stressed the sharp division in the powers and functions of two co-equal sovereignties as a basis for classifying systems of government as federal. Wheare's definition was derived primarily from his analysis of the American constitution and, in particular, its formally sharp division of powers between national and state governments.

Wheare also compared the constitutions of governments with their actual workings in order to classify such governments as federal or non-federal in practice. He found that only three then existing constitutions met his criteria of "federal"—the United States, Australia and Switzerland. Canada, the fourth system that he analyzed in depth, did not qualify as a "federal constitution" primarily because the powers of disallowance and reservation of provincial legislation accorded the federal government effectively nullified the co-equal status of the provincial governments. Wheare then turned to the actual workings of these governments, and found that the governments of the United States, Australia, Switzerland and Canada all more or less fulfilled his criteria

---

[1] K. C. Wheare, *Federal Government*, 4th Ed., (London, Oxford University Press, 1963). The first edition was published in 1946.

* From *World Politics*, Vol. XX no. 4, July 1968. Reprinted by permission of the author and publisher. The author wishes to acknowledge his indebtedness to Professors Robert J. Jackson and Donald C. Rowat of Carleton University and Mr. Peter H. Solomon, Jr., of Columbia University, for their comments on his paper and to the students in his seminar on *Federalism* at Carleton.

MICHAEL STEIN – Associate Professor of Political Science, McGill University.

of a working federal government. Wheare justified his inclusion of Canada as an operative federal system by noting that the powers of disallowance and reservation had been very infrequently applied, especially since the turn of the century.

Wheare recognized that his criteria of coordinate, but independent, status for the two levels of government, and his implicit notion that the functions of government should somehow be carried out independently by the two different levels of government were only components of an ideal-typical definition. His discussion of the evolution of a preponderant financial position of the federal government over provincial governments as a result of depression and post-war economic strains reveals this.[2] Nevertheless, Wheare was optimistic that the approximate coordinate and independent relationship between the two levels of government would continue into the post-World War II period, with some modifications in the financial and administration sphere. He also was confident of the continuing utility of federal forms of government in post-World War II conditions. His ideal-typical definition of federalism became the most widely accepted basis for a classificatory scheme and for comparing federal systems of government in such problem areas as financial and administrative relations between the two levels of government, relationships between the court system at both levels, and the composition of legislatures at the two levels of government.

Wheare, however, neglected several important problem areas which are vital to the working of any federal government. Among them are the party system, and the role of pressure groups and political movements, and the effect of political attitudes on the system. Probably the most important, as both W. H. Riker and Aaron Wildavsky have argued, is the political party system. The relationships between the two levels of government are dependent on the kinds of relationships which members of political parties at both levels establish with each other. Often in a federal system the members of the political parties operating governments at the regional level are co-partisans of those operating governments at the federal level. In such instances informal party relationships became important to federalism. At other times members of the governing parties at the regional level belong to opponent parties of the governing parties at the national level. The rivalry between the parties can be an important factor in determining legislative and administrative relations between the two governments. The federal structure of government also affects the pattern of organization of these different parties, the relationships between the extra-parliamentary party and the parliamentary caucuses at both levels of government, and the organization of election campaigns. The parties in turn not only affect the pattern of relationships between the two levels of government through the internal relationships of their members, but also the patterns of party finance from region to region. These are only a few of the similarities

---

2 *Ibid.*, Chapters 6-8.

between the pattern of relationships of political parties operating within federal structures which can be illuminated by comparative analysis.

For almost two decades Wheare's definition of federalism stood unchallenged in the textbooks of political science, and in numerous government documents. However, not long after his book first appeared, several scholars began to cite some shortcomings in what seemed to be an overly narrow definition of federalism, based on legal and juridical writings. Several of these often neglected essays, written in the 1950's and early 1960's, are reprinted in the first three sections of Aaron Wildavsky's *American Federalism in Perspective*. One of them by W. S. Livingston is worthy of special attention.

Livingston's critique was directed at the limitations which a formal-legal definition of federalism imposes on the kinds of problems with which students of federalism concern themselves. In his perceptive view,

> . . . the essential nature of federalism is to be sought for, not in the shadings of legal and constitutional terminology, but in the forces— economic, social, political, cultural—that have made the outward forms of federalism necessary. Federalism, like most institutional forms, is a solution of, or an attempt to solve a certain kind of problem of political organization . . . . [F]ederal governments and federal constitutions never grow simply and purely by accident. They arise in response to a definite set of stimuli; a federal system is consciously adopted as a means of solving the problems represented by these stimuli.[3]

According to Livingston, the stimuli for the outward forms of federalism were the forces which he described as "the federal quality of the society". A federal society is one in which diversities are grouped territorially.[4] Where societies exist in which diversities are grouped in some other way, then the society is not federal, and there is little likelihood that its political institutions will be federal in form. On the other hand, where diversities are grouped territorially, the likelihood is that these territories will be assigned functions appropriate to their diversities, and federal forms will be established.

Livingston was careful to point out that these diversities may not be precisely translated into political forms which follow the strict boundary lines of the principal geographic cleavages in the society. Administrative and historical considerations generally weigh most heavily in determining how such political boundaries defining the regional units in a federal system should be drawn. For example, in Canada the federal form of government established in 1867 was primarily the product of a compromise between French-and English-speaking groups in the then united Province of Canada. Two separate provinces, Ontario and Quebec, were established in which each of the two principal language groups comprised a majority. Nevertheless, there were large minorities of both

---

[3] W. S. Livingston, "A Note on the Nature of Federalism", *Political Science Quarterly*, Vol. LXVII no. 1 (March, 1952), pp. 83-84.
[4] *Ibid.*, p. 85.

groups concentrated along the borders of each province. The provincial boundaries were not redrawn to encompass them.

Livingston did not make clear precisely what kinds of diversities he thought were crucial in defining his concept of "federal society". He seemed to be speaking of differences in language, religion, ethnicity or historical tradition, which distinguish groups of people living in one concentrated area from those of neighbouring areas. These differences form the basis of federalism when such groups attain sufficient power to permit their political representatives to insist upon retaining important functions in those areas in which they constitute an overall majority.

Can Livingston's concept of "federal society" be made more precise? Can one distinguish between a society which is "federal" and one which is not? And what utility is there in identifying a "federal society", assuming some consensus can be reached on what is meant by the term?

It seems to me that some degree of consensus has already been reached on the meaning of "federal society". Several other students of federalism, including R. L. Watts and Aaron Wildavsky, have adopted Livingston's terminology and applied it in their own writings. Watts limits Livingston's use to "that segment of the spectrum [of societies] in which the pressures for unity and diversity are fairly closely balanced".[5] Watts introduces here a notion of equilibrium, which is absent in Livingston's analysis. He defines federal society as that kind of inclusive social system in which social forces making for diversity among differentiated communities are in approximate balance with forces making for unity. He does not, however, suggest indices which might permit the student of federalism to identify the kind of society and the type of equilibrium which he envisages. Nor does he provide a list of criteria which distinguish "federal societies" from other kinds of societies. Are the United States and Australia, despite the comparative homogeneity of social groups in their respective societies, to be characterized as "federal societies"? If not, what kind of societies are they? And how does one account for the adoption and continued operation of federal political forms in these systems?

Aaron Wildavsky deals with this problem. He distinguishes between what he calls "structural federalism" and what he refers to as "social federalism".[6] For Wildavsky, "structural federalism" exists today in societies like Australia largely because a structural framework of federalism was originally adopted and has created vested interests which support its retention rather than because of the social makeup of territorially based groups. The political framework of federalism is no longer a minimum condition for the survival of Australia as a nation-state, as it apparently once was.

---

[5] R. L. Watts, *New Federations, Experiments in the Commonwealth* (Oxford, Oxford University Press, 1966), p. 95.
[6] Aaron Wildavsky, "Party Discipline Under Federalism: Implications of the Australian Experience", Aaron Wildavsky (ed.), *American Federalism in Perspective* (Boston, Little, Brown and Co., 1967), p. 178.

Surprisingly, Wildavsky considers the United States, despite the relative homogeneity of its territorially concentrated communities in terms of language religion, and historical experience, to be a type of "social federalism" rather than "structural federalism". Wildavsky disagrees with writers such as Riker, who see the United States as sufficiently integrated at present to abandon federalism if its national political leaders choose to do so. The disagreement between Wildavsky and Riker demonstraes how imporant it is to define the concept of "federal society" with greater precision.

It seems to me that the concept of "federal society" can be most usefully applied if it is confined to a society which is conterminously both "polyethnic" and multilingual in makeup. The major cleavage defining societies of this type is a product of ethnic and linguistic differences. Where a society is constituted of territorially based communities which are clearly differentiated by language and ethnicity, then one can expect to find a federal society. The cleavage defining such a "federal society" may be reinforced by other factors such as religion, geography and economics, which also help to create a sense of belonging to distinctive communities. However, the ethnic and linguistic factors are determining factors in the decision concerning the nature of the larger political order which each community wishes to establish in union with other communities. If the aforementioned social conditions are present, then the political leaders of the distinctive communities will "bargain" for sufficient autonomy for themselves and their followers to prevent the establishment of a system more centralized than a federal union.

Once the "federal bargain is struck", to use William Riker's phrase, then forces in the society will again operate on and be shaped by the political structure.[7] Here the concept of "federal political system" becomes relevant. The first student of federalism to use the concept "federal political system" in conjunction with "federal society" was R. L. Watts. Watts borrowed the concept from the writings of David Easton and others. He extends K. C. Wheare's definition of federal government to subsume all political systems in which jurisdictions and functions are divided between central and regional governments, so that neither is totally subordinate to the other. He includes systems in which one level of government is stronger or more powerful than the other.[8]

Watts does not really apply the concept "political system" in a systematic manner. He focuses almost exclusively on the formal structures of government which manifest federal features. He does not include those political or power relationships outside the formal structures of authority which ultimately produce authoritative decisions for the members of a society. In particular, he does not deal systematically with those aspects of political parties, interest groups, elite groups and political attitudes which are shaped by, and in turn shape the operation of federal political systems.[9]

---

[7] William H. Riker, *Federalism: Origin, Oporeation, Significance* (Boston, Little, Brown and Co., 1964).

[8] Watts, *op. cit.,* p. 13.

[9] Watts was hamstrung by lack of information about informal political processes within the new federations. This point is made below, p. 37.

Watts also does not distinguish between the more inclusive aspects of a society's political behaviour encompassed by the concept "political system", and those aspects which are peculiarly influenced by and influence the federal structure. The concept "federal political system" is narrower in meaning and scope than is the general concept of "political system".

A "federal political system", then, in my view is that form of political system (of a nation-state) in which the institutions, values, attitudes, and patterns of political action operate to give autonomous expression to both the national political system and political culture and to regional political subsystems and subcultures (defined primarily by ethnic-linguistic factors). The autonomy of each of these systems and subsystems is counterbalanced by a mutual interdependence. This balance maintains the overall union.

The concepts used by Livingston and Watts can be fruitfully combined with those of William Riker. Riker focuses on the specifically "political" variables in any federal arrangement. A mutual desire among negotiating communities for territorial expansion by means other than conquest, and a mutual interest in security against an outside neighbour are for Riker the two major factors producing a "federal bargain". Once the "bargain" is struck, a number of other variables come into play in maintaining the federal system. Riker explores the relationship between fiscal and administrative arrangements (which he refers to as the "administrative theory of federalism"), the influence of the federal institutions of government, and the pattern of political attitudes (which he describes as "patriotism") as they relate to the maintenance of federalism. He concludes that none of these factors is crucial to the maintenance of federalism. Rather, the pattern of relationships operating within the party system is the key factor preserving the federal bargain over time. In his words,

> Whatever the general social conditions, if any, that sustain the federal bargain, there is one institutional condition that controls the nature of the bargain in all the instances here examined and in all others with which I am familiar. This is the structure of the party system, which may be regarded as the main variable intervening between the background social conditions and the specific nature of the federal bargain.[10]

Riker considers his approach to be a more purely political one, in opposition to the sociological approaches adopted by such writers as Karl Deutsch.[11] However, there is nothing in my opinion which prevents a synthesis of the two approaches in comparing certain federal systems. The concept "federal political system" can incorporate both pure power political relationships and more inclusive socio-political patterns of action.[12] The patterns of political relation-

---

[10] Riker, *op. cit.*, p. 136.

[11] *Ibid.*, p. 16.

[12] The distinction between pure power political relationships and socio-political patterns of action is often blurred in the literature. By socio-political patterns of action I mean all those behaviour patterns which directly or indirectly contribute to authoritative decision-making in a society. Pure power political relationships are those which specifically involve power, authority and rule, defined in a coercive sense.

ships in polyethnic federal systems which are comparable are those which operate within the limits set by the federal bargain. They also emanate from comparable territorially based cleavages in these societies. Thus, in the same way as one speaks of the interactions between societies and their political systems, one can speak of the interaction between the "federal" or polyethnic factors in a society and the "federal" patterns of power political relationships which operate in any federal political system.

By "federal" patterns of power political relationships I mean simply those bargains, compromises and balances in power relationships between the representatives of the major ethnic-linguistic communities which operate within the formal and informal structures (such as the executive, legislature, judiciary, political parties and political groups). Within the legislature a compromise might be arranged through special representation provisions, or through linguistic guarantees. Within the executive a bargain may exist in the representation of different regions in cabinet decision-making. Within the judiciary the scope of different legal systems and the representation of judges from the different communities and legal traditions strengthens the bargain. Within political parties, an agreement to give representation on party executives to the members of different communities, and an arrangement to separate national and regional party structures in parties which bear the same name and are part of the same tradition, also involves implementation of the federal bargain. These delicate compromises are worked out in part through mutual adherence to the strict terms of the original constitution and in part through informal understandings between the representatives of the member communities in the federal society.

It seems to me that R. L. Watts, implicitly rather than explicitly, has confined his concepts and his analyses to just such types of federal systems and societies. Watts compares societies which manifest aspects of federalism both in their social structure and in their political structure. The patterns of political relationships are sufficiently similar to lend themselves to comparison. Thus Watts selected such widely divergent political systems as India, Pakistan, Malaysia, Nigeria, the Federation of Rhodesia and Nyasaland, and the West Indies Federation for comparison.

Watts has applied the concepts of "federal society" and "federal political system" in answering two major questions: 1) what causes new nations to adopt federal forms, and 2) how well have these forms worked once they have been adopted? The focal point of his analysis of the first question is the "federal society", or the forces of unity and diversity in these six societies which influenced them to strike a "federal bargain". These forces include a balance in desire and capacity for both unity and diversity between different ethnic-linguistic groups; a balance in economic goals and capabilities between the negotiating communities; a balance between shared historical traditions and those historical memories making for differentiation between these communities; a balance of the desire to achieve political independence from the colonial power and of the realization of the limited possibilities of achieving such independence except under a federal system, and so forth. After comparative analysis, Watts argues that the factors making for federation in the six societies he compares vary from federation to federation.[13] Despite the large number of factors which he lists, Watts' analysis of the forces in a federal society is, in my opinion, still incomplete. It is not sufficiently multi-dimensional to encompass other social factors which might have been even more important in producting the federal bargain. For example, a balance in social and economic transactions and a balanced set of mutual perceptions between the negotiating communities may also have influenced them to negotiate the bargain. Karl Deutsch gives these factors special prominence in his discussion of the preconditions for security-communities, of which a federal system is one sub-type.[14]

Watts also neglects to weight his factors in terms of their relative importance. Riker gave two factors, the desire for security from external attack and the desire for territorial expansion through diplomatic negotiation, a major place in his analysis. This may be true for some communities but not for others.[15] Wheare, Watts and Deutsch all emphasized non-political factors, which may be more important than the political factors as preconditions for the bargain in some federal systems. What is needed, then, is a technique for measuring the relative weight of the variety of factors impinging on the federal bargain.

In his second question, namely how well the forms worked once applied in practice, Watts claims to focus on the interactions within what he calls the "federal system". In fact, however, because so little information is available about the federal institutions of these new federations other than those falling strictly within the formal governmental sphere, Watts was forced to confine his analysis to the formal distribution of legislative and executive authority in these new federations.

Political scientists have now come to include the informal political structures in their analyses of political systems. Concepts have been developed in comparative politics which give some precision to such institutions and patterns of action as political parties, pressure groups, political movements, cliques and factions; competing elites; and political cultures and subcultures. This is particularly the case in developed and westernized political systems, where the informal institutions, informal patterns of political action, and the patterns of political attitudes which comprise the infrastructure of any political system show striking similarities, particularly as they relate to the federal political structure.

What kinds of questions might one ask about the relationship between the aforementioned patterns of action and the federal structure? I have already listed several problem areas involving the relationship between political parties

---

13 Watts, *op. cit.*, pp. 65 ff. 90ff.

14 K. W. Deutsch, *et al.*, *Political Community and the North Atlantic Area* (Princeton, Princeton University Press, 1957), p. 58.

15A. H. Birch makes this point in his excellent review of Riker. See "Approaches to the Study of Federation", *Political Studies*, Vol. XIV no. 1, 1966, pp. 15-33.

and the federal structure. In the case of pressure groups and other competitive structures, one might investigate the following: What kinds of pressure groups and political movements are formed with the specific purpose in mind of representing one of the ethnic-linguistic communities? How do they act on the central and regional decision-making centers? Are their activities in influence concentrated more on the central government or on the regional governments? How intense are these pressures on the two levels of government? What is the internal structural pattern of these groups, unitary, federal or confederal? How well represented are the different ethnic-linguistic communities in the internal decision-making processes of such groups? What overall role do such groups play in preserving or destroying the federal bargain?

With regard to competing elites, one might explore the following: Are the ethnic-linguistic communities equally represented within the society's "power elite"? When their representatives join the "power elite", do they continue to champion their community's interests? Or do they abandon their community ties and become part of a "national" political community? What role do they play in decisions made by the central government affecting the demands and interests of the ethnic-linguistic communities? Are they deliberately recruited from their ethnic-linguistic community in order to strengthen the federal bargain?

Finally, one can investigate some questions relating political cultures and subcultures to the federal structure. What are the major subcultures within the federal society? Do they correspond with the various ethnic-linguistic communities? What are the comparative loyalties felt towards the central and regional governments of the federal political system? How efficacious a role do the individual members of the major communities feel they perform in the national and regional political systems and subsystems? How do changing perceptions about the national and regional governments affect the behaviour of the various ethnic-linguistic communities towards these governments?

In which federal systems might these questions be investigated? There are several contemporary federal systems which fall easily into the category of "federal societies" (defined in terms of polyethnicity and multilingualism) which also have federal governmental structures. Most of them, however, have very little experience as operative political systems. Among the mature federations, Switzerland and Canada are the most outstanding examples. The former system has achieved a considerable success as a model of stable federalism. The latter is now experiencing serious strains after one hundred years of what seemed to most outside observers to be a highly stable and durable federalism as well. I shall use Canada then as a laboratory for applying some of the concepts which I have discussed above.

At present, after one hundred years of what seemed a firmly established and stable federal political system, Canada is undergoing what the Royal Commission on Bilingualism and Biculturalism aptly referred to as a "crisis in the Confederation partnership" in its Preliminary Report published just over two years ago.[16] There has been a growing realization among politically aware Canadians that the Commission's diagnosis was correct. The federal bargain between French- and English-speaking Canadians struck one hundred years ago is in serious danger of coming unhinged.

What tools can political scientists apply to explain why this bargain is now endangered? Why has it been maintained for one hundred years without seemingly a threat to its continued existence? What are the possibilities for its future maintenance, if reforms are introduced? Where are the changes most needed, at the constitutional level, within the formal govermental institutions, or within informal political institutions such as the political party system, the pressure groups, and in the political attitudes which French- and English-speaking Canadians have towards each other?

As has been previously mentioned, Riker argues that the crucial factor maintaining the federal bargain in any political system is the party system. In the case of Canada, I think this is correct. However, writers on Canadian federalism had not given much attention to the relationship between the Canadian party system and federalism. We know very little about the power relationships and bargains struck between French- and English-speaking Canadians within the parliamentary caucuses and extra-parliamentary parties, between members of each language group belonging to the same political party at the provincial and national levels, etc. Such aspects are just beginning to be systematically studied by these political scientists. But their study can be facilitated by the application of some of the hypotheses suggested in the Wildavsky reader by Truman and Grodzins in the case of the American party system, by Wildavsky and Davis in the case of the Australian party system (which, because Australia has a parliamentary cabinet type of government, is more similar to the Canadian case than is the United States), by Muller in the case of the Canadian system itself, and by Riker.[17]

It seems to me that one of the prime factors which will determine whether the "federal bargain" will endure in Canada is the accommodation that will be worked out between French- and English-speaking Canadians in the two major parties at the federal and provincial levels, and also that between French- and English-speaking Canadians in the minor parties, the New Democratic Party and the Social Credit Party. If, for example, accommodations can be made for French-speaking Canadians living outside the Province of Quebec so that they can be educated in and retain their own language (and these accommodations are negotiated both within the cabinet and upper levels of the administration and within the caucuses of the federal and provincial parliamentary parties),

---

[16] *A Preliminary Report of the Royal Commission on Bilingualism and Biculturalism* (Ottawa, Queen's Printer, 1965), p. 13. The Preamble reads: "Canada, without being fully conscious of the fact, is passing through the greatest crisis in its history. The source of the crisis lies in the Province of Quebec." It is also interesting that the Commissioners describe Canada as a nation-state containing "two societies".

[17] Wildavsky, *op. cit.,* pp. 23-24, 51-59, 81-181.

then the possibilities for maintaining the federal bargain are enhanced. This assumes that the major negotiating communities, the French- and English-speaking communities, are willing to maintain their electoral confidence in these long-standing parties, and the leading partisan representatives of both major communities are also willing to preserve the federal bargain.

In a similar manner, the internal composition, structure and bargaining within the leading pressure groups will affect the durability of the federal bargain. For example, the major union in Canada, the Canadian Labour Congress (CLC) is a confederation of provincial and locally organized unions. One of these provincial unions is the Quebec Federation of Labour (QFL), which represents a substantially larger proportion of the working class in Quebec than their major competitors, the Confederation of National Trade Unions (CNTU). The latter, however, has adopted a more radical stance with regard to the role of Quebec in Confederation. Consequently it has expanded its membership at the expense of the QFL. This has caused the members of the QFL to demand a more sympathetic attitude on the part of Canadian labour as a whole to such questions affecting the French-Canadian community as its representation in the decision-making processes of the union, use of the French language at work, and so forth.

Other subjects of crucial importance in this negotiating process are the entire array of federal and provincial powers and the linguistic and regional composition of the federal and provincial courts, the ethnic-linguistic composition of the federal administration, and the bicultural composition of a national capital district.

However, all this assumes that the two dominant ethnic-linguistic communities retain their confidence in the traditional parties and pressure groups. The existence of different types of structures of political competition such as political movements within French Canada opposed to the existing bargain threatens to undermine the prospects for a negotiated settlement. Here the analysis of the major right- and left-wing political movements dedicated to the independence of Quebec becomes relevant. Comparative analysis has something to contribute to the question of whether such movements of independence can make sufficient headway in the Province of Quebec to undermine the federal bargain.

It has been found by students of political movements that under severe conditions of deprivation (of an economic, status, or other sort) and psychological strain, individuals in any society will seek outlets in the form of some episodes of collective protest behaviour.[18] In the case of two party systems in which one party has been dominant for a long period of time, so that the major opposition party is no longer seen as a credible alternative to the dominant

---

18 Neil J. Smelser, *Theory of Collective Behaviour* (New York, Free Press of Glencoe, 1962), p. 14 ff. Also Maurice Pinard, "One-Party Dominance and Third Parties", *Canadian Journal of Economics and Political Science,* Vol. XXXIII no. 3 (August, 1967), pp. 358-73.

party, the individuals in that society will tend to vote for the third party alternatives which appeal to their attitudes of discontent.[19] In the case of Quebec, the independence parties of the right-and the left-wing, the Ralliement Nationale and the Rassemblement de l'Indépendence Nationale, have competed in one provincial election, in 1966, and together gained only about 10% of the vote.

The Union Nationale, one of the major parties provincially, is at present still committed to maintaining the Confederation pact, although it seeks significant reforms in the federal structure. It succeeded in capturing power from the Liberals, which had also pledged to maintain the bargain. Federally all the major and minor parties have agreed to support the Confederation settlement. Much depends, then, on whether the two major parties provincially can hold their electorate to a program of reform within the existing federal structure. The condition of the electorate depends largely on the fluctuating economic and social conditions in the province. If conditions worsen, French-Canadians may feel themselves attracted to parties opposed to the existing system. For, given the fact that a predominance of force is held in federal hands, the most likely way that independence can be achieved for Quebec is by election to power of an independence party (or the achievement by such a party of sufficient bargaining power through a balance of power position to win the major parties away from their pledge to maintain the bargain).

Alternatively, one of the major provincial parties might unilaterally decide to opt out of the federal bargain. It seems to me that this is not at present a likely possibility. Premier Johnson of Quebec, leader of the Union Nationale, has expressed his desire to maintain the Confederation pact if certain reforms favourable both to the Province of Quebec and to French-Canadian interests are enacted. The provincial Liberal party, the other major party, has recently had a showdown within its ranks in which the *indépendentistes,* led by the colourful René Lévesque, were defeated in their bid to commit their party to separatism. The party now appears to be firmly under the control of those pledged to retain the federal bargain.

What would be the signs of changing French-Canadian attitudes towards the federal pact? Clearly, public opinion polls and studies of changing attitudes of Quebeckers towards the federal pact are an important indicator. A recent public opinion poll revealed that, whereas 70 per cent of Quebeckers favour some constitutional change, only 7 per cent are committed to outright separatism.[20] Of course the attitudes of English-speaking Canadians towards implementing the kind of reforms which French-speaking Canadians are now demanding must also be studied.

The use of these tools of analysis cannot give us more than a very rough

---

[19] Pinard, *op. cit.,* p. 361.
[20] This poll was conducted for the Canadian Broadcasting Corporation in October 1967.

approximation of what is likely to occur in Canada. We cannot know for sure whether the bargain will be maintained or not. Its preservation will depend on the willingness of French- and English-speaking Canadians to retain their trust in the federal pact. This trust rests ultimately on mutual understanding and confidence on the part of the leading representatives of both communities. They must agree that their welfare can best be enhanced through a willingness to let the members of the other community live in the enjoyment of their "full personality as a community" (to use a common French-Canadian phrase). It seems to me probable that such a confidence will be maintained over the long run in Canada.

The questions concerning the relationship between the informal political structures of a society and federalism are, as stated earlier, relevant to other systems besides that of Canada. In particular, where modern societies have ethnic-linguistic cleavages which reinforce each other, creating distinct communities along territorial lines, similar problems related to the structure of the political system arise. If such societies have adopted federal forms as a minimum condition for the formation of political communities, then it is likely that conflicts will arise which will translate themselves into federal political problems. Ethnic-linguistic differences between separate communities tend to polarize around the federal structure because political power, both potential and actual, exists for these communities within the spheres of jurisdiction and functions assigned them by the federal legal-political structure. Thus the problems that have been discussed in relation to the "federal society" and "federal political system" of Canada, exist in similar form in other clearly "federal societies" such as Switzerland, Yugoslavia, the Soviet Union among developed systems, and India, Pakistan, Nigeria, among some less developed systems.

It is also possible to apply these concepts comparatively to multicultural societies which do not have federal structures (for example, Belgium), in order to assess the possibilities for adoption and workability of federal forms. And comparatively homogenous societies with federal structures, such as Australia and the United States, can be analyzed to assess whether federalism can survive over the long run in a system which lacks the solid underpinnings of multicultural societies within federal structures.

4 Federalism and the Public Policy Process*

Donald V. Smiley

The major concern of this study is the making and implementing of public policy within the framework of Canadian federal institutions. It is focused primarily on relations between executive officials, both elected and appointed, of federal and provincial governments. Under the circumstances which have developed, each jurisdiction retains responsibilities for broad areas of public functions but there are an increasing number of situations in which the action of each in pursuing its objectives impinges on the activities of the other. The ways by which the central and regional administrations respond to this kind of mutual dependence have been neglected by students of the Canadian and other federal systems.

Traditional discussions of federalism emphasize the co-ordinate and independent powers of federal and regional governments rather than their interdependence. According to the juridical analysis found in the textbooks of law and political science, there are three possible ways of legally organizing a particular territory. The first alternative is unitary—the government whose jurisdiction includes the whole territory is sovereign and whatever other public authorities there may be are legally subordinate to it. At the other end of the spectrum is the confederacy where the powers of the central jurisdiction are held at the discretion of the regional governments. The third alternative is federalism and there would be broad agreement among constitutional scholars that a federal constitution has these characteristics:

1. The totality of governmental powers which can legally be wielded within a territory are divided by a written constitution between a central and two or more regional governments.

2. Those parts of the constitution which delineate governmental power are not subject to interpretation or amendment by the unilateral action of the executive or legislature of either level of jurisdiction.

3. At least one of the legislative chambers of the federal government is chosen by popular election.

4. Individual residents of the federation are directly subject to the laws of both the central and the regional governments.

---

* From Donald V. Smiley, *Constitutional Adaption and Canadian Federalism Since 1945* (Ottawa, Queen's Printer, 1970), pp. 1-8. Volume IV of the Documents of the Royal Commission on Bilingualism and Biculturalism. Reprinted by permission of the author and Information Canada.

DONALD V. SMILEY – Professor of Political Science, University of Toronto.

The kind of definition given above is static and concerns the formal constitutional features of federal systems regardless of how these systems operate. Using this defintion one could read the constitutions of various countries and intergovernmental associations and quickly and mechanically determine which qualified as federations. In most cases, however, the actual workings of political systems diverge widely from what one would expect by a literal reading of their constitutions. K. C. Wheare, whose influential book emphasizes the co-ordinate authority and mutual independence of central and regional governments as the essential features of federalism, recognizes this difficulty and makes an important distinction between "federal constitutions" and "federal governments."[1] According to Wheare's analysis, the Canadian constitution is only "quasi-federal" because of the powers conferred upon the federal executive to disallow provincial legislation and to appoint the provincial lieutenant-governors and judges of the principal provincial courts. Examining the actual practices of Canadian government, however, he concludes that, ". . . although the Canadian constitution is quasi-federal in law, it is predominantly federal in practice. Or to put it another way, although Canada has not a federal constitution, it has a federal government."[2] This conclusion seems to be deficient because the somewhat facile dichotomy between the law of the constitution and the practices of government allows one to avoid analysis of the intricate relationships between the two kinds of matters when studying particular political systems. Furthermore, the undue emphasis on the co-ordinate and independent relationships of the central and regional governments predisposes the student either to ignore patterns of interactions between the two levels which are so much a part of the workings of established federations or to consider these interactions as somehow a deviation from the federal principle.

Federalism may thus usefully be considered as a continuing process by which governmental powers are exercised. In his recent work Carl J. Friedrich contrasts federalism as "consensual world order" with imperialism as "coercive world order" and he states:

> . . . Federalism should not be considered a term for a static pattern, designating a particular and precisely fixed division of powers between governmental levels. Instead, "federalism" seems the most suitable term by which to designate the process of federalizing a political community, that is to say the process by which a number of separate political organizations, be they states or any other kind of association, enter into arrangements for working out solutions, adopting joint policies and making joint decisions on joint problems.
>
> Conversely, federalism is the process by which a hitherto unitary political community, as it becomes differentiated into a number of separate and distinct political communities, achieves a new organization in which the differentiated communities, now separately organized, become

---

[1] K. C. Wheare, *Federal Government,* 4th Ed. (London, 1963), Chapter II.
[2] *Ibid.,* p. 20.

capable of working out separately and on their own problems they no longer have in common. It is not only a matter of decision-making, but of the entire range of power and its exercise. . . . The federalizing process accompanies, so to speak, the communal development as its organizational counterpart. If values, interests and beliefs exhibit a stable and structured pattern in which the commonly shared values, interests and beliefs are counterbalanced by values, interests and beliefs that are not shared, though territorially distributed, then a federal development becomes possible.[3]

Friedrich regards as an essential element of federalism the constitutional protection of each level of the political order against the other. His definition thus excludes instances of international relations or senior-local authority relations where such legal protection does not exist. A recent book on the American federal union concludes with the most useful definition of federalism from the public-policy-process viewpoint that I have found:

Federalism is a system of government in which central and regional authorities are linked in a mutually interdependent political relationship; in this system a balance is maintained such that neither level of government becomes dominant to the extent that it can dictate the decisions of the other, but each can influence, bargain with, and persuade the other. Usually, but not necessarily, this system will be related to a constitutional structure establishing an independent legal existence for both central and regional governments, and providing that neither shall be legally subordinate to the other. The functions of government will be distributed between these levels (exclusively, competitively, or co-operatively, initially perhaps by a constitutional document, but thereafter by a political process, involving where appropriate the judiciary; in this process the political interdependence of the two levels of government is of the first importance in order to prevent one level absorbing all effective decision-making power.[4]

Established federal systems are characterized by the growing importance of the relations between the executives of the central and regional governments. Several interrelated influences contribute to the development of what might be called "executive federalism."

1. The constitutions of most federations have proved somewhat resistant to evolution through amendment or changing patterns of judicial review. Amending procedures in most established federal systems are inflexible, i.e. small minorities can block attempted changes in the text of the constitution. For several reasons the courts in several federations now play a more restricted role than previously in maintaining the federal balance. Thus political and administrative processes have become the chief instruments of change.

2. The increasing interdependence of modern social and economic life makes it impossible for the regional governments to carry out their responsibilities in the absence of appropriate action by the other regional jurisdictions

---

[3] C. J. Friedrich, *Man and His Government* (New York, 1963), pp. 594-95.
[4] M. J. C. Vile, *The Structure of American Federalism* (Oxford, 1961), p. 199.

and the federal authorities. Maurice Lamontagne wrote of Canada a decade ago ". . . . l'attribution de responsabilités exclusives aux différents gouvernements n'est pas possible parce que la politique économique et sociale est devenue quasi indivisible."[5]

3. Nationalist and egalitarian sentiments focused on the federations as such have propelled federal governments into collaboration with regional governments to establish minimum country-wide standards in public services regarded as being within the social minimum. Under the constitutions of most federations the regional authorities are assigned the primary responsibilities for health, welfare and education. The only way that this circumstance can be reconciled with the demand for equal services on a national basis is through intergovernmental collaboration.

4. Contemporary rates of taxation and the deliberate use of fiscal policy to provide for economic stability and growth mean that particular tax and spending policies of one level have consequences for the other. The central and regional jurisdictions increasingly compete for tax sources. Federal governments, like other national governments assume responsibility for over-all economic direction. This direction will be ineffective if appropriate actions are not taken by regional and local authorities. In Canada, as in other federal systems, the fiscal relations between the central and regional governments have become increasingly complex and increasingly crucial for the stability of the federation.

5. The widening scope of public activity gives rise to an increasing number of situations where federal and regional objectives must be coordinated if intolerable stresses on the system are not to result. The old classical federalism in which each level carried out the functions assigned to it by the constitution in relative isolation from the other had some relevance to a period when governmental responsibilities were limited in scope and importance. It has no relevance today.

The relations between the executives of the federal and regional governments are extraordinarily complex in most federations. Many of these interactions are of an informal and *ad hoc* nature. Furthermore, in many matters the significant decision-making units are not the federal and regional administrations but functional groups constituted across jurisdictional lines. Edward W. Weidner after several intensive studies of federal-state relations in the American system wrote about functionalism in this way:

> It is a thesis of the present discussion that in the federal system in the United States there are relatively few direct clashes or compromises between state and national governments on large issues of domestic policy. Furthermore, in the administrative sphere positive cooperation is the pattern rather than aloofness or conflict. The disagreements and conflicts that do arise and that may be encourged by federalism's structural features are not basically clashes between state and national

---

[5] Maurice Lamontagne, *Le Fédéralisme canadien* (Quebec, 1954), p. 245.

governments. Instead, they are clashes between much smaller groups of people and the opposing groups are concentrated within a single governmental level as often as not.[6]

Similarly, in a 1963 study I found that in the administration of federal conditional grants to the Canadian provinces the attitudes and interests of programme specialists and financial officials were very different and that conflicts related to the grant-in-aid arrangements characteristically resulted in divisions along these lines rather than between federal and provincial governments as such.[7]

Although the analysis of public policy processes seems to me a useful focus for studying contemporary federalism, it is a partial approach. It concentrates on a relatively small number of executive officials who devise and implement public policy. However, political scientists increasingly question the validity of studying the law and practices of government in isolation from the attitudes, social groupings, economic structures and so on which condition and are conditioned by governmental activity.[8] This study examines how policy is made and implemented in the Canadian federal system. Another more difficult kind of investigation would concentrate on the sociology and politics of Canadian federalism. An American scholar has asserted: "The essence of federalism lies not in the institutional or constitutional structure but in the country itself. Federal government is a device by which the federal qualities of a society are articulated and protected."[9] In all developed societies there are groups striving to secure governmental actions that they perceive to be favourable to their aspirations and interests. Federal governments can be sustained only in societies which are themselves federal, that is societies where people believe that their interests in respect to a number of important matters are specific to geographical divisions of the country rather than to the country as a whole. On the other hand, federalism has little relevance if the major incidences of political differentiation relate to class, religious, occupational or other groupings which are not territorially located. In his study of four Latin-American republics with federal constitutions (Mexico, Argentina, Brazil and Venezuela) William S. Stokes concludes that certain economic and cultural features make federalism as government in the usual sense impractical in these countries:

> Most Latin Americans are conditioned by their historical traditions and social and economic institutions to understand and accept con-

---

[6] E. W. Weidner, "Decision-Making in a Federal System", in Arthur W. Macmahon (ed.), *Federalism, Mature and Emergent* (New York, 1955), p. 363.

[7] D. V. Smiley, *Conditional Grants and Canadian Federalism* (Canadian Tax Foundation, Canadian Tax Paper no. 32, Toronto, 1963), pp. 37-42.

[8] One of the most distinguished efforts in this direction is the Little, Brown series in Comparative Politics under the editorship of Gabriel A. Almond, James S. Coleman and Lucien W. Pye. See particularly G. A. Almond and Sidney Verba, *The Civic Culture* (Princeton, 1963) and the abridgement under the same name in the Little, Brown series (Boston, 1965).

[9] W. S. Livingston, *Federalism and Constitutional Change* (Oxford, 1956), p. 2.

centrated, centralized power, usually of a highly personalized sort. The strong, frequently exalted role of the father in the family, the importance of the elite in the class system, the honor, dignity, power and influence of the *doctor* from the *aula* (lecture hall), the significance of centralized leadership in the Church, the paramountcy of the "general" in politics, and the position of the public and private monopolist in the economic system — these characteristics of Hispanic culture all suggest powerful, centralized government. In addition, the political experience and traditions of hundreds of years were with a powerful monarchy operating by means of a centralized administrative hierarchy. The modern constitutions all provide for "interventionist" states.[10]

Federal governmental institutions to be stable must correspond with particular kinds of social structures and cultural predispositions so that regionally-based particularisms can find an outlet while making possible common action in respect to matters where these particularisms are of less importance.

The sociological and governmental aspects of federalism are thus intimately related. When relatively stable federal systems have been established, some groups come to press their claims primarily through the federal government and others through the states or provinces. In the United States, for example, those hostile to the public regulations of business usually favour "states' " rights while those striving for civil rights for the Negro look to action from the federal legislature, executive and courts. If most of the influential groups in any federation came to look exclusively to either one level of government or the other it is not likely that federalism could long survive, although the federal rituals might remain. But once the division of legislative and executive powers between the central and regional governments is established, there are influences at work to sustain the federal quality of the society itself and they create new country-wide and regional centres of influence where none existed before. The Report of the Committee on Manitoba's Future published in 1963 stated:

> The Province of Manitoba is more than a political division of the nation. During the more than 90 years since its establishment a distinctive social and economic entity has been developed within the essentially artificial political boundaries. When the Province joined the Canadian Confederation, "Manitoba" was not much more than a block of land surrounded by lines on the map. In the intervening years, however, it has become an organic unit; trading patterns have developed, transportation systems have been established, educational and administrative systems have been organized, and all the other social, economic and political institutions of a modern society have evolved. The people of Manitoba, now, therefore, are responsible for dealing with many of their own problems. . . .[11]

---

[10] W. S. Stokes, "The Centralized Federal Republics of Latin America", in G. C. S. Benson *et al., Essays on Federalism* (Claremont: California, Institute for Studies in Federalism, 1961), p. 93.

[11] Committee on Manitoba's Economic Future, *Report* (Winnipeg, 1963), p. 111.

The establishment of important centres of political power thus provides the setting for the growth of other influences within the same territorial limits and social and governmental federalism reinforce one another. Conversely, a federation under great stress may be expected to feature tensions in both its public and private institutions. The drives for provincial autonomy in contemporary Quebec have corresponded with influences toward a greater measure of independence for the French Canadian elements in nongovernmental organizations. These influences in some cases (such as those involving university students, the Junior Chambers of Commerce and the municipal associations) have culminated in the withdrawal of the French-speaking members.[12] In the period immediately preceding the outbreak of the American Civil War many formerly national organizations such as churches and political parties separated into northern and southern components.

There has been almost no systematic examination of the kinds and distributions of popular attitudes which are compatible with the maintenance of federalism in government. Some years ago J. A. Corry spoke of the "stresses and conflicts" in the Canadian federal system "which need to be negotiated and compromised (by the governments) in *ad hoc* arrangements, particularly where the electorates do not seem disposed to say clearly whether they are federal or unitary in spirit."[13] Does contemporary cooperative federalism require widespread popular attitudes which are pragmatic and equivocal as to the appropriate level of government for carrying out particular public responsibilities? It seems unlikely that the federation could survive if the prevailing attitudes came to the point of considering one or the other level more legitimate in respect to all public activities believed important. If there were a consensus throughout the country about this matter the system might either disintegrate in a peaceful and orderly way or evolve into a unitary state. It is more likely, however, that no such agreement will be established and if the conflicts about legitimacy are pushed to the limits we have a "recipe for civil war."

It is common to assign the political parties a central role in the maintenance of federal systems. The usual analysis in Canada and the United States has been that these unions can be sustained only if there are country-wide parties drawing strength from all regions.[14] In examining eight established federations the American political scientist William H. Riker addresses himself to the question, "What maintains federalism?" and systematically dismisses the

---

[12] Professors Vincent Lemieux and John Meisel have undertaken a study of the bicultural aspects of certain non-governmental associations in Canada for the Royal Commission on Bilingualism and Biculturalism.

[13] J. A. Corry, "Constitutional Trends and Federalism", in A. R. M. Lower *et al.*, *Evolving Canadian Federalism* (Durham, N.C., 1958), p. 141.

[14] See, for example, Herbert Agar, *The Price of Union* (Boston, 1950) for a presentation of this hypothesis as it relates to the United States. In Canada, Frank Underhill has been the most persuasive apologist for the bi-national parties. See *In Search of Canadian Liberalism* (Toronto, 1960) and *The Image of Confederation: The Massey Lectures, 1963* (Toronto, Canadian Broadcasting Corporation, 1964).

arguments that the crucial elements are the sharing of administrative responsibilities, dual citizen loyalties or the existence of dissident provincial patriotism.[15] He concludes:

> Whatever the general social conditions, if any, that sustain the federal bargain, there is one institutional condition that controls the nature of the bargain in all the instances here examined and in all the others with which I am familiar. This is the structure of the party system, which may be regarded as the main variable intervening between the background social conditions and the specific nature of the federal bargain.[16]

According to Riker's analysis, a federation is centralized or "peripheralized" to the degree that "the parties organized to operate the central government control the parties organized to operate the constituent governments."[17] Although federal-provincial party relationships have received little systematic attention in Canada,[18] my tentative conclusion is that executives of the federal and provincial governments, working in isolation or in collaboration, have assumed the crucial role in effecting changes in the political system. On the other hand, the influences pushing these executives towards federal-provincial integration are not reinforced by corresponding pressures on the party organizations. Because of this cooperative federalism may fail.

The preceding brief analysis of the sociology and politics of federalism is meant to suggest only that the public policy approach is a limited one and that executive federalism cannot realistically be considered in isolation from the other influences impinging on the maintenance of federal institutions. The underlying assumptions of this study are, first, that federal systems, like other institutions, must have the capacity to adapt to changing circumstances if they are to survive and, second, that it is more doubtful than most of us would have believed a few years ago that the Canadian federation can develop the necessary resources of adaptability. For analytical purposes, I make a distinction between two kinds of processes of evolution. The first I call "devices of adjustment"—the procedures by which the respective powers, resources and responsibilities assigned to the federal and provincial governments by the original constitution are dynamically redelineated as new circumstances arise. The second category of processes is named "devices of articulation"—the procedures through which the activities of the two levels are related to one another by their respective executives. It seems reasonable to believe that a

---

[15] W. H. Riker, *Federalism: Origin, Operation, Significance* (Boston, 1964), particularly pp. 135-36.

[16] *Ibid.*, p. 136.

[17] *Ibid.*, p. 129.

[18] For one of the few systematic efforts in this direction see E. R. Black, "Federal Strains within a Canadian Party", *Dalhousie Review*, XLV (1965), pp. 306-23. More recently Khayyam Paltiel has made a provocative analysis of the relation between party finances and the maintenance of Canadian federalism, "Federalism and Party Finance: A Preliminary Sounding", in Committee on Election Expenses, *Studies in Canadian Party Finance* (Ottawa, 1966), pp. 1-21.

federal system could not survive under modern circumstances unless it developed resources of flexibility through both kinds of devices. We have only the crudest of measures to determine whether a federation is responding effectively to the demands made upon it. In a negative sense one might judge that the resources of adaptability in a particular federal system were being strained if any or all of the following circumstances existed:

1. If no political party were able to draw significant strength from all regions of the country. In any federation much of the political conflict at the federal level will revolve about divergent regional interests. When at least one of the parties comprehends these interests, however, tolerable compromises can ordinarily be worked out through the procedures of intraparty accommodation. When no such inclusive party exists these procedures cannot be used for this purpose.

2. If there were widespread public attitudes which attribute to the inherent nature of federal institutions those deprivations that people feel strongly about. Federations, like other human institutions, can survive only if people regard them as legitimate.

3. If most of the politically influential elements of the country sought their objectives exclusively or almost exclusively through one or the other level of government. Such a situation attenuates the tension between national and regional interests necessary to the maintenance of federalism.

Part Two

Canadian Federalism: An Overview

5 The Five Faces of Federalism*

J. R. Mallory

Canadian federalism is different things at different times. It is also different things to different people. This is not the result of widespread error but of simple fact, for political institutions which accommodate diversity will reflect the dimensions which are vital to the actors who work them.

In the past century it is possible to see five different forms of Canadian federalism which may be described roughly as follows: the quasi-federalism (to use Dr. Wheare's description) which was most marked in the Macdonald era; federalism of the classic type characterized by the co-ordinate and autonomous relationship of the central and regional organs; emergency federalism, most obviously in being during the periods of extreme centralization in wartime; the co-operative federalism which reached its zenith in the period since 1945; and the "double-image" federalism which includes both the straight-forward central-regional relationship between the central and provincial organs and a special relationship between French and English which to some extent transcends the other. While these various forms can be made to fit approximately into different historical periods, they overlap one another and do not in fact conform to a clear stage-by-stage development.

QUASI-FEDERALISM

In 1867, the new Dominion of Canada did not begin to operate as a full-blown federal structure. There were several obvious reasons for this. Canadians are always sensitive to the influence of the United States, and the American federal system was at that time in some disarray. The peril of state's rights and secession was manifest, and there were not a few of the Fathers of Confederation who noted with concern that state's rights afforded an opportunity for such democratic excesses as the spoliation of the vested rights of property. The new federal government in the first blush of its power in Ottawa was both a national coalition and a concentration of political talent which was bound to leave little political weight in the provinces. Furthermore, the opening of the West led to the creation or admission of new provinces whose early relationship with Ottawa was a colonial one.[1]

---

[1] An excellent discussion of the theme that the relationship was essentially colonial is found in V. C. Fowke's *Canadian Agricultural Policy* (Toronto, 1947).

* From P.-A. Crepeau & C. B. Macpherson (eds.), *The Future of Canadian Federalism* (Toronto, University of Toronto Press, 1965), pp. 3-15. Reprinted by permission of the author and the University of Toronto Press.

J. R. MALLORY – Professor of Political Science, McGill University.

The influence of the forms of government on political action should never be underestimated. The "colonial" relationship with the provinces was a natural one—much more natural than the "co-ordinate and autonomous" relationship more appropriate to a federal system. Macdonald and his ministers had grown up politically in a system in which the governor still played a role as an imperial presence difficult to appreciate today. Most of them had been in politics long enough to remember when the governor still actively participated in policy discussion with his council, and before the cabinet had completely split off from the formal executive. For a wide range of matters that were beyond the reach of local self-government or were ones in which there was an imperial interest, they were accustomed to the idea that the governor possessed power as well as influence. In the British North America Act, the lieutenant-governor was just as much an agent of the federal government as the governor general was an agent of the British government.

It therefore seems more appropriate to think of the dominion-provincial relationship at that time as similar to the relationship of the imperial government with a colony enjoying limited self-government. This was most obviously true in provinces like Manitoba and British Columbia where the weakness of political parties and the lack of political and administrative experience meant that the provincial governments were in a state of tutelage. The difference between these provinces and the older provinces in this matter was a difference of degree.

Dr. Wheare, in discussing the nature of Canadian federalism, attaches some importance to the ambivalent role of the lieutenant-governor and concludes that the Canadian constitution is in form only quasi-federal.[2] During the first couple of decades after Confederation, when the federal government frequently resorted to disallowance and reservation to curb the growth of provincial powers of self-government, "quasi-federal" understates the case. The relationship was much more like that of mother-country and colony, and the institutions of control were essentially those of colonial rule. But there was the inescapable fact that the constitution was indeed federal, and the federal distribution of power nourished the strength of the provinces as the strains brought about by race, religion, economic exploitation, and the sheer impossibility of running such a disparate country further diffused power in the system.

Nevertheless, this quasi-imperial relationship was a long time dying. The long retention by the federal government of administrative control over the natural resources of the western provinces emphasized their colonial status. The rise of agrarian populism through the progressive movement was a revolt against the exploitation of the west by the banks, the railroads, and the tariff-protected industries of the east. When populism went too far, as it did under William Aberhart's Social Credit administration in Alberta, it was curbed by the old imperial remedies of reservation and disallowance.

[2] K. C. Wheare, *Federal Government,* 3rd Ed. (London, 1953), pp. 19-21.

CLASSICAL FEDERALISM

A federal constitution is in essence a division of jurisdiction between equally autonomous bodies. But no constitution can express, in precise detail, a distribution of authority so exact that no doubts can arise about which of the two legislative structures, central and regional, is within its powers in a particular regulatory statute. Some agency, external to both legislatures, must hold the balance between them. It was natural in Canada, as it was in the United States, that this role should be assumed by the courts, for both countries are part of a constitutional tradition that insulates the judicial process from the politics of the day. Furthermore, disputes of this kind— about the powers of constituted authorities—are justiciable.

This is not the place to consider this large and intricate subject, but only to make some general observations on its effect on the system and the boundaries within which it operates. There is one important difference between the role of the Supreme Court of the United States and the role of the Judicial Committee of the Privy Council, and that is in their approach to the problem of adjudication. Following the bold initiative of Chief Justice Marshall, the Supreme Court has approached its role in a spirit of constructive statecraft. "We must never forget," said Marshall in *McCulloch* v. *Maryland,* "that it is a constitution we are expounding."[3] Accordingly the Court has not hesitated to reverse itself in the light of changed circumstances, and to play the major role in adapting the constitution to the changing needs of succeeding generations.

A Canadian court might well have followed the same path. Much of the law is experience, and Canadian judges would no doubt have been more sensitive to the strains and the changing patterns of Canadian life that the Privy Council.[4] To the remoteness of the Privy Council and its reluctance to engage in judicial statecraft was added a further difficulty—the inability of English judges to understand the basic fact about federal constitutions, i.e., that a distribution of power written into the constitution is fixed and almost unalterable. In the United Kingdom it was a perfectly proper exercise of judicial self-restraint to take the view that, if the purpose of Parliament was frustrated by lack of foresight in drafting so that the courts found a section to be meaningless, it was not the business of the courts to interpose themselves and say, "This is what Parliament meant to accomplish by this act, and we shall interpret it accordingly," but rather to interpret the words narrowly and as they found them. If this is not what Parliament wanted, then it has the right to amend the act itself. This is all very well in a unitary state, but in a federal system, a construction of the constitution which is too narrow, or wrong-headed, may do great harm, since constitutional amendment is extremely difficult.

---

[3] Wheat, 316, at p. 407 (1819).
[4] This has often been argued, but never more persuasively than by Alexander Smith in *The Commerce Power in Canada and the United States* (Toronto, 1963) where by reference to early cases he shows the Canadian courts appealing to history and experience in a way which would horrify "black-letter" lawyers.

There is no general agreement about the general effect of the interpretation of the Canadian constitution by the Judicial Committee of the Privy Council. It has been argued that the very wide meaning given to property and civil rights, together with the emasculation of the federal power of trade and commerce and the relegation of the "peace, order and good government" concept to a wartime emergency power, was clearly contrary to the intention of the Fathers of Confederation to create a strong central authority and to confine the provinces to local matters.[5] Whether this was the result of ignorance or high imperial policy is no longer of much importance. It is more than likely that the narrow construction placed on federal powers was the only reaction which could have been expected from common law judges in a period when the courts, in the United States as well as the United Kingdom, were responding sympathetically to the litigious pressure of powerful economic interests intent on resisting the growing role of the state in limiting economic liberty.[6] In any event, by the inter-war period the courts by using a "watertight compartment" theory of jurisdiction, had succeeded in interdicting effective action by the federal authorities to deal with the economic problems of the depression.

Whatever its consequences, what had evolved was federalism of the classic type, if I may borrow Principal Corry's phraseology, in which power is allocated to the central and provincial authorities so that each enjoys an exclusive jurisdiction, with disputes about the margins of power settled finally by the courts. This has certain advantages. It entrenches provincial rights, and at the same time it confines the provinces to their sphere. Disputes are settled by the impartial arbitration of the courts, as guardians of the constitution. It has its disadvantages. Since federal constitutions are notoriously hard to amend, the only dynamic element is the extent to which the courts are able to adjust the meaning of the constitution to face the facts of social change. That is what Dicey meant when he said that federations substitute litigation for legislation. But the courts are not the first to perceive the outlines of social change. And while the Supreme Court of the United States has shown considerable capacity to "follow the election returns," the Judicial Committee of the Privy Council was so deficient in both sense and sensibility that the allocation of power in the constitution, by the end of the 1930's, had achieved a remarkable incongruity between the resources, capacities, and responsibilities of the federal and provincial governments.

---

[5] Thus Sir John A. Macdonald said, "The primary error at the formation of their constitution was that each state reserved to itself all sovereign rights, save the small portion delegated. We must reverse this process by strengthening the General Government and conferring on the Provincial bodies only such powers as may be required for local purposes." Sir Joseph Pope, ed., *Confederation Documents* (Toronto, 1895) p. 14, n. 4.
[6] Cf. J. R. Mallory, *Social Credit and the Federal Power in Canada* (Toronto, 1954), *passim*.

EMERGENCY FEDERALISM

But the Canadian constitution in one respect was totally lacking in the rigidity of its federal arrangements. This had not been by design, for there is nothing in either the Confederation Debates or the BNA Act itself which addresses itself to the distribution of power in an emergency. It was the courts themselves which made this dangerous opening in the system. Nobody before 1914 foresaw the effect of modern war on constitutional government or on the settled Victorian not'ons of propriety about the role of government in economic affairs. But when war came and Parliament abdicated to the executive the vast powers to make regulations for the peace, order, and good government of Canada, the federal government assumed a wide range of powers over matters of civil rights and property which in peacetime belonged to the sacrosanct powers of the provinces. And the courts gave their blessing to the proposition that the federal distribution of power was a peacetime luxury which must be foregone in wartime. Building on a dictum of Lord Watson in the *Local Prohibition Case,* they found that wartime was a situation which transcended the terms of sections 91 and 92 altogether and one which, in effect, made Canada a unitary state for the duration.

When the First World War was over the courts hurriedly began to erect a fence around this dangerous doctrine, to the exasperation of many Canadian lawyers during the depression years, and they stubbornly refused to seek a more flexible formula which would allow the central authorities power to deal with lesser emergencies. For the trouble with the emergency doctrine was that it went too far. It seemed to be all or nothing. And it went so far that it is not difficult to sense their reluctance to apply it. This is no doubt why Lord Haldane was led into the entertaining speculation in the *Snider Case* that the Judicial Committee had upheld federal jurisdiction in *Russell* v. *The Queen* only on the assumption that the country was confronted by such an epidemic of intemperance as to constitute a national disaster.

The emergency doctrine, in the form in which Lord Haldane left it, is one that we can well do without. For events have shown that it was of little value in conferring necessary jurisdiction on Parliament except in wartime and in the short period necessary to wind up wartime controls after the end of hostilities. From this difficulty we were extricated by the unexpected wisdom of Lord Simon who demonstrated, in the *Canada Temperance Federation Case,* that "emergency" is not just a rather frightening source of absolute federal power in wartime, but rather an aspect of things. Categories of the constitution are not absolutes which are mutually exclusive, as between the federal and provincial authorities. Each in its own way, and for its own purposes, may legislate about things which properly concern it. The facts have always been this way, but they have sometimes been neglected. For example, the courts early rejected the idea (in *Bank of Toronto* v. *Lambe*) that a province could not tax a bank just because it was a bank and therefore under federal jurisdiction.

In any event, the elaborate reasoning of the emergency doctrine may have been unnecessary since Parliament has exclusive power to legislate for defence, and it is obvious today that this is a concept that goes far beyond military arrangements for defence against an enemy. It is concerned with a very wide range of economic activity and, in these days of subversion on a massive scale, with internal order as well. It is noteworthy that the Essential Materials (Defence) Act (1950-51) was founded on a broad view of the defence power, and so was its successor, the Defence Production Act of 1951. In the federal constitutions of Australia and the United States the defence power has turned out to be the most powerful centripetal force in the constitution.[7]

One of the most striking developments of the past quarter of a century has been the decline in the role of the courts as arbiters of the balance of the federal constitution. "The courts are retiring, or being retired, from their posts as the supervisors of the balance," as Principal Corry notes in a perceptive analysis of modern Canadian federalism.[8] He attributes this change to an alteration in the interests and attitude of the business élites. The central role of the courts in the half-century before was brought about, as I have argued elsewhere,[9] by the persistent resistance of the business community to regulation by the state. Great aggregations of economic power have a strong vested interest in stability; they have come to accept the primacy of the federal government in regulating their affairs, and they find it better to exert influence at the summit of the political system rather than to fight every extension of state power in the courts. Since they cannot beat the welfare state, they have decided to join it.

CO-OPERATIVE FEDERALISM

At the same time there has been, as a result of a spectacular refinement of the techniques of economic and fiscal policy since the war, a quiet revolution in the structure of Canadian federalism. A whole new set of institutional arrangements has grown up under the name of "co-operative federalism." In spite of the separate and co-ordinate division between the authority of the provinces and the central government enunciated in the law of the constitution, the demands of modern government and the immense financial resources of the central authority have forced an incestuous relationship in which administrative co-operation has become an effective device for control and initiative from the centre. This system is the only effective answer to the size and complexity of modern economic institutions and everyone now has such a strong vested interest in this system that no one, Dr. Corry argues, can afford to rock the boat.

The essence of co-operative federalism in Canada is this: while the central and regional legislatures nominally retain their separate jurisdictions over different aspects of the same subject, there is close contact and discussion beween ministers and civil servants of both levels of government so that even changes

---

[7] Cf. Bora Laskin, *Canadian Constitutional Law*, 2nd ed. (Toronto, 1960), pp. 242-43.
[8] J. A. Corry, "Constitutional Trends and Federalism," in Paul Fox (ed.), *Politics: Canada* (Toronto, 1963), p. 36.
[9] *Social Credit and the Federal Power in Canada.*

in legislation are the result of joint decisions. Since 1945, says Professor Smiley, the most obvious characteristic of Canadian federalism has been "a process of continuous and piecemeal adjustment between the two levels of government, which is still going on. To an overwhelming degree, these adjustments have come about through interaction between federal and provincial executives."[10] There are three principal areas of co-ordination. The first is through continuous consultation of officials on joint programs. In these consultations there appears to be a surprising degree of harmony, partly, no doubt because there is a broad consensus among the economists about the goals of economic policy and partly because all officials are inclined to see problems in a practical and pragmatic way. The second area of co-operation is through the delegation by Parliament of regulatory functions to provincial agencies, a technique which gets around the bar against delegation of legislative authority from one level of government to another. The third "device of flexibility" is through federal spending on matters which fall within provincial and/or municipal jurisdiction.

The advantages of these arrangements are apparent. The "artificial" division of powers in the constitution, conceived before the dawn of the welfare state, can be ignored in achieving progress and uniformity comparable to that normally realizable only in a unitary state. The higher administrative skills and deeper purse of the federal government result in better schemes. Finally, the obstruction to geographical mobility imposed by tying the citizen—like a medieval serf—to the area of land from which his pension, his hospitalization, and his other welfare benefits come, is removed.

The benefits of co-operative federalism are not achieved without serious costs. The joint-cost schemes involve the federal government in very heavy fixed commitments, though, since the Dominion-Provincial Conference at Quebec in April 1964, discussions have begun for ultimate federal withdrawal from some of them. A further disadvantage is that the financial and constitutional context of the arrangements has made it impossible to take into account differing provincial fiscal capacity so that, while rich provinces can participate readily, the poorer provinces must divert a substantial share of their resources to providing their share of the cost. Lastly, the main drift of these programs has been in the direction of health and welfare services.

The result has been seriously to limit provincial autonomy. Provincial priorities are distorted by the inability of a province to forgo, for political reasons, a program which may inhibit financing its other obligations. The result has been to starve areas of provincial jurisdiction in which the federal government is not, for various reasons, interested. While a vast amount of time is spent in intergovernmental consultation, it nevertheless remains true that provinces find long-term budgeting virtually impossible, because they cannot forsee where the lightning of federal generosity will strike next.

---

[10] D. V. Smiley, "The Rowell-Sirois Report, Provincial Autonomy, and Post-War Federalism", *Canadian Journal of Economics and Political Science,* Vol. XXCIII no. 1, p. 54.

A reaction against these cosy arrangements is now in train. Significantly it is led by Quebec, but Quebec is not alone in seeking to reverse the trend to centralize all economic and social policy in Ottawa. It is not improbable that the practical advantages of centralization, which English-speaking Canadians would probably accept, would have led—as it had done in the United States and Australia—to the growing obsolescence of federalism. But Canada is not the same kind of federal state as the United States or Australia, where the growing homogeneity of the population is likely to lead inevitably to national integration. The difference is what is now usually described as the French-Canadian fact.

DOUBLE-IMAGE FEDERALISM

The survival of French Canada as a fact has depended more on a sustaining national myth and on political power than it has on constitutional guarantees. For the Canadian constitution does not, except to a very limited extent, support the claims which French Canadians regard as necessary to their survival as a distinct group. In the matter of their rights in the Manitoba school question, or in their claim to retain French as a language of instruction in Ontario separate schools, they were either over-ridden by an unsympathetic majority or told by the courts that minority educational rights in the constitution were essentially questions of religion and not of language.

Indeed, one of the most striking things about French-Canadian rights and aspirations in the constitution is that the courts have played little or no role in protecting them. This is one of the striking differences between the American and Canadian constitutions. Where the American constitution extends its guarantees across the whole range of the social order, so that it is the Supreme Court which is presiding over the orderly assimilation of Negroes to full equality as citizens, the Canadian constitution provides no such protection. It confines itself essentially to the distribution of power between two levels of sovereign legislatures, and has little to say on any other rights than the rights of legislatures. In this respect it is indeed a constitution "similar in Principle to that of the United Kingdom." As de Tocqueville said of the British constitution, "elle n'existe point."

It is for this eminently practical reason that French Canadians have adopted as a national strategy the building up and guarding of the security of their fortress-province. The constitution has made such a strategy unavoidable, and the only possible defence against the aggressive nationalism of the dominant English-speaking majority. For even the most liberal of English-Canadians have seldom accepted the "French fact" as more than a transitory source of trouble and discomfort.

There has been among English-speaking Canadians an element of deep-seated Protestant suspicion of the Roman Catholic Church, a feeling that the French tongue is an anomaly in an English-speaking continent, a feeling that the French are both backward and reactionary and therefore an enemy to the forces of progress, and a touch of the North American radical belief that a good state could be built in the New World only by destroying the cultural roots of "foreigners" who must be assimilated in order to build a new Canada.

Against this persistant pressure the French-Canadian reaction was to husband their political strength, to limit as far as possible the impact of the twentieth century on the *habitant* whose backwardness and ignorance—it was thought—would be a solid political barrier against the secular and integrating forces of urban industrial society. Thus Duplessis pursued a policy of immobilism, staying aloof from federally sponsored welfare programs, leaving the educational system in a state of inanation on the grounds that it was bound to develop the kind of social leadership which would destroy him, and harrying those organizations, such as the trade unions, that seemed to be enemies of the traditional centres of community authority.

And yet in the end he could not stem the tide. At his death an irreversible political change began. The most striking change is the alteration in the pattern of power relations in the French-Canadian community. New élite groups of managers and technicians are challenging the traditional leaders. The intellectual of an earlier generation could accept the romantic myth of the mystical virtue of subsistence agriculture as the source of the political and moral strength of French Canada. The intellectual of today has no patience with a dream of bucolic *survivance*. The French-Canadian community has developed a new set of expectations from government, and looks to the power of the state to satisfy their new wants and to bring the economic development which will enlarge opportunities for all. For them, these things must be done by their own French-Canadian state of Quebec, and not by Ottawa. For this there are two reasons: the new élites wish to share in the management of the new society, and —as they say—Quebec has much ground to make up in order to pull level with the rest of Canada.

It is these new forces which have created the latest crisis in Canadian federalism. The growing centralization of the past fifty years created no great problems in Quebec as long as the province was seeking to contract out of the twentieth century. But with the French-Canadian community determined to use to the full the resources of the provincial government to achieve a national revival a whole range of problems has emerged in Canadian federalism which will require substantial readjustments in the system. The mechanics of this readjustment will not be easy, and the issues at stake are very large indeed.

The federal government must not lightly weaken its fiscal and monetary powers, for it alone has the capacity and the constitutional right to deal with problems of major economic policy—foreign trade, stability, economic growth. It alone can prevent us becoming, as Mr. Pearson said, "a country of developed and underdeveloped areas—Cadillac areas and cart areas."[11] So it must confront the provinces by clear-headed and hard-headed negotiations, but with a sympathetic and imaginative grasp of the difficulties which confront them.

---

[11] Canada, *House of Commons Debates* (unrevised) April 14, 1964, p. 2142.

This is, in the last analysis, not a political problem at all, but one that can be solved by the ingenuity and sophistication of the economists.

There must be, at the same time, some recognition that Quebec is not a province like the others. Section 94 of the BNA Act already does so by providing for uniformity of laws relating to property and civil rights in all provinces except Quebec—a tacit recognition that the different needs of Quebec must in any event be accomplished within a conceptually different legal system. This is the contracting-out formula in reverse and should give some comfort to those who regard any special treatment of Quebec as both immoral and unconstitutional. For Quebec must always rate somewhat special treatment from the facts of counter-vailing power.

However, one of the lessons of constitutional government in its federal form is that the protection of interests by political means is a source of instability and uneasiness. The atmosphere is better if these basic interests become constitutional rights, so that conflicts about them become justiciable. It is difficult in these days not to admire the broad sweep of the American constitution which extends its protection not only to states but also to people. We should consider seriously a similar extension of our own constitution to include rights—including individual rights—to language and within reason to access to the courts and other community services in one's mother tongue whether it be French or English.

This will perhaps require a reconsideration of our present judicial structure to ensure adequate machinery for a constitution which protects not only the rights of government organs but also the rights of individuals and of minorities. It may be that a constitutional court, more fully representative than the present Supreme Court, should be created. A good case on practical grounds can also be made for limiting appeals in civil law questions, unless they raise important questions of public and constitutional law, from the courts of Quebec. Common lawyers cannot get their minds around the concepts of the civil law and, since the function of a court of appeal is to clarify the law, it seems obvious that where possible civil law should be dealt with by civilians.[12]

There is a major danger in the present situation, which is the calculated risk inherent in the public discussion of anything. French Canadians, excluded for so long from the power élite except at the price of becoming wholly English-speaking and operating in a wholly English-speaking environment, tend to attach enormous importance to symbols. The extent to which the debate about the refusal of Trans-Canada Air Lines [Air Canada] to adopt the Caravelle dominated Quebec politics, is a case in point. It is perhaps not surprising that Hon. René Lévesque got into the act, but he was not alone. Just as ministers of the Crown and newspaper editors adopt extreme positions about status sym-

---

[12] Anyone who doubts this should contemplate the effect of a century of House of Lords decisions on modern Scots law. Whatever the gains in apparent uniformity with English law they were more than offset by a blurring of concepts and a misunderstanding of the system.

bols, those outside the fringes of power will show their frustration by reacting more violently.

Meanwhile, as they read in their newspapers of the latest outrageous speech or act from Quebec, English-speaking Canadians will become increasingly impatient and will in turn say things which moderate men will later regret. And as a consequence the fund of goodwill towards French Canada, founded on lack of interest and ignorance, will slowly be dissipated and the climate for negotiation slowly congeal. There is a too easy assumption about that what is needed to solve outstanding misunderstandings is a "dialogue." These exchanges are not a dialogue. Dialogue there must be. But first there should be some agreement on the subject matter.

It needs to be said that the crisis is real. One cannot turn one's back on two centuries of history. French Canadians have survived as a distinctive group by a series of overt and tacit acts. Canada is in fact a country based on the co-existence of these two cultures, and is the better for it. There has been a delayed revolution within the social structure of French Canada, and this social revolution has political implications. There will have to be some readjustment of the machinery of the constitution. We may even have to modify some of our out-of-date symbolism because symbolic gestures are important as an earnest of good faith. Just because the position of French Canada within confederation has never been clearly defined it is bound to be a source of unease in a group which is a permanent minority. There has been a comfortable and, on the whole, mutually satisfactory liaison between French and English for all these years, and we should not complain too much if one partner would now prefer more formal marriage lines.

Federalism, of all the forms of government, is the most difficult to work. The fact that we have been able to work it at all for nearly a century should be a matter of pride, and sustain our belief that it will continue to work. The fact that the Canadian federal system has materialized in so many forms is proof of its essential vitality, but the survival of any system depends on a consensus that it is worth while and worth paying for.

6 The Rowell-Sirois Report, Provincial Autonomy, and Post-War Canadian Federalism*

Donald V. Smiley

On May 3, 1940, the Royal Commission on Dominion-Provincial Relations presented its report to the Prime Minister of Canada. This report, along with the specialized studies undertaken by direction of the commission, constitutes the most comprehensive investigation of a working federal system that has ever been made. In spite of the scope and quality of the commission's work, its analysis of federal-provincial relations has had surprisingly little influence on the directions that the theory and practice of Canadian federalism have taken since 1945. More specifically, the concept of provincial autonomy which is central to the commission's argument has been denied explicitly or implicitly by such influential writings on the Canadian federal system as the so-called Green Book proposals submitted by the federal government at the Dominion-Provincial Conference on Reconstruction in 1945,[1] the Report of the Royal Commission on National Development in the Arts, Letters and Sciences,[2] Mr. Maurice Lamontagne's book, *Le Fédéralisme canadien*,[3] and the Report of the Quebec Royal Commission on Constitutional Problems,[4] as well as by the actual developments in federal-provincial relations since the Second World War.

At the present time of uncertainty in the Canadian federal system it seems desirable to re-examine the perspectives of the Rowell-Sirois Report.[5] This paper attempts to analyse one of these perspectives—provincial autonomy in the fields of health, welfare and education.

---

[1] *Submissions and Discussions* (Ottawa, King's Printer, 1946).
[2] (Ottawa, King's Printer, 1951).
[3] (Quebec, Les Presses de l'Université Laval, 1954).
[4] (Quebec, Queen's Printer, 1956).
[5] *Report of the Royal Commission on Dominion-Provincial Relations* (Ottawa, King's Printer, 1940) reprinted 1954, Bk. II, p. 80. All page references in this paper are to the 1954 reprint, hereafter cited as *Report*.

---

* From *Canadian Journal of Economics and Political Science*, Vol. XXVIII no. 1, February 1962, pp. 54-69. Reprinted by permission of the author and publisher. This paper was presented at the annual meeting of the Canadian Political Science Association in Montreal on June 9, 1961.

DONALD V. SMILEY – Professor of Political Science, University of Toronto.

Provincial Autonomy in the Rowell-Sirois Report

The emphasis on provincial autonomy in the performance of a very wide range of public functions which pervade the analysis of the Rowell-Sirois Commission has given rise to much less comment than the commission's relatively few but significant proposals for transferring particular provincial responsibilities to the federal authorities and for sharing functions previously the exclusive concern of the provinces between the two levels of government. Indeed, viewed against the constitutional impasse of the 1930's the report is a somewhat cautious document.[6]

It is fundamental to the commission's analysis that the highly integrated nature of the Canadian economy makes it appropriate for the provinces to perform a very wide range of public functions without the direct involvement of the federal authorities.

> As striking as the economic interdependence of Canadian provinces is their political, social and cultural individuality. The Commission's recommendations are based, in accordance with its terms of reference, on the economic and financial analysis it has made. But the Commission appreciates the existence of many non-economic and non-fiscal factors, and its recommendations are not those which might have been made for a more homogeneous country. No allocation of jurisdiction, over education and social services, for example, would be satisfactory which did not take full account of the existing loyalties to provincial traditions and institutions. The Commission's plan seeks to ensure to every province a real and not an illusory autonomy by guaranteeing to it, free from conditions or control, the revenues necessary to perform those functions which relate closely to its social and cultural development.[7]

It appears implicit in the commission's analysis that the desirability of provincial autonomy to safeguard regional particularisms is more pressing in relation to health, education, and welfare services than to the regulatory activities of government. In regard to welfare the report states, "provincial responsibility for social welfare should be deemed basic and general; Dominion responsibility, on the other hand, should be deemed an exception to the general rule, and as such should be strictly defined". It was recommended that welfare responsibilities be transferred from the provinces to the federal level only in relation to unemployment and contributory old age pensions, and then only after the commission had taken some pains to demonstrate that there would be substantial disabilities to provincial action.[8] Of health services it asserted, ". . .

---

[6] It might be argued that the Report was conditioned by the commission's terms of reference which directed it in part to ". . . express what in their opinion, subject to the retention of the distribution of legislative powers essential to a proper carrying out of the federal system in harmony with national needs and the promotion of national unity, will best effect a balanced relationship between the financial powers and the obligations and functions of each governing body, and conduce to a more efficient, independent and economical discharge of governmental responsibilities in Canada." *Ibid*, Bk. I, p. 10.

[7] *Ibid.*, Bk. II, p. 80.

[8] *Ibid.*, Bk. II, pp. 24-28 and 40-42.

there are pronounced regional differences in Canada in social philosophy which are bound to affect public health legislation. Centralization of jurisdiction might not, therefore, conduce to progressive action in public health, or to national unity in general".[9] As in welfare, federal activity should be limited to a relatively few residual functions whose limits should be carefully defined— research, statistical and other staff services, activities ancillary to other federal responsibilities, leadership in establishing uniform standards where such are desirable, and leadership in co-ordinating provincial activities to avoid over-lapping and deficiencies in health services.[10] The commission rejected the many proposals made to it in regard to federal aid for general education on the ground that "a free hand in something so important to the social and cultural life of the people seems to us to be vital to any provincial autonomy worthy of the name";[11] the commission did, however, give cautious approval to small annual Dominion grants to the Canadian universities.[12] Thus full provincial responsibility in the fields of health, welfare, and education, with the exception of a relatively few federal residual responsibilities, was seen by the commission to be essential to the maintenance of those provincial particularisms which were strategic in the establishment of the Canadian federal system and whose continuing existence made necessary the preservation of that system.

The Commission had a precise idea of what it meant by provincial autonomy. A province has genuine independence only if it has the revenues at its disposal to carry out those functions for which it is responsible, free from federal control in respect to those functions; the master-solution of the report was aimed at ensuring that each province was put in a financial position to provide, if it chose, a level of provincial services at average national standards without sub-jecting its citizens to provincial taxation above the national average.[13] The commission implicitly rejected the notion that has been propagated by latterday defenders of provincial rights that provincial autonomy is genuine only if the provinces have exclusive access to the more lucrative fields of direct taxation. The commission also rejected the position that the federal government had a direct responsibility for the standards at which particular provincial services were rendered; this was to be in the last analysis the duty of the respective pro-vincial electorates. In rejecting proposals for federal grants-in-aid to education the commission argued, ". . . the representations appear to us to go too far in denying the right of each province to decide the relative importance of expendi-ture on education and expenditure on other competing services. . . . Our financial proposals aim at placing every province in a position to discharge its responsibilities for education (on a scale that is within the means of the people of Canada) if it chooses to do so. Once this position is established it seems to

---

9 *Ibid.*, Bk. II, p. 34.
10 *Ibid.*, Bk. II, pp. 34-35.
11 *Ibid.*, Bk. II, p. 50.
12 *Ibid.*, Bk. II, p. 52.
13 See *Ibid.*, Bk. II, "Abstract of the Leading Recommendations", pp. 269-76.

us best that education, like every other form of welfare service in a democratic community, should have to fight for its life, and that a generous provision for the education of the children of the nation should depend, not on any arbitrary constitutional provision, but on the persistent conviction of the mass of the people that they must be ready to deny themselves some of the good things of life in order to deal fairly by their children. . . ."[14] Along the same lines the Report stated in relation to the proposed national adjustment grants to the provinces:

> It should be made clear that while the adjustment grant proposed is designed to enable a province to provide adequate services (at the average Canadian standard) without excessive taxation (on the average Canadian basis) the freedom of action of a province is in no way impaired. If a province chooses to provide interior services and impose lower taxation it is free to do so, or it may provide better services than the average if its people are willing to be taxed accordingly, or it may, for example, starve its roads and improve its education, starve its education and improve its roads. . . . But no provincial government will be free from the pressure of the opinion of its own people and if, when it applies for an increased adjustment grant on the basis of need, it has to produce figures which indicate that although it might, without specially heavy taxation, have provided better education but did not do so, it has, of course, to justify this to its own voters.[15]

The kind of solution the commission recommended thus relieved the federal authorities of the responsibility for guaranteeing the standards of particular provincial services or of influencing the priorities the provinces set in relation to the functions assigned to them.

The commission had little enthusiasm for "co-operative federalism" through the device of federal grants-in-aid of particular provincial activities. An astute and closely reasoned analysis of the conditional grant procedure was made following in the main the trend of Professor J. A. Corry's specialized study "Difficulties of Divided Jurisdiction", and the commission pointed out what appeared to them to be the inherent defects of this technique in the Canadian setting.[16] There are almost inevitable rivalries between federal and provincial authorities involved in administering joint programmes; under the cabinet system with its union of politics and administration these rivalries can be resolved only at the political level and thus irrelevant partisan considerations are introduced into the implementations of these programmes. Federal supervision of shared activities is seldom effective and is usually restricted to checking on the regularity of provincial expenditures; this leads to further differences between federal and provincial officials as the former are characteristically Treasury and auditing personnel preoccupied with protecting the federal purse while the latter are involved with the provision of particular services. In practice too, it is rarely practical for the federal authorities to withdraw a grant from a prov-

---

[14] *Ibid.*, Bk. II, p. 51.
[15] *Ibid.*, Bk. II, p. 84.
[16] *Ibid.*, Bk. II, p. 84.

ince which fails to adhere to the conditions imposed by the federal authorities in respect to that grant. The general conclusion is that, "The experience with conditional grants leads us to doubt whether joint administration of activities by the Dominion and a province is ever a practical way of surmounting constitutional difficulties. Where legislative power over a particular subject is divided it is ordinarily desirable that these powers should be pooled under the control of a single government in order to secure unified efforts in administration".[17] The report does, it is true, give cautious and qualified approval to the use of federal conditional grants where the amounts of money involved are relatively small and where the programmes can either be routine or subject to scientific standards of performance which eliminate differences between the federal and provincial officials involved.[18] However, in most situations the aim was a clearcut delineation of the respective responsibilities of the federal and provincial governments and the unified control of particular programmes by one or the other. Furthermore, the commission's emphasis on the desirability of a mutual power of delegation between provinces and Dominion and between Dominion and provinces[19] suggests a procedure by which particular functions might be transferred completely from one to the other as an alternative to joint arrangements in the implementation of these programmes.

In summary, provincial autonomy is fundamental in the commission's concept for a viable Canadian federal system. Such autonomy was justified on three grounds—cultural, political, and administrative: (1) It is necessary for the preservation of provincial particularisms; (2) It makes possible the effective accountability of provincial public authorities to provincial electorates, particularly in relation to the respective priorities that are placed on provincial programmes; (3) It makes possible the unified control over the administration of particular provincial functions necessary to the vigorous implementation of public policies relating to such functions.

To the commission, then, the major implications of the integration of the national economy lay in the desirability of giving the federal authorities exclusive access to the major field of direct taxation with the corresponding responsibility of affecting some redistribution of financial resources among the provinces rather than the alleged need for federal involvement in the range or standards of provincial functions. Further, in the commission's view the fact that particular problems have come to have more than provincial significance does not by itself justify federal action in respect to those problems; in perhaps its most striking sentence the report asserts in respect to health functions, "Mere importance of a service does not justify its assumption by the Dominion".[20] It is this last judgment which most sharply distinguishes the underlying philosophy of the commission from much of the more recent thinking about Canadian federalism and the directions that the Canadian federal system has taken.

---

[17] *Ibid.*, Bk. I, pp. 257-59.
[18] *Ibid.*, Bk. I, p. 257.
[19] *Ibid.*, Bk. II, pp. 72-73.
[20] *Ibid.*, Bk. II, p. 34.

Developments in Federal-Provincial Relations Since 1945

The final breakdown of the Dominion-Provincial Conference on Reconstruction in May, 1946, signalled the second failure in five years to evolve a comprehensive settlement of the relations between the two levels of government and no subsequent attempts have been made. The rejection of a solution on the general lines proposed by the Rowell-Sirois Commission can be attributed to the obstruction of the governments of Ontario, Alberta, and British Columbia. However, the character of the so-called Green Book proposals presented by the federal Government at the opening of the Conference on Reconstruction in the spring of 1945,[21] with their emphasis on shared programmes and their rejection of the principle of equalization, indicates that by that time the federal authorities had, for whatever reasons, turned their back on the broad solution of the Rowell-Sirois Report and accepted an alternative which would have reduced the provinces to a subordinate and dependent role in the Canadian federal structure.

Canadian federalism as it has developed since 1945 has not patterned itself according to either of the comprehensive solutions sponsored by the federal Government at the conferences of 1941 and 1945-46 respectively. Rather, the action of the federal authorities after the latter conference in attempting to negotiate tax-sharing arrangements with each of the provinces was the beginning of a process of continuous and piecemeal adjustment between the two levels of government, which is still going on. To an overwhelming degree, these adjustments have come about through interaction between federal and provincial executives—the tax-sharing arrangements, the various kinds of shared cost programmes, the activities of the Continuing Committee on Federal Provincial Fiscal and Economic Relations and other *ad hoc* and standing committees, and so on—rather than through formal constitutional amendment or through an evolving pattern of judicial interpretation of the British North America Act. Thus any discussion of contemporary Canadian federalism which revolves about the traditional concerns of students of federal systems—residual powers, judicial review, procedures of constitutional amendments, and other matters relating to the formal constitutional structure—is somewhat unprofitable. The federal aspects of the Canadian constitution, using the latter term in its broadest sense, have come to be less what the courts say they are than what the federal and provincial Cabinets and bureaucracies in a continuous series of formal and informal relations determine them to be.

The Canadian constitution has in fact become a more flexible instrument than those who faced the impasse of the 1930's could have visualized. There is a recognition of this actual or potential flexibility in much of the recent writing on the Canadian federal system, a recognition that significant developments in federal-provincial relations can come about without either a change in the pattern of judicial interpretation of the BNA Act or of amendment to that Act. The

---

[21] *Submissions and Discussions,* pp. 55-108, pp. 111-18.

Green Book proposals contemplated sweeping and permanent changes in the Canadian federal system; although the Minister of Labour mentioned, almost in passing, the desirability of a constitutional amendment making possible mutual delegation between Parliament and the provincial legislatures which would apply to industrial relations and other matters,[22] the delegation amendment was not central to the Government's plan, as it was in the Rowell-Sirois Report; and the Minister of Health and Welfare, a constitutional lawyer in his own right, asserted of the Government's comprehensive programme for national health insurance, "It is believed that none of these proposals involves any change in the constitutional jurisdiction or responsibility of federal and provincial governments under the British North America Act".[23] The Massey Report envisages almost a new dimension in the responsibilities of the federal authorities with its sweeping proposal for federal involvement in cultural development; there is no hint in the report that the implementation of any or all of these recommendations would necessitate any amendment of the BNA Act, and the laboured argument made to justify federal responsibility in cultural matters ends with the astounding, and from the constitutional point of view, question-begging assertion that "If the Federal Government is to renounce its right to associate itself with other social groups, public and private, in the general education of Canadian citizens, it denies its moral and intellectual purpose, the complete conception of the common good is lost and Canada, as such, becomes a materialistic society".[24] The continuing debate over a more appropriate procedure for constitutional amendment also reflects an underlying assumption of the possibilities of significant constitutional development by other means. The debate in the 1930's was an intensely serious one because those who supported reform were clearly bent on important amendments, particularly those which would increase the scope of federal jurisdiction in matters of economic regulation and social welfare; during the last decade or so, if I have understood the situation, the impulse for a new amending procedure has sprung very largely from the symbol of colonial status represented by the existing arrangements rather than from any sense of urgency relating to the need for substantive changes in the BNA Act. It has, of course, proved possible to effect amendments transferring significant fields of jurisdiction to Parliament after unanimous provincial consent, as the amendments of 1940 and 1951 relating to unemployment insurance and old age pensions respectively have demonstrated. More important in dispelling the previous sense of urgency, however, is the recognition that significant changes can and do come about in delineating the respective responsibilities of Ottawa and the provinces without formal amendment of the British North America Act.

There are three major procedures for adjustment on what one might call the

---

[22] *Ibid.*, pp. 75-76.
[23] *Ibid.*, p. 89.
[24] *Report of the Royal Commission on National Development in the Arts, Letters and Sciences* (Ottawa, King's Printer, 1951), p. 8.

executive side of federal-provincial relations—co-ordination through *ad hoc* and standing committees of the federal and provincial cabinets and bureaucracies, the delegation of federal powers to provincial executive agencies, and the exercise of the federal spending power on objects usually regarded as provincial and/or local responsibilities. Of these the third device, the use of the federal spending power, has the most direct implication for provincial autonomy.

Contemporary Canadian federalism has seen the growth of a very large number of *ad hoc* or standing committees of federal and provincial executive officials. In 1957 Dr. K. W. Taylor, the Deputy Minister of Finance, made a tabulation of sixty-four federal-provincial committees "more or less formally constituted, and that have either continuing terms of reference, or terms of reference that will keep them operating for a considerable period of time".[25] In generality of function these range from the Continuing Committee on Federal-Provincial Fiscal and Economic Matters to the Co-ordinating Agency on Diseases of the Beaver. Most of these committees meet in Ottawa and the chairman and secretary are provided by the federal government. A recent article by Professor Richard Leach reveals the extent of inter-provincial executive relationships, most of them of an informal and continuing nature.[26] The establishment of the Federal-Provincial Relations Division in the Federal Department of Finance, the Continuing Committee on Federal-Provincial Fiscal and Economic Matters, and the Quebec Department of Federal-Provincial Relations, along with the various *ad hoc* and standing committees on more specialized matters, appears to indicate a more profound emphasis than in the past on the executive aspects of federalism.

Legislation enacted by Parliament in 1949 and 1954 delegating federal authority to executive agencies operating under provincial legislation signals another device for delineating federal-provincial responsibilities apart from constitutional amendment or judicial review of the BNA Act. In a 1951 decision the Supreme Court affirmed a series of earlier cases that inter-delegation between Parliament and provincial legislatures was invalid.[27] However, it appears that there is no constitutional objection if delegation is made by Parliament to an executive agency operating under provincial legislation.[28] Thus the Agricultural Marketing Act of 1949[29] authorized the Governor-in-Council to delegate to any agency which under provincial law had the authority to regulate intra-provincial trade in agricultural products the power to exercise regulatory responsibilities over the extra-provincial and international aspects of agricultural

---

[25] "Coordination in Administration" in *Proceedings of the Ninth Annual Conference of the Institute of Public Administration of Canada*, pp. 253-59.

[26] "Interprovincial Cooperation", *Canadian Public Administration* Vol. II, no. 2 (June, 1959), pp. 83-99.

[27] *A. G. Nova Scotia v. A. G. Canada*, [1951] S. C. R. 31. For a criticism of the decision see John R. Ballem, *Canadian Bar Review*, Vol. XXIX (1951), pp. 79-86.

[28] *P. E. I. Potato Marketing Board v. H. B. Willis Inc. and A. G. Canada*, [1952] 4 D. L. R. 146.

[29] *Revised Statutes of Canada*, 1952, c. 6.

marketing. Similarly, the Motor Vehicle Transport Act of 1954[30] authorized provincial regulatory boards to exercise powers over the interprovincial and international aspects of commercial road transport.

The third device lending flexibility to our constitutional arrangements is the exercise of the federal spending power on objects traditionally regarded as being within the exclusive concern of the provinces and/or local governments. In some circumstances payments have been made directly to individuals (family allowances) and to private groups (Canada Council grants). Unconditional grants to the provinces have been made under the tax-sharing agreements and supplementary subsidies to the Maritimes. In other cases payments have been made to local governments through grants in lieu of taxes on federal properties and grants for land assembly and winter works programmes. Particular capital projects over which the provincial legislatures have exclusive responsibility like the St. Mary's and South Saskatchewan developments and the Canso Causeway have been aided by federal funds. Most importantly for provincial autonomy, a very large number of federal conditional grants to the provinces, and these increasingly involve local governments also, have been established, particularly in the fields of health, welfare, and vocational education.

The exercise of the spending power provides a means by which the federal government can by unilateral action involve itself in many matters which under traditional understandings of the constitution have been the exclusive concern of the provinces. Although it is not within my competence to judge the constitutionality of the various uses of this power, which have been justified as an exercise of an inherent prerogative power of the federal Crown to disburse its revenues as it chooses subject only to prior parliamentary authorization and as exercises of Parliament's jurisdiction over "The Public Debt and Property", it appears to a layman to be the most superficial sort of quibbling to assert that when Parliament appropriates funds in aid of say, vocational training or housing, and enacts in some detail the circumstances under which such moneys are to be available that Parliament is not in fact "legislating" in such fields.[31] There are four limitations faced by the federal authorities in augmenting their power through this mechanism. First, the provincial and local governments have the unchallenged right to participate or not in shared programmes, although federal financial inducements combined with popular and perhaps internal bureaucratic pressures may in many circumstances make this alternative illusory. Second, the federal government cannot in most cases oust the provinces from the primary administrative responsibilities in the fields assigned to them by the constitution; that is, federal and provincial objectives must be implemented through provincial or local agencies. Third, conditional grants have little relevance to the sharing of power in respect to regulatory functions. Fourth, in line with current understandings of the BNA Act,[32] the federal

---

[30] *Statutes of Canada*, 1953-54, c. 59.

[31] It must of course be admitted that in the case of conditional grants federal legislation is inoperative in the absence of provincial and/or local action.

[32] There are some unresolved constitutional ambiguities in this area. The only case deal-

Parliament is precluded from contributing to a particular provincial activity from the proceeds of a federal levy made for that purpose. Within these limits, however, the exercise of the federal spending power provides an important device for overcoming the rigidities in the division of responsibilities between the federal and provincial authorities delineated by the BNA Act as judicially interpreted.

What criteria have been used to justify the expenditure of federal funds on behalf of particular provincial functions? Most of the argumentation proposing or upholding such actions in Parliament and elsewhere amounts to no more than assertions that the matter in question is of vital importance to someone or other and *ipso facto* Ottawa should do something about it; proponents of particular measures do not ordinarily feel obliged to demonstrate why provincial or local action has been inadequate—whether these governments lack the financial resources to support the function, or contrariwise whether they have the resources and choose not to give the activity a sufficiently high priority in their expenditure patterns. Thus the dominant consideration dictating federal involvement has been the assumed significance of a particular function in contradiction to the principle enunciated by the Rowell-Sirois Commission that "mere importance of a service does not justify its assumption by the Dominion"[33] and to any acceptable theory of federalism.

The following generalizations can be made about the existing conditional grant programmes:

First, several of the existing arrangements embody what appear to be permanent obligations for the federal government. When Dr. Luella Gettys investigated the seven existing programmes of federal conditional grants to the provinces in 1937-38 she discovered that only two, those related to old age pensions and employment offices, were regarded as of a continuing nature.[34] Several of the largest current schemes, more particularly those related to hospital services, welfare, and operating expenditures for vocational training, can reasonably be viewed as continuing commitments assumed by the federal government.

Second, the federal authorities have in most cases chosen to share in only part of the provincial and local costs incurred in particular aided functions. In most cases administrative costs are not shareable. Under the Hospital and Diagnostic Services Act federal grants are paid on behalf of patients under-

---

ing directly with such a situation was *A. G. Canada* v. *A. G. Ontario*, [1937] A. C. 355, in which the Judicial Committee declared the federal *Unemployment and Social Insurance Act* of 1955 invalid as an invasion of provincial jurisdiction over property and civil rights. See also Leon Mercier Gouin and Brooke Claxton, *Legislative Expedients and Devices Adopted by the Dominion and the Provinces,* Ottawa, 1939, Ch. 3, "Grants in Aid for Objects not Under Dominion Jurisdiction"; and the evidence given by F. P. Varcoe, Deputy Minister of Justice, to the Joint Committee of the Senate and House of Commons on Old Age Security, *Minutes of Proceedings and Evidence* (Ottawa, King's Printer, 1950), pp. 1161-72.
[33] *Report,* Bk. II, p. 34.
[34] *The Administration of Canadian Conditional Grants,* Public Administration Service (Chicago, 1938).

going treatment for mental illness and tuberculosis only if such treatment is given in a general hospital. In the Trans-Canada Highway programme costs of acquiring rights-of-way are not shareable. Other examples could be given. Also, grants are sometimes made for relatively narrow functions as is the case with the nine existing grants for specific provincial health programmes and grants for forest inventories, forest fire protection, and reforestation. Thus federal action can reasonably be viewed not only in terms of federal support for particularly provincial activities but also in terms of Ottawa's desire to limit its contributions, for reasons which are often not easy to discover, to particular aspects of these programmes.

Third, the financial arrangements relating to particular programmes have been designed with little apparent concern for the relative fiscal capacities of the provinces or their respective financial needs in respect to particular functions. The general rule has been for the federal government to pay the same proportion to all provinces of the shareable costs incurred in grant-aided functions. There have been refinements. Under the Hospital Insurance and Diagnostic Services Act the federal contribution to particular provinces is related both to national average *per capita* costs and to the average *per capita* costs in those provinces. Under a 1956 amendment to the Trans-Canada Highway Act the federal government will contribute ninety per cent of the shareable costs incurred by each province in building one-tenth of its approved mileage while maintaining its fifty per cent contributions to the costs of other mileage as provided for in previous legislation. Some of the federal grants for vocational education are related to the numbers of persons between fifteen and nineteen years of age in the respective provinces. A proportion of the health grants for tuberculosis control and child and maternal health are allocated on the basis of the relation between provincial population and deaths from tuberculosis and infant mortality respectively in the previous five-year period. However, there has been relatively little effort devoted to evolving sophisticated measures of either the needs of provinces in relation to particular services or of over-all provincial fiscal capacities which have characterized some of the central government grants to local authorities and many of the federal grants-in-aid to the American states.

Fourth, in most of the major shared cost programmes the conditions of federal and provincial participation, including the standards of acceptable provincial performance, are evolved through protracted negotiations between officials of the two levels of government. Federal standards are thus seldom determined by unilateral action and it must be remembered that in some of the grant-aided functions the provinces have at their disposal a much larger supply of specialized skills than does the federal government; and in these circumstances the justification for central control that is operative in many instances of provincial-local relations where the receiving jurisdictions are deficient in expertise, is absent.[35]

---

[35] For circumstances relating to provincial-local relations see my article "Local Autonomy and Central Administrative Control in Saskatchewan", *Canadian Journal of Economics and Political Science,* Vol. XXVI no. 2 (May, 1960), particularly pp. 303-306.

Fifth, the bias of the conditional grant system is towards health and welfare services. It is estimated that in 1961-62 the federal government will disburse $415,898,000 to the provinces for these functions, including hospitalization. This is 75.6 per cent of the total estimated for conditional grants for all purposes.[36]

The Nature and Relevance of Provincial Autonomy

The existing conditional grant programmes pose a direct challenge to provincial autonomy as that concept was defined in the Rowell-Sirois Report. Provincial discretion is limited in four directions by the programmes:

First, the present arrangements distort the priorities that the provinces would otherwise give to particular functions. Perhaps the most significant decisions a provincial government can make and can be held responsible for are budgetary ones—decisions relating to the respective priorities in the expenditures of available resources on schools, roads, welfare and health services, on vocational as against general education, curative as against preventive health services, the direct provision of services by the province as against subventions to the local authorities. We can deduce that under existing arrangements total provincial expenditures, including proceeds from conditional grants, are distributed among public functions rather differently than if the provinces had the same resources with no conditions attached to their use. We can also assume that the distribution of the resources available to the provinces from sources other than conditional grants is different from what it would be if no such grants were available; it is reasonable to conjecture than the existing policies influence the more prosperous provinces to spend less from non-grant sources on grant-aided services than they would otherwise do and the poorer provinces more. To put this in another way, if federal assistance is available on behalf of a service which a prosperous province would otherwise provide at the same or almost the same cost, the grant in effect is an unconditional subsidy which the province may use either to pay for other services or to hold taxes at a lower level than otherwise, while in a poorer province which conceivably might not provide the services at all if there were no federal help available, the provincial proportion of the cost might be met either by higher provincial taxation or by using provincial moneys which would otherwise be spent on non-grant-aided services. If this general argument is valid, one of the effects of the present grant arrangements is to increase the disparities between the abilities of the wealthier and poorer provinces to finance non-grant-aided services like secondary highways and elementary education. At any rate, the priority-determining function of provincial cabinets and legislatures is restricted by conditional grant programmes and there is no evidence that the federal authorities in inaugurating such programmes have had regard for their implications for the over-all pattern of provincial services or the impact of these programmes on the abilities of the provinces to perform other functions.

---

[36] *House of Commons Debates* (unrevised), July 11, 1961, p. 7915.

Second, existing policies place limits on the discretion of the provinces in formulating objectives related to particular shared functions and in implementing these objectives. For example, present arrangements in the field of welfare might make it difficult for a province to embark on policies either of eliminating categorical assistance programmes in favour of assistance based on need regardless of the circumstances occasioning such need or of implementing categorical programmes different from those supported by the federal government. In the field of senior citizens' housing the policies of Central Mortgage and Housing Corporation and provincial welfare officials in regard to the relative usefulness of hostel accommodation and self-contained dwellings for senior citizens' housing have sometimes been different. In these kinds of circumstances the formulation and implementation of programme objectives by the provinces is restricted by action and it is yet to be demonstrated that federal judgment has been, according to any reasonable criteria, "better" than that of the provincial authorities.

Third, provincial discretion is restricted by the uncertainties of future federal policies in relation to shared functions. Provinces are almost inevitably frustrated in long-term budgetary and programme planning when any such plans may be upset by federal action. Much of this uncertainty relates of course to the failure of the two levels of government to evolve stable divisions of tax sources and revenues. Provincial uncertainty as to federal actions in shared programmes has to some degree been mitigated, however, in those fields where there has grown up a tradition of prior consultation between Ottawa and the provinces in respect to new programmes or to changes in existing programmes and where long-term agreements relating to particular functions have been signed. It is probably true that provincial uncertainty is occasioned more by the continuing possibility of the federal government's sponsoring new programmes, to take advantage of which would impose new burdens on provincial revenues, than by the possibilities of changing federal policies in relation to existing programmes. Although consultative procedures have become more widespread and constructive in the past decade, Premier T. C. Douglas's complaint at the 1950 Federal-Provincial Constitutional Conference is not altogether inapplicable to the present and it is significant that Mr. Douglas spoke as the leader of an administration more committed than most to long-term budgetary and programme planning:

> Without consultation with the provinces it [the federal government] is vacating the field of rental control, after permitting substantial rent increases, and thus thrusting upon the provinces the responsibility of meeting a social crisis.
>
> Without consultation with the provinces, it has announced a comprehensive irrigation scheme, which we now learn must be supported by substantial provincial contributions.
>
> Without consultation with the provinces, it has announced the construction of a Trans-Canada highway, and it is later found that the provinces will not only have to stand fifty per cent of the cost of construction but also the entire cost of the right-of-way.

Without consultation with the provinces, it has decided upon a housing program for which every province must contribute twenty-five per cent of the cost, without regard to its ability to pay.

By these unilateral decisions, the federal government has embarrassed the provinces in respect to their capital programs and has virtually dictated policies to which their consent has not been obtained.[37]

Fourth, several of the existing programmes restrict the provinces in dealing as they choose with the local authorities within their boundaries. The traditions and practices of provincial-local relations differ profoundly among provinces and much is to be gained by preserving these differences in this complex and rapidly changing field. However, several of the federal grant programmes —those relating to hospital construction and hospital insurance, vocational education, low-rental housing and urban land assembly, municipal winter works, and others—involve local authorities directly or indirectly and must inevitably have some impact on provincial objectives in relation to particular local functions. Further, such federal involvement complicates the attempts of at least some of the provinces to base their subventions to local governments on some objective standards of local fiscal need and to evolve a more rational allocation of responsibilities and revenue sources between provincial and local governments.

Provincial autonomy finds its justification in three major sets of considerations: (1) the desire to preserve certain territorially-defined particularisms; (2) the desire to disperse political power and to make those who exercise such power effectively accountable to those over whom such power is wielded; (3) the desire to promote vigour and effectiveness in the implementation of public policies.

The relation of the division of powers between the federal and provincial governments and the maintenance of territorially located particularisms has not been systematically examined; perhaps here is a fertile field for collaboration between the political scientist and the cultural anthropologist. In regard to these particularisms in their most critical form, the existence of English-speaking and French-speaking cultures in Canada, I should rather summarily reject two extreme points of view. The first is that of the Tremblay Report whose essential argument is that governmental as well as all other human activities are culturally determined and that therefore most significant exercises of federal power are a challenge to the minority cultures.[38] This point of view forgets that there are values other than the protection of cultural particularisms to be sought through federalism and that there are some exercises of federal power, say for example in the regulation of weights and measures or agricultural research, which have few cultural connotations. At the other extreme it might be asserted that the minority culture has adequate protection if the guarantees in the BNA Act relating explicitly to minority rights are upheld;

---

[37] *Proceedings,* p. 23.
[38] Quebec Royal Commission on Constitutional Problems, *Report,* Vol. II part 3 (Quebec, Queen's Printer, 1956), especially Ch. I, "Culture, Nation, Society."

this position overlooks the existing scope of federal activity, particularly in the fields of health, welfare, and education, and the possible implications of such activity for French-speaking Canadian society. However, the kinds of restrictions on provincial autonomy that I have described above bear both upon Quebec and the other provinces, although it is understandable that Quebec's suspicion of shared programmes should be more profound than that of other provinces.

Provincial autonomy, indeed federalism itself, finds its major justification in liberal views about the desirability of dispersing political power and of making those who hold such power effectively accountable to those over whom power is exercised. Alan Barth forcefully states part of this aspect of the Western political tradition in the first sentences of his *Government by Investigation*: "Political liberty consists of limitations upon the authority of governments. It is in the nature of power to expand and seek its own aggrandizement. Through a variety of rationalizations—in the name of efficiency or economy, in the name of public welfare, in the name of national security—power presses always at the boundaries prescribed for it and can be held within these boundaries only by countervailing power.[39] Thus federalism, in Professor Arthur Macmahon's words, "lessens the risk of monopoly of political power by providing a number of independent points".[40] This dispersal of political power can, of course, take place along other than territorial lines,[41] although in Canada with its size and regionally based diversities there have been strong influences from the first for the allocation of significant public functions to regional units. There is the desirability not only of dispersing power but of making those who hold it effectively accountable. The parliamentary system operating under circumstances where there is both cabinet and party solidarity provides an effective mechanism by which those who wield executive and legislative power can be made accountable. Accountability, however, is attenuated when functions are shared between two or more levels of government.

Provincial autonomy is necessary for the vigorous and effective implementation of public policy. The Rowell-Sirois Commission made a perceptive analysis of the impact of joint federal-provincial control over the administration of particular public functions.[42] Essentially the argument is that effective administration requires unified direction, which is almost inherently impossible in shared programmes in the Canadian setting except in those few circumstances where objective and agreed-upon standards of performance can be evolved.

The kinds of consideration which I have described would, at least in my scale of preferences, have to give way if it could be demonstrated that the

---

[39] (New York, The Viking Press, 1955), p. 3.
[40] Quoted in "On the Theory of the Federal State" in Sigmund Neumann, *The Democratic and the Authoritarian State* (Glencoe, Ill., Free Press, 1957), p. 220.
[41] See the analysis of Arthur Maass on the distinction between the "areal" division of power and the "capital" division of power in Arthur Maass (ed.), *Area and Power* (Glencoe, Ill., Free Press, 1959), pp. 9-25.
[42] *Report*, Bk. I, pp. 257-59.

provinces would not in fact provide the functions allocated to them in an effective manner. Such an argument might have two bases. First, it might be asserted that the provincial elected and appointed executives have neither the competence nor the integrity to perform adequately. This proposition would I think be difficult to demonstrate, particularly in view of the substantial advances in establishing the merit system that have been made since the Second World War in most of the provincial bureaucracies. A second and more serious argument might be that some or all of the provinces are too small to make feasible the employment of the specialized personnel and equipment necessary for the adequate provision of particular provincial services. This objection could not be met without careful empirical investigation. However, on the surface it appears that all but one or two of the provinces are at least potentially viable units for the provision of most services allocated to them, particularly if the federal authorities are imaginative in providing a range of research and other specialized staff services which may be made available to the provinces without significantly limiting their autonomy.

Provincial autonomy is obviously incompatible with the claim that Canadian citizens as such have the right to *defined* standards of health, welfare, and education services and the corollary of this proposition that the federal authorities have in the last analysis the responsibility of securing these rights. Apart from the provision of Section 93 of the BNA Act relating to denominational schools, the appropriateness of Ottawa's interposing its judgment between Canadians and their duly-elected provincial and local governments is by no means self-evident. However, the devising of explicit standards of provincial performance by the federal authorities, in consultation with the provinces or otherwise, and the enforcement of these by the federal government in connection with conditional grant programmes is only one of the possible procedures for attaining adequate performance by the provincial and local government in respect to particular functions. Assuming that a government has the financial resources permitting the provision of a particular service at adequate levels, the level at which the service will actually be provided will be determined in the long run by popular views about acceptable performance in respect to that activity. These views will in turn be determined by a complex and little-understood interaction between the public and the standards evolved by groups professionally involved in the provision of particular services— roads, education, welfare, hospitalization, and so on. Thus, where there are large numbers of people who change their residences from province to province, where there are relatively easy means of communication, and where there are close and constructive relations among persons professionally engaged in particular public functions, we can expect that popular expectations will tend to become more uniform as time goes on. From this point of view then, the federal government can, without inhibiting provincial autonomy, do much to equalize the standards at which provincial and local services are provided by ensuring that the provinces have the financial resources to provide, as they choose, adequate levels of service, by undertaking research and other staff activities relating to provincial and local functions, and by fostering fruitful contacts among officials throughout Canada engaged in the provision of particular services through such groups as the Dominion Council of Health and the various other advisory committees to the minister of health and welfare on specialized health matters.

Can the existing conditional grant arrangements with their restrictions on provincial autonomy be defended as egalitarian devices? As has been pointed out the bias of the conditional grants as a whole is towards health and welfare services and a very strong argument can be made that total provincial expenditures for these functions, including the proceeds from federal conditional grants, are greater than if the provinces had equivalent financial resources available with no strings attached as to their use. Further, federal participation in social assistance and hospitalization has aided enormously in resolving the residence problem to the egalitarian end that needy persons are not denied access to benefits because of their failure to establish legal residence in particular local or provincial jurisdictions. However, the present shared cost programmes have serious deficiencies as equalization devices among the provinces. In spite of the refinements previously mentioned, most of the programmes pay little regard to the relative fiscal capacities of the provinces or their particular needs in respect to particular functions. Further, it may be surmised that the increased expenditure in aided functions in the less prosperous provinces has been induced by the federal government partially at the expense of provincial and local services in which Ottawa does not share, and thus has increased the inequalities among provinces in respect to those latter activities.[43] The present arrangements give the federal authorities relatively little scope of channelling federal money into those expenditures where deficiences in particular functions are most acute, and Ottawa moneys can be and are used to support facilities in some provinces at a level which others will not attain in the foreseeable future.

The case for provincial autonomy in health, welfare, and education is somewhat different than where the purely regulatory functions of government are concerned. Speaking broadly, in an integrated national economy the existence of different provincial practices is more disadvantageous in regulatory matters than where service activities are concerned. However, in line with the Rowell-Sirois analysis, there is much to be said for a clear-cut delineation of responsibilities between the two levels of government in both kinds of situation.

Unless international crisis makes federalism wholly irrelevant, provincial autonomy as that concept was defined in the Rowell-Sirois Report continues to be a worthy value to be sought through the Canadian federal structure. In the existing Canadian setting there seems no reason to think that we must make the hard choice between the broad social and political values which provincial autonomy can foster and the effective provision of particular provincial and local services.

---

43 See the surmise of Premier Shaw of Prince Edward Island at the Dominion-Provincial Conference of July, 1960, when he said in speaking of the conditional grants "There remains the doubt . . . whether the improvement in certain fields may not in some provinces have been purchased at the cost of some stagnation or retardation of improvement in other fields, such as education", *Proceedings of Dominion-Provincial Conference* (Ottawa, Queen's Printer, 1961), p. 75.

7 A Different Perspective on Canadian Federalism*

Edwin R. Black
Alan C. Cairns

Traditional interpretations of Canadian federalism have stressed constitutionalism, legalism, the powerful influence of economic factors, and the impact of distinctive geographic and ethnic communities. These interpretations are clearly inadequate. The constitutional approach, with its structural emphasis, fails to explain political behaviour. While closer to real life, the conventional economic wisdom has been too obsessed with the centralist assumptions implicit in attempts to enlarge Ottawa's historic role in managing the economy. Regional aspects of the traditional interpretations seem to be viewed either as self-evident facts whose continued existence requires no further explanation or as inconvenient impediments to national unity which really ought to go away. It seems essential, therefore, to investigate neglected elements of regionalism in order to explain contemporary developments. The deficiencies thus far suggested have been compounded by two divergent ethnic traditions of scholarship. While English-speaking scholars stressed the challenges of nation-building across vast distances, their French-speaking colleagues concentrated on problems associated with "la survivance".

The construction of more adequate explanations requires a fresh perspective which recognizes these salient characteristics of the Canadian polity:

1. Almost regardless of the impact of the "French fact" on the state as a whole, the maintenance of a federal form of government is required by the diversities of the English-speaking communities.

2. Since 1867 Canadians have been engaged in more than the construction of a new state; they have been building provinces and complex series of relationships between governments and societies as well.

3. Economic and social factors respond to political forces just as political forces respond to them.

4. The survival of a federal system depends upon the flexibility of its constitutional process in accommodating demands unforeseen at its birth.

* From *Canadian Public Administration*, Vol. IX no. 1 (March, 1966), pp. 27-45. Reprinted by permission of the authors and publisher. This paper was prepared initially for one of a series of radio lectures and for publication in Louis Sabourin (ed.), *Le Système Politique du Canada: Institutions fédérales et québécoises* (Ottawa, University of Ottawa Press, 1968).

EDWIN R. BLACK – Associate Professor of Political Studies, Queen's University.
ALAN C. CAIRNS – Associate Professor of Political Science, University of British Columbia.

A general preoccupation with discovering forces tending to create an impressive nation-state led many to ignore the creation and effects of social, political, and physical communication networks within the provinces, the growth of regional economies with international as well as national ties, and the burgeoning provincial bureaucratic and other elites which confidently manage state systems bigger in scope, competence, and importance than some foreign sovereignties. It is suggested that adding these perspectives to the more usual approaches will provide better explanations of Canadian politics than those to which we have been accustomed.

Federal systems are characterized by a division of lawmaking and administrative authority between a central government and several regional governments. Each type of government controls some significant aspects of public activity and is supreme within its own jurisdictional sphere. The difficulty of distinguishing boundary lines between governments has customarily required court arbitration the results of which were bound to displease at least one party and its supporters. For much of the past century the Judicial Committee of the British Privy Council had ultimate authority to determine the precise meaning of the powers distributed by the British North America Act. Thus arose the popular Canadian sport of lambasting British jurists who were usually accused of misinterpreting the clear meaning of sections 91 and 92, and particularly the relationship between the peace, order, and good government clause and the enumerated subjects following it. In essence, the British law lords were being asked to settle political questions arising from a changing, pluralist society whose governments were federally organized by a legal document. Much of the legal writing on Canadian federalism seems, however, to demand interpretation of the constitution according to technicalities encrusting the legal framework within and around which the actual system operates.

"Legal answers," Professor Livingston reminds us, "are of value only in the solution of legal problems. And federalism is concerned with many other problems than those of a legal nature."[1] Federalism is translated into governmental forms when a particular constellation of forces leads men to create institutions permitting diverse territorial groups to express themselves politically and to resist incorporation into the homogenizing framework of a unitary state. Logically, then, it is more important to analyse the federal nature of society than to analyse the legal framework it uses to achieve its diverse public goals.

The value of a socio-political approach is emphasized by the experience of Confederation's first three decades. John A. Macdonald and his colleagues had provided the federation with a highly centralized framework. That the new state was a most reluctant federation is shown by the division of functions and revenues and by the superior-inferior legal relationships contemplated between the central and the provincial governments. The concessions made

---

[1] W. S. Livingston, *Federalism and Constitutional Change* (Oxford, Clarendon Press, 1956), p. 1.

to the pressures of geography, ethnic identities, and previous histories were restricted to as few as possible while the political institutions of the central government took on a strong majoritarian bias. In reflecting the principle of representation by population, the House of Commons was, and is, a highly majoritarian body. The Senate's organization displayed greater fidelity to regional considerations, but its general power and, in particular, its ability effectively to articulate the interests of the provinces was seriously inhibited from the outset. The chief executive officer of the provincial governments was a central government appointee, and the federation's Supreme Court owed its creation in 1875 to the central Parliament. The majoritarianism and centralization built into the legal structure of Canada can scarcely be denied.

It is highly significant that even though Macdonald, its chief architect, presided over this structure for a quarter of a century, it still proved incapable of resisting provincial assertions of local independence. One satisfactory explanation for this development may be found within the context of a new federal regime lacking even as much legitimacy as the former colonies had enjoyed. Confederation was the accomplishment of a small group of elites who neither sought nor obtained popular support for the new undertaking; this aspect of its origins effectively denied the new central government that widespread feeling of patriotic sentiment which it required to struggle successfully with recalcitrant provinces. The Fathers had gambled that the new policy would win legitimacy by its performance, particularly in terms of economic growth and rising standards of living throughout the country. That gamble failed. Within a few years of the union celebrations, economic depression set in and lasted almost three decades; only with the opening up of the prairies and the resultant wheat boom did that prosperity arrive which had been hoped for thirty years earlier. An inevitable consequence of this initial absence of legitimacy was the central government's inability to withstand strong pressures for enlarged areas of provincial self-assertion. From the '80's on, constitutional decisions began to favour the provinces, thus confirming the underlying realities of Canadian society. By 1896, when Laurier assumed office, the political system was established as thoroughly federal in nature—whatever might have been the intentions of the Fathers and their legal draughtsmen.

The course of Canadian federalism has displayed cyclical swings from centralization to decentralization and back again. One should beware, however, of equating centralizing periods with times of social integration. Centralization has been primarily a product of emergencies such as the years of birth, of war, and of depression when the very survival of the country was thought to be at stake. During the two world wars, Canada was largely run as a unitary state with the provinces subordinating their separate claims for a temporary period. But even war did not provide a completely effective solvent of internal differences. While English-speaking Canadians generally answered Ottawa's demands for complete support in the face of external crises, French Canadians were more hesitant; with their much longer identification with North America and the consequent weakening of their ties with Europe, the French-speaking people saw little justification for the demands put upon them by the majority.

Both wars were marked by conscription crises which deepened the cleavages between the two main racial groups. The First World War decimated Conservative support in Quebec, with damaging effects on the party system as a whole, while the Second World War was skilfully exploited by Duplessis, whose reactionary regime helped isolate Quebec from the rest of Canada. If the war periods brought the English communities closer together, they did so at the expense of seriously weakening French Canadians' identification with the federal government. The unifying effects of the depression of the 1930's have also been miscalculated. While intellectuals of English expression were fond of arguing that the fluctuations of modern industrialism made federalism obsolete, federal governments at Ottawa were characterized by timid leaderships in considerable contrast to the demagogues elected to power in Quebec, Ontario, and Alberta who were volubly hostile to any accretion of power by the central administration. Thus, even when the facts of social crises seemed to indicate an imperative need for centralized political direction, Canadians have shown little disposition to scrap their regional political systems.

On the whole, Canadian experience gives little credence to the belief that federalism is a transitional stage on the road to a unitary state. While federalism has changed significantly in response to new demands, its basic features of two levels of government each wielding important powers seems to be durable. Indeed, at the present time, the question is not whether provincial governments can withstand centripetal pressures which would diminish their significance, but whether the federal system can successfully contain the powerful recentralizing pressure welling up from below without losing its essential character.

To survive and to thrive politically, a federation must be flexible enough to adapt to radical changes in circumstances over time. The presence of permissive political styles and of effective techniques for making short-run experimental adjustments in areas such as federal-provincial relations is especially helpful. But federations are dependent in their structures on legal distributions of authority, and constitutional adaptation is generally thought to require legal rather than political or customary procedures. Such legal procedures tend to be cumbersome, time-consuming, and rigid. During the '30's, structural changes were widely desired but neither of the major legal avenues of adaptation —formal amendment or judicial reinterpretation of the constitution—proved to be fruitful directions in which to seek desired reforms. The amending process was too difficult and too permanent, while the courts, dependent on the fortuitous arrival of appropriate cases, were much too unpredictable in their decisions. Lacking the expertise in assessing modern society with which political decision-makers are furnished, the courts exhibit great difficulty in giving shaded responses in complex problem areas, and in Canada they have been largely restricted to the black-and-white approach of ruling legislation either *intra vires* or *ultra vires*. In contrast with the American Supreme Court, which effectively kept the U.S. constitution abreast of societal shifts, the Canadian jurists were unwilling to consider political or sociological aspects of a case, and preferred to rule according to the technicalities of legal construction.

The "constitutional impasse" referred to so frequently in the literature of the '30's reflects a despair of ever achieving structural changes in a federal system apparently tied to legal procedures. The courts specialized in delineating boundaries just at the time that public interest seemed to require blurring the boundaries. For these reasons, the courts and the formal amending process have been increasingly bypassed as mechanisms for resolving conflicts in the federal system.

All the more remarkable then, in the face of inadequate legal provisions for adaptation, is the occurrence of more important changes in Canadian federalism during the past quarter century than those of the preceding seventy years. The depression's revelations of the perils of an unregulated economy combined with the war years to foster an enhanced peacetime role for the state. Although the process is not completely clear, an increase in public economic control and much wider public provision of welfare services have been generally correlated in the western democracies with the type of dramatic speedup in industrialization and urbanization that Canada experienced during the 1940's. The exigencies of fighting the war had left the federal government to assume many of the normal provincial powers, but when the war ended Ottawa proved most reluctant to return these powers to the provinces. Immediately after 1945 federal politicians were seeking votes with fresh fervour, the electorate was demanding more extensive government services, egalitarian sentiments were growing, and the public was largely indifferent to constitutional niceties of federal-provincial dividing lines. No wonder, then, that postwar federal governments exploited their overall dominance in the taxation field in an effort to orient the federation more or less permanently in a centralist direction. Previous concern for provincial autonomy was probably reduced, and an enhanced rate for the federal government was legitimized by the ineffectiveness of provincial governments during the depression which stood in stark contrast with the federal government's much touted efficiency during the war years.

For the reconstruction period a series of highly centralist programs was drafted by senior civil servants at Ottawa. Presented as a package at the Reconstruction Conference, these policy proposals were vigorously rejected by provincial politicians, and the federal cabinet had to settle for achieving its objectives for postwar federalism on an *ad hoc* basis. Although the long-term direction of change was generally understood to be centralist, federal politicians were content to operate in the short run. They had, so they thought, developed a going concern. The anticipated postwar depression had not materialized. The country was prosperous. The prairie revolt of the '30's had subsided into agrarian reformism in Saskatchewan and conservative business administration in Alberta. Duplessis had amassed large electoral majorities in Quebec, but his antipathy to Ottawa was an irritant rather than a threat to the developing centralization. The Liberals at Ottawa seemed possessed of almost permanent tenure on the government side of the House of Commons, and to many observers the system seemed stable almost to the point of boredom. That these halcyon days are separated from the political excitement and uncertainty of the present by only ten years appears scarcely credible.

The federal structure had adjusted to the wartime crisis chiefly by monarchical *force majeure* with the emergency-powers legislation finding retroactive approval from the courts which evoked a defence-of-the-realm power said to be implicit in the constitution. Alternatives to the formal amending and judicial instruments of flexibility were found after the war in the new networks of bureaucratic and political collaboration which blurred jurisdictional lines between governments. A host of committees brought specialist civil servants together to develop and administer intergovernmental agreements and to discuss extensions of joint endeavours to solve problems outside any single jurisdiction. Periodic tax rental conferences provided a forum wherein federal and provincial ministers decided the allocation of the federation's total tax resources for the next five-year period. By these mechanisms[2] views were exchanged, tensions eased, and significant changes introduced into the federal system by short-term agreements capable of ready alteration should circumstances require it. In short, the practical workings of the federal system in the postwar decades came to be decided more and more by politicians and administrators who shared a common interest in making the system work rather than in determining its internal dividing lines. The result was an intertwining of the activities of ten (later eleven) governments through cooperative arrangements which made the British North America Act a less and less accurate guide for the determination of which government provided which service.

The many changes in the working constitution which developed in the postwar period are all the more remarkable when contrasted to the relatively slight impact on the system made by formal and visible changes to the founding document. The levelling of jurisdictional barriers resulted in a "fused federalism" characterized by involvement of the federal administration in virtually all of the provincial areas of "exclusive" jurisdiction: natural resources, social welfare, highway building, higher education, local government, and so on. The Sirois Commission had proclaimed earlier that the "mere importance of a service does not justify its assumption by the Dominion", but this opinion in no wise inhibited the federal government's diligence in discerning some kind of national interest in a great many provincial services in order to justify its intervention. The intervention was primarily accomplished through the mechanism of conditional grants. Close analysis of the conditional grants programs provides little compelling evidence that any consistent definition of the national interest was involved in their development.[3] On the contrary, they seem to have resulted from a series of complex bureaucratic and popular pressures and the desire of federal politicians to gain political capital by aiding popular causes directly. Most striking, however, of all the postwar changes was the virtual

---

[2] J. H. Aitchison, "Interprovincial Cooperation in Canada", in J. H. Aitchison (ed.), *The Political Process in Canada* (Toronto, University of Toronto Press, 1963); a summary of federal-provincial taxation arrangements may be found in the Canadian Tax Foundation's *The National Finances, 1962-63,* Toronto, p. 117.

[3] D. V. Smiley, *Conditional Grants and Canadian Federalism,* Canadian Tax Paper no. 32 (Toronto, Canadian Tax Foundation, 1963).

solution of the constitutional impasse of the '30's. The most important instruments in its solution besides conditional grants were the tax-rental agreements. These pacts while informal and legally unenforceable,[4] effected a massive shifting of provincial taxation powers to the federal government in return for huge transfer payments without strings attached. Both conditional and unconditional grants programs were accomplished by political agreements supported by a liberal use of the central government's spending power and did not require either constitutional reallocation of functions or formal transfer of fiscal rights from one level of government to another.

Critics of cooperative federalism in this period have seen it as largely a one-way street. While consultations did take place in some areas, the federal government launched conditional grant sorties into provincial fields quite often without even informing those provincial administrations which were supposed to help finance the federal initiatives. The selective nature of federal financial inducements often distorted priorities which the provinces had set up for their own fields of constitutional authority, but there was no *quid pro quo*; the provinces whose policy-making autonomy was effectively diminished by Ottawa's manoeuvres were not compensated with any influence over the exclusive federal areas of policy-making. These tendencies led Professor J. A. Corry to observe in 1958 that the most a province could then hope for was "freedom for minor adventure, for embroidering its own particular patterns in harmony with the national design, for playing variant melodies within the general theme. . . . It is everywhere limited in the distance it can go by having become part of a larger, although not necessarily a better, scheme of things."[5] The determinants of this kind of federalism he located primarily in an interdependent economy requiring national regulation, the growth of large and powerful enterprises whose attention was focused on the federal government, and to a nationalizing of sentiment, especially among elites.

The pressures toward extension of federal government involvement came almost entirely from English Canada, a sign of potential trouble that was either unnoticed or ignored even when the federal prime minister was a French Canadian. "Pressures towards new federal initiatives are quite indiscriminate," Professor Smiley has observed, pointing out that English-speaking Canadians came to demand leadership and money from Ottawa for a great variety of matters they regarded as worthy national purposes. To this he adds:

> Anglo-Canadians have ordinarily not felt it necessary to demonstrate the administrative or other disabilities of exclusively provincial action or the constitutional appropriateness of their proposals; the case usually goes no further than a demonstration that the subject under discussion is of great importance and *ipso facto* Ottawa should do something about it.[6]

---

[4] Bora Laskin, *Canadian Constitutional Law*, 2nd Ed. (Toronto, Carswell, 1960), p. 659.
[5] J. A. Corry, "Constitutional Trends and Federalism", in A. R. M. Lower, F. R. Scott, *et al.*, *Evolving Canadian Federalism* (Durham, N. C., Duke University Press, 1958), p. 108.
[6] D. V. Smiley, "Two Themes of Canadian Federalism", *Canadian Journal of Economics and Political Science,* Vol. XXXI no. I (February, 1965), p. 86.

A number of English-speaking elite groups continued to behave as they had during the war—as if they lived in a unitary rather than a federal state. While their actions were influenced by lack of concern rather than any design to destroy federalism, the consequences were clear—a kind of centralization by indirection.

In 1955 Parliament was ramrodded by a cabinet that felt strong enough to seek the indefinite retention of over-riding powers almost the equal of those it had enjoyed during the war.[7] Today the pressures for decentralization have been so fired up by resurgent provincialism that many have questioned the very survival of the federal government as a decisive body. The factors lying behind this change are not easily deciphered because of its recency but some indication of the more important causes can be suggested. Popular commentators have been prone to attribute the change to the new Quebec, but such attribution is incomplete at best. French Canada has made a significant impact on the federalism of the '60's, but, even if Quebec had remained quiescent, it is likely that pressures for change emanating elsewhere in the system would have had an almost similar impact.

Relevant factors in the swing from centralization back to decentralization include:

1. A return to peace-time normalcy.

2. An important diminution in the legitimacy of the governing party at Ottawa, especially with respect to any proposed federal initiatives outside its constitutional sphere of jurisdiction.

3. A mid-century decline in the importance of the powers constitutionally assigned to Ottawa and a corresponding magnification in social importance of the provincial powers.

4. A relatively great increase in the competence and confidence of provincial administrations and a consequent growth in elites who identified their prospects with the fortunes and favours of the provincial governments.

The period of centralization from which the country is rapidly receding was in large part the aftermath of war, depression, and a degree of collectivism inspired by them. As the influence of these crises waned, so did the justification for federal political dominance. The provinces, in continually asserting their needs and rights to more tax money, have had the obvious justification that they and not Ottawa are constitutionally entrusted with authority over most of the expanding areas of government activity. In 1939, federal, provincial, and municipal governments shared almost equally in total government expenditures in Canada. Under wartime pressure the federal share rose to 87 per cent in 1944. By 1963 the federal share had dropped to 46 per cent, the provincial share had risen to 26 per cent, and the municipal was 28 per cent.[8] One recent analysis indicates that if there are no major changes in defence spending and no major reallocation of functions between governments, each

---

[7] For a discussion see John Meisel, *The Canadian General Election of 1957* (Toronto, University of Toronto Press, 1962), p. 7.

[8] Canadian Tax Foundation, *The Provincial Finances, 1965* (Toronto, 1965), p. 3.

level of government will be spending about one-third of the total by 1980—a return to the pre-war division.[9] Given provincial responsibility for municipalities, such a trend would put two-thirds of the total government expenditures in Canada under provincial jurisdiction.

Much of the federal government's current dominance in the taxation system has been justified by the size of defence expenditures and the need for Canada-wide economic stabilization and growth policies. But in recent years the use of fiscal policy to counter economic fluctuations appears to have declined in significance. The Conservative government's willingness to let the tax rental system expire in 1962 was a major indication of this change. Professor Hood has observed:

> Anti-recessionary fiscal policy is now less capable of providing support for monetary policy than at any time since the war. This feeling derives essentially from the fact that the provinces have so strategic a role in both tax and expenditure policy by virtue of the relative weights of their budgets and from the fact that much of the initiative for changes rests with them.[10]

Canadian defence expenditures are also declining dramatically from their peaks of ten and twenty years ago, and in this connection it might be suggested that defence expenditures today are unlikely to lead to the same degree of voter support for the federal government as equivalent expenditures on education, roads, and even sewers elicit for provincial and local governments.

The federal government's ability to offer uncompromising resistance to provincial pressures for decentralization has been seriously reduced. The capacity of the party system to contain the country's major centrifugal forces and to reconcile them was impaired by the social crises of war and depression,and it has never really recovered. The Diefenbaker revolution of 1957-58 was a climatic revelation of the traditional party system's failure to bring together and give effective expression to the new postwar mixture of disparate social forces demanding recognition. While restructuring is obviously taking place, informed opinion is virtually unanimous that no federal party effectively incorporates the interest and allegiance of the new bureaucratic and political elite in power in Quebec. A by-product of these changes in the party system has been the failure of a legislative majority to emerge in the House of Commons to legitimate the work of the last two governments. The continued lack of majority support has clearly sapped the nerve of the once-confident Liberal Party leaders and diminished the authority which formerly supported federal cabinet ministers in their forays into provincial fields. The atmosphere of

---

9 David Ivor, "General Expenditure Analysis", in Canadian Tax Foundation, *Report of Proceedings of the Fourteenth Annual Tax Conference* (Toronto, 1960), p. 103. For a similar analysis see Eric J. Hanson's discussion on municipal tax problems in the Canadian Tax Foundation's *Report of Proceedings of the Seventeenth Annual Tax Conference* (Toronto, 1963).

10 William C. Hood, "Economic Policy in our Federal State", *Canadian Tax Journal,* Vol. XII no. 6 (November-December, 1964), p. 394.

uncertainty engendered by this situation inevitably pervades the psychological context of federal-provincial relations. Since the beginning of the '60's, federal political leaders have been unable to radiate a meaningful sense of Canadian purposes with which their citizens could identify. In decided contrast to this central government weakness has been the decisive leadership of the provincial premiers. Most provincial ministries are faced with ineffectual oppositions, and many have enjoyed exceptionally long tenure. While some of it can be described only impressionistically, the combination of federal weakness and provincial strength has undoubtedly strengthened the hands of the provinces in their negotiations with Ottawa.

One's assessments of the Canadian state as a whole should not be too much influenced by the preceding judgments about the relative weakness of governments at Ottawa in the '60's. For nearly a century Canadians have undergone the common experience of living together within the same political community, and in the process something of a common identity and habit of cooperation has emerged. The populace is bound together by numerous country-wide institutional arrangements, both formal and informal, in government, politics, economics, and socio-cultural matters. The importance of the political system as a whole in determining the life opportunities of Canadians from coast to coast and in providing the framework of law and regulation within which men work, struggle, and live has helped to create an identity which, if it be not strongly based on emotion, finds its roots in a curious combination of rational interest and customary self-identification. Rising standards of living and improved communications have widened the range of contact for many Canadians far beyond that of a century ago. Less and less do people live out their lives within the confines of a single community or province; as their experience of other districts and other people expands, so do the standards change by which they assess the performance of particular political systems.

The process of state-building has given rise to a concept of Canadianism which seeks to minimize the disabilities which attend the accidental location of birthplace. This concept, which is a particular expression of egalitarianism, has facilitated satisfaction of some of the poorer provinces' claims, whether stimulated by a sense of historical injustice or by simple envy. Whatever the source of grievance, voters in the poor regions have been unwilling to accept the consequences of poverty in terms of public services. The interaction of inequalities in provincial revenue capacities with the widening frames of reference within which people judge their lot resulted in pressures for federal action to redress the perceived inequities. Funds were transferred from the wealthy to the less fortunate provinces with the federal administration performing the redistribution. Such recent attempts to reduce regional differences in public services, and consequently to minimize the price Canadians pay for their federal way of politics, are but modern manifestations of conventions and understandings which have been fashioned during the past century for promoting the welfare of the various provincial communities. That regional grievances are satisfied, at least partially, through the transfer of funds from the centre outwards rather than by the consolidation of functions at Ottawa reveals the persistent resistance to centralization. It is not for us to assess the degree to which that resistance is based on the hostility of provincial elites to any reduction in their roles, as distinguished from the tenacity of community identification.

The institutional protection of the provinces at the federal capital, originally a task of the politically enfeebled Senate, has been assumed by the cabinet whose members not only are responsible for their government departments but are spokesmen as well for the interests of their home provinces. Appointments to the Supreme Court, the Board of Broadcast Governors, the Board of Transport Commissioners, and numerous other central government institutions reflect to a greater or lesser extent the division of Canada into a number of regional societies and interests whose explicit recognition is essential to the legitimation of central government activities.

The distinctive regional interests and identifications underpinning the federal structure have long been thought to be temporary aberrations from the norm, and doomed to eventual disappearance. Many have agreed with Professor Alexander Brady who argued that the "socio-economic forces of modern industrialism tend to quicken the pace from federation to legislative union".[11] Professor Corry claimed that an independent economy with its nationally oriented big businesses would inexorably drive Canadian federalism in a centralist direction; American students like Karl Deutsch have argued similarly that regional emotional identifications become progressively weaker as transcending relationships are created by the forces of economic integration.[12] The thesis that federalism would disappear under the impact of modern economic development has been a popular one, but its application to Canada's experience encounters serious difficulties and must be reappraised.

The continuing power and influence of the provincial governments in Canadian federalism is intimately related to the importance of their considerable economic functions. The budgets of Ontario and Quebec together came close to equalling one-third of the federal budget, and the expenditures of all provincial governments exert a weighty influence on the country's economy as a whole. All but three of the provinces cover vast land areas whose lavish natural resources are exploited at the sole discretion of the provincial cabinets. The boom in most of the northern hinterlands is subject to their exclusive jurisdiction. Large numbers of frontier towns and communities are spread across Canada from Quebec westward, and their citizens are well aware that their immediate future is tied much more closely to the provincial capitals than to the federal. Such settlements have ever had their eyes focused on provincial legislatures because of their primary responsibility for most elementary and essential services—particularly those of local political organizations, health and sanitation, and communications (at first railways and now highways). The

---

[11] Alexander Brady, "Report of the Royal Commission on Dominion-Provincial Relations", *Canadian Historical Review* Vol. XXI no. 3 (September, 1940) p. 247.
[12] Karl Deutsch, *et al., Political Community and the North Atlantic Area* (Princeton, University Press, 1957) Chs. 2 and 3.

provincial orientation of frontier communities is given extra significance by the distribution of legislative representation which favours the rural districts to a greater extent in the provincial assemblies than in the House of Commons.

Even though the decline in the agricultural portion of the labour force is ironing out some of the differences in the provincial economies, they remain dissimilar in several important aspects. Canada's generally heavy dependence on foreign trade is reflected in the substantial connections which the regional economies have with international markets as well as with each other. The importance of these international links helps to explain the growing international role of the provincial governments, especially with regard to the expansion of their economies. Provincial missions to foreign capitals seeking trade, investment, and technical knowhow are becoming commonplace. Many of these regional enterprises are virtually independent of the country's finance capitals and are able to attract sizeable investment funds from abroad. The large funds which the Canada Pension Plan will make available to the provincial treasuries will augment even the smaller provinces' autonomy from the centre.

That socio-political structures need not be dictated by the alleged integrating effects of an evolving economic system seems to be quite clear. It is worthwhile noting the frontal assault being made on this primitive version of economic determinism in Quebec. From the French-Canadian viewpoint, economic interdependence poses a serious challenge to a distinct culture and must therefore be countered by an even greater emphasis on the provincial government—the only one which French Canadians control. Political integration is not an inevitable consequence of urbanization, industrialization, and rising standards of living. The Canadian experience suggests that whatever integrating effect industrialism does exert is a function of the degree to which the internal economy is interlocking and approaches self-sufficiency. The Canadian economy falls far short of optimum conditions in this respect.

The disparate regional economies are complemented by the existence of distinguishable socio-political communities at the provincial level. The Canadian population is dispersed widely, and the provincial boundaries are still geographically meaningful except on the prairies. Despite improved communications, the country's great distances still require bureaucratic and political decentralization and seriously inhibit the ready dissolution of parochial identifications. While the psychological fibres may be weak in some of these provincial societies, they are sustained not only by their relative geographic isolation from each other but by networks of economic, cultural, and political self-interest. Their identities are reinforced by a large number of institutions organized along provincial lines. Many of these, such as political parties and associations of school teachers and school trustees, can be explained by the need of influencing the provincial political institutions. There are, however, many other organizations with few if any obviously public functions which organize within the same limits: churches, fraternal groups, ethnic associations, model railroaders, and other hobby and handicraft groups. There seems to be no obviously political need for organizing the Junior Red Cross League and the

United Nations Associations along provincial lines, but that those associations are so structured is witness to the perceived naturalness of provincial boundaries for such purposes.

What this reveals is that since 1867 Canadians have been engaged not only in state-building but in province-building as well. The existence of separate provincial governments automatically elicits a more intense pattern of communications and associational activity within provincial boundaries than across them. Mechanisms set in motion by the creation of political institutions permit provinces such as Saskatchewan and Alberta which possessed little sociological legitimacy at their birth to acquire it with the passage of time and creation of a unique provincial history.

Probably the most important aspect of province-building concerns the growth of influential provincial elites in politics, administration, and resource-based industries. Recent writings on federalism have often remarked on the nationalization of elites as a factor in attenuating provincialism. Such nationalization is based on the high degree of geographical mobility of elites and the tendency of professionals to identify with their counterparts across the country. They belong to national organizations, read the same journals and attend frequent conferences tending to build up horizontal ties of loyalty. They belong to sub-cultures based on particular skill endowments and seem to have no geographical reference points. While these are important factors, they can be over-emphasized, for it is certain that not all elite groups possess an undiluted national orientation; in fact, elite groups exist which furnish potent incentives and supports for the expansion of provincial power against that of the federal government.

Members of the political elites, and particularly those involved in minor parties with only remote hopes of success in the federal field, may well see the province as the main arena for the pursuit of power. Capable people who are not at all interested in the preoccupations of federal policy-makers are often attracted by the type of activities in which provincial governments engage. The attractiveness of provincial politics for the public-spirited may be enhanced by statistical factors as well. Although the financial rewards are slighter and the duties less demanding the provincial legislatures make available more than twice the number of seats to be found in the House of Commons, and the chances of an able man winning a post in the provincial cabinet are infinitely better than they are at Ottawa.

For many of the new professional groups and some of the old engaged in public service the provincial administrations are almost the only source of employment. Professional educators, forest biologists, electrical power generation specialists, highway engineers, public safety inspectors and scientists, social workers, and large numbers of skilled program administrators find their lives intimately bound up with the size and prosperity of provincial governments. Professor Guindon's provocative interpretation of the new Quebec in terms of a bureaucratic revolution[13] seems especially to the point here. He

---

[13] Hubert Guindon, "Social Unrest, Social Class, and Quebec's Bureaucratic Revolution", *Queen's Quarterly*, Vol. LXXI no. 2 (Summer, 1964) pp. 150-62.

indicates that the chief sources of dissatisfaction with confederation are found among intellectuals who, in French Canada, provide the legitimating ideas for political movements and among members of the postwar middle class located in the bureaucratic organizations that evolved to meet the problem of mass migration from country to city. In French Canada the bureaucrats are found overwhelmingly in the public and semi-public sectors, and their personal progress and prosperity have depended upon a rapid expansion in the scope and tempo of provincial government activity. Their demands for greatly expanded public support of their activities helped bring on a political crisis in federal-provincial relations that still exists.

The marked improvement in the competence and confidence of the public bureaucracies in almost every province has been a factor of peculiar influence in the course of federal-provincial relations during the past ten years. Civil service reforms, the elimination of patronage, entrance by competition, and security of tenure were introduced first at the federal level but began to spread at a slow pace to the provincial governments. Today the process is almost complete and it is no longer safe to assume that administrative competence resides only in federal hands. In many cases of public activity the real expertise is found only at the provincial level. In the fields of education, natural resource administration, municipal affairs, roads, law enforcement, and local economic promotion, the provincial civil servants will be found to be more numerous and generally more competent than the federal.

The improved quality of their civil services helps to invalidate the assumption, present at confederation and not yet dead, that the provinces should be entrusted with functions of only secondary importance. The traditional English-Canadian view of the federation as a pyramid of hierarchy becomes anachronistic with the location of superior administrative talent within the provincial rather than the federal functional departments. This redistribution of administrative competence has removed much of the paternalism from federal-provincial relations in specific areas, and we can expect provincial administrators and their political superiors to become even less likely to accept federal leadership as they grow more aware of their own capacities.

New political orientations within provincial cabinets are combining with this growing administrative competence to revolutionize the management of regional economic resources. During the 1950's it seems clear that provincial cabinets formulated their budgets with inadequate views of the future and were seldom prepared to make hard choices allocating different priorities to different services. That picture has changed. More and more cabinets plan their public policies within a broad context of long-range projections and expectations of economic development. Every example of *ad hoc* federal intervention in provincial fields becomes more difficult to tolerate because of the disruption in provincial planning; federal-provincial cooperation, requiring as it now does the fitting together of many governments' plans and expectations, grows more difficult to achieve. Saskatchewan's premier was the first to complain of such federal government disruptions, while the Quebec government, to take another case, has opposed conditional grants programs not only on principled grounds but because it wished to establish its own policy priorities within a coherent development program free of any environmental disturbances caused by federal activity.

The Quebec government's official demands for a general withdrawal of the federal programs in provincial areas and for radical increases in the province's effective fiscal capacity are clearly of major importance for the federal system. Within four or five years the Lesage government demanded and secured more changes in federal-provincial relations than Premier Duplessis had brought about in twenty years. Quebec's silent revolution of the '60's involved a major political breakthrough by a new and influential class which Duplessis had treated with indifference despite its special degree of concern for the consequences of government decisions. The Lesage electoral victory permitted a virtual seizure of power by these once-scorned bureaucrats of the middle class, and a dramatic change in public attitudes toward the role of the state was set in motion.

Under the old regime there had been a widespread distrust of the state. Both Taschereau and Duplessis were hostile to what they regarded as paternalism, while French-Canadian Catholic thought displayed a general preference for private rather than public action to ameliorate social conditions. In any case, the grossly inadequate provincial administration could not possibly have played any role other than the negative one. Bureaucracy, in Weber's sense, simply did not exist, for neither Taschereau nor Duplessis appears to have tried to separate governmental from private affairs. The corruption, nepotism, and incompetence of the provincial government suffered neither electoral disapproval nor moral stigma except in a few relatively ignored journals of opinion.

By contrast, the present government gives state power a positive emphasis as the main collective instrument of modernization and as the main instrument for controlling an economy whose ownership and managerial positions are largely in "foreign" hands. Governmental power is now being used in Quebec with a vigour and élan which makes most other provincial governments and the federal administration seem insipid by comparison. Since maximum exploitation of potential provincial powers requires expanded financial resources and the fullest possible arena for provincial legislative action, demands for more "tax room" and for federal withdrawal from provincial jurisdictions were both logical and inevitable.

Little general attention has been paid to province-building in Canada, or even to the related aspects of regional communication patterns, provincially oriented elites, and the development of overall planning approaches by a number of provincial cabinets. The natural desire of provincial elite groups to reduce planning uncertainties caused by outside interests such as the federal government contains implicit dangers of movements toward provincial autarchies. While speculation is hazardous, the possibility of accentuated economic regionalism must be scouted and guarded against if the federal system is to retain any significant control over its economic future.

While outside our immediate concerns, the recent emergence of the federal-provincial conference as an institution of unique influence in Canadian affairs must be noted. This institution must, in fact, be accounted the only effective instrument available today for the authoritative resolution of some of the federation's most insistent political questions. Some of the probable consequences of this development for the various elected bodies can already be discerned. At the very least, it seems, even further reductions may be expected in the effectiveness of Canadian parliaments as controllers of national and provincial policy-makers. What more may come in connection can only be guessed at.

The capacity of political systems to maintain their legitimacy over a long period of time is not easily addressed. As we have noted, the formal structure of Canadian federalism is reflected and reinforced in scores of other associational patterns both public and private. Political federalism is not the simple creature of existent, social, economic, and geographical forces, but is itself a creative influence. Governments within the system tend to create their own supports through a variety of methods; among them are the charisma surrounding all distant authority, the identification of particular groups with the fortunes of particular governments, the socializing of men to accept their political environment as the natural one, and the complex intertwining of modern government with society that endows any major proposal for change with widespread and often unforeseen consequences for all parts of the structure. This reciprocal relationship between federalism and the society it serves infuses both levels of government with durability and continuity by sustaining the divided system of loyalties that a working federalism requires. But the supports that governments build for themselves remain largely invisible. One level of government may appear to be much the more soundly underpinned by public loyalty until, perhaps, some dramatic event serves to thrust public sentiments for the "neglected" government to the fore. Certainly there lay beneath the apparently stable, centralized federalism of the postwar years a number of potent factors leading to a divergence between the system's form and the demands being put upon it. As we have seen, these demands have overwhelmingly favoured a relaxation of central authority and an increase in the provincial. So insistent has the pressure become that Canadian federalism is undergoing the greatest crisis since its inception.

Prediction of future developments is especially hazardous because for the first time since the depression Canadians are discussing the basic features of their federalism with passion and vigour. This renewed concern for fundamentals and its attempts to find guiding principles is one of the most important manifestations of the changing climate. The Laurendeau-Dunton Commission, the proposals for amending and delegation procedures, the swelling critique of conditional grants and the consequent opting out provisions, the ending of tax rentals, and the frequent demands for a new constitution are all indicative of a revised concern for the basic ground rules governing Canadian federalism. At the time of writing most of the basic issues appear to be open, but how long they will remain so is uncertain.

A new consensus on the purposes and structures of the Canadian state is clearly needed. The continued appropriateness of the federal form of government has been suggested by the analysis presented here. But if the state is to survive as a federation, it must embody a delicate balance between the forces of centralization and decentralization, a balance that obtains not only within the country as a whole but within each region as well. Tension arises not from changes in the relative significance of the push-pull pressures in the system as a whole but primarily from interregional disagreements about their relative importance. The centrifugal forces in Quebec and British Columbia cannot be offset by the centripetal forces in Ontario. That is a recipe for civil war.

To discuss Canada's federal system primarily in legal and economic terms is to misunderstand it from the beginning, and to discuss its problems in terms of ripping up the B.N.A. Act and beginning again from scratch is to hand over the decision to the separatists both east and west. The present structure has exhibited a marvellous degree of flexibility, but if the assumption gains currency that this structure must be scrapped and a new constitution written in both form and substance, then the prospects will not be hopeful. Rewriting constitutional documents is neither a mere exercise in legal logic nor a simple process of transforming a few accounts from this side of the ledger to that. In rewriting such documents one embarks on the reshaping of the entire set of interdependent relationships between government and peoples which has evolved during a full century. If necessary, Canadians will undoubtedly undertake this complex task, but for them to attempt it lightheartedly and without a full understanding of the present system would be an act of political immaturity for which succeeding generations would long curse their ancestors.

8 The Dynamics of Federalism in Canada*

A. W. Johnson

The Conflicting Elements in Federalism

The adjustments that must be made in a federal state in response to change take their form from the very nature of federalism, which—simply and without gloss—is a form of government designed to get the best of two worlds; the advantages of a unified state and the benefits of the diversity which is inherent in the peoples and the regions which make up the state. The compromise between these two conflicting elements in a federal country is institutionalized in a constitution, the centrepiece of which is a division of the power to govern between the central government and provincial authorities. If there is not much governing to be done, the compromise is not too complicated, and if the societies being governed are static, the compromise is likely to be lasting and stable. But remove these two conditions—static simplicity—and the federal state encounters difficulty. The equilibrium between the machinery which fosters unity and that which preserves diversity is upset; the values attaching to unity or to diversity themselves are changed; and even the meaning of unity and the meaning of diversity may be altered.

These two conflicting elements of federalism are found in an exaggerated degree in Canada, for the objectives of diversity are rather two-dimensional here. The first dimension arises out of the linguistic-cultural duality of our country. This has meant that the first and most obvious goal of diversity is the preservation and the promotion of the French culture on the one hand and the cultures of English-speaking Canada on the other, including now not only the culture of the other founding race, the British, but also the heritages of many other peoples.

The second and less obvious dimension of diversity embraces all the other objectives of classical federalism, most of them having to do with the goals of a pluralistic society. In such a state a diversity of values and interests and social units is to be found, with the institutions of government having been

* From *Canadian Journal of Political Science,* Vol. 1 no. 1 (March, 1968), pp. 18-39. Reprinted by permission of the author and publisher. A paper presented to the annual meeting of the Canadian Political Science Association at Ottawa on June 8, 1967. The text has been revised in detail but not in substance and does not take account of major developments in federal-provincial or Ottawa-Quebec relations since June 1967. The author wishes to acknowledge the very direct and substantial contribution of his colleague, Edgar Gallant, director of the Federal-Provincial Relations Division of the Department of Finance, to the development and presentation of the ideas contained in this paper.

A. W. JOHNSON – Assistant Deputy Minister, Department of Finance, Canada.

designed to preserve this diversity. Federalism is one such institution. The development of a monolithic state is less to be feared where federalism prevails; the citizen is able to turn to one government to counteract the actions of another. The ability of the individual to control or to influence government policy is enhanced by virtue of the existence of more than one level of government. Regional and sectional differences are more likely to be preserved as are the historical differences between groups and units of government within that society. Similarly differences in economic interests can more adequately be represented in the formulation of public policy where regional governments as well as representatives in national organs of government speak for these interests. All of these elements of pluralism in a federal state are to be found in the several provinces of Canada.

These two dimensions of diversity in Canada have been more or less constant, with the one, the preservation of two languages and two societies, having been the more obvious and the more persistent, and the other, the preservation of a pluralistic society, having been less tangible and rather more fluid.

The objectives of unity, on the other hand, are more or less obvious depending upon the times in which one lives. In times of international crisis, the importance of a common defence against external threats becomes more self-evident. In times of economic crisis, the importance of strong central management of the economy becomes more apparent to the average citizen. In times of political or cultural crisis, the requirements of unity, or at least the cost of disunity, become more evident.

During periods of calm, on the other hand, the objectives of unity are less apparent, more likely to be obvious primarily to those who are expert on or have occasion to concern themselves with the functioning of the country. In times of economic equilibrium it is more likely to be the specialist who understands the importance to all of Canada of the central measures for maintaining economic stability, for increasing the productivity of labour and capital across the country, for enlarging rather than compartmentalizing markets for Canadian products. In times of prosperity it is more the technocrat who understands the underlying mechanism of income redistribution measures, by which the citizen in one part of the country is persuaded to pay taxes to relieve the poverty of others in other parts. In times of comfort and ease, it is the artist or author who is more likely to perceive the importance to Canadian cultural achievements of measures which defend the country against external assaults of a cultural kind. Only if these mechanisms of unity were to cease functioning for an extended period is it likely that the full realization of their importance would be borne in on every citizen.

These conflicting elements of unity and diversity are to be found in any federal state—an obvious proposition, perhaps. The process by which they are reconciled is probably equally apparent—that of shifting power as between the central and the provincial governments or *vice versa*. But to understand fully the mechanisms of adjustment, it is helpful to consider the adjustments to which a country is exposed or may be called upon to undergo.

The Environment to which Canadian Federalism Must Adjust

The extent of the changes which Canada currently is undergoing may appear to be obvious, but I found that an inventory of them gave me a better sense of their magnitude and complexity, and of their effect upon federalism in our country. The dominant change, of course, has been the decision of French Canadians to participate fully in Canadian and North American society and to share in its economic benefits, while at the same time preserving and promoting their unique culture. The price of this change—from the earlier and easier course of preserving the French-Canadian culture through isolation—is profound adjustments, both for French- and English-speaking Canadians. Within English-speaking Canada there have been changes of another sort: the dilution, the adaptation, even the weakening, of the British culture brought about by the immigration since the Second World War of almost two million persons of European and other stock. Within both English- and French-speaking Canada the shifts of population from rural to urban areas, and the substitution in so many regions of industrialization for agriculture, have brought technological, social, and cultural changes which have further disrupted the earlier patterns of life.

Along with these changes there has been a growing obsolescence of the old bonds and the old symbols which united Canadians—both as between English- and French-speaking Canadians and as between the peoples within each of these two societies. The Union Jack, the Commonwealth, the church, the frontier, even connections with one's motherland have little appeal as symbols of unity for the younger people of today. And the institutions which have united us and have the potential for uniting us have come to be taken for granted or have lost their unifying force—the CBC, transcontinental railways, Air Canada, even the common denigration of Toronto and the shared suspicion of Ottawa.

Changes in the Canadian economy also have worked to force adjustments in the machinery of federalism. The balance between the various sectors of the economy has changed substantially: manufacturing and processing have developed to a point that they now outrank by two to one the contribution to Canadian production of agriculture, mining and logging. The regional balance has shifted, too, with much of the West having joined Ontario in the club of the wealthy, leaving the Maritimes and to a lesser extent Quebec striving to achieve their rate of growth. The infrastructure of the economy—transportation, energy, communications, social capital—has been elaborated, and has become a more important if more complicated element in Canada's economic development. Financial markets have grown and developed to the point that national and international capital flows, through a network of financial intermediaries, now provide substitutes for branch banking and direct foreign investment as sources of capital for growth and development.

Along with these social, cultural, and economic developments there has been a significant change in the social ethics of Canadians, and in their tendency to use government to achieve their ends. Governments now are expected to see to it that the economy is kept fully employed, to ensure that it grows at a satisfactory rate and somehow to enable all regions to share in the growth. They are expected, too, to contribute to the well-being or even the efficiency of the several sectors of the economy and to the infra-structure and the financial markets which serve them. In the field of social policy, income redistribution, through taxes and transfers, has replaced relief cars as the vehicle by which higher-income people contribute to those in lower income brackets. And income redistribution now is supplemented by state welfare measures. In addition, Canadians have added medical and hospital care to education as services which should be removed from the market and purchased by the state for the citizen. And public services generally are thought to be important enough that the residents of richer regions are called upon to contribute to the governments of poorer ones.

These are the changes brought about by internal forces in the Canadian society. Increasingly international pressures too will force—are forcing—changes on Canadian society. The protected domestic market is giving way to larger market areas. The small company is giving way to the international corporation. International capital markets are replacing small and insulated local ones. External influences upon domestic monetary and fiscal policy are being brought to bear through international consultations, as well as through international markets. The concept of equalization is being broadened so that individual Canadians are contributing not only to other Canadians, and to other provincial governments in Canada, but also to the poorer nations of the world. Culturally, the development of satellite communication is bringing and increasingly will bring to Canada the cultures of many nations—not only American—and will subject our cultural development to international tests.

The Forces of Diversity and the Forces of Unity: a State of Disequilibrium

Curiously, despite the nationalization and even the internationalization of the technological and economic environment in which Canada lives, the forces of diversity have gathered force relative to those of unity. This, of course, is not peculiar to Canada. Provincial functions have grown in importance relative to the functions of the central government: expenditures upon education and health, upon roads and urban development, have multiplied at the very time that economic management, income redistribution, and defence have been losing their glamour. Efforts on the part of the federal government to assume control or at least a measure of influence over provincially administered programs have been stoutly resisted by Quebec, the consistent champion of provincial rights. Other provinces have taken similar positions intermittently, as political personalities or government ideologies or simply concern over centralized decision-making have changed over time.

With these changes, the fiscal power of the provinces has increased relative to that of the federal government, this being the result not only of higher provincial and municipal taxes but also of very large fiscal transfers from the federal to provincial governments. The economic power of certain provinces has increased too, with the consequence that British Columbia, Alberta, and Saskatchewan, in addition to Ontario, now have the fiscal as well as the constitutional independence to pose as antagonists of the federal government as and when they wish.

The engines of unity, on the other hand, have tended to weaken. The threat of external aggression no longer unites Canada, and carping about the personal characteristics of Americans or Englishmen is no real substitute. The British Crown has long since ceased to be looked upon as a protector of the rights of French Canadians and now is regarded as a symbol of unity largely among those English-speaking Canadians who belong to an older generation. Other symbols of Canadian unity, and common institutions across the country, have, as I have said, tended to weaken or to be taken for granted. New engines of unity, in the form of common public services such as nation-wide social security programs and projects like the Trans-Canada Highway, have in no small measure been transformed into provincial enterprises in the eyes of the public, as provincial governments have learned how to turn conditional federal grants to their advantage.

Paralleling, and partly as a consequence of, this growth in the relative power of those engines of diversity, the provincial governments, has been a growing conflict between the two levels of government. The role of the state has so increased that it is scarcely possible for the federal government to exercise its powers without affecting provincial programs, or for provincial governments to occupy their jurisdiction without affecting federal policies. The federal government cannot use monetary and fiscal policies to stabilize the economy without employing taxes which the provinces want for their purposes or without affecting through monetary policy the rate at which the provinces and their municipalities must borrow. It cannot seek to influence the rate of economic growth through the use of tariff, tax, and expenditure measures without affecting the regional industrial development measures of the provinces. It cannot use the tax-transfer mechanism—a combination of income tax and income maintenance measures such as family allowances and old age security payments —to redistribute income without its having an effect on provincial welfare programs.

The provinicial governments, in their turn, cannot, because of their very fiscal power, make tax and expenditure and borrowing decisions without affecting the stability of the Canadian economy. They cannot exercise their jurisdiction over education, over their resources, or over the various aspects of property and civil rights—be it health, welfare or the regulation of financial institutions— without affecting the rate of growth of the economy. Nor can they undertake regional economic development programs without having an effect upon the allocation of resources in Canada, and an indirect influence upon parallel federal measures.

The inevitable frictions which accompany the side-by-side existence of federal and provincial programs have been exacerbated by alleged invasions of provincial jurisdiction by the federal government and *vice versa*. The federal power has been used, knowingly and intentionally, to alter provincial priorities. It has sometimes been used, too, unknowingly and unintentionally, in such a way as to affect the very administration of provincial programs. Similarly the provinces, or certain of them, have sought by hard political pressure and negotiation to lay claim to jurisdiction long accepted as being federal—the mineral rights of Hudson Bay, for example, and certain aspects of international relations.

These are some of the general tensions in present-day Canadian federalism. To them must be added the paramount pressure upon our federation: the presence in Canada of a French-Canadian minority which is no longer prepared to accept a subordinate role in Canadian society. Here one finds the strongest desire for diversity. Here one finds the smallest attachment to the symbols of unity. Here one finds language and culture adding inflammation to the common suspicion of Bay Street and St. James Street, Westmount and Ottawa. Here one finds a determination to protect the integrity of the French-Canadian social entity from the erosion which would be the product of an unthinking drift toward centralization.

Somehow, in the face of and out of all these social and economic changes, all these federal-provincial and Quebec-Ottawa frictions, must come a new balance between the conflicting elements of unity and diversity in our Canadian federation. The question is which way to go.

Alternative Directions for Canadian Federalism

There is no shortage of prescriptions. But there are, it seems to me, only four main alternatives. One is to move toward more centralization of government, on the assumption that diversity must ultimately suffer anyway as we become more a part of the North American and ultimately of the international community. The second is to strengthen the regionalization of government, generally, on the assumption that the advantages of unity can be preserved even through a weakened federal government, with perhaps some buttressing from inter-governmental machinery or agreements. The third alternative is to provide for a greater regionalization of government in Quebec only, on the assumption that a higher degree of centralization would prevail in the rest of Canada, and the parallel assumption that the advantages flowing from this centralization would not seriously be diminished by the Quebec decentralization either for the country as a whole or for Quebec in particular. The fourth alternative is somehow to marry the stronger regional governments and a strong central government—the role of government as a whole having increased—on the assumption that strong federal and provincial governments can somehow reconcile and harmonize their priorities, policies, and administrative practices.

I shall consider each of these alternatives in turn, not with a view to determining which of them is to be preferred, but rather with a view to identifying the essential characteristics of each alternative and the questions or the problems which seem implicit in it. It should then be possible better to consider how these alternatives would function in balancing the forces of unity and diversity in Canada, not only now but in the future.

The Alternative of Centralization

The case for greater centralization, on the face of it, is very strong. There *is* greater interdependence as between the provinces of Canada, today, however much it may be obscured by the very complexity of the mechanics of interdependence: and the growing interdependence of the nations of the world will likely strengthen intra-national interdependence before the national state is eroded by the growth of the international community. The structure and the scale of Canadian industry is geared to Canadian markets and to Canada's trade and other policies. The infrastructure of our economy has been developed to serve the country as a whole, not just a group of more or less discrete regions. The social ethics of Canadians have developed on a national basis too: the citizen now is contributing to the welfare of other citizens 3,000 miles away, not just to his neighbour. The institutional structure serving Canadians —governmental, private and professional—is to a considerable extent country-wide in character. Above all, Canada is an open economy and an open society, vulnerable to external pressures of all kinds; to subdivide the Canadian community would be to make it even more open and more vulnerable.

Having said this, I think it is now generally accepted that progressive and general centralization simply will not work in Canada. The accumulation of steps in this direction, such as those which resulted from the programs of post-war reconstruction and from the social reform of the last two decades, has contributed to friction and disequilibrium in our federation. Quebec would rather separate than be submerged, and the peoples and the premiers of English-speaking Canada would have to become uncharacteristically submissive before a substantial centralization of government could be realized. Indeed, when carried to its logical conclusion, centralization defeats the very objective of federalism—pluralism; by its nature it cannot be expected to demonstrate those characteristics of flexibility which are so important in a diverse and divergent country.

The Alternative of General Decentralization

The second alternative, the progressive decentralization of government powers throughout Canada, has many attractions too. It would meet the demand of Quebec governments that more of the powers of government be concentrated in Quebec City, thus better enabling Quebeckers to be "maîtres chez nous". Equally, it would enable other provincial governments to pursue more vigorously the regional or provincial economic development programs to which all of them now are committed. It would lend itself to the preservation of cultural and historical differences, the strength of which is manifest to anyone who travels across Canada. It would make it easier for all provinces to develop their own priorities and to adapt their public services to the peculiar needs of their people. Conflicts with national economic and social policies would be minimized by virtue of the diminished role of the federal government.

But the cost of this alternative, too, is high. In economic terms, the vehicles of national economic policy would tend to remain static, or be diminished, as provincial economic powers grew. Federal fiscal policy would decline in importance as the fiscal resources of the central government were progressively transferred to the provinces; increasingly the voluntary participation of provincial governments would be essential to the development of a meaningful national fiscal policy. Monetary policy would come to have more effect upon provincial financial and developmental policies, as reliance upon this tool of policy grew and as the scale of provincial fiscal activity was enlarged; increasingly the provinces would expect to be consulted at least on the direction if not on the details of credit policy. Trade policy, too, would tend to become the subject of federal-provincial discussion, and perhaps negotiation, as the provinces sought to adapt this instrument to their several development goals. Provincial regulation of financial institutions would proliferate, and there would be a strong temptation to shape the investment policies of these institutions to serve provincial ends.

The potential economic cost of general and progressive regionalization is the most evident cost of this course for Canadian federalism. A coherent and an effective national economic policy would be possible only through intergovernmental agreement. Decisions on fiscal and monetary matters, difficult enough in a large central apparatus, would tend to become halting, uncertain and muddied by compromise, as the several governments sought a consensus. Regional economic policies would tend to proliferate and the misallocation of resources would tend to increase, as each region pursued its own development. The Canadian government would be less and less able to speak with authority and assurance in international councils, with all this would imply for international confidence in Canada's ability to manage her own economic affairs.

Socially and culturally the same fragmentation would tend to emerge. As the provinces pursued independent social and education policies, there would be less and less sense of being a Canadian. As people moved between provinces they would be irritated by substantial differences in public services and their feeling for Canada would diminish as their irritation increased. Independent broadcasting and communications policies would weaken the sense of cultural unity in the country. The diminished sense of Canadianism would test the willingness of British Columbians and Ontarians to contribute toward equalization payments to the poorer provinces, and ultimately, perhaps, even to income maintenance payments to individuals. This would be the consequence not only of a decline in the sense of mutual responsibility, but also of a suspicion that the transfer payments were not being used wisely or that they were being used to enhance the competitive position of the recipient provinces.

I think social scientists would agree that the equilibrium between the forces of unity and diversity must lie somewhere between these two extremes of centralization and decentralization. The consequences of these alternatives, however, should be borne in mind, for they illustrate vividly some of the problems and the pitfalls which must be avoided if other approaches are to be successful.

Special Status for Quebec

The third way to balance the forces of unity and diversity in Canada—the first of the two which lie between the extremes of centralization and decentralization—is to provide for a greater regionalization of government in Quebec only. This increase in regionalization could take the form of a special status for Quebec within the present federal structure, or it could call for giving to that province associate state status. In either case a substantial measure of centralization would be expected to prevail in the rest of Canada.

The appeal of *statut particulier* is understandable. Quebec is *not* a province like the others, however much the other nine may differ from one another, and one should reasonably expect therefore a differentiation in particular government programs as between that province and the rest of Canada. Moreover, if progressive regionalization in the whole of Canada would seriously weaken the central government, it does not follow logically that the same price would be paid if that course were to be followed only in Quebec. The questions to be asked, therefore, are of a different order, having to do largely with the major shifts which would be involved under *statut particulier* in the burdens and benefits of confederation, and in the patterns of influence inherent in our machinery of government.

There are four elements to *statut particulier,* if I understand this approach to federalism correctly. First, under this proposal the government of Quebec would assume full responsibility for most if not all federal-provincial programs and would receive from the federal government a fiscal transfer which would fully compensate the province. The government of Quebec would similarly be compensated for new federal-provincial programs—such as medicare—whether or not the province undertook a program similar to that required in other provinces. Secondly, the government of Quebec would under this approach assume responsibility for certain purely federal programs, principally the family allowance and old age security income maintenance programs, and again would be compensated by means of a fiscal transfer from the federal government. Thirdly, the government of Quebec would be given the right to be consulted in respect of other federal policies, including fiscal, tariff and trade policies, and probably monetary policy. I am not entirely clear from what has been said by the proponents of this approach just how many areas of policy would be involved in these consultations or precisely what the process of consultation would entail. The importance of what *is* meant in terms of the constitutional arrangements called for will be self-evident. Fourthly, the government of Quebec might expect to assume certain aspects of federal jurisdiction, such as the right to conclude international arrangements, at least in fields of provincial jurisdiction and certainly to develop something of an international personality. These I think are the principal propositions which have been advanced at one time or another by the people advocating *statut particulier.*

This approach to the balancing of the forces of unity and diversity in Canada is one of the important alternatives being considered in Quebec; as such it deserves serious discussion in the rest of the country. I content myself here with an attempt to identify some of the questions which would arise, the problems which would be encountered, if an effort were made to adapt Canadian federalism to this model. I realize that in so doing I display one of the more wearisome traits of the civil servant, that of cocking a critical eye at a new idea. I can only plead that it is in the very nature of my training to search out the consequences of proposals in order adequately to examine their feasibility. Moreover the capacity of this structure to adapt itself to the shifting forces, indeed the shifting requirements of unity and diversity, in Canada can only be judged by this kind of evaluation.

The first question I have identified has to do with the effect of *statut particulier* upon the efficiency of economic policy in Canada, and upon the distribution in different parts of the country of the benefits and the burdens of economic policy. As conceived by its authors, the effect of *statut particulier* on fiscal arrangements would be to transfer 100 per cent of the individual income tax and anywhere between 50 and 100 per cent of the corporation tax to the government of Quebec. This would mean that the effect of federal tax measures, whether used for stability or for growth, would be felt largely in the provinces other than Quebec, while the economic benefits of these measures would be felt across the whole country. Quebec's use of its extra share of the income taxes would also be felt across the country, albeit indirectly, but the Quebec legislature, not the Parliament of Canada, would be the organ of government responsible for these policies. To the extent, therefore, that federal policies continued to be relied upon as the balance wheel of the economy, the people and the governments of the other provinces would have to be prepared to accept the application of these policies in their part of Canada, though not in Quebec, and rely upon the voluntary co-operation of the government of Quebec for the application of similar policies in that province. The same reasoning would apply, of course, to the expenditure side of fiscal policy, given the additional expenditures that would be financed in Quebec from that province's extra share of the income taxes.

Federal monetary and trade policies, unlike fiscal policy, would continue to apply in the whole of Canada, one gathers. However, they would be formulated in the context of special consultations with Quebec, unless, of course, the other provinces were to insist upon similar rights. A good deal would turn upon the meaning of consultation. If it were to mean that Quebec, or in the alternative any provincial government, were to have the right to express its views on federal economic policy, the situation would not be too dissimilar from the present. If on the other hand, there were to be some moral or constitutional obligation upon the government of Canada to gain the consent of Quebec—as is sometimes suggested by the provinces with respect to the level of federal income taxes—then it is difficult to visualize any region in Canada being prepared to give Quebec a priority voice in these economic policies. If this analysis is sound, then *statut particulier,* in these areas of economic policy, would tend to lead to general regionalization, the consequences of which I have already considered.

The same analysis would apply to regional economic policies. *Statut particulier,* according to its authors, would call for Quebec's exercising full control over all federal regional development policies, including, presumably, ARDA, ADA, and similar federal measures. Some draw the further inference that to make economic sense Quebec should also have a voice in general economic policies—fiscal and credit, tariff and trade, and manpower training and mobility—since regional economic measures can function properly only if they operate in harmony with these general policies.

Special status in the field of regional economic policy, therefore, could come to mean the use by the government of Quebec of a whole range of special powers for the purpose of influencing its industrial and resource development: its larger share of the corporation tax, its control over special federal regional measures, its right to consult with the central government on federal economic policy, as well as the more familiar loan, guarantee and industrial estates programs to be found in all provinces. The question implicitly raised by such a regime will be obvious: given the different economic interests of the several provinces of Canada, and given the keenness of competition between them for industrial and resource development, would *statut particulier* be acceptable to the people and the governments of the other provinces or would it lead instead to general regionalization?

A second important question about *statut particulier* is its effect upon social policy and upon the distribution of the benefits and burdens of the several federal and federal-provincial programs involved. Shared-cost programs in the fields of health and welfare already have been the object of a good deal of discussion; indeed Quebec now enjoys special status in respect of the well-established programs in this field—at least until other provincial governments take advantage of a federal offer under which they too could assume full fiscal responsibility for the major health and social assistance programs. New federal-provincial programs, on the other hand, have not provided any special option for Quebec: that province like all others must start a universal and public medical care program, to use this example, in order to qualify for the new federal medical care grants. And Quebec like the other provinces has been told by the federal government that when its medical care program is well established, new fiscal arrangements will be considered under which it could assume full fiscal responsibility for its program. To give Quebec special status in respect of new programs such as this would mean offering to the government of that province full federal compensation, whether or not a qualifying program were started. For this system to work, however, the other provinces would have to refrain from asking for similar treatment, and Parliament would have to be prepared to legislate accordingly. For to offer the same option to all provinces would in effect be to offer them unconditional grants—some $360 million in the case of medical care, a temptation I can scarcely see the provinces resisting—or Parliament to withdraw the offer altogether. Put more generally, the logical conclusion of the system proposed is either for Parliament to refrain altogether from trying to stimulate new country-wide health and welfare programs or for Parliament to extend an unconditional fiscal benefit to Quebec only.

The extension of *statut particulier* to social policies which are purely federal—essentially the income redistribution measures—would raise a different aspect of the benefit-burden question. Here the proposal is that the government of Quebec would become the sole agency responsible for income redistribution measures in Quebec, with federal income maintenance programs such as family allowances and old age security pensions being replaced by Quebec government measures. The only official proposal which has been made calls for the transfer to the government of Quebec of most federal income redistribution measures—including both the family allowance and old age security payments to persons, and federal equalization and other payments to the provincial government—and provides that the government of Quebec would be compensated by the transfer to it of 100 per cent of the federal income tax on persons and much of the tax on corporations.

The advocates of this form of particular status recognize that tax revenues from the rest of Canada would have to continue to flow into Quebec, in one way or another, if taxes in that province were not to rise as a result of the assumption by the provincial government of full responsibility for income redistribution within its borders. It is well known that income in Quebec is below the national average, with the result that federal income redistribution measures, which apply automatically across Canada, now result in a net inflow into Quebec of some $200 million a year (1967-68 figures). The suggestion is, therefore, that the Parliament of Canada should continue to be responsible for making payments to the government in Quebec (preferably by means of tax transfers), but that it should forego any constitutional right to make payments to persons in Quebec. Thus the disposition of the contributions of taxpayers outside of Quebec toward income maintenance within Quebec would be solely within the discretion of the government of the province. The question, it will be evident, is whether Canadians outside of Quebec would willingly accept the proposition that they ought to make contributions to maintain the revenues of the *government* of Quebec, but that they ought not to make contributions to maintain the incomes of the *people* of Quebec.

The second question raised by this aspect of *statut particulier* also concerns Canadians outside of Quebec. Would the politicians in other provinces refrain from asking for the same privilege Quebec politicians would be receiving, namely the right to write and send all family allowance and old age security cheques? If they did not—if they too wanted to assume responsibility for these programs—the federal government's role in income redistribution gradually would be dismantled. Such a prospect raises even more fundamental questions than does *statut particulier*. For income redistribution, through a combination of taxes and transfer payments, has come to be considered one of the principal characteristics of nationhood and to the citizen one of the more obvious evidences of citizenship; it is doubtful that this tax-transfer mechanism could be dismantled without jeopardizing one of the unifying strands of the Canadian community.

The third question that particular status for the government of Quebec could raise would develop from the accretion in the fiscal power of the province, resulting from the transfer to it of certain federal powers such as those just discussed. Currently the federal government equalizes and stabilizes the revenues of *all* provinces, under a kind of fiscal income test, universally applied. Such an arrangement is consistent with a form of federalism under which all provinces have similar constitutional powers. Under *statut particulier,* however, the government of Quebec would have superior constitutional powers in relation to those enjoyed by other provinces—for example, its special ability to influence Canada's economic policy and its competitive advantages in the field of industrial and economic development. One is driven to wonder whether these present intergovernmental arrangements would persist in the face of this new balance of power. Would there arise in the minds of other provincial governments, for example, the question as to whether Quebec was in a position to combine its special fiscal status with the equalization payments, toward which the citizens of the other provinces contributed, to finance competitive tax or expenditure incentives to industry? Put more generally, would intergovernmental arrangements, under which all provinces benefit and contribute equally, persist or would special fiscal status enjoyed by one provincial government force a readjustment designed to bring into balance the fiscal power and the fiscal responsibilities of all governments?

The particular status approach to federalism would raise questions concerning the machinery of government in Ottawa, as well as those concerning intergovernmental arrangements. Under the system proposed, as I understand it, Parliament would no longer have jurisdiction, so far as the people of Quebec were concerned, with respect to income redistribution measures, new federal-provincial programs, or regional economic development, to take three examples. Moreover, under some formulations the Quebec government would be recognized as the responsible spokesman for the views of Quebeckers on purely federal economic policies. In effect, therefore, cabinet ministers in the Quebec government would have replaced Quebec members of Parliament as the responsible spokesmen for the views of Quebeckers on a wide range of matters which had been federal, and which would remain under federal jurisdiction in respect of the other provinces. What adjustments would be required in the machinery of government to make it consistent with these new arrangements is a complicated question, which I leave to constitutional experts. But it seems evident to the layman that the Parliament of Canada would come to legislate on two classes of questions: those in which it had jurisdiction throughout Canada and in which Quebec MP's had a vote, and those in which the opposite was the case. The broader the range of responsibilities transferred to the government of Quebec, the more Parliament would be legislating in respect of the nine provinces only, with the Quebec legislature legislating in respect of Quebec. The effect of this transfer of powers, if carried to the conclusion advocated by some, would be a relatively independent Quebec, associated with the rest of Canada to the extent that it was advantageous to do so. Parliament would legislate for the two parts of Canada only in respect of such matters as tariffs and trade, currency and monetary matters, and presumably defence.

This leads to my final, and to me the most fundamental question about this direction for Canadian federalism. What would be the reaction of Canadians to the diminution in the degree of pluralism implied under *statut particulier,* by comparison with that provided for under the present constitutional division of powers? For Quebeckers the new regime would mean a shift to their provincial government of certain powers which now lie within the central government's domain or are shared with the federal government. Such a shift would imply both that Quebeckers would to a greater degree be "maîtres chez nous," and correspondingly that they would be the subjects of what would be more like a unitary provincial state. For Canadians in other provinces, too, *statut particulier* likely would lead more in the direction of a unitary state, as it became easier and more convenient to centralize powers in Ottawa. Quebec would no longer be in the vanguard of the forces of diversity, and of the remaining provincial governments so many are so small that it would be difficult for them to oppose any trend toward centralization.

So Canada might well be faced with a paradox: in an effort to strengthen the forces of diversity in Canada, through greater regionalization of government in Quebec, the nation might end up by diminishing the forces of pluralism.

The Associate State

This result is almost explicit, I would think, in the other variant of greater regionalization of government in Quebec—the associate state proposal. The essence of this alternative, if I understand it correctly, is to create two virtually sovereign states, one English and one French, and then to provide for the delegation by them to a new confederal body of certain defined and limited powers. Some of the advocates of this approach would assign to the confederal body roughly those powers given up by the members of the European Common Market; others would assign it broader powers, including trade and monetary policy and international relations. Whatever the case this approach seems to assume a centralization of powers in both states—a kind of "dual centralism".

Most of the questions which arise in respect of *statut particulier* would be resolved under the associate state approach. For there would no longer be a federal state or federal machinery, as we know it, within which a new balance would have to be found between the influence of Quebeckers and the people of other provinces. According to the authors of this proposal each state would influence equally the common economic policies; they would be developed through negotiations within the new confederal apparatus. Each state would have its own regional development policies, subject of course to the agreed economic policies. Each would have its own income redistribution system and its own social security measures. In short, under this approach the machinery of government would be adjusted in a quite fundamental way: by substituting for the federal Parliament and government of elected representatives a confederal apparatus operated by delegates appointed by the government of the two member states. Mutual self-interest would be relied upon to force a reconciliation of the conflicting interests of the two states.

The associate state approach poses, not the problems of adjustment within a federation if this understanding of the proposal is correct, but rather the question as to whether the needs of mutual interdependence would be sufficient to guarantee, in the face of the influence of our single powerful neighbour, the creation and then the survival of a new confederal country. A common economic market is assumed, for example. With such a major division in the country, however, the proponents of the associated states would have to consider whether British Columbia and the Prairie provinces would not prefer a common market with the United States to one which included Ontario and possibly the new state of Quebec. And they would have to consider too whether the old ties of the Atlantic provinces to the New England states would not impel these provinces in the same direction. In the field of social policy, it would be equally logical to consider whether the English-speaking state would continue to feel under an obligation to provide equalization payments or transfer payments to the state with which it now had to negotiate common economic policies. Or would English-speaking Canadians consider that Quebec under these circumstances was too independent a nation to qualify for equalization and too rich to qualify for foreign aid? It seems to me, in other words, that the preoccupations of the new states would not be those of today; they would be with their new status in relation to one another and in relation to an increasingly interdependent world.

Supposing, however, that the two states *were* to be established and were to function as their advocates suggest, the second question is whether the new state of Quebec would in fact gain the degree of independence its authors anticipate. The economy of Quebec would be more exposed to external influences than Canada's now is; economic logic would suggest that the governors of the new state would discover that control over monetary and fiscal policy would not be sufficient to enable them to follow a truly independent economic policy. Similarly they could be expected to find that control over the institutional repositories of Quebec savings would be subject to external contraints: rigid regulation of Quebec financial institutions might well reduce the inflow of capital from Canada and the United States, even to the extent that total investment in Quebec might decline. More important, the advocates of the associate state might find that the limitations of an open society could extend even to the promotion of the French language and culture—that the government of Quebec might be more inhibited than it has been, for example, about legislating with respect to the use of the French language in private business. For unless the rate of economic growth were to increase in Quebec —and it could indeed decline if it were subject to more protection or more direction—per capita income would decline relative to that elsewhere in North America, and increasing numbers of Quebeckers might choose to migrate to English-speaking areas. Only a return to a closed society, this line of reasoning suggests, would insulate Quebec from the constraints of an open economy and an open society. It is even possible that the presence as neighbours of 215 million English-speaking people might impose similar if less powerful constraints on the development of the French-Canadian culture within Quebec, bearing in mind that the new English-speaking Canada would no longer have any sense of obligation concerning the protection or preservation of that culture. Similar but more powerful constraints could be expected to operate in respect of Quebec's influence in international affairs.

Pursuing this logic, the new English-speaking Canada would be faced with similar constraints upon its independence. But its will to survive would have been weakened, in part because of the greater similarity between the cultural traits of English-Canadians and those of their American neighbours, and in part because of the newly exaggerated or newly emphasized divergence between the economic interests of Ontario and those of eastern and western Canada. Even the advantages of regional diversity might not be preserved if the nine remained together; the preoccupation with survival would almost certainly require a greater centralization of power, and this would militate against even this advantage of survival.

The creation of associated states, then, if this analysis is sound, would not be the product of a shift in emphasis between the forces of unity and those of diversity *within* Canadian federalism. Rather it would involve the termination of confederation, and the creation of two new states, one of them a unitary state and the other either a unitary or a federal state, but with the two federated as closely as negotiations within the confederal apparatus would allow. Such an approach, it will be evident, really falls outside my framework of analysis, which was to examine how an equilibrium is established between the forces of unity and diversity within a single federal state.

Strong Regional Governments and a Strong Federal Government

Statut particulier, then, remains as one of the two alternatives which lie between progressive and general regionalization and progressive centralization of government in Canada. The other alternative which is being currently advocated is a marriage between a strong federal government and strong or stronger provincial governments. At first sight this proposition appears to be self-contradictory; if regional governments are to grow in strength, it must surely be at the expense of the central government. The advocates of this alternative point out, however, that this need not be the case: the role of government generally has grown so greatly that it is possible to have a federal government as strong as it has been, or as it is, while at the same time strengthening the role of the provincial governments.

It must be acknowledged that the marriage of governments, like the marriage of people, is the untidiest of all solutions. The respective powers of husband and wife, even if spelled out in some detail in a marriage contract, will vary over time as the family grows, as the huband's occupational responsibilities increase, as the wife's interests change and expand, and as both are thrown together again when the children leave the home. Nor will their responsibilities be mutually exclusive: the husband's decisions concerning his job will affect the family's finances and hence the manner in which the children are reared; the wife's decisions concerning the family will in turn affect the family's finances and hence the husband's occupational aspirations. Only if the family becomes monolithic—if either husband or wife somehow submerges the personalities of the other members of the family—does it become unequivocally clear how marriage works.

So it is with central and provincial governments in a changing federal state, argue the advocates of this fourth approach to Canadian federalism. No matter how carefully, or recently, the division of powers has been drawn, the exercise by the central government of its powers inevitably will affect the activities of provincial governments and *vice versa*. Constitutional lawyers perceived this long ago, it is pointed out, when they developed the "aspect theory": there will be aspects of provincial legislation which will touch upon federal powers and *vice versa*; only the "central tendency" of the legislation can be used as a guide to its constitutionality. The only escape from this untidiness is a unitary state—achieved in Canada either by centralization or by separation.

The advocates of the strong central-strong regional government approach hold that the present division of powers, with some modification, is capable of serving as a satisfactory framework within which the forces of unity and diversity could adjust over time. Some would modify the division of powers fairly substantially, through constitutional amendment; others less so. But whatever the case, most advocates seem to hold that the division of powers must be stated generally enough to make possible adjustments over time, as society and technology change, as the role of government grows, and as the forces of internationalization advance.

This approach to federalism calls, secondly for a reversal of the cumulative influence the federal government has come to have, through shared-cost programs, over provincial government decisions. And it calls for a greater respect on the part of the federal government than it has often displayed in the past for those areas of provincial jurisdiction which are critical to the preservation and the promotion of cultural diversity, in particular education. The recent proposal of the federal government to transfer to the provinces fiscal resources to enable them to assume full responsibility for well-established health and social assistance programs, and the new program of fiscal assistance in respect of higher education, illustrate the mechanisms by which this shift in emphasis would be accomplished.

It is not entirely clear what the strong central-strong regional government advocates would do about new federal-provincial programs. Some of them argue that the federal government should refrain altogether from using its spending power to induce the provinces to undertake new programs within their jurisdiction—that it should use this power only to make unconditional grants to the provinces. Others argue that it should initiate new federal-provincial programs only when a clear provincial consensus in favour of them has emerged. Still others argue that federal-provincial programs remain one of the important vehicles by which the forces of unity are renewed in Canada and that the federal government should employ this vehicle when Parliament has decided that it is in the national interest to do so. Whatever their views about the manner in which the spending powers should be used, the proponents of this approach would avoid a cumulative centralization of powers by transferring to the provinces full fiscal responsibility for continuing federal-provincial programs once they had become well established.

Thirdly, the powers of the central government, to look at the other end of the balance, would also be strengthened under this approach to the adjustment of the forces of unity and diversity in Canada. Its authors point out that adherence by the federal government to the spirit of the constitution would give it a stronger base from which to resist provincial invasions of federal jurisdiction. The constitution would be used both ways, in other words; as a basis for resisting federal raiding of provincial jurisdiction, and *vice versa*. One important element in the strengthening of the federal power would be a return by the federal government to that primary principle of public finance and of government which holds that "the government which spends is the government which should tax"; under such a regime, the provinces would have to increase their income taxes whenever they needed the revenues rather than expect the federal government progressively to reduce its income taxes.

A fourth element in the strong central-strong regional government approach is the suggestion that the federal government would be expected to adapt more of its programs to regional needs and regional differences. The principle that all federal measures must be capable of equal and similar application in all regions is rejected by the spokesmen for this approach as being invalid in certain areas of public policy: they point out that, in fact, there have been regional programs for years, such as the Prairie Farm Rehabilitation Act and the Maritime Marshlands Reclamation program. Thus the federal government would and should as a matter of policy adapt its institutional structure to the important differences which exist in the country.

Finally, the advocates of strong central-strong regional government propose as part of their system that the federal government should adopt an even more vigorous bilingual-bicultural policy in governing Canada. The federal civil service should be bilingual, in Ottawa and in other areas where Canada's two languages are spoken; the nation's capital should be made a model of bilingualism and biculturalism; French should be the language of instruction in those schools in Canada where there are enough French-Canadians to warrant it; and French or English should be taught in schools throughout the country as second languages.

These, I think, are the principal elements in the strong central-strong regional government approach to federalism.

While the advocates of this approach seem neither to be disposed to generalize nor to advance their views in the form of a general theory, there are, I think, certain generalizations which emerge from what they say. They are arguing, with respect to the first dimension of diversity in Canadian federalism, the preservation of pluralism, that the provinces should continue to enjoy similar constitutional powers, and that the federal government should continue to exercise constitutional jurisdiction evenly across the country. They are suggesting, moreover, that the powers of the provinces should be such that each province is able to develop its own particular status, but that none should be able to do so at the expense of the others. As for the federal government's role in the preservation of diversity, it is argued that the central government should ensure, through the exercise of its economic and other powers, that personal incomes and provincial government revenues are maintained at reasonable levels across the country, thus enabling the people and the governments of the several provinces to preserve and develop their own regional and cultural characteristics. It is argued, further, that the federal government can also contribute to the goal of diversity by refraining from unnecessary intervention in the affairs of provincial governments, and, more positively, by adapting its own programs to the unique needs and characteristics of the several regions of Canada. As for the second dimension of diversity in Canada—the duality of language and culture—the advocates of the fourth approach are contending that the preservation of the language and cultural rights of French Canadians is as much a job for the Parliament of Canada as it is for the legislature of Quebec. They argue that these rights should be properly protected throughout the country; that Canada as a whole, not Quebec alone, should be the homeland for the French Canadians. The question, they seem to be suggesting, is not whether the government of Quebec should be given particular powers because five-sixths of all French Canadians live in that province but rather whether the French-Canadian society should enjoy the same rights in English-speaking Canada as the English-speaking society enjoys in Quebec. Turning to the forces of unity in Canadian federalism, the advocates of the strong central-strong regional government approach point out that under their regime the federal government would remain a strong national government, able to perform the responsibilities normally associated with a central government. Parliament's powers would remain unimpaired; provincial "raids" upon its jurisdiction would be resisted. It would continue to be responsible for external affairs, defence, the principal elements of economic policy, and those common social and cultural policies which are essential to nationhood.

As with the particular status alternative, a number of questions arise out of any attempt to evaluate this approach to Canadian federalism. First, can the existing division of powers between the federal and provincial governments withstand the strains to which it is currently being subjected? Differences of opinion as to what the constitution means, or ought to mean, are in constant evidence, particularly as between English- and French-Canadian constitutional authorities. Competing generalizations are common, for example, as to what economic powers would be the 1967 equivalent of those which were known or were assigned to the central government in 1867. Controversy persists as to what would be the 1967 equivalent of the education power which was assigned to the provinces a hundred years ago. To generalize, the question which arises is whether the constitution must be modernized if it is to contribute to a resolution of today's frictions, or whether, alternatively, today's frictions would be exacerbated if an effort were made to rewrite the constitution.

The second question raised by the strong central-strong regional government approach is whether federal and provincial programs can exist side-by-side and can be harmonized by intergovernmental consultation or whether a clearer compartmentalization of powers is required to solve current differences between the federal and provincial governments. If the latter is to be preferred, is a greater compartmentalization of powers possible in today's interdependent society? Or must one reconcile oneself to the expectation that the exercise of exclusive jurisdiction by the federal government will nearly always affect some provincial program or *vice versa?* If this is so, if the muddier course of attempting to harmonize federal and provincial programs must be accepted, coupled with some doctrine of paramountcy where a definite locus of responsibility must be fixed, what shape should the machinery for harmonization or consultation take? When will consultation imply simply the development by each government of an adequate understanding of the interests and the policies of the other governments? When will it centre upon the shape or even the details of particular programs, with each government accepting responsibility for consulting the others as to how a particular policy or program ought to be fashioned, in order to take account of parallel or related programs? And when should consultations be expected to influence the choice as between competing priorities *within* governments and legislatures in an effort to rationalize decisions on priorities as *between* governments and legislatures?

This leads to the obvious but often overlooked question as to whether consultation has to do with influence or control. Should federal-provincial conferences have as their objective the attempt on the part of provincial governments to influence federal ministers and *vice versa* or should these meetings be looked upon as forums in which *decisions* are made? If the latter were to be the case, what would be the machinery for determining when a sufficient consensus had been reached to be binding on all participating governments and what changes would be required in the relationship of governments to their legislatures if the decisions of federal-provincial conferences were to be binding? If influence is to be the goal of intergovernmental consultations, what would be the appropriate form for such consultations? What machinery would be required to ensure that an adequate and an adequately equal opportunity were open to each government to attempt to influence the others in their decisions?

The third question that emerges when one considers this approach to Canadian federalism is whether the use of the federal spending power needs to be reviewed; whether it confers upon the central government an unintended *de facto* power over the provinces; whether it is a necessary vehicle for the practical expression of national aspirations or for the practical resolution of national problems. The spending power has been used so widely and with such great effect by the federal government that it can scarcely be ignored: it is the primary basis for income maintenance payments to persons, for industrial incentive payments to industry, for unconditional equalization payments to the provinces, and for conditional or shared-cost grants to the provinces. Its use by federal governments for influencing provincial priorities through shared-cost programs has raised in the minds of certain authorities the question as to whether the spending power has not come to rival in importance the division of powers in determining the effective role of the federal government. This being so, the question must be considered, with respect to the spending power as with respect to the division of powers, whether or not an attempt to clarify the intent of the constitution would contribute to a reduction in the tensions in our federation.

A fourth and more fundamental question which must be faced in considering the strong central-strong regional government approach to federalism is whether its premises are sound. Is pluralism a realistic goal in modern society, or must one reconcile oneself to the gradual centralization of government—in the Canadian context to the development of two relatively centralized states? If gradual centralization is inevitable, is it reasonable to expect that pluralism could be expected to persist in the North American context—that an English-Canadian society and a French-Canadian society could be expected to flourish in a US-dominated North America—if this is an unreasonable expectation within the Canadian context?

If there remains a place for pluralism in modern society and if it is a reasonable premise that two societies can flourish within a single federation, is it a reasonable expectation that this country can be made a homeland for both French and English Canadians? Or must one expect the French-Canadian society to expire except in Quebec? This is probably the fundamental question which must be answered by Canadians. For the French Canadian the question is whether a return to isolation—and separation is essentially a modern version of isolation—is the price he is prepared to pay to protect his culture or whether indeed this is the way in which his culture will flourish. For the English Canadian, on the other hand, the question is whether French Canadians are to be forced into the isolation of Quebec and ultimately perhaps into separation by a refusal on the part of English Canadians to give to the French-Canadian society equal status wherever this is possible, by a refusal to embrace the advantages of a second society in Canada.

These are the questions which become apparent when one attempts to evaluate critically the strong central-strong regional approach to federalism in Canada. It will be only too evident that this approach, like that of particular status, carries with it its own questions and poses its own problems. This should scarcely be surprising given our starting proposition that the essence of federalism is a delicate balance between the engines of unity and the engines of diversity, and a vigilant concern that the balance is maintained as the environment changes and the role of government evolves.

Conclusion

This brings me to the most difficult part of this paper—the end. I say this because, while one normally expects a speaker to come to a conclusion, a civil servant is not supposed to come to conclusions—at least not audibly or noticeably and certainly not in public. But there are a few things I would like to say.

The proposition with which I began was a simple one: that federalism is a compromise between the conflicting elements of unity and diversity within a single state. Except in a society which is both simple and static the equilibrium between these forces will be subject to constant change, with the mechanism of adjustment being the shift in power, or in the exercise of power, as between the central and provincial governments and *vice versa*. I went on to examine the several ways in which the forces of unity and diversity in Canada might be brought into a new balance, given the state of disequilibrium which presently prevails in our federation and the forces of change with which we are yet confronted.

It is not for me to make a choice between the alternative models of federalism. But I venture to suggest some of the conditions which I hope will apply in the making of the choice. We need a fuller and a more rigorous account of how these several approaches to federalism would function. We need a more critical analysis of their consequences and of their implications. We need to weigh carefully the quantum of change which Canadians may be expected to withstand before adjustments in the name of equilibrium might be transformed into forces of disequilibrium. We need to consider the relative contribution to the debate over Canada's future both of constitutional principle and of social and economic analysis. And we need to consider the importance to this debate of a clear understanding of the processes of government and how they function. In all of this the attention and the talents of Canada's social scientists are urgently required.

9 Political Parties and Elite Accommodation: Interpretations of Canadian Federalism

S. J. R. Noel

In Canada, as in all federations, there exists a complex reciprocal relationship between those political forms which are constitutionally defined and those which are not; and of the latter political parties are certainly the most conspicuous and have long been regarded as the most important. The purpose of this paper is to show that the models, theories, or metaphors most commonly used to explain the role of political parties, and the political process generally, in the operation of the Canadian federal political system are in a number of important respects either defective or inadequate, and to suggest a possible alternative.

S. J. R. NOEL – Professor of Political Science, University of Western Ontario.

Three models in particular are chosen for discussion, either because they are widely found, explicitly or implicitly, in Canadian historical and political writing, or because they purport to provide a general theoretical framework which is applicable to the Canadian federal system.

1. The Brokerage Model

The main function of Canadian political parties, according to this model, is to act as agents of political integration, combatting and neutralizing the notoriously fissiparous tendencies of Canadian society by providing for the representation within each party of every significant interest group. The underlying assumption is that the Canadian federation, being bound together by neither a transcending nationalism nor by the fact of being an inevitable economic or geographical unit, is far too fragile a creation to survive political conflict between parties which are basically dissimilar in composition or behaviour. Canada, the brokerage theorists point out, is a country divided by formidable social cleavages based upon language, ethnicity and culture, as well as by potentially disruptive regional economic differences. Its national political parties, therefore, must be 'omnibus' or 'department-store' parties, composed of similar coalitions of interests, which act as brokers (or 'interest aggregators'), reconciling the conflicting claims of different social groups. In the words of R. MacGregor Dawson:

> The parties are the outstanding agents for bringing about co-operation and compromise between conflicting groups and interests of all kinds in the nation; for as a rule it is only by a merging of forces that these can hope to become powerful enough to secure office.[1]

According to another textbook, party politicians

> are always arranging deals between different sections of opinion, finding compromises that "split the difference", and thus concentrating votes behind the programme of their political party. As long as the sovereign electorate is of numerous diverse opinions, this is the only way majorities can be constructed and power gained to push through any political programme in a democracy.[2]

The authors were referring not only to Canadian but to American parties as well, which points to a second basic assumption underlying the brokerage model: that the Canadian Liberal and Conservative parties are analogous to the Democratic and Republican parties of the United States, and can therefore be understood in the same terms. In other words, there is a *North American type* of political party which functions in a similar way in both countries, and can be similarly analysed.[3]

---

[1] *The Government of Canada,* 4th Ed. rev. by Norman Ward (Toronto, 1963), p. 454.

[2] J. A. Corry and J. E. Hodgetts, *Democratic Government and Politics,* 3rd Ed. (Toronto, 1959), p. 223.

[3] A book which appears to have had considerable influence on Canadian writers on politics in the 1940's and '50's is E. Pendleton Herring's *The Politics of Democracy* (New York, 1940).

The difficulties in this interpretation (for there are certain differences between Canadian and American political parties which are too obvious to be ignored) are usually explained historically in terms of Canada's British connection:

> Our North American environment (writes the historian F. H. Underhill) makes for fundamental resemblances between Canadian and American politics. Our cabinet system of parliamentary government makes for parties on the British model. And like most other Canadian institutions and habits, our Canadian parties show the constant interplay between North American environment and British inheritance.[4]

In other words, although in both countries the parties operate in essentially the same way because of the influence of their shared environment, there are also differences between them which result from the different constitutional frameworks within which they operate. The latter, however, affect mainly appearances and are not fundamental.

In the American system of presidential-congressional politics the brokerage functions of the parties are performed openly, and indeed amid considerable publicity. At the presidential level, the process through which an aspiring candidate bargains for the support in primary elections and in the nominating convention of the heterogeneous elements of his party is a matter of public knowledge and comment. In Congress, the legislative process likewise tends to emphasize the open interaction between parties and interest groups.[5]

The Canadian system, by contrast, is 'closed'; like the British, it operates behind a screen of constitutional conventions which normally shades its crucial areas of bargaining and decision-making from the public gaze. Moreover, the requirements of the unwritten part of the Canadian constitution, which defines the role of the Crown, cabinet and Parliament (and, through the convention of ministerial responsibility, of civil servants), also drastically limit our knowledge of how the political process actually works. It is significant that there are no studies of this aspect of Canadian politics comparable to the large American literature on governmental decision-making, interest group behaviour, and the analysis of roll-call voting in Congress.[6] This is not simply the result of an unfortunate oversight on the part of Canadian political scientists. The fact is that either the data upon which such studies might be based are for the most part not available in Canada (for example, almost nothing is known of the operation of cabinet committees, or of the interaction between interest group representatives and ministers and senior civil servants) or of little practical use (for example, an analysis of the voting record of M.P.'s in House of Commons divisions is hardly likely to illuminate the role of the parties as interest aggregators—however much

---

[4] F. H. Underhill, *Canadian Political Parties* (Canadian Historical Association Booklet No. 8, 1964), p. 11.
[5] See V. O. Key, Jr., *Politics, Parties, and Pressure Groups*, 5th Ed. (New York, 1964).
[6] For an attempt to apply the terminology of American legislative studies to the Canadian House of Commons see Allan Kornberg, *Canadian Legislative Behavior* (New York, 1967), which is a study not of how M. P.'s behave but of their personal and political backgrounds and attitudes.

it might show about the strength of party discipline). The one Canadian party institution which might appear at first sight to be amenable to the same sort of analysis as its American counterpart is the party leadership convention. Here, it might be argued, the attempts of leadership aspirants to build nation-wide coalitions in support of their candidates make these conventions very like the American parties' presidential nominating conventions. While superficially there is much to support such a view, (particularly in recent years when the television cameras have tended to turn the Canadian conventions into 'media-events', complete with American-style floor demonstrations by supporters of the various candidates), in reality there are fundamental differences between the two types. To mention only the most important, in the American convention voting is open and by state delegation; in Canada the *individual delegates* vote by secret ballot. This may mean only that our knowledge of the details of party brokerage and coalition-building is deficient in the Canadian case—or it may mean, as Donald Smiley concludes, that "the voting rules of the Canadian leadership convention preclude the deliberate creation of the kind of presidential coalition that is so central to American national politics."[7] The point is, however, that here too the Canadian system is relatively 'closed', and the type of analysis that is so enlightening in the study of American politics is therefore largely inapplicable.

There remain the Liberal and Conservative party platforms, which, it is commonly remarked, are typically constructed on the principle of 'something for everyone'. A study of the actual party platforms, however, does not show that this is the case, at least not in the American sense of being a list of promises designed to appeal specifically to different groups. Rather, the Liberal and Conservative platforms in the twentieth century have tended to be more like the election statements of the British Conservative Party; i.e., designed to appeal widely but not reflecting the outcome of some prior bargaining process.[8] They show, in fact, little more than that both parties are, or aspire to be, national parties; what they do not show is *how* they actually operate.

The brokerage theorist therefore is forced to make the assumption that Canadian parties function in the federal political system in much the same way as American, even though (because of certain constitutional 'peculiarities') they cannot be observed doing so! This, of course, may be the case. But it is not shown to be the case merely because the claims of conflicting and competing groups do in fact appear to be accommodated fairly successfully in the Canadian political system, for the means of accommodation may be drastically different. But even if they are not, even if the Canadian parties perform in the secrecy of their parliamentary caucuses a brokerage function similar to that performed more or less openly by the American parties, the brokerage model, as applied to Canada, remains no more than a dubiously useful analogy, for virtually all of its empirical underpinnings must be drawn from American experience.

---

[7] D. V. Smiley, "The National Party Leadership Convention in Canada: A Preliminary Analysis", *CJPS,* Vol. 1 no. 4 (December, 1968), p. 380.
[8] See D. Owen Carrigan, *Canadian Party Platforms, 1867-1968* (Toronto, Copp Clark, 1968).

2. The Systems Model

A second model that has been employed in the analysis of Canadian parties and politics is the familiar systems model of David Easton.[9] This has the considerable merit of relating the political process to the functioning of political institutions, and is not difficult to apply plausibly, as long as it remains at a high level of abstraction. The usual inputs, outputs, conversion process, feed-back arrow, etc. can all be identified in a general way, and to this extent the model is pedagogically valuable. Beyond this, however, it provides few new insights into the way in which the Canadian federal system operates. To take an obvious example, it is undoubtedly useful for certain purposes to emphasize that the federal cabinet is a vital part of the 'conversion process', but it does not get around the fact that this vital part of the conversion process operates under an effective convention of secrecy. Even more serious is the difficulty in using an input-output model to explain the complexities of intergovernmental relations in a federal system where not only much of the conversion process but also much of the input side lies in a political *terra incognita*. There is perhaps no *intrinsic* reason why the subtleties and complexities of federal-provincial relations, including the relations of federal and provincial parties to one another and to the interest groups which operate within the respective jurisdictions, could not be illuminated by the application of a sufficiently sophisticated systems model, but it is as well to recognize that the *practical* difficulties are immense. Engelmann and Schwartz, in discussing in general terms the relatively simple questions of interest articulation and aggregation as inputs at the national level, and the interaction of interest groups and national parties, are forced to admit when it comes to applying their analysis to the hard world of political reality, that

> it would require the kind of empirical research bordering on military intelligence work to obtain a full picture of the extent to which interest groups seek access to parties on their way to the governmental structure.[10]

In summarizing their findings they conclude unhelpfully that "political parties may or may not be involved in carrying interest demands to the governmental structure".[11]

This of course does not mean that system analysis as a technique may not be useful in certain circumstances—only that the circumstances have to be carefully chosen. And in the case of Canada it would appear that the system itself does not produce as one of its outputs the data on the basis of which a satisfactorily rigorous and sophisticated systems model could be applied.

There is, however, a useful by-product of systems analysis in the Canadian context: it helps direct the attention of Canadian political scientists outward, away from their traditional concerns and towards those relatively unexplored

[9] See David Easton, *A Framework for Political Analysis* (Englewood Cliffs, N.J., 1965).
[10] F. C. Engelmann and M. A. Schwartz, *Political Parties and the Canadian Social Structure* (Scarborough, Prentice-Hall, 1967), p. 107.
[11] *Ibid.*, p. 110.

intra- and extra-societal environments which interact with the formal and informal mechanisms of government. While the application of systems analysis has not notably advanced our understanding of that interaction, it remains to be seen whether other models might be applied, or new ones developed, which could be used to greater advantage. One as yet untried approach which appears to hold considerable promise—the European 'elite-accommodation' model—is discussed in Section 5.

3. The Federal 'Bargain'

To question the utility of the brokerage model as applied to Canada is not, it should be made clear, to deny the existence of a strong predisposition towards compromise and the peaceful resolution of conflict in the Canadian political culture (or cultures). In this respect, Canada is probably not very different from other democratic polities, whether their parties are of the brokerage type or not. In Austria, Sweden, Switzerland, the Netherlands, and Finland, to take but a few examples, the political process would certainly appear to be no less a process of compromise. The phrase 'brokerage politics', however, as normally used, implies something more than 'compromise'; it implies not merely the existence of a cultural norm but also the existence of a pattern of political behaviour, a *way* of doing this politically that can be distinguished from other ways. Hence to point out the importance of compromise in Canadian politics, or to suggest that "it is no accident that the three Prime Ministers with the longest terms in office—Macdonald, Laurier, and King—have all been conspicuous for their willingness to make concessions, their skill in avoiding awkward or hasty decisions, and their ability to bring together people of diverse-interests and beliefs"[12] is to say hardly more than that Canadian politics are democratic and that some party leaders have been more successful than others. It tells us very little about the role of political parties or the way they perform that role.

The theory of the 'federal bargain', as advanced most recently and succinctly by W. H. Riker, contains a further model that merits examination in its application to Canada. Riker argues that federal systems result from a mutual desire of the member states or communities for greater security in the face of external threats, and for economic or territorial expansion. Once the bargain is struck it is maintained over time by a variety of factors, the most important of which is the party system:

> Whatever the general social conditions, if any, that sustain the federal bargain, there is one institutional condition that controls the nature of the bargain in all the instances here examined and in all other ways with which I am familiar. This is the structure of the party system, which may be regarded as the main variable intervening between the background social conditions and the specific nature of the federal bargain.[13]

---

[12] R. MacGregor Dawson, *Democratic Government in Canada*, rev. by W. F. Dawson (Toronto, 1963), p. 125.

[13] W. H. Riker, *Federalism* (Boston and Toronto, 1964), p. 136.

In the United States the type of bargaining which takes place especially within the parties, tends to confirm the validity of the brokerage model. As Riker notes, "the life of a President . . . is one of constant bargaining—to get the votes to get nominated, to get the votes to get elected, to get the votes to get bills through Congress, to get the votes to get re-nominated, etc., etc."[14] In Canada, on the other hand, the type of bargaining which is most central to the federal system takes place not within or even between parties, but between the federal and provincial *governments*. And even when these governments are controlled by a single party (or more accurately, by federal and provincial parties bearing the same name) it would be highly misleading to suggest that the party therefore acts as a broker between federal and provincial interests. Rather, "even within the Liberal party, provincial prime ministers look to Liberal leaders in Ottawa, not for leadership, but for bargaining concessions of exactly the same sort that might be gained by Social Credit or Union Nationale provincial ministries."[15]

Riker, indeed, nowhere claims that brokerage-type national parties, or brokerage-type politics on the American model, are essential to the making or maintenance of a federal bargain. What he does claim is that the degree of centralization or decentralization in a federal system will vary "according to the degree to which the parties organized to operate the central government control the parties organized to operate the constituent governments".[16] It will also vary, he suggests, with the strength of popular identification with the federal state itself or with its constituent territorial units.

The first hypothesis has not been tested in the Canadian case by any empirical study designed specifically for this purpose, but the most extended recent treatment of the fluctuations in the level of centralization in the Canadian federation suggests that the internal structure of parties is not among the most important determinants.[17]

The second hypothesis, while also untested, nevertheless does appear to be confirmed by one of the most generally recognized features of the Canadian federation: the persistence within it of strong regional identities.

4. Regionalism and 'National' Consensus

That Canada is a country without a strong sense of 'national identity' is a truism repeated *ad nauseum* in both old and new analyses of Canadian politics. While almost any statement of it would serve equally well, the following by John Meisel puts it succinctly and in contemporary terms:

> The most significant feature of Canada's value system, and the one with the most far-reaching consequences for the political process and the operation of the party system, concerns the almost total absence of a

---

[14] *Ibid.*, p. 93.
[15] *Ibid.*, p. 118.
[16] *Ibid.*, p. 129.
[17] Paul W. Fox, "Regionalism and Confederation" in Mason Wade (ed.), *Regionalism in the Canadian Community, 1867-1967* (Toronto, 1969), pp. 2-29.

national fervor. Canada must, in many respects, be the least nationalistic country in the world. The French-speaking population has a highly
developed sense of national cohesion when "national" refers to its own
cultural group, but the country as a whole is almost totally lacking in
a genuinely shared set of symbols, heroes, historical incidents, enemies,
or even ambitions. Canada, in short, lacks a fully developed secular
political culture, and the many divisions which are inevitable in a country
of its extent and variety cannot be mediated within the context of a
shared and similar complex of national values and emotions.[18]

The fact that even within English Canada there are a number of strong regional
identities ('regional' being used here as a close synonym for 'provincial') is
typically regarded as a major contributing cause of Canada's national weakness
(or problem, crisis, etc.). Implicit in such a view is a comparison with the
United States: what is missing north of the border is an over-riding sense of
pan-Canadian identity. Hence the nation-building process has been thwarted
and Canada remains essentially a hope unfulfilled.[19] The popular nation-
building school of Canadian history, as is well-known, has tended to divide
historical figures into nation-builders (good guys: Macdonald, Laurier) and
provincialists (bad guys: Mowat, Duplessis).[20] Recently, however, it has been
suggested that 'province-building' also might be considered a legitimate feature
of Canadian federalism[21], and the historians Ramsay Cook and J. M. S.
Careless have called attention to the significance of "limited identities" in
seeking to define the nature of the Canadian experience. Some of that
experience, Careless remarks,

> is doubtless common to all as citizens in one political sovereignty, with
> many economic and social interconnections besides. But much of it
> surely lies in the "limited identities" of region, culture and class. . . .
> These represent entities of experience for Canadians no less than the
> trans-continental federal union; indeed, it is largely through them that
> Canadians interpret their nation-state as a whole.[22]

Cook suggests further that while "our over-heated nationalist intellectuals" find
this situation lamentable, "it might just be" that Canadians in general find it
"quite satisfactory".[23] In the case of English Canada it is neither class nor
culture, but above all the province, which forms the basis of the strongest

---

18 John Meisel, "Canadian Parties and Politics" in R. H. Leach (ed.), *Contemporary
Canada* (Durham, N.C., 1968), p. 134-135.
19 See e.g., S. M. Lipset, *The First New Nation* (New York, 1963).
20 See e.g., Arthur R. M. Lower, *Colony to Nation,* 4th Ed. rev. (Toronto, Longmans.
1964).
21 Edwin R. Black and Alan C. Cairns, "A Different Perspective on Canadian Federalism"
in J. Peter Meekison (ed.), *Canadian Federalism: Myth or Reality* (Toronto, Methuen.
1968), pp. 81-97.
22 J. M. S. Careless, "Limited Identities in Canada," *CHR,* Vol. I no. 1 (March, 1969),
p. 3.
23 Ramsay Cook, "Canadian Centennial Celebrations", *International Journal,* Vol. XXII
no. 4 (1967), p. 663.

"limited identities". Careless advances a number of reasons for this, including metropolitanism (which in Canada gave the provinces strong urban centres of economic and political leadership), patterns of immigration and social class, and the values inherent in the political cultures:

> As for English Canada, the habitual emphasis on particularized social groupings rather than mass citizenship, on pragmatically nearer community interests instead of some generalized, idealized, national way of life, effectively ministers to strong identification with regions or provinces delineated by geography, economics, and history.[24]

The result, according to Careless, is (if we would but see it) to make of Canada a distinctive nation-state characterized by "pluralism, constraints, and compromises":

> A key word is articulation. What has been sought, and to some degree achieved, is not really unification or consolidation, but the articulation of regional patterns in one transcontinental state.[25]

Careless does not attempt to explain how, or through what institutions or mechanisms, the Canadian political system as a whole has managed to produce such an outcome, but his observation that federal leaders have tended to deal with provincial demands "pragmatically, rather than seek some broad, national counter-response"[26] is suggestive, and his general regional approach helps to cast the problem in fresh perspective.

The typical response of political scientists, when faced with the Canadian paradox of strong "limited identities" (or "weak national identity") existing within a federal system which for over a century nevertheless managed to maintain its existence by peaceful means, has been to turn to the concept of 'consensus' and particularly to view the national political parties as the promoters and vehicles of consensus. In other words, the political parties are seen not only as brokers between interests but also as being instrumental in creating a mass national consensus without which the Canadian federal system could not survive.

Consensus, however, is not a simple concept (as I. L. Horowitz has pointed out, it contains at least six ambiguities or "dimensions")[27], but the usage which seems most generally favoured in writings on national identity is to treat it as a cultural term, meaning agreement on, or acceptance of, a generalized set of values, opinions, expectations and orientations towards national institutions and symbols. Unlike Britain, where a high degree of national consensus arises naturally out of a culturally homogeneous community, in Canada it must be artificially cultivated or "nurtured"—and this is a function of political parties.

---

24 *Ibid.*, p. 6.
25 *Ibid.*, p. 9.
26 *Ibid.*, p. 5.
27 I. L. Horowitz, "Consensus, Conflict and Cooperation: A Sociological Inventory", *Social Forces* (December, 1962), pp. 178-82.

As John Meisel puts it:

> For the parliamentary system to function smoothly and, consequently, for the party system which has grown up in association with it to function effectively, a high level of cohesion and consensus is required. In a country lacking a strong national political culture and the institutions fostering it, political parties have a special role to play as agencies for the creation of national symbols, experience, memories, heroes, and villains, not to mention national favours, benefits and concessions. . . . An absolutely latent function of the party system in Canada is, therefore, the role it plays in the development and fostering of a national political culture,; it must play a vital role, in fact, in generating support for the regime. So few other institutions do so and, in the event, few are as well suited for this task as the parties.[28]

Paul Fox posits as one of the chief factors explaining the growth of provincial powers the lack of consensus "in Canadian opinion coming to bear at Ottawa". On the role of parties he comments:

> If parties are to fulfil the role that political science traditionally assigns to them, namely the function of being a unifying force by acting as a national broker to bring diverse and opposing interests together and by securing a consensus, then each of the parties must be agreed within itself on the fundamentals of its existence.[29]

Whether Canadian political parties do now, or have ever, fulfilled the role of creating a popularly shared national consensus, however, is a question to which the answer is far from clear. Presumably a consensus must be a consensus *on* something, and if this is the case it should be possible to establish empirically the strength and composition of such a consensus. The most thorough and systematic attempt to date to discover the content of the Canadian consensus, and to define the role of parties in promoting it, is to be found in Mildred Schwartz's exhaustive review of the data from twenty years of public opinion polling.[30]

After examining responses to a broad range of questions relating to national "problems" (external, internal and symbolic) the author concludes, as might be expected, that the level of consensus is low, and, moreover, that to "the proverbial average man, in this case a Canadian, the significant concerns are those which relate to his economic well-being. Neither the symbols nor the substance of national independence have troubled him unduly."[31] Thus, it would appear, while the study does not explicitly confirm Cook's view that Canadians by and large have found their "limited identities" quite satisfactory, it is perfectly consistent with it.

---

[28] John Meisel, "Recent Changes in Canadian Parties" in Hugh G. Thorburn (ed.), *Party Politics in Canada,* 2nd Ed. (Scarborough, Prentice-Hall, 1967), p. 34.
[29] *op. cit.,* p. 15.
[30] Mildred A. Schwartz, *Public Opinion and Canadian Identity* (Berkeley and Los Angeles, University of California Press, 1967).
[31] *Ibid.,* p. 231.

And although the study throughout places particular emphasis on the role of parties as instruments for the nurturing of consensus, the conclusion suggested by its data is that either Canadian parties do not seek to perform this task, or if they do, they perform it badly. Schwartz therefore concludes by questioning the basic assumption underlying the party-as-consensus-builder view:

> To see in Canada specific categories of voters consistently differentiated by a large percentage margin could only be interpreted as indicating a lack of national consensus, at least on the issues surveyed. Yet Canada has existed in its present political form for almost one hundred years, and it is probably safe to assume that during most of that period consensus on similar issues has never been appreciably greater. We have explored the reasons why the major cleavages, the regional-economic and the regional-ethnic, have such a great impact on opinions and, correlatively, why political parties are restricted in their contributions to national integration. This investigation has suggested that countries such as Canada may provide alternatives to a general consensus.[32]

While it may be that Canadian survey research has simply never asked the right questions which would enable it to identify a national consensus, if this is not the case, and if therefore the search for an underlying national (i.e., mass) consensus in Canada is indeed a search for a chairman, several conclusions would appear to follow.

First, the lack of a national consensus has not necessarily been a hindrance to the survival and operation of the Canadian federal system; secondly, it has not been incompatible with the successful functioning of parliamentary democracy; and thirdly, Canadian political parties have not performed at least one of the roles (consensus nurturing) that political scientists have traditionally attributed to them. Indeed, it may well be that the importance of parties in the Canadian political system has been (and is) greatly exaggerated (partly, no doubt, because we still know so little about their operation that large, and perhaps false, assumptions about them are easily made and difficult to challenge).

It would, of course, be absurd to claim that political parties are of no importance in the political process. At the very least they remain the essential instruments for the recruitment of personnel for the elective offices of the system. But there are nevertheless numerous reasons for believing that they are less important in the operation of the *federal system,* or, assuming that their role was once greater, that their importance in this regard has diminished. In another terminology, though they perform the vital function of political recruitment, they are not similarly dominant in the performance of the functions of interest articulation and aggregation. Two developments would appear to be particularly responsible for this, one in the decision-making process of the federation and the other in the nature of provincial economies.

First, there has been a growing tendency over the past decade for decision-making in Canada to become a matter of federal-provincial consultation and negotiation, not only at the highest level of premiers and cabinet ministers but

---

[32] *Ibid.,* p. 248.

also down through various levels of the federal and provincial civil services. The effect has been to exclude parties from any significant role in the process.[33]

Secondly, the economies of most provinces, whether based on manufacturing or resource-exploitation, or a combination of both, are now extremely complex and dominated by large American corporations. (It is remarkable how often discussions of the effects of American-owned industry in Canada overlook the fact that these industries exist *in provinces,* and often have their economic stakes heavily concentrated in one province only.) While these corporations no doubt provide substantial financial backing for the old national parties, I would suggest that they do so less in the manner of a business transaction (payment for services rendered or to be rendered) than in the manner of taking out an insurance policy: by their campaign contributions the corporations seek to insure themselves against the possibility of ideologically unacceptable or unsympathetic persons winning control of the federal government. That is to say, they are primarily concerned that the parties should continue to dominate the recruitment function, and less concerned with parties as interest articulators or aggregators. The old provincial economic structures on the other hand, were dominated by relatively simple regional interests (agriculture in its various forms, fishing, lumbering, locally-owned secondary manufacturing, etc.) whose demands, while often difficult to reconcile at the national level, were also relatively simple (concerning, for example, tariffs, market regulation, public works); hence the M.P.s of the national parties could to some extent represent and mediate between them.

In contrast, modern corporate interests operate within a sophisticated framework of governmental and self-imposed constraints, understandings, and "rules of the game"; they are affected by complicated international taxation, trading, and resource-sharing arrangements; and they engage in capital transactions which frequently involve special government concessions or guarantees. In their normal day-to-day and year-to-year operation they do not seek to promote their multifarious interests through the national political parties, for the parties as such are not for the most part directly involved in the relevant decision areas.[34] Instead, they adopt a 'non-partisan' stance, cultivate a 'responsible' image, and endeavour to place their executives on government regulatory and advisory bodies. Their associations employ professional representatives and spokesmen, and maintain regular channels of communication with federal officials and ministers. A 'lobby' campaign directed at party M.P.s is nowadays a sign that an interest group lacks influence where it really counts, or that the normal process of interest group representation has broken down. The parties are left to dispose of the dwindling 'small change' of local

---

[33] This point is discussed in John Meisel, *"Recent Changes in Canadian Parties",* loc. cit, pp. 35-37.

[34] The degree of party involvement in particular decision areas is not easily determined. In general, however, I think there is a valid distinction to be made between the involvement of a party *as a party* and the involvement of, for example, a cabinet minister in *his ministerial role* even though he is of course also a party figure.

patronage, but this should not be confused with interest articulation and aggregation.

It therefore remains to be asked whether there are social or political mechanisms instead of or in addition to parties which have enabled the Canadian federal system to achieve at least the minimum level of harmony between its regional components necessary for its survival, and if there are, whether they are still capable of functioning effectively.

5. Consociational Democracy and Elite Accommodation

It is only natural that Canada should most frequently be compared with the United States, and that models, metaphors and theories of the political system that are applicable to the one should be assumed to be applicable to the other. There are certain indisputable similarities: both are federations, both span the North American continent, both are affluent Western democracies, and both exist within the common economic framework of modern capitalism. These and other similarities, however, too often obscure the significance of those differences which do exist, or cause similarities which exist with other countries to be neglected. This is particularly true of European countries, even though it would appear to be the case that Canadians, with their attachment to regional identities, and their strong linguistic and cultural differences, have a good deal in common with at least some Europeans. This is not to say that Canada is more European than American. It is merely to suggest that there may be some advantages to be gained from occasionally viewing Canadian politics from a European perspective.

It used to be the case that European political studies were almost entirely historical or legalistic, but this is no longer so. Contemporary European writing on politics is distinguished by a new interest in empirical theory and model-building. The primary emphasis, moreover, is not on the 'developing' countries (as is the case with much contemporary American theory) but on the economically developed modern democracies of Western Europe. A number of these countries, like Canada, lack an overriding national identity or mass consensus and are characterized by strong limited identities, yet they nevertheless manage to function as stable and effective political entities. A theory which attempts to explain their successful operation is therefore of considerable interest to the student of Canadian politics. One such theory is the theory of "consociational democracy" developed by the Dutch political scientist Arend Lijphart.[35]

Lijphart's starting point is the inability of American empirical theory to deal adequately with the reality of politics in a number of West European democracies. In particular he argues, neither pluralist theory nor structural

---

[35] See Arend Lijphart, "Consociational Democracy," *World Politics,* Vol. XXI no. 2 (January, 1969), pp. 207-25; *idem,* "Typologies of Democratic Systems," *Comparative Political Studies,* Vol. I no. 1 (April, 1968), pp. 3-44; *idem, The Politics of Accommodation: Pluralism and Democracy in the Netherlands* (Berkeley and Los Angeles: University of California Press, 1968).

functionalism nor communications theory can deal with the politics of "fragmented but stable democracies" (such as the Netherlands, Austria, Belgium, and Switzerland) other than by treating them as 'deviant' cases.[36] In none of these societies is there a situation of "cross-cutting cleavages" or national consensus such as American theory holds to be necessary for the successful functioning of democratic government, yet each must be regarded as an effectively functioning democracy.

The explanation, Lijphart suggests, is to be found in the role played by political elites in these countries in deliberately overcoming the effects of cultural fragmentation. Hence, even in the absence of a national identity or consensus, if there are strong limited identities or subcultures it is possible for the political leaders of these units consciously to practice accommodation at the elite level in order to maintain the political system and make it operate effectively. For this to take place, however, it is necessary that within each subculture the political elite should possess the confidence of their respective societies. Lijphart's model of a consociational democracy may be portrayed diagramatically, as in Figure 1.[37]

Figure 1

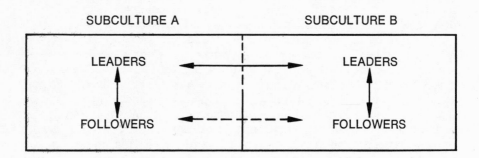

SUBCULTURE A   SUBCULTURE B

LEADERS   LEADERS

FOLLOWERS   FOLLOWERS

For the system to function successfully the elites (leaders) must have the following abilities or qualities:[38]

> (1) they must be able to accommodate the divergent interests and demands of the subcultures;

---

[36] Arend Lijphart, "Typologies of Democratic Systems," *loc. cit.*, pp. 14-17.
[37] *Ibid.*, p. 26.
[38] *Ibid.*, pp. 22-23.

(2) they must be able to transcend cleavages and join in a common effort;

(3) they must be committed to the maintenance of the system; and

(4) they must understand the perils of political fragmentation.

For the masses (followers) the requirements are only that they be committed to their own subcultures and that they trust and support their respective political elites. Lijphart maintains that the less contact between the masses of the subcultures the less friction there will be between them. "Hence, it may be desirable to keep transactions among antagonistic subcultures in a divided society—or, similarly, among different nationalities in a multinational state—to a minimum."[39]

In the perfect (i.e., most extreme) case of consociational democracy each of the units in the system would be perfectly encapsulated. There would therefore be no horizontal communication whatever at the mass level. Instead, there would be only vertical communication between mass and elite within each unit, and communication across subculture boundaries would be entirely a function of the political elite. However, in actual political systems, even when the subcultures are separated by a language barrier, there is always a certain amount of horizontal communication at the mass level (as well as a certain amount of communication between the elite of one subculture and the mass of the other). Consocionality, therefore, must be understood as a relative term. Moreover, even in societies with a fairly high degree of cultural homogeneity, such as Britain, there will be certain consociational features; e.g., the Welsh and Scottish representatives in the cabinet. In a consociaional democracy such as the Netherlands, on the other hand, such features as subcultural representation in the Social and Economic Council are crucial to the maintenance and effective operation of the political system.

Theoretically, also, it is possible that a consociational democracy could function satisfactorily even if among the masses of the different subcultures there was absolutely no attachment to the national political system and no sense whatever of a national identity. In actual systems, however, some popular national sentiment is always present. What distinguishes a consociational political system from other types of political systems is the relative weakness of its mass national sentiments and the overcoming of this weakness through accommodation at the elite level. Thus, not only does Lijphart's model suggest parallels between Canada's experience and the experience of a number of other countries, it also offers a possible explanation of the way the Canadian political process operates. First, in broadest terms, it suggests that the lack of a pan-Canadian identity combined with strong regional subcultures is not necessarily a dysfunctional feature in terms of the successful operation of a federal political system, as long as within each subculture demands are effectively articulated through its political elite. Secondly, it suggests that in the relative absence of a national mass consensus, Canadian federalism has

---

[39] Arend Lijphart, "Consociational Democracy," *loc. cit.*, pp. 220-21.

been maintained and made to work mainly through a process of accommodation at the elite level.

The fact that Canada is a federal system presents certain difficulties that Lijphart does not consider in the application of the model to European countries. The most important, perhaps, concerns the definition of the political elite. In Canada this could be defined, for example, as either the holders of the most important national political offices (federal cabinet ministers) or the holders of the most important federal and provincial political offices, or, more broadly still, it could be defined to include not only politicians but also senior civil servants and the members of the most important boards and commissions at either or both levels. Likewise, the definition of 'subculture' could be applied only to English Canada and French Canada, or it could be applied to a number of regions with distinct identities: Newfoundland, the Maritimes, Quebec, Ontario, the Prairies, and British Columbia; or it could be applied to each of the ten provinces. These difficulties, however, are not insuperable. One possible method of operationalizing the concept of elite is demonstrated in Rodney Stiefbold's recent application of the consociational model to Austria.[40] Using a "reputational and positional method", Stiefbold distinguishes both between levels of elites, and between socio-economic and political elites. There is no reason why a similar classification could not be used in applying the model to Canada.

The significance of various elites (political, economic, bureaucratic, etc.) in Canadian society has been frequently noted. The landmark in the field of elite studies in Canada is of course John Porter's *Vertical Mosaic,* but Porter's main concern was apparently to show the extent to which elite recruitment in Canada is 'closed' (i.e., membership in the elites is not based on merit). Indeed, his entire work can be read as a sustained argument in favour of meritocracy, having as its unstated assumption the validity and paramountcy of meritocratic values, which are identified with democracy. Hence, factors which promote such goals as "equality of opportunity" and "social mobility" are regarded as good, and the obstacles to such goals are regarded as bad. It is this perspective which colours Porter's analysis of Canadian federalism. Cultural particularism and regionalism are treated by Porter as barriers to the achievement in Canada of a more perfectly democratic (i.e., meritocratic) society. He maintains that the federal system is based on "doubtful sociological assumptions"[41] and inhibits the development of "creative politics",[42] and deplores the absence in Canadian society of "a clearly articulated system of values, stemming from a charter myth or based on an indigenous ideology."[43] It is not surprising, therefore, that an approach so fundamentally unsympathetic to the regional factor in Canadian political life should attach little value

---

[40] Rodney P. Stiefbold, "Elite-Mass Opinion Structure and Communication Flow in a Consociational Democracy (Austria)," paper presented at the American Political Science Association, Washington, 1968.

[41] John Porter, *The Vertical Mosaic* (Toronto, 1965), p. 385.

[42] *Ibid.,* p. 383.

[43] *Ibid.,* p. 558.

or significance to the role of the political elite in maintaining Canada's existence and in enabling the political system to function even in the absence of "a charter myth" or mass consensus.

A better approach to the understanding of Canadian federalism is surely to start with the Canada that has existed and now exists, and to seek to explain the institutions and processes that have enabled so fragmented a country to achieve accommodation without integration. In other words, to begin with Careless's hypothesis that "the implicit aim of every regional community has been maximum autonomy for itself consonant with the maximum advantage to be gained from an overriding central regime."[44] Empirical studies (along the lines suggested by Lijphart's model of consociational democracy) into such subjects as elite-mass and inter-elite communication could well add a new dimension to our understanding of the Canadian political process. A possible adaption of the model to Canadian circumstances is suggested in Figure 2.[45]

The implications of viewing the process of political communication and accommodation in the Canadian federal system in terms of such a model are several. First, it implies that, at the federal level at least, the political and bureaucratic elites whose members are drawn from the provincial sub-cultures agree *in their federal roles* on the desirability of maintaining the system. Moreover, if the federal political elite is regarded as consisting of federal cabinet ministers, there are ample historical cases, from Joseph Howe onwards, of provincial politicians with no more attachment to the federal system than the mass of their constituents being transformed in Ottawa into cabinet ministers intent on making the system work. The study of the contrasting provincial and federal political careers of cabinet ministers would almost certainly prove a rewarding exercise for the student of consociational democracy. (In the present cabinet, for example, a case that would merit attention is that of the Newfoundland representative and Minister of Transport, Donald Jamieson, who in 1948-49 was one of the leading figures in the campaign to keep Newfoundland *out* of Confederation.)[46]

Secondly, it implies that the mass of people in the provincial communities trust their political elites and continue to support them in spite of their absorbtion into the "Ottawa milieu".[47] On the other hand, it could be maintained that it is because their representatives are successful in reaching

---

[44] J. M. S. Careless, op. cit., p. 9.

[45] To simplify the diagram only two provinces are included. Also, the model inevitably oversimplifies or omits certain patterns of communication. In particular, a more fully developed model might well include a pattern of direct communication between provincial political and bureaucratic elites — a pattern which in recent years appears to have developed considerably.

[46] See Richard Gwyn, *Smallwood: the Unlikely Revolutionary* (Toronto, McClelland Stewart, 1968), pp. 102-103.

[47] The relative ease with which new arrivals from the provinces develop 'national' perspectives upon assuming office in Ottawa suggests that political scientists concerned with 'socialization' might do well to include in their researches not only children but also federal politicians.

Figure 2

ELITE ACCOMMODATION MODEL OF THE CANADIAN FEDERAL SYSTEM

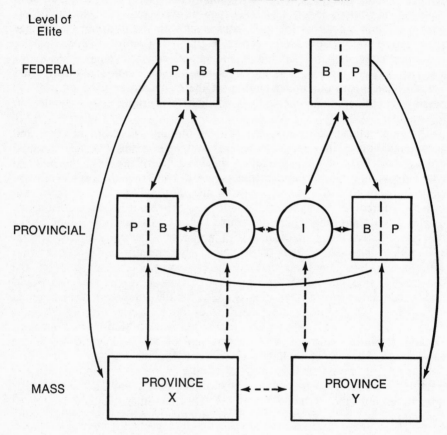

THE ARROWS INDICATE THE DIRECTION AND STRENGTH OF THE
FLOW OF COMMUNICATION

P = POLITICAL ELITE

B = BUREAUCRATIC ELITE

I = INTEREST GROUP / SOCIO-ECONOMIC ELITE

accommodation, and so enabling the system to produce certain desired material outputs, that the masses support them, (i.e., the masses are reasonably satisfied with the outputs of the system while remaining unattached to its symbols or substance).[48]

Thirdly, it implies that a key role in the working of the Canadian system must be accorded to provincial political and bureaucratic elites and interest groups. Given the division of powers in the Canadian constitution, it is inevitable that federal-provincial patterns of interaction and communication should be very complex, and that the articulation of demands should take place through a variety of channels. Provincial premiers are particularly important in articulating the demands of their respective communities to the federal government. This is not a process that takes place primarily within a political party, but is rather a transaction that takes place between different elite levels regardless of the party labels of the individual actors involved.[49] Specialized interest groups and corporate or socio-economic elites occupy a crucial role which places them in close communication with political and bureaucratic elites at both the federal and provincial levels.[50] Hence, it would appear to be necessary for a consociational system to survive in combination with federalism that the middle-level elites too be committed to the maintenance of the process of accommodation.

Fourthly, the model implies that in the system of responsible cabinet government, as it operates at both the federal and provincial levels, the political and bureaucratic elites are closely interlocked. This, however, is not to suggest that their functions are indistinguishable. It would appear to be the case in the Canadian system that the political elites at the federal and provincial levels are primarily responsible for the accommodation of broad cultural and regional interests, whereas the bureaucratic elites at both levels are increasingly important as the normal means through which the specific demands of interest groups are aggregated.

Finally, if some of the recent developments in Canadian politics are viewed in terms of the elite accommodation model a number of conclusions emerge. First, the decline of 'elitism' in Canada and a growing popular acceptance of the Jacksonian myth of popular or 'participatory' democracy may be detrimental to the maintenance of Canadian federalism if it leads to a situation in which the mass of the people are unwilling to accept the inter-elite accommodations made by their political leaders. If inter-elite accommodations must be popularly ratified they may be impossible to achieve. Secondly, 'national' policies aimed at promoting bilingualism and biculturalism may be

---

[48] This is certainly not unique. See the discussion of the German political culture in Gabriel A. Almond and Sidney Verba, *The Civic Culture* (Boston and Toronto, 1965).
[49] See W. H. Riker, *op. cit.*, p. 118.
[50] And hence, it might be added, potentially in a position to play one government off against another.

misguided in the sense that they may increase friction between separate communities that previously paid little attention to one another. It may be that a system of consociational federalism works best when the "two solitudes" are preserved.[51] Thirdly, the emergence within any one subculture of new elites who, for nationalistic, economic, ideological, or any other reasons, are unwilling to provide "overarching cooperation at the elite level with the deliberate aim of counteracting disintegrative tendencies in the system",[52] will make the system inoperable, for there exists no mass consensus to which its defenders may appeal. Consocionality combined with federalism, however, creates the possibility of a conflict between federal and provincial elites within the same subculture, and so would appear to make the outcome more uncertain.

For the student of Canadian politics, the elite consensus model thus provides an alternative way of viewing the political process which has the advantage of requiring him to posit neither the chimerical notion of an 'underlying' national identity nor to regard the national parties as 'builders of consensus' and 'aggregators of interests' even though they are evidently not very active or are unsuccessful at such tasks. Though the model was originally applied by Lijphart to actual political systems only in the most general and theoretical way, the successful application of it by Stiefbold in his detailed and original analysis of Austrian politics indicates that it can be used as a framework for systematic empirical research. In the case of Canada, in view of the inadequacies of other theories, and the presence of factors that in Europe are conducive to consociational democracy and elite accommodation, there is reason to believe that the application of Lijphart's model would prove equally insightful.

---

[51] This view would appear to be supported by David Easton also. See *A Systems Analysis of Political Life* (New York, 1965), pp. 250-51.
[52] Arend Lijphart, "Typologies of Democratic systems," *loc. cit.*, p. 21.

Part Three

The Constitution

10   The Living Canadian Constitution

Alan C. Cairns

The dustbin of recent history is littered with discarded constitutions cast aside after brief and withering exposure to reality. Constitutions capable of responding and adapting to the perils of change have sufficient scarcity value to be treated with the deference appropriate to rare achievements. All the more curious, therefore, has been the detached, unappreciative Canadian attitude to one of the most durable and successful constitutions in the world.

A partial explanation is found in the nature of the British North America Act. It is a document of monumental dullness which enshrines no eternal principles and is devoid of inspirational content. It was not born in a revolutionary, populist context, and it acquired little symbolic aura in its subequent history. The movement to Confederation was not a rejection of Europe, but was rather a pragmatic response to a series of economic, political, military and technological considerations. There was no need for the kind of political theorizing which accompanied the American experience of creating a new political entity, and which exercised a spell on subsequent generations. With the important exception of the federal system, Canada was endowed "with a Constitution similar in Principle to that of the United Kingdom." Constitutional monarchy and responsible government in a parliamentary setting were already part of the Canadian heritage which was approvingly translated to the larger sphere of action which the new Dominion created. No resounding assertions of human rights accompanied the creation of the new polity. The British tradition precluded any approach to their protection premised on comprehensive declarations of principle.

The absence of an overt ideological content in its terms, and the circumstances surrounding its creation, have prevented the BNA Act from being perceived as a repository of values by which Canadianism was to be measured. Further, the first thirty years of its existence were troubled by depression, threats of secession, and constant bickering over its terms. These scarcely constituted the circumstances for the Act to become the symbolic focus for the nascent political system. Consequently, a conscious ideological adherence and loyalty to the BNA Act and the constitution of which it was a part never became overt integral components of the Canadian civil identity.

An additional factor in the Canadian lack of appreciation for the consti-

* From *Queen's Quarterly*, Vol. LXXVII no. 4 (Winter Issue, 1970), pp. 1-16. Reprinted by permission of the author and *Queen's Quarterly*.

ALAN C. CAIRNS – Associate Professor of Political Science, University of British Columbia.

tution is a confused understanding of the meaning of age and time for institutions.

With the passage of time the intentions of the Fathers unavoidably became an increasingly artificial concept with an ever attenuated contact with reality. Their visions were responses to the problems they faced in the light of prevalent conceptions of the role of government. Many of the conditions to which they addressed themselves faded away, to be replaced by conditions they could not predict. In such circumstances deference to their intentions became impossible, for they had none. Nevertheless, the BNA Act, which represents a consolidation of some of their intentions, remains an important constitutional document. This raises the question of how relevant for a contemporary evaluation of the Canadian constitution is the fact that the BNA Act is a century old.

At the most abstract level of institutional analysis, age has a double significance. Positively, a functioning institution of ancient origin acquires the special credibility that derives from its continuing utility for the attainment of one or more specified human goals. In the Darwinian process of institutional competition for survival it has emerged triumphant. Negatively, it is placed on the defensive by the fact that the contemporary circumstances to which it now applies are significantly different from the circumstances to which it was originally a response. Hence, it appears to be tinged with mortality. The graveyard, sooner or later, is its inevitable destination.

To continue the discussion on this level, however, is to grant to the question of age an undeserved importance and a spurious relevance. Institutions do not have a natural life span. They are, when wisely constructed and carefully tended, evolving human arrangements for avoiding the ravages of time by flexibly responding to the demands which confront them. Therefore to discuss the relevance of an institution in terms of its age, defined by the lapse of time since its first beginnings, is to misconceive what an institution is.

Canadian understanding of the constitution would have been much improved had it been consistently viewed in the significant American phrase as a "living constitution."[1] The wise admonition of Holmes reveals a perspective sadly lacking in Canada:

> The provisions of the Constitution are not mathematical formulas having their essence in their form; they are organic living institutions transplanted from English soil. Their significance is vital, not formal; it is to be gathered not simply by taking the words and a dictionary, but by considering their origin and the line of their growth . . . . When we are dealing with words that are also a constituent act, like the Constitution of the United States, we must realize that they have called into life a being the development of which could not have been forseen completely by the most gifted of its begetters. It was enough for them to realize or

---

[1] For an excellent American discussion of the living constitution, see K. N. Llewellyn, "The Constitution as an Institution", *Columbia Law Review* (1934), p. 34.

to hope that they had created an organism; it has taken a century and has cost their successors much sweat and blood to prove that they created a nation. The case before us must be considered in the light of our whole experience and not merely in that of what was said a hundred years ago.[2]

It is the virtual absence of this understanding of a living constitution which has produced the mistaken belief that the constitution is a century old, that it has already outlived its allotted life span, and that *younger* means *better* and *older* means *worse*. Given this belief it is possible to advocate a new constitution simply because the BNA Act was drafted a century ago. The rather trite conclusion automatically follows that a constitution, or a constitutional document, so heavy with years must be out of date.

In the 1960s there has been a recurrence of the criticism of the constitution as obsolete which was so widespread in the Depression of the thirties. In that troubled decade, the constitution as judicially interpreted was roundly condemned by centralists for the barriers it placed in the way of decisive action by the federal government. The contemporary attack has different roots. One source is the spurt of nation building and constitution making which followed the demise of Western imperialism. In much of the Third World, constitution making became a normal political activity interrupted by secession movements, coups, assassinations, and civil war as the new states struggled to overcome appalling problems and to find a framework for modernization. Whatever the justification for their endemic efforts to resolve their constitutional difficulties, and there are many, only a masochist would find their experience worthy of emulation.

An additional source is the French-Canadian view of recent years that the existing constitution restricts the process of nation building in Quebec. Hence Marcel Faribault, the late Premier Daniel Johnson, Father Ares, Professor A. Dubuc, and numerous others have issued clarion calls for a new constitution to usher in the new age of emancipation which is part of the rhetoric of the Quebec nationalist intelligentsia. Their search for a new constitution is sustained by English-Canadian writers such as Peter O'Hearn, who finds the "battered hulk of the British North America Act and its train of amendments" unacceptable.[3] Other English-Canadian support is found in politicians who capitalize on any groundswell of opinion, or who naively assume that to be progressive requires a repudiation of the past, at least at the level of oratory. They sympathize with T. C. Douglas, whose own party is more trapped by the shibboleths of the nineteenth century than any other Canadian party, when he states: "The time has come for Canadians to free themselves

---

[2] Cited in Archibald MacLeish and E. F. Pritchard, Jr., (eds.), *Law and Politics: Occasional Papers of Felix Frankfurter* (New York, Capricorn Books, 1962), p. 71. The eloquence of Holmes can be supplemented by Marshall's famous description of "a constitution intended to endure for ages to come, and consequently, to be adapted to the various crises of human affairs".

[3] Peter Joseph Thomas O'Hearn, *Peace, Order and Good Government* (Toronto, Macmillan of Canada, 1964), p. 6.

from the dead hand of the past and forge a constitution that will enable Canada to keep its rendezvous with destiny. . . . I do not think that the dead hand of the past should be allowed to stay the onward march of progress. Human rights are sacred but constitutions are not."[4]

In an age when rapid obsolescence is viewed as the natural and inevitable end for every man-made product, such a thesis quickly finds attentive receptive hearers. Superficially it has compelling force, for clearly the conditions of 1867 have passed away. It logically follows that decisions made in the light of those conditions must become increasingly irrelevant with the passage of time.

Crucial to this widespread position is the belief that the constitution is by and large what the Fathers bequeathed to us a century ago. From this perspective the constitution emerged in 1867 in the form of the British North America Act and its accompanying understandings, the product of a small political élite, the Fathers of Confederation, and barring formal amendments, is now what it was then. The confusion is subtle. To view the constitution in terms of what the Fathers intended and immediately achieved fails to see that the constitution is a continuous creation. It accords too much deference to the constitution as it existed in 1867, and too little attention to the contribution of subsequent generations to its evolution.

The Canadian constitution is the body of understandings defining the basic institutions of government and the relationships between them, plus the relationships between governments in the federal system, and between the citizens and those governments. At any given point of time the content of the constitution is a series of living practices which has been worked out by successive generations. It is a product of continuous selection, rejection, and addition. It is always, in a practical sense, contemporary. It is a living instrument of government, wider in scope than the BNA Act, and not restricted to the 1867 intentions of the Fathers. It is an evolving institution which has responded to pressures and flexibly accommodated itself to a variety of needs and changing demands.

The distinction between the constitution as an institution and the key statute that went into its formation is cogently described by Llewellyn in his discussion of the American constitution:

> The discrepancy between theory and fact found in private law is exaggerated in the constitutional field, because under a code of rigid words no easy and gradual rewording of outmoded rules, in such manner as to hide the changes made in their content, is possible. The consequences is that with growing age all force in the actual words of a code withers and dies. What is left, and living, is not a code, but an institution. Many of the institution's roots trace back through time into the code. *Many do not.* But the living institution is neither the dead code nor its interpretation." It is not even by any parthenogenesis descended from its great-grandmother code alone. It is new, it is different, it is growing; and

---

[4] *Globe and Mail* (Toronto, April 13, 1966), p. 7.

in its blood run so many other streams that resemblance to the code is seldom strong and always confined to single traits.[5]

Evidence on the living nature of the constitution is ubiquitous. The settlement of 1867 was only a beginning. It has been under constant transformation since that time. The major evidence is as follows:

1. The instruments of federal control—disallowance, reservation, and refusal of assent by the Lieutenant-Governor—have fallen into virtual desuetude. If not entirely dead, there is no likelihood that they will ever again be used in the coercive fashion of the early post-Confederation years.

2. The transformation of Empire into Commonwealth—from "Colony to Nation"—has reduced the ties to Great Britain until all that remains is an increasingly attenuated emotional link, a similarity in the institutions of parliamentary and monarchical government, and an embarrassing leftover in the continuing (entirely formal) role of the British parliament in the amending procedure.

3. As is well kown, the division of powers in the BNA Act was importantly affected by the Judicial Committee of the Privy Council. While its decisions aroused much resentment and may or may not have been appropriate to Canadian needs, it cannot be denied that they made a fundamental contribution to the constitution evolution Canadians actually experienced.

4. The division of powers was also transformed by the massive engine of the federal spending power and the conditional grants mechanism. Once again the evaluation may be favourable or unfavourable, but it is clear that the result was a marked change in the practical significance of Sections 91 and 92 of the BNA Act. Perhaps the spending power was used indiscriminately. Perhaps its use should have been (or should be) more tightly controlled, but that is not the issue here.

5. The proliferation of federal-provincial meetings of administrators and politicians, culminating in conferences of premiers and prime ministers has added, as many have pointed out, an important new mechanism of coordination for the federal system.

6. Since the onset of Word War II the fiscal system has not been the chaos of clashing taxing jurisdictions which it was in the Depression. Further, as part of a succession of fiscal agreements, huge equalization grants have been paid to the less well-endowed provinces. The original compulsory federal subsidies have been rendered financially trivial by comparison.

7. The parliamentary system has been transformed by the development of the party system, the institution of party discipline, the emergence of third parties and their recognition, the institution of research staffs for the opposition parties, etc. Recently we have been told that before our very eyes the parliamentary system is being transformed into a presidential system without the requisite checks and balances. The truth of this latter statement is irrelevant for our purposes. What is relevant is that the parliamentary half of the Canadian wedding of parliamentary government and federalism has not stood still.

---

[5] Llewellyn, *op. cit,* p. 6 *n.*

8. Even prior to the passage of the Diefenbaker Bill of Rights, the Supreme Court, and particularly Mr. Justice Rand, began to develop a court-supported jurisprudence for the protection of civil liberties. Basing their decisions largely on the flimsy constitutional basis of the preamble to the BNA Act which stated that Canada was to have "a Constitution similar in Principle to that of the United Kingdom," the court enunciated an important series of civil liberties decisions.

9. Finally, there were the formal amendments to the Act which contributed to its evolution.

Even in the cryptic fashion expressed above, these changes have been of momentous significance in the evolution of the Canadian constitution.

The agents of these changes were largely the politicians and civil servants of both levels of government responding to the demands and opportunities which the possession of office imposed on them. To examine the above list is to have it confirmed that the constitution never has been, and is not now, only what the courts say it is. The evolution of the constitution has been largely guided by successive generations of political leaders and their influential bureaucratic advisers. Admittedly they did not have a clean slate to work with. Admittedly the result has been evolution rather than revolution. Admittedly certain key parts of the constitutional framework remain, in form at least, as they were originally established in 1867. It is also true that a different beginning would have produced a different outcome, but that is true of all human experiments. The point is not that what happened in 1867 did not matter, but that the decisions then made did not constitute a cake of custom which has held subsequent generations of Canadians in unwilling thralldom in a world they never made. The point is that the constitution has worked and grown in response to the shifting conditions thrown up by the passage of time. A constitution which had accommodated for a century the often competing demands of two ethnic groups, which had survived through depression and war, the transformation of a rural society into an urban society, the settlement of the West, and the technological revolution of recent years might have been appreciated in more prosoic times for its real practical virtues, rather than as was so often the case, being scorned for its absence of symbolic appeal, and criticized for a non-existent inflexibility. In the words of Eugene Forsey, "There is no point in change for its own sake, or just for the sake of having the very latest thing in constitutions. (What matters in a constitution is not how new it is but how good it is, how well it works.) The bigger the change, the heavier the onus upon those who propose it to prove that it is necessary, or even useful."[6]

It may be taken for granted that the Canadian constitution, like any other, prejudices some and fosters other public policy outputs. Any constitution,

---

[6] "Constitutional Monarchy and the Provinces", *Ontario Advisory Committee on Confederation: Background Papers and Reports* (Toronto, Queen's Printer, 1967), p. 180. Ronald I. Cheffins, *The Constitutional Process in Canada* (Toronto, McGraw-Hill, 1969) provides a well-argued defence of the existing constitution. See especially Chapter 1 and pp. 150-51, 167.

particularly a federal one, will regularly prevent some group of office holders from attaining some of their policy objectives. To criticize a constitution because it entails this consequence, however, is similar to criticizing the law of gravity. The more precise and relevant question is comparative, whether or not the existing constitution erects more barriers to desired governmental output than would its successor. The answer depends on the nature of the particular new constitution that is advocated. Until that information is available, it is entirely proper to note the flexibility of the existing constitution.

All of the changes noted above are obvious and well known. Why then has so little heed been paid to the message they contain about the flexibility of a living constitution? What explains the constant confusion implicit in the attacks on the constitution because of its age? First, there is sometimes failure to distinguish between the BNA Act and the constitution. Then the relative paucity of formal amendments, especially dealing with the division of powers, has produced a misleading impression of stability belied by our actual experience even in that area. Much of the change which has occurred has not been formally designated as constitutional, and it has not been accompanied by fanfare. It has simply represented the handiwork of busy men attempting to work an on-going system of government.

A good part of the explanation simply lies in a compartmentalization of the minds of the critics and analysts. While all the changes have been recognized and noted, they have frequently co-existed with the assumption that the constitution is a century old. The absence of the concept of a living constitution has aided in this compartmentalization. The confusion has been deliberately sewn by propagandists who have undertaken partisan attacks on the constitution because it stood in the way of their pet panacea. No century-old document (or constitution), they contend, should be allowed to stand in the way of the people. At the opposite pole, blindness on the part of some constitution-worshippers, who have been reluctant to believe that their god could be affected by anything so mundane as the passage of time, has had some influence.

Finally, the scholarship of historians and lawyers, and to a lesser extent of political scientists, has been obsessed with discovering the true meaning of 1867. Centralists and provincialists, compact theorists and their opponents, have all fought over the BNA Act in an attempt to discover its true meaning and often to further their partisan objectives. By so doing they have exaggerated the importance of the original agreement of 1867 and have downgraded the changes it underwent in its subsequent expression.

In view of the preceding, two frequent tendencies in the discussion and evaluation of the Canadian constitution have been based on dangerous misunderstandings. It is simply mistaken to attack the existing constitution because of the age of the BNA Act, one of the key documents which went into its making a century ago. Llewellyn describes a working constitution "as being in essence not a document, but a living institution built (historically, genetically) in first instance *around* a particular document."[7] "With every passing

---

[7] Llewellyn, *op. cit,* p. 3.

decade," stated Carl Brent Swisher, "a constitution written long ago provides less and less guidance for its own interpretation amid patterns of social change and with sheer change in the dictionary meanings of familiar terminology."[8] It is equally fallacious to transform the constitutional settlement of 1867 into a measuring rod against which subsequent deviations can be assessed and their perpetrators chastised. Two American authors describe the "intentions of the framers" as a "filio-pietistic notion that can have little place in the adjudicative process of the latter half of the twentieth century. . . . A nation wholly different from that existing in 1787, facing problems obviously not within the contemplation of the Founding Fathers, can scarcely be governed—except in broadest generality—by the concepts and solutions of yesteryear."[9] The same point was lucidly expressed by Chief Justice Hughes of the United States Supreme Court: "It is no answer to say that this public need was not apprehended a century ago, or to insist that what the provision of the Constitution meant to the vision of that day it must mean to the vision of our time. If by the statement that what the Constitution meant at the time of its adoption it means today, it is intended to say that the great clauses of the Constitution must be confined to the interpretation which the framers, with the condition and outlook of their time, would have placed upon them, the statement carries its own refutation."[10] To attack the constitution on grounds of age is to fail to see its living nature. It is the same failure which produces the description of post-1867 changes as deviations.

This latter approach was very widespread in discussions of judicial review, particularly in criticisms of the Privy Council. Since lawyers constitute the professional group which has arrogated specialized expertise to itself in this matter they have an important responsibility for the misconceptions which heavily influence our constitutional discussion. I do not forget that one category of legal criticism of the Judicial Committee was based on the alleged failure of British judges to treat the BNA Act as a living instrument of government. It is true that to this group Lord Sankey, with his "living tree" analogy, was the closest thing to a judicial hero that is found in the law periodicals. However, the other major group of criticisms was specifically based on the unacceptable conduct of the Judicial Committee in departing either from the intentions of the Fathers, or the clear meaning of the BNA Act in which those intentions were presumably embodied. Further, the "living tree" school of Canadian criticism typically also reproached the Privy Council for leading Canada down the provincial path away from the limited, centralized federalism so wisely chosen in the sixties of the nineteenth century. This was partly because those critics willing to overtly discuss the constitution in terms of current need were usually centralists. Consequently, they could not resist appealing

---

8 *The Supreme Court in Modern Role,* rev. ed. (New York, New York University Press, 1965), p. 192.
9 Arthur S. Miller and Ronald F. Howell, "The Myth of Neutrality in Constitutional Adjudication", *University of Chicago Law Review,* 27 (1960), p. 683.
10 Cited in Paul Abraham Freund, *The Supreme Court of the United States* (Cleveland and New York, Peter Smith, 1965), p. 20.

to the Fathers and their original creation as the touchstone of constitutional wisdom.

In general, the basic language of both constitutional case law and its Canadian critics stressed fidelity to an ancient document. O'Connor, the author of the classic fundamentalist statement that judges should apply the Act in terms of the meanings deliberately embodied in it by its creators, strongly attacked the Judicial Committee for "most serious and persistent deviation . . . from the actual text of the Act." He was highly critical of Lord Watson's "assumption of the guardianship of the autonomy of the provinces. His proper function was merely that of an interpreter of the meaning of the words of a statute."[11] This position reflected the British tradition which instructs judges to apply statutes literally. Thus, jurisprudence in Canada, both in the language of courts and that of their critics, has not devised adequate criteria to guide judges in the employment of the discretion they unavoidably possess. This has been unfortunate, for it has meant that much constitutional advocacy has been, literally, meaningless. It has also contributed to the misunderstanding of what a constitution is.

The critics of the Privy Council frequently asserted that its failure rested on an unwillingness to use the variety of historical evidence available to throw light on the intentions of the Fathers, and thus clarify obscurities in the BNA Act. This approach was always fraught with difficulties, but with the passage of time its desirability became increasingly questionable. This was recognized by Professor Strayer in a recent publication. He noted the "very limited" evidence available on the formation of the Act and, more important, questioned its utility in principle. "Conditions have so drastically changed since 1867," he pointed out, "that the particular context in which the Act was passed may have little bearing on the context in which it is now expected to operate."

This position represents a marked change from the obsessive concern with the intentions of the Fathers in the decades prior to the abolition of appeals to the Privy Council. Yet Strayer is still caught in a historical quagmire of his own making. The obligation to appeal to the past is irresistible. His argument continues: "The more crucial question now is: What would the framers have intended had conditions been in 1867 as they are today? Even if the courts could now be induced to make use of external evidence as to the conditions of that time such evidence would be of limited value in answering this hypothetical question."[12]

Unfortunately, we are not told what evidence would be helpful. Given the impossibility of deciding how to undertake this pseudo-historical quest, one wonders why it should be undertaken at all. The assertion of Learned Hand

---

[11] *Report Pursuant to Resolution of the Senate to the Honourable the Speaker by the Parliamentary Counsel Relating to the Enactment of the British North America Act, 1867, any lack of consonance between its terms and judicial construction of them and cognate matters* (Ottawa, King's Printer, 1939), 11, Annex 1, p. 47.

[12] Barry L. Strayer, *Judicial Review of Legislation in Canada* (Toronto, University of Toronto Press, 1968), p. 156.

is as valid for Canada as for the United States: "It is impossible to fabricate how the 'Framers' would have answered the problems that arise in a modern society had they been reared in the civilization that has produced those problems. We should indeed have to be sorcerers to conjure up how they would have responded."[13]

In the evolution of a constitution, it is evident that the passage of time does and should reduce the weight to be given to the views and desires of the Fathers or of influential moulders of the constitution at other points of time. As time transforms the conditions to which the constitution must be responsive, the search is not for what was originally intended, but for what can be creatively extracted from a constitutional heritage of which the BNA Act is only a part. The search for the contemporary meaning of the constitution does not consist in minute examination of what was said or intended or achieved a century ago. Such an approach would deny to constitutional unfolding the benefits which a century of experience has given us. This generation, its predecessors and successors, partially have and certainly should view the constitution for what it is, a developing responsive tradition neither to be lightly departed from nor to be casually obeyed.

The arrangements of 1867 were never a sacrosanct body of holy writ. Approaches which so regarded them constituted a disservice to the Canadian polity and rested on a misunderstanding of the nature of a constitution. They inhibited change and thus reduced the flexibility essential for survival. Equally important, they blinded their possessors to the changes which did occur. Realistically, all working constitutions are living constitutions springing from, but not bound and gagged by, history. Inadequate recognition of this truth is a significant cause of the constitutional morass in which we now find ourselves. Cryptically we might say that the constitution has not failed us, so much as we, by our inadequate understanding of its living nature, have failed it. In a living constitution all generations are simultaneously Fathers and Sons, by necessity even if not by choice. King, Bennett, Diefenbaker, and their provincial counterparts were in their own way Fathers as were Macdonald and Cartier. Like Macdonald and Cartier they were also sons in that they built on the achievements of their predecessors. There can be no quarrel with the fact that each succeeding generation of Canadians has decided what parts of the constitution they received were viable and worthy of continued life, and which were not. However, we can quarrel with those who, either blinded by a deification of the past, resist new departures because the Fathers intended otherwise, or propose a new constitution on the mistaken grounds that the existing one, because of its time or origin, is necessarily an inflexible, incompetent instrument for new conditions. The first approach makes us prisoners of the past. The second approach deprives us of the benefits which a rich tradition provides.

---

[13] Learned Hand, *The Bill of Rights* (Cambridge, Mass., Harvard University Press, 1958), pp. 34-35.

To view a constitution as a living constitution has important consequences. It is to recognize that the processes of constitutional change are manifold and unpredictable. The process of formal amendment and judicial review are neither the only nor the most important vehicles for change. The constitution is constantly interpreted and modified by the men who work it. No new division of powers can prevent the intermingling of the activities of both levels of government in modern conditions. Predictable, clear-cut procedures for change can be obtained in the area of formal amendment, but nowhere else. The Supreme Court can be revamped in various ways, but "the history of judge-made law invites no other view than this: that the parties to the original federal 'bargain' can never be certain that the words in which they have clothed their intentions can ever be more than a rough guide to political activity, or that the range of permissible activity at any time after will bear any exact relation to their intentions."[14]

The terribly difficult problem, frequently overlooked because of obsession with the written text and the more blatant methods of change by amendment and judicial review, is how to devise conventions and understandings by which the other less obvious methods of change can be brought within a framework of constitutionalism. The main weakness, for example, of the compact theory as a set of criteria for constitutional change did not lie in its hotly contested validity, but in the restricted scope of its intended operation. Even if whole-hearted agreement to its terms had existed, this would have represented no more than a control of the amending procedure, one of the least important methods of constitutional change in Canadian history.

This problem is, of course, recognized by influential Quebec spokesmen. The late Premier Daniel Johnson, for example, stated in 1967:

> Canada today is faced with a whole series of problems which the Fathers of Confederation . . . could not conceivably have foreseen . . . . Therefore, when a new problem arises in Canada, we are more and more likely to base each government's responsibilities for it, not on constitutional principles, but on considerations of the moment which, in turn, derive from a variety of factors such as relative capacity to act, financial resources or merely the political power wielded by a given area of government. Hence even though there is a written document called the British North America Act from which we may expect some light to be cast on such traditional fields as education and municipal institutions, the allocation of new tasks among governments has not been guided by this document but by decisions mainly based on exigencies of the day. . . . Our present Constitution, perhaps admirable during the age of steam trains, no longer suits Canada's needs in this era of interplanetary rockets.[15]

---

[14] Rufus Davis, "The 'Federal Principle' Reconsidered", in Aaron B. Wildavsky, (ed.), *American Federalism in Perspective* (Boston, Little, Brown, 1967), p. 14.
[15] *The Confederation of Tomorrow Conference: Proceedings* (Toronto, Queen's Printer, 1968), Appendix B, p. 8.

At the 1966 Federal-Provincial Conference on taxation, Johnson stated:

> Having reached what it considers a turning point in its history, Quebec expects some specific things from the present constitutional system. First, it wants proof that the division of powers written in the constitution is not mere window-dressing and that, accordingly, it can count on the fiscal and financial resources it requires in order to discharge its obligations properly. . . . Quebec also wants assurance that it can exercise, fully and without interference from any quarter, all its power under the present constitution. It wants the Government of Canada to withdraw from fields which are not federal or in which the provinces have priority.[16]

Essentially the same point was made by Professor Dubuc who asserted that a century of change had rendered the BNA Act "too far removed from the basic structure and values of . . . [contemporary] . . . society to remain the touchstone for the division of powers," with the consequence that the "most important conflicts are settled on the political level and become confrontations of power; these are the conditions of political chaos."[17]

The general cogency of these critiques can be accepted. The question, however, is what can be done about them. To Johnson and Dubuc the obvious answer is a new constitution whose division of powers reflects the worked-out results of a contemporary agreement, responding to today's conditions, as to what the responsibilities of each level of government should be. Assuming for the moment that agreement could in fact be reached on a new constitution, the contribution that this would make to the solution of the problem which troubles Dubuc and Johnson is debatable. Obviously, if Quebec were to be granted greatly enhanced jurisdictional authority, the seriousness of the problem from Quebec's viewpoint would be greatly diminished. The problem would still exist, but its scope would be less extensive. If, however, as seems more likely, a new division of powers did not deviate markedly from the existing division, we would be little better off. It is not entirely clear that an ancient division of powers is more likely to produce "decisions mainly based on exigencies of the day" than is a division freshly minted at a constitutional conference. To some extent the problem arises from the impossibility of devising a comprehensive catalogue of powers into which all proposed legislation can be easily fitted. The operations of modern governments are too complex, the future is too unpredictable, and words are too full of imprecision and ambiguity for such an achievement. Further, the very political processes which Johnson and Dubuc decry for the uncertainties they generate can be seen as the instruments to produce the concordance between the division of powers and contemporary requirements which they seek. If such processes did not

---

[16] *The Federal-Provincial Conference, Quebec — Federal-Provincial Tax Structure Committee* (Ottawa, Queen's Printer, 1966), pp. 56-57.
[17] Alfred Dubuc, "The Decline of Confederation and the New Nationalism", in Peter Russell, (ed.), *Nationalism in Canada* (Toronto, McGraw-Hill for the University League for Social Reform, 1966), p. 131.

exist, we would really be in a bad way. The difficult problem, as suggested earlier, is to find ways by which they can be brought within a framework of constitutionalism.

The assault on the existing constitution has led to a process of constitutional review out of which a new, or at least a drastically modified, constitution is supposed to emerge. Unfortunately, the justification for this review does not reside in any self-evident likelihood that a new and better constitution can be created. The existing constitution was caught in a barrage of criticism based on its age, which is largely a fraudulent consideration, and a confused battery of French-Canadian demands to break with the past and stake out for themselves a status in Canadian federalism superior to what was apparently possible under the constitution as they perceived it.

From the evidence which is available, there is little possibility that a new constitution will emerge. Most of the political leaders engaged in constitutional review are dutifully going through the motions with little hope or desire that any major changes will transpire. If their pessimism is correct, Canadians will be left with the existing constitution whose limited sanctity has been further eroded by the criticism to which it has been subjected in the process of review. Its claim to our continued allegiance may come to rest on the flimsy basis that it is the only constitution Canadians have.

The perspective on the constitution adopted in this essay is a reminder that a constitution is not merely a piece of paper. It is a set of relationships between governments and between governments and peoples which has become embedded in the evolving habits and values of successive generations of Canadians. Tinkering with constitutional documents in an era of *laissez faire* might have left the mass of the citizenry unaffected. However, when governments increasingly involve themselves in the nooks and crannies of our lives, dramatic constitutional change presents a less attractive and less plausible face. It is only necessary to observe the difficulties of successfully introducing major policies, such as medicare or tax reform, to question the feasibility of attempting to change a large part of the very constituional framework from which governments derive their authority and by means of which citizens deal with government.

A new constitution can be no more than a point of departure. The day after it is proclaimed its evolution away from the agreement just reached will commence. The new settlement will inevitably be subject to the informal processes of change and growth which helped "undermine" the BNA Act. The security and control of the future which can be obtained from a written document are only relative. Further, if a new constitution is created, the shortrun result of its implementation inevitably will be an increase in uncertainty and insecurity until the text is fleshed out by the actions of men struggling to make it work. This, of course, is in addition to the uncertainties automatically generated by the simple fact of change from the old constitution to the new. Given these corollaries of a new constitution, we might consider whether constitutions are not like wine—much better when well aged. Perhaps, however, 1867 was not a good year for constitutions.

11 Federalism for the Future*

Lester B. Pearson

The Government of Canada rejects both centralization and fragmentation as alternatives to federalism. Centralization, a trend toward a unitary state, would be inconsistent with Canada's character—with its cultural diversity, with a geography which calls for the extensive decentralization of government, and with the freedom which is characteristic of states where the powers of government are not concentrated in the hands of a few.

The opposite course—a loose association of political units in which the effectiveness of the national government is dependent upon the will of provincial governments—is equally incompatible with Canada's goals. It would jeopardize the ability of the federal government to contribute to rising living standards for the people of Canada; it would weaken the willingness of individual Canadians to contribute toward the well-being and progress of their fellow citizens in other provinces; and it would threaten the very existence of our country in a world where size as well as excellence count in the struggle for economic, technological and cultural achievement.

Canadian federalism must be a balance between these extremes, and we should expect to find this sense of balance expressed in our constitutional arrangements. We should expect to find this sense of balance in the constitutional guarantees of the rights of Canadian citizens including their linguistic rights—balanced as to the rights of individuals and their obligations to one another and to society, and balanced as to their rights as members of one of Canada's linguistic communities and their concern for those who are members of the other. We should expect to find central institutions of Canadian federalism capable of ensuring a balanced representation in the governing of the nation—representation on the basis of population where the general power to legislate is concerned and representation related to Canada's regions and linguistic groups where the power to legislate is particularly concerned with identity and the rights of these regions and groups. We should expect to find a balanced division of the power to govern between the federal and provincial governments—balanced in the powers it assigns to each and balanced in its concern for the needs of the present and those of the future.

---

* From *Federalism for the Future,* a White Paper published by The Right Honourable Lester B. Pearson, Prime Minister of Canada (Ottawa, February, 1968). Reprinted by permission of Information Canada. The document was published for the Constitutional Conference held in Ottawa, February 5, 6 and 7, 1968.

LESTER B. PEARSON – Professor of International Affairs, Carleton University. Prime Minister of Canada, 1963-1968.

Having formulated these goals and these guiding principles, the Government of Canada believes it is appropriate for it to present to the people, the Parliament and the Provinces of Canada its general views on Canada's Constitution.

The Rights of Citizens and Canada's Linguistic Duality

The first goal of the Canadian federation, in the opinion of the Government of Canada, is the protection of the rights of the individual. This means to begin with, the guarantee of individual human rights for all Canadians. This is a fundamental condition of nationhood; take these rights away and few Canadians would think their country was worth preserving. In a country such as ours, with its two founding linguistic groups, the preservation of individual rights also must mean the guarantee of the linguistic rights of both groups. For language is at once the extension of the individual personality and an indispensable tool of social organization: fail to recognize the linguistic rights of either French or English speaking Canadians and their will to preserve Canada will be seriously weakened, if not destroyed.

The rights of the individual—human and linguistic—are so fundamental to the will of the nation to survive, that the Government of Canada suggests as the first step in reviewing Canada's Constitution the guarantee of these rights in the fundamental law. For this purpose we propose the incorporation into Canada's Constitution of a Charter of Human Rights as quickly as the federal and provincial governments and legislative bodies can agree. For the same purpose we propose that the recommendations in Book I of the Royal Commission on Bilingualism and Biculturalism be considered by this Conference, and that each government here represented agree now to the declarations of principle and of objectives set forth in the recommendations, and set in motion the machinery for realizing these goals as soon as possible.

A Canadian Charter of Human Rights

An important forward step was taken when the Parliament of Canada enacted in 1960 a Bill of Rights which guaranteed the rights of Canadians, to the extent that Parliament could do so by statute. The same can be said about the provincial enactments which guaranteed some of the rights of the citizens in certain of the provinces of Canada, again to the extent that such guarantees can be given by statute. But we do not yet have in this country a comprehensive Charter of Human Rights which assures to Canadians all of the rights they believe to be fundamental, nor do we have a Charter which would prevent these rights from being infringed by the legislative bodies of Canada. This can be achieved only by placing a Charter of Human Rights in the Constitution of our country. Such a Charter, unlike most proposed constitutional amendments, would not involve a transfer of legislative power from one government to another. It would not, for instance, affect provincial jurisdiction over property and civil rights any more than federal jurisdiction over criminal law and procedure in criminal matters. Instead, it would involve a common agreement to restrict the power of all governments.

Central Institutions of Canadian Federalism

The guarantee of the rights of individual Canadians, including linguistic rights, would be the first step in adapting Canada's constitutional and governmental arrangements so as better to achieve the goals of our federation. The second step, in our view, would be the adaptation of our national institutions of government so as to ensure that they too were making their most effective contribution toward the realization of these goals.

The Government of Canada believes that the central institutions of government must be designed to ensure that the essential character of the country is preserved. Federalism is not just a matter of dividing up the powers of government between the federal and provincial governments in the hope of achieving an appropriate balance between the forces of unity and diversity in the nation. The division of powers is, of course, a central element of federalism, and it must be fully considered at the Conferences which are to follow. But it should not be finally decided until the central institutions of federalism provided for in the Constitution have been re-examined.

The Parliament of Canada

The first such institution is the Parliament of Canada. The Constitution provides for two kinds of representation in Parliament; representation on the basis of population in the House of Commons, and representation on a regional basis in the Senate. But because Canadians gradually have come to believe that the Senate should not be able to overrule the will of a popularly elected body, the House of Commons, the Upper House has almost ceased to use its right of veto. This has imposed an effective limitation on its exercise of legislative power.

There are of course other important if informal methods by which Canada's diversity is represented in the national organs of government. We refer to the representation in federal cabinets of the several provinces of Canada, or both of the country's basic linguistic groups, and of much of the diversity in religion and culture in the nation. Similarly the major political parties in the House of Commons have organized so as to ensure in their caucuses and otherwise that these interests are adequately represented.

We believe, however, that the role and the powers of the Senate should be reviewed. It might well be reconstituted so as to enable it to play a new role in representing the federal character of our country. It might, for example, be called upon to make a special contribution in securing the rights of Canadians and in protecting the bilingual character of Canada. It might also be expected to reflect better than it does now the regional interests of our country.

If the role and the powers of the Senate were to be changed, it would also be appropriate, in the judgment of the Government of Canada, to consider changes in the method of appointment. For the method of selecting Senators clearly should be related to the particular role and functions of an Upper House in a federal form of government.

The Supreme Court

Another essential element of federalism is the system under which disputes as to the meaning or application of the Constitution are adjudicated. There have been serious discussions in Canada concerning the composition, jurisdiction and procedures of our final constitutional court, the Supreme Court of Canada; these properly should be considered in any review of the Constitution. For example, the Supreme Court both as a general court of appeal and the final court in constitutional matters now operates under an ordinary statute of the Parliament of Canada. It has been urged that its Constitution and role should be set forth in the fundamental law.

The Government of Canada will be prepared to discuss questions such as these at the constitutional meetings to follow. At this time, however, we would set forth the fundamental principles which in our view should guide us in such discussions. First, there is a functional need, in a federal system such as ours, for a body to settle the jurisdictional conflicts and uncertainties to which all federal Constitutions inevitably give rise. Secondly, if such a body is to enjoy the respect and authority which it needs in order properly to discharge its functions, it must retain a judicial character and be able to perform its functions impartially. Thirdly, the independence of the judiciary is a fundamental principle of the Constitution which must be protected accordingly.

These principles, we acknowledge, are self-evident; they are essential if Canada is to continue to be governed by the rule of law. Unquestionably they would guide both federal and provincial governments in their review of the Supreme Court of Canada.

The Public Service of Canada

The public service of Canada should also be looked upon as one of the institutions of federalism. This means, as the Royal Commission on Bilingualism and Biculturalism has said, that English and French must be the languages of work in the federal public service, particularly in Ottawa and other areas where both languages are spoken. It also means that in its composition the public service should in a general way reflect the character of the nation.

The fact that the Government recognizes the public service as an institution of federalism was evident in its announcement almost two years ago of its intention to make the public service progressively bilingual, and its determination to increase the numbers of French-Canadians in the service. A great deal of progress has been made in this direction, and more can be expected as our capacity for language instruction improves, and as our ability to attract to the public service French-Canadians, and Canadians from all regions and walks of life in the country, increases. The problems we face are not constitutional; they are very practical. Canada's public servants are the products of Canada's educational systems, and if the educational systems have not produced bilingual graduates public servants cannot be expected to be bilingual. There are therefore very difficult problems of adjustment, for the Government and for the public servants. We intend protecting as a matter of justice civil servants who have rights to security and expectations for advancement under past language practices. But we are resolved, while according such protection, to make the required changes. To this end we are providing extensive language training facilities for civil servants who are not bilingual. For the future, it is the provincial governments which can contribute most of this change by making available to all students the opportunity of learning to speak French as well as English.

The National Capital

If the organs of government in Ottawa should reflect the federal character of the country, the nation's Capital should be a symbol of Canada. Ottawa and the Capital region should be a model of what we think Canada should be—in particular, as our capital, it should be a model of bilingualism and biculturalism. The Government of Canada has begun discusssions with the Provinces of Ontario and Quebec under whose jurisdiction the Ottawa/Hull area falls, on arrangements which could be made to achieve this goal. These discussions will have to take into account both the jurisdictional and the municipal interests which are the proper concern of the Provinces of Ontario and Quebec. We are pleased that the Prime Ministers of these Provinces have been so ready to discuss this question with the Government of Canada.

Canada in the World

Before turning to the third element of Canada's Constitution which we would expect to discuss in the series of constitutional conferences we have proposed, the Government of Canada feels special mention should be made of Canada's international presence.

Canada can have only one international personality. We think that Canadians generally want and expect their country to be seen abroad as a single united country—as Canada. This requires, in our view, that the Government of Canada continue to have full responsibility for Canada's foreign policy and for the representation abroad of Canada's interests.

This is not to deny the interest that provincial governments have in international matters which touch upon their own jurisdiction. This interest can be recognized and protected by ensuring that the Government of Canada exercises its international responsibilities in the proper manner, and by co-operative arrangements between the federal and provincial governments in international matters of mutual concern. There is no evident need to provide the Provinces with special powers in this field. Indeed no federal state has found it necessary or desirable to confer independent treaty-making powers on its provinces or states, or, with the single exception of two of the republics of the USSR for very special reasons in 1945, to allow for a separate presence in international bodies or independent diplomatic representations. The reason is obvious. Such powers or representation would divide or fragment a federal union into separate international entities. In Canada's case, it would destroy our influence and our presence abroad, and undermine our unity at home.

This would not only be tragic; it would be unnecessary. The Government of Canada has been seeking progressively to ensure—in its foreign policy and in all its actions abroad—that it reflects the bilingual character of the country and that it takes into account the proper and developing interests of the Canadian provinces in various international activities. For example, delegations to international conferences where provincial interests are affected increasingly contain a provincial component; provincial desires to benefit from co-operation and interchanges with foreign states are fully recognized and assisted; the provincial governments can, where it is necessary, make agreements with other jurisdictions, with Federal Government agreement; and provincial interests in other forms of international co-operation are also facilitated. Indeed any provincial requirement that calls for some international action can be met by the federal government, save of course for actions which would undermine the ability of the Government of Canada to represent the country abroad. The Government intends, in full co-operation with the provinces, to continue to pursue and develop this policy.

Canadians will understand that talk of separate international personalities or a divided presence abroad is not just academic talk of interest to constitutional lawyers. It strikes at the roots of our existence as a country. Indeed the achievement of independent status for Canada rested a great deal on gaining for our country a separate international voice. To extend this right and power to the provincial governments could mean the same result for them: separate foreign policies, separate relations with other states, separate representations in the U.N. and other agencies, and separate ambassadors and embassies. But it would mean more than that. Separatism abroad would lead to separatism at home. We should make no mistake about it.

The Division of Powers

The third important aspect of Canada's Constitution which should be reviewed is the division of the powers of government between the federal and provincial governments. It is the part of the Constitution over which most differences between governments arise: inevitably it will occupy a major part of our attention in the course of the constitutional conferences we have suggested.

This is understandable and desirable. It is understandable because of the enormous growth in the role of government, federal, provincial and municipal. As the scale of government has increased, the tendency of governments to propose policies or undertake measures which affect the policies or measures of other governments also has increased. Concern as to whether governments'

taxing powers match their spending responsibilities has increased correspondingly. And as the range of government activities and programme planning has
widened, there has been a growing tendency on the part of governments to
extend their planning to cover the activities of other governments operating
in the same area.

It is important that the federal and provincial governments review seriously
the consequences of proposed constitutional adjustments in this field, in view
of the differences which currently divide them. We should be frank about these
differences. The governments of the provinces believe that their powers of taxation are too limited; the federal government believes that provincial taxing
powers are virtually as great as its own. The governments of some provinces do
not believe the Parliament of Canada should use the spending power in the way
it has; but in fact, the use of this power has been responsible for much of
Canada's social and economic progress. There have been demands for whole-
sale transfers of taxing and spending powers from the Parliament of Canada; the
federal government has replied that transfers to the province of powers of such
magnitudes would make it impossible for it to discharge its responsibilities for
the whole country.

All of these differences are serious. And all of them stem from genuine differences of opinion over how the powers of government are or ought to be divided
between the Parliament of Canada and the legislative assemblies of the
provinces. The Government of Canada has concluded that the point has been
reached where the federal and provincial governments should meet to discuss,
formally and fully, the whole question as to how the powers of government
should be divided in Canada. We should examine the claims that are made for
the transfer or the clarification of powers, and the consequences of these claims.
These meetings would, of course, involve difficult discussions of complex and
sensitive questions, including the division of powers, the spending power, the
residual power, and the power of delegation. But meetings on these questions
would be preferable, in our opinion, to dealing with forever recurring disputes
over particular powers, in a partial or a piecemeal fashion.

Discussion on the division of powers should take place, in the opinion of the
Government of Canada, after the constitutional conferences have considered the
other principal elements of the Constitution—the rights of individual Canadians,
including linguistic rights, and the central institutions of federalism. We
say this because provincial interests and the interests of Canada's two linguistic
groups are not and cannot be represented simply through the device of transferring powers from the federal government to provincial governments. These
interests are and must be reflected as well in constitutional guarantees and in the
central institutions of federalism. It follows that a balanced judgement as to
the powers required by the provincial governments for the primary purpose of
protecting linguistic or provincial interests can only be made in the perspective
of the constitutional guarantees and the representation of such interests in
the central organs of government. To jeopardize the capacity of the federal
government to act for Canada, in the name of protecting linguistic and
provincial rights, when what is essential could be accomplished through

constitutional guarantees and the institutions of federalism, would be to serve Canadians badly. Furthermore, the division of powers between orders of government should be guided by principles of functionalism, and not by ethnic considerations. Such principles can best be applied after issues concerning the protection of linguistic rights have been settled.

The Government of Canada would propose, therefore, that discussions on the division of powers take place at subsequent conferences. However, in anticipation of these discussions, and as a guide to the direction of the Government's thinking, we believe we should place before the Conference some of the principles by which we feel would have to be guided.

First, we are committed to the view that Canada requires both a strong federal government and strong provincial governments. The field of government now is so wide, and the problems of government are so many, that it is not a contradiction to speak in these terms. Governments themselves confirm this view when they argue that their spending responsibilities exceed their ability to raise revenues. There is another reason for achieving a balance between the powers of the federal and provincial governments: the freedom of the individual is more likely to be safeguarded if neither order of government is able to acquire a preponderant power over the citizen.

Secondly, the Government of Canada believes that there are certain areas of responsibility which must remain with the federal government if our country is to prosper in the modern world. The Parliament of Canada must have responsibility for the major and inextricably inter-related instruments of economic policy if it is to stimulate employment and control inflation. It must have control over monetary and credit policy, the balance-wheel role in fiscal policy, tariff policy, and balance of payments policy. It must be responsible for interprovincial and international trade. It must be able to undertake measures for stimulating the growth of the economy, some of which inevitably and some of which intentionally will affect regional economic growth. Without such powers Canada's federal government would be unable to contribute to many of the central objectives of federalism, including the reduction of regional disparity.

We believe that the Government of Canada must have the power to redistribute income, between persons and between provinces, if it is to equalize opportunity across the country. This would involve, as it does now, the rights to make payments to individuals, for the purpose of supporting their income levels —old age security pensions, unemployment insurance, family allowances—and the right to make payments to provinces, for the purpose of equalizing the level of provincial government services. It must involve, too, the powers of taxation which would enable the federal government to tax those best able to contribute to these equalization measures. Only in this way can the national government contribute to the equalization of opportunity in Canada, and thus supplement and support provincial measures to this end.

The Government of Canada believes it must be able to speak for Canada, internationally, and that it must be able to act for Canada in strengthening the bonds of nationhood. We have said what we think this implies in international matters. Internally it seems to us to imply an active federal role in the cultural and technological developments which so characterize the 20th century. We acknowledge, of course, that the nourishment of Canada's cultural diversity requires imaginative provincial programmes, as well as federal ones. But there is a role for the Government of Canada, too; indeed cultural and technological developments across the country are as essential to nationhood today as tariffs and railways were one hundred years ago.

These are central areas of responsibility essential to the apparatus of the modern sovereign state—economic policy, the equalization of opportunity, technological and cultural development, and international affairs. There are among these, of course, areas of responsibility which are shared with the provinces—including cultural matters, regional economic policy, and social security measures. However to catalogue these now, or federal powers generally, would be to depart from a statement of guiding principles and to anticipate the discussions of future conferences.

The third principle which would guide the Government of Canada in discussions concerning the division of powers is that most services involving the most immediate contact between the citizen and the government, and those which contribute most directly to the traditions and heritages which are uniquely provincial, should generally be provided by Canada's provincial governments. Strong provincial governments, able to adapt public services to the particular needs of their people, are as essential to meet the facts of diversity in Canada as a strong federal government is to the preservation of Canadian unity.

The governments of the provinces have responsibility for education, and their own power to support technological and cultural development—so often associated with educational institutions. These powers play an important part in the flourishing of Canada's linguistic groups, and of the diverse tradtions to be found in our country. We acknowledge, of course, that many of the institutions involved serve the nation as well as the province but this fact should not be allowed to diminish the capacity of the provinces to perform their role.

The Government of Canada believes that the provinces must have the power to provide health and welfare services. For instance, the provincial governments rather than the federal government should operate hospitals or public health clinics and determine the needs of persons requiring social assistance. Provincial administration of services such as these makes possible the variation of levels of service to accord with local priorities. The role of the federal government should be to provide for those transfers of income between people and between provinces which generally support the incomes of people and the services of governments in the different provinces.

The Government of Canada recognizes too that the provinces should continue to have the constitutional powers required to enable them to embark upon regional economic development programmes. Provincial programmes inevitably will affect national policies for economic growth, and vice versa, and the programmes of the several provinces may well be competitive with one another. But the aims and the expectations of people in the several provinces should find expression in provincial as well as federal economic measures. The provinces must continue, too, to have responsibility for the many intra-provincial matters which call for local rather than national action.

The Government of Canada holds the view that in the exercise of these responsibilities—which under the present division of powers are at least as wide ranging as those of the federal government—each province should be able to develop its own unique approach. The range of powers we would expect the provinces to have would extend, as they do now, into the areas which are vital to the preservation of Canada's several cultural and regional identities.

We believe, finally, that the provincial governments like the federal government must have taxing powers sufficient to enable them to finance their responsibilities. However, we suspect that in assigning to governments the power of taxation—the capacity for financing public services in Canada—the principle of access to tax powers will supersede the principle of an exact division of tax fields. We would do well to remember that it is as difficult to predict what technological or social or international changes will have increased the role of the provincial or federal governments in 30 years as it would have been to predict the changes between 1938 to 1968.

The fourth generalization we would advance concerning the division of powers has to do with the effect each government's activities inevitably will have upon the activities of the others. This applies both to individual programmes and to the totality of government activity. For example, federal income redistribution measures inevitably have an effect upon provincial social welfare programmes and provincial resource development policies inevitably affect the rate of growth of the nation's economy. Similarly the aggregate use by the provinces of their spending and borrowing powers inevitably affects federal fiscal, and monetary and balance of payments policies, and the use of the federal spending power affects provincial policies in different ways. Obviously the total volume of spending by each order of government affects the priorities of the other.

We question whether it is any longer realistic to expect that some neat compartmentalization of powers can be found to avoid this. Instead we suspect that the answer is to be found in the processes by which governments consult one another and by which they seek to influence each other before decisions are finally taken. This remedy has been prescribed so often as to appear commonplace. But there is much to be done even in coming to understand the processes of intergovernmental influence, to say nothing of perfecting the machinery by which intergovernmental consultation takes place. Nor will we find the "participation" of provincial governments in federal government decisions, and vice versa, to be an easy answer to the problems of consultation. The federal government must remain responsible to Parliament, and the provincial governments to their legislatures: federal-provincial conferences must, it seems to us, occupy themselves with the art of influence rather than the power of decision-making.

Both federal and provincial governments will recognize, too, the unresolved question as to whether there should be a federal government role when there is a "national interest" in provincial programmes (or the lack of them), or whether there should be a provincial government role when there is a "provincial interest" in national programmes (or the lack of them). Examples abound: What the provinces do or do not do about urban development unquestionably affects the national interest, and what the federal government does or does not do about tariff policy affects the provincial interest. We have to consider seriously whether there should be a way for the federal government to seek to influence the provinces in cases where a national interest is involved, and a way for provincial governments to seek to influence the federal government when a provincial interest is involved.

There are, we think, no easy solutions. What is required is a comprehensive review of the federal-provincial conferences and committees which now exist, how they function, and how their work is co-ordinated. We must be prepared, it seems to the Government of Canada, to give more systematic recognition to these new forms of federalism.

We must be prepared to consider new methods for bringing provincial influence to bear on developing federal policies, and federal influence on developing provincial policies, before decisions have finally been taken. We must be prepared for innovations in the machinery of government which will enable us to preserve the essence of Canada's two great governmental traditions—federalism and parliamentary government.

12 Judicial Review and the Division of Powers in Canada*

Martha Fletcher

One of the most obvious consequences of judicial review is that political questions often come to the courts clothed as legal, constitutional questions. The most notable political questions in federal systems are usually those involving the constitutional division of powers between the two levels of government. The constitutional framework within which the Canadian federation operates and from which judicial adjustment within it proceeds is the British North America Act, 1867 (B.N.A. Act). There the powers of government are divided between the Dominion[1] and the provinces, with section 91 of the Act containing the scope of central government power, and section 92 containing

---

[1] Though in recent years the term "federal government" has been the proper designation for the government in Ottawa, the term "Dominion" has been used in this study. Since it is less ambiguous than "federal" and was the term used by the courts in referring to the central authority in nearly all of the cases discussed here, it was felt that greater clarity would result from its use.

---

* Published by permission of the author.

MARTHA FLETCHER – Doctoral Candidate in Political Science, Duke University.

that of the provinces. Yet, because even the most carefully drawn language is subject to multiple interpretations, and because the context in which the arrangements operate changes over time, the division of powers presents to those who govern a continuing problem of adjustment. It is in these areas of adjustment that the choices made by the courts are of political importance, since they may determine which governments may carry out which activities and whether, indeed, some activities may be carried out at all. Thus, judicial review has considerable significance for the way in which the political process responds to the demands placed upon it.

As the court of final appeal for Canada until 1949, it was the responsibility of the Judicial Committee of the Privy Council, sitting in London, to adjudicate conflicts over the division of powers in the Act. Composed of some of the most eminent jurists of the United Kingdom and, later, of the Empire and Commonwealth, the Judicial Committee is technically not a court but rather an advisory body to the Crown, though its "advice" is invariably taken. During much of the time it ruled on Canadian cases it was criticized for its remoteness from the political system and the facts of Canadian life. It was felt by many that an indigenous court would have made different, more "realistic" decisions. The demand for a final court of appeals within Canada ultimately led to the abolition of appeals to the Judicial Committee in 1949 with the Supreme Court of Canada assuming the role of final constitutional arbiter.

Two problems arose in the interpretation of the Dominion and provincial powers conferred by the Constitution under sections 91 and 92. One was the changing definition of what matters are of national concern. The second was the sharp difference of opinion between the courts (particularly the Judicial Committee of the Privy Council) and Canadian political leaders and legal scholars concerning both what had been meant in 1867 by the specified functions contained in these sections and how they should be applied to current problems. Further, because the B.N.A. Act has the legal status of merely another statute of the British Parliament, the judges took the view that they were not to go outside the contents of the Act in determining its meaning.

Within sections 91 and 92, four of the constitutional powers which have often been the legal clothing for political disputes concerning the division of powers between Dominion and province are the powers of the Dominion parliament to legislate for the peace, order, and good government of Canada and to regulate trade and commerce; and the powers of the provinces to control property and civil rights in the provinces and to legislate on all matters of merely a local or private nature in the province. Though the litigation involving these powers does not by any means comprise the totality of decisions concerning the federal division of powers, it can serve as an example of the impact of the judicial review on the framework of the federal system, for the interpretation of the boundaries of these powers has been perhaps one of the conspicuous areas in which the courts have played the role of arbiter in the federal system.[2]

---

[2] For a discussion of the ways in which constitutional cases come before the courts see J. A. C. Grant, "Judicial Review in Canada: Procedural Aspects", *Canadian Bar Review*, Vol. XLII (1964), pp. 195-224.

The Location of the Residuary Power

The residuary power—the general grant of legislative authority to the Dominion on all matters not assigned specifically—is a useful example for the study of the impact of judicial review on the working of the federal system. This is true both because the residuary power can be used to legitimate expansion of governmental authority if the court is sympathetic to that expansion and because its expansion or contraction is a sign of the courts' view towards the "proper" division of powers in the federation. Thus it is important both as a source for legitimization of a changing balance of power in the federation and as a sign of the judicial attitude towards such an alteration.

The residuary power in the British North America Act is normally considered to reside in the Dominion authority granted in the opening paragraph of section 91:

> It shall be lawful [for Parliament] to make laws for the peace, order, and good government of Canada, in relation to all matters not coming within the Classes of Subjects by this Act assigned exclusively to the Legislatures of the Provinces; and for greater certainty, but not so as to restrict the Generality of the foregoing Terms of this Section, it is hereby declared that (notwithstanding anything in this Act) the exclusive Legislative Authority of the Parliament of Canada extends to all Matters coming within the Classes of Subjects hereinafter enumerated . . .

The meaning of this grant has been, however, a subject of considerable litigation for nearly a century, and its interpretation in relation to the totality of legislative powers granted in sections 91 and 92 of the B.N.A. Act has varied over time, with the result that other sections at times have taken precedence over it.

From the standpoint of legal interpretation, the meaning of the peace, order, and good government clause can be understood only in the context of the two sections which comprise the division of legislative powers between the Dominion and provincial legislatures, and one must begin with an analysis of the grammar of the two sections. In the *Parsons* case, the Board identified the following grammatical construction as the correct one, and this opinion has been shared by many later writers on the Canadian constitution.[3]

The opening clause of section 91—"It shall be lawful [for Parliament] to make laws for the peace, order, and good government of Canada, in relation to all matters not coming within the Classes of Subjects of this Act assigned exclusively to the Legislatures of the Provinces;"—states that the Dominion it to have authority over *all matters* not specifically enumerated in section 92. The next clause—"and for greater certainty, but not so as to restrict the Generality of the foregoing Terms of this Section,"—emphasizes that this general grant of power is not restricted by the enumerated heads that follow.

---

[3] *Citizens Insurance Co.* v. *Parsons* (1881), 7 A. C. 96 at 107-108. For others who agree with this grammatical interpretation see Bora Laskin, *Canadian Constitutional Law*, 2nd ed. (Toronto, Carswell, 1960), pp. 65-66; W. R. Kennedy, "The Interpretation of the B.N.A. Act", *Cambridge Law Journal*, Vol. VIII, 1943, pp. 146-59; Fredrick P. Varcoe, *The Distribution of Legislative Power in Canada* (Toronto, Carswell, 1954), pp. 18-22.

The words in parentheses—"notwithstanding anything in this Act"—serve to make explicit that the power of the Dominion to make laws for peace, order, and good government takes precedence over the enumeration in section 92. The final words of the sentence—"the exclusive Legislative Authority of the Parliament of Canada *extends* [emphasis supplied] to all Matters coming within the Classes of Subjects . . . enumerated"—implies that the general grant is the sole authority given to the Dominion and that the authority exercisable under the enumerations comes from the one general grant of power rather than from a separate source to which the general power is merely supplementary (as subsequent decisions were to maintain).

The final paragraph of section 91, coming after the enumerations, says that "any matter coming within any of the Classes of Subjects in this Section shall not be deemed to come within the *class of matters* [emphasis supplied] of a local or private nature comprised in the enumeration of the Classes of Subjects by this Act assigned exclusively to the Legislatures of the Provinces." The significant point in the understanding of this paragraph's place in the Act is to note that the word "class" in the phrase "class of matters" is singular. When read in conjunction with section 92, grammatically, the phrase can only refer to section 92, head 16—"generally all matters of a merely local or private nature in the province."

In summary, it is argued here that the peace, order and good government clause was intended to give to the Dominion all subjects of legislation not covered in the provincial list of powers in section 92. The enumerations in section 91 neither add to nor subtract from the Dominion's residuary power over all subjects other than those in the section 92 list, since they are examples of the sorts of powers contemplated in the general grant rather than powers in their own right. The closing paragraph of section 91 was intended to make clear that the mere fact that a matter was of a local or private nature did not remove it from Dominion jurisdiction when it also came within the enumerations of that section. Thus, none of the enumerated heads in sections 91 could, by definition, be considered a provincial matter under any circumstances.

The interpretation of the application of the power to legislate for peace, order, and good government by the Dominion in specific situations has, however, been considerably different from the grammatical reading presented above. In an early landmark case, *Russell* v. *The Queen* (discussed below), the Committee based its decision on a similarly broad interpretation of the Dominion's residuary power. But this view was soon considerably altered by the decisions which followed.

The decisive point in the interpretation of the powers of the Dominion conferred by section 91 came with the *Local Prohibition*[4] case in 1896, in which Lord Watson presented what was to become the prevailing Judicial Committee interpretation of section 91. Watson's decision set out that the power of the Dominion to legislate for the peace, order, and good government of Canada was merely supplementary to the primary power of the Dominion given in the

---

[4] *Attorney-General for Ontario* v. *Attorney-General for Canada*, (1896) A.C. 348.

enumerations in section 91. Moreover, the power granted in the section 91 enumerations was not absolute. The closing words of section 91 did not contemplate that the authority of the Dominion under all matters enumerated in section 91 was absolute in its application to local and private matters coming within those subjects, but was merely an authority to legislate on local and private matters when such legislation was necessarily incidental to the exercise of the power over the Dominion as a whole. "It appears to their Lordships that [the closing words of section 91 were] not meant to derogate from the legislative authority given to the provincial legislatures . . . save to the extent of enabling the Parliament of Canada to deal with matters local or private in those cases where such legislation is necessarily incidental to the exercise of the powers conferred upon it by the enumerated heads of clause 91."[5] And, the Board declared, Sir Montague Smith was in error in the *Parsons* case when he declared that the closing words of section 91 applied only to head 16 of section 92. "It appears . . . that the language of the exception in section 91 was meant to include and correctly describe all the matters enumerated in the sixteen heads of section 92."[6] Thus was ruled that the Dominion could not consider its powers listed in the enumerations as paramount over any of the powers given the provinces in section 92. The opening words of section 91 that "(notwithstanding anything in this Act) the exclusive Legislative Authority of the Parliament of Canada extends to all Matters coming within the Classes of Subjects hereinafter enumerated . . ." were ignored rather than explained. The power of the Dominion to legislate for the peace, order, and good government of Canada was ruled to be a supplementary power which gave the Dominion authority to legislate "on such matters as are unquestionably of Canadian interest and importance" but it could not in so legislating "trench upon provincial legislation with respect to any of the classes of subjects enumerated in section 92".[7]

What this view of the peace, order, and good government power would mean became clear in the *Insurance Reference,* where Lord Haldane made more explicit what Lord Watson had begun. "It must be taken to be now settled," Haldane said, "that the general authority to make laws for the peace, order, and good government of Canada . . . does not, unless the subject matter of the legislation falls within some one of the enumerated heads which follow, enable the Dominion Parliament to trench on the subject matter entrusted to the provincial legislatures by the enumerations in section 92."[8] Thus only if the matter is not mentioned in section 92 can the Dominion legislate outside the enumeration of section 91 concerning a province. As Frank Scott put it, "the examples swallowed up the rule".[9] The idea of a general power to legis-

---

[5] *Ibid.,* p. 359.
[6] *Ibid.,* p. 359.
[7] *Ibid.,* p. 360.
[8] *Attorney-General for Canada* v. *Attorney-General for Alberta* (1916), A. C. 588 at 595.
[9] F. R. Scott, "The Development of Canadian Federalism", *Papers and Proceedings, Canadian Political Science Association,* Vol. III (May, 1931), p. 247.

late for peace, order, and good government which would take precedence over provincial claims in section 92 when matters falling under the section became of national importance was rejected. The general power of legislation disappeared into the enumerated heads of section 91 and reappeared as a provincial power in head 16 of section 92.

As the Dominion power to legislate for peace, order, and good government lost its original significance the Judicial Committee developed a new role for the phrase, while attempting to demonstrate that this interpretation was consistent with previous decisions. The most notable of the cases which the Board had either to refute or re-interpret if the new use of peace, order, and good government was to stand was *Russell* v. *The Queen*,[10] decided in 1882. Here the court had ruled that the pith and substance—what the act was actually intended to do—determined whether it was to be viewed from the Dominion or Provincial aspect and the section into which it would fall.

The act in question, the Canadian Temperance Act of 1878, provided, according to its preamble, uniform legislation on the subject of temperance throughout the Dominion: "the objects and scope of the law are general—to promote temperance by means of a uniform law throughout the Dominion". On this ground the Dominion felt the measure properly fell under "peace, order, and good government" and not under the class of subjects "property and civil rights". The fact that the act was applied individually to each particular place could not alter its character as general legislation.[11] The Board agreed with this view of the Act, saying that "their Lordships cannot think that the Temperance Act in question properly belongs to the class of subjects property and civil rights". Instead, they said that it was very similar to laws placing restrictions on the sale of poisons and drugs, emphasizing that while such items are property, their character is such that their sale and custody can be regulated by the Dominion on the grounds that their use is dangerous to public safety. This sort of regulation, they insisted, does not deal with those items as they are viewed under section 92, head 13. "What Parliament is dealing with is not a matter in relation to property and its right, but one relating to public order and safety," their Lordships maintained. It is the aspect of public order and safety with which the Dominion is concerned, and its overriding interest is not negated by the fact that property is incidentally interfered with. The purpose of the Act is not to interfere with property but to protect public safety, and the section of the B.N.A. Act under which it falls depends on what the Act in question is basically intended to do.[12] As for the local option section of the law, the Board again insisted that the basic intent of the Act was decisive, and this intent was that there should be uniform legislation in all provinces respecting the traffic in intoxicating liquors. "Parliament does not treat the promotion of temperance as desirable in one province more than

---

[10] (1882), 7 A. C. 829.
[11] *Ibid.*, p. 829.
[12] *Ibid.*, pp. 837-39.

another. . . . The objects and scope are still general. . . ."[13]

With the redefinition of the Dominion's general power, however, the decision of the Board in the *Russell* case and the meaning of the opening words of section 91 took on new connotations. In the *Board of Commerce* case in 1922[14] Lord Haldane suggested that the decision in the *Russell* case was made to deal with an abnormal, *i.e.,* emergency, situation. Otherwise, the general Dominion powers could not have been called into play. It was in *Fort Francis Pulp and Paper Co.* v. *Manitoba Free Press*[15] two years later that this emergency doctrine was clearly and systematically stated. Here measures taken under the War Powers Act of 1914 were held *intra vires* Dominion authority not under the general powers of peace, order, and good government conferred in section 91, but under an emergency power "discovered" by the Committee. In the event of an emergency, national survival may depend upon the use of exceptional means. It would be suicidal to say that the Dominion could not provide for its own survival, said the Board. Therefore, the interests of the individual might have to be subordinated to those of the community and the Dominion permitted to act under power to legislate for the peace, order, and good government of Canada.

Their application of this heretofore unknown doctrine, however, resulted in some rather unusual legal reasoning. In 1925, basing its opinion on the two earlier Haldane decisions (see above), the Board declared the Industrial Dispute Investigation Act of 1907 *ultra vires* the Dominion on the ground that its subject matter was not among the enumerated subjects of section 91, and its powers trenched upon section 92, head 13, concerning property and civil rights in the provinces.[16] In specifically rejecting the decision in *Russell* v. *The Queen* that an act could be held *intra vires* simply on the grounds that it was to the general advantage of Canada, the court hypothesized in the following terms as to the true grounds upon which the *Russell* case had been decided:

> Their Lordships think that the decision in *Russell* v. *The Queen* can only be supported today, not on the footing of having laid down an interpretation such as has sometimes been invoked of the general words at the beginning of section 91, but on the assumption of the Board, apparently made at the time of deciding the case of *Russell* v. *The Queen,* that the evil of intemperance at that time amounted in Canada to one so great and general that at least for the period it was a menace to the national life of Canada so serious and pressing that the National Parliament was called upon to intervene to protect the nation from disaster. An epidemic of pestilence might conceivably have been regarded as analogous.[17]

---

[13] *Ibid.,* p. 841.
[14] *In Re The Board of Commerce Act, 1919* (1922), A. C. 191.
[15] (1923), A. C. 695.
[16] *Toronto Electric Commissioners* v. *Snider* (1925), A. C. 396.
[17] *Ibid.,* p. 412.

To this rather incredible statement by their Lordships came the following Canadian reply:

> I [said Mr. Justice Anglin of the Supreme Court of Canada] cannot find anything in the judgment delivered by Sir Montague E. Smith in the *Russell* case suggestive of such a view having been entertained by the Judicial Committee. On the contrary, the whole tenor of the judgment seems to me inconsistent with its having proceeded on that basis. I should indeed be surprised if a body so well informed as their Lordships had countenanced such an aspersion on the fair name of Canada even though some hard-driven advocate had ventured to insinuate it in argument.[18]

The peace, order, and good government power, then, was to apply in only two very limited cases.[19] First, in normal times, it was limited to only those items which did not fall into either the enumerations of section 91 or 92 (and these instances were rare indeed).[20] Secondly, it would override the provincial powers in section 91 in times of extreme emergency, with the question of whether the situation was a sufficient emergency to justify the use of the power in this fashion to be determined by the courts.

In 1929, however, a less restricted view of the B.N.A. Act was taken by Lord Sankey, when, in ruling on whether women could be called to the Senate, he said: "The British North America Act planted in Canada a living tree capable of growth and expansion within its natural limits. . . . Their Lordships do not conceive it to be the duty of this board . . . to cut down the provisions of the Act by a narrow and technical construction, but rather to give it a large and liberal interpretation. . . ."[21]

The Sankey "living tree" concept also seemed to carry over in the *Radio* case, decided in 1932, which interpreted the power of the Dominion to implement the International Radiotelegraphy Convention of 1927. Taking notice of the fact that those involved in radiotelegraphy "must so to speak be kept in order by legislation and the only legislation that can deal with them all at once is Dominion legislation", the Board stated that control of the field was *intra vires* the Dominion under the general power of Parliament to legislate for the peace, order, and good government of Canada, rather than being divided between Dominion and province, provision by provision, according to the heading in section 91 and 92 under which each fell.[22]

In 1937, however, court decisions on the scope of the Dominion general power reverted to the extreme of the *Snider* opinion (1925) with the decisions of the Judicial Committee concerning the Bennett "New Deal" legislation.

---

18 *The King* v. *Eastern Elevator Company* (1925), S. C. R. 434 at 438.
19 Laskin, *op. cit.*, p. 267.
20 One of the few examples is the incorporation of companies with Dominion objects. *Great West Saddlery Co.* v. *The King* (1921), 2 A. C. 91.
21 *Edwards* v. *Attorney-General of Canada* (1930), A. C. 136.
22 *In Re the Regulation and Control of Radio Communication in Canada* (1932), A. C. 304 at 312.

These enactments were perhaps some of the most crucial ones, both economically and politically, to come before the Board during the years in which it ruled on the B.N.A. Act. This legislation was introduced in an attempt to cope with the problems of the great Depression and dealt with a wide variety of subjects.[23] Three of these acts—the Weekly Rest and Industrial Undertakings Act, the Minimum Wages Act, and the Limitation of Hours of Work Act—were defended before the courts both as coming under the Dominion power to implement treaties (since they were enacted in compliance with agreements of the International Labour Organization) and also under the general power of the Dominion to legislate for the peace, order, and good government of Canada.[24] The Board, however, ruled that neither of these grounds was sufficient to bring the legislation under the power of the central government.

To the argument that treaty legislation as a category was a Dominion affair both under section 132 and under the peace, order, and good government clause, their Lordships said: "While the ship of state now sails on larger ventures and into foreign water she still retains the water-tight compartments which are an essential part of her original structure".[25] Rejecting the use of the general power as it had been applied in the *Radio* case, they stated that the true ground of the *Radio* decision was that the legislation fell under the general clause only because it could not be fitted under any of the enumerations in sections 91 and 92.[26]

Finally, to the plea that an emergency situation existed and therefore the acts were valid under power to legislate for the peace, order, and good government of Canada, their Lordships replied that in their view no such overriding emergency existed and ruled the Dominion acts *ultra vires*. In their view,

> It is only necessary to call attention to the phrases in the various cases, "abnormal circumstances," "exceptional conditions," "standard of necessity" (*Board of Commerce* case [1922] 1 A.C. 191), "some extraordinary peril to the national life of Canada," "highly exceptional," "epidemic of pestilence," (*Snider* case [1925] A.C. 396), to show how far the present case is from the conditions which may override the normal distribution of powers in sections 91 and 92.[27]

---

[23] For a general discussion on the new deal see J. R. H. Wilbur (ed.), *The Bennett New Deal: Fraud or Portent?* (Toronto, Copp Clark, 1968).

[24] *Attorney-General for Canada* v. *Attorney-General for Ontario* (Labour Conventions Case) (1937), A. C. 327.

[25] *Ibid.*, p. 354.

[26] *Ibid.*, p. 351. That this interpretation is a patent misreading of the *Radio* decision is shown by quoting from the decision itself: "As their Lordships' views are based on what may be called the pre-eminent claims of section 91, it is unnecessary to discuss the question whch was raised . . . whether, if there had been no pre-eminent claims as such, broadcasting could have been held to fall either within 'property and civil rights,' or within 'matters of a merely local or private nature' ". *Radio Reference* (1932) A. C. 302 at 312.

[27] *Ibid.*, p. 353.

The Employment and Social Insurance Act was also ruled *ultra vires* the Dominion on the ground that the general powers of the Dominion did not apply here any more than in the previous case and that the Act trenched on section 92, head 13, property and civil rights.[28] With these cases, the height of the emergency doctrine was reached, as bitter Canadians noted that the only emergencies which the Privy Council had recognized were World War I and the "public drunkenness" sufficient to a national emergency read into the *Russell* case.

In 1946, however, the Privy Council showed sings of retreat from the position taken in the "New Deal" cases. In another test of the temperance legislation which had been in question in *Russell* v. *The Queen*, the Board was asked specifically to rule on the meaning of that case. There Viscount Simon expressly repudiated the reasoning of *Toronto Electric Commissioners* v. *Snider* which had postulated the emergency doctrine in its fullest form. To quote him,

> ... the British North America Act nowhere gives power to the Dominion Parliament to legislate in matters which are properly to be regarded as exclusively within the competence of the provincial legislatures merely because of the existence of an emergency. Secondly, they can find nothing in the judgment of the Board in 1882 which suggests that it proceeded on the ground of emergency; there was certainly no evidence before the Board that one existed. The act of 1878 was a permanent, not a temporary Act and no objection was raised to it on that account. . . . [T]he true test must be found in the real subject matter of the legislation: if it is such that it goes beyond local or provincial concern or interests and must from its inherent nature be the concern of the Dominion as a whole . . . then it will fall within the competence of the Dominion Parliament as a matter affecting the peace, order, and good government of Canada, though it may in another aspect touch on matters specially reserved to the provincial legislatures. . . . It is the nature of the legislation itself, and not the existence of emergency, that must determine whether it is valid or not.[29]

While liquor legislation was considered to be a matter of such general interest to the Dominion as a whole as to fall under the peace, order, and good government clause, the regulation of hours of work of employees of hotels run by the Canadian Pacific Railway was considered, as late as 1950, to be "substantially" a matter of property and civil rights in the provinces rather than of general interest to Canada.[30]

In 1951 the Judicial Committee again utilized the reasoning of the *Labour Conventions* cases, ruling that legislation controlling the manufacture and

---

[28] *Attorney-General for Canada* v. *Attorney-General for Ontario* (Employment and Social Insurance Act Reference) (1937), A. C. 355.

[29] *Attorney-General for Ontario* v. *Canadian Temperance Federation* (1946), A. C. 196 at 205-206.

[30] *Canadian Pacific Railway* v. *Attorney-General for British Columbia* (1950), A. C. 123 at 142.

importation of margarine in the interest of protecting and encouraging the dairy industry throughout Canada could not be justified by appealing to the sufficient interest rule so recently stated in the *Canadian Temperance Federation* case. Without countering the reasoning in that case, Lord Morton quoted the contrary view found in the *Labour Conventions* opinion as controlling in this instance and made no further comment.[31] Thus the final decisions of the Judicial Committee left the matter of the scope of the peace, order, and good government clause in considerable doubt, and the Supreme Court of Canada (which became the court of final appeal in 1949) was presented with a considerable variety of precedents to follow in interpreting the clause.

The Supreme Court was presented with an opportunity to decide on the scope of the general power soon after the Court became Canada's final constitutional authority. The case was a reference on the validity of the Wartime Leasehold Regulations which were adopted during World War II and carried over into the post-war era.[32] The precedent which the Court used in unanimously upholding the validity of Dominion rent controls came directly from the "emergency" doctrine of *Fort Francis Pulp and Paper Co.* v. *Manitoba Free Press.*[33] In deciding that the Act was valid, the Justices emphasized both the "abnormal" and "emergency" situation arising out of the war and its aftermath and the explicitly temporary nature of the legislation. Nothing that in normal times the subject of rent control lay exclusively with the provinces through their power over property and civil rights, the Court emphasized that "the rights of the provinces are not . . . permanently suppressed, and their jurisdiction temporarily suspended . . . flows afresh when the field is finally abandoned".[34] In a spirit unlike that which animated the Judicial Committee in the "New Deal" cases, however, the existence of the emergency in this instance was attested to both by "common sense" (an expression of Mr. Justice Taschereau) and by the view expressed by Kerwin and others that its existence as asserted by the Dominion could only be disregarded in the light of "very clear evidence" or "clear and unmistakable evidence that the Government was in error".[35] Nowhere in the decision was the reasoning of the more recent *Canadian Temperance Federation* case considered worthy of more than passing mention, with Taschereau explicitly denying its applicability.

The second case in which the Supreme Court ruled on the scope of this power in the post-Privy Council era was *Johannesson* v. *West St. Paul,*[36] which harks back strongly to the reasoning and tone of the *Aeronautics* and *Radio* references of the early 1930's. Quoting the *Aeronautics Reference,* Mr. Justice Rinfret echoed the view of a unanimous court in declaring aerial navigation

---

[31] *Canadian Federation of Agriculture* v. *Attorney-General for Quebec* (1951), A. C. 179 at 198.
[32] *Reference Re the Validity of the Wartime Leasehold Regulations* (1950), S. C. R. 124.
[33] (1923), A. C. 695.
[34] *Wartime Leasehold Reference* (1950) S. C. R. 124 at 140.
[35] *Ibid.,* p. 135.
[36] (1952), 1 S. C. R. 292.

to be a "class of subject which has attained such dimension as to affect the body politic of the Dominion".[37] Thus municipal legislation controlling the erection of airports was invalid as encroaching on the power of the Dominion to legislate for peace, order, and good government. Once the determination is made that the subject falls under the Dominion general clause, the Court said, the powers of the provinces over property and civil rights and matters of merely a local or private nature in the province have no standing, even if the Dominion has not exercised its jurisdiction over the matter. In his opinion Mr. Justice Locke quoted approvingly the words of Lord Sankey in the *Aeronautics Reference*:

> While the courts should be jealous in upholding the charter of the Provinces as enacted in section 92, it must be borne in mind that the real object of the Act was to give the central government those high functions and almost sovereign powers by which uniformity of legislation might be secured on all questions which were of common concern to all the provinces as members of a constituent whole.[38]

It took nearly fifteen years for two more cases on the general residuary power to arise before the Supreme Court, and these, like the other two cases from the post-Judicial Committee period, upheld the power of the federal government to act for the "peace, order, and good government of Canada". In the first of these two—a case involving the power of the federal government to expropriate land in Ontario near Ottawa to create a green belt surrounding the national capital—Mr. Justice Cartwright, speaking for a unanimous court, rested the decision firmly on the more generous construction of the *Radio Reference, Johannesson* v. *West St. Paul,* and the *Canadian Temperance Federation* case. Noting that the subject matter of the National Capital Act (the creation of a national capital with the appropriate setting) was not mentioned in either section 91 or 92, and citing both *Johannesson* and the *Radio Reference* as precedents, he concluded that ". . . such legislation [*i.e.,* legislation not mentioned in ss. 91 and 92] falls within the general words at the opening of section 91. . . .[39]

The second ground for the decision, however, followed the slightly different tack of the *Temperance Federation* case. There the reasoning was in the tradition of *Russell's* case, holding that the relevant test was whether the subject matter of the legislation did or did not go beyond local or provincial concern. Again the Court's answer was unequivocal: "I find it difficult to suggest a subject matter of legislation which more clearly goes beyond local or provincial interests and is the concern of Canada as a whole than the development, conservation and improvement of the National Capital Region. . . ."[40] And, to the objection that the Act trenched on civil rights in the provinces, the Court answered in the same vein: "once it has been determined that the matter in

---

[37] *Ibid.,* p. 303, quoting the *Aeronautics Reference* (1932), A. C. 54 at 77.
[38] *Ibid.,* pp. 327-28, quoting the *Aeronautics Reference,* p. 70.
[39] *Munro* v. *National Capital Commission* (1966), S. C. R. 663 at 670.
[40] *Ibid.,* p. 671.

relation to which the Act is passed is one which falls within the power of Parliament, it is no objection to its validity that its operation will affect civil rights in the provinces".[41] There is hardly a more unequivocal statement in support of the Dominion's general power in the entire history of Canadian constitutional interpretation.

The most recent case dealing with the residuary power also supports the Dominion. In the *Off-Shore Mineral Rights Reference,* decided in late 1967, a unanimous court held that the control and exploration of minerals in the lands under Canada's territorial seas was the sole responsibility of the Federal government, not the provincial government (in this case British Columbia). Basing the judgment squarely on a wide view of Dominion authority, the Court, having found that the lands in question did not fall within the historical boundaries of the provinces and therefore were federal territory concluded that control of mineral rights must be "regarded as a matter affecting Canada generally and covered by the expression "the peace, order, and good government of Canada' ".[42] Since the lands did not fall within the boundaries of the province they could not, logically, fall within the subjects of section 92. Moreover, the court ruled, "The mineral resources of the lands underlying the territorial sea are of concern to Canada as a whole and go beyond local or provincial concern of interests".[43] Thus even if the lands had been within the boundaries of the province, their resources would have been of sufficient concern to the nation as a whole to take them out of the ambit of "matters of a merely local or private nature in the province".

With these decisions, the pattern of interpretation of the peace, order, and good government clause would seem to have come full circle to the position taken in *Russell* v. *The Queen.*

Although there have been only four cases from the era of Supreme Court autonomy dealing with the residuary power, the consistency with which the justices have upheld the wider interpretation and the variety of tests they have used in doing so suggest that the Dominion may now be able to reply with some measure of confidence on "peace, order, and good government" as a standard against which to measure proposed legislation.

The Scope of "Trade and Commerce", Section 91(2)

The facts of the peace, order, and good government clause and of the enumerated heads of section 91 were, certainly, closely interrelated. With the interpretation of the closing words of section 91 to mean that the Dominion enumerations could extend only to necessarily incidental control of matters of a local or private nature (this phrase being defined as including the totality of section 92) and the eclipse of the *non obstante* clause, the authority of the Dominion

---

[41] *Ibid.*
[42] *Reference Re Ownership of Off-shore Mineral Rights,* 65 D. L. R. (2nd) 353 at 376.
[43] *Ibid.*

under those enumerations was clearly circumscribed in comparison with what it had previously been.

The trade and commerce power of section 91, head 2, which on its face would seem to have the widest scope of any Dominion enumeration, however, received a still more restrictive interpretation than the other enumerated powers in section 91. Thus it was doubly restricted: first by the generally restrictive interpretation of the relation of section 91 to section 92, and also by a narrow reading of the meaning of the words "the regulation of trade and commerce" themselves. The potential usefulness of this heading to centralists as a device for moving the control of the nation's economy from the provinces to the Dominion as Canada entered her industrial phase can hardly be exaggerated. (This is especially notable when the application of the commerce clause in the United States is compared to the role of its somewhat more forcefully stated counterpart in Canada.) As one observer has noted, there is considerable irony in the fact that the United States has done so much with so little while Canada has done so little with so much.[44] The expansion or contraction of this power has, of course, fundamentally influenced the way in which the federation has approached the crucial issues growing out of the development of a national economy.

The narrowing of the potential scope of the trade and commerce power began the first time the clause was considered by the Judicial Committee in *Citizens Insurance Company* v. *Parsons* in 1881.[45] There the Board rejected the contention of the appellants that the words "trade and commerce" were meant to be "the most generous words which can be used, and include every kind of business which can pòssibly be carried on". Their Lordships asserted that the Act could not have contemplated such a wide meaning, or several other classes of subjects enumerated in section 91, such as banking, bills of exchange and promissory notes, and weights and measures would not also have been mentioned.[46] Instead, their Lordships speculated that the true intent of the words of head 2 correspond to those used in the Act of Union between England and Scotland which allowed differing controls and rules of trade in those two kingdoms.[47] "Trade and commerce" in the meaning of the B.N.A. Act, their Lordships said, "would include political arrangements in regard to trade requiring the sanction of Parliament, regulation of trade in matters of inter-provincial concern, and it may be that they would include general regulation of trade affecting the whole Dominion". The Board ruled, however, that the phrase did *not* support legislation regulating contracts of a *particular* business or trade carried on in a single province.

When the Supreme Court of Canada had considered the matter, Mr. Justice Taschereau had also maintained that the power of the Dominion parliament

---

[44] Alexander Smith, *The Commerce Power in Canada and the United States* (Toronto, Butterworth, 1963), p. 4.
[45] (1881), 7 A. C. 96.
[46] *Ibid.,* p. 100.
[47] *Ibid.,* p. 112.

to incorporate companies was derived from the trade and commerce power, but Sir Montague Smith suggested that this power was more correctly derived from the general power of the Dominion to legislate on all matters not expressly given to the provinces.[48] The *Parsons* case, then, set several precedents. First, the words trade and commerce were not to be taken in their common meaning, for such an interpretation "would all but destroy the autonomy of the provinces". Secondly, the Dominion could not regulate the contracts of particular business in a single province. Finally, the tentative definition of the power was that it encompassed political arrangements for trade, interprovincial trade, and perhaps general trade affecting the whole Dominion.

Some of the ramifications of the *Parsons* case became evident in the *Local Prohibition* case. Citing *Parsons* as precedent, the Board confirmed that the Dominion power over trade and commerce did not extend to intraprovincial trade itself. Here the Judicial Committee, however, went beyond that holding and also limiting the power of the Dominion to regulate local trade and commerce even as a part of a general regulation of these activities.[49]

While their Lordships noted that "the provisions of the Act of 1878 [involved in the *Russell* case] were in all material respects the same with those which are now embodied in the Canada Temperance Act of 1886 [being tested in this case]",[50] they ruled that it could not also be sustained under the trade and commerce power but only under peace, order, and good government. The reason for this holding, Lord Watson explained, was the distinction between regulation and prohibition:

> A power to regulate, naturally, if not necessarily, assumes, unless it is enlarged by the context, the conservation of the thing which is to be made the subject of regulation. In that view, their Lordships are unable to regard the prohibitive enactments of the Canadian statute of 1886 as regulations of trade and commerce.[51]

Thus the general power to regulate trade and commerce could not include prohibition as a means of regulation.

Again, in the *Insurance Reference,* the Judicial Committee restricted the scope of the commerce powers, declaring that not only were contracts of particular businesses operating in a single province beyond the scope of the power (as held in *Parsons*) and regulation by prohibition invalid, but the regulation

---

48 *Ibid.,* p. 116.
49 In *Russell* v. *The Queen* the Board had emphasized that, while the prohibitory liquor legislation there in question was primarily to be upheld under the peace, order, and good government power, this "must not be understood as intimating any dissent from the opinion . . . that the Act, as a general regulation of the traffic in intoxicating liquors throughout the Dominion, fell within the class of subject 'the regulation of trade and commerce' . . . and was, on that ground a valid exercise of the legislative power of the Parliament of Canada.
50 (1896), A. C. 348 at 362.
51 (1896), A. C. 348 at 363.

of particular *trades* whether local or interprovincial by a licensing system was also beyond the competence of the Dominion.[52] This limiting trend reached its logical conclusion in 1922, when in the *Board of Commerce* case Lord Haldane concluded that interference with particular trades and businesses (such as insurance) in any way, was not consistent with a power limited to general regulation of trade (that is, general commercial intercourse), *not trades.*[53]

A more sweeping, if not more serious, limitation on the ambit of section 91(2) came in a series of cases which culminated in *Toronto Electric Commissioners* v. *Snider.* As early as 1912 the Judicial Committee implied that the limitations placed on the peace, order, and good government clause which restricted its application   to only those situations where it supplemented a power enumerated in section 91 were also to apply to the trade and commerce clause.[54] It was not until ten years later in the *Board of Commerce* case, however, that this view was expressed explicitly. There Lord Haldane suggested that the trade and commerce power could *only* apply when used in conjunction with another Dominion power, particularly the general power over peace, order, and good government.[55] Thus the trade and commerce clause was not even to have the status of an ordinary enumerated head, but, because of the generality of its terms, the Board ruled that it had to be buttressed by a more explicit, additional authority as well.

In *Toronto Electric Commissioners* v. *Sniders,* Lord Haldane stated the point succinctly, saying:

> It is, in their Lordships' opinion, now clear that, excepting so far as the power can be invoked in aid of capacity conferred independently under other words in s. 91, the power to regulate trade and commerce cannot be relied on as enabling the Dominion Parliament to regulate civil rights in the Provinces [in this case the settlement of industrial disputes].[56]

Far from being the most far-reaching of the enumerated Dominion powers, trade and commerce was seen as nothing more than a weak relation.

It was not long, however, until the Judicial Committee beat a retreat from the extravagance of this opinion. In a 1931 opinion Lord Atkin spoke for the Board, saying:

> Their Lordships merely propose to disassociate themselves from the construction suggested . . . in the judgment in the *Board of Commerce* case under which it was contended that the power to regulate trade and commerce could be invoked only in furtherance of a general power

---

[52] *Attorney-General for Canada* v. *Attorney-General for Alberta* (1916), A. C. 588.

[53] *In Re The Board of Commerce Act, 1919* (1922), A. C. 191.

[54] *Montreal* v. *Montreal Street Railway* (1912), A. C. 333 at 344. See also *John Deere Plow Co.* v. *Wharton* (1915), A. C. 330.

[55] (1922), A. C. 191 at 197-98.

[56] (1925), A. C. 396 at 410.

which Parliament possessed independently of it. . . . The words of the statute must receive their proper construction where they stand as giving an independent authority to Parliament over the particular subject-matter. . . .[57]

And again, in the *Aeronautics Reference,* heard the following year, the Board intimated that the trade and commerce power might have been a ground for upholding Dominion regulation of aeronautics, had not the treaty power given in section 132 been sufficient ground in itself.[58] The argument that the authority of the trade and commerce clause was supplementary became a dead issue with the *Trade Mark* case (1937), in which Ontario questioned the Dominion's power to established a national trade mark. In answering the question affirmatively, the Board made it clear that this was an appropriate exercise of the trade and commerce power unaided by any other power of the Dominion. In its view, "there could hardly be a more appropriate form of the exercise of this power than the creation and regulation of a uniform law of trade marks".[59]

But though the extravagance of the "supplementary" view of the trade and commerce power had been discarded, the restrictions of narrow reading of the words and the understanding that none of the enumerations of section 91 could reach farther than a necessarily incidental interference with the provincial matters in section 92 remained. A crucial test of the extent to which these views still applied came with the reference of the Dominion's Natural Products Marketing Act to the courts (also in 1937.[60] The Act was part of the Bennett Government's "New Deal" legislation through which the Dominion sought to cope with the marketing problems of the Depression by claiming sweeping federal authority to regulate time and place of selling and, when necessary, prohibit marketing of any product. This the Board declared wholly *ultra vires* the Dominion on the ground that aspects of the scheme which controlled inter-provincial and international trade were so intermixed with control of purely local transactions that the whole scheme was invalid as an infringement of section 92(13). Said the Board, ". . . the regulation of trade and commerce does not permit the regulation of individual forms of trade or commerce confined to the Province".[61]

It was nearly fifteen years before the Judicial Committee was again called upon to comment on the meaning of the trade and commerce power. In 1951 Section 5A of the Diary Industry Act was referred to the courts for an opinion as to whether it was valid for the Dominion, in an effort to support and develop the dairy industry, to prohibit the manufacture and sale of margarine

---

57 *Proprietary Articles Trade Association* v. *Attorney-General for Canada* (1931), A. C. 310 at 326.
58 (1932), A. C. 54 at 73.
59 *Attorney-General for Ontario* v. *Attorney-General for Canada* (1937), A. C. 405 at 417.
60 *Attorney-General for British Columbia* v. *Attorney-General for Canada* (1937), A. C. 377.
61 *Ibid.,* p. 387.

throughout Canada. Again, noting that the Act prohibited these activities even when carried on solely within the boundaries of a single province, the Board (appealing to the considerable precedent for the view) ruled that such a measure was an invalid encroachment on property and civil rights in the province. In their final word on the subject before appeals were ended, the Board summed up the Judicial Committee view:

> . . . [T]he present case is typical of the many cases in which the Board had felt bound to put some limit on the scope of the wide words used in head 2 of section 91 in order to preserve from serious curtailment, if not from virtual extinction, the degree of autonomy which, as appears from the scheme of the Act as a whole, the provinces were intended to possess.[62]

The end of appeals to the Judicial Committee of the Privy Council left the Supreme Court with a considerable bulk of precedent for a narrow construction of the meaning of section 91, head 2. In 1957, with its first opportunity to rule as the final court in a case involving the commerce power, however, it took a more venturesome tack. The matter in question was the validity of the Ontario Farm Products Act, which was designed to regulate the sale of farm products throughout Ontario.[63] Seven of the eight justices sitting in the case pronounced it *intra vires* the province, but the case was seized as an opportunity to comment on the meaning of trade and commerce as stated in section 91 and the problem of setting the limits of geographical areas of jurisdiction in an integrated economic system. Questioning the validity of considering trade and commerce a part of the power of the provinces over property and civil rights, as it had so often been in the past, Mr. Justice Rand commented: "The production of goods as an economic activity does not take place by virtue of positive law or civil right, it is assumed as part of the residual free activity of men upon or around which law is imposed. It has an identity of its own recognized by section 91(2)."[64] Trade, the Court said, was not static but "dynamic, the creation and flow of goods from production to consumption . . . as an individualized action". Thus, the boundaries of the province and the bounds of provincial authority over trade were not to be considered coextensive. In matters of trade and commerce within the province but with effects beyond the province, the Dominion power under section 91(2) was held paramount. But, though the use of the provincial boundary as the mark of the division of jurisdictions has now been at least temporarily discredited, it is not clear what formula or test of jurisdiction will take its place.

Murphy v. *Canadian Pacific Railway,* decided in the next year, however, offered a more clear-cut test of the Court's view of the commerce power.

---

62 *Canadian Federation of Agriculture* v. *Attorney-General for Quebec* (1951), A. C. 179 at 194.
63 *Re The (Ontario) Farm Products Marketing Act* (1957), S. C. R. 198.
64 *Ibid.,* p. 211.

There Mr. Justice Locke, writing for himself and for Justices Taschereau, Fauteux and Abbott, specifically upheld the Canadian Wheat Board Act. He ruled that the Act was a valid regulation of trade and commerce and added: "the fact that . . . it [necessarily] interferes with property and civil rights in the province . . . is immaterial".[65] To the argument that the Dominion did not have the power to regulate the activities of a particular trade (as held in the *Insurance Reference*), the Justices replied that the Act did not regulate just one trade but several, and since their activities were directed to the export of grain from the province, the provincial governments were powerless to control them. Though no general trend can be safely inferred from the two rulings of the Supreme Court on trade and commerce since the abolition of appeals to the Judicial Committee, the difference of approach between the Privy Council and the Court is evident. How far the potential of the pragmatic approach to the matter of whether trade is in fact merely local or interprovincial in import will be developed, awaits the arrival of similar cases before the court.

Summary and Conclusion

The impact of judicial review on the legal framework within which Dominion and provinces operate, then, has been substantial. The peace, order, and good government clause was transformed from a general residuary power to legislate on all matters not specifically excepted by section 92 to a supplementary power operating (1) only on those matters not covered by either of the enumerated lists, (2) as a supplement to powers possessed independently in section 91, and (3) in time of emergency, when it could temporarily override the normal jurisdiction to save the nation from catastrophe. From the early 1930's until 1949, decisions by the Judicial Committee wavered back and forth between this restrictive interpretation and the broader scope given the clause prior to 1896. Thus, at least until recently, the courts failed to produce even the clarity and certainty as to the meaning of the law which is one of the prime functions of the judiciary.

The interpretation of the trade and commerce power followed a similar pattern. The scope of the power was limited first by a narrow reading of the meaning of the words, then by an interpretation of its relation to section 92 which settled that it could not extend into the realm of the powers given the provinces in section 92 and, finally, by an interpretation which declared it to be operable *only* as a supplement to another federal power. Again, as in the case of the residuary power, the courts retreated from the extremities of their position in the early 1930's only to return to them in the later years of that decade.

After the Supreme Court became the final arbiter of the federal balance in 1949, it began to throw its weight behind broader interpretations of the scope of these two powers. Twice in the past two decades, the Court has shown itself

---

[65] (1958), S. C. R. 626 at 632.

willing to repudiate sharply the more restrictive and abstract elements in the earlier interpretation of the trade and commerce clause. Similarly, in the case of the residuary power, the Court has found it possible to uphold Dominion legislation enacted under the government's authority to provide for the "peace, order, and good government" of Canada, at first tentatively and then with broader sweep. One must proceed cautiously, however, in advancing these trends as settled interpretations, both because of the small number of cases involved and because of the wide fluctuations in interpretation common in the past.

The result of the judicial interpretations of the boundaries of legal authority between Dominion and province with regard to the crucial powers in question here, however, has been primarily to enlarge the provincial area of power and to restrict that of the Dominion. Thus the legal framework has operated as a centrifugal force in the federation, dividing jurisdiction and thwarting attempts to centralize control in important areas of economic and social concerns. There can be little doubt that for much of its history the Judicial Committee brought a "states' rights" bias to its interpretive task. The decisions based on this normative position could not fail to have significant repercussions on the policy-making process in Canada, and thus important consequences for political life. Perhaps the Committee's invalidation of the "New Deal" legislation is the outstanding example of their Lordships' determination to give the provinces their rights—whether they wanted them or not. In this, as in several other areas, judicial decisions made it more difficult for Canada's governments to cope with their problems than it might otherwise have been.

One of the most important functions of a court which adjudicates constitutional questions in a federal system is to provide flexibility in the allocation of responsibilities between governments, so that the system may adjust, over time, to changing economic, social and political realities. The absence of a settled amendment procedure has made this function particularly important in Canada. The initial rigidity of constitutional interpretation and the unpredictable fluctuations in interpretation which followed have no doubt played their part in discrediting the judicial review process. Among the consequences of this loss of faith are an increase in the use of informal mechanisms of adjustment and, perhaps, a decline in the legitimacy of the courts as arbiters of the federal balance.[66] Bora Laskin sums up the situation as follows:

> It is as if a stalement has been reached in the legal relations of Canada and the Provinces, but with no legal, no judicial means of resolving current conflicts. In fact, there are such means. But what has been evident for many years is that the mood of our political leaders is less and less for acquiesence in a judicial order of constitutional change through reinterpretation of the division of legislative powers. The courts themselves cannot, of course, force such a mood; their jurisdiction must be activated by the initiative of private litigants or by

---

[66] See J. A. Corry, "Constitutional Trends and Federalism," in A. R. M. Lower, F. R. Scott, *et al., Evolving Canadian Federalism* (Durham, Duke University Press, 1958) pp. 117-18.

governments; and above all, the exercise of jurisdiction must be founded on actual or proposed legislation as the subject of challenge.[67]

If, as Professors Corry and Laskin suggest, the courts are no longer a major mechanism for constitutional adjustment, certainly at least part of the explanation of this apparent lack of faith of governments and other potential litigants in the results of judicial decision-making lies in the record of past performance.[68]

13   The Supreme Court Since 1949: Contemporary Issues*

Peter H. Russell

The Supreme Court's elevation in 1949 to a position of true judicial supremacy did not either then or later make the Court a major focus of public attention. Canadians traditionally have not been inclined to regard the organization of their country's judicial system as being as influential in their system of government—or as malleable—as its legislative, executive, and political institutions. This is generally the result of conventional views as to the independence of the judiciary and its duty to interpret, rather than make the law. Also, in the case of the Supreme Court, neither the Canadian constitution nor its judicial system imposes on Canada's ultimate appellate court as distinctive or as consequential a set of responsibilities as are imposed, for instance, on the United States Supreme Court. Nevertheless, the attainment of judicial autonomy did intensify the interest of a small, although

---

[67] Bora Laskin, "Reflections on the Canadian Constitution After the First Century," *Canadian Bar Review*, Vol. XLV no. 3 (September, 1967), pp. 395-96.
[68] Other factors than the trends in interpretation have obviously also played a part in the decline in the role of the Court as arbiter of the federal balance. As Richard Jones points out, one such factor is the doubt that Supreme Court justices, selected solely by the central government, can act as unbiased arbiters in conflicts between the two levels of government. See Richard Jones, *Community in Crisis: French-Canadian Nationalism in Perspective* (Toronto, McClelland and Stewart, 1967), p. 103.

---

* From Peter H. Russell, *The Supreme Court of Canada as a Bilingual and Bicultural Institution*. Volume 1 of the Documents of the Royal Commission on Bilingualism and Biculturalism (Ottawa, Queen's Printer, 1969), pp. 43-58. Reprinted by permission of the author and Information Canada.

PETER H. RUSSELL – Professor of Political Science, University of Toronto.

potentially influential, group of Canadians in some of the basic questions relating to the Court's role in the Canadian system of government. The Court's actual performance since 1949 has increased this interest, as has the growing concern with bicultural and federal problems. . . .

For purposes of analysis three distinct kinds of concern can be distinguished: the federalist, the bilingual and bicultural questions which are of special concern to Quebec, and the general interest in the Supreme Court's capacity for national judicial statesmanship. While no doubt in practice there is considerable overlapping of these concerns, it seems worthwhile to consider them separately for they raise different kinds of questions for research and point to different kinds of possible reform.

A. Federalist Concerns

From the perspective of federalism, the chief point of interest in the operations of a federal Supreme Court concerns its role of arbiter or umpire of the federal system. Advocates of "classical" or "pure" federalism argue that the institution which settles disputes between the constituent parts of the federal state and the national government should not, in principle, be subject to the exclusive control of either level of government. In the words of K. C. Wheare, one of the foremost expositors of the principles of federal government, "what is essential for federal government is that some impartial body, independent of general and regional governments, should decide upon the meaning of the division of powers."[1] As has already been noted above, one of the primary points of criticism raised by the Tremblay Commission, Quebec's Royal Commission on Constitutional Problems, was the contention that this principle was violated by the existing organization of the Supreme Court of Canada.

While this particular point of criticism might be taken up by any thoroughgoing adherent of "pure" federalism, it would appear that since 1949 only Quebec spokesmen have been prominent in expressing this argument. However it may be that the recent reluctance of a number of provincial governments to submit to the Supreme Court the question of whether jurisdiction over off-shore mineral rights is a provincial or federal concern stems, in part, from the same kind of distrust voiced by Quebec representatives.

The essential element in this distrust is the central government's control over the appointment and dismissal of Supreme Court judges. The inference which sustains this distrust is that judges who are appointed by the federal government and can be removed by the federal legislature, are apt to favour the federal level of government in federal-provincial disputes.[2] Presumably, although this is not spelt out by those who adopt this argument, the centralist

---

[1] K. C. Wheare, *Federal Government,* 3rd Ed. (London, 1955), p. 66.

[2] The following extract from the submission made by La Presse étudiante nationale to the Royal Commission on Bilingualism and Biculturalism is fairly typical of the popular expression of this viewpoint: "In regard to those matters which concern the powers of the provinces, agreement of the local governments is required in order to amend our constitution. However, it should be noted, that if there is total impossibility of agreement between the federal and provincial governments, the case will be referred to the Supreme Court. . . . However, the judges of the highest Court in the land are nominated by the federal government exclusively and without ratification by the provinces. . . .

bias would result from the kind of men a federal government is most likely to choose in making Supreme Court appointments, or else from the influence which the federal level of government might have on Supreme Court justices after their appointments. The latter suspicion would have to be based primarily on the informal rather than formal influence which federal agencies might exercise, for Supreme Court judges, once appointed, hold office on good behaviour and can be removed only by the Governor General on address of the Senate and House of Commons.[3] Still, this does mean that the federal Parliament possesses the exclusive power to remove Supreme Court judges. Also, there is the possibility that the conditions of tenure, because they are provided for in federal legislation, rather than in the Constitution, could be altered unilaterally by the federal legislature. Besides the rather remote possibility of the federal government influencing the Supreme Court through the exercise of these legal powers, there is the larger possibility of the judges' outlook being shaped by the federal environment in which they work and live. But this kind of influence could not be overcome simply by altering the method of appointing Supreme Court judges.

It should be noted that provincial opposition to the central government's control over the Supreme Court appointments and dismissals is not based on actual manifestations of the centralist bias which, it is alleged, such control might produce in the constitutional decisions of the Supreme Court. K. C. Wheare, the federalist expert, whose opinion has been cited here and is so often cited as grounds for the federalist critique of the Canadian Supreme Court, has commented on this point. After pointing out that "in most federal governments the settlements of disputes about the meaning of the division of powers is confided to a body appointed and dismissable by the central government," he goes on to observe that "in spite of the formal dependence of the supreme courts on the executive and legislature of the general government, they have exhibited a considerable impartiality in the exercise of their function as interpreters of the division of powers.[4] Whether or not Wheare's generalization holds true for Canada, one does not find that recent provincial critiques of the inherent centralist bias of the Supreme Court turn on real indications of this in the Court's decisions.

Continued   •

Hence, the powers already acquired by the provinces are, to a certain extent, as far as their existence is concerned, controlled by what in principle is a hostile authority. (Submission 240-71, no. 172, 48-9.) (Original French: "Dans les matières qui concernent les pouvoirs provinciaux, l'accord des gouvernements locaux est requis pour amender notre constitution. Toutefois, on note que, s'il y a impossibilité totale d'entente entre les gouvernements fédéral et provinciaux, le cas sera référé à la Cour Suprême. . . . Cependent, les juges de la plus haute cour de notre pays sont nommés par le fédéral exclusivement et sans ratification par les provinces. . . . Les pouvoirs déjà acquis par les provinces sont donc, dans une certaine mesure, soumis, quant à leur existence, à une autorité hostile, en principe.")

[3] Supreme Court Act, 1961, s. 9 (2) provides that judges automatically retire on reaching age 75.

[4] Wheare, *Federal Government,* p. 63.

When one actually examines the Supreme Court's record in constitutional adjudication, one finds that in the one period when the Supreme Court was most vulnerable to the charge of favouring the federal government, this complaint was not a significant ingredient of public discontent with the Court. The period referred to was, of course, during the Court's earliest years when it had not yet become thoroughly controlled by Privy Council precedents and, in one or two instances as we pointed out earlier, when it had demonstrated a concern for upholding federal power, particularly in the field of trade and commerce. Following these early decisions and up to 1949, the Supreme Court's subordination to the Privy Council was such that it could scarcely be accused of having taken an initiative on the basic issues of constitutional law that was clearly centralist or provincial. There were, it is true, occasional instances when the Supreme Court, or at least some of its members, showed an independence of the Privy Council's modes of reasoning; but in their disagreements, the Canadian judges were, as often as not, on the provincial rather than the federal side.[5] What was surely more important than any of the concrete differences between the tenor of the Supreme Court's constitutional decisions and those of the Privy Council in shaping popular attitudes was simply the fact that the Privy Council, as the supreme arbiter of the Canadian constitution, was independent of both the provincial and federal governments. When you add to this the generally acknowledged tendency of the Privy Council's critical decisions to strengthen provincial powers, it is not surprising that provincial spokesmen, after 1949, might suspect that a final constitutional arbiter subject to exclusive federal control would tend to move in the opposite direction.

---

[5] For an extensive analysis of the Supreme Court's captivity by Privy Council precedents in constitutional law, see F. E. Labrie, "Canadian Constitutional Interpretation and Legislative Review", *University of Toronto Law Journal*, Vol. VIII (1949-50), p. 298. Chief Justice Anglin was perhaps the best example of a Supreme Court judge who differed openly with the Privy Council's interpretation of the B. N. A. Act and, in so doing, took a position more favourable to federal legislative power. See his opinion in *In Re The Board of Commerce* (1920) 60 S. C. R. 467; and his attack on Viscount Haldane's reasoning in the *Snider* case in *The King* v. *Eastern Terminal Elevator Co.* (1925) S. C. R. 438.

A strictly quantitative analysis makes it difficult to argue that the Supreme Court has been inherently pro-Dominion. In thirteen cases concerning the division of powers the Privy Council reversed the Supreme Court's decision. In six of these the Privy Council's decision granted the provinces legislative power which had been denied by the Supreme Court (The *Manitoba Public Schools Act* case, 1892; the *Local Prohibition* case, 1896; the *Bonanza Creek* case, 1916; and three cases involving provincial tax measures — the *Fairbanks Estate,* 1928; the *Atlantic Smoke Shops* case, 1943; and *A. G. B. C. v. Esquimalt and Nanaimo Ry. Co.,* 1950). On the other hand, in four others the Privy Council invalidated provincial laws declared valid by the Supreme Court (*Cotton* v. *The King,* 1914; *Ottawa Separate Schools Trustees* v. *Ottawa Corp.,* 1917; *Great West Saddlery* v. *The King,* 1921, and the *Winner* case of 1954). In the remaining three, Supreme Court decisions denying the Dominion jurisdiction were overruled by the Privy Council (*The Aeronautics Reference,* 1932; *Croft* v. *Dunphy,* 1933; and one part of the Dominion Trade and Industry Commission Act in the "New Deal" Reference of 1936-37, *A.-G. Ont.* v. *A.-G. Can.* (1937) A. C. 405).

Since 1949, the Supreme Court has not embarked on a revolutionary departure from the Privy Council's approach to the division of powers. It is true that in the *Johannesson*[6] case a majority of the Court supported a less restrictive view of the federal legislature's general power than that developed by the Privy Council, and again the Court's judgments in both the *Ontario Farm Products Marketing Act Reference*,[7] and the *Murphy*[8] case, pointed to a larger conception of the federal trade and commerce power.[9] But, on the other hand, in a number of cases challenging provincial statutes, the Court was willing to uphold the provincial legislation and, in effect, carve out a larger area in which the provinces could act concurrently with the Dominion.[10] It may be true that in the post-1949 period the provincial legislatures have certainly had more of their Acts invalidated by the Supreme Court than has the federal Parliament. But this is more likely a reflection of the greater tendency of contemporary provincial régimes to venture into new spheres of activity than a reflection of a federal bias among the members of the Supreme Court. In any event, it is not the phenomenon which appears to have provoked federalist objections, especially in Quebec, to the Supreme Court.

Those objections, as we have stressed, are based primarily on the principle that federal equity demands either the supreme constitutional tribunal's complete independence of both levels of government, as was the case with the Privy Council, or else its bilateral dependence on both levels. Expressed not as a sense of distrust of the existing Court, but more as a positive proposal for strengthening the provinces' and particularly Quebec's confidence in the constitutional decisions of a Supreme Court, this position insists above all on provincial participation in the appointment of Supreme Court judges. A number of proposals have been made for implementing this principle. One approach is to have the provincial governments directly appoint or nominate some of the judges of the Supreme Court or of a special constitutional court.[11] Proponents of this scheme have usually contemplated that for this purpose the provinces be grouped in accordance with the regional divisions of the Senate. Of course, those in Quebec who have recently been pressing for a more dualistic constitution for Canada would go much further than this and insist that the part of Canada representing the French culture enjoy equal

---

6 (1957), S. C. R. 292.

7 (1957), S. C. R. 198.

8 (1958), S. C. R. 626.

9 For a survey of the Supreme Court's decisions on the division of powers since 1949 see Peter H. Russell, "The Supreme Court's Interpretation of the Constitution Since 1949", Paul Fox (ed.), *Politics: Canada*, 1st Ed. (Toronto, 1962).

10 For a discussion of some of these decisions, see W. R. Lederman, "The Concurrent Operation of Federal and Provincial Laws in Canada", *McGill Law Journal*, Vol. IX (1963), p. 185.

11 See, for instance, the recommendations of the *Tremblay Report*, III, Bk. I, Chap. X, 389. See also recommendations of Antonio Perrault, "La Cour suprême du Canada", *Relations*, XIII (January 1953), pp. 19-20.

rights with the English section in selecting the members of the tribunal that interprets the constitutional compact.[12] But this position goes considerably beyond federalist concerns, for it entails a binational rather than a federal approach to institutional reform. A more indirect way of involving provincial representatives in the process of making Supreme Court appointments is to have one of the national institutions, most likely a reconstructed Senate, which is especially designed to represent provincial interests, have some power of ratification over Supreme Court appointments. Those federal states which place some restrictions on the central government's control over appointments to the highest constitutional court, namely the United States and West Germany, use this type of mechanism.[13] Short of either of these approaches, there is another remedy which could be regarded as a minimal way of reducing provincial suspicions of federal control over the Supreme Court. This would entail subscribing some of the key clauses of the Supreme Court Act governing the appointment and tenure of judges—and possibly the jurisdiction of the court—in articles of the written Constitution not subject to unilateral amendment by the federal legislature. This extension of constitutional status to the crucial qualities of the Court might include the clause in the Supreme Court Act requiring that at least one-third of the nine Supreme Court judges be from Quebec.[14]

It is not our intention here to follow through all the implications of carrying out any of these proposals. Nor in our study of the Supreme Court's work since 1949 will we be paying special attention to its interpretation of the B.N.A. Act. These matters, as we have indicated, are more directly concerned with federal rather than bicultural issues. Only where the Supreme Court's constitutional decisions may impinge directly on a bicultural question, especially in the field of civil liberties, will the quantitative and qualitative analyses of the Supreme Court's decisions touch these federal matters. In addition, the detailed study of the Court's procedures will examine the representative character of the Court's composition, and this may shed some light on the Court's capacity for serving federalist values.

Outside the realm of constitutional law, the wide scope of the Supreme

---

[12] There is apparently some support for this position outside Quebec. See submissions of the Board of Directors of the Student Christian Movement of Canada (750-485, no. 41), and of the Communist Party of Canada (750-430, no. 159), to the R. C. B. & B.

[13] In the United States, the Senate which gives equal representation to each state must consent to the President's appointments to the Supreme Court. In West Germany, half of the 24 members of the Federal Constitutional Court are elected by the federal parliament *(Bundestag)* and half by the federal council *(Bundesrat)* which gives direct representation to the state governments. For detailed comparative studies of judicial structures of federal states, see Robert R. Bowie and Carl Friedrich (eds.), *Studies in Federalism* (Boston, 1954). Study no. 3 in this volume compares Australia, Canada, Germany, Switzerland, and the United States. Also W. J. Wagner in *The Federal States and Their Judiciary* (The Hague, 1959) compares federal judicial organizations in the United States, Canada, Australia, Switzerland, Argentina, Brazil and Mexico.

[14] See Peter H. Russell, *The Supreme Court of Canada as a Bilingual and Bicultural Institution,* p. 60.

Court's appellate jurisdiction in ordinary areas of law raises another issue which may be a source of federalist discontent. The fact that from the very outset the Supreme Court has been vested with authority to hear appeals in cases dealing with matters subject to provincial legislative jurisdiction, as well as those falling under federal jurisdiction, has meant that there is no division of judicial authority paralleling the division of legislative powers in Canadian federalism. As we pointed out above, the Judicial Committee's decision in 1947 which removed any constitutional obstacles to Parliament's abolishing all Canadian appeals to the Privy Council, consolidated the unitary nature of Canada's judicial structure. This decision confirmed the federal legislature's power under Section 101 of the B.N.A. Act to assign final appellate authority in all legal matters—federal and provincial—to a federal appeal court created and regulated by the federal Parliament.

This failure to extend the federal principle from the legislative to the judicial sphere is not an unusal feature of federal states. Indeed, of the classical federal countries, only the United States comes close to having a dual system of courts, one set to apply and interpret federal law and another to apply and interpret state law. And even there, of course, the jurisdiction of each set of courts is far from being exclusive of the other.[15] It is difficult enough to classify the subject matter of a complex piece of legislation under national or local heads of power. It is much more difficult, again, to take the myriad questions which crop up in all the lawsuits which are constantly being fed into the country's system of courts and sort them into matters coming under national or local spheres of jurisdiction. Certainly any attempt to work out a federalist division of jurisdiction in handling a country's legal disputes would be bound to confront some enormously complex jurisdictional tangles.

In Canada, those who have favoured a division of judicial jurisdiction closer to the federal division of legislative powers have usually only gone as far as to propose cutting off appeals from provincial courts to the Supreme Court in cases which involve only provincial law issues. This proposal, it should be noted, would not go very far towards realizing a federal division of judicial authority. It would leave the provincial courts with original jurisdiction over most aspects of federal law; for ever since the decision was taken in the first few years after Confederation not to press ahead on a large scale with the development of additional federal courts for the enforcement of national laws, the national legislature, like its counterpart in Australia and Switzerland, has relied mainly on provincial courts for the application of its

---

15 For instance, Henry M. Hart Jr., analyzing the relations between state and federal courts in the United States, writes that "State courts are regularly employed for the enforcement of federally-created rights having no necessary connection with state substantive law while federal courts are employed for the enforcement of state-vested rights having no necessary connection with federal substantive law." "The Relations between State and Federal Law" in A. W. MacMahon (ed.), *Federalism: Mature and Emergent* (New York, 1952), p. 184.

laws.[16] There is no indication that even the staunchest federalist would be interested in reversing this trend; nor, at this stage in the country's history, that he would call for the establishment of what would have to be a very extensive system of federal courts to deal with all disputes—including the broad fields of criminal and commercial law, which are affected by federal legislation. Besides this, the federal pattern of organization is further violated in the Canadian judicial system by the fact that the national government appoints all the judges of the Superior, District and County Courts in the provinces.[17]

It may be that this latter point raises the element in the existing system which is most vulnerable to the federalist point of view. A fairly large degree of overlapping in the jurisdiction of regional and national courts is probably an inescapable feature of a workable federal system. But exclusive national control of all senior judicial appointments—at both national and provincial levels—is not. K. C. Wheare, for example, after acknowledging the compatibility of the former situation with federalism, goes on to state that "on the other hand, the case of Canada, where the appointment of all judges is in the hands of the general government, is an example of a system which contradicts the federal principle."[18] The substantial responsibilities of provincial judges in federal law matters make some federal participation in their appointment appropriate. By the same token, it could certainly be argued that provincial governments should be involved in the appointment of all provincial court judges and, possibly, on the basis of the same logic, in the appointment of those federal judges (i.e., of the Supreme Court of Canada) who have a final appellate control over provincial law matters. An incidental benefit of such an approach might also be the removal of fetters on the development of provincial administrative tribunals which the judicial construction of Section 96 of the B.N.A. Act has imposed on the provinces.[19]

Again we must stress that the research we have carried out on the Supreme Court's development since 1949 does not bear directly on the federalist critique of the Court's jurisdiction over provincial law matters. What we have been aiming at here is simply to untangle the principal points of view from which the Supreme Court might be evaluated in order to single out the particular aspects of the Court that are related to bilingual and bicultural considerations. As for the relationship between the federalist concerns which we have discussed, and the bilingual and bicultural questions which we deal with below, two points should be made. First, the issues raised by the federalist criticism of the Supreme Court are taken up mainly by Quebeckers. We have already

---

[16] That is not to say, of course, that no federal courts have been established under Parliament's power in Section 101 of the B. N. A. Act to provide "additional courts for the better administration of the Laws of Canada". Among such courts are the Exchequer Court, the Board of Transport Commissioners, the Tariff Board, the Income Tax Appeal Board, and the Court Martial Appeal Court.

[17] Section 96 of the B. N. A. Act.

[18] Wheare, *Federal Government*, p. 71.

[19] See Morris C. Shumiatcher, "Section 96 of the British North America Act Re-examined", C. B. R., Vol. XXVII (1949), p. 131.

noted this fact in relation to the Supreme Court's role as a constitutional umpire. Again, in relation to the Supreme Court's review of provincial law matters, not too many outside of Quebec would be apt to argue that "because of the greater familiarity of local judges with the relevant social context,"[20] provincial judges should control the shape of the law in crucial fields of provincial law. This argument obviously has special relevancy to Quebec with its very distinctive private law system. And, indeed, the desire for some degree of legal uniformity, which is the point most often made for the retention of national appellate review of provincial law questions, is likely to be least convincing to Quebec opinion.[21] The second point, however, that should be made about the relationship of federal to bicultural concerns, is that the very fact that the points of criticism raised by a federalist analysis of the Supreme Court have the largest following in Quebec, and indeed tend to spill over into the special concerns of French Canadians in Quebec, suggests that one way of dealing with the special concerns of Quebec would be to adopt general federal solutions. Although it is clear that if such a course were adopted and all the provincial governments were given a voice in judicial appointments; or all appeals to the Supreme Court in matters relating to "property and civil rights," were terminated, it is likely that such measures would be regarded as far more meaningful in Quebec than in any of the other provinces.

B. Bicultural Concerns

Besides evaluating the Supreme Court in terms of federal principles, the position of the Court can also be examined from the point of view of French-English relations in Canada. In so far as the interests of French culture in Canada are represented by Quebec, then, to that extent the federal concerns which we examined above might overlap and contain the bicultural needs and aspirations of French Canada. But it also seems worthwhile, one might even say mandatory in the context of the Royal Commission on Bilingualism and Biculturalism for which this study was undertaken, to isolate for detailed study those aspects of the Court's contemporary organization and work which have a direct bearing on bicultural questions. When this is done, it is possible to distinguish three distinct areas of investigation: bilingualism in the Court's proceedings, the dualism of private law systems (the English common law and the Quebec civil law), and the broader clash of cultural values along a bicultural axis. Most of the quantitative and qualitative examination of the Court's decisions since 1949, which we have undertaken, focused on various phases of these issues. But as a preface to our report of that study, we wish

---

[20] Albert S. Abel, "The Role of the Supreme Court in Private Law Cases", *Alberta Law Review*, Vol. IV (1966).

[21] For a discussion of the Supreme Court's function in securing uniformity of law in Canada, see John Willis, "Securing Uniformity of Law in a Federal System", *University of Toronto Law Journal*, Vol. V (1944), P. 352. As Professor Willis acknowledges and as s. 94 B. N. A. Act implies, uniformity of laws related to property and civil rights is a value which only the common-law provinces are likely to accept.

to state the questions which seem paramount in each of these areas.

First, as far as bilingualism in the Supreme Court is concerned, the main contention is simply that since only three of the nine Supreme Court judges come from Quebec, it follows that the majority will not speak or understand French well enough to give French-speaking counsel the same opportunities to use their first language before the Court as English-speaking lawyers enjoy. The Junior Bar Association of Montreal's brief to this Commission presents a contemporary expression of this viewpoint. After concluding that "the Courts and Board of Quebec, especially in the Montreal area, are satisfactorily bilingual," the brief continues as follows:

A similar situation however does not exist in the federal courts. Despite Section 133 B.N.A. (1867) which permits a French speaking lawyer to use his own language before the Courts, this in fact has not been possible or practical. Up to the present, the majority of judges on the Supreme Court could not understand French. If a lawyer wished to convince the judges, he would have to draft his factum in English and argue in English. This was necessary if he was to serve the best interests of his client. On the other hand, there has never been a French speaking judge on the Supreme Court who could not understand and speak English. It seems that bilingualism has been a requirement for French speaking judges but not for their English speaking counterparts.[22]

This charge will be investigated in the first part of our detailed study. The extent to which both languages are and can be used in the Court's proceedings and records will be examined. In the light of this examination, possible methods of increasing the bilingual quality of the Court will be considered. Finally, in looking at the Court's decisions since 1949, we shall single out any cases in which the legal issue before the Court has confronted the Court with a bilingual problem, and see how the Court treated such problems.

It should be noted here that the complaint about the difficulty of using French in the Supreme Court has customarily been much less significant than anxiety about the Supreme Court's effect on Quebec's legal culture. In the historical narrative we traced the early expressions of this protest when there was some tendency to assume that the members of the Judicial Committee possessed a higher degree of linguistic versatility than the English-speaking members of the Supreme Court. However, with the passing of time, much less was heard of this complaint and French Canadian opinion focused more on the question of legal biculturalism. But this latter concern cannot, as Girouard argued over 75 years ago,[23] be entirely separated from the question of bilingualism. If one wants to preserve Quebec's civil law as a distinctive system of private law, enriched by the great body of French legal doctrine that is associated with that legal tradition, then it is likely that the pursuit of such a goal requires a bar and bench capable of mastering and contributing to the

---

[22] Submission no. 740-270 to the R. C. B. & B., 8.
[23] See Peter H. Russell, *The Supreme Court of Canada as a Bilingual and Bicultural Institution*, p. 71.

French-language scholarship which sustains that legal system. It is at this point that the linguistic capabilities of the judges who sit on the final court of appeal might well be a critical factor in the over all influence which that court has on Quebec's civilian jurisprudence.

The fate of Louisiana's French[24] civil-law system may be instructive on this point for those concerned about the preservation of Quebec's system. There seems little doubt that without any formal legislative change, Louisiana's civil-law system has over the years been thoroughly impregnated with common-law influences, so that it is now possible for a competent student of that system to conclude that "it must be admitted that Louisiana is today a common law state."[25] Now in Louisiana's case, the erosion of its distinctive legal tradition cannot be traced to the federal Supreme Court's ultimate appellate authority over that system, for with the dual system of courts operating in the United States, control over the interpretation of Louisiana's civil code would, for the greater part, rest in the hands of local judges. But on the state level, the absence of a pervasive French culture has been one of the most obvious factors at work in the Anglicization of the state's legal system. Professor Ireland in his study of the evolution of Louisiana's legal system, reports that "use of the French language before and by the courts though perhaps not unlawful, has been unheard of for many years, and three-quarters of the bar of Louisiana are probably unable to read the French commentators in their own tongue."[26] Another Louisiana jurist, Sidney Herold, anxious to see Louisiana retain its unique legal system, insists that its bar and bench must be able to read French sources of their code on the grounds that "one cannot know the history and background of the Articles of the Louisiana Code without at least a working knowledge of reading French.[27]

In Quebec there has been little anxiety as to the extent to which French sources are taught in its law schools and used by members of the provincial bar and bench. However, if the charge referred to above were well founded so that not only were a majority of the Supreme Court's members unable to mine French sources, but also French Canadian lawyers were discouraged from citing such sources before the Court, then the experience of Louisiana might well be regarded as a warning signal to French Canadian jurists concerned about preserving the purity of their legal system. But a careful investigation of the influence which the linguistic limitations of the Supreme Court might have on Quebec's system of civil law, would have to go beyond the mere study of the Court's procedures and personnel. It would require above all an extremely painstaking examination of the Court's jurisprudence in relation to the Civil Code, which would far exceed the capacities of this project. Nevertheless, this relationship between the use of language in the Court and the Court's impact on Quebec's Civil Code, must be acknowledged

---

24 There are also, of course, Spanish elements in the Louisiana civil-law tradition.

25 Gordon Ireland, "Louisiana's Legal System Reappraised", *Tulane Law Review,* Vol. XI (1937), p. 596.

26 *Ibid.,* p. 595.

27 Sidney Herold, "The French Language and the Louisiana Lawyer", *Tulane Law Review,* Vol. V (1931), p. 176.

as a possibility, even if it is one upon which this particular study cannot shed much light.

Turning to the second area of bicultural concern—the Supreme Court's treatment of the dualism of common law and civil law—we confront what has undoubtedly over the years been the most persistent source of Quebec discontent with the Supreme Court. In the historical section we traced how as early as the Confederation Debates French Canadians voiced their fear that the vesting of the highest appellate powers over all matters of law, including the civil law of Quebec, in a Supreme Court containing a majority of common-law judges, would eventually result in the large-scale infiltration of common-law principles into Quebec's civil law. At all the stages of debate through which the Supreme Court has passed right up to the present day, this has continued to be a main theme of French Canadian criticism of the Court. It has usually stimulated the advocacy of two alternative types of reform: either the termination of all appeals from Quebec courts to the Supreme Court in cases dealing with the Civil Code (or more broadly with property and civil rights in the province); or else, as an alternative approach, the reorganization of the Supreme Court to ensure that in all such Quebec appeals the civilian judges on the Court have a controlling voice.

Our study of the Supreme Court's decisions touches on this critical question in two respects. In our quantitative analysis we have attempted to provide simply a statistical account of the degree to which the non-civilian members of the Court have played a decisive role in Quebec appeals during the various periods of the Court's existence. In the section following this which presents a more jurisprudential analysis of leading cases, we examine, among other things, some of the recent cases in which the Court has divided on the lines of civil law and common law in matters relating to Quebec's civil law. These parts of our research, it is hoped, will provide some indication of the over-all weight which common-law judges have had in reviewing the decision of Quebec judges, and provide some illustrations of the kind of Quebec lawsuit which might pit the common-law judges on the Court against their civilian brethren. Obviously, however, it cannot pretend to provide anything approaching a definitive assessment of the common-law influence on Quebec's civil law which has resulted from the Supreme Court's exercise of its appellate authority. Such an assessment would have to be based on an extensive examination of the way in which the Supreme Court has shaped Quebec's civil law—both in terms of substantive legal precepts and general judicial techniques. In order to isolate and comprehend the Supreme Court's influence such a study would have to compare the Supreme Court's own contribution to Quebec law with that of the Privy Council and that of the Quebec courts themselves. Already a number of French Canadian scholars have made substantial contributions to this kind of study, but there is still much that remains to be investigated.[28]

---

[28] See the works cited in Peter H. Russell, *The Supreme Court of Canada as a Bilingual and Bicultural Institution* (notes 132-56, 246-49), in the historical account of French Canadian Attitudes to the Court contained in Chap. 1.

While this detailed legal scholarship is unquestionably the indispensable step in revealing the full extent of common-law influences on Quebec's civil law, what perhaps is too often left out of account are the alternative ways of *evaluating* this influence once it is revealed. Of course, one's objection to the Supreme Court's review of Quebec decisions dealing with civil-law matters may be based primarily on principle. One might argue that regardless of the actual ways in which the Supreme Court's treatment of civil law has affected Quebec society and changed its legal culture, it is wrong in principle to give a federal court, containing only a minority of Quebec judges, the power of revising the decisions of Quebec courts in matters relating to Quebec's distinctive system of private law. From this point of view, the citation and analysis of actual cases can only provide corroborating evidence for an already well-formed judgment. At the level of popular, political discourse this rather ideological attitude to the question has been most prevalent.

It is possible, however, to take a more pragmatic approach which requires a close study of actual judges and actual cases. To begin with, one would want to ascertain, more carefully than has been done to date, the extent to which common-law judges lack competency in handling civil-law matters. It may be that given appropriate methods of consultation and collaboration on the Court, plus enlightened appointments, Supreme Court judges not formally trained in the civil-law tradition can, in a reasonably short perod of time, acquire enough knowledge to justify their reviewing the judgments of the highest Quebec court. Secondly, once the particular forms of common-law influence on Quebec's civil-law system are ascertained and traced to Supreme Court judges, a number of further questions might be asked. How have these "distortions" of Quebec's Civil Code affected the particular rights of Quebec litigants and, more generally, legal relations in Quebec society? Are these effects just or unjust, beneficial or adverse? Is there a "comparative law advantage" in any of these common-law infiltrations of the Civil Code? On the other hand, has the presence of civilian judges on the Supreme Court had a counter-balancing effect on the law of the common-law provinces? Again, have these been beneficial effects? Of course, the answer to any of these questions must hinge on the values one holds both in relation to various areas of social policy as well as in relation to alternative patterns of legal development. But the point is that once the discussion of the Supreme Court's impact on the civil law of Quebec passes the essentially ideological point, they are questions which can only be answered candidly by first defining the values and premises upon which one's answers will be based.

The third area of bicultural concern which we have defined revolves around those legal issues which come before the court and which would, at least potentially, appear to turn on a conflict of French as opposed to English values. Since 1949 a large number of cases have been brought before the Supreme Court involving potentially bicultural issues in such areas as family relationships, morals, religious beliefs, education, and civil liberties. A number of these cases, especially in the field of civil liberties, have concerned questions of great public importance. Many of them have been appeals from decisions of the Quebec courts and, in some of the most prominent of these cases, the Supreme Court of Canada has reversed the decision of the Quebec courts. All of this has produced a heightened awareness of the possibility of bicultural conflicts across a broad range of legal issues adjudicated by the Supreme Court.[29]

Our research on the Supreme Court's post-1949 decisions has tried to ascertain the extent to which this possibility is an actuality. In the quantitative part of our study we have first carried out a comparison of the Supreme Court's disposition of Quebec appeals in various categories of legal issues with its disposition of appeals from the other provinces. Also, by analyzing voting patterns we have tried to see whether or not ethnic blocks are operative in the Court's decision-making. Secondly, we have looked closely at a variety of cases in which there would appear to be at least a possibility that differences among the judges might hinge on differences in their ethnic or religious backgrounds. In these cases we have endeavoured to answer two questions: (a) is there any evidence in the judges' opinion to suggest that their ethnic or religious attitudes have been a significant factor in influencing their conclusions? (b) where judicial disagreements do appear to reflect French-English, or possibly Roman Catholic-Protestant differences, how has the Court resolved these differences?

One crucial point should be made here as a qualifying note to the general public discussion of bicultural divisions on the Court and to our investigation of this matter. In this area of discourse, it may be too readily assumed that the Quebec judges on the Supreme Court, or at least the French-speaking Quebec judges, represent French Canadian cultural values. It may also be questionable to assume that judges who sit on Quebec's Court of Appeal, and whose decisions can be reversed by the Supreme Court, are also representative of French Canadian culture. Neither of these assumptions may be correct. If we set aside the whole problem of identifying a French Canadian (or for that matter, an English Canadian) consensus on the values involved in these "bicultural" lawsuits, and assume that something approaching a prevailing French Canadian attitude to these issues exists, it still does not necessarily follow that Quebec judges share and apply these prevailing attitudes. Indeed, given (a) the fact that the federal government appoints both Quebec provincial judges and Quebec judges on the Supreme Court, and (b) the fact that once appointed Quebec judges usually remain on the Court until retirement at age 75, it is possible that these Quebec judges in their basic value orientations might be quite out of step with the prevailing tone of French Canadian society in Quebec—particularly at a time when that society is passing through a very dynamic period of social change.

Even if this were the real situation, and Quebec's representatives on the

---

[29] One of the scholars who has been most sensitive to this development is Prof. Edward WcWhinney. See, for example, his article on "Federalism, Pluralism and State Responsibility-Canadian and American Analogies", *New York University Law Review*, Vol. XXXIV (1959) 1079. See also his *Comparative Federalism* (Toronto, 1963).

Supreme Court, or even her own provincial judges, were in a significant way unrepresentative of the main stream of her cultural life, this in itself might not diminish the seriousness from a bicultural point of view of the recent divisions on the Supreme Court on important bicultural issues. The very fact that such issues come before the Court and seem from their very subject matter to embrace questions upon which the country's two major cultural groups have different attitudes, might in itself suggest to the exponent of bicultural equality that the Supreme Court's structure should be seriously reformed. The obvious directions that such reform would take would be to organize the Court so that, at least in dealing with those areas of law sensitive to a bicultural division of opinion, French Canadian judges are equal in number to English Canadian judges. Also, if one were concerned about the degree to which French Canadian or Quebec judges now represent the prevailing values of their society, one might advocate altering the system of appointment or tenure to ensure that such judges are more truly representative.

C. The Search for Judicial Statesmanship

Since 1949 a number of professional commentators, especially in English-speaking Canada, have expressed a desire for the Supreme Court to play a more creative and statesmanlike role in developing Canada's legal system. This feeling embraces a number of different points of view and focuses on a number of different aspects of the Court's behaviour. Although the considerations which this body of opinion entails are not per se concerned with bicultural or bilingual questions, they do raise issues which must be taken into account in appraising the Court's capacity for dealing with such questions.

The three phases of the Court's performance on which this general current of thought has focused most frequently are its adjudicative posture, its decision-making techniques, and the character of its work load or docket. While each of these aspects is a large subject in itself, a few general remarks on each in turn may be worthwhile here, in order to indicate what, from a rather professional, as opposed to a federalist or bicultural point of view, might be regarded as some of the Court's shortcomings as the country's highest judicial organ.

The most common point of criticism within this frame of reference is what is considered to be the overly conservative character of the Court's adjudicative posture. In particular, the jurists of the Supreme Court are accused of having adopted too rigid an adherence to the principle of *stare decisis*, and too narrow a conception of the principle of legislative supremacy and the constraint which that principle imposes on their own law-making functions. Dean Horace E. Read, in a perceptive study of the judicial process in common-law Canada, concluded that "in the first half of the twentieth century the rigor of *stare decisis,* and the doctrine of legislative supremacy as applied in Canada, combined to produce a static and mechanical operation of law."[30]

---

[30] Horace E. Read, "The Judicial Process in Common Law Canada", *C. B. R.* Vol. XXXVII (1959), pp. 279-80.

While Dean Read applied this indictment to all of the courts in common-law Canada, he and those who share his view, have looked to the newly emancipated Supreme Court to lead the way towards the development of a more creative and, for Canadian society, a more appropriate style of jurisprudence.

It has been easier for this body of critics to state what they find wanting in the Supreme Court's traditional pattern of adjudication than it is for them to indicate the precise ways in which these shortcomings might be overcome. The one common expectation or hope that they share is that the Supreme Court, now that it is at the apex of Canada's judicial structure, will adopt Canadian law more effectively to the changing needs of Canadian society. Such a wish stems directly from the main grounds for advocating judicial autonomy for Canada. The minimal requirement for the fulfilment of this hope is that the Supreme Court would be willing to diverge from English decisions when by doing so it could adjust the law more appropriately to changing Canadian circumstances. Gilbert Kennedy echoed the feelings of many thoughtful Canadian lawyers when, in 1955, after criticizing the Supreme Court for a particularly uncritical adoption of an English precedent, he went on to say: "May I suggest that our Supreme Court faces the very great challenge to develop over the next few years, not merely the law in a few individual cases, but the approach to law in this country for years to come? Any attitude which ties us blindly to the House of Lords is, I suggest, merely the green light for a continuance of the stagnation in Canadian legal thought and development of which many of us are all too aware."[31]

But beyond this general injunction to avoid a stultifying subservience to *stare decisis* and develop a more distinctive Canadian jurisprudence, it is not easy to state in precise terms the necessary ingredients of the desired judicial approach. What is called for is, above all, a state of mind in which the Court fulfils its function of making the law, as distinguished from merely applying it. Those who subscribe to this general position are quick to insist that they do not wish to see the Court usurp the position of the legislatures. But their basic contention is that in the process of adjudicating disputes by applying the law to particular instances, the Supreme Court, like any other court will, by virtue of the ambiguities, generalities or silences of the statutory laws of precedents, be forced to make law, at least in the sense of applying established legal rules to unforseen circumstances. When this occurs what is advocated is that the Court acknowledge the significant discretionary power which is inescapably thrust upon it, and seek not only the most appropriate modes of legal reasoning, but also knowledge of the most relevant kinds of social facts which might enable it to act wisely.[32]

---

[31] Gilbert D. Kennedy, "Supreme Court of Canada — *Stare Decisis* — Role of Canada's Final Court", *C. B. R.* Vol. XXXIII (1955), 66. 340 and 632.

[32] There is nevertheless little indication in Canadian literature of how judges might best acquire knowledge of societal facts, or how such knowledge might be related to the outcome of their deliberations. For a discussion of some of these questions and references to relevant American literature, see Read, *The Judicial Process in Common Law Canada,* pp. 290-91. See also Edward WcWhinney, *Judicial Review in the English-Speaking World,* 2nd Ed. (Toronto, 1960), pp. 203-12.

At a more practical level of criticism, the actual techniques and procedures followed by the Supreme Court in its decision-making process have been found by some to reduce seriously the Court's capacity for providing Canada with effective judicial leadership. Two related aspects of the Court's methods have caused most of the adverse comment—the lack of consultation in the process of arriving at decisions, and the Court's custom of seriatim opinion writing. On the first point, what is advocated is a more systematic use of judicial conferences in order to seek a consensus, or, where that is impossible, to identify clearly the significant points of difference. The absence of sufficient collaboration in decision-making would appear to be the main reason for the practice, in many cases, of individual judges writing their own judgments, even when there are no major points of difference between the various opinions. This practice is criticized on the grounds that it results either in mere repetition, or worse, in hopeless confusion, if it is impossible to identify one line of reasoning adhered to by a majority.[33]

Finally, it can also be argued that the commonplace character of the bulk of the Supreme Court's business mitigates against the Court's assuming a role of distinctive judicial leadership. Only a small minority of the cases which come before the Court are likely to raise legal issues of fundamental importance to the country. Most of its work load concerns rather mundane points of law which arise in private lawsuits. This is principally the result of the statutory rules governing the Supreme Court's jurisdiction, and the Court's own treatment of those rules.[34] In particular, the provision of appeals as of right in cases involving over $10,000 accounts for at least half the cases on the Supreme Court's docket, and thus has a decisive effect on the nature of the Court's work load.[35] On the other hand, in some instances where important questions of civil liberties have been at issue, the Court has assumed a rather restrictive attitude with regard to its own powers of granting special leave to appeal.[36] Unlike the United States Supreme Court, which by carefully selecting the cases it will hear, confines its attention to cases which raise questions of great significance, mainly in the public law field,[37] the Canadian Supreme Court exercises relatively little control over the shape of its own docket, and spends far more of its time dealing with technical points of "lawyer's law" than with questions of larger public concern.

---

[33] Bora Laskin, "The Supreme Court of Canada: A Final Court of Appeal of and for Canadians," *C. B. R.* Vol. XXIX (1951), pp. 1047-48.

[34] See Peter H. Russell, *The Supreme Court of Canada as a Bilingual and Bicultural Institution,* pp. 41 and 118-20.

[35] *Ibid.,* see Table IV. 1, p. 116, for a quantitative analysis of the types of cases and sources of cases on the Supreme Court's docket since 1949.

[36] For a detailed examination of this tendency, see John Cavarzan, "Civil Liberties and the Supreme Court: The Image and the Institution" (Master of Laws thesis, Osgoode Hall Law School, 1965), pp. 37-57.

[37] At one time a large number of cases reached the U.S. Supreme Court as a matter of right. But a series of statues culminating in the Judiciary Act of 1925 gave the court a large measure of control over its own docket so that it can concentrate on crucial questions of nationwide concern.

What should be borne in mind with regard to the points which we have very briefly canvassed here is that they represent another vantage point from which the Court's capacity for dealing with both bicultural and federal issues might be appraised. The conservative style of the Supreme Court's jurisprudence means, at the very least, that the Court's judgments on important questions touching bicultural or federal relations have usually been phrased in a technical, legalistic manner, making it difficult to detect any real policy choices which the Court may have confronted. The lack of systematic consultation and discussion in decision-making has likely reduced the opportunities for negotiating agreements between judges representing different values or traditions, so that the outcome of a case has simply been determined by mechanically adding together the separate conclusions of individual justices. And the relatively shapeless, undistinguished nature of the Court's work load has not conditioned either the Court's bench or its public to recognize the Court's function in determining questions which have an important bearing on French-English or federal relations.

It would take us far beyond the bounds of this study to investigate the possible reforms to which this mode of analysis might point. What should be noted is that any steps taken to increase the Court's capacity for concentrating in a deliberate way on the settlement of legal issues touching questions of great public importance are likely to intensify bicultural or federal concern about the Court. Indeed, it may be that the very judicial conservatism, which the Court's realist critics have attacked, by hiding the real value cleavages implicit in some areas of the Court's work, has muted these sources of anxiety. Now as legal realism becomes a more pervasive outlook, it is likely to produce a heightened sensitivity to the role which the background and social assumptions of judges might play in shaping their decisions. This, in turn, is apt to make French Canadian or federalist critics of the existing Supreme Court set-up more eager for something approaching bicultural or federal-provincial parity in the composition of the Court, particularly if the Court concentrates on those areas of law in which the opportunities for judicial law-making are numerous and prominent.

14 Federalism and Reform of the Senate: A Commentary on Recent Government Proposals*

E. Donald Briggs**

The perennial, time-worn question of Senate reform has again come to the fore in Canada. Like many of his predecessors, Prime Minister Trudeau promised reform of the upper house when he first took office. Since that time Senate Government Leader Paul Martin has on several occasions indicated that he is anxious to see its role in government recognized and extended. Moreover, some official suggestions for reform have already been put forward. These are contained in the white paper, *The Constitution and the People of Canada*,[1] published in February 1969.

The suggestions are of two sorts. First, on the organizational side, it is proposed that a review of the distribution of Senate membership be undertaken; that the term of office for Senators be reduced to a set number of years, (perhaps six, with a possibility of reappointment); and, probably most important, that Senators be "partly appointed" by the provincial governments. Second, on the functional side, it is suggested that the Senate's powers be curtailed in some respects and extended in others. The curtailment would result from providing that "in the general legislative process" the House of Commons would be enabled to over-rule rejection of a bill by the upper house. (p. 32) The extension would come from giving the latter "special responsibility" in dealing with legislative measures concerning human rights and the official languages, as well as the right to approve appointments to the Supreme Court, ambassadorial positions, and the chairmanship of cultural agencies. Over these specific matters it is proposed that the Senate should have an absolute veto.

These proposals are under consideration by the Continuing Committee of Officials on the Constitution established by the Constitutional Conference of February 1968, and have been published for "the consideration and comment" of the people of Canada. So far, little public comment of any kind has been made on them.

In putting the proposals forward the Government has been motivated by

---

[1] *The Constitution and the People of Canada* (Ottawa, Queen's Printer, February, 1969).

* From *Queen's Quarterly*, Vol. LXXVII no. 1 (Spring, 1970), pp. 56-71. Reprinted by permission from the author and *Queen's Quarterly*.
** The author wishes to thank his colleagues, Professor K. G. Pryke and C. L. Brown-John, for helpful suggestions during the preparation of this article.

E. DONALD BRIGGS – Vice-Dean, Division of Social Science, University of Windsor.

more than the desire to "improve" the Senate. Senate reform and the re-
vitalization of Canadian federalism are apparently seen as closely linked, and
the purpose of the suggested changes is stated to be to enable the Senate "to
play a more vital role in reflecting the federal character of our country."
(p. 28) In these and other suggestions for constitutional change, however,
the Government was also concerned with maintaining the customary responsibility of the cabinet to the House of Commons alone—hence the rejection of
such ideas as that for a directly-elected Senate. The proposed Senate changes
are consequently described as providing "the best balance between the
principles of responsible and representative government and the need in a federal
state for the adequate protection of regional and cultural interests." (p. 32)

There are, however, a number of things about these proposals which are
both surprising and puzzling. In the first place, it is not entirely obvious that
changes in the method of handling many of the matters over which it is proposed to give the Senate special power are either necessary or desirable in and
of themselves. To most Canadians the manner in which ambassadors, for
instance, have been appointed has been unobjectionable. It is not easy to see,
either, how these proposals are related to, or can be expected to solve, the
principle problems of federalism, or what value there may be in them if they
do not tend in this direction. Finally, the extent to which they would be effective in reforming or upgrading the Senate may also be questioned, particularly
since the new duties proposed for the upper house are plainly of no great
significance in terms of the general governmental burden of the central
administration.

These considerations are not equally relevant to the organizational proposals, of course, but it may be argued that the latter are unlikely to be
effective in improving the position or reputation of the Senate either, unless
the functional changes succeed in transforming it into an obviously important
body. Each of the proposals has its own weaknesses, however, and they are
consequently better discussed individually than collectively.

The proposal which by itself seems likely to cause least difficulty is that
of a specific term of office for Senators. Sinecures for life or even to age
seventy-five have only one thing to recommend them: They ensure that
once Senators are appointed they will be relatively immune from pressure
by the appointing authority. That this is a principle of paramount importance
with respect to judicial and perhaps some other offices is obvious, but its
applicability to legislators is considerably more doubtful. It may be argued,
in fact, that if the Senate is to become even partly a provincial or regional
instrument, then Senators should be to some degree responsive to the wishes
or policies of their provincial governments. In general, too, a less static
membership for the upper house would probably be advantageous. Whether
it would prove to be equally desirable to have federally-appointed Senators
subject to pressure from the federal cabinet is more problematic, but this
problem will be taken up more fully below.

In much the same way, the proposal to review the distribution of Senate
seats seems, on the face of it, reasonable enough. As the white paper points

out, no such review has been undertaken since confederation, though the original regional balance was upset by assigning Newfoundland an extra six seats when it became a province in 1949. There are admitted inequalities—or at least peculiarities—in the present distribution. Not only does the Atlantic region have thirty seats as compared with twenty-four for each of the other regions, but there are inconsistencies as between individual provinces, particularly between those in the east on the one hand and those in the west on the other. It is difficult, for instance, to reconcile New Brunswick's ten senatorial seats with British Columbia's six when the former has fewer than seven hundred thousand people and the latter close to two million.

It may be argued that since representation in the Senate has always been on a regional basis, comparisons of individual provinces in this way are not relevant. Once the possibility of redistribution is raised, however, such inequalities become a legitimate subject for consideration, particularly as the Government in this case has not revealed the basis on which it thinks redistribution should be undertaken. The fact that some Senators are to be appointed by the provinces also promises to make provincial as against regional representation more important than in the past.

Representation in second legislative chambers, of course, especially in federal systems, is not normally on the basis of population; witness the fact that each state in the United States has two Senators when they vary in population from Alaska's two hundred and fifty thousand to New York's seventeen million. Rather, the idea is that interested blocs or geographical areas should be represented to provide a balance with the population-based representation in the lower house. The simplest and perhaps the most logical way of accomplishing this is to give equal representation to each of the federated units, as has been done in the United States. A Canadian Senate composed of ten representatives from each province would therefore be logical, were it not for the fact that this would mean reducing Quebec's share of the total seats from approximately 23.5 per cent to a mere 10 per cent at precisely the time that province is demanding recognition of its special linguistic and cultural position within confederation. Granting, then, that Quebec should be accorded special recognition, other difficulties also appear. The west, for example, and perhaps the Maritimes as well, would be less than happy if their strength were to decline in relation to Quebec's. Ontario might also be a problem, but might feel less strongly about it than the west provided a reasonable balance were maintained between French and English Canada as a whole.

Given such difficulties, however, one is tempted to suggest that it might be better to leave things as they are. In view of the Government's declared intention of making the Senate the guardian of regional and cultural interests, however, this would not be without difficulties either. To date, the Senate has not been of any great importance to any of the provinces, and hence the distribution of its seats has not been of much importance in their eyes either. But, obviously, if it is to be rededicated to their use, this will no longer be the case, and redistribution will almost inevitably be demanded by one or more of them.

It was undoubtedly recognition of this fact that led to the Government's somewhat tentative inclusion of such a review in its proposals. Needless to say, the same factors which are likely to make review necessary will also intensify the difficulties of achieving it.

With a minimum of good will on all sides, however, a solution should not be beyond the ingenuity of our collective political leadership. Two formulas might be suggested as containing at least some of the elements out of which a solution might be constructed. The first would be to provide for a ninety-seat house in which Quebec would be given one-third or thirty seats, with the remaining two-thirds being divided equally among the other three regions (twenty seats each). The second, and perhaps from the aesthetic point of view the better, formula would again allow Quebec thirty seats, but out of a total of one hundred and twenty, with each of the other nine provinces having ten. In the first case all three "English" regions would lose strength relative to Quebec, but provided the blocks were equally distributed among the eastern and western provinces (five each) the most glaring inequalities between the provinces of these regions would be eliminated. Under the second formula, Quebec would retain approximately the same proportion of the total seats as she has now (actually a gain of 1.5 per cent), while relative to her the east would make a slight gain and the west a considerable one. Ontario would obviously be the big loser relative to all the other regions, but it may be doubted whether there is any good reason for treating her differently from the other largely English provinces. Either of these formulas, or some variation thereon, would be more logical and would reflect existing political realities more precisely than present arrangements.

Theoretically, therefore, redistribution presents no great problem, and it would certainly seem to be desirable from a number of points of view. Of the organizational proposals, however, both the most substantive and the most uncertain in result is that of making appointments partly provincial. Two obvious and interrelated questions arise from this proposal. First, what does, or should, "partly" mean? Second, why, when the declared object of Senate reform is to create a house which will reflect more precisely "the federal character of our country," are the provinces to be allowed to appoint only some of the Senators but not all of them?

The white paper gives no indication whatever of what the Government may have in mind by "partly," but it does indicate the Government's feeling that while it is necessary to give expression to provincial interests, "the interests of the country as a whole should continue to find expression in the Senate to maintain there an influence for the unity of Canada." (p. 30). Presumably it is that portion of the Senate which will continue to be appointed by the federal cabinet which is expected to be such an influence.

One may sympathize with the objective of giving expression to the interests of the country as a whole, but whether the federal appointment of some Senators is necessary to achieve this, or whether Senators so appointed would actually constitute an influence for unity is questionable. The Government appears to anticipate that provincially appointed Senators will be so preoccupied with parochial interests that unless some counter-balance is provided chaos or deadlock or some such catastrophe will result. It should not be forgotten, however, that the Senate is and will continue to be only the second legislative chamber, with no independent existence or mandate of its own. Legislation will continue to be initiated largely by the cabinet and discussed by the Commons from a predominantly national viewpoint, and it will be the duty of the Senate to take the traditional "sober, second look" at what is passed to it from the lower house or directly from the cabinet. As long as cabinet and Commons do their work effectively, therefore, there is little chance that "the interests of the country as a whole" will be neglected or that these interests could be ignored by even the most parochially-minded Senate. It is true that provincially-oriented Senators may be inclined to be more critical of federal legislative proposals, and critical from a different point of view, than present ones, but this would seem to be precisely the purpose and value of having them in the Senate in the first place; they would bring a new and different perspective to the work of the central government, and hopefully by so doing would pave the way for better understanding and more co-operation between the different levels of government.

What the Government means by unity, and what the connection is between it, the presence of federal appointees in the Senate, and the expression of "national" interests, are far from clear in any case. Is it unity within the Senate which is sought? Or concurrence of the Senate with the "national" view of the federal cabinet? One might be excused for suspecting that it is the latter which concerns the Government most, since there seems little reason to assume that the provincial or regional orientation of its members would necessarily mean inability to achieve at least sufficient unity to reach decisions in the upper house. Apart from anything else it is reasonable to suppose that voting would ultimately resolve differences in a provincially-oriented Senate as elsewhere in democratic institutions.

The degree to which federal appointees might be able to act as catalysts in reconciling conflicting provincial viewpoints is also doubtful. Federal no less than provincial appointees must be from somewhere, and even if they should in theory be selected at large rather than on a regional or provincial basis, a reasonable distribution over the country would be necessary. When and if federal and provincial views should conflict, minority groups of federal appointees would be likely to find themselves caught between two pressures: to act in accordance with their provinces' interests or views on the one hand, or to conform to the central government's view on the other. If they should tend to lean to the latter, they would be less likely to exert influence in the direction of unity than to form simply another faction within the chamber—a "they" group against which opposition might even solidify. If they should tend to "go provincial" on the other hand, any advantage of federal appointment, except that of patronage, would be lost. In neither case would they contribute to Senate unity in any obvious way.

Assuming the validity of this line of reasoning, and assuming that it could not have been overlooked by the drafters of the reform proposals, it follows that the provision for the continued appointment of some Senators by the federal government is likely to have been intended not only to provide patronage but also a means of preventing or discouraging excessive divergence between the Senate and the cabinet. However, both the need for and the wisdom of attempting to "build in" unity in this fashion must be questioned. Undoubtedly the primary responsibility for governing the country must continue to rest on the federal cabinet and the directly-elected representatives in the House of Commons and consequently the forceful expression of their views must be guaranteed. But as it was pointed out above, there is little danger that this would cease to be the case even if the Senate were entirely devoid of "national " spokesmen. Moreover, it must be remembered in this context that except with regard to a very few, not very significant matters, the "new" Senate is not to have a deciding voice in any case: the Commons is to be given power to overrule it in all "general legislative matters." While this is not a power which should be resorted to on any regular basis, it would provide a means whereby the government could, if necessary, ensure that its view of the country's interests would prevail.

Use of this procedure, furthermore, would at least be honest. It would bring differences between federal and provincial authorities into the open and provide an issue upon which voters could ultimately pass judgement. This would be less true if federally appointed Senators, either because of their numerical superiority (we are not told that they will not be numerically superior, though we might hope that the Government's intentions are more honourable than that) or for some other reason, were able to circumvent differences within the Senate itself. An "arranged" unity, however, would obviously be no unity at all, and a Senate so constituted as to provide an appearance of unity would, from the point of view of federalism, be no advance over present arrangements. Unfortunately, indications are that the Government is not yet ready to face that fact. But since the Government does not propose giving the Senate sufficiently important functions to cause the provinces to take a very active interest in its deliberations or the performance of its members, all of this becomes somewhat beside the point. The "new" Senate, as it materializes from the present proposals, is simply never likely to be sufficiently concerned with, or important in relation to, the major issues of federalism to make federal-provincial confrontations within it a serious threat to harmony on Parliament Hill. This, of course, makes the Government's concern for unity even more unnecessary.

These factors are of immediate and practical as well as long-term and theoretical importance. Apart from anything else, if the proposed changes in the Senate are to be successful at all, it is essential that the provincial governments should be satisfied that they, or their appointees, will have a real and significant role to play in the new institution. If they are not convinced of this from the outset they are unlikely to take seriously such appointive responsibilities as they are finally accorded, and as a result the quality of Senate membership is likely to give far more legitimate cause for concern than it has to date. The white paper obliquely recognized the importance of this when it expressed the hope that federal and provincial governments "would engage in healthy competition" to ensure that the best men available would be appointed to the upper house. (p. 34)

Provincial attitudes are likely to be determined largely by two factors: the proportion of Senate membership to be appointed by them, and the importance of the functions to be performed by the house. The first is self-explanatory in that there is a direct relationship between the number of representatives and the importance of their role. On the other hand, numbers alone mean little if the functions of the house are unimportant. We must consequently turn now to an analysis of the proposals for functional reform. These, unfortunately, are perhaps even more open to criticism than the organizational ones.

The proposal to accord the Senate "special responsibility" with respect to legislation affecting civil rights and the official languages may seem unobjectionable and natural given the special interest which Quebec in particular has in some of these matters. In terms of the extent of the national government's powers and legislative responsibilities, however, it cannot be said to be particularly significant, nor are civil and language rights matters with which the provinces, with the exception of Quebec, are either especially concerned or especially competent to deal.

Moreover, in view of the Government's intention to entrench a comprehensive Charter of Fundamental Rights in the constitution, it may be questioned whether legislative safeguards are necessary even from Quebec's point of view. The proposed Charter is to contain guarantees of linguistic as well as the customary legal and human rights, and once it has been enacted all of these matters will presumably be protected by the courts against legislative encroachments. It is true, of course, that it may be some time before the Charter comes into being, while it may be possible to reform the Senate more quickly in the case of possible encroachment than the cumbrous judicial system. It may also be argued that one cannot be too careful where such fundamental matters are concerned, but it is nevertheless difficult to become very excited about this power which is to be conferred upon the new second chamber, and it is doubtful if the majority of the provinces will be excited about it either.

Much the same can be said for the confirmation powers which are proposed. On the one hand they seem unlikely to elate the provinces with the opportunities they present for participation in the essentials of the governing process at the national level, and on the other their inherent value also seems open to question.

The proposal to have ambassadorial appointments, for instance, approved by the Senate will almost certainly come as a surprise to most Canadians. Many, it seems safe to say, will find the reasons behind the proposal puzzling, and the benefits to be derived from such a procedure—for the Senate, the provinces, the country, or the diplomatic corps—perhaps even more so.

For example, it is unlikely that the confirmation procedure is intended as a safeguard against arbitrary or excessive executive power, as it is in the

United States. In the latter, of course, the Senate's cherished prerogative of reviewing the President's major appointments is part of the system of legislative checks on executive power made necessary by the fact that the two exist and operate virtually independently of one another. But in a system such as ours where the executive is part of, and continuously responsible to, the legislature for all its actions in any case, such checks have never been considered necessary, and it is doubtful if the Government considers that they have become so now. Moreover, even if they were, there are cabinet prerogatives of far greater potential danger than the right to appoint ambassadors or, for that matter, judges of the Supreme Court, and these proposals would therefore be of comparatively little significance in that connection.

It seems equally improbable that the intention is to improve the quality of ambassadorial appointments, or that the confirmation procedure would necessarily have this effect in any event. In the first place, while occasional ex-cabinet ministers or the like have received such appointments on a patronage basis (London and Paris are the two posts which have most frequently been filled in this way), the vast majority of ambassadors have been appointed from the professional foreign service on the basis of professional criteria. While individual appointments from time to time have undoubtedly been open to criticism, it is far from clear what would be accomplished by throwing the matter into the legislative arena—an arena, moreover, composed in this case partly or even largely of legislators with provincial rather than national orientations. Finally, it is hardly conceivable that the power of confirmation would confer upon the Senate any substantial glory or prestige. Rarely are more than ten or fifteen ambassadors appointed in any one year, and since it is to be hoped that most confirmations would be more or less automatic, the process would neither engage the Senate for very long nor attract much public attention.

One would not have thought, either, that the provinces would have any great interest in participating in the appointment process. With the possible exception of one, in fact, it seems safe to say that they are not. Quebec, however, has in recent years developed a well-publicized penchant for dabbling in international affairs, and Ottawa has been understandably disturbed for the obvious reason that Canada can hardly continue to be a state if her constituent elements act independently in the international realm.

It is plainly here that the *raison d'être* for the confirmation proposal is to be found. While it is by no means clear that Quebec would consider indirect participation in the appointment of ambassadors (and/or, for that matter, the heads of cultural agencies) a satisfactory substitute for the freedom of action which, as a "nation," she claims as her necessary right, it is clearly something of this kind that the Government hopes to achieve. Though the Government would undoubtedly deny it, it is true that the proposal to have ambassadorial appointments confirmed by a provincially-oriented Senate constitutes a tacit admission that in Canada the central administration does not, and cannot, have any natural or other monopoly of jurisdiction in the realm of foreign affairs. This is a considerable (and perhaps a dangerous) concession of principle which might go far toward appeasing Quebec City, at least temporarily. But even if it did not, the confirmation procedure might be argued to be advantageous from the federal point of view in that it would considerably strengthen Ottawa's hand in dealing with Quebec demands. It would be possible to claim that appointees so confirmed represented, and had the backing of, the whole country in a much more complete sense than at present. Having had a voice in the selection of Canadian representatives, it would be more difficult for Quebec to insist on the need for separate representation because such insistence would be less creditable both within the country and outside it.

In another recent white paper, "Federalism and International Realism," published in 1968, the Government presents a strong defence of traditional federal prerogatives in the international area, despite the fact that a variety of minor encroachments into this realm by many provinces has long been quietly ignored by Ottawa in order to avoid unnecessary confrontations on the ambiguous ground of the BNA Act. Nevertheless, to institutionalize provincial participation in even such a relatively minor matter as the appointment of ambassadors is surely to concede that the provinces have some legitimate interests in the international field, and such a concession could make additional encroachments more difficult to resist.

The proposal that appointments to the Supreme Court also be subject to confirmation by the Senate has a similar origin and is undoubtedly expected to yield similar advantages. Quebec has also long contested the competence of the Supreme Court to decide constitutional issues between the provinces and the central government, feeling, presumably, that as it is federally appointed it is automatically biased in favor of the latter. She has suggested accordingly, that the provinces should either have the right to appoint some of the judges, or that a separate constitutional court should be established, with respect to which they would enjoy a similar right. What the Government is now proposing is a compromise, which, as in the case of ambassadors and cultural agencies, concedes the principle but refuses to go the distance.

It seems clear, in fact, that the Government's whole design for Senate reform has been motivated primarily by, and is aimed primarily at providing a solution to, the "Quebec problem." Individually and collectively the suggested changes make sense only within that context. The Government has not set out, as one might have supposed from the references to the necessity of reflecting more accurately "the federal character of our country" and giving expression to "the interests of the provinces," to provide a means of dealing more effectively with the broad complex of problems arising from the interrelationship of the various levels of government. There is, for example, little if anything in the proposals to indicate that the new Senate is conceived as a means of coping, except perhaps in the most incidental way, with what former Manitoba Premier Walter Weir on several occasions referred to as the growing provincial "alienation" from Ottawa, or with the type of problems which dominated the February 1968 constitutional conference. Since it is in these areas that the interests of the majority of the provinces plainly seem to lie, one might, in the light of the Government's declared objective, have expected some greater attempt to accommodate them. One might also conclude that in the absence of such accommodation the majority of the provinces will at best be unlikely to take very seriously their responsibilities in the selection of Senators, and, at worst, will feel confirmed in whatever feelings of alienation they already have.

It may equally be argued that the Government has shown little real interest in Senate reform *per se*. While at least some of the proposed organizational changes (for example, the suggestion of a set term of office for Senators) may be regarded as desirable in themselves, it is also true that for the most part they are necessary concomitants of, and prerequisites to, the peace-offerings to La Belle Province. What is more important, however, is that the proposed changes, organizational and functional collectively constitute only very minor surgery which is at best calculated to cure some peripheral ills rather than the inherent feebleness of the patient.

By far the most serious and insistent criticism of the present Senate is that it serves no useful function. Unfair as this criticism is in a number of respects, it may be argued that it is the first problem with which reform measures should deal, and that measures which fall short of this goal are not reform in any real sense at all. Since the special tasks visualized for the new Senate are largely ritualistic, and since its power is to be largely confined to these tasks, it seems unlikely that the position or the reputation of the upper house will be substantially improved by the proposed changes.

Both these problems could, at least in principle, be fairly simply solved, and without making the Senate into a rival of the Commons in any significant sense. All that would be necessary would be to convert the Senate into what I have elsewhere called a "House of Provinces,"[2] which would be composed of representatives of the provincial governments, and which would be given the power of approving all measures falling within the area of joint federal-provincial responsibility. Such an arrangement would give the Senate the obvious *raison d'être* it has always lacked, and at the same time ensure the continuing interest of more than one province in its operations.

Machinery for federal-provincial co-operation in some areas has already been approved in principle and is presumably in the process of being worked out in detail. At the constitutional conference of June 1969, the federal government agreed that the provinces should have the power to block federal spending in provincial areas of jurisdiction (i.e., cost-sharing programmes). The means, however, by which the provinces would exercise this power was not spelled out. According to press reports,[3] Prime Minister Trudeau had suggested an arrangement under which any two of the four senatorial districts could veto federal spending in areas of provincial jurisdiction, but this, along with alternative formulas proposed by the provinces, was referred for further study to the continuing committee of federal-provincial officials

[2] "The Senate: Reform or Reconstruction?" *Queen's Quarterly,* Vol. LXXV no. 1 (Spring, 1968), pp. 91-104.
[3] See *Globe and Mail* (June 13, 1969).

established earlier to deal with matters of constitutional change. The communiqué issued at the end of the conference stated simply that "there was agreement that the Parliament of Canada and the provincial Legislatures would be appropriate bodies to determine whether a consensus exists, and there was general agreement that the regional character of the country should be recognized in some way."[4]

There seems to be here an obvious opportunity to combine the search for appropriate machinery for federal-provincial co-operation with the movement to make the Senate an instrument of federalism. Why should the upper house not become the continuing federal-provincial conference which could thresh out such matters as well as take responsibility for such specific tasks as are contained in the proposals under discussion here? Would not such an arrangement be simpler and more generally advantageous than a variety of different means of dealing with matters which are undeniably of provincial concern but which, for reasons of efficiency, economy, or national unity, should be handled at the national level?

It may be objected, however, that the provinces would be unlikely to find such a plan acceptable. From their point of view it would mean relinquishing to the Senate rights which have only recently and with considerable difficulty been won—e.g., those conceded at the June conference—and which are considered vital by every one of them. Even effective control over the composition of the chamber could well not be enough to make this palatable, since under the proposed appointment system there could be no guarantee that Senators would not act independently rather than in accordance with the wishes of their "home" governments. It must be remembered that if, through Canadian history, federal governments have been less than enthusiastic about the idea of making the Senate into a powerful body, the provinces have been no more inclined in this direction since such an institution would be a rival to their authority as well as to that of the federal cabinet. In present circumstances these fears are, if anything, likely to be accentuated.

Yet again, it seems possible that this difficulty could be circumvented without too much trouble. The key would be to ensure senatorial responsiveness to provincial policies, and this could be accomplished by seconding members of provincial governments to the Senate on whatever basis individual provinces might think desirable. There would thus be no specific term of office for Senators at all (except perhaps for federal appointees, if these should still be regarded as necessary), and perhaps no specific membership as such. This would provide the maximum of flexibility from the provincial point of view, while the importance of the senatorial responsibilities would at the same time ensure that careful consideration would at all times be given to selecting suitable representatives. From the federal point of view such a Senate would be powerful, but with a provision that the Commons could overrule except with regard to matters designated as of legitimate provincial concern, its effective strength would be sufficiently channelled so that the authority of the House

---

[4] *Ibid.*

of Commons and the cabinet's primary responsibility to it would also be preserved.

Nevertheless, there is no doubt that this would be a radical departure from the traditional concept of the Senate and of second chambers generally, and it is not easy to predict all the consequencies which might follow if it were adopted. While it would almost certainly bring the Senate publicity and recognition of the kind it has never before enjoyed, it would not be the type of recognition which Senator Martin and some others have been urging and it is perhaps not even certain that a "House of Provinces" of this type could to the same extent carry on the kind of work for which these spokesmen consider it to deserve recognition. As they have rightly pointed out, the Senate at present makes a considerable contribution to the governing process by its extensive committee work, and by giving detailed and in some cases first-instance study to legislative proposals, thus saving much time for the hard-pressed House of Commons. They believe that these functions could and should be extended still further, and it would undoubtedly be useful if they were. Would a House composed largely or entirely of untenured ambassadors of the provinces be able to perform such functions?

The answer is not clear one way or the other, but whether this is the most important consideration may be questioned in any case. The point is that because of a variety of pressures from a variety of sources means have to be found to institute a new kind of federalism. At the same time, for equally varied reasons, Senate reform seems to have been accepted as desirable and necessary. The first is inevitably going to require considerable, even radical, changes in both our thinking and our governmental machinery. The era in which federal and provincial levels of government could operate more or less independently of one another or in which the provinces could be expected to defer to the wisdom of Ottawa has obviously gone and cannot be expected to return. The only real question now is whether changes are going to come about in a piecemeal and haphazard manner in response to provincial demands which are always seen individually rather than as a part of a single whole, or whether there is still hope for a more imaginative and less *ad hoc* approach such as has been suggested here.

Much the same sort of questions must be raised with regard to Senate reform. Is it to be reformed, or is it, in a phrase recently used by Senator Keith Davey on the CBC, merely to be "tinkered with?"[5] Is it to be made a genuine instrument of federalism and protector of provincial and regional interests, or merely a device for spiking the guns of Quebec? The white paper does not give much ground for encouragement on either score. Certainly if the "reforms" are instituted as proposed the result will be that the Senate will be far worse off than before. Its effective power will have been curtailed and confined to a few largely ritualistic tasks, a fact which will not fail to impress the public as confirmation of its inherent uselessness. The quality of its membership is likely to decline since provincial regimes can hardly be

---

[5] CBC interview with Bruno Gerussi (August 28, 1969).

expected to devote much energy or care to the selection of people to perform tasks of little direct importance to them, and since political debts at the provincial level are unlikely to be owed to individuals who are very familiar with or interested in federal affairs. Consequently, not even the traditional functions of the Senate referred to above could be expected to be performed as well as at present. Neither, of course, is all this likely to do anything whatever for the state of Canadian federalism in any general sense.

Real Senate reform cannot be accomplished without giving it something of obvious importance to do. Neither can the real needs of Canadian federalism be accommodated by the Senate without giving it authority over matters of substance. Both mean making the Senate powerful in at least some respects. If that is not a prospect which the Government can accept, it would perhaps be better to leave the Senate as it is, concentrate on extending and publicizing its traditional functions, and look elsewhere for solutions to the problems of federalism. It will certainly be unfortunate however, if some more serious attempt is not made to solve both problems with one blow by turning the Senate into something approaching a "House of Provinces."

15   Federal — Provincial Grants and the Spending Power of Parliament*

Pierre Elliott Trudeau

The Spending Power: What It Is and How It Has Been Used

Ordinarily one thinks of the "spending power" of governments simply in terms of the spending they do on particular programmes, under the authority of legislation passed by their legislative bodies. Constitutionally, however, the term "spending power" has come to have a specialized meaning in Canada: it means the power of Parliament to make payments to people or institutions or governments for purposes on which it (Parliament) does not necessarily have the power to legislate. The best example, perhaps, is the grants to provincial governments to assist in the provision of free hospitalization across Canada: Parliament does not have the power under the Constitution to establish general hospitals or to regulate them or their use; but under its "spending power" it is generally conceded that Parliament can make grants to the

* From Pierre Elliott Trudeau, Federal-Provincial Grants and the Spending Power of Parliament (Ottawa, Queen's Printer, 1969). Reproduced by permission of Information Canada.

PIERRE ELLIOTT TRUDEAU – Prime Minister of Canada. Minister of Justice, 1967-68.

provinces to assist them in financing provincially operated hospitalization programmes.[1]

The spending power provisions of the Constitution of Canada are less precise than those of other federations. They flow from, and are a part of the general distribution of powers, and can best be understood in this context. The British North America Act divides the power to legislate between the Parliament of Canada and the legislatures of the provinces, principally in Sections 91, 92, and 93 to 95, and gives to the Parliament of Canada the residual legislative power. It follows that there are certain specific heads upon which Parliament may not legislate, namely those in Sections 92 and 93, and others upon which provincial legislatures may not legislate, principally those in Section 91.

In addition to the powers of the Parliament of Canada to legislate, the Constitution as it has been interpreted by the Courts gives to it the power to spend from the Consolidated Revenue Fund on any object, providing the legislation authorizing the expenditures does not amount to a regulatory scheme falling within provincial powers. The constitutional basis for this spending power is to be found in Section 91 (3) of the B.N.A. Act, which gives the Parliament of Canada the power to raise money by any mode of taxation, and Section 91 (1A) which gives Parliament the right to make laws respecting public debt and property, the latter having been construed to include every kind of dominion asset, including the Consolidated Revenue Fund.

A judgment in the Supreme Court of Canada said of these provisions:

> . . . Parliament, by properly framed legislation may raise money by taxation and dispose of its public property in any manner that it sees fit. As to the latter point, it is evident that the Dominion may grant sums of money to individuals or organizations and that the gift may be accompanied by such restrictions and conditions as Parliament may see fit to enact. It would then be open to the proposed recipient to decline the gift or to accept it subject to such conditions. As to the first point, it is also undoubted, I conceive, that Parliament, by properly framed legislation may raise money by taxation, and this may be done either generally or for the specific purpose of providing the funds wherewith to make grants either before or after the conferring of the benefit.[2]

On appeal, the Privy Council stated the general principle in this way:

> That the Dominion may impose taxation for the purpose of creating a fund for special purposes, and may apply that fund for making contributions in the public interest to individuals, corporations or public authorities, could not as a general proposition be denied.

---

[1] This latter statement must be qualified both in legal terms and in terms of the generality of the support for this view of the Constitution. See pp. 12 and 14, *infra*.

[2] *Reference re Employment and Social Insurance Act* (1936) S. C. R. 427, Duff, C. J. at p. 457.

The qualification of this general proposition was stated as follows:

> But assuming that the Dominion has collected by means of taxation a fund, it by no means follows that any legislation which disposes of it is necessarily within Dominion competence.

> It may still be legislation affecting the classes of subjects enumerated in s. 92, and, if so, would be ultra vires. In other words, Dominion legislation, even though it deals with Dominion property, may yet be so framed as to invade civil rights within the Province, or encroach upon the classes of subjects which are reserved to Provincial competence.[3]

It cannot be said that there is universal agreement among constitutional lawyers in Canada as to the precise meaning of these and related decisions. Some argue that they mean Parliament may make conditional or unconditional grants for any purpose, even if the purpose falls within exclusive provincial legislative jurisdiction, providing only that the programme involved does not amount to legislation or regulation (see for example Bora Laskin and Gerard V. La Forest).[4] Others, such as Quebec's Tremblay Commission, argue that the qualifications the Privy Council attached to the spending power mean that Parliament has no power to make grants of any kind in areas of exclusive provincial jurisdiction—even unconditional grants.[5] Others seem to suggest, when discussing federal grants to provincial governments, that Parliament might properly make unconditional grants to the provinces, but not conditional grants.[6]

In fact, there seems to have been little disposition on the part either of the federal or the provincial governments to seek further judicial clarification of the matter. Federal governments consistently have taken the position that Parliament's power to spend is clear,[7] while provincial governments generally have limited themselves to criticism of the *use* of the spending power by Parliament—in particular to its use to start new federal-provincial shared-cost programmes, or to terminate old ones, without the consent of the provinces.[8] Only governments of Quebec have advanced the more general proposition that it was constitutionally improper for Parliament to use its spending power to make grants to persons or institutions or governments for purposes which fall within exclusive provincial jurisdiction.

---

[3] (1937) A. C. 355 at 366.
[4] Bora Laskin, *Canadian Constitutional Law* (Toronto, The Carswell Co. Ltd., 1966) p. 666; and Gerard V. La Forest, *The Allocation of Taxing Power under the Canadian Constitution* (Toronto, The Canadian Tax Foundation, 1967), pp. 36-41.
[5] *Report of the Royal Commission of Enquiry on Constitutional Problems*, 1956 Vol. II, pp. 217-23.
[6] See, for example, the reference in Jacques Dupont, "Le pouvoir de dépenser du gouvernement fédéral: 'A Dead Issue?'," in *Cahiers de Droit* (Laval University), Vol. 8, footnote 63.
[7] See in particular a speech by Prime Minister Louis St. Laurent in 1957. *Hansard*, January 29, p. 754.
[8] See the Proceedings of Federal-Provincial and Dominion-Provincial Conferences of the past 10 or 15 years.

The Spending Power and Federal-Provincial Programmes:
Provincial Government Criticisms

The governments of the provinces have advanced three criticisms of Parliament for its use of the spending power to establish new federal-provincial programmes:

(1) That the Government and the Parliament of Canada are deciding, without the formal participation of the provinces in such decisions, as to when federal-provincial programmes ought to be started.

(2) That shared-cost programmes force upon provincial governments changes in their priorities.

(3) That "taxation without benefit" occurs when the citizens of a province whose provincial government has refused to participate in a shared-cost programme are required to pay the federal taxes which finance the federal share of the programme.

Each of these criticisms is examined in the paragraphs which follow.

Provincial participation in the decision to establish shared-cost programmes. It is argued by many provincial governments that the Government of Canada ought not to, or perhaps ought not even have the right to, initiate, change or terminate shared-cost programmes without first obtaining some kind of consensus among provincial governments in favour of doing so. The rationale for this argument is essentially this: where exclusive provincial jurisdiction is involved, federal-provincial shared-cost programmes can only be established and operated by the provinces; therefore, the Government of Canada ought not to proceed with any plan to contribute to such programmes without first obtaining some kind of agreement from among the provinces. (The counter-argument has been that no provincial government is constitutionally obliged to enter into shared-cost agreements with the Government of Canada; and that what really is being criticized, therefore, is the political pressure which is imposed upon provincial ministers to participate in Canada-wide programmes.)

Provincial priorities. Secondly, the provincial governments point out that, because they feel obliged to enter into new federal-provincial shared-cost programmes, they are forced to alter their spending and taxing priorities. Moreover, because shared-cost programmes cost the provinces only 50 cents for each dollar they spend (the usual ratio), there is a greater incentive to allocate provincial funds toward these as opposed to purely provincial programmes, and a smaller incentive to economize in administering them. (The response to this argument has been that in the very purpose of shared-cost measures is to achieve a country-wide priority for certain programmes, and that in the absence of some such vehicle common priorities across Canada would be highly unlikely.)

"Taxation without benefit". Thirdly, some provincial governments are arguing that their citizens ought not to be forced to contribute toward the

federal share of shared-cost programmes which do not operate in their province, by reason of the decision of their provincial government. Alternatively, it is argued, the federal government ought to pay over to the provincial government the equivalent of what the taxpayers in the province are contributing toward the federal share of the programme, or the equivalent of what they would have received in benefits had the province embarked upon the programme. (The counter-argument has been that the taxpayers of each province are represented in Parliament as well as in provincial legislatures, and that they have participated, through their M.P.'s and their Senators, in Parliament's decision to offer to spend from the Consolidated Revenue Fund for the purpose of contributing toward new shared-cost programmes.)

The Spending Power and Payments to Persons and Institutions

In addition to the arguments which are made concerning federal-provincial shared-cost programmes, the Government of Quebec, as has been noted, has generally argued against the use by the Parliament of Canada of its spending power for the purpose of making payments to persons and institutions. The rationale for this position is different, generally speaking, than that concerning shared-cost programmes. New provincial programmes are not required as a consequence of federal payments to persons or institutions; most adaptations might be called for in the related federal and provincial programmes to achieve the best results for the citizen. Provincial government priorities remain unaffected; again the most which might be called for would be programme adaptation (usually involving reduced obligations on the provincial treasury). Finally "taxation without benefit" does not occur.

The argument against federal grants to persons and institutions is based more upon a particular approach to the Constitution, and upon what might be called "the case for programme integration". The constitutional argument is straightforward: Parliament ought not to have the power to spend except where it has a specific power to regulate. The programme argument is that a single authority is better able to integrate different programmes in the same or related fields—for example income redistribution and social security—than are two authorities. Further, the single authority, if it is the provincial government, would be able to adapt every programme to the specific demographic, income and regional structure of the province, without taking into account the situation in the rest of the country. This approach is based on the assumption, of course, that a province would be put in the financial position, by Parliament, of being able to finance the federal programmes it took over, including, if it were a lower income province, higher equalization payments.

It is not possible to enter into a discussion of this particular proposition without considering the whole of the structure of Canadian federalism, including the totality of the distribution of powers. There are two reasons for this. First, programmes which involve payments to persons and institutions and which are excluded from Parliament's jurisdiction under the propositions submitted by the Government of Quebec, include income redistribution measures, possibly certain economic development programmes, contributions to Canada's cultural development, and research and technological development measures—all of which the Government of Canada considers to be important powers of Parliament. This view was advanced by the federal government at the first meeting of the Constitutional Conference, when it was argued that Parliament ought to retain explicit powers in these fields. Secondly, to achieve the programme and fiscal transfers called for in the Quebec propositions relating to these matters would be to weaken very substantially the powers of Parliament across the country, or to call for special status for the National Assembly of Quebec. In either case the structure of Canadian federalism would be fundamentally altered. For these reasons the Government of Canada does not believe it would be appropriate to discuss the Quebec propositions concerning federal payments to persons and institutions until all propositions concerning the distribution of powers have been received by the Secretariat of the Constitutional Conference, and until their effect upon the structure of Canadian federalism has been fully evaluated by all governments.

Federal Contributions to Provincial Programmes: The Rationale for the Spending Power

The case for a federal spending power for the purpose of enabling Parliament to contribute toward provincial programmes in fields of provincial jurisdiction is to be found in the very nature of the modern federal state—in its economic and technological interdependence, in the interdependence of the policies of its several governments, and in the sense of community which moves its residents to contribute to the well-being of residents in other parts of the federation. To understand these characteristics of an industrialized, Twentieth Century federal state is to understand the rationale for the spending power of the Parliament of Canada.

The Interdependence of the Modern State—The modern industrial state is so interdependent, particularly in technological and economic terms, and its population is so mobile, that it has become quite impossible to think of government policies and programmes as affecting only the people within the jurisdiction of the particular government responsible for those policies. There are benefits which flow to the people of the whole of Canada from certain of the services of provincial governments, when such services take into account national as well as provincial interests, and there are costs which are borne by the people of the whole or of parts of Canada when the programmes of a particular province fail to take into account the extra-provincial effects. The effectiveness of pollution control, for example, affects the people of neighbouring provinces; provincial educational systems contribute to or fail to advance the economic growth of Canada as a whole; and the equality of opportunity across the country, or the lack of it, affects the well-being of Canadians generally. Moreover the mobility of Canadians—increasing year by year—itself creates a kind of interdependence: a person in almost any part of Canada, accustomed to the expectation that he or his children will sooner or later move to other parts of the country, develops an interest in the public services in other provinces as well as the services of his own province—the obvious examples being hospital and medical care.

The extra-provincial or national effects of certain provincial public services would pose no problem if the interests of each individual province always coincided with the interests of other provinces and of the country as a whole. In such a simplified state, a provincial government would automatically be serving the national interest when it was doing its job of serving the provincial interest. But this is not always the case. And when it is not—where provincial interests would be better served by one kind of programme and the national interest by another—the provincial legislature which does its job of meeting the needs of its constituents will not be meeting the protential needs of other Canadians. There is nothing new or unusual about this: the problem of differences between the interests of the "provincial constituency" and those of the "national constituency" has been very real in the history of Canadian federalism, as indeed it has been in the history of other federations. Only a few examples need be given to illustrate this problem—some of which have involved the use of Parliament's spending power and some of which have not.

First, the *terms of reference* by which a provincial government is guided differ necessarily from those which the Government of Canada must take into account. The criteria which are used by the provinces and their municipalities in determining the amount they will borrow each year, for example, are necessarily different than those employed by the Government of Canada. The provinces and municipalities are guided by their views as to the proportion of capital expenditures they think ought to be borne by present as opposed to future generations, their judgment as to the amount which can be borrowed in different capital markets, and the needs of their respective economies. The Government of Canada is guided, on the other hand, by its judgment as to the total demands which are likely to be placed upon the supply of resources and capital in the economy as a whole, including those by the provinces and municipalities, the desirable balance between fiscal and monetary policy, and other related considerations. The harmonization of fiscal and financial policies of governments, therefore, in the interest of the national as well as of regional economies, requires some vehicle for bringing the national perspective to the attention of the provinces, and vice versa. (It is for this purpose, among others, that the Ministers of Finance and Provincial Treasurers meet each year before their annual budgets are completed.)

Secondly, the *priorities* imposed upon provincial governments by their constituencies are almost certain to be different, in some measure, to the priorities which might be suggested by the needs of the "national constituency". For example, the transportation requirements of the people of most if not all provinces suggest naturally that intra-provincial roads and streets should take precedence over inter-provincial highways. It is scarcely surprising, therefore, that the Trans-Canada Highway was built as a result of a federal-provincial programme under which provincial governments were able to meet a national need without foregoing unduly their local priorities.

Thirdly, the *objectives of provincial policies and programmes* are naturally directed more to the needs and the interests of the provincial constituency than to those of the national constituency. French is not required as a second language in many provinces of Canada, for example, and it is not surprising therefore that it has not been taught as a living language in the schools of these provinces. Yet it is in the interest of the country as a whole that English-speaking Canadians receive an adequate "base" in the nation's other language, and in particular it is in the interest of the young people who leave English-speaking areas to go to areas and jobs where both languages are required or are desirable, that they have such a "base".

Fourthly, the *consequences of provincial policies* must be judged by politicians largely in terms of their provincial constituency. Provincial industrial development programmes, for example, are designed primarily to increase the rate of growth of the economy of the individual provinces. Their extra-provincial consequences—in terms either of their effect upon the efficient allocation of labour and capital in the economy as a whole, or in terms of their impact on development programmes in other provinces—are understandably a second rather than a first consideration in the decision-making process. Another example could be given in the municipal field: each urban municipality tends to establish its own building codes, under the authority delegated to it by the province, in terms of its own local interests or objectives. But taken together, a multiplicity of municipal building codes increases considerably the cost of housing in Canada.

This point is perhaps best illustrated by considering the *national consequences of inaction* on the part of some or all provinces. To take an extreme, if one or more provinces were to provide, for whatever reason, quite inadequate education, health and housing services, the rest of the country could be expected sooner or later to bear some of the "cost" of this inaction. A larger proportion of the labour force in those provinces would tend to be unemployed, the capacity of people to seek employment opportunities in areas where jobs were available would be more limited, and income would tend to be lower. In consequence the nation as a whole would be called upon to redistribute income to the people of those provinces, to provide equalization payments to their provincial governments, and to contribute to the economic development of the regions or areas involved.

The essential difference between the influences which enter into provincial decision-making and those which are a proper part of national decision-making is clearest when considering *the costs and benefits of providing services*. Provincial governments cannot be expected to assume unduly heavy burdens, or to impose upon their taxpayers considerably higher costs, for the purpose of providing benefits to other provinces or their residents. Pollution control and technical education are the most obvious examples.

The governments of upstream provinces are not likely to be disposed to impose very heavy burdens upon their municipalities and industries where the benefits of pollution control will be felt largely in a neighbouring province. Not will a largely agricultural province be likely to initiate expensive technical and professional training courses, the graduates of which can only be employed in manufacturing enterprises. It might have been expected, therefore, that federal-provincial programmes such as the Technical and Vocational Training Agreements, under which the whole of Canada bore a part of the cost of the training facilities, would be the vehicle for initiating technical and vocational training institutes across the country.

The Interdependence of Government Policies—A further reason for shared-cost programmes, in addition to the "national interest" coming to attach to certain provincial programmes, is the need for some vehicle for harmonizing programmes where "mixed" federal and provincial jurisdiction is involved. However clear and however tidy the division of legislative powers, the complexity of today's society and the scale of government activity will inevitably result in both orders of government having an impact upon certain public policy problems. Again, this phenomenon is not unique to Canada: it is common to all federations. Urban development provides a good example. The provinces are responsible for establishing and regulating municipal government; but the Parliament of Canada has jurisdiction over rail and air transport and over harbour facilities, and the Government of Canada, including its Crown agencies, is a leading "resident" of most of Canada's urban centres. Moreover, the exercise by the Government of Canada of its responsibilities for certain economic policies, including credit policies, has an important influence upon housing and municipal development. In these circumstances there must be some vehicle by which the provinces can influence the federal government in the exercise of its jurisdiction and vice-versa. Federal-provincial shared-cost programmes are one such vehicle.

Technological change over the years to come can be expected to increase rather than decrease the interdependence of federal and provincial policies and programmes. Health care, to take one example, is less and less a matter which can be identified with small defined local areas. Certain highly specialized and expensive facilities serve whole regions, if not the whole of Canada. And medical records—even diagnostic techniques— are increasingly coming to involve computer technology and communications facilities which are national rather than local in scope. The Constitution must be flexible enough to enable Canada's governments to adapt to changes such as this: to eliminate the possibility of federal-provincial shared-cost programmes would be to move in the opposite direction.

The Sense of Community in a United Country—The sense of community that exists in Canada provides the third essential reason for a federal spending power. Canadians everywhere now feel a sufficient sense of responsibility for their compatriots in other parts of the country that they are prepared to contribute to their well-being. They do so in a great many ways, the principal of which will always be income redistribution payments directly to the people of other parts of Canada. But one of the most important ways of giving expression to this concern is by the provision to every citizen, wherever he lives, of adequate levels of public services—in particular of health, welfare and education services. Again, some vehicle is required by which Canadians can achieve this goal—by which the "national interest" in the level of general provincial public services or of a particular public service can be expressed.

The Spending Power and Other Aspects of the Constitution—It can be argued that the Constitution should be contrived so as to avoid any need for a spending power—that each government ought to have the revenue sources it needs to finance its spending requirements without federal assistance, and further that where the national interest comes to attach to a certain matter within provincial jurisdiction the Constitution ought to be amended to transfer that matter to federal jurisdiction. The difficulty with this "tidy" approach to federalism is that it does not accord with the realities of a Twentieth Century state.

It is quite true that in the ideal state provincial governments ought to have access to enough tax fields that they themselves can discharge their responsibilities. But in fact the tax-raising potential of Canada's provinces differs very markedly across Canada, because of the differing levels of income and economic activity in the country. One percentage point of personal income tax, for example, yields about $3.14 per capita in Ontario, $2.98 in British Columbia, $2.21 in Quebec, $1.89 in Saskatchewan, $1.27 in New Brunswick and 91 cents in Prince Edward Island (1968-69 figures). Similarly one point of corporation income tax yields $3.40 per capita in Ontario, $3.29 in British Columbia, $2.39 in Quebec, $1.82 in Saskatchewan, $1.38 in New Brunswick and $1.00 in Prince Edward Island. It is evident from these figures that federal grants to the lower income provinces are essential if these provinces are to provide adequate levels of public services at levels of taxation which are not too far out of line with those in the higher income provinces.

It is also true, to deal with the second argument, that when technological, economic and social changes have the effect of transforming a purely local or provincial matter into a national or quasi-national one, it can be argued that the Constitution should be amended to give Parliament jurisdiction. This is obviously valid where the change is so marked as to warrant giving one order of government full legislative jurisdiction where it had none before. But this "either-or" approach—either it is federal jurisdiction or it is not—does not meet the situations so less prevalent in today's society, where there is a valid national interest in certain provincial problems or policies, but not such a "total" national interest as to call for the transfer of jurisdiction to the Parliament of Canada. It is for these "in-between situations"[9] that some such vehicle as federal-provincial programmes, involving on occasion the spending power, is required.

---

[9] See pp. 222-24, *supra*.

The Role of the Parliament of Canada—If the interdependence of Canadian society which has been described in earlier paragraphs is acknowledged, and if it is accepted that there may be a national or extra-provincial interest in certain provincial problems or programmes, it remains to determine what vehicle would be most appropriate for communicating that national interest to the provincial governments concerned, and for achieving the desirable adaptations in the provincial programmes involved. What is involved here, it should be emphasized, is sometimes only a matter of identifying the extra-provincial or national interest which is seen to exist, and communicating it to the provinces concerned, and sometimes also a matter of compensating these provinces for the cost—measured in dollars or in disruption of priorities—of adapting the programmes involved to serve the national as well as the provincial interest.

It might be argued that because provincial jurisdiction is involved, provincial governments themselves ought to assume this responsibility—that the Provincial Premiers' Conference rather than Parliament ought to be the body through which this "national interest" in provincial public services might be expressed. Where intergovernmental grants were involved, this argument would go, the provincial governments rather than the federal government ought to be responsible for making the grants. Thus the Premiers' Conference would decide what equalization payments would be contributed by the higher income provinces to the lower income provinces, for the purpose of ensuring adequate levels of provincial public services across Canada. Similarly, it would be the Premiers' Conference which would decide when and whether Canadians in certain provinces could or ought, because they were benefiting from or were being affected by the programmes of other provinces, to contribute to the governments of those other provinces for the purpose of bringing about an adaptation, in their interests, of the programmes involved. Federal-provincial programmes would become interprovincial programmes, in other words, and federal-provincial grants would become interprovincial grants.

Neither the governments of Canada nor students of government in Canada —except those advocating the replacement of federalism by "confederalism" —have suggested this approach. There are very practical reasons for this. First, there exists in a federal state a Parliament which has been chosen by all citizens, and which because it has been directly elected is uniquely able to represent the "national interest" of the citizens—as distinguished from their "provincial interests". Only in a "confederal state", where the directly elected Parliament is replaced by intergovernmental conferences of state ministers or other delegates, is it necessary to define the national interest by political negotiation rather than by public election. It is in the nature of federalism, in other words, for the citizen to look to Parliament for an expression of his national or extra-provincial interests.

This is not to suggest that interprovincial meetings cannot play a useful role in harmonizing provincial programmes, or in providing a forum for the communication of extra-provincial interests in respect of many provincial problems. But it is to suggest that the nationally elected Parliament has a unique and a legitimate role to play in determining the national interest, even where provincial jurisdiction is involved. And it is to suggest, further, that Parliament is the appropriate body to make grants to the provinces for the purpose of equalizing provincial public services and for the purpose of compensating the provinces for adapting their programmes to meet national as well as provincial needs.

Having said this, it must be emphasized that this reasoning does not lead to the conclusion that because Parliament is elected by all Canadians it has or ought to have the power to invade provincial jurisdiction any time it perceives some national interest in a provincial programme. Nor does it mean that Parliament ought to have the power to enlarge its constitutional powers at the expense of the provinces by unilateral, *de facto* action. This would make a mockery of a federal constitution, which has as one of its purposes the definition and protection of provincial jurisdiction, making it subject to change only by constitutional amendment. Rather, the correct conclusion is that because the people of Canada will properly look to a popularly elected Parliament to represent their national interests, it should play a role, *with* the provinces, in achieving the best results for Canada from provincial policies and programmes whose effects extend beyond the boundaries of a province.

Federal Contributions to Provincial Programmes: A Possible Approach in a Revised Constitution

If the rationale for federal government contributions toward provincial government programmes is accepted, and if at the same time some validity is recognized in the provincial criticisms of the use of the federal spending power for this purpose, the problem is to find a method of meeting these criticisms, while at the same time retaining a sufficiently strong spending power. *To this end the Government of Canada has attempted to develop certain principles which it could tentatively advance to the Constitutional Conference as a basis for reviewing this aspect of the Constitution. They are these:*

(1) The constitutional power of the Parliament of Canada to contribute toward the public services and programmes of provincial governments should be provided for explicitly in the constitution;

(2) The power of Parliament to make unconditional grants to provincial governments for the purpose of supporting their programmes and public services should be unrestricted;

(3) The power of Parliament to make general conditional grants in respect of federal-provincial programmes which are acknowledged to be within exclusive provincial jurisdiction should be based upon two requirements: first, a broad national consensus in favour of any proposed programme should be demonstrated to exist before Parliament exercises its power; and secondly the decision of a provincial legislature to exercise its constitutional right not to participate in any programme, even given a national consensus,

should not result in a fiscal penalty being imposed upon the people of that province.

It will be evident that a firm proposal for defining the federal spending power in this way is impossible until the revised distribution of legislative powers is known. If Parliament's powers to *legislate* in the national interest are reasonably broad, its freedom to *spend* to this end, where provincial jurisdiction is involved, could be limited. If on the other hand, its powers to legislate were narrow in relation to present and potential national needs, the freedom to spend would have to be relatively untrammelled. *It follows that the principles here suggested for defining the federal spending power, and the specific proposal which will subsequently be advanced for realizing them, are subject to the adoption of a distribution of legislative powers which will ensure a strong federal government as well as strong provincial governments. During the course of the discussions on the Constitution, and before the coming into force of a revised distribution of powers, including any suggested limitation on the federal spending power, the Government of Canada would propose to exercise the spending power under the present Constitution with the kind of restraint which the Prime Minister indicated during the course of the Second Meeting of the Constitutional Conference.*

Unconditional Grants

These proposed principles would give to Parliament the unlimited power to make unconditional grants to the governments of the provinces, in support of programmes falling within exclusive provincial jurisdiction. This would provide the constitutional basis for federal equalization payments to the provinces, much as the present Constitution does. The case for such payments has not been questioned by any province (though the Government of British Columbia has suggested that if the minimum annual income of individual Canadians were high enough equalization payments to provincial governments would become unnecessary). Without federal equalization payments, disparities in provincial public services would be wider and would widen, and any existing feelings of disaffection with Canada in the lower income regions, would be aggravated. Moreover, greatly inferior public services in certain areas of the country would undermine the efficiency of the Canadian common market, by making more difficult the mobility of labour and capital within it. It follows, in the view of the Government of Canada, that Parliament must retain its unqualified spending power for the purpose of making unconditional grants to provincial governments.

Conditional Grants for General Federal-Provincial Programmes

The proposed principles would establish two limitations on the use by Parliament of its power to make conditional grants for general federal-provincial programmes—first the existence of a "broad national consensus" in favour of any programme, and secondly the assurance that a "fiscal penalty" would not be imposed upon the people of non-participating provinces. The Government of Canada would suggest the following method for giving effect to these two requirements:

(1) The determination as to when the national interest or extra-provincial interests warranted a new shared-cost programme between the Government of Canada and the governments of the provinces would be arrived at jointly by Parliament and the provinical legislatures, in the manner described below[10], instead of by Parliament alone.

(2) Where a consensus had been reached that a new shared-cost programme was desirable, the provincial governments whose legislatures had voted *for* the consensus would receive conditional grants for the programme, once it was started by them. In the provinces whose legislatures had voted *against* the consensus, the people of the province would be paid grants equivalent in the aggregate to the average per capita amount paid to the participating provinces (multiplied by the population of the non-participating province). (See pp. 230 and 231.)

The introduction into the Constitution of these two requirements would meet all of the provincial objections to the present procedures for initiating shared-cost programmes. Parliament would no longer have the power to decide unilaterally when a shared-cost programme ought to be initiated: a provincial consensus would be required. The payment of grants to the people of the provinces whose legislatures had voted against the consensus would meet the "taxation without benefit" argument. The two principles taken together would ensure that the priorities of any provincial government would be changed only if its legislature had supported the consensus. They would also mean that Parliament would not be able to give effect to its judgment that the national interest had come to attach to some problem or programme within provincial jurisdiction unless enough legislatures had voted their agreement, and it would be able to do so only in the provinces where the legislatures had voted for Parliament's proposal.

Determining the Consensus—The first step in determining whether there was a consensus in favour of a new shared-cost programme would be the presentation to the Parliament of Canada by the federal government of a resolution proposing the programme.[11] If Parliament approved the resolution, it would be transmitted to the provincial governments for submission to their legislatures. The legislatures, in turn, would approve or reject the resolution. The determination as to whether there was a provincial consensus

---

10 See pp. 230 and 231, *infra*. Note also the qualification concerning the role of the Senate.
11 This would be a money resolution preceding a Bill which would be considered if and when a consensus was reached. Special procedures likely would be required by Parliament for the consideration of such a resolution.

in favour of the shared-cost programme would be made by reference to the Senate divisions provided for in the Constitution.

For the purposes of this proposal the Senate could be regarded as having four divisions under the present Constitution, namely Ontario, Quebec, the Maritime Provinces and Newfoundland, and the Western Provinces.[12] The affirmative vote of the legislatures in at least three of these Senate divisions would be required before Parliament could proceed with the proposed shared-cost programme. The vote of the legislatures in the Atlantic region would be considered to be in the affirmative if the legislatures of provinces having at least 16 of the 30 Senate seats of that region were to vote for the resolution (two of Nova Scotia, New Brunswick or Newfoundland). The vote of the legislatures of the Western region would be considered to be in the affirmative if the legislatures of provinces having 12 of the 24 Senate seats of that region were to vote for the resolution (two of the Western Provinces).

An affirmative vote on the part of the three Senate divisions would represent a provincial consensus in favour of Parliament's proposal. In the event of a negative vote—two or more Senate divisions voting against a proposal— Parliament could re-transmit its resolution to the governments of the provinces whose legislatures had voted against the proposal, within one year, to determine whether the legislatures wished to change their decision given the results of the votes in other legislatures. Subsequently Parliament could not re-submit its resolution to the provinces more often than once every two or three years.

This method of determining a consensus is based upon the present constitutional provisions regarding the Senate. If the Senate were to be reformed in such a way as to increase the representation of provincial interests (that is, by the appointment of a proportion of the Senators by the governments of the provinces), another alternative for determining the provincial consensus could be considered, namely by a special vote of the Senate (using the Senate division voting procedures suggested). Whatever the decision as between these two alternatives—a vote of the legislatures or a vote of a reformed Senate—it would not be appropriate to give the provinces a "double veto", once by a Senate in which provincial governments were directly represented, and once by provincial legislatures. It should be noted that any revision in "the basis of distribution in the Senate as among the various regions and provinces" (which possibility the Government of Canada has suggested should be considered) might call for a review of the formula for determining a provincial consensus.

Provinces whose legislatures had voted for the consensus. In the event of a provincial consensus in favour of the proposed programme the Government of Canada could begin making payments to the provincial governments

---

[12] The Newfoundland seats have been added to the Maritime Provinces division referred to in Section 22 of the B. N. A. Act.

whose legislatures had voted for the consensus, once the shared-cost programme had been started by them. To ensure the participation in the programme of the required number of provinces, personal grants in lieu of programme grants would not be paid in any province whose legislature had voted in favour of the proposal but whose government either had failed to start the programme or rescinded it once it was started.

Provinces whose legislatures had voted against the consensus. In the event of a favourable provincial consensus, and after a prescribed lapse of time, the Government of Canada would begin making personal grants in lieu of programme grants in the provinces whose legislatures had voted against participation. During this interval the legislatures which had voted against the consensus would have an opportunity to reconsider their decision given the results of the votes in other legislatures, and the governments of the participating provinces would be engaged in establishing the programme. The personal payments might begin, for example, three months after the end of the fiscal year in which the shared-cost programme had been started by the required minimum number of provinces. The payments would continue until the provinces concerned established a qualifying programme: the Government of Canada would not have the right to re-transmit Parliament's resolution to the non-participating provinces any more often than once every two or three years.

Other aspects of the determination of a consensus. To ensure that all legislatures had an opportunity to express themselves on proposed shared-cost programmes, and did in fact vote upon the proposals, a constitutional obligation would be imposed upon provincial governments to submit Parliament's resolutions to their legislatures at the current or the next session, and upon provincial legislatures to vote upon the resolutions within one year of their receipt by the provincial government. A constitutional obligation of this kind would not be unique: an obligation upon the provinces to hold annual sessions of their legislatures and to dissolve their legislatures for a general election at least every five years has also been suggested. It would be open to the legislatures, of course, to amend the proposals submitted by Parliament. A major amendment by any legislature, which was unacceptable to the Government of Canada, would be taken to be a negative vote. Minor amendments acceptable to the Government of Canada would be discussed with the provincial governments whose legislatures had voted in the affirmative, to determine the acceptability of the amendments to the provinces.

Grants to Persons in the Non-Participating Provinces—The aggregate amount of the grants to persons in the non-participating provinces would be calculated by multiplying the average per capita payment to participating provinces by the population of the non-participating province. The alternative basis of calculation—the taxes paid in support of the shared-cost programme by the people of the non-participating provinces—would not be feasible, since it is impossible to trace with any accuracy the tax contribution to the federal treasury from each province.[13]

The allocation of the aggregate amount as between persons in the non-participating provinces, and the method of distributing the refunds would have to be determined by Parliament. Clearly it would not be feasible to make this allocation on the basis of the taxes paid by each taxpayer in the province, because of the impossibility of making such a calculation. Nor would it be reasonable to require that the refunds be based upon the amount of the individual income tax contributed by each taxpayer—the one tax where the amount paid by each person is known. To do so would be to act upon the fiction that all federal-provincial programmes were or could in reality be financed solely from this source of revenue . In fact federal expenditures of whatever kind—excepting those paid from insurance funds, such as unemployment insurance—are financed from *all* of the taxes paid by the people of Canada to their federal government, and no bookkeeping device would obscure this fact.

It is recognized that the arrangement here proposed for calculating the aggregate amount to be paid to the people of the non-participating provinces, and for distributing it among them, would involve some redistribution of income, both as between provinces and as between taxpayers. But this is true of all taxes and expenditures. More particularly, it is necessarily true of federal payments to provincial governments, since federal taxes fall more heavily upon high income areas than upon low ones, and because contributions to provincial services frequently result in greater benefits to low income as opposed to high income provinces. It follows that the redistributive effects of the arrangements proposed might reasonably be accepted as simply one of the side effects of an arrangement under which federal-provincial programmes could be established in the provinces which wanted them. Moreover the redistributive effect of federal-provincial programmes could be said to be undesirable only if it were suggested that the particular government measures, and the taxes used to finance them, ought somehow to be based, in the participating provinces, strictly upon the benefits each family was likely to receive from the programme, and, in the non-participating provinces, strictly upon the contribution each person was making to the federal treasury in the taxes he was paying to it, directly or indirectly. Neither proposition would be practical, nor, in the view of the Government of Canada, desirable.

Payments to the governments rather than to the people of the non-participating provinces would seem, at first glance, to be a reasonable alternative to the approach here proposed. Upon reflection, however, it is evident that such a suggestion would be inconsistent with the underlying

---

[13] Shared-cost programmes are financed out of the Consolidated Revenue Fund, which is made up of personal income tax, sales and excise taxes, customs duties and other revenues. It is not possible to determine, province by province, the true source of many of these revenues.

reason for a payment of any kind to non-participating provinces. The basic principle underlying such payments would be this: no provincial government ought to feel obliged to exercise its constitutional powers in a particular way for the reason that a fiscal penalty would be visited upon its people if it took a contrary view. The objective, therefore, clearly must be to keep the *people* of non-participating provinces from paying a penalty: it follows that any payment must logically be made to them.

There is another way of stating this principle which may make the proposition clearer. Every provincial government ought to be free to accept or reject federal-provincial programmes proposed by the Government of Canada. Once the decision finally has been made by a province to reject a proposed programme—once a provincial government has said it wants nothing to do with the programme—it ought not indeed be expected, or expect, to participate in any way. It remains only for Parliament to return to the people of that province—to its taxpayers—an amount which bears some relationship to the taxes they have contributed toward the programme, or the amount they would have received through the programme had their provincial government decided to participate.

There is, in short, no reason in principle for Parliament to pay to the government rather than to the people of a non-participating province the amount it would be obliged under the Constitution to pay. Nor is there any compelling administrative reason to do so. In an age when virtually all citizens have contact with the government, in one way or another, and when computers can be used to do things which earlier would have been impossible, it is not too difficult to develop a system under which the compensatory payments to non-participating provinces would be paid directly to the citizen.

Amendment and Termination of General Shared-Cost Programmes—A brief note should be added about the amendment or termination of general shared-cost programmes. The resolution concerning each programme proposed undoubtedly would contain provisions for the termination, lapsing or amendment of the programme. Major amendments to the programme not provided for in the original resolution (presumably those requiring statutory amendment) would require Parliamentary approval, and the consent of the participating provinces (the minimum consensus required would be the same as that provided for in the Senate division voting procedure described previously).

Conditional Grants in Support of Federal-Provincial Programmes Involving Fewer than Ten Provinces

The proposed outlined above would not apply to regional programmes, that is to say shared-cost programmes which involved some or all of the provinces of one or two Senate divisions. Such programmes would continue to be negotiated directly between the Government of Canada and the governments of the provinces concerned. Further, because regional schemes by their nature usually require the participation of all provinces affected in order to be viable, and because the taxpayers in the other parts of Canada would be required to contribute toward such schemes without either programme benefits or compensatory personal grants, no personal grants in lieu of programme grants would be paid in provinces which were invited to participate in a regional plan but whose governments decided against doing so. It is difficult to visualize a shared-cost programme which would be applicable to the provinces of three Senate divisions, but it would have to be decided whether the scheme for general shared-cost programmes or that for regional plans ought to apply in these circumstances, in case that eventuality were to arise in the future.

This proposal for a new approach to the federal spending power in a revised Constitution is based upon the belief that federalism in a modern state must provide for joint federal-provincial action, sometimes initiated by Parliament, and upon the further belief that a federal constitution must always provide for the integrity of the regions or provinces which make up the state. It is hoped that the Constitutional Conference will find this proposal helpful in beginning its task of reviewing the distribution of powers in the Constitution of Canada. It remains to be said of this Working Paper, as the provinces have said of the papers they have submitted, that the Government of Canada will not feel bound by the particular proposal which is here presented. More specifically the Government will feel obliged, as was said previously[14], continually to review its position as discussions on the distribution of legislative powers proceed.

---

[14] See p. 227-28, *supra*.

16   Constitutional Reform in Canada

J. Peter Meekison

The purpose of this paper is to present various ideas on the process of constitutional reform in Canada. It is not the intention of the author to assess the several positions which have been presented at the Constitutional Conferences. While one might be tempted to develop a new theory of federalism or federal bargaining from what has taken place in Canada during the past three and one half years, the more modest goal of reviewing the process is all that is attempted.

1   Background

It is difficult to give an exact date to the beginnings of constitutional reform, since this process has in one way or another been in existence since Confederation. What distinguishes the current exercise from earlier ones is its all-encompassing nature. Nevertheless one might argue that governments in Canada have been more than normally conscious of certain flaws in the Canadian federal system since the Depression, and as such have endeavoured to correct these imperfections. One need only cite the terms of reference of the Rowell-Sirois Commission, and the discussions of its report to be aware of this fact. Or one can mention the O'Connor report in which the author reviewed with considerable disfavour the interpretations of the British North American Act by the Judicial Committee of the Privy Council. Another major review of the federal system or at least certain aspects of the division of powers took place in 1945 at the Reconstruction Conference. In his opening statement to the Conference, The Right Honourable W. L. Mackenzie King said:

> What exactly is the relationship we are seeking between the Dominion and the provinces? Let me first make very clear what we are not seeking. The federal government is not seeking to weaken the provinces, to centralize all the functions of government, to subordinate on government to another or to expand one government at the expense of others. Our aim is to place the Dominion and every province in a position to discharge effectively and independently its appropriate functions. In other words, we believe that the sure road of Dominion-Provincial cooperation lies in the achievement in their own spheres of genuine autonomy for the provinces. By genuine autonomy, I mean effective

J. PETER MEEKISON – Associate Professor of Political Science, University of Alberta.

financial independence, not only for the wealthier provinces but also for those less favourably situated.

To put it very briefly, we regard autonomy and co-operation as essential means of achieving satisfactory Dominion-Provincial relations.

What then are the aims or objectives for which we are seeking the best possible Dominion-Provincial relations? To express them also very briefly, we are asking the provinces to go into partnership with the Dominion in a broad programme for the development of our national heritage, and the promotion of the welfare of the Canadian people.[1]

Despite the fact that Mr. King was concerned with immediate post-war problems his words continue to have contemporary relevance.

This conference dissolved without any agreement as to how this partnership might be achieved. Why? In essence the provinces and the federal government had differing perceptions as to their respective roles in the federal system and of federalism itself. Despite the lack of agreement at this particular conference, the idea of the federal-provincial conference as the forum for resolving disputes and where the conflicting views of each government could be presented has persisted. At first conferences were held every five years with the principal agenda item being the renegotiation of the financial agreements between the federal and provincial governments.[2] In the sixties, however, they became far more frequent and the range of agenda items covered was far more extensive. For example, agenda for the 1965 Conference contained the following items: social security, economic development, tax structure committee report, transportation, inland water resources, liaison and secretariat arrangements and other matters.[3]

At this point a number of observations should be made before proceeding with the discussion of the current constitutional conferences. First of all the main concern of most of the post-war conferences was the entire range of federal-provicial financial relations. Thus, in addition to discussing the tax-sharing arrangements, major programmes, which involved the committment and expenditure of large sums of public funds, were also subject to the scrutiny of the participants at these conferences. Included in this latter category were programmes such as the Canada Pension Plan, Medicare and Aid to Higher Education. A second factor which requires mention is the change in the style of negotiations or bargaining. Professor D .V. Smiley describes

---

[1] *Dominion-Provincial Conference, 1945, Dominion and Provincial Submissions and Plenary Conference Discussions* (Ottawa, King's Printer, 1946), p. 5.

[2] After the dissolution of the Reconstruction Conference, the next conference was in 1950. This was followed by conferences in 1955, 1957, and 1960. The five year sequence was broken in 1957 with the changeover in governments. Mr. Diefenbaker convened a conference shortly after assuming office to review the tax sharing agreements which had been negotiated two years earlier and which had just come into effect. See *Dominion-Provincial Conference, 1957* (Ottawa, Queen's Printer, 1956).

[3] *Federal-Provincial Conference, Ottawa, July 19-22, 1965* (Ottawa, Queen's Printer, 1968), p. 4.

this tranformation as the transition from "joint" to "consultative" federalism.[4] At the recent conferences the provinces have asserted themselves and have resisted federal encroachment into their sphere of authority. In other words the co-operation federal system which Mr. King advocated took on a much different character.[5]

What is the significance of all of this negotiation and bargaining which has been the predominant feature of Canadian federalism since 1945? Two points come to mind. First is the obvious imbalance between financial needs and financial capacities of the provincial governments. This dilemma has brought the provinces to the conference table each time with the expectation that their fiscal positions might be improved as a result. The second is that — implicity or explicitly — much of the discussion, given the fiscal problems of the provinces has been related to the division of powers. Through its exercise of the spending power, particularly since the Second World War, the federal government has effected certain changes in provincial policies and priorities and as a result, the division of powers. A casual perusal of the agendas of the conferences held in the late sixties suggests that a quasi-constitutional review was already underway.

What had become obvious as a result of the continuing negotiations between the federal and provincial governments was that a degree of interdependence had developed which did not conform to traditional theories of federalism. Statements by many of the premiers and prime ministers, starting with King, stressed autonomy, while at the same time governments were developing new means and techniques for co-operation and as a consequence a mutual dependence evolved. The eleven governments, if one adds up the meetings of officials, ministers, and first ministers, were in almost permanent session while the range of topics discussed became even more extensive. Moreover the mechanism of the conference began to develop an existence and identity of its own. This development is very noticeable at the 1963 meeting when the following procedure was introduced:

> It may be desirable to set up committees of the Conference to which certain individual subjects or groups of subjects could be referred for detailed examination and recommendations to the plenary Conference in due course. It is proposed, however, that decisions concerning the establishment of specific committees be left to the Conference itself. While the plenary meetings of the Conference will be devoted to the discussion of the main items on the agenda, and of the broad principles

---

4 D. V. Smiley, "Public Administration and Canadian Federalism", *Canadian Public Administration,* Vol. VII, no. 3 (Sept. 1964), pp. 371-88. See also his article entitled, "The Rowell-Sirois Report, Provincial Autonomy, and Post-War Canadian Federalism," *Canadian Journal of Economics and Political Science,* Vol. XXVIII no. 1 (Feb. 1962), pp. 54-69.

5 For an excellent review of the transition in provincial attitudes during this period see, Edwin R. Black and Alan C. Cairns, "A Different Perspective on Canadian Federalism", *Canadian Public Administration,* Vol. IX no. 1 (March, 1966), pp. 27-45.

governing federal-provincial relations in various fields, the Conference might decide in due course to establish committees to consider such specific problems as, for example, hospital insurance costs and operation, categorical assistance programmes, national agricultural marketing boards, the administration of Indian and Eskimo affairs, etc.[6]

The summit meeting or first ministers' conference became an accepted part of the Canadian political process and a political group outside of the traditional structure of parliamentary government.

What finally triggered the present review? One can list a series of events which took place in the mid-sixties which finally precipitated the review. The obvious explanation, but not the only one, was the changing relationship between Quebec and Ottawa. Others have written on this subject and only a few remarks are necessary at this point. The impact of the Quiet Revolution can be demonstrated by the statement of Premier Jean Lesage in his 1963 budget speech, in the rejection by Quebec of the Fulton-Favreau formula in 1966 and in the working paper prepared for the Quebec Liberal Party Convention in the fall of 1967.[7] In addition to those influences the Royal Commission on Bilingualism and Biculturalism in its *Preliminary Report* warned the Canadian public of the growing schism between French and English in Canada. In its report the Commissioner's said:

> The Commissioners, like all Canadians who read newspapers, fully expected to find themselves confronted by tensions and conflicts. They knew that there have been strains throughout the history of Confederation; and that difficulties can be expected in a country where cultures exist side by side. What the Commissioners have discovered little by little, however, is very different and they have been driven to the conclusion that Canada, without being fully conscious of the fact, is passing through the greatest crisis in its history.
> The source of the crisis has been in the province of Quebec . . . .[8]

---

[6] *Federal Provincial Conference, 1963* (Ottawa, Queen's Printer, 1964), p. 7.

[7] See Jean Lesage, *Budget Speech* (Quebec, Queen's Printer, 1963), pp. 55-64. In his speech Mr. Lesage said, *"whichever party is elected on April 8,* and I repeat *whichever party is elected on April 8,* will have taken advantage of the twelve months to meet Quebec's requirements . . . ." p. 64, (italics in original.) For the letter from Mr. Lesage to Mr. Pearson announcing that Quebec could no longer support the amending formula see Paul Fox, (ed.), *Politics: Canada,* 2nd Ed. (Toronto, McGraw Hill, 1966), pp. 146-47. He said in part, "It is contended, in fact, that under the formula any province could prevent the extension of the powers of another province. Needless to say if that interpretation were to prevail, the evolution of our constitutional system in the direction desired by Quebec might become very difficult. . . ." p. 147. For the Quebec Liberal Party Working see, J. Peter Meekison, (ed.), *Canadian Federalism; Myth or Reality* (Toronto, Methuen, 1968) pp. 367-78.

[8] *A Preliminary Report of the Royal Commission on Bilingualism and Biculturalism* (Ottawa, Queen's Printer, 1965), p. 13.

Had the question of Quebec-Ottawa relations been the only issue one could ask whether or not constitutional reform in its present form would have been initiated. Certainly the non-acceptance of the suggested amending formula and any revision of its wording by Quebec would have required discussion with the other provinces as would any changes to the British North America Act relations to the position of Quebec. What forced the federal government to consent to a constitutional review was the increasing tension within the Canadian federal system which was not solely attributable to Quebec.

The "consultative" phase of Canadian federalism apparently unleashed certain forces which have yet to be contained. "It is prudent to realize the limits of consultative procedures;" Professor Smiley warned because "they do not provide any means of reconciling interests which are incompatible."[9] One must review the bargaining and disputes over the Canada Pension Plan and Medicare to illustrate the fact that Quebec was not alone in her criticism of the federal government. Perhaps the catalyst, apart from the situation in Quebec, which precipitated the review was the 1966 Tax Structure Conference in which the federal government took a strong stand in opposition to provincial demands for a larger share of the tax dollar. The federal Minister of Finance, The Honorable Mitchell Sharp stated:

> . . . the problem is not lack of access to revenue sources, but rather the difficulties the provinces form in company with the Federal Government in raising taxes that are already high.
>
> The conventional approach to this problem during the post-war period has been to argue that the Federal Government should reduce its taxes so as to give the provinces more "tax room".
>
> What I am suggesting then, is that we must get away from what is tending to become a conventional notion that the Federal Government can and should be expected to give greater tax room to the provinces, when they find their expenditures rising more rapidly than their revenues. This has been possible and has been done, in the past decade, but it cannot be accepted as a general duty. Our basic duty is the ancient one—to tax no more than we need, and to reduce taxes when we can and should.[10]

In addition to the above statement Mr. Sharp also told the provinces the federal corporation tax would be continued because of its national characteristics. He added that the federal government would "maintain a substantial position in the personal income tax field" because through this tax "equity is achieved between the rich and the poor across the nation."[11] This strong stand on the part of the federal government may have been an incentive for some provinces to see constitutional reform as a means of gaining the revenues they deemed necessary for their responsibilities.

---

[9] Smiley, "Public Administration and Canadian Federalism", *op. cit.*, p. 387.
[10] *Federal-Provincial Tax Structure Committee* (Ottawa, Queen's Printer, 1966), pp. 24-25.
[11] *Ibid.*, p. 25.

2 Constitutional Review

It was under these circumstances that Prime Minister Robarts of Ontario convened the Confederation of Tomorrow Conference in Toronto in November of 1967. In his opening remarks to the Conference, Mr. Robarts commented on the strains in the federal system but added that governments in Canada were . . . making a series of decisions that subtly, but nonetheless forcibly, were changing the political and economic character of Canada.[12] In particular he was concerned that these:

> . . . decisions, which were largely of a fiscal nature, . . . were being made not in the democratic glare of our legislatures but in the closed-door sessions of many federal-provincial conferences. These decisions were often in response to short-term, specific, and very important problems, rather than the result of a set of commonly-agreed principles and a knowledge and awareness of clearly-defined purposes.[13]

While Mr. Robarts was apparently concerned with the substance of the decisions he also questioned the manner in which they were made, a challenge which struck at the very core of co-operative arrangements then in existence. This, of course, helps to explain why this meeting and the subsequent constitutional conferences have been televised.

The publicity given to this conference by the media and the expressions of concern over the future of the federal system throughout the meetings prompted the federal government to call a constitutional conference for February, 1968. While an ordinary federal-provincial conference had been suggested by the Right Honourable Lester B. Pearson to discuss the *Report on Official Languages* of the Royal Commission on Bilingualism and Biculturalism and the possibility of entrenching a bill of rights in the constitution, the agenda was expanded and the conference in fact became the first meeting of a continuing Constitutional Conference.[14] A crisis atmosphere surrounded these two conferences, with the obvious problem being the future position of Quebec in the Canadian federal system. Throughout the discussions at both of these meetings the immediate problems facing governments were presented by the participants. Interspersed with these expressions of the day-to-day concerns were broad statements of principle relating to the federal system and its future. Thus the debate did not focus completely on either long-term or short-term considerations and as such, specific proposals for reform were not forthcoming. The general conclusion of both meetings was that a complete review of the constitution was necessary and should be undertaken immediately.

---

[12] *The Confederation of Tomorrow Conference: Proceedings* (Toronto, Queen's Printer, 1968), p. 1. See also the pamphlet.
[13] *Ibid.*
[14] See the Forward by the Right Honourable Pierre Elliott Trudeau, in *Constitutional Conference: Proceedings, First Meeting, February 1968* (Ottawa, Queen's Printer, 1968), p. 4.

How was this review to be carried out? In the closing hours of the February 1968 Conference this matter was discussed.[15] It was agreed that the review would take place on three levels. The following diagram shows the groups engaged in the discussion.

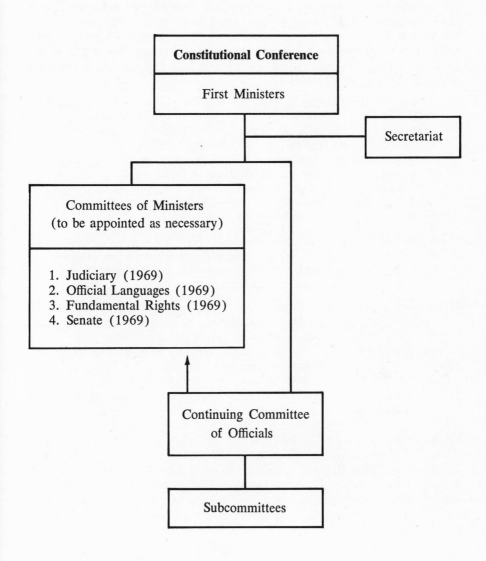

15 *Ibid.*, pp. 515-37.

The permanent body established to discuss the constitution was of course to consist of the eleven first ministers who would discuss general principles and could delegate, if need be, specific assignments to the other two groups. The major justification given for this structure and in particular for the creation of the Continuing Committee of Officials (C. C. O.) was that "heads of government have pretty busy lives these days."[16] While the accuracy of this statement cannot be challenged its ready acceptance suggests that constitutional reform was not the number one priority problem of the heads of government, despite the professed urgency. Moreover, it meant that much of the preliminary work and negotiating was to be left to experts. Mr. Pearson in referring to the C. C. O. said:

> That committee would facilitate our tasks by examining in a preliminary way policy questions referred to them, by coordinating research work, and by preparing material for the conference. Because a review of the Constitution requires an understanding of both the institutions of government and how they function, as well as a very broad knowledge of the functions of government, we would expect, and I am sure you would agree, that the committee would be made up of general advisers of government from the Privy Council or executive council officers, the federal provincial affairs departments, the departments of the attorneys general, and the provincial treasuries. In other words, it would be composed of members who would be in close touch with their respective governments as officials. Naturally, it is the responsibility of each government to decide on the membership of this committee so far as a particular province is concerned.[17]

The possible problems which this structure presents will be discussed later.

To service this entire structure a Secretariat was created to handle administrative details including such matters as reports of conference proceedings, circulation of documents, etc. The federal government offered to set up the Secretariat but provincial governments were encouraged to assist with its staffing. The establishment of a continuing constitutional conference did not mean that the use of federal-provincial conferences to discuss other matters would be discontinued. Indeed the Tax Structure Committee which had been reporting to federal-provincial conferences was expected to work on certain aspects of the review.[18] The machinery of inter-governmental relations had become even more complex with those additions, which were seen as continuing bodies. Although the personnel involved were the same there was a distinction made between the federal-provincial conferences and the constitutional conferences.* The differentiation in roles would be difficult to realize, since the issues brought before each kind of conference are, in fact, intertwined.

---

[16] *Ibid.*, p. 519.

[17] *Ibid.*

[18] This directive is found in the statement of conclusions of the second meeting of the conference. *Constitutional Conference: Proceedings, Second Meeting, February 1969* (Ottawa, Queen's Printer, 1969), p. 397.

With the machinery agreed upon the last act of the 1968 Conference was to determine the scope of the review. Initially six items were proposed for consideration.

These were:
(a) Official languages;
(b) Fundamental rights;
(c) Distribution of powers;
(d) Reform of institutions linked with federalism, including the Senate and the Supreme Court of Canada;
(e) Regional disparities;
(f) Amending procedure and provisional arrangements.[19]

A seventh item was suggested by Premier Robarts, "mechanisms of federal-provincial relations." Once again he voiced his concern over the role of conferences in the political system. His comment was that, "Federal-provincial conferences and their place in the total scheme of things in Canada have grown rather like Topsy in the last few years on an *ad hoc* basis."[20]

Although agreement had been reached on the machinery and scope of constitutional reform little thought was given to the goals and objectives of the exercise. This task was to be left to future meetings. In particular, what was not resolved was whether the conference should draft a completely new constitution or modify the existing one.

For the second meeting of the Constitutional Conference, held in February 1969, Prime Minister Trudeau in *The Constitution and the People of Canada* outlined what he saw as the four objectives of Confederation. These were:

1. To establish for Canada a federal system of government based on democratic principles.
2. To protect basic human rights, which shall include linguistic rights.
3. To promote national economic, social and cultural development and the general welfare and equality of opportunity for all Canadians in whatever region they may live, including the opportunity for gainful work, for just conditions of employment, for an adequate standard of living, for security, for education and for rest and leisure.
4. To contribute to the achievement of world peace and security, social progress and better standards of life for all mankind.[21]

These objectives or goals of Confederation are certainly worth pursuing and few people would challenge or find fault with them. Their achievement, however, is a different matter and it is here that problems develop. While one finds agreement amongst the eleven governments in Canada that a federal system is both necessary and desirable, significant differences of opinion continue to exist over the nature of the federal system and their role within it. It is due to these differing perceptions of federalism that one very quickly encounters difficulty with constitutional reform.

---

[19] *Constitutional Conference, First Meeting.*
[20] *Ibid.*, p. 527.
[21] The Right Honourable Pierre Elliott Trudeau, *The Constitution and the People of Canada* (Ottawa, Queen's Printer, 1969), pp. 4-14.

Assuming for the moment that federalism implies a certain degree of diversity within the political system one should not expect constitutional bargaining to be a routine matter. There may be a tendency to believe that the circumstances present at the time of Confederation approximate those surrounding the current dialogue on reform and will as a result lead to a similar solution. While there are a number of interesting parallels one significant difference exists and that is that the change is coming after a federal system has been operating for over one hundred years. Any change will for the most part be determined by the ambitions, anxieties, and attitudes of governments which have become conditioned to operating with certain powers and within certain limits. Consequently, to expect that ready solutions will be forthcoming is to be mistaken.

What are some of the conflicting views? While no attempt is made to classify them by province at this point, one can see a number of distinct general areas of contention, which in turn influence stands taken on specific reform proposals. Cleavages have run along the following dimensions:

1. Attitudes relating to a strong versus a weak central government.
2. Have versus have not provinces.
3. Regional versus national goals.
4. Importance attached to the review.
5. Fundamental versus expedient or *ad hoc* changes.

These are rough or approximate guides which may be used to categorize the attitudes of both the federal and provincial governments. To a great extent these positions are not mutually exclusive but rather they represent the areas of concern which have appeared during the negotiations to date. The problem is, whether these positions are reconcilable given the task at hand.

One finds considerable variation among the provincial governments over the degree to which they are willing to have Ottawa make decisions. Thus on the question of provincial autonomy there is little consensus for the simple reason that the provinces are not equal nor do they approach the bargaining table with similar objectives. While provinces are equal in legal terms (although one might argue that Quebec is an exception) they are certainly not equal in size, population, wealth, resources or economic potential. The cultural aspirations of Quebec and the influence this force has on the negotiations cannot be ignored and must be added into the matrix which determines the boundaries of the process. These differences produce widely divergent reactions to constitutional reform in general and provincial autonomy in particular.

It may be contended that this type of presentation is too simplistic but these are the obvious conflicting positions. To a great extent provincial positions are determined by their ability and/or determination to meet their constitutional obligations. Another way of expressing this idea is the degree of co-operation which provinces are willing to promote with Ottawa. The resolution of this dilemma brings into sharper focus the other positions mentioned above.

The difficulty of resolving these differences is perhaps best illustrated by a statement of Premier Robichaud's at the December 1969 Conference. After a long debate over the method of determining a consensus of provinces for approving new federal spending programmes along the lines of Medicare he said:

> I would certainly veto any proposal made by any province that would demand the right to veto—I would veto that . . . . I would exercise that right of veto before they have it because then they would veto everything that some of the provinces [would want] . . . . These provinces would be losing, or could in the future lose.[22]

The February 1969 Conference agreed on an "accelerated" review but with the complete lack of consensus on goals or a timetable for review itself how this speeded up examination could be accomplished was left in abeyance. Judging from remarks made at the December 1969 Conference, presumably all the discussions to date are in anticipation of a meeting some time off in the future when the hard bargaining will take place. That such a conference is contemplated was suggested by Prime Minister Trudeau. In closing the debate on the exercise of the federal spending power he said:

> Well, I think the subject has been sufficiently aired. There is obviously no agreement on whether there should be a formula for consensus or just an obligation to consult. . . .
>
> The different formulae have been explored at the official level, and I do not think there is anything to gain at this time by referring it back to them. I suggest that we just report whatever progress we have made and go on with the next item. It is obvious that this, as many other items, will have to be returned to in due course when we try to look at the overall picture which we have been drawing of the Constitution at that time.[23]

Other indications that a future conference when the serious negotiating will take place is found in the discussions on regional disparities. In December, 1969 when the Maritime provinces were pushing the federal government to consent to a constitutional obligation to recognize the problem of regional disparities, they were unable to obtain any committment from the federal government other than a promise of a clause in the preamble to a revised constitution, a legally non-enforceable provision. Premier Campbell of Prince Edward Island even went so far as to suggest that "we might draw some conclusions or even propose making a decision. . . ." His pleadings were to no avail. Instead, the federal government through the Minister of Justice, the Honorable John Turner, argued that the issue required more study. In other words no final decision on this (or any other) matter would be made at that conference.

Given the obvious problems associated with reform the question presents itself is this approach the only alternative? The December 1967 Conference

---

[22] *Constitutional Conference: Proceedings, Third Meeting, December 1969* (Ottawa, Queen's Printer, 1970), p. 133.
[23] *Ibid.*, pp. 141-42.

not only demonstrated the cleavages but it also indicated that the enthusiasm for constitutional reform was diminishing. Indeed, the concerns of many of the provinces, apart from specific changes to particular parts of the constitution, appear to be related to more immediate problems. For example, Premier Thatcher was more concerned with possible effects of the White Paper on Taxation and discriminatory freight rates than the great principles of reform. If these immediate concerns, which do relate to the division of powers and how governments use their powers, can be resolved then constitutional reform might progress more quickly. If so, one must ask: should the process continue? If so, in what form? Assuming that this exercise cannot be terminated as easily as it started, then what options are open to the eleven governments?

3 Problems and Alternatives

Perhaps the most obvious conclusion which can be drawn from the proceding analysis is that to revise the constitution through a series of *ad hoc,* infrequent discussions is tantamount to folly. Historically, constitutions have not been written in this fashion. This, of course does not mean they cannot be but certain problems arise. One difficulty which has already been encountered, is that the personnel at the conferences, and consequently views expressed, has undergone continuous change. If the review is to continue over the next few years then the probability of more changes is very high. The effect this may have on the results of the conference is all too evident. It may require every decision to be reviewed once more, to see if a consensus still exists. Moreover, new governments are usually concerned with matters other than constitutional reform. Since the review started in 1968, eight changes in first ministers have occurred, and only four of the original first ministers remain at the bargaining table.[24]

---

[24] To May 1971 the following changes have taken place in the composition of first ministers:

	1968	Reason for Change	1971
Canada	L. B. Pearson	(retired from office 1968)	P. E. Trudeau
Nova Scotia	G. I. Smith	(electoral defeat 1970)	G. A. Regan
New Brunswick	L. J. Robichaud	(electoral defeat 1970)	R. J. Hatfield
Quebec	Daniel Johnson	died in office, 1968)	
	J. J. Bertrand	(electoral defeat 1970)	Robert Bourassa
Ontario	John P. Robarts	(retired from office 1970)	W. J. Davis
Manitoba	Walter Wier	(electoral defeat 1969)	E. Schreyer
Alberta	E. C. Manning	(retired from office 1969)	H. E. Strom

The four original members of the conference are W. A. C. Bennett, Ross Thatcher, Alan Campbell and Joey Smallwood.

Another difficulty which develops is the continued interjection into the constitutional arena of matters which are currently of pressing importance to the governments involved in the process. For example, the White Paper on Taxation has been discussed, powers on pollution are under consideration, western alienation has been voiced. A final problem related to the review itself is the possible undermining of the legitimacy of the present constitution. Televised conferences and repeated reference to shortcomings of the constitution and the need to reform certain areas could have deleterious effects over the long run. While Canadians do not venerate the British North America Act (or for that matter the Fathers of Confederation) its position in the political system has never been seriously challenged. Continual buffeting could weaken considerably the constitutional fabric of the country by the implication that the constitution is obsolete or not in keeping with the times.

Given the lack of consensus on the meaning of federalism, other than what is expressed in very general terms, attempts to renegotiate the distribution of powers will in all probability lead nowhere. The lack of success over the last thirty-five years to achieve an amending formula is indicative of the problems involved. Changes in the distribution of powers will involve either the provinces relinquishing certain responsibilities, the federal government relinquishing certain responsibilities or greater use of concurrent powers.

Will the provinces give up some of their existing responsibilities to the federal government? Will we witness, to some extent, a repetition of the 1867 agreement when the central government assumed the great or important functions of government and the provinces assumed the minor functions. Provincial governments appear most reluctant to see their powers diminished in any way if the discussions which have taken place over the past three years are indicative of their feelings. Instead some provinces are asking for more responsibilities, some stress securing their financial position while some are anxious to prevent what is seen as further federal encroachments into what is considered provincial jurisdiction.

If the provinces are unwilling to decrease the scope of their responsibilities is the federal government willing to reduce its powers? Again the answer is no. For example, both Mr. Pearson and Mr. Trudeau indicated that the federal government must have authority to expand, control, develop and/or regulate the economy.[25] In the paper, *Federalism and Foreign Relations* the federal government stressed the unity of Canadian foreign policy. In the paper, *Federal-Provincial Grants and the Spending Power of Parliament,* Mr. Trudeau argued that the federal government had the power to spend money for provincial purposes, in the form of either conditional or unconditional grants.[26] The justification for the continuance of the spending power was the interde-

---

[25] For the federal government's position on this particular point see The Right Honourable Lester B. Pearson, *Federalism For the Future* (Ottawa, Queen's Printer, 1968) and Trudeau, *The Constitution, and the People of Canada.*
[26] The Right Honourable Pierre Elliott Trudeau, *Federal-Provincial Grants and the Spending Power of Parliament* (Ottawa, Queen's Printer, 1969).

pendence found in the modern federal state. The principal modification to the existing practices was that in a new constitution a provincial consensus would have to be achieved which was based on the existing Senate divisions.[27] Provinces which disagreed with the programme, could by legislation opt out, ensuring a measure of flexibility. The requirement of obtaining a consensus was seen by the federal government as a major concession on its part and overcomes many, but not all, of the criticisms of the spending power expressed by provincial governments.[28] Other than this policy proposal there is no evidence to suggest that the federal government plans to reduce its responsibilities. This position is not particularly surprising given the demand for federal action in so many areas.

With the obvious interdependence of governments the principal difficulty is in devising a rationale, or basis for the distribution of powers. The responsibilities of government are not sufficiently tangible to be carved up as one would divide money or land. To devise a formula for dividing functions of government would be an impossible task.[29] Either the conventional categories of

---

[27] The suggested formula is as follows: "The determination as to whether there was a provincial consensus in favour of the shared-cost programme would be made by reference to the Senate divisions provided for in the Constitution.

For the purposes of this proposal the Senate could be regarded as having four divisions under the present Constitution, namely Ontario, Quebec, the Maritime Provinces and Newfoundland, and the Western Provinces. The affirmative vote of the legislatures in at least three of these Senate divisions would be required before Parliament could proceed with the proposed shared-cost programme. The vote of the legislatures in the Atlantic region would be considered to be in the affirmative if the legislatures of provinces having at least 16 of the 30 Senate seats of that region were to vote for the resolution (two of the Western Provinces).

An affirmative vote on the part of three Senate divisions would represent a provincial consensus in favour of Parliament's proposal. In the event of a negative vote — two or more Senate divisions voting against a proposal — Parliament could re-transmit its resolution to the governments of the provinces whose legislatures had voted against the proposal, within one year, to determine whether the legislatures wished to change their decision given the results of the votes in other legislatures. Subsequently Parliament could not re-submit its resolution to the provinces more often than once every two or three years.

This method of determining a consensus is based upon the present constitutional provisions regarding the Senate. If the Senate were to be reformed in such a way as to increase the representation of provincial interests (that is, by the appointment of a proportion of the Senators by the governments of the provinces), another alternative for determining the provincial consensus could be considered, namely by a special vote of the Senate (using the Senate division voting procedures suggested). Whatever the decision as between these two alternatives — a vote of the legislatures or a vote of a reformed Senate — it would not be appropriate to give the provinces a "double veto", once by a Senate in which provincial governments were directly represented, and once by provincial legislatures." *Ibid.*, pp. 40, 42.

[28] For a detailed examination of this proposal see D. V. Smiley and R. M. Bruns "Canadian Federalism and the Spending Power: Is Constitutional Restriction Necessary", *Canadian Tax Journal,* Vol. XVIII no. 6 (November-December, 1969), pp. 468-82.

[29] For a good account of this problem see Rufus Davis, "The 'Federal Principle' Reconsidered, Part II", *Australian Journal of Politics and History,* Vol. I (1955), pp. 223-44.

governmental activity, such as justice, health, agriculture, etc. must be refined to the point where some minimum agreement can be reached over who should be responsible for what or else the debate would continue forever. Since most of the discussion at federal-provincial conferences has focused on specific policy proposals rather than general policy considerations this approach might be feasible. Its main defect, however, is that the revised constitution would contain a detailed division of powers which would be unparalleled and the federal system would in all probability lose its elasticity. The decision as to which government would be responsible for what, would still, of course, be subject to bargaining. With the conflicting views already in existence this kind of suggestion has dubious validity.

Underlying much of the discussion on the division of powers is the assumption that the finished product will contain two exclusive lists of powers. Moreover, the positions adopted suggest a high degree of competition between the two orders of government and a suggestion that the two can operate independently of each other. While this type of situation is not to be unexpected given the nature of political bargaining, it is unrealistic to anticipate much in the way of change through this approach. With the obvious interdependence of governments in the modern federal state, to concentrate on exclusive lists of powers overlooks the actual as opposed to the theoretical functioning of the system. The probable reason that the review to date has accomplished little is that governments have failed to consider seriously the existing relationships within the federal system and are operating from a traditional theory of federalism.

One possible solution, which certainly recognizes and forces interdependence is greater use of concurrent powers. While this approach is perhaps more feasible than the use of exclusive lists the problems of what is to be shared remains. That this approach is possible is indicated by discussions in pollution control. Even then the conflict between technology and jurisdiction was evident in that some provinces wanted to wait until there had been more experience in dealing with pollution control.[30] An even more difficult question to be

---

[30] The "Statement of Conclusion" issued at the end of the third working session of the Constitutional Conference in February, 1971, had the following clauses on pollution control:

"In particular, the First Ministers considered a federal proposal that there should be a new concurrent power for Parliament and the provincial legislatures to make laws in relation to the control of pollution of air and water. Under this proposal, if there were a conflict between a federal law made under this power and a provincial law made under it, the federal law would prevail when it applies to control pollution which has, or if permitted would have, significant international or interprovincial effects, but in other circumstances the provincial law would prevail over the federal law.

Some First Ministers expressed interest in this proposal. Another view, however, was that new provisions could better be considered after there has been more experience in dealing with pollution; in the meantime, it would be preferable to rely on improved arrangements for coordination and cooperation between governments based upon existing constitutional provisions. A further view was that areas of exclusive federal and provincial jurisdiction would be preferable to the general concurrency which has been proposed."

resolved is the one of paramountcy or expressed another way which government has the final say in the event of a conflict in laws in an area of concurrent jurisdiction. When this matter was discussed in December 1969 with regard to public retirement insurance, the provinces were adamantly opposed to giving the federal government the last word.[31]

Another problem, which relates to the above discussion and the review process itself, is that many individuals at the official level, who are involved in the day-to-day decisions relating to the administrative aspects of federalism, are also involved in the discussions on reform. Presumably their attitudes and ideas on reform are influenced by their administrative activities and consequently their positions will affect their views expressed at meetings of officials. This thinking is also reflected in much of the discussion at the constitutional conferences themselves.

The question of reform at this point in time requires less concern with the administrative details of the future federal system and more concern with what is politically feasible. The final document will probably not be a perfect constitution but perhaps one which is more acceptable. (This statement assumes that at least some minimal change is deemed both desirable and necessary.) In other words the test that any changes must meet is that they are politically acceptable rather than administratively feasible. This suggestion is not intended to belittle the importance of administrative problems but presumably the revised constitution must be sufficiently general to provide for the flexibility necessary to permit governments to resolve both policy and administrative differences which may arise. The current review was not a response to administrative difficulties but a result of political problems and pressures.

In summary I would argue that the present review is in fact failing to resolve the dilemmas of the federal system because the views presented to date at the bargaining table indicate that major revisions to the constitution are virtually impossible to achieve. If only minor changes are required then something may be accomplished but this type of reform is not what has been suggested is necessary. An alternative course of action would be to de-emphasize the functional features of the federal system and give more attention to its structural aspects.

The interdependence, which has become so noticeable in the past few years, has produced a highly complex and completely unstructured network of federal-provincial communication links. In 1968 Mr. Pearson reported that, at that time, 170 federal-provincial committees were in existence.[32] What may be required, therefore, is that formal recognition be given to the machinery of intergovernmental relations or if one prefers, to the structure of the bargaining process. The federal-provincial conference is an already accepted

---

[31] See *Constitutional Conference, Third Meeting, op. cit.* See the discussion beginning on p. 102 when Premier Robarts said, "I have a little difficulty with the word paramountcy. I do not know quite what that means."

[32] *Constitutional Conference, First Meeting, op. cit.,* p. 529.

body and it is here that consultation and negotiation can take place on particular problem areas. If the experience of the past few years have taught us anything it is that there is a greater likelihood of the success of the *ad hoc* approach to the division of powers than the comprehensive approach. The federal position paper on the spending power and its suggestions for consultation and consensus give recognition to the fact that whatever reforms are adopted, intergovernmental discussions and negotiations are expected to continue in the future.

Of equal significance are the suggested reforms for the appointment of Senators and changes in the Senate's role. Provincial and regional viewpoints would be taken into consideration to a greater extent than in the past. Provincial participation in federal policy development would be done on a continuous rather than on an occasional basis.

Modification of these two structures will obviously produce a different constellation of checks and balances within the federal system. If provinces are given a greater say in the development of federal policies it is possible that a greater degree of co-operation could emerge over time. A third structural alteration which is required, is to find an acceptable amending formula which will permit formal changes being made to the constitution. The first ministers at their second working conference in September 1970 decided that early agreement on an amending formula was essential, and that this formula had to be found soon. In February 1971 a formula was given tentative agreement subject to "further [analysis of] all the juridicial and other implications." In other words the door was left open for individual provinces to suggest changes in the formula or more probable to make its acceptance conditional on acceptance of other modifications in the constitution.[33] Related to this provision is the need for a clause in the constitution permitting the temporary delegation of responsibilities from the federal to the provincial governments and *vice versa,* an item which has not yet been discussed.

The significance of both the amending formula and the new approach to determining a consensus on federal spending proposals is considerable. Each formula, while requiring a majority of provinces, recognizes the *regional* features of the country, a phenomenon which, other than for appointment of senators, has had no particular legal importance. It is too early to tell what the impact of this apparent new approach to solving federal-provincial disputes will be.

----

[33] The suggested formula is as follows:
   "The Amending Formula —
   The Constitutional Conference has considered the nature of the formula which would be adopted to permit the Canadian Constitution to be amended wholly within Canada. The First Ministers agreed that the following formula was a feasible approach:
   I. *General Procedure*
   All constitutional amendments in future, except those covered in II and III, would require a resolution of consent at the federal level plus consent of the legislatures of a majority of the provinces of Canada including:

If agreement on the structure of the federal system can be resolved, the functional problems, while not disappearing, will at least be subject to a more systematic review. Since change in any political system is inevitable, it must be anticipated, and the constitution must provide the instruments or permit the flexibility through which reforms can be accommodated. Recognition of this fact and creation of the machinery for discussion and consultation at the political level means that alterations to the constitution, such as the addition of a Charter of Human Rights, are much more probable. In essence then, constitutional reform should be seen as a continuing phenomenon and not as a periodic exercise.

Continued

(a) the legislature of any province now containing at least 25% of the population of Canada, and of any other province that hereafter contains 25% of the population of Canada; and

(b) the legislatures of at least two provinces west of Ontario providing that the consenting provinces comprise 50% of the population of the provinces west of Ontario and the legislatures of at least two provinces east of Quebec.

II. *Federal and Provincial Constitutions*

Sections 91(1) and 92(1) would be repealed and replaced by a section giving the Parliament of Canada and the legislatures of the provinces power to amend their respective Constitutions except with regard to the following matters when the general procedure set out in 1 would apply:

(a) the functions of the Queen, Governor General and Lieutenant Governors;

(b) need for annual sessions;

(c) maximum period between elections;

The above three would apply to the legislature as well as to Parliament; the following would apply to Parliament only.

(d) principle of proportionate and minimum representation of members of Parliament from the provinces in the House of Commons.

(e) the number and residence qualification of Senators representing each province, and the powers of the Senate.

III. *Amendments of Concern to Canada plus One or More but not All Provinces.*

Such changes would require a resolution of consent at the federal level plus the consent of the legislatures of the provinces concerned.

Part Four

Intergovernmental Relations

17 The Machinery of Federal-Provincial Relations*

Edgar Gallant

Let me say at the outset—before it becomes obvious—that I have come to the field of federal-provincial relations only recently. I came to it from work in other fields including that of international trade relations where I have had the opportunity to observe intergovernmental consultation in international organizations.

We are all aware of the growing importance of consultation between the federal and provincial governments in Canada, in this age of "cooperative federalism," and I should like to begin with an indication of this growth. Some of you no doubt remember an address given by Dr. K. W. Taylor at the Ninth Annual Conference of this Institute in 1957 on the subject of "Coordination in Administration."[1] The list of federal-provincial committees which he appended to his paper contained 64 items. At the Federal-Provincial Conference of Prime Ministers and Premiers last July, a calendar of federal-provincial conferences and meetings for 1965 was distributed. There are 125 items in this list. To judge by these comparisons, the number of conferences and committees doubled over a period of eight years!

This rapid growth, it could be observed, is not out of line with the striking development of international machinery for intergovernmental consultation. Since the Second World War we have witnessed the birth of several new international organizations, and new ones seem to appear every now and then. If independent countries have found it in their interest, in this age of growing interdependence, to set up such elaborate machinery for intergovernmental liaison, should it not be expected that different levels of government within a federal country would provide machinery for even closer consultation?

Before I attempt to analyse the federal-provincial machinery we now have, it might be useful to reflect briefly on the need for consultation as it has developed in the past and as it is now evolving.

---

[1] *Proceedings of the Sixth Annual Conference of the Institute of Public Administration of Canada,* Toronto, 1954, p. 253

* From *Canadian Public Administration,* Vol. VII, No. 4, December, 1965, pp. 515-26. Reprinted by permission of the author and the Institute of Public Administration of Canada.

EDGAR GALLANT – Deputy Secretary to the Cabinet (Federal-Provincial Relations).

The Need for Consultation

In theory there would appear to be two types of federal state: one in which all fields of responsibility are precisely defined and properly allocated, requiring little machinery for intergovernmental consultation; and one in which many fields of responsibility are shared by two levels of government, requiring much more elaborate machinery for coordination. The Canadian constitution did provide for a fair amount of abutting or overlapping jurisdictions—for example, in the fields of agriculture and immigration. Nevertheless, I would suggest that the Fathers of Confederation intended to establish the first type of federal state. Over the years, however, as Canada evolved into a modern and increasingly complex industrial economy, and as the role of government underwent drastic changes, our federal system evolved into the second type.

In the early days of confederation there was not much need for federal-provincial consultations. At the beginning, relations between the federal government and the provinces were of a formal legal character, with the Secretary of State and the Lieutenant-Governors being the channels of communication. Subsequently there were periods when federal-provincial relations played an important role at the political level, and other periods when they subsided. Since then, increased use of financial power has expanded fields of influence and concern of the federal and the provincial governments. Through the use of such devices as shared-cost programs, and grants and loans to institutions under provincial jurisdiction, the federal government has considerably expanded its field of influence, though not its field of jurisdiction. Parallel to this growing role of both levels of government, and as a consequence of it, there has been an increasing crowding of the tax fields. Obviously, given such a large scale of government activity, together with this high degree of interaction between levels of government, effective intergovernmental consultation has become a basic requirement.

It is in matters relating to the over-all management of the economic affairs of the country that this requirement is becoming, in my opinion, particularly pronounced. Like other modern industrial countries, Canada seems to be paying increasing attention to the use of government economic policies for the achievement of basic social and economic objectives. While, broadly speaking, the citizens of a country will tend to look to their national governments for leadership in reaching such goals, we have to recognize that in Canada all levels of government are active in matters having definite implications for the economy as a whole. Let me try to illustrate this with a few obvious examples.

Consider first the objective of economic growth. It goes without saying that the behaviour of the public sector as a whole has a definite impact on the growth of the national economy. This applies not just to the sheer magnitude of government activity — and total government expenditure amounted to 31 per cent of the G.N.P. in 1964—but also to the priorities given to the different functions of government, the timing of public expenditure, and the means by which the funds are raised. In all of these decisions, governments may stimulate or retard growth.

When one considers that the provincial-municipal governments spent $8.1 billion in 1964, compared to $6.5 billion spent at the federal level (excluding intergovernmental transfers), and that provincial-municipal expenditures have grown by over 200 per cent in the last ten years compared to 56 per cent for federal expenditures, it becomes more than obvious that the management of government financial transactions to maximize economic growth is a matter of concern for all levels of government in Canada. We can also illustrate this point by passing from the aggregate activity to individual government measures, particularly those specific programs relating to economic growth, in which both levels of government are active. Think, for instance, of the many programs relating to the provision of trained manpower—the technical and vocational training programs, the financing of institutes of technical training and higher learning, the rehabilitation of disabled persons, and so on. Think, also, of the programs for development of primary resources—the dual roles in agriculture and fisheries, ARDA, PRFA, roads to resources, etc. One could mention also many undertakings involving both levels of jurisdiction in such important fields as energy, transportation, communication, and industrial development.

Now let us consider some further illustrations by referring to economic stabilization. Generally speaking, governments can alleviate the effects of short-term fluctuations in the economy by building automatic stabilizers into the fiscal system or by making discretionary fiscal changes. An important automatic stabilizer is, of course, the personal income tax with its basic exemptions and progressive rates. We are all aware of the recent developments in the sharing of this revenue source, and the growing importance of the provincial shares. On the expenditure side of the budget, we have an example of automatic stabilizers in unemployment insurance and other programs of assistance to the unemployed—the one involving the federal government, and the others involving the provincial and federal governments.

Turning to the ability of federal and provincial governments to implement discretionary stabilization policies, as opposed to automatic ones, an examination of the 1964 National Accounts shows that provincial and municipal governments spent over $5.6 billion on goods and services in that year while the federal government spent about $3.0 billion. One could also note that expenditures of a capital nature, which are generally more susceptible to changes in timing, are estimated to be about five times as great at the provincial-municipal level as at the federal level. Clearly, there is more potential for implementing discretionary stabilization policies through the timing of purchases in the provincial-municipal sphere than in the federal.

I have mentioned a few examples to establish the point that the two levels of government are both intimately involved in many matters which bear heavily on economic policy. This is just one, although a very important one, of several areas of joint federal-provincial concern, but it serves to illustrate, I think, the increasing need for consultation which our machinery will have to meet.

The Machinery for Federal-Provincial Relations

I now move back to the machinery. I mentioned previously that there are now (1965) some 125 committees and conferences. These do not, of course, encompass all federal-provincial consultations. There are many informal or *ad hoc* meetings to deal with particular problems. Also, and this is perhaps even more significant, individual contacts between officials and between ministers, by letter, telephone, or visits, appear to be increasing. Therefore, when one speaks of the machinery for federal-provincial relations, one has in mind much more than just the formally constituted bodies with a more or less continuing role in facilitating federal-provincial consultations and coordination. In this paper, however, I intend to analyse mainly this ensemble of federal-provincial committees.

The first point that strikes me about this machinery is a notable difference between it and that which exists for intergovernmental liaison at the international level. At the international level, we have, as I said earlier, a vast structure of international organizations and specialized agencies, conferences and committees, covering a very broad range, if not all areas of governmental activity. In addition, we have a large network of diplomatic sessions which, it should be noted, was established well before the rapid growth of specialized agencies and specialized missions.

In our federal-provincial relations, our machinery has evolved in a reverse order. We have first developed numerous committees and conferences at a specialist level. We have not had a comparable network of intelligence concerned with the total picture of intergovernmental relations. While Canada has over 400 professionals engaged in international relations, we still have very few engaged full-time in a professional way in federal-provincial relations, and our machinery makes relatively little provision to ensure continuous liaison with respect to the over-view of matters which concern both the federal and provincial governments.

The central body of our federal-provincial machinery is the Plenary Conference of Premiers and Prime Ministers. It seems to me to have been concerned more with specific policy issues than with the continuous over-view of federal-provincial matters. It began meeting sporadically in the early years of Confederation, but only in recent years has it taken on the role of a more continuing body for federal-provincial consultations. It now meets at least annually.

The rest of the machinery reflects the concentration on special program areas that I mentioned. As would be expected, this machinery tended to develop first where the constitution provides specifically for concurrent roles, notably in the agricultural sector. Then, as the country matured and the activities of government increased, we witnessed a growing interdependence between the programs of the federal and provincial spheres. Associated with this was the growth of shared-cost programs and the appearance of new consultative machinery to facilitate coordination in the areas where federal and provincial activities were coming together. This machinery sometimes developed at the ministerial level, and sometimes it involved deputy ministers or other officials. Several different committees, at different levels, have evolved within particular fields to meet specific needs.

This process has taken us to the point where in 1965 there are some 125 committees and conferences meeting on federal-provincial matters. They have taken so many different forms that a simple, concise description of the machinery becomes difficult. However, I think it will contribute to our understanding of the subject if I attempt a brief description. Before I do, I should make the point that federal-provincial machinery by no means included every body which exists to facilitate coordination of government activity in Canada. There is also a substantial body of interprovincial machinery committees and conferences which bring provincial representatives together to deal with matters of purely provincial concern. And there are the intragovernmental machinery devices which operate within one government for the purpose of dealing with federal-provincial matters. They include cabinet committees, interdepartmental committees of officials, and specialist federal-provincial relations divisions. The latter exist in the federal government, and in some if not all of the provinces. They aid in developing the positions which are taken at conferences, and in facilitating communication between conferences.

Taking all of these together, we have a large package of committees; and there are those who still disparage the committee as a device. They belong to the school of thought which defines a committee as "a collection of people who individually believe that something must be done and who collectively decide that nothing can be done," or which says of a committee's labours, "Never have so many spent so much time to accomplish so little."

The Federal-Provincial Conferences and Committees

When one is faced with the task of describing a collection of many entities, one seeks first a convenient system for classifying them. I see several different possible classifications for these committees and conferences: the broad structure, the participants, the subject matter, and the broad purpose or type of consultation. I think it could be illuminating to give a little attention to each of these possibilities.

1. The Broad Structure

Under the heading of what I call, for lack of a better word, the broad structure, I would identify seven groupings.

a. *Federal-provincial committees as such.* These, I think, are what we would normally think of first when considering the subject of federal-provincial machinery. I consider them to be federal-provincial bodies in the truest sense of the word. They are composed of ministers or officials from the federal and provincial governments, who come together as official representatives of their governments to work on matters of mutual concern. Note first that they are definitely committees of government. Note next that they are made up by the participation of individual governments, each in its own right. The federal government by virtue of its central position usually provides the chairman and secretarial services. I would place most of the committees—approximately 100, including sub-committees—in this category, and I would offer, as examples, the Plenary Conference of Prime Ministers and Premiers, the Conference of the Ministers of Welfare, the Continuing Committee on Economic and Fiscal Matters, and the meeting of Federal and Provincial Directors of Vocational Education.

I should note, also, that committees may be national in scope, involving all provinces, such as the examples I have given, or they may be regional in nature, with representation from only a few provinces plus the federal government. Of the 100 noted above, about 30 could be considered to be regional in nature. The Atlantic Fisheries Committee is one example.

These federal-provincial committees are established with varying degrees of formality. Some annual meetings are called as a matter of tradition, some are handled more casually, being called together as circumstances dictate.

b. _Federal advisory councils_. A compilation of federal-provincial committees and conferences has to include certain councils which are appointed under federal statute or order-in-council to act as advisory bodies to federal ministers. As such, they would not appear to belong in a classification of federal-provincial bodies. However, their composition, with representation from all provincial governments, is such, that they do, in effect, function as federal-provincial committees to a large extent. The process is roughly as follows. The council deliberates on a matter with the benefit of the provincial points of view. When it decides to recommend something to its ministers, this means that its provincial members are in agreement or go along with the decision and will be ready to advocate acceptance in their provinces. If the minister accepts the advice of his council and gains the approval of the federal government, he can then make a proposal to the provinces with reasonable prospects for ready acceptance. In effect, then, this body has been instrumental in facilitating the development of federal-provincial policy.

Examples of these advisory councils include the Dominion Council of Health, the National Advisory Council on Rehabilitation of Disabled Persons, the Technical and Vocational Training Council, and the National Council of Welfare.

These councils all have members not only from the governments, but from outside organizations, as well. The wide representation means they tend to become quite large, and they look as if they could be somewhat cumbersome to handle. It is interesting to speculate on the reasons for their formation. Are they needed primarily as a source of ideas, or as a public relations device to satisfy all interest groups by giving them a voice? Or are they meant to serve primarily as a device for federal-provincial consultation, but with these other elements thrown in for good measure? Whatever the answer, it seems clear that their federal-provincial role has been substantial.

c. _Quasi-independent associations_. There are certain bodies which are made up wholly, or almost wholly, of ministers or civil servants, and which are supported by government, but which are not federal-provincial committees in the usual sense of the term. They are constituted as associations and function to some extent as professional organizations or special interest groups. Their stimulus comes more from within themselves than from the governments, and the participants function more as association members than as representatives from governments. And yet, because they do bring together people in a particular field from all governments, they serve to some extent as a vehicle for federal-provincial consultation and coordination.

Examples of bodies I would place in this category include the Canadian Council of Resource Ministers, which has its own letters patent and its own staff, the Canadian Association of Administrators of Labour Legislation, and the Association of Canadian Fire Marshals.

d. Interprovincial conferences. A relatively new but in my view very significant development in intergovernmental liaison in Canada is the growth of the interprovincial machinery for consultation. One compilation, which may be incomplete, indicates that there are now about 60 formally constituted interprovincial bodies, some of which could be defined as quasi-independent or independent associations. They convene for the purpose of discussing matters of interest primarily to the provinces, or perhaps for agreeing on a joint approach to the federal government, and the provinces usually take turns acting as host to them. These conferences and committees at ministerial and official levels have a definite impact on federal-provincial relations. Indeed, they can be regarded as essential for the effective functioning of the country. I mention them here in this classification of federal-provincial devices because some do in fact assume a considerable federal-provincial role.

The Provincial Ministers of Mines Conference is an interesting example. One of the things the provincial ministers do at these conferences is to agree on the substance of a brief to be submitted to the federal government. However, the federal minister or his representatives are present as observers so that, when the provincial ministers make their formal presentation a few months later, the federal minister has had time to consider their conclusions and is in a position to discuss them.

Other examples in this category include the Conference of Provincial Premiers, which was held in Winnipeg this year, the Trade and Industry Council, and the Conference of Provincial Deputy Ministers of Public Works. (I think I should like to be invited as an "observer" to the Motion Picture Censor's Association Conference—at least I should if they compare cuttings.)

e. Subcommittees. Perhaps I can complicate the picture somewhat now by noting that there are also subcommittees. Committees seem to have two tendencies which are sometimes thought to be unfortunate: they tend to live forever, and they tend to produce offspring. The former possibly suggests something angelic about their nature; the latter, however, might be taken to invite a description of their activities which is really too uncharitable to be used here.

There are about 30 committees in my list which I would call subcommittees because they seem to have a direct reporting relationship to some other committee. They are usually at a technical level, with terms of reference requiring them to give attention to a specific problem area. The Dominion Council of

Health has several such committees reporting to it, for example. Sometimes a description of the organization becomes difficult. For example, I would describe the Committee on Technical and Vocational Training as a federal-provincial committee since it works to achieve coordination of technical and vocational training programmes at an administrative level. However, it is considered to be subordinate to the Technical and Vocational Training Council, a federal advisory body.

f. Provincial advisory committees. At the risk of extending this list excessively, I should note that in individual provinces there are some provincial committees with federal representation created to advise on matters relating to federal-provincial programs. They may be formed and chaired by provincial authorities but can be initiated on the basis of a federal proposal. Examples are the Coordinating Committees on Indian Affairs and the ARDA Joint Advisory Committees.

g. Non-government associations. There are some organizations which are quite independent of government, unlike the quasi-independent associations noted earlier, but which play an important role in federal-provincial relations nevertheless. Some associations have a substantial number of members representing governments across the country and are interested in subjects relating directly to some area of government activity. When the membership comes together to discuss its area of interest, it is inevitable that ideas will be born, thinking influenced, and policy eventually affected. The Canadian Good Roads Association is a notable example of this type of organization. Perhaps I might be so bold as to suggest that the Institute of Public Administration is another.

I have attempted so far to describe the federal-provincial machinery under a classification I have called "the broad structure." This became complicated enough, but I am now going to compound the problem by introducing a number of other possible classifications. I shall deal with them more briefly, however.

2. The Participants

The first of these I call "the participants." One could classify the federal-provincial meetings by the people who attend them. When I group them by hierarchical levels, I come up with the following count (excluding non-government associations):

Level	No. of 1965 Conferences & Committees
Prime Ministers and Premiers	2
Ministers	13
Deputy Ministers	14
Directors	27
Professional and Technical	65

I should explain that this was a rough classification involving arbitrary judgments about the level of meetings, and that the picture is frequently not clearly defined. Deputy Ministers may attend meetings which are primarily technical in nature, and so on.

I might also note that when Dr. K. W. Taylor did this exercise in 1957 he counted 5 conferences at the Ministers level, 13 at the Deputy Ministers level, 18 at the Directors level, and 28 professional or technical meetings. He, also, was modest about the absolute validity of his figures.[2]

This classification does not match up in any way with the broad structural classes previously defined. To take the ministerial conferences only, some of them could be defined as federal-provincial committees as such, while some are interprovincial, and at least one, the Resource Ministers Council, I have described as a quasi-independent association. Ministers may also meet at non-government organizations such as the Canadian Good Roads Association. Technically, it would be possible for provincial ministers to appear on some of the federal advisory councils, since the composition of some councils includes representation from some organizations to which provincial ministers belong.

3. The Subject Matter

Another obvious classification which may be used is based on the subject matter discussed by the committee. In the lists of conferences and meetings I have referred to, the committees are grouped under headings of Agriculture, Finance, Health and Welfare, and so on. As one would expect, the largest number of committees occurs in those fields where the activities of both levels of government overlap the most. For example, in the 1965 calendar of meetings the two areas with the most committees listed are Health and Welfare with 21 and Agriculture with 16.

It is of interest to note that there is a wide variety in the character of the committees which have developed for each class of subject matter. Some sectors have ministerial conferences, others do not. Some have advisory councils, others do not. Some have an extensive network of technical sub-committees, while others do not.

4. The Broad Purpose or Type of Consultations

One might also attempt to group the committees according to broad categories of purpose. Some, such as the Plenary Federal-Provincial Conference, have very broad terms of reference. Others obviously have a restricted field of activity, as, for example, the National Potato Breeding Committee. Some have elaborately spelled-out terms of reference, perhaps as a part of a formal constitution, requiring them to work toward uniformity of legislation across Canada in their field, or toward objectives of comparable significance. Others have no terms of reference other than to provide an opportunity for an exchange of views on matters of mutual interest. Some are created to advise a minister, others to advise other committees, and so on.

---

[2]*Proceedings of the Sixth Annual Conference of the Institute of Public Administration of Canada,* Toronto, 1954, p. 255.

One might define a range of the different kind of purposes which have to be served by intergovernmental consultation in Canada. I should like to suggest the following spectrum of purposes:

a. Public relations. I use the term "public relations" here, even though the public is not involved, to designate the process of getting to know one's counterparts in other governments, to the extent that a sense of *rapport* and conviviality is established. This presumably helps to oil the channels for smoother intergovernmental consultations in future.

b. Professionalization. There are some areas of specialized activity which lie almost entirely within the governments, and the specialists involved tend to want to express themselves as a professional group. A federal-provincial meeting sometimes serves as the vehicle for such expression. This type of gathering does much to advance an area of specialization through the exchange of ideas, and it also permits the development of a brotherly feeling of togetherness.

c. Advancement of knowledge. The exchange of information is a frequent purpose behind the function of a committee. Also, some federal-provincial technical committees are created specifically to inquire into a problem area to learn more about it or to encourage research for this purpose. I believe these committees have convincingly demonstrated the truth in the old adage that eleven heads are better than one.

d. Harmonization. I use this word to describe the process by which purposes are explained, suspicions are assuaged, and conflicts are removed.

e. Coordination. This is a step farther than harmonization. It implies a conscious effort to work together toward some mutually acceptable goal. In our more sceptical moments, we might describe it as the process by which activities which would otherwise be completely unintelligible become merely muddled.

f. Persuasion. This type of consultation is getting closer to the policy level. Governments may use a committee to attempt to influence the actions of others in directions deemed to be desirable.

g. Negotiation and decision-making. At this end of the spectrum is the consultation which results in a decision being reached either through agreement or through compromise. This may sound impressive. Sometimes, however, the decision may be to refer the matter to another committee.

The wide diversity in the committees' terms of reference and the problem in some cases of determining what the terms of reference are, if there are any, would make it a difficult exercise to attempt to assign present committees to these categories. For that matter, many of the committees probably work at some or even most of these objectives at some time or another. However, one might speculate that a more consistent committee structure could be established if it were formed on the basis of an accepted definition of purposes.

Concluding Observations

I hope that the approach I have taken of outlining a number of possible classifications of the federal-provincial committees will have left a reasonable overall impression of the formally established machinery which exists. By way of conclusion I would like to make a few observations on the relationship between the *need* for consultation between the provinces and the federal government—about which I spoke earlier—and the *machinery that exists* for this consultation. Is the present machinery adequate to meet present and future needs, and how might it be improved?

I think one could say, first of all, that machinery exists in most of the individual program areas where both levels of governments are active. I will go even further and say that in most if not in each of these individual program areas consultation seems to have been reasonably effective. Certainly, if these consultations have had anything to do with the rapid growth in shared-cost programs, I am impressed with their success.

I would say secondly, however, that we have to take a close look at our provision for coordination of this machinery. When a complexity of devices exists to permit consultation on a multitude of intergovernmental activities, we run the risk, unless there is adequate provision for coordination, of having a situation in which the right hand does not know what the left hand is doing. More than once I have seen this happen in international organizations. It is not inconceivable to me that it could happen in federal-provincial relations and that the position taken by the representative of one government at one federal-provincial meeting may not be wholly consistent with the position taken by another representative of the same government on a related question at another meeting.

Another and related observation that could be made on the relationship between the need and the machinery for consultation has to do with the basic economic objectives I have referred to earlier in this paper. The various federal, provincial and joint programmes may be proceeding satisfactorily, taken individually, but how do we assess their combined effect on the economy, or determine which area should receive emphasis relative to another at a particular time? Similarly, what machinery exists to facilitate consultation and coordination with regard to other areas of fiscal and economic management? I note that the federal and provincial ministers of finance and provincial treasurers held a pre-budget meeting for the first time last December. If this new ministerial committee holds annual meetings, as I hope it will, it could well develop into a body which meets this need, at least in part.

Finally, I would like to raise a question concerning the direction in which the process of federal-provincial relations is evolving. At the start we relied largely on the connections built up within the political parties representing Canadians in the House of Commons and in the provincial legislative assemblies. This machinery proved to be not entirely adequate: it was not always reliable, it was often not available when needed, and governments could not hold it responsible. Over the years we developed a considerable number of committees and other devices for consultation. The majority of these provide for contacts among specialists in a wide range of specific areas of government activity. We appear to see now the need for more frequent contacts among those who see the over-all picture of federal-provincial relations. The establishment of units responsible for federal-provincial relations in a broad way in some provinces and within the federal government indicates that our governments are responding to this need. The question which I would like to raise is this: where does this evolutionary process lead us? How far are we going to go in providing machinery for improving intelligence and coordination in Canadian federal-provincial relations?

18 Intergovernmental Liaison on Fiscal and Economic Matters: Proposals*

Institute of Intergovernmental Relations

The institutions and methods of co-operation in a federal system are heavily dependent on a federation's constitutional form and particularly on the division of powers and responsibilities. With a concentration of authority in the hands of the central government there would be little need for any elaborate machinery of intergovernmental relations. On the other hand, if extensive decentralization were to be accepted, the provinces would have limited incentive for liaison with the centre, although the federal government would have a very real need of provincial co-operation if it were to fulfil any national purpose. Special status of one form or another would bring with it other problems which need not concern us here.

While flexible enough to meet the requirements of most situations, our approach to the problems of liaison in fiscal and economic matters is based on what seems to us to be a realistic acceptance of the facts as they are and as they must be if we are to preserve the Canadian nation in recognizable form. This form, we believe, is that of a strong central government working in tandem with strong regional governments in the growing place of the public sector in today's society.

The Co-ordination of Policy

In our examination of these federal-provincial fiscal and economic relations we have attempted to understand why the deficiencies in the most important areas of mutual interest have occurred. We believe that the answer lies to an important extent in the difficulty of adjusting changing pragmatic interests often highly political in nature with the basic responsibilities of the constitution, sometimes not too clearly defined and understood.

In our liaison proposals we attempt to meet this within the present governmental structure but the limits are clear. We must acknowledge that the

*From *Report: Intergovernmental Liaison on Fiscal and Economic Matters,* (Ottawa: Queen's Printer, 1969), pp. 255-301. Reprinted by permission of Information Canada.

success of the approach depends to a great extent upon the willingness of the partners to accept the obligations as well as the advantages of such operations.

Under existing conditions the fiscal and economic content of the federal-provincial relationship must remain of predominant interest. Obviously the highest level of policy responsibility must be involved in matters which so vitally affect all governments as well as the state of the total economy. The plenary federal-provincial conference has been used for this purpose and will continue to have a primary role. But we should consider how its part can be re-designed so that it can operate to better effect and to this end another institution enters into our basic proposals. This is the committee of Ministers of Finance and Provincial Treasurers. While distinct in operation and membership the fields of responsibility of these two groups are complementary and both are fundamental to the development of an effective system of intergovernmental relationships.

A. The Federal-Provincial Conference of Prime Ministers and Premiers

While in theory at least a meeting of first ministers, the plenary conference has become a general gathering increasingly cumbersome in size. This had been dictated in large measure by its concern with a number of detailed objectives which have required a widely representative group of ministers and advisers from the various governments. It is likely that over two hundred ministers and officials were present at the last plenary conference.

A conference of this size, regardless of the fact that there are few active participants, is not a good medium for free discussion of basic issues. Further, its size raises important questions of the ability to maintain the confidential nature of the proceedings where this is desirable. We found a strong body of opinion in favour of smaller confidential meetings, especially where negotiations are involved.

But we should not reject the advantages of public education and interest that go with access to such discussions. There is growing acceptance of the idea of open meetings following the success of the Confederation of Tomorrow Conference in Toronto in November 1967 and the Constitutional Conference in Ottawa in February 1968. The answer may lie in separating the work of the plenary conference into two parts, one concerned with matters of high policy determination often involving negotiations of a political nature, the other taken up with a more general coverage of matters of principle and opinion.

1. The Committee of First Ministers

We propose that a top-level policy meeting, formally constituted, should be held at least annually consisting of the federal prime minister and the prime ministers and premiers of the ten provinces. The objective would be to examine in confidence the whole range of matters of current mutual interest in principle, with regard to their effect rather than to the detail of their operation, with a view of determining what joint objectives might be sought and what means might be employed in seeking them. This group would not concern itself with detailed programme development but with the direction and course of government and the delineation and reconciliation of objectives. A major concern would undoubtedly be the determination of the general nature of priorities within and between governments and in relation to the state of the economy and in this the close relationship with the finance ministers could be of great importance.

As the first ministers would be dealing with matters of high principle rather than of detailed substance, limited support at the meetings of advisers, ministerial and official, would be both desirable and practicable. We emphasize the value of direct and private personal exchanges in such situations and these are not usually convenient in crowds. In many respects this committee could follow the general pattern of the present Provincial Premiers' Conference, with emphasis on vital matters of mutual interest. The nearest parallel in other federations would be the Premiers' Conference in Australia.

2. The Federal-Provincial Conference

The first ministers will undoubtedly decide that certain matters require the wider consideration which can best be provided by a plenary conference of the kind to which we have become accustomed. In fact while the first ministers might be able to deal with a number of issues, part of their concern would be with the question of just what matters should be referred to the plenary sessions and what to functional groups. For example, questions of principle in matters of wide interest and concern such as the federal-provincial fiscal arrangements or the constitutional questions that currently concern us could be of the kind for plenary treatment.

We do suggest, however, that every effort should be made to limit the agenda of these conferences. In the past where a broad and varied agenda has been put forward, the demands of time have meant that inadequate attention was paid to the important parts of it in many cases. The use of functional sub-conferences has much to commend it and we will deal with this further. An agenda concentrated on matters of broad impact is the only one that should concern a plenary conference. If there are many topics demanding attention, better results would come from several meetings with only those directly concerned present on each occasion.

If the plenary conferences concern themselves with matters of broad principle and opinion and leave detailed negotiations for more confidential surroundings, the advantages of public access to such conferences should be recognized. While there is certainly not enough evidence in the response to the two open meetings held so far to indicate a sustained public interest over time, the advantages of public involvement in fundamental matters of national importance warrant further experience with direct access. There may be an additional bonus in that given such a forum, participants may feel less impelled to provide the public through the press with their own views for political purposes regardless of the effect such statements may have on the course of the discussions. We repeat, however, that we do not believe public meetings are the appropriate media for specific and detailed negotiations between interested parties. The reasons are much too obvious to require re-statement here.

B. The Committee of Ministers of Finance and Provincial Treasurers

In the organization of most Canadian governments, federal and provincial, the departments of finance or the provincial treasuries have certain broadly based responsibilities which place them apart from other ministries. This is particularly so with respect to our interest in fiscal and economic matters and it is for this reason and in this context that we preserve a special place for the finance ministers' committee. This committee should operate primarily as a staff arm of the conference of first ministers and the plenary conference even though it would also have certain functional responsibilities. Its basic purpose would be to advise on the harmonization of fiscal and economic policies and to deal with those matters which the first ministers referred to it for action or advice. This committee would be concerned particularly with such matters as fiscal and monetary problems, the projection over the longer term of government revenues and expenditures, the development of long-term budgeting for both capital and current expenditure, technical methods for the control of expenditure and the more effective collection of public revenue, public borrowing, harmonization of budgetary accounting and financial statistics practices and all matters related to the fiscal and economic problems of governments.

We fully appreciate that in some cases other departments of government will be intimately concerned in these processes. We see no reason why their ministers should not continue to participate in the proceedings when it is appropriate that they should do so.

This committee would be called upon to assume most of the responsibilities which have been carried out by the Tax Structure Committee and the existing finance ministers' committee in the immediate past.

C. Functional Committees

An examination of the existing structure suggests that a good deal more consistency could be introduced into federal-provincial functional relationships. What we have, in many cases, seems to have developed from responses to individual situations rather than from any organized attempt to deal with functional areas of related interest.

In most areas of the public sector there are interests of sufficiently widespread importance to warrant representation from both levels of government. We found, in the course of our study, a substantial body of opinion in favour of this mutual involvement even where the strict constitutional position did not seem to require it. There was a point of view that favoured a wide federal participation as providing a cohesive force which operated to the advantage of all. Experience in other federations would seem to lend support to the approach.

We propose, therefore, that there be established in support of the Federal-Provincial Conference, a series of functional standing committees of ministers, representing the Government of Canada and all ten provincial governments. Such committees would be created to deal with matters in broadly defined functional areas and while they would generally follow the accepted division of ministerial responsibilities, they would not necessarily have to conform to them. Such functional areas could include: agriculture and rural development; labour, manpower and training; health; welfare; national resources; and we suggest, even education, which might include the manpower and training function. Ministerial committees in some of these areas already exist. Clearly the membership of such functional committees would have to be fluid with the appropriate special sub-committees on particular topics, but continuity could be maintained through a permanent representative from each member government, though its secretariat, and perhaps by a standing chairman.

In certain cases interprovincial gatherings would also be required where matters of purely regional interest were involved. Such groups could meet independently of the functional committees but there would often be advantages of continuity and economy in meetings held prior to or subsequent to the related federal-provincial gatherings.

D. Support Groups (Officials)

An examination of the inventory in the appendix indicates that ministerial meetings have been strongly supported in some cases by committees of officials, sometimes on a continuing, sometimes on an 'ad hoc' basis. This is as it should be for in many instances the matters dealt with are of a detailed and technical nature. There has often been, however, a lack of form and structure with the result that it has been frequently difficult to relate the growth of these various bodies to any consistent programme of federal-provincial co-operation.

But as the problems of our intergovernmental relations become more complex and the solutions more sophisticated, the old methods will not always serve. In recognition of the broad increased responsibilities that will fall on ministerial bodies, we offer the following support organizations, emphasizing the need for a close and continuing relationship between policy and administrative groups:

(1) A continuing committee of senior officials in support of the Federal-Provincial Conference of Prime Ministers and Premiers and the Federal-Provincial Conference.

Under the present system the main continuing official-level support for the Federal-Provincial plenary conferences has come from the Federal-Provincial Continuing Committee on Fiscal and Economic Matters. If we examine the history of this relationship we find that it stemmed from the preoccupation of the plenary conference with fiscal and economic matters, particularly those connected with the financial agreements.

With a strong and continuing central role for the conference of first ministers and the Federal-Provincial Conference, a new official support group should be established. Such a group would be made up of the most senior policy advisers. Who these would be would, of course, vary as between governments, but in each case there would have to be a close and continuing relationship of the individual members with their first ministers. To an important extent there should be a common element of membership between this support committee and the existing Federal-Provincial Continuing Committee on Fiscal and Economic Matters. The use of alternate or associate delegates on these two committees would likely be essential in achieving effective co-ordination between their activities.

Before proposing the formation of the new group we gave careful attention to the role of the Federal-Provincial Continuing Committee on Fiscal and Economic Matters as it has developed since 1956. We wished to determine whether or not it might fulfill the support functions in relation to the Committee of First Ministers that it has for the Plenary Conference in the past. We have come to the conclusion that with the increased complexity of the demands on the liaison structure and the growing tendency to centre federal-provincial activities around the head of government in most cases, the Continuing Committee would have to assume a dual personality in its relationships with the first ministers and the finance ministers. In fact, it has already had to do this, on occasion. Under the circumstances and taking into account the increased responsibilities of the Continuing Committee, if the Tax Structure Committee is dissolved as we propose, it seemed only sensible to accept the situation as it would almost certainly exist in practice and to provide for the new senior officials' committee, always recognizing its very close community of interest and responsibility with the Continuing Committee.

We put a good deal of emphasis on the need for such a senior officials' committee to be formalized and of a continuing nature meeting regularly and as circumstances require. Like all federal-provincial committees it could not take decisions itself nor could it assume a policy role, but it would not serve its proper purpose if it were merely ancillary to the ministers it served and was without identity and purpose of its own.

(2) The Federal-Provincial Continuing Committee on Fiscal and Economic Matters.

While composed for the most part of finance deputies, since its inception in 1956 and increasingly over the years a number of other government officials have been associated with it in areas of their special interests when circumstances made this advisable.

As we have already noted, the Continuing Committee would lose some of its present authority as the senior officials' committee with the formation of the proposed group. But its duties as the working arm of the finance ministers' committee would involve important alternative responsibilities, particularly as they develop under the proposed re-organization. This would apply particularly with respect to the work of the kind undertaken by the Tax Structure Committee which we have proposed the finance ministers should undertake. It was as the operational group for that organization that the Continuing

Committee had its most sustained period of activity since the early years of its existence.

This Committee would become the clearing-house for all technical matters which were of fiscal and economic content and in this responsibility it would have to act as the co-ordinator in the application of many policies in functional areas of government where there were fiscal and economic interests. Its relationships with the senior officers' committee in the co-ordination of fiscal and economic matters within total intergovernmental relationships would be of vital importance.

(3) Committees of Officials Subordinate to the Functional Committees.

The series of functional committees of ministers with its appropriate structure of sub-committees, has an important place in the proposed liaison structure. In order that they may perform to the best advantage in the various areas of interest, they should be supported by the necessary subordinate committees of officials as the particular matter under consideration requires. Logically the subordinate group should function in preparation for the ministerial meetings and in harmony with them. To the extent necessary, each such subordinate group should be capable of further division where the participation of technically qualified officers could be available. As an example of what we mean, the Federal-Provincial Continuing Committee on Fiscal and Economic Matters has on occasion found itself dealing with questions of high technical content. In the past it has not always developed the necessary detailed approach. We understand that this has now been recognized and that special sub-committees are being formed to deal with special problems such as that of the integration of activities related to programme budgeting and its procedures.

We are of the opinion that the system of committee relationships which we have outlined would make superfluous in the intergovernmental context those advisory groups and quasi-independent organizations which have come into being over the years. The purpose of an intergovernmental organization is to reconcile the policies and activities of the different governments. This is a proper responsibility for ministers and officials. What assistance from the outside governments may use in developing policies is something else again. We are not in any way suggesting that independent advice should not be sought where it could be helpful in advancing the public interest.

E. The Secretariat

The intergovernmental structure we have outlined, if complex, is still more logical and a good deal tidier than that which is now employed. If it is to work to the best advantage, however, we believe it must be served by a full-time secretariat.

If the duties of such a body were purely mechanical, the arranging and servicing of conferences and meetings and the like, a continuing organization would not be required and the practice of having these tasks performed through a federal office could continue, although the increasing burden of work would unquestionably warrant a more specific allocation of adequate resources. We believe, however, that the responsibilities involved in the structure we have proposed could not be served on a casual basis. As we see it the work of such a group would include not only serving the conference of first ministers and the plenary conference but that of co-ordinating the activities of all other conferences and committees which form the inter-governmental system.

Such duties would be important and extensive and would include the tasks of arranging meetings, drafting agendas, keeping and circulating records of proceedings, etc. To meet the requirements which are called for, it would be essential that the secretariat undertake duties beyond those of a purely routine nature. If it is to be a positive force, it will have to provide back-ground material, preparing it where it was not otherwise available, maintain active communication between members of conferences and committees and, where necessary, originate activities which follow logically from the respon-sibilities of its place in the structure of liaison. It should be competent to co-ordinate studies if so instructed and aid in their preparation if this is required. We do not recommend that the secretariat should assume responsi-bility for original research involving positive policy proposals as this could be detrimental to its relationship with member governments. It should be qualified however to suggest any projects it considered necessary and be able to see them carried out either through member governments or by special contract arrangements.

We believe that as the secretariat developed it would be of great support to the conferences and committees in the assistance and guidance it would be able to give in its role as a trusted intermediary, as a vehicle for the communi-cation of information and as an agent in the promotion of understanding and co-operation among member governments.

In view of the special place proposed for the finance ministers' committee, we considered whether or not a special secretariat should be organized to serve that body. We do not think these responsibilities can be met without adequate staff support. Rather, however, than constitute such support as a separate entity the resource would be better provided as part of the main secretariat with necessary specialist personnel assigned to fiscal and economic duties. This is consistent with the close association of the finance ministers with the first ministers which we see as essential to effective fiscal and economic liaison.

We do not propose that a special permanent secretariat be established for the functional committees. Necessary secretarial requirements can be supplied through member governments as they now are in most cases, and co-ordinated by the main secretariat which can assume the responsibility for consolidation and analysis of reports in the broad policy contexts for the purposes of the first ministers and the finance ministers. Members of functional committees, as all others, would continue to report individually to their own governments.

Much, of course, will depend on how the functional committees develop. This will vary and some may become centres for specialized study and research. In such cases the proposed staffing is not likely to be adequate and the situation will have to be re-assessed. We would urge, however, that the creation of special continuing staff bodies should be approached with caution as a proliferation of secretarial organizations attached to functional groups might solve one problem at the expense of creating a more serious one—the development of a new bureaucratic structure in the Canadian governmental system.

Organization and Responsibility

Answers to the questions of the need for a continuing secretariat, its form of organization and its responsibilities have been hard to find. A number of problems arise which to our knowledge have not been answered in any of the various proposals that have been made from time to time in this connection. Involving as they do not only its effective performance but its acceptability as an objective instrument of intergovernmental co-operation, they cannot be ignored or left to settle themselves. No such organization can operate usefully unless it knows what it is supposed to do and where the lines of its direction lie. If it does not know the tendency will be for it to accomplish little of a positive nature, or at the other extreme, to take to itself authority which it was never intended it should have.

Accepting the view that the proposed secretariat must be responsible to some person or some body, we have concluded that in principle this must be the Committee of First Ministers which we regard as the focal point of all intergovernmental concerns. At the same time we recognize that first ministers are not always readily available and that there will be many questions of a more or less administrative nature where guidance will be needed. We believe that common sense dictates that such matters should be referred by the secretariat to the senior officials' committee which we have proposed. In both cases the requirements of convenience suggest that communication will in routine matters be through the chairman of the committee. But we would emphasize that acceptance of this as a practical method should in no way inhibit direct communication with individual committee members where the situation seems to call for it. We do not see any real difficulty in this as presumably any person appointed to head the secretariat would be sufficiently astute to judge where such situations existed and to act accordingly. If he did not always judge correctly his errors would soon no doubt be made known to him.

This inevitably brings up the matter of the chairmanship of the committees and conferences. We see no reason why the rather distinct position of the federal government should not continue to be recognized as it has been in the past and the meetings of the first ministers and the plenary conferences presided over by the Prime Minister of Canada. We have encountered no objections to this in principle and it is supported by logic and concept as well as by tradition. We would go further and suggest that it would likely be the most suitable practical solution to have all permanently established federal-provincial conferences or committees chaired by the permanent representative of the national government. As the secretariat would almost certainly be located in Ottawa, the advantages of convenience in such an arrangement argue in favour of it, regardless of any principles that might be involved. The alternatives of a rotating chairmanship or of an independent chairman from outside government do not seem to provide a satisfactory alternative either in principle or practice.

What we have sought to provide in our proposal is a secretariat that will assist in the development of effective co-operation between governments but which will not develop for itself an identity that will intrude upon or replace the essential political processes of the federal-provincial relationship. In this respect the central organization of international bodies has not provided the necessary guidance. The role, for example, of the Secretary-General of the United Nations does not seem appropriate in the federal context. We are not dealing with distinct and separate political entities which have agreed to consult on their common interests. We are dealing with what are essentially the individual parts of an organic whole whose political relationships are close and continuing.

Responsible as it is to all the people of the nation, the central government has a position and an obligation distinct from that of the individual states of a federation. Essentially the basic responsibility to preserve and promote the unity and cohesiveness of the country belongs to it and while the states can and will contribute to these ends in many important aspects through the influence of their assigned powers, they do not have the same fundamental purpose. If this were not the case the whole reason for the federation would in itself be suspect.

In the past it has been the practice for the Government of Canada to supply the conference with the necessary secretarial services. For example, the Privy Council Office has serviced the plenary conferences. The Federal-Provincial Relations Division of the Department of Finance has looked after the needs of the finance ministers' meetings and those of the Federal-Provincial Continuing Committee on Fiscal and Economic Matters. If the responsibilities of a secretariat are limited to the more mechanical aspects of the job, we see no reason why such arrangements should not be continued. But if the responsibilities are more extensive, as we propose that they should be, some more independent arrangements will be required.

There are two possible alternatives. The most practicable, in our opinion, would be for the secretariat to be supplied from the resources of the Government of Canada, with the concurrence of the provinces on organization and personnel. This we understand is now being done for the Constitutional Conference. We see no reason why this should not prove satisfactory in practice, provided the federal government would be prepared to establish the organization on a continuing and independent basis outside the influence of its policy and direction. The secretariat in such a case would be strengthened by the seconding to it of Provincial personnel from time to time.

The second alternative would be for a completely independent secretariat to be organized, perhaps along the lines of that which operates for the Canadian Council of Resource Ministers. This approach lacks the clarity and the simplicity of the first with respect to problems of tenure and finance but these are certainly not insurmountable. Insofar as the relationship to the conferences and committees which it serves are concerned there does not seem to be any important practical difference from a federally supported but independent group although a matter of principle may be involved, the importance of which is a matter which can only be assessed by those directly concerned.

We are quite conscious of the objections that can be raised to the creation of an independent bureaucracy outside the scope of existing government organization. While they are valid, we would not attach sufficient weight to them to void the proposal if an independent secretariat is considered desirable in principle. We would, however, urge that as far as possible an independent secretariat should be staffed from the public services with officials seconded by their governments for reasonable terms. This would go some way at least toward reducing the influence of any third-tier bureaucracy which concerns many people. It would at the same time provide a more knowledgeable organization and might usefully broaden the experience and even raise the level of tolerance of the individuals concerned.

The question of the financing of the secretariat has been raised. We see no reason why the continuing costs of the operation (other than salaries and related benefits of seconded provincial personnel) should not be borne by the Government of Canada as part of its national responsibility. However, if some sharing of costs is thought desirable either in the case of a federally appointed body or one fully independent, there should be no serious obstacle to agreement on a reasonable method of pro-rating the amount involved.

F. Research Organization

No one is likely to question seriously the claim that research in the field of fiscal and economic matters where intergovernmental interests are involved has been less than adequate. While the situation has improved in recent years with a substantial growth of interest in these problems on the part of the universities and other independent organizations, the greater part of the effective work in applied research is undertaken within government departments, especially those of the federal government. Valuable as much of it is, it is always open to challenge on the grounds of its objectivity, rightly or wrongly.

Except in the case of the Tax Structure Committee, federal-provincial co-operation in fiscal and economic research has not been very productive. Even there the difficulties of objective research by intergovernmental bodies in areas of mutual interests were unfortunately only too clearly illustrated.

Most government research, at least within departments, tends to be related to practical situations and solutions. Unavoidably, the necessary information is often classified and unavailable to outsiders. This is probably as it must be, although sometimes classification seems to be carried to rather unlikely extremes. In any event this seems to indicate that a close relationship to government is an essential if effective applied research is to be fruitful in these areas. In such cases the responsibilities of the secretariat would be confined to the organization and co-ordination of material prepared within governments.

But this does not mean that all fiscal and economic research in intergovernmental areas must be carried on only within governments. There is an urgent need for more to be done in the general and theoretical fields of all aspects of Canadian federalism including intergovernmental liaison in all its aspects. We strongly recommend that greater encouragement and attention should be given by all levels of government to such studies. This can best be done by supporting the work of independent individuals and organizations as was done in certain areas of the Tax Structure Committee's work. In some cases this might be appropriately dealt with through the secretariat, in others it would be better to have special studies commissioned by individual governments where there was a special interest, with the work co-ordinated for the purposes of the intergovernmental committee or conference through the secretariat.

But the situation seems to warrant something more specifically designed for the purpose. In our reference to the United States we made mention of the useful work of the Advisory Commission on Intergovernmental Relations, a body established by Congress but widely representative of various interests, national, state and local. We think that a similar organization set up under Act of Parliament with provinces having an effective voice in the selection of members, would be of great value in the examination of many of the serious problems with which we continuously will be concerned.

G. Economic Advice

The Economic Council of Canada, while broadly based in its representation, is nevertheless a legal creation of Parliament. It is not a body in which the provinces can feel any substantial or direct involvement. Some provinces do have economic bodies very roughly equivalent to the Economic Council, but in most cases they appear to be neither active nor influential. The relationship of these bodies to the Economic Council has not proved a very effective one despite the efforts of the Council to make it so.

One possible answer to the need for a wider involvement in long term economic research commends itself to us as being worthy of greater consideration than it appears to have had. At a conference of provincial premiers in Victoria in 1962, a proposal was made by the Premier of Manitoba, Mr. Roblin, that an economic advisory council should be established representative of both levels of government. Presumably such a council would not be directly representative of the individual provinces and Canada but would be selected from a slate of candidates put forward by the various governments. This would form a quasi-independent advisory group for all governments in much the same way as the Economic Council does for Canada. Such a council would tend to be regionally oriented rather than representative of various interests in the economy but it would serve the same basic purposes.

There are obvious difficulties in implementing such a system but if the structure of federal-provincial liaison is to be formalized some such advisory body for the first ministers and the finance ministers would be an essential element in the same way that an advisory group in intergovernmental relations could serve a different or related need. We suggest therefore that the present structure and status of the Economic Council should be re-examined to see whether or not it would be profitable to convert it into an intergovernmental advisory council for problems of the longer term rather than one that is solely the responsibility of the Government of Canada.

H. Legislative Committees

While this area could be regarded as somewhat marginal to our terms of reference, we have encountered enough interest in the subject to lead us to believe it is of sufficient importance to warrant attention.

To the best of our knowledge neither in Parliament nor in any of the provincial legislatures is there any involvement of members through committees of the various houses especially charged with the consideration of intergovernmental relations. This is in contrast to the U.S. experience where a committee in each of the houses of Congress has a continuing interest in such matters.

As things now are, private members can become involved in these important matters only when specific bills or motions are up for consideration, during such debates as those on the Throne Speech or the Budget or in the examination of Estimates. The careful surveillance that could come from the work of a standing committee in which private members could play some continuing part is not available.

We attach particular importance to this because we fear that there is sometimes an inclination on the part of most governments to take to themselves a responsibility for long-term decisions on broad issues of principle in which the electorate has had no voice. Some aspects of constitutional amendment provide a case in point where a broader consensus of public opinion seems called for. The value of a legislative involvement would be in its function as a counter-weight to the over-vesting of interests by governments in themselves. Through the use of standing committees and the examinations that they might conduct in public hearings, interested and informed members of the general population would have an opportunity to be heard that is not easily available to them under present executive control. We strongly recommend that any reorganization of the legislative process for Parliament or any of the provincial legislatures should provide for standing committees of Parliament or the legislatures in the field of intergovernmental relations. An informed and involved body of opinion in the legislative branches might go some way to resolving some of the artificial issues which can develop when political interests conflict with more fundamental requirements of the country.

I. Bilateral Arrangements

In a country as large and as diversified as Canada, there will frequently be economic situations which concern the federal government and one or more but not all the provinces. In such cases the structure of liaison that we have proposed will need to be modified.

Provided that bilateral or non-inclusive arrangements are not used where the interests of all parts of the country are involved, we see such instruments as 'task forces', as having a useful role to play. Conferences or committees assigned to deal with particular situations can also be valuable in special circumstances. But such situations should be clearly explained to those governments not directly concerned so that no misunderstandings follow. Where there are situations which touch upon the interests of all provinces, all members of the federation should be consulted through the established machinery we have proposed.

In the economic fields in particular, certain bilateral programmes are entered into from time to time with continuing involvement of the parties concerned. In such cases the device of a crown corporation reflecting federal and provincial interests in the manner of the Cape Breton Development Corporation would seem to be worth serious consideration. This device contains the freedom of action of the corporation with the joint responsibility of intergovernmental agreement and might be more widely applied, particularly in special situations.

J. Regional Arrangements

Earlier in this report we discussed some suggestions that would have had federal representatives stationed in each provincial capital and conversely provincial representatives permanently located in Ottawa.

On the surface these two ideas may seem complementary. We regard them as serving quite different purposes. The federal government has a national responsibility which it can only perform adequately if it is conscious of the different attitudes and needs of the different regions of the country. It is an admitted fact that the Government of Canada sometimes is not well informed as to the developments in areas of provincial government responsibility where there is a national influence, until the situation has hardened to such an extent that the problems of reconciliation are multiplied. Such a situation is not lightly tolerated in international affairs although it may occur and while we accept the fact that the situations are not parallel, we see sufficient similarity to warrant further consideration. We recognize the objections, not the least of which is the danger of confusing normal channels of communication and authority, but the potential benefits under the right approach seem to offset them.

In theory, federal ministers and members from the different regions of Canada have performed this liaison function, but we doubt that in the depth and breadth of their national responsibilities they can or should continue to do so. A department for regional affairs has just now been announced. We are not as yet entirely clear as to its intended responsibilities but presume that its purpose is to co-ordinate federal programmes with respect to their regional and national effects. Such a department can contribute a great deal to the improvement of liaison with the provinces if it has as one of its purposes the relating of national policies to the needs and wants of the various regions of Canada. There are, however, some potential hazards here of undue interference with the established processes of administration which suggest that any such agency must be handled with extreme care, intelligence and diplomacy.

All this, of course, is tied in to the need for greater regional authority in government departments within the carefully established limits of consistent policy. This subject was dealt with, if briefly, in the Third Annual Review of the Economic Council of Canada. Regional interest of the kind proposed could, we think, do a great deal to pull together the isolated threads of federal government authority in the regions so that they become part of a more effective fabric of governmental activity. If this is not a function of the new department, we suggest that consideration should be given to the setting up of regional representatives in provincial capitals for this purpose responsibile to the intergovernmental co-ordinating organization within the central government.

The advantages advanced with respect to provincial representation in Ottawa are not nearly so evident. The provinces are not charged with a co-ordinating responsibility and, while there would be occasional advantages in the convenience of communication that could result, we agree with most provincial people with whom we talked that introducing a further link between federal and provincial operating departments is superfluous. The resulting complications would far outweigh the benefits.

K. Internal Organization

It has been evident to us that one of the most important factors determining the effectiveness of intergovernmental liaison is the quality of internal organization of governments themselves. This applies throughout the whole structure from the policy-making machinery itself to the operating departmental organization.

Although there have been noticeable changes for the better in recent years, governments generally have been content to leave matters involving intergovernmental relationships to the departments directly concerned. Co-ordination as part of total government policy has often been lacking. If any evidence of this is needed, a reference to the list of intergovernmental committees, etc., should provide it. Where the co-ordination has existed it has been more as part of the financial process than as any part of the structure of total government operation.

Those governments which do not have the cabinet committees and related interdepartmental committees of officials would find it valuable to establish and use them. But in the growing complexity of the process this may not be enough. Some governments, notably that of Quebec and in a somewhat different way, Ontario, have found a special department or agency desirable in the central co-ordinating responsibility for federal-provincial matters. How far and how specialized the approach should be will depend on the extent co-ordination demands, the size of the government and the degree of control considered desirable. All governments may not consider an organization so influential as the Quebec Department of Intergovernmental Affairs necessary. But some co-ordinating unit should exist and should be placed in the special position which will enable it to deal with these matters of mutual involvement in a way that will eliminate much of the confusion which has been so typical of the situation in the past without interfering with the established flow of business which is carried on directly between federal and provincial departments. Certainly we believe that a strong central authority in the Government of Canada is called for, preferably as a part of the Prime Minister's organization.

It has been common practice in the past for the finance departments to have a principal influence in these matters in both the federal government and the provinces. This is a recognition of the importance of the fiscal fact in federalism. We believe that it is essential that this continue and with particular weight in the matters of our direct concern, fiscal and economic policy. But so important are the questions of intergovernmental involvement that any central authority must be directly responsible to the office of the first minister and not merely be another department of government. Unless this relationship to the first minister is clearly established, the authority might better remain with the finance department. Regardless of how this is handled, the relationship of any such organization to the finance department would have to be very close.

But internal organization will, like intergovernmental organization, be no better than the people that run it. We have become very conscious in this study of wide differences in the resources that different governments are prepared to devote to their part in the liaison process. It must be recognized, although apparently it not always is, that the effectiveness of a province's representations will depend as much on the quality of its representatives as on the merits of its case. While ministers and officials have usually made every effort to meet their responsibilities, the fact is clear that in some provinces inadequate provision has been made for the necessary support. Unless they are prepared to provide it, they are handicapped and have little cause to complain if their cause is dependent on the goodwill of others rather than on the merits of their case.

L. Procedural Matters

Questions of operating procedure may not be fundamental and in most instances will not involve any important changes in structure or organization. Nevertheless they can be of great importance, for while they do not provide final answers in themselves, attention to them may have a substantial influence in improving liaison arrangements.

Such matters can be divided into three interrelated sections: vehicles of co-ordination, personnel and procedures.

(1) *Vehicles of co-ordination*:

(a) 'task forces' of federal officials visiting the provincial government departments to work out details and adjust differences in programmes or policies in advance of formalization and subsequently for administrative harmony, should be given greater emphasis than they have in the past.

(b) 'consultants' on the staffs of federal departments should be made available to the provinces in matters of fiscal and economic significance as well as in programme areas where special knowledge is available. This is already done to some extent in special fields. In certain cases the service could flow in the opposite direction.

(c) senior officials at both levels of government should make greater efforts to visit the various regions of Canada so that they may be better informed and consequently better able to assess situations with which they must deal. This applies particularly to federal officials in what might be termed broad policy areas, including officers of such organizations as the Bank of Canada.

(d) modern communication techniques involving the use of such devices as 'Telex', the 'Ampliphone' and perhaps closed-circuit television, should be considered as possible substitutes for meetings of limited importance which while sometimes desirable nevertheless may not justify their costs in time, money or inconvenience.

(2) *Personnel:* As all governments presumably are interested in the same ultimate end, that of providing the best public service at the least possible cost, every effort should be made to avoid unnecessary conflict and competition. This is increasingly important in the field of intergovernmental personnel practices. The supply of competent staff particularly at policy advisory levels is limited and should be used to the best advantage. For this reason co-operation should be sought not only through recruiting standards but through training programmes and facilities. We do not suggest an all-Canada public service, although it might have some real advantages in certain fields, but we do believe there should be much greater interest in the mobility of trained public personnel either by loan or by transfer so that the available sources may be used in the greatest public interest.

(3) *Procedures*:

(a) Improved conference 'housekeeping' with respect to such matters as the preparation and distribution of agendas, documents, background papers, and the like, would add substantially to the effectiveness and harmony of meetings. If a full-time secretariat is organized this should be covered automatically.

(b) More attention should be given to the intangibles of co-operation in the more ready acceptance of the process as one of partnership rather than rivalry, avoidance of unnecessary rigidity in established positions in negotiation, 'one-upmanship' in the use of press releases and public interviews, leakages of information in advance of formal agreement or understanding, the presentation of the 'fait accompli' when negotiation was expected. All these, often minor in themselves, contribute to misunderstanding and resentment and make true cooperation doubly difficult.

(c) It has not been the practice in federal-provincial meetings for votes to be taken either on matters of substance or procedure. Suggestions have been made occasionally that this should be changed and as an example the practice of one of the most effective intergovernmental institutions, the Australian Loan Council, has been given. Voting in intergovernmental bodies within a federal state raises a number of difficulties. The question of the relative power of the central voice as compared to those of the provinces or states is one of these. The relative weights of the different regional governments is another. All these might eventually be settled, although the process could raise other issues equally hard to resolve. But essentially the course of action rests on the fact that a federal-provincial conference or committee is not a decision-making body but a forum for seeking a consensus amongst governments, each of authority within its own defined limits. Under the circumstances the present procedure would seem to be the proper one.

(d) Some thought might be given to a more equitable method of sharing conference costs among governments. Present practices tend to penalize those provinces geographically distant from Ottawa as compared to those relatively near. Greater consideration might also be given to holding more meetings away from the national capital. The advantages of the central location are obvious and in certain cases an Ottawa meeting is essential but in some situations the difficulties could be overcome and a more central meeting place chosen. There is precedence for this in a number of cases in meetings of special groups. We do not however suggest that meetings of the first ministers should be held outside the national capital except under exceptional circumstances.

Concluding Remarks

The problems we have had to face in trying to develop a system of intergovernmental liaison in the broad field of fiscal and economic matters has been how to make possible a workable system of consultation and co-operation without interfering with the basic constitutional powers and responsibilities as they exist under our present system.

We have proposed an extensive network of communication which we think is structurally more logical and direct than that which now exists. It involves the creation of certain new intergovernmental bodies, which we believe will be assuming, in most cases, responsibilities now carried on less effectively in other ways. The net dollar cost should be no more and could be less. The benefits that flow from this restructuring should in any case more than justify any expense that may be incurred.

We are confident that the changes we have proposed are consistent with

Canada's present constitutional structure and will enable it to adjust more easily to today's changing need. We also believe the resulting structure will be flexible enough for any changes that are likely to take place in the foreseeable future.

Throughout the study we have emphasized that we have been speaking of the co-ordination of information and of co-operation, not of joint decision-making. We do not regard this either as being consistent in most cases with assigned constitutional responsibilities in a federal state or with the responsibility of the government to its electors. Nor is it likely to be effective in most practical aspects.

While consultation should be extended to its fullest reasonable limits, we appreciate that such limits do exist. Governments will not always be able to consult fully in every aspect of their policies and activities even though the influence may sometimes be wide spread. Even when they have consulted they will still have to be prepared to assume the full responsibilities which are theirs. Thus we do not believe that the federal and provincial governments can act jointly responsible in all aspects of fiscal and economic policy. Certain major parts of it must be federal. Other important aspects are clearly provincial. It is incumbent upon each government to make its decisions on the basis of its own best judgment and consistent with its responsibilities within the federation and its duties to its people.

But nevertheless we emphasize that it is incumbent upon each to consult with the others before a course of action is decided upon whenever it is appropriate and possible and to co-operate to the fullest extent when this has been done. Even in areas where the mutual interest may be more actual than legal, as say in the control of air transport policy from the federal side or in education from the provincial, the obligation remains. Both the national and the local interest will require that all factors be given proper weight in the policy-making process.

Very briefly what we regard as essential to a working federation can be summed up in the following requirements.

(1) as clear as possible a definition of constitutional powers and responsibilities,

(2) an effective internal organization of government for relating policies and programmes in different functional areas within a total policy framework,

(3) a systematic structure of intergovernmental relationships with the purpose of all possible co-ordination of individual jurisdictional responsibilities, but stopping short of formal joint decision-making,

(4) a political acceptance of mutual involvement and obligations which are inherent in any co-operative approach to federalism.

No structure of liaison can be more than a means to an end. Its ultimate value will depend on the use that is made of it and upon the degree of trust that is placed in it, always accepting the practical limits of differing political interests. As J. A. Corry has said, "All significant problems of federalism are political in the deepest sense." This being so, what governments will get out of this mutual relationship will be pretty much in line with what they are prepared to put into it.

Note on the Chart of Proposed Organizational Relationships

Any attempt to chart the involved relationships between government organizations, particularly as between governments, is clearly open to having more read into it than is really there.

We have attempted to show in simple form the sort of lines of communication and authority that would exist under the proposals, but obviously there will be many cross-references, both informally and within the structure, that cannot be illustrated by a few boxes and lines. For example, in the text we have stressed the close relationship of the membership of the Senior Committee of Officials with that of the Continuing Committee on Fiscal and Economic Matters but this does not show on the diagram.

With such reservations, the chart may offer useful assistance in an understanding of the structure of the proposed relationships.

Chart of Proposed Organizational Relationships

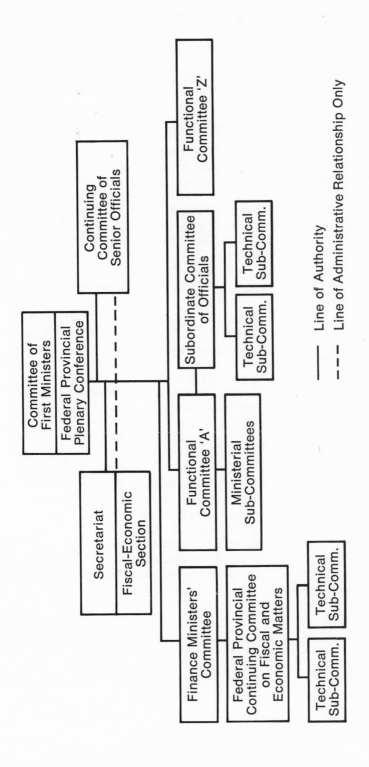

Committee of First Ministers
Federal Provincial Plenary Conference

Continuing Committee of Senior Officials

Secretariat
Fiscal-Economic Section

Functional Committee 'Z'

Subordinate Committee of Officials

Technical Sub-Comm.
Technical Sub-Comm.

Functional Committee 'A'

Ministerial Sub-Committees

Finance Ministers' Committee

Federal Provincial Continuing Committee on Fiscal and Economic Matters

Technical Sub-Comm.
Technical Sub-Comm.

——— Line of Authority
– – – Line of Administrative Relationship Only

19 Attitudes Towards Financial Relations
a) The Federal View*

Mitchell Sharp

The Objectives of Canadian Federalism

It is evident to us that the federalism of the future must recognize even more than the federalism of the past that intergovernmental arrangements must serve the two purposes which concerned the Fathers of Confederation. One was to establish a federal system which would define the roles of the federal and the provincial governments in the management of the public affairs of Canada. The other purpose was to provide the means for promoting the social and cultural development of our two societies, a goal which has come to include the cultivation of the enriching heritages that have come to us from other lands. In this twofold purpose lies the uniqueness both of the spirit of Canadian federalism and of the intergovernmental arrangements which our system calls for.

It will be equally self-evident, I think, that the economic and social developments of our first century have changed substantially the roles both of the federal and the provincial governments, and the inter-relationship between these roles. The Depression, the war and then the years of reconstruction taught governments everywhere that they must assume the new and difficult task of managing their economies, in the interest both of full employment and balanced economic growth, and the Federal Government assumed the primary responsibility for this role in Canada. These years taught us, too, that Canadians everywhere want and expect certain basic government services wherever they live, and that they expect their federal and provincial governments to find the methods by which this can be achieved.

It was during these years too that the role of the provinces was similarly enlarged, by the expectations imposed upon them by the people of the provinces, by the technological changes and urban developments which created new needs, and by the renewed realization of provincial potential by provincial politicians. So the responsibilities of provincial governments grew both in scale and in scope, involving programmes in the fields of health and welfare, education, urban development, transportation, and resource and economic development.

---

* From *Federal-Provincial Tax Structure Committee* (Ottawa, Queen's Printer, 1966), pp. 12-27. Reprinted by permission of Information Canada. This statement was presented to the Tax Structure Committee, September 14, 1966.

MITCHELL SHARP – Secretary of State for External Affairs, Minister of Finance, 1965-1971.

Out of these developments emerged still another and a different role for the Federal Government, and new interpretations of the role of the provinces. The Federal Government assumed the responsibility for ensuring that the poorer provinces should, through a system of equalization payments, be put in a position to finance their new and heavier responsibilities. The provincial governments in turn, exercised both their taxing and spending powers in such a way and on such a scale as to increase, in practical terms, both their fiscal powers and their influence over the nation's economy. In the process of these changes, many of the programmes of the federal and the provincial governments, each of them acting within its own constitutional domain, have come to overlap, with the consequent need for harmonization of government plans and programmes.

These are the forces the federalism of the future must accommodate. We must somehow fashion machinery which will permit a strong Federal Government to accomplish the economic and social responsibilities which properly belong to it, but without impairing the fiscal freedom and responsibility of the provinces. We must on the other hand fashion machinery which will strengthen the ability of the provinces to provide the greatly expanded and improved public services which are expected of them, but without at the same time hobbling the Federal Government or forcing it to have different laws for different parts of Canada—differences which might have the effect of obscuring or weakening its proper role as a government which governs all Canadians and protects equally the interests of all of them.

We in Canada, in other words, cannot solve the problems of twentieth century federalism by subordinating one level of government to another. Nor can we do so by adopting a kind of compartmental federalism, under which the federal and provincial governments would attempt to function in isolation. We must find another way.

Any general appreciation of the objectives of federalism in Canada, such as this, must lead to a statement of the guiding principles which flow from it, if it is to be useful in discussions such as those we are about to begin. The following, then, are the principles by which we believe we should be guided in trying to develop a system of federal-provincial fiscal arrangements which will be consistent with the federalism of the future.

(1) The fiscal arrangements should give both the federal and provincial governments access to fiscal resources sufficient to discharge their responsibilities under the constitution.

(2) They should provide that each government should be accountable to its own electors for its taxing and spending decisions and should make these decisions with due regard for their effect on other governments.

(3) The fiscal arrangements should, through a system of equalization grants, enable each province to provide an adequate level of public services without resort to rates of taxation substantially higher than those of other provinces.

(4) They should give to the Federal Government sufficient fiscal power to discharge its economic and monetary responsibilities, as well as to pay

its bills. In particular they should retain for the Federal Government a sufficient part of the income tax field in all provinces—both personal and corporate — to enable it to use variations in the weight and form of that tax for economic purposes and to achieve a reasonable degree of equity in the incidence of taxation across Canada.

(5) They should lead to uniform intergovernmental arrangements and for uniform application of federal laws in all provinces.

(6) The fiscal arrangements should seek to provide machinery for harmonizing the policies and the priorities of the federal and provincial governments.

These then are the principles or the objectives which have guided us in formulating our approach to the new fiscal arrangements. I would like now to say something about the fiscal environment in which these principles would operate during the next five years, before discussing their application to the four main elements of fiscal relations—equalization arrangements, the use of shared-cost programmes, tax-sharing, and intergovernmental liaison on fiscal and economic matters.

The Fiscal Outlook for the Next Five Years

Since the early 1950's provincial and municipal expenditures have increased from an amount equal to less than one-half of federal expenditures to an amount greater than the total amount the Federal Government now spends. The provincial use of major tax fields has grown correspondingly. All provinces now receive twenty-five per cent of the personal income taxes paid and Quebec receives an additional twenty-three per cent in return for assuming equivalent additional expenditures under the contracting-out arrangements. The ten provinces taken together receive almost twenty-five per cent of all commodity taxes, including about the same percentage of general sales taxes, some fifty per cent of liquor taxes (or mark-ups), and virtually one hundred per cent of gasoline taxes. And the provincial/municipal governments collect virtually all of the property taxes and natural resources levies paid in Canada.

Federal revenues and expenditures are growing too, but at a slower rate. Indeed the Federal Government was able in the past, because its revenues had been growing more rapidly than its expenditures, to facilitate the rise in provincial revenues through the progressive reduction or abatement of certain federal taxes.

The outlook for the future according to studies made for the Tax Structure Committee indicates a number of trends. First, provincial/municipal expenditures will continue to rise more rapidly than those of the Federal Government. Secondly, provincial and municipal expenditures will also rise more rapidly than will their revenues from existing taxes. Thirdly, federal government revenues from existing taxes, on the other hand, are expected to grow at a rate more nearly equal to the pace at which its expenditures will increase.

These are the fiscal prospects which we have had to take into account in the application of our guiding principles.

Equalization arrangements are one of the four central features of federal-provincial fiscal relations. They represent one of the dividends of Canadian unity, designed as they are to enable all Canadians to enjoy an adequate level of provincial public services. Where circumstances — whether natural or man-made—have channelled a larger than average share of the nation's wealth into certain sections of the country, there should be a redistribution of that wealth so that all provinces are able to provide to their citizens a reasonably comparable level of basic services, without resorting to unduly burdensome levels of taxation.

To accomplish this goal and in the spirit of the principles I spoke of earlier, we have concluded that we must undertake a fundamental reform in our equalization arrangements. We should seek in the future to measure the whole revenue or fiscal capacity of the provinces — to develop a comprehensive "prosperity index" if you will — in place of the partial measure now in use. Instead of selecting certain taxes and equalizing them to the level of the top two provinces, we should take into account all of a province's revenues and equalize them to the national average. This would be a good deal more expensive to the federal treasury but far more equitable. Secondly, the arrangements should be sensitive to the revenue requirements of the provinces, taken together — that is, they should grow as provincial responsibilities increase — and they should be equally responsive to changes in the tax capacity of individual provinces. Finally, to develop a formula that meets these requirements, we must take into account objective factors only, recognizing at the same time the need to deal with any special problems which may arise in the transition from the present to the new arrangement.

The proposed formula is estimated to cost the federal treasury about $490 million, about $140 million more than the present one. These estimates are based upon the hypothetical application of the proposed formula to 1966-67 revenues. They also take into account transitional arrangements which it was recognized from the beginning would be required if there were substantial reductions in the payments to any province under the new formula, as compared with the old. The results, for individual provinces, are [found in Table 1].

The Joint Use of Tax Fields

The major element of federal-provincial fiscal relations, by far the most important one in the post-war period, is the division and use of tax fields by the federal and provincial governments. What this has come to mean to most of us is periodic federal-provincial disputes over what share of personal income tax should be federal and what share provincial. We have come to the conclusion that it is time to try to recast this whole question of tax sharing in broader and more comprehensive terms. I say this both because negotiations over tax shares have increasingly tended to be divisive rather than unifying forces in Canadian federalism, and because this conventional approach to the use of tax fields is misleading.

The real problem confronting us, if we are to take seriously the projections of government revenues and expenditures our officials have presented to us, is how the federal, provincial and municipal governments — and particularly the provincial and municipal governments — are going to finance their continually rising expenditures. This in turn leads to the difficult question as to whether the provinces have access to sufficient revenue sources to finance these increasing expenditures, for unless they do we would be forced to the conclusion that they do not possess that measure of fiscal strength which is an essential element of twentieth century Canadian federalism.

An examination of the tax sources now being used by the provinces reveals that these governments do in fact have access to revenue fields capable of yielding the required revenues. The real question is not whether they have access to such sources but rather whether there are practical considerations making it difficult for them to use their taxing powers. Under the constitution the provinces have access to the income tax fields, both personal and corporate, just as the Federal Government has. Indeed their use of these fields has risen substantially since the war: from five per cent of personal income tax fifteen years ago to twenty-five per cent now, and from one tenth of the corporation income tax to about one quarter today, They are now levying taxes on commodities at the consumers level, while the Federal Government levies such taxes at the manufacturers level. As I have indicated earlier the provinces now collect some forty per cent of all commodity taxes imposed in Canada, including nearly forty per cent of the general sales taxes, some fifty per cent of liquor taxes, and virtually a hundred per cent of gasoline tax. The provinces have full access as well to the asset tax field; they and their municipalities now receive close to a hundred per cent of all the property taxes collected, and seventy-five per cent of estate taxes or succession duties. The provinces also have access to resource revenues, as does the Federal Government; indeed provincial resource revenues now represent close to one hundred per cent of the revenues from this source. Only the customs duties can be said to be exclusively collected by the Federal Government.

The conclusion seems clear: the problem is not lack of access to revenue sources, but rather the difficulties the provinces face — in company with the Federal Government — in raising tax levels that are already high.

The conventional approach to this problem, during the post-war period has been to argue that the Federal Government should reduce its taxes so as to give the provinces more "tax room". This is an understandable argument if federal tax yields are rising more rapidly than required. But when federal revenues are required to meet federal expenditures, or to reduce a deficit or create a surplus for economic reasons, then this approach is unhelpful and even misleading. For the Federal Government would not

Table 1

ESTIMATED EQUALIZATION PAYMENTS TO PROVINCES
UNDER FEDERAL PROPOSALS OF SEPTEMBER, 1966
AND UNDER PRESENT ARRANGEMENTS
(Using 1966-67 figures for illustrative purposes)
(All figures estimated)

Province	Total Payment			Per Capita Payment			Payment as Percentage of Provincial Revenues from Own Sources[2]		
	Present Arrangements[1]	Proposed Arrangements	Change	Present Arrangements[1]	Proposed Arrangements	Change	Present Arrangements[1]	Proposed Arrangements	Change
	$000'000	$000'000	$000'000	$	$	$	%	%	%
Newfoundland	37.2	59.8	+22.6	73.96	118.89	+44.93	49.9	80.3	+30.4
Prince Edward Island	10.6	10.8	+0.2	98.15	100.00	+1.85	73.1	74.5	+1.4
Nova Scotia	50.2	69.0	+18.8	66.14	90.91	+24.77	46.7	64.1	+17.4
New Brunswick	44.6	60.3	+15.7	71.25	96.33	+25.08	46.6	62.9	+16.3
Quebec	149.5	235.3	+85.8	26.08	41.04	+14.96	10.7	16.9	+6.2
Ontario	—	—	—	—	—	—	—	—	—
Manitoba	27.5	29.1	+1.6	28.68	30.34	+1.66	14.5	15.4	+0.9
Saskatchewan[3]	33.2	27.2	-6.0	34.84	28.54	-6.30	13.2	10.9	-2.3
Alberta	—	—	—	—	—	—	—	—	—
British Columbia	—	—	—	—	—	—	—	—	—
Total	352.8	491.5	+138.7	—	—	—	—	—	—

Notes: 1 The amounts shown for present arrangements include the Atlantic Provinces Adjustment Grants.
2 "Provincial revenues from own sources" consists of provincial net general revenues less all transfers from the federal government (based on D.B.S. statistics), i.e., it includes all provincial revenues from taxes, licences, fees, fines, etc.
3 The payment to Saskatchewan under the proposed arrangements is a transitional payment which would be paid in 1967-68, and would decline during 1967-68 to 1971-72.

be justified in these circumstances in reducing   one of its taxes simply to make it easier for the provinces to increase the same tax. What would be involved would be a reduction in one federal tax to enable the corresponding provincial tax to be raised and then an increase in some other federal tax to restore the necessary budgetary position. The end result of this process would be a net increase in this other tax, with the Federal Government having imposed the increase. The provinces would get the extra money. Surely a more appropriate course would be for the provinces to finance their expenditure increases by increasing the taxes they think should be increased, just as the Federal Government is expected to do in financing its expenditure increases.

The proposition that the Federal Government should reduce its taxes to ease increases in provincial levies must, in circumstances such as those I have described, be based on the assumption that Parliament is appropriating money for purposes less important than those being served by provincial expenditures. That governments should reduce expenditures is a proper subject for argument—taxpayers make it regularly, and apply it equally to federal, provincial and municipal governments. But we cannot accept as a general principle that federal expenditures are less important than provincial ones. The principle that _does_ call for recognition is a different one: namely that both Parliament and provincial legislatures must accept their financial responsibilities and that each should look to its own electors for direction as to what money should be raised and how it should be spent.

This is not to say that the Federal Government rejects the notion of federal-provincial consultation concerning public policy priorities. We must have such consultations and increasingly so, in order to ensure a proper concern for the taxpayers' interests. Consultations involving discussions about the size and direction of revenues and expenditures must be a two-way street.

What I am suggesting then, is that we must get away from what is tending to become a conventional notion that the Federal Government can and should be expected to give greater tax room to the provinces, when they find their expenditures rising more rapidly than their revenues. This has been done, in the past decade, but it cannot be accepted as a general duty. Our basic duty is the ancient one — to tax no more than we need, and to reduce taxes when we can and should.

The second convention of federal-provincial fiscal relations that must be questioned is that there is some particular share of income tax and estate taxes and succession duties, the so-called "shared taxes", which is rightly federal or rightly provincial. The fact is that both have constitutional rights in these fields.

What we must share now is the responsibility for the total taxes imposed on Canadians, taking into account what each other is doing. We must find ways of harmonizing federal and provincial tax actions, to ensure that the interests of the taxpayers of Canada are protected, both in the way and the extent to which the several tax fields are used. This must include the determination of what taxes tend to have national as opposed to provincial characteristics. The corporation tax is one of these, because corporation profits may be earned elsewhere than in the province where the head office is located and profits recorded. I submit too that the Federal Government must have a predominant share of this tax field by reason of the importance and the peculiar value of this tax as an instrument of national economic policy — as we saw in this year's federal Budget.

There are also compelling reasons for the federal government to maintain a substantial position in the personal income tax field. This is the principal tax by which equity is achieved between the rich and the poor across the nation. This implies that a substantial share of this tax should continue to flow to the national government. This tax, too, is one of the central instruments for regulating total demand in the economy, and Canadian governments must not allow total federal income taxes to be abated so much that they can no longer be used for this purpose. This means that the Federal Government must maintain a strong position in this field, despite the pressures it will continue to face for reducing its share in favour of the provinces. We have already made arrangements with Quebec which have enabled that Province to bring its tax to levels equalling those of the federal tax. We have made proposals here which would enable the other provinces gradually to reach the Quebec position. The position that will have been attained under those proposals is, we think, a reasonable one for the provinces, and leaves the Federal Government with a personal income tax adequate to serve the purposes of equity and economic policy.

For these reasons we have concluded that we must look elsewhere than to the further and continuous abatement of federal income taxes for the solution to provincial fiscal problems. We must look instead, I think, to provincial access to all tax fields in provincial jurisdiction. For access can be limited by practical as well as legal obstacles.

Provincial use of the personal income tax field has been impeded and provincial responsibility for the use of this tax has been diluted by the designation under federal-provincial tax arrangements of a certain provincial income tax rates as being the "standard rate". This standard rate, now 24 per cent, has been used in determining equalization payments, and in determining the extent to which the federal personal income tax would be abated. The provinces have been free to impose any rate they chose, but they have had to recognize that any rate above the standard rate would expose them to the charge of "double taxation". In fact, where provincial rates do exceed the standard rate, the excess has been called a "surtax".

It is a nice question as to whether the Federal Government should by inference or otherwise suggest the rate of provincial tax it considers to be appropriate. We have concluded that it should not. In saying this we recognize, as I have said, that each of us should take into account in our fiscal decisions the levels of the other's taxes. But this need not and should not extend to the point that either of us states or implies the level of taxes appropriate for the other. We therefore propose to recommend to Parliament the elimination of reference to "standard rates" (of personal income tax) in the Income Tax Act. This would be done at the time of any major revisions to this Act pursuant to the recommendations of the several Royal Commissions on Taxation. I should note that the equalization formula proposed will similarly make no reference to "standard rates", but will use instead actual average provincial rates.

I should emphasize that this action would in no way weaken the incentives which exist in present fiscal arrangements for uniform tax laws, and should not therefore lead to different definitions of income or other differences in our tax laws. Canadians are justly proud of their accomplishments in achieving uniform income tax laws across the country, and the Federal Government will continue to bend every effort to maintain this uniformity. For this purpose, tax collection agreements will be offered again to the provinces in the period 1967-72, without any charge being made for the collection of provincial taxes under them. The one condition will be that the form of the provincial tax laws must accord with the model Act, a requirement of present tax collection agreements.

In all of this I have scarcely mentioned the details of our tax structure, or the impending Royal Commission reports which may, with the Quebec Royal Commission report, propose extensive changes in it. This is not because I attach little importance to the form and the burden of taxes in Canada, but because I felt the first question to occupy our attention should be a new approach to tax sharing. This, indeed, has always been the aspect of taxation most considered at federal-provincial meetings, and is one upon which the Commissions were not asked to make recommendations.

I regret, as I know some provincial representatives do, that we were unable to have before us at this meeting the report of the Royal Commission on Taxation, for it would enable us to view our problems in the wider perspective which a broad study of this kind makes possible. I hope that this committee will be meeting next year to discuss changes in our tax laws arising out of the revisions that will be undertaken in the light of the commission's report.

I would hope, in the meantime, that the Tax Structure Committee will give serious consideration to the new approach to the joint use of tax fields which I have outlined. I believe it is the approach best suited to the long-term requirements of the provinces and their proper desire for fiscal freedom and responsibility. It equally will serve to preserve the ability of the Federal Government to act effectively on matters of national importance.

b) Ontario's View*

Charles S. MacNaughton

This meeting is as important to the future of Canada as any federal-provincial confrontation since World War Two. We can no longer afford simply to affirm platitudes about co-operation and co-ordination or indulge in the luxury of theoretical speculation. We have some explicit questions and we expect un-equivocal and logical answers. We believe these questions must be answered at the outset if the items on the agenda of this Conference are to have any meaning.

Our whole purpose, in this exercise, is not to debate which government must face the issue of raising taxes but, rather, to define the best route to a viable Canadian federalism, given the fact that the provinces and their municipal partners account for such a high proportion now of the governmental financial and economic activity in this country. We insist that, whereas the federal government is the central government, it cannot afford to place its own problems ahead of those problems which confront Canadian federalism and Canada as a nation.

1. Does the federal government believe in approaching our financial problems in a spirit of partnership?

2. If so, does this not imply that we must look at the structure and problems of government finance at all levels taken together?

3. Will the federal government continue to insist that the provinces should go their own way, raise their own taxes, and concern themselves only with their own responsibilities, without regard to the needs or requirements of governments as a whole? Is this what you really want? Is this your view of Canadian federalism? Is this your view of the extent of the federal government's responsibility for the financial and economic future of this country?

4. Do you really wish to have a tax jungle? Do you really wish to have a balkanized economy? Do you really wish to have ten separate economic principalities in Canada? Do you really feel that the federal government can ignore the spirit engendered by the provinces in recent years for greater co-ordination and joint planning?

5. Does the federal government realize that its most recent budget, by adopting an elaborate device to avoid sharing an increase in income tax revenues with the provinces, has made it very difficult for provinces like

---

* From *Federal-Provincial Conference of Ministers of Finance and Provincial Treasurers, Ottawa, November 4-5, 1968* (Ottawa, Queen's Printer, 1969), pp. 9-12. Reprinted by permission of Information Canada.

CHARLES S. MACNAUGHTON - Treasurer and Minister of Economics, Province of Ontario.

Ontario to follow the federal government's advice and raise its own income taxes? Does it know that the social development tax, announced prior to this tax-sharing conference, will impose the equivalent of a 9 per cent increase in total income tax collection? What room will this leave us to make provision for those critical needs of education, health and economic development?

6. Does the federal government not believe, as we do, in a more progressive tax structure?

7. Does it realize that by urging the provinces to meet their expenditure responsibilities by raising their own tax revenues, it is encouraging greater reliance on regressive tax fields?

8. Does it believe that the provinces can independently raise their taxes without creating problems in turn for the federal government? Only recently, our increase in the tax on aviation fuel has caused concern to the federal government. Is this not a small, but significant, indication of what could lie ahead?

9. Does the federal government believe, as many of its ministers have stated, that the big expenditure problems of the future lie in our cities?

10. Does it believe, as was concluded by the Smith and Select Committees on Taxation in Ontario, that the plight of the municipalities should be relieved not by greater reliance on the regressive property tax but by revenues originally obtained through the personal income tax and passed down through the provinces?

11. Does the federal government really believe that the problem of expenditure controls relates only to a few shared-cost programs? Or should a discussion of such controls not apply to all government expenditures, federal, provincial, and municipal? If the federal government believes that the institution of shared-cost programs leads to irresponsibility in spending, why is it introducing the medicare program in the present manner? If the federal government believes provincial governments should be in a position to act responsibly and set their own priorities in expenditure, is it prepared to turn over to us the fiscal equivalence of its budgeted medicare cost so that we can apply the money to our highest expenditure priorities?

12. If the federal government believes that all governments should work together in advance of their budgets to achieve co-ordinated views and take appropriate action, does it not seem strange that for the third year in a row the federal budget has been timed to come just before these financial discussions rather than just after, thereby effectively pre-empting our position? Is this now the pattern of federal-provincial co-operation?

13. Is the federal Minister of Finance prepared to sit down with his provincial counterparts in December or January to discuss the scope of the total government finance problem, our preliminary plans for all of our budgets, and to change its own plans in the light of the discussions that we have?

14. If we correctly understand your apparent course and if you are determined to follow it, do we understand, then, that we are to go back and plan our own future in our own way? Is that what you wish? If that is the case, we are prepared to do it and we are prepared to do it vigorously but

we want to know, we want the people of this country to know and, in particular, we want the people of our own province to know exactly why we are being advised to go in this direction, and why we have been obliged to embark upon the course of self-determination in the provincial economy which we must then follow.

15. Can this pattern also be taken as a guarantee that the federal government will not intrude in the future in the provincial jurisdiction, not withstanding recent evidence of increasing federal interest in matters such as securities legislation, educational broadcasting, certain aspects of transportation policy, and so on? If so, do you really think that you will be able to ignore the policies and the activities upon which the provincial governments might be obliged to embark?

16. What assurance is there of any future consistency in federal financial policies? We find it ludicrous and incongruous that the Minister of Finance should, in the same budget speech, urge fiscal restraint, point the finger of blame at rising costs of provincial programs in which the federal government participates, and then insist on going ahead with medicare while saying that costs in that field are now under control. How does this reconcile with the table prepared recently in the Department of Finance which projects rapidly rising medicare costs over the next few years? What guarantee have we that, in a few years from now, the federal government will not dump the full responsibility for this program on the provinces and close off or limit its contributions after it has obliged the provinces to embark on this slippery slope?

It is obvious that the social development tax is a premium for medicare. In turn this coerces the Ontario taxpayer into a program, within the provincial jurisdiction, which the Ontario Government does not believe to be required as a government scheme when nearly 95 per cent of the people of the province already enjoy some form of medical care insurance. The fact that the federal tax increase is of an amount at least equivalent to the current federal estimate of its contributions to medicare in a full year is a clear indication of the federal intentions. We also regard it as nothing short of effrontery that this act should have been taken on the eve of a conference to discuss medicare, a conference which was urgently requested by all the Premiers during their meeting in Saskatchewan last summer.

We therefore insist that this money be turned back to us unequivocally from January 1, 1969 so that we may then embark upon our own course of public medicare at an appropriate time, support the public forms of medicare presently underway or assign this money to those matters which we regard as having greater priority.

We are not prepared to pass judgment on the policies of the other provinces where circumstances vary greatly. Let us merely note how the federal government's determination to persist with this program in Ontario, where corporations are now making considerable contributions to medicare for their employees from corporate funds, will shift the burden to individuals as taxpayers and thereby, once again, follow a regressive path from corporations to individuals.

We would point out to the federal government that we are undertaking an examination of the cost structure of all provincial programs and the means of controlling expenditures in those realms, with firm measures to follow. We would like to know what the federal government proposes doing about costs within its own jurisdiction. In view of the failure of the federal government to anticipate the mounting pace of costs, what confidence can we have that it will not only anticipate where it is going but do something about the direction?

In Canadian federalism today, nothing is more compelling than the plight of the municipalities. It is in the municipalities and the urban areas that the great need for government support is required. We are determined to help our municipal partners but we cannot do it alone. By insisting that we go our own way, is the federal government not turning its back on municipal problems? Does this mean that the federal government has no concern for municipal and urban problems and is unwilling to do anything about them? Does the federal government believe that the provinces should say to their municipalities what the federal government has said to the provinces: "If you need more revenues, raise them yourself?" Or does the federal government intend to break some of its own principles of federalism and offer money directly to the municipalities? Since the federal government can only help the municipalities through the provinces, where the constitutional responsibility for the municipalities lies, unwillingness to co-operate in meeting the financial needs of the province is tantamount to an unwillingness to help the municipalities. Surely, this is an unacceptable and irresponsible course for a federal government to adopt in Canada today. We believe that it can only be described as "unjust federalism".

We have come here to put these questions and we expect to receive answers. We have come here in the belief that the future of Canadian federalism rather than the future of the federal government is at stake. We have come here to insist that financial problems are as important a matter for national unity as any matters in the general area of constitutional concern. No distribution of spending powers will have much meaning unless it is accompanied by a like distribution of revenue powers. If the federal government refuses to take these problems seriously, we want there to be no mistake about where the responsibility will squarely lie.

c) Quebec's View*

Jean-Jacques Bertrand

On several occasions in the past, I have had the opportunity to attend federal-provincial or interprovincial conferences. It is the first time however that I attended such a conference as Prime Minister of Quebec. The health of our Minister of Finance did not permit his presence here and I have decided to come myself for two main reasons. First, because of the extreme importance of the questions to be discussed and, second, because of the many current issues on which Quebec's opinion can perhaps best be expressed by Quebec's Prime Minister.

All those who know me can bear witness to my belief in a renewed Canadian federalism. They know the interest I have shown in the solution of our constitutional problems. They can also testify to the hope I have placed in Canadian solidarity—a solidarity which would respect the rights of Quebec and of the French-Canadian nation. I have never fought shy of delicate and difficult questions and I am used to speaking my mind loud and clear. And this is what I intend to do at this conference, in all deference to my friends of the federal government and of the other provinces.

I Federal encroachments: their costs and dangers

What have we seen happening lately, more particularly during the last few months? I am sorry to say that we have seen the federal attitude becoming arrogant, and imperialistic, as the Government of Canada has begun intruding directly or indirectly in an astonishing number of provincial matters.

We need only reflect on its desire for a larger hand in regional and urban development, securities regulation, scientific research, educational radio and television, cultural affairs. We can recall the last federal budget which, without any prior consultation with the provinces, changes many features of our fiscal structures in matters of great interest to Quebec. Then there are fields of action where the federal government wants a head start for fear the provinces might get in first. Or medicare and the imposition by the federal government of a tax which goes by the provocative name of "social development tax" and which—whatever anyone may say about it—will actually be used to implement a social security program that clearly falls within the

---

* From *Federal-Provincial Conference of Ministers of Finance and Provincial Treasurers, Ottawa, November 4-5, 1968* (Ottawa, Queen's Printer, 1969), pp. 13-17. Reprinted by permission of Information Canada.

JEAN-JACQUES BERTRAND - Leader of the Opposition, National Assembly, Quebec. Prime Minister of the Province of Quebec, 1968-70.

provinces' constitutional jurisdiction. How many other fields will, in the future, witness similar federal intrusions? Our past experience prompts us to ask the question.

What are the short- and long-term effects of this federal encroachment which, however gradual, is plain for all to see.

In the short run, the central authority creates new financial obligations which serve as excuses for not vacating taxation fields to leave room for the provinces. The process also leads to duplication and misallocation of resources, needlessly adding to the Canadian taxpayer's burden.

But, in the long run, something much more fundamental will be involved—Canadian federalism itself. The present federal government appears to be reliving the old political dream of twenty years ago, thinking centralization, a policy which Quebec as well as all other provinces have grown to resent. The Canadian government is now acting as if it meant to achieve two objectives: generally speaking, to reduce the provinces to the rank of regional administrations totally lacking real power and, more particularly, ignoring one of Canada's essential sociological realities, to prevent Quebec from asserting her presence as a distinct entity. Finding themselves under a sort of guardianship, the provinces will necessarily have to react strongly, a situation that will lead to instability in the very structure of the entire country's administrative and political organization. Is this the desire of the federal government?

I could not help being amazed at recent federal announcements. I fondly hope that they came as a result of passing unawareness, but at times I fear that they actually stem from a considered and deliberate policy. If such were the case, I am afraid that consequences could be disastrous. Quebec wants to co-operate, but she also wants her rights to be concretely recognized. Quebec wants to adopt a positive attitude but, whatever pretext the federal government may invoke, she does not want to sit idly watching the gradual erosion of her constitutional prerogatives.

Having lived through the centralizing federalism of twenty years ago, to "new federalism" ten years later, and "co-operative federalism" five years past, Quebec will not tolerate a switch to domineering federalism now.

We sincerely want to work at improving and renewing our federal system, but it would be serious indeed if, just when we have started this difficult but necessary task, the federal government were to alarm us by putting us in a financially, administratively and politically untenable position.

In that context, Quebec finds itself confronted with one specific problem: medicare and its accessory, the "social development" tax. We have every intention to have medicare in Quebec, but at the time and in the manner which we will choose for ourselves. We cannot tolerate that the federal government should feel free to levy additional taxes on our citizens in order to finance programs, outside Quebec, which we know to fall within provincial jurisdiction. Such a behaviour is unacceptable. The Government of Quebec cannot tolerate to be hustled financially and administratively in order that the federal government might fulfill its electoral promises. *This is why I want to declare immediately that we formally ask the federal government not to apply the new tax to Quebec citizens, and that from the moment of its proposed implementation on January 1st, 1969.*

I would like now to come to the fiscal arrangements devised two years ago. At that time, it was obvious that several of the participating governments were not at all satisfied with the results and had strong misgivings about the state of this country's public finances. It was decided then that the clauses of the arrangements would be reopened after two years and a new attempt made to reach an agreement. Last August, in Waskesiu, the provincial Premiers have reminded the federal government of that understanding. And we are here today to determine the best ways to prepare that review of existing arrangements.

II The rise of public expenditures

The work of the Tax Structure Committee has hardly been used. More specifically, the projections of expenditures and revenues showed a gradual deterioration in the financial situation of the provinces. Rather than correct the balance, hold a tight rein on the expansion of the cost of existing programs, and slow down the creation of new programs, the federal government has been unable to curb certain expenditures and unwilling to cancel some of the costliest of its announced new programs.

Thus all spheres of government have been forced to increase taxes considerably and will have to do so again if our disorganized fiscal structure remains unchanged. That some rise in taxation should be necessary when public needs increase sharply is understandable. But we have collectively reached a point where we have to raise taxes too steeply and at times that are inappropriate for a proper balance of the economy. In fact, completely disregarding the dictates of economics or common sense, we have continued to the point where tax increases only reflect the total lack of coordination and management in the public sector of our economy.

Because we have never agreed or even tried to agree on what the priorities should be, because the federal government has competed with the provincial governments in developing programs, we have reached a point where the most sombre appraisals of the Tax Structure Committee with respect to the future now appear to understate the facts.

The present fiscal arrangements between governments are not only unrealistic but are conducive to a disorderly management of public finances.

The late Prime Minister of Quebec, Mr. Johnson, had suggested that a committee regularly examine the total investment requirements and policies of major government spenders and crown corporations, so that public investments be better adapted to the current needs of the economy. Nothing came of the proposal.

More recently, the Prime Minister of Canada attacked the provinces for the rapidly rising cost of post-secondary education as if the Bladen Report had never been published and as if this rate of increase had not been forecasted years ahead by the governments responsible for this field of action. What are we to think of this attitude? Should the federal government question the educational policies followed by the provinces? Perhaps, but if so, then national defence expenditures must also come under scrutiny. It is as legitimate for the provinces to raise questions about the share of the federal budget taken by our defence policies as it is for the central government to question the increase in the costs of post-secondary education.

For all these reasons, I believe that we should attempt to achieve one very definite purpose: a fiscal and financial structure that will, thanks to a net transfer of resources to the provinces, allow each order of government to carry its present responsibilities as efficiently as possible.

In the view of the Quebec government, all fiscal negotiations should be based on a few essential principles.

III Basic principles

(a) Governments should determine from time to time what the total tax burden should be, and share at least some of the tax fields among themselves.

(b) Governments that are ultimately responsible for given fields of activity, must have access to resources that they can handle as they see fit and allocate in the way they want to carry out their responsibilities. Thus all government funds must be such that they can be spent unconditionally. Successive Quebec Governments have stressed this point and the present government is determined to follow the same policy. Conditional grants, subsidies or transfers are wholly unacceptable since they earmark resources for purposes that may run counter to the policies which the government concerned has adopted. We have seen too many examples of such conflicts in the past and have no intention of witnessing any more in the future. Indeed the Quebec government recognizes that other provincial governments might find it convenient, for a variety of reasons, to participate in shared-cost programs. But it will not accept them for itself.

(c) All governments in Canada should periodically survey the priorities that have emerged in their budgets. We should from time to time review together the programs that we have embarked upon.

(d) Finally much closer cooperation should be established between governments in certain fields of strategic importance, so as to ensure a proper management of the economy. It seems odd—nay, irresponsible—not to have attempted any coordination at all in areas such as public investment or wages in the public sector. Provinces and municipalities now account for more than 20 per cent of all public investment in this country. The direct or indirect wage component of provincial budgets is close to 50 per cent. In municipalities, it sometimes reaches 65 per cent, while in the federal budget the direct wage bill does not make up more than 18 per cent of total expenditures. These are all elements that must be taken into account in our discussions.

On the basis of the principles and considerations that I have just stated, I therefore suggest that the present conference call upon the Continuing Committee on fiscal and economic matters to study the possible solutions to the problems that have been raised.

IV Mandate of the Continuing Committee on Fiscal and Economic Matters

The mandate given to the Continuing Committee could include the following points:

(a) Study of the budgetary situation of the various governments, so that we may have an idea of the cost of present commitments in relation to the existing tax rates.

(b) Preparation of budgetary projections for the next three years, in order to determine the level of taxation and borrowing that will be needed.

(c) Evaluation of the share of the total economy taken by the public sector and of the consequences thereof on economic growth.

It could also be useful to ask the Continuing Committee to report on possible new forms of coordination, particularly as regards public investment and wages policies. As far as equalization is concerned, the Government of Quebec is satisfied with the existing formula, although it would not oppose its revision in order to allow for a catching-up operation where it is warranted.

On the basis of such information, a meeting of Ministers of Finance could be held in January to work out an agreement on our new fiscal arrangements for the period April 1969 to April 1972. No doubt the studies that have been carried out on tax reform will have an impact on the solutions which each government will propose. However, the fact that tax reform has not yet taken place should not be an obstacle to establishing new fiscal arrangements.

Conclusion

In concluding, I would like to say once again how important these negotiations are for Quebec. In the last two years, we have been forced to increase taxes considerably. The brunt of these new taxes has been largely borne by individuals, even though we have taken definite steps to achieve a better distribution of the tax burden.

We have therefore an urgent need of a more equitable tax-sharing. This is not to be achieved today nor tomorrow. And this is why we have suggested that a positive result of our meeting would be to give the Continuing Committee a precise mandate in preparation for a January conference.

In a country as complex as ours and in the present state of public opinion, anything that results in a weakening, let above a subjection of the provinces—and of Quebec in particular—can only lead to useless conflicts and major failures. Modern Quebec believes in the coordination of efforts in a common spirit, but not in subordination nor in unitarism.

Canadian federalism still remains to be invented. To identify it too closely with existing formulas, or with foreign federal systems, or to confine it within the concepts to which we have been accustomed or to relate it to ideas which are now obsolete, would only sterilize our brand of federalism and imprison its members in a strait-jacket inhibiting the spirit of evolution and adaptation which should characterize our federal system.

Canada needs a federal system that is imaginative, creative and able to renew itself. The fiscal arrangements that we will be discussing next January will be the test, the necessarily successful test, of a truly Canadian federalism —a federalism which accepts the decentralization required by our changing society.

It is only through governments which are strong, free and equal, which are respectful of the others' jurisdiction and which are ready to work in harmony for the solution of their common problems, that we will finally achieve Canadian solidarity.

d) Nova Scotia's View*

Robert Stanfield

Although this federal-provincial conference is called primarily to discuss fiscal matters, it would appear that discussion of fiscal matters may relate very closely to the fundamental nature of Confederation. It is clear that certain problems have developed within the framework of Confederation which must be given the most careful consideration.

This is not the first time in our history of almost 100 years when stresses and strains developed within the framework of our federal system of government. Indeed it may be said that stresses and strains within the colonies of British North America contributed in no small measure to the creation of this nation. Certainly, these stresses and strains became very evident in the Province of Nova Scotia immediately following Confederation, resulting in at least two attempts by well-meaning, public spirited citizens to take the Province of Nova Scotia out of Confederation. However, moderation prevailed, and the strength of the framework of Confederation was preserved. . . .

Nova Scotia, in 1867, made sacrifices in order to play its full part in creating a new nation. It held grievances for many years and some of them are still with us, but we are citizens of Canada as well as Nova Scotians and we intend to do everything within our power to preserve this nation and to solve our difficulties and differences in a modern reasonable manner around the conference table.

Nova Scotia, in 1867, supported a federal system of government as opposed

---

* From *Federal-Provincial Conference, 1963* (Ottawa, Queen's Printer, 1964), pp. 51-54. Reprinted by permission of Information Canada.

ROBERT STANFIELD – Leader of the Opposition, House of Commons, Canada. Premier of the Province of Nova Scotia, 1956-1967.

to a unitary state and in 1963 we still hold the same belief. However, a federal constitution must be so framed as to serve all the citizens of the nation and not just those who happen to live in certain geographical parts of the nation. Each of us has a responsibility to his own province but surely each of us has a greater responsibility to the nation as a whole.

Nova Scotia believes in a federal system of government but we do not believe in a form of federalism which creates a central government with no ⋇ responsibility for the social and economic well-being of the various parts of the nation, or a central government charged with the responsibility but without the means to discharge that responsibility. Some government in Canada must be charged with the responsibility of assuring to Canadian citizens a national standard of essential services and that responsibility can only be discharged effectively by the federal government.

In fact, that responsibility has been accepted by successive Governments of Canada. The proposals presented to the federal-provincial conference in 1945 by the Government of Canada contained the following statements:

> These proposals assume a broad federal responsibility in co-operation with provincial governments for establishing the general conditions and framework for high employment and income policies and for support of national minimum standards of social services . . . . The third requirement of post-war financial arrangements is that they should make possible at least an adequate minimum standard of services in all provinces while not denying to any province the advantages which its resources give to it nor the freedom to establish its own standards. The fourth requirement is that the dominion-provincial financial arrangements must be such as to strengthen, not weaken, the federal system established in our constitution.

The Prime Minister of Canada, addressing the federal-provincial conference on October 3, 1955, stated:

> Our present problem is twofold—to achieve some method of sharing of the revenue available from the direct tax field and some reasonable degree of equity and stability in the revenue of the various provinces. The latter involves some recognition of the fiscal need of those provinces whose tax potential is less than others—payment of subsidies in one form or another. There is nothing repugnant to the spirit or the letter of our constitution in this; the original British North America Act provided what was then substantial subsidies and recognized fiscal need. Throughout our history the forces of economics and geography have been tempered by some measure of national consciousness and solidarity. But this process requires judgement and discretion and due regard to the interest of the nation as a whole.

The Prime Minister discussed very briefly the history of the tax rental agreements and went on to say:

> The present government had no intention of abandoning the objective of the tax rental agreements which is to make it financially possible for all the provinces, whatever their tax base, to perform their constitutional

functions themselves and to provide a reasonable Canadian level of provincial services without an abnormal burden of taxation. That is the
foundation of the policy of Federal government. This is the principle of
paying an element of fiscal need subsidies to provinces with lesser tax
potential than others.

The Prime Minister of Canada at the federal-provincial conference, July 25,
1960, in somewhat different terms, reaffirmed the objective of the Government
of Canada when he stated:

> Again I wish to emphasize that the federal government remains firmly
> committed to the principle of equalization and of financial assistance to
> those provinces in which incomes and taxable capacity are below those
> of the richer provinces. . . . The Government believes that the principle of
> fiscal aid and equalization to assist the less wealthy provinces stands on
> its own feet and is accepted on that basis, and is quite separate from the
> question of tax rental or tax sharing.

The Government of the Province of Nova Scotia assumes that the Government of Canada is still committed to those objectives.

The need for subsidization of one government by another government is not
to be desired and every effort should be made to eliminate the conditions
which create the need. Nova Scotia is making a determined effort to improve
the economic life of the province and it is having a measure of success. It has
joined with the Provinces of New Brunswick, Prince Edward Island, and
Newfoundland to form a conference of Atlantic Premiers to deal with matters
of mutual concern. As a committee of that conference, the Atlantic Provinces
Research Board was constituted to study and analyze the factors which have
contributed to our economic disabilities and to consider ways and means
whereby those disabilities can be overcome.

Atlantic House in London has been established to represent the trade
interests of the four provinces. Nova Scotia has established Industrial Estates
Limited as an agency through which industry can be attracted to our province.
Nova Scotia has embarked on a program of Voluntary Economic Planning
designed to achieve the maximum rate of economic growth and thereby create
a higher rate of employment, higher incomes, better social and public services.
Nova Scotia wants to mobilize the knowledge, skill, energy and creativity of
all its people and to increase its rate of economic growth without regimentation
or compulsion.

The Government of the Province of Nova Scotia believes that our efforts
will be productive but it all takes time and in the meantime, we must look to
the Government of Canada for assistance so as to achieve and maintain a
national standard of service for the citizens of Canada domiciled in the
Province of Nova Scotia.

Someone may suggest that an attempt to establish a national standard of
services is impractical and that each province should provide only a standard
of services which its own economy can support. The Government of the
Province of Nova Scotia suggests that there are some services which as a

nation we can ignore or maintain at a sub-standard level in some provinces, only at the peril of all Canada, namely, education, social welfare and public health. We repeat, at the peril of all Canada, because in these days of mobility of population, the problems created by sub-standard services in one province will inevitably spill over into the other provinces of Canada. As a nation, we must assure to our youth equality of educational opportunity and for the ill and needy a degree of assistance which recognizes the dignity of each Canadian citizen.

We recognize that great demands are being made upon the financial resources of all governments in Canada but we respectfully suggest that the establishing and maintaining of national standards in the fields of education, public welfare and public health are matters of national concern.

The Government of the Province of Nova Scotia suggests that the present fiscal arrangements cannot achieve the objective of enabling each province to provide a national standard of essential services. The present fiscal arrangements and our share of the Atlantic Provinces Adjustment Grants have benefited greatly the Province of Nova Scotia. However, the Government of the Province of Nova Scotia asserts that fiscal arrangements incorporating an equalization factor based only on the returns from income tax, corporation tax, succession duties and natural resources revenue completely disregard the fact that the tax return from these tax sources or the tax return from these sources plus the equalization amount furnish but a portion of the required revenue of each province. The Province of Nova Scotia must raise the major portion of its requirements from other tax sources.

Any plan which recognizes tax deficiencies in limited tax fields and which disregards tax deficiences in all other tax fields will not enable some of the provinces to furnish a national standard of essential services without imposing an excessive burden of taxation.

We wish to point out that based on 1963-64 estimates, the portion of our revenue coming from individual income tax, corporation tax, succession duties and natural resources is approximately $18,960,000. This is about 21 per cent of the total amount we raise from our own sources of revenue. In short, under the present fiscal arrangements, about 21 per cent of our revenue is equalized to the national average and 79 per cent is not. Under this arrangement, national standards of services cannot be maintained in all fields without imposing an abnormal burden of taxation. Some services will have to suffer; in fact, without the Atlantic Provinces Adjustment Grant, we would not be able to maintain even our present standard of services. Nova Scotia is making a determined effort to encourage and stimulate our economic growth, but an excessive burden of taxation could nullify all our efforts.

The Government of the Province of Nova Scotia wishes to state again the principles on which it believes federal-provincial fiscal arrangements must be based if all Canadians in all provinces are to have a reasonable standard of essential services.

First: that the constitutional responsibilities of each government in Canada must be coupled with financial ability to discharge those responsibilities.

Second: that in the light of the disparity in natural resources and economic development in the various provinces, the federal government must retain a sufficient portion of the tax fields in Canada to enable it to discharge its direct constitutional responsibilities and to assist provinces with low tax potential so as to enable them to furnish a national standard of services of the Canadian citizens residing within their boundaries.

We recognize that through conditional and shared cost programs, the Government of Canada has participated in the development of programs which are under provincial jurisdiction but we do not oppose that participation although we would welcome consultation before the Government of Canada initiates programs involving participation by the provinces.

For the federal government to simply withdraw from certain tax fields or to turn over a lump sum of money to each province without regard to the tax potential of each province, or without regard to the future costs of existing shared cost programs, would be virtual abandonment of federal objectives which have been stated clearly since 1945.

Whatever plan is proposed, it must recognize the necessity of providing for standards of services not only for the present but also the future. It must recognize the financial inability of some provinces to provide a reasonable standard of essential services without imposing an excessive burden of taxation.

The Province of Nova Scotia helped to create this Confederation of Provinces and we want to preserve it. We know that few countries in the world present greater problems of government than does Canada with its great variance in natural resources and regional rates of economic development.

The Government of the Province of Nova Scotia is not seeking through equalization grants a standard of services comparable to the richest provinces in Canada. It is seeking to obtain the necessary financial resources to maintain a good average standard of services without imposing an abnormal burden of taxation.

20 Co-operative Federalism*

Jean-Luc Pepin

To my mind, co-operative federalism is the best answer to the two main
political problems which Canada must solve to guarantee her political future:
the problem of relations between the central government and the regional
governments, that of Quebec in particular; the problem of relations between
French-speaking and English-speaking Canadians. These two problems are
intimately related.

Any political system involves 1) a philosophy, that is, a concept of man,
society and political action . . . ; 2) a technique of government. Technique is
useless without philosophy . . . and vice versa.

Co-operative federalism does not escape this rule.

The philosophy of co-operative federalism

. . . First of all, after several others, I would like to warn my fellow French
Canadians against the *cult* (I mean the excessive concern) for the particularities of race, language, culture, nation and state . . . . All these particularities
which some people delight in over-stressing, in dramatizing (to such an extent
that we are given the impression that, for example, between the French culture
and the English culture there is a gap which cannot be bridged, that English
institutions are totally incompatible with the French mentality), . . . have their
importance, but only a relative one: they are useful only inasmuch as they
serve man.   And then, not exclusively, as every language, every culture and
every nation is largely made up of borrowings.   Voltaire, who before
Montesquieu and de Tocqueville and others since them, had studied the Anglo-
saxons carefully, writes: "The English have taken good advantage of the works
in our language; we should in turn borrow from them, having loaned so much
to them.   The English and ourselves came only after the Italians who in everything were our masters, and whom we have surpassed in a few things.   I do
not know to which of the three nations we should give preference, *but
fortunate is he who can gauge their various merits."*   Therefore, there should
be no question of opposing cultures, languages, and nations within Canada. We

* From a translation in *The Canadian Forum*, Vol. 44 no. 527 (December, 1964), pp.
206-10. A speech to the Conférence de l'Institut canadien des Affaires publiques, September 12, 1964, by the author who was then the member of Parliament for Drummond-
Arthabaska and Parliamentary Secretary to the Minister of Trade and Commerce. Reprinted by permission of the author and the publisher. Italics are the author's.

JEAN-LUC PEPIN – Minister of Trade and Commerce, former Parliamentary Secretary to the Minister of Trade and Commerce.

should rather seek to link them, achieving a synthesis mindful of their rights and obligations of each of them.

Let us therefore guard ourselves against exaggeration. We French Canadians, should not switch from a stupid inferiority complex to a stupid superiority complex: we should not let our lazy shyness of yesterday be converted into pretentious arrogance. *The assertion of oneself does not compel us to deny the rights of others.* The value of our quiet revolution stems from the fact that it is revolt against ourselves, against our past deficiences, and especially a will to become competent, to achieve progress for the future. Let us therefore assume with vigour, assurance and enthusiasm our rightful place in Canadian and world society.

It seems to me that the particularities respectful, protected and constantly enriched, the building of a co-operative federal state can allow Canadians of French, English and other origins to give the world a fine example of political wisdom and human brotherhood.

Otherwise, what the devil are we doing in Cyprus and Rwanda?

May I also raise my voice against "Quebec sovereignism," a concept which stems from the old principle of nationalities of the 19th century according to which every nation, every association which is sociologically homogeneous is entitled to political independence.

Mr. Pierre E. Trudeau magnificently deflated the balloon of "Quebec National Sovereignism" in the April, 1962, issue of the *Cité libre,* showing that a large number of contemporary States are bi- and multi-national and do not fare worse than the uni-national States, and that an appeal to the principle "one-nation-one-state" would immediately unleash a hundred wars throughout the world. . . .

We can defend Quebec's autonomy, the "politique de grandeur" and the principle of "maîtres chez nous" without advocating the national sovereign Quebec State. Several times last evening, we heard that sovereignty was a totally outmoded concept as the interdependence of peoples and governments has now become evident. We fool people by intimating that once independence is won, everything will be peace, happiness and prosperity in the State of Quebec. The philosopher Locke shows us that the people, who in his time struggled over religious matters, would easily find other reasons for fighting against neighbouring peoples and even among themselves unless they first acquired a spirit of tolerance. The internal division of the RIN are a good example of this truth.

Thus, co-operative federalism aims at and allows us to achieve political bi-nationalism in Canada.

One last excerpt from my creed. It has almost become fashionable in our province to denounce in the name of purity, compromises, pragmatism, package deals, "constitutional laxity" and "political horsetrading," to quote Jean-Marc Leger, as if all this were immoral and disgusting.

You know as well as I do, ladies and gentlemen, that politics, in a federal State as in a unitary State, in a State with a mainly written constitution as in a

State with a mainly customary constitution, in a latin society as in an anglo-saxon society, yesterday in Athens and Rome and today in Istanbul and in the Vatican, politics, I say, is the art of achieving the greatest possible common good for the whole community by applying wisdom, caution, and also charity, to the solution of conflicts which are *unavoidable,* since we are all stained by the original sin, in the relations between individuals and groups.

Under these conditions, the political man, and politicians, since we must call a spade a spade, improvises, must improvise and cannot help improvising in conformity with the image which the society he governs and himself are making of harmony, justice and happiness. He is constantly looking for equilibrium, the immediate solutions which do not contradict long term objectives, the happy medium (where Aristotle places virtue) between equally inaccessible extremes. Negotiation, haggling, compromise, package deals . . . are his stock in trade. As every good craftsman, he is proud of his tools. "Compromise," said the honourable Guy Favreau, "is the meeting-point between the thought of two intelligent beings."

May the Lord allow great men of compromise to be born into Canada in order to assure the success of co-operative federalism!

Let us recapitulate: co-operative federalism, as any other federalism, "calls on the virtues which have given birth to civilization, the sense of human brotherhood, Christian charity, the spirit of tolerance, the art of compromise, the desire to build collectively great works, the hope of making a better world where peace and justice shall prevail." If my lyricism amazes you may I specify that my past paragraph was taken from the brief of the Saint Jean-Baptiste Society of Montreal to the parliamentary committee for the constitution at the Quebec Legislative Assembly, page 22.

The technique of co-operative federalism

Co-operative federalism is also a set of rules, techniques, and government institutions.

We should take time to situate this co-operative federalism in our constitutional history, to compare it to previous forms of Canadian federalism, to trace its origins; we should above all describe the present social, economic and political situation which has made it possible and even necessary. But it would no doubt be more useful to seek this evening to define it with a few key statements. Here again, I should like to be able to draw generously from the text of recent laws and the recent speeches of Federal and Quebec leaders in order to demonstrate that there is among them a broad consensus of opinion concerning the nature and the implications of co-operative federalism.

What are these propositions?

1. Economic decentralization and bi-nationalism

Co-operative federalism can be defined on the basis of a few forceful ideas. Some of them are *philosophical*; I singled out a few of them a while ago (for example, the relative value of particularism, the necessity of compromise . . .).

Others are related to *economy*. For example, there is no doubt that the recent popularity of economic decentralization helps to justify co-operative federalism, which advocates a much greater dose of political decentralization. In the *cultural* field the vitality of French culture in general (I am thinking especially of technology) and the progress of science, arts and letters in French Canada contribute in supporting the political arguments of Quebec.

In the *socio-political* field, *the theory of two nations,* whether true or false in the eyes of history, is now recognized by the best Canadian constitutionalists and political leaders, leaders in both nations; Mr. Pearson first, Mr. Diefenbaker, somewhat behind. Canadian society is bi-national; the Canadian state is the result of at least a moral agreement between the two founding nations.

Here is a fact which, if not new, has at least been recently accepted. Henceforth, the question runs as follows: *How shall we transpose to the Government level this socio-political reality of bi-nationalism?* In other words, how will the presence of a French-Canadian nation affect the rules, the techniques and the political institutions of Canada?

Some people do not want such a transposition: the *separatists,* English and French speaking; some deny it partially: the bi-statists and the *confederalists*; some believe that this transposition is possible within the framework of a revised Canadian federal State: these are the *co-operative federalists.* We note that there are among the defenders of this idea varying views as to the methods and amount of economic and political decentralization which are possible and the methods and desirable amount of recognition of the French reality and the Quebec reality.

2. "To each level of Government according to its aptitudes"

As "Canada is a vast continental domain—too big, too spread out, too cut up to be governed exclusively, or even dominantly, from one centre" (Mr. Pearson, May 26, 1964), co-operative federalism proclaims, against separatists and centralizers alike, *the necessity of two orders of government in Canada.* But how shall be divided the responsibilities between them?

The traditional *criterion,* the 1867 criterion, of the division of function— that is, matters of general interest will be attended to by the central government and matters of local interest by the provincial governments, is not worth much. Everything can in some way be of general interest: agriculture, highways, education . . . temperance!

We must therefore replace the former criterion with two others drawn from common sense and from the Act of '67: 1) *the criterion of aptitude*: We must allot to each order of Government what it is particularly able to do well in principle and in the present situation (Mr. Hirsch said last night that each decision should be taken at the level where it can best be made); 2) *the criterion of agreement between the two nations*: we must not assign to the central government matters over which there is clear-cut dissension between the two nations. The reports of the Tremblay Commission also stated this principle, extrapolating it from the Act of 1867.

I admit that these two criteria do not provide an easy solution to all problems. The concepts of "aptitude" and "agreement" are themselves relative. A socialist does not think of "aptitude" like a conservative in the manner of social legislation. A French Canadian does not have the same philosophy of education as an English-speaking Canadian. Nor is it always easy to know whether French Canadians agree among themselves: tonight's meeting is sufficient proof of this!

Thus, encounters and conflicts cannot be prevented. We will always need discussion and compromise.

I do not have enough time to state in which fields of government activity Ottawa is more competent *in principle,* and in which fields *in principle* the provinces are more competent. I underline "in principle" because, in practice, we have already seen provinces, including Quebec, refuse, due to a lack of personnel or merely a lack of will-power, to take over fields of jurisdiction which were, in principle, rightfully theirs.

3. Unavoidable overlapping: inevitable interdependence

Without denying the usefulness of dividing as accurately as possible the duties between Ottawa and the provinces, we must observe the unavoidable overlapping of central and regional authorities in most segments of Government activity, especially in a period of interventionism as the present one and the next one. I hear Messrs. Lesage, Kierans and others assert that the provinces should participate in the determination of Canada's tariff policies, in her transportation policy and even her monetary policy, her trade policy, her tax policy, etc. I agree wholeheartedly. Co-operative federalism leaves room for consultation, co-operation and co-ordination even in these traditionally federal fields. I could read you, only as an example, a speech made by Mr. Sharp and speak to you of the Federal-Provincial conferences on international trade promotion, where the participation of the provinces is not only accepted but solicited. However, the provinces, especially Quebec, cannot claim a kind of right to be consulted in sectors of jurisdiction which are considered as "exclusively" *federal* (i.e. monetary policy) while refusing a similar right to Ottawa in sections of jurisdicton whch are considered to be "exclusively" *provincial* (i.e. highways).

The inevitable overlapping, the overall interdependence is thus a reality which has to be acknowledged.

Hence, it is not possible anymore, in my view, to divide clearly and once and for all the fields of activity. *The sharing of power* between Ottawa and the provinces is no longer the sole major problem of Canadian federalism. The true key problems are: 1) the establishment of *priorities of action*: the decisions as to what must be done first and how, it being understood that everything cannot be done at the same time; 2) *pre-consultation and continuous co-operation* in the establishment of priorities of action as well as the implementation of measures which have been adopted jointly.

4. Provincial priorities

Another key proposition of co-operative federalism: the claim by the provinces, especially Quebec, and the acknowledgement by Ottawa of the priority, not in principle, but "actual" (Mr. Lesage, himself, used this word), i.e. in the social, economic and political situation in which we Canadians are now living *of certain provincial requirements:* education, social security, highways and economic development. Once again I repeat, these priorities are essentially relative; the situation could change (unfortunately, a world war is not impossible), the order of priority also. But we can say that co-operative federalism *is essentially a decentralizing force,* that it brings about a certain decrease in Ottawa's role, at least the gradual withdrawal by the central government from esentially provincial sectors. Ottawa's offer to hand over to the provinces a large number of joint plans, announced today, is but one of several proofs.

5. The division of income: "to each according to its needs"

The distribution of government income and especially the powers of taxation between Ottawa and the provinces has been going on since 1957 and especially since 1961, not by virtue of the powers of taxation or methods of taxation described in the British North America Act, but, on the basis of the above-mentioned propositions, by virtue of the responsibilities accepted by each level of government at a given period. "To each order of government according to its needs." There is agreement between Ottawa and the provinces in this respect.

The provinces have submitted their financial needs to the central government, especially in their acknowledged fields of priority as of now. The central government has acknowledged the merits of these claims and for some years has been making major tax concessions to the provinces. Mr. Diefenbaker boasted the other day in the House of Commons that he had paid to the provinces from 1957 to 1961, $439 million more in unconditional subsidies and $698 million more in conditional subsidies than the previous government. The agreements concluded following the Federal-Provincial Conferences of November 1963 and April 1964 resulted in an additional displacement during the years 1963-64 to 1966-67 of $523 million in favour of the provinces including $323 million in favour of Quebec. *Tax decentralization is already a reality.* The provinces have recently obtained a larger share of the individual income tax and of the estate tax. The equalization formula has been improved. Other federal laws: assistance for technical and vocational training, assistance to municipalities, youth allowances, the submission of federal crown corporations to provincial taxes, student loans, especially the transfer to the consenting provinces of certain joint plans with a corresponding share of the powers of taxation and, what is more important, the capitalization now contemplated for the pension fund, which will apparently make no less than $4 billion (and probably more) available to the provinces within the next ten years, . . . all this is contributing not only toward making funds but also additional powers available to the provinces. Mr. Laporte said "we must reverse steam": it is obvious that steam has already been reversed.

6. The repatriation of joint programs

Few commentators deny the theoretical unconstitutionality and the practical difficulties of several joint plans although most of them recognize the past and future usefulness of the device "in certain circumstances" (Mr. Lesage). We have just said so: co-operative federalism recommends "that the provinces which so desire be entrusted with the full responsibilities of certain well-established programs which at any rate are presently administered by the provinces" (Mr. Gordon) and "which entail relatively stable, annual expenditures," with, of course, the equivalent financial resources or better still the equivalent powers of taxation.

This very day, it was announced that twelve joint plans will be offered to the provinces.

Co-operative federalism also recommends that Ottawa should not introduce any more joint plans unless it has the provinces' consent.

7. Co-operation and co-ordination

As a result of all that we have said, co-operative federalism proclaims the necessity of consultation, co-operation and co-ordination on a permanent basis between the two levels of Government. You will tell me that this principle was violated in some cases. That is true, and by both sides. However, the over-all progress is no less evident. Mr. Lesage has acknowledged that there has never been so much co-operation between Ottawa and the provincial capitals as now. Agreed, but we must do better still . . . .

In the event of irreparable conflicts of ideology or interests, co-operative federalism acknowledges that the provinces have 1) a right of *option*: i.e., to a different method more respectful of provincial autonomy, of putting into practice a law which stems mainly from the Federal Government; 2) the right of *contracting out*; i.e., the right to waive all participation in a federal-provincial plan: (i.e., assistance to universities), without being penalized.

Instruments of co-ordination are already in place and others will be created to make common action more efficient: a federal-provincial secretariat, a joint economic committee, etc.

8. The particular status of Quebec

Co-operative federalism acknowledges the right of the French Canadians, a "minority not like the others," the right of Quebec, "a province not like the others," to a particular status.

All we have just set forth makes possible a particular status for *Quebec* within Canadian federalism if, for example, it wants to take advantage of options, "contracting out," and withdrawal from joint plans.

Other questions will arise. I agree for my part that the lieutenant-governor could be appointed by the Provincial Governments; I am sure that the right of the provinces, especially Quebec, to diplomatic or quasi-diplomatic action within the purview of its traditional jurisdiction will soon be acknowledged.

The rights of *French Canadians* are partially acknowledged by the text of 1867; the only thing to do is to make the facts comply with the act . . . and to draw from its texts certain implications. It is the purpose of the Laurendeau-Dunton Commission to have the French language acknowledged everywhere in Canada where this is possible; it is the objective of the Pearson Government to have bilingualism recognized within the federal civil service. If they succeed, as I think they will, major constitutional amendments will have been achieved since Section 133 of the Act of 1867 does not go so far.

9. Constitutional pragmatism

How did the recent changes come about and how will future changes be carried out? Will we have to rewrite the Canadian Constitutional text? Here we have conflicts of mentality, a rift between the formalists, who are not all French Canadians, and the pragmatists, who are not all English Canadians. . . .

A study of Canadian federalism shows that *circumstances* explain its original formulation as well as the subsequent changes, and the judicial interpretation, conventions of the constitution, ordinary legislation and in rare cases, formal amendment have been used in the past *to legalize changes*.

From now on, we cannot rely too much on formal amendments and judicial interpretation: major changes, present and future, are and will be legalized by constitutional practice and by ordinary acts adopted by the federal and by the provincial governments following consulation and federal-provincial agreements. For example, it should be observed that the recent tax arrangement between Ottawa and the provinces constitutes a de facto revision of sections 102 to 120 of the British North America Act.

At this time, a complete redrafting of the Act of 1867 seems to me, considering the present discussions and the nebulousness of the situation, not only impossible but dangerous even if co-operative federalism does not discard it for the future.

You will tell me that I am anglicized, that co-operative federalism is an Anglo-saxon philosophy and technique. I will reply that even some great jurists of France do not think otherwise about the usefulness of written constitutional documents. We could benefit from reading the article written by George Burdeau in *Les Etudes en l'honneur de Achille Mestre,* an article entitled: "A Survival: the idea of a Constitution." For Burdeau real powers exist which are infra, supra and para-constitutional, but which are not liable of perfect integration in a constitutional text. He writes:

> Considering the forces of this type, it would seem that the *idea of the constitution is outmoded*. Politics is similar to an instinctive or internal function in that it admits only the law of possibility and requirements. The truth is that constitutions do not encompass the manifestations of political life. The latter evolves *independently of their provisions* and that is what explains the favour now being enjoyed by studies in political science.

Unfortunately, to my mind, too many French-Canadian politicians are suffering from *legalitis* especially with regard to our constitution. They seem to want to settle problems by fabricating legislation. Fortunately, in practice, the pragmatism of the majority overrides them.

Conclusions

Thus, here are the key propositions which I might use to define Canadian co-operative federalism:

1) profitability, even from the economic standpoint, of economic and political decentralization;
2) the existence of two nations and the necessity of transposing this fact at the political level;
3) the division of taxation between the central and regional governments according to the principle "to each according to its ability" to find a better solution for such and such a problem;
4) the unavoidable overlapping of activity between the two levels of government;
5) the present "actual" priority of provincial authority in certain fields;
6) the distribution of tax income and taxation powers between Ottawa and the provincial capitals according to the principle "to each level of government according to its requirements";
7) the necessity of constant co-operation and co-ordination between the central and the regional governments;
8) the particular status of the French Canadians and of Quebec;
9) pragmatism, empiricism, in the legal formulation of the new system.

Someone underscored last evening the need for world federalism. Very well. But before offering the formula to the world, let us try to prove that federalism can work in Canada.

21 "Co-operative Federalism" in the New Face of Centralisation*

J. M. Leger

Next week, under the sign of "co-operative federalism", the federal-provincial conference season will open. On September 9, business begins with a meeting devoted to the proposed Canada-wide social security followed by the conference on main highways, and, in November, the first of a series of meetings on the division of fiscal resources. It is quite likely that other meetings will be added to this already very busy schedule.

* Translation of "le 'fédéralisme coopératif' ou le nouveau visage de la centralisation" which appeared in *Le Devoir* (Montreal, Tuesday, September 3, 1963). By permission of the author and *Le Devoir*.

J. M. LEGER – *Le Devoir*.

The expression "co-operative federalism", first used by Ottawa a few months ago, has become exceedingly popular in certain quarters and has especially been taken up by the English-language press. Let us first note the redundancy in this expression: he who says 'federalism' also says that co-operation for federalism is impossible unless the parties involved want to co-operate, have the means to guarantee co-operation, and finally intend to respect each other's areas of jurisdiction. The fact that the 'co-operative' aspect of Canadian federalism is being stressed today can only indicate that Canadian federalism has failed, that it has become only a pious wish, or that it is time to offer condolences on its passing.

What then is "co-operative federalism"? What ideas and desires behind this formula allow it, according to certain of our politicians, to be considered a universal panacea? This so-called new kind of federalism is presented to us as the firm indication of an historic turning-point in relations between Ottawa and the provincial capitals, as the dawn of a new day, and as the unstated recognition on the part of the federal government that too often it has acted as if the provinces did not exist. Politically, the formula would have made sense and would have been acceptable (despite the redundancy in its name) if the federal government also decided to intervene no longer in areas controlled by the provincial governments and to abandon without delay those areas where it is presently acting but where it actually has no jurisdiction.

A New Name But Nothing Changed

Now what do we see? Exactly the opposite. "Co-operative federalism" has been accompanied by a new and vigorous assault against certain prerogatives of the provincial governments and by a reappearance of the philosophy of centralisation which, in truth, underlies the British North America Act of 1867, and which various governments in Ottawa have repeatedly endeavoured to encourage.

Thus the conference that took place at the end of last July and the agreement that followed have been greeted as an expression of "co-operative federalism". However, despite the various modifications and adjustments, despite the alternative choice offered to Quebec in particular, no one can deny that this is another advance toward centralisation and another violation of both the spirit and the letter of the B.N.A. The federal government, via winter works programmes and the fight against unemployment, has entered the area of municipal affairs. It was again in the name of co-operative federalism that a conference was called to deal with the federal general retirement fund by which Ottawa continued to control the important area of social security. In a year or so, following the same plan, Ottawa will invite the provincial government to study a proposed system run by the federal government to grant scholarships to students at university and in community colleges, etc.

To summarize, Ottawa wishes "to help the provinces fulfill their obligations" by assuming control over some of the provinces' areas of jurisdiction, in the name of "national unity", the "Canadian common weal", efficiency and uniformity.

From Promoting Co-operation with the Provinces . . . to Centralisation

The ploy is clever: to have the provincial governments lay down their powers one by one and on their own, and under the guise of co-operation and by means of general and in depth consultation, to link them with the federal government's insidious and patient efforts to achieve centralisation. Of course, two times out of three, Ottawa will have to revise its original plan, to agree to arrangements, to allow options, particular options for particular provinces. However, this will not matter for the desired end will have been achieved; Ottawa's right to intervene will have been admitted, albeit with bad grace, and the control apparatus will have been set up. The rest will be only a matter of time, of political sense, of pressure at the appropriate moment, of financial arrangements.

In the Canadian federation, Ottawa has already assumed control over external affairs as well as over a great deal of internal affairs. Obviously it intends (as it has amply shown since 1945) to take over by stages those areas of internal government which it does not yet control. Initially it tries to bring about joint rule with the provinces in their areas of jurisdiction. Eventually it takes over completely.

It is only in the areas falling under provincial jurisdiction (municipal affairs, social security, education, labour, health, planning, land management, etc.) that Ottawa discovers the virtues of co-operative federalism, that is, of a formula which allows it to intervene where it has not formerly done so. We are witnessing the initial stages of the strongest campaign for centralisation ever unleashed by Ottawa, of a campaign which is even more dangerous since it goes under the title of co-operation. Ottawa might say: "We are not forcing anything upon you. Rather, we are offering you help in facing up to your duties. We shall share your terrible burden and your difficult tasks and provide you with financial and technical aid and, if you so desire, even a legal framework . . . what is of importance here is not to waste time in petty discussion of resource sharing and areas of authority, but rather to work together for the common good of all Canadians. And who would not admit that the federal government is the best equipped in every way to fulfil this purpose in all areas, with, of course, the 'co-operation' of the provinces?"

The Only Fool is He Who Wishes to be a Fool

Obviously "co-operative federalism" is only another clever and deceptive name for centralisation. With upsetting naivety, many good people wish to see the beginning of a new era in Ottawa's increasing the number of conferences with the provinces. According to these people, centralisation is dead and gone and Ottawa will consult with the provincial governments in future. But in what areas does Ottawa consult with the provinces? The federal government makes new incursions into areas under provincial jurisdiction or increases its meddling in sectors where it has already entered. Could one imagine for a single moment that Ottawa would call a federal–provincial conference to study the federal government's retirement measure under the social security plan, to discuss its surrendering control over direct taxation, or, again to examine Canada's foreign policy? The answer to that question is obvious. "Co-operative-federalism" has only one meaning and goes in only one direction. Without doubt, it will be one of the greatest deceptions of the century.

Ottawa's action is encouraged by the false image that many people, both in Quebec and elsewhere, have of the federal system, which they see as a pyramid with Ottawa at the top. In this simplified vision, naturally supported by those in favour of centralisation, the municipalities are at the bottom, with next the provincial and regional governments, and finally the central government, Ottawa, which is responsible for the well being of all Canadians. It is evident that the great majority of English-speaking Canadians have in actual fact accepted this idea; for them, Ottawa is the "national government" and naturally has priority over the provinces and in almost all areas.

Centralisation is found in our constitution, it is supported by English-speaking Canada, it is sought after by the government in Ottawa as well as by the federal public service. Unless it collapses under an avalanche of *ad hoc* measures (something which is, alas, not impossible) the Quebec government will have to realize that it is engaged in a vital and continuing battle. This struggle will become more and more difficult and will expand to include all sectors; it will end only when the present federation falls apart completely or when a new constitution, more suited to a confederation, is adopted.

22   Co-operative Federalism: An Evaluation*

Donald V. Smiley

Cooperative federalism is in essence a series of pragmatic and piecemeal responses by the federal and provincial governments to the circumstances of their mutual interdependence. We will try in this article to evaluate this evolving system of relations in answer to three kinds of general questions.

First, what are the general preconditions of success in cooperative federalism?

Second, what are the relative possibilities of cooperative federalism and

* From Donald V. Smiley, *Constitutional Adaption and Canadian Federalism Since 1945*. Volume 4 of the Documents of the Royal Commission on Bilingualism and Biculturalism (Ottawa, Queen's Printer, 1970), pp. 111-28. Reprinted by permission of the author and Information Canada.

DONALD V. SMILEY — Professor of Political Science, University of Toronto.

explicit constitutional reform in meeting the demands for change in the Canadian federal system?

Third, what are the possibilities of the ongoing procedures of cooperative federalism in meeting the demands of English and French Canadians and of securing the survival of the Canadian federal union?

A. Circumstances of Success

1. Public policy effectiveness

There can be little disagreement with the general proposition that if liberal-democratic institutions are to survive they must somehow find ways of dealing with the very great number of varied and often contradictory demands made upon them, and that only by demonstrating such effectiveness can enough support be generated among the politically influential elements of democratic communities to ensure the long-run continuance of these institutions. In federal systems the individual jurisdictions must not only learn to respond effectively to demands upon them but must also evolve adequate means of central-regional articulation to cope with the circumstances of the interdependence of the two levels. Such articulation can take two forms, coordination and consultation.

Coordination is the process by which a complex of public activities is ordered according to some set of goals or priorities. Coordination relates both to the ranking itself and the subsequent actions to implement these decisions.

Consultation is the process by which officials and public agencies, with some significant degree of both independent discretion and mutual inter-dependence, communicate to each other their respective perceptions of situations and their judgements of the appropriate way of dealing with these situations. Coordination will be facilitated by effective procedures of consultation but does not always result from them.

Coordination and consultation in respect to public policy are of course easier to achieve when only one jurisdiction is involved and when, in principle at least, activities can be ordered through one hierarchical structure of authority than when, as in a federal system, the participants have legal and political safeguards for their independent positions. Within a hierarchical system authorized channels of communication are usually provided, although other patterns grow up through deliberate design or otherwise. Hierarchy also provides formal procedures by which solutions may be imposed in the absence of agreement and, as J. A. Corry pointed out many years ago, the very existence of these procedures may inhibit "bickering."[1] The relations between the federal and provincial governments cannot of course proceed within a pattern of hierarchical authority. On the surface, it would seem that

---

[1] J. A. Corry, *Difficulties of Divided Jurisdiction: A Study Prepared for the Royal Commission on Dominion-Provincial Relations* (Ottawa, 1940), p. 10.

the processes of joint decision-making which characterize cooperative federalism must lead almost inevitably to delays and frustrations in the framing and implementation of public policy.

Despite the inherent difficulties in working the institutions of cooperative federalism, it is significant that in the past two years a very large volume of public policy has resulted from the collaborative procedures. Agreements of fundamental importance have been reached in respect to contracting-out, public contributory pension plans and important aspects of economic direction and control. Important changes appear to be coming in the fields of medical insurance and public assistance. The agreement to set up the Tax Structure Committee was a major achievement in this direction and one can be reasonably optimistic that this committee will have some measure of success in attaining the ambitious objectives set out in its terms of reference. I am not here stating that these actual and anticipated policies resulting from the processes of cooperative federalism were the appropriate responses of the governments concerned to the demands upon them. Rather, I would argue that the record indicates that these procedures of joint decision-making have not in the recent past imposed insuperable barriers to the formulation and implementation of public policies of fundamental importance.

Consultative procedures leading to federal-provincial policy coordination are extraordinarily subtle and one cannot predict with any assurance the form which the most effective of these procedures will take. What seems reasonably certain, however, is that the establishment of administrative machinery, even though ingenious, will not of itself bring about constructive relations. The following general points can be made:

1. Consultation leading to effective coordination will be facilitated when the participants can speak authoritatively for their respective governments. This does not mean that the officials involved have received explicit "instructions" from their governments on every matter under discussion; such a formal requirement would inhibit effective consultation. What is necessary is that the participants perceive each other as persons closely in touch with the perspectives of their respective administrations and with some degree of influence in determining these perspectives. There is also the requirement, that is probably not completely fulfilled in any of the governments, that effective procedures of cabinet and treasury control be maintained so that programme agencies and programme goals are subordinated to more comprehensive goals. As we saw in Chapter VII, a complex pattern of functional relations has developed between counterpart agencies of the two levels and in some circumstances those involved in these relations may resist attempts to subsume their activities under less particularistic goals. Although the effective articulation of federal and provincial objectives involves these functional interactions being sustained and in some cases strengthened, effective relations concerning more comprehensive kinds of public policies require greater measures of overhead control than have been developed in some jurisdictions.

2. Consultation and coordination will be facilitated when the participants come to share as much of a common frame of reference as is compatible with their continuing loyalty to their respective governments. Federal-provincial collaboration in respect to a very large number of specific programmes and projects has been possible largely because those involved were members of the same professions or sub-professions. Such membership characteristically means not only the common possession of specialized knowledge and techniques but also commitment to certain public-policy preferences. When matters of more fundamental political and economic choice are at issue it is unreasonable to expect that federal-provincial agreement can be reached in terms of such professional criteria, although agreement on matters of economic policy is more likely than otherwise if the elected and appointed officials involved are relatively sophisticated in the ways of contemporary economic analysis. However, a prolonged period of constructive relationships between the elected and appointed officials of the federal and provincial governments can be expected to result in a kind of community being developed, a community with its own characteristic perspectives and procedures and with its own subtle ways of distributing status and influence among its members. This development will of course be encouraged if the membership in such a group becomes relatively stable and if there is some movement of personnel among the governments involved. It is obvious that the growth of community is dependent upon the politicians of the federal and provincial governments continuing to support such kinds of collaborative behaviour.

3. Consultation and minimum levels of coordination will be facilitated if the participants are more committed to the substantive results of particular policies than to enhancing the influence of their respective governments. Cooperative federalism requires a high degree of pragmatism, even opportunism, among those officials involved in federal-provincial relations as to what functions each level should perform. Thus any assumption by federal officials that decisions by the central government are somehow inherently "better" or more legitimate than those of the provinces is clearly incompatible with effective federal-provincial collaboration. Conversely, if some or all of the provinces carry out a persistent policy of attempting to extend their range of discretion at the expense of the federal authorities, the prerequisites of cooperative federalism are challenged in the most fundamental way. Any effective system of federal-provincial relations must of course deal with circumstances in which there are conflicts between the interests of the governments involved. It is only realistic to recognize that these differences characteristically arise from the divergent responsibilities these jurisdictions have assumed rather than from the perversity of the authorities of one level or the other. However, no government can be a constructive collaborator in the enterprise if its over riding objective is to decrease its dependence on the others regardless of the consequences of such actions for the substantive results of public policy.

4. Effective consultation leading to at least limited measures of coordination will be facilitated if the participating governments are predisposed to include the objectives of the others within their own priorities. Let us take a simple example. Assume federal-provincial discussions about a proposed measure where the result would be to increase municipal borrowing for capital purposes. Assume further that the primary objectives of the federal authorities relate to the income and employment aspects of these expenditures and that the first aim of the provinces is to safeguard the financial solvency of the municipalities. If each government presses its primary aim to the exclusion of the concerns of the other it is likely that these will prove incompatible, to a greater or lesser degree. But let us make more optimistic assumptions that either before or as a result of intergovernmental consultations (a) the provinces recognize both that the increase in aggregate demand expected to result from the measure is desirable and that the federal authorities have a legitimate interest in ensuring full employment, (b) the federal government shows a genuine interest in the continuing financial stability of the municipalities and a sympathetic appreciation of provincial concern for this objective. Under such circumstances effective consultation can lead to a solution which includes both federal and provincial aims, a solution agreed upon against a background of mutual respect among the governments concerned for the constitutional responsibilities of each other.

5. Consultation will be facilitated when for the most part it takes place within a framework of confidentiality and when both formally and informally the governments come to share with each other information about situations and their appreciation of these situations which are not available to the public. It does not seem necessary to argue that the processes of federal-provincial collaboration and consultation about fundamentals cannot be successful unless to some considerable degree they can take place without publicity until agreements are reached. The sharing of information and views among the officials must be continuous and it is impossible to defend the situation which existed in the past where the federal authorities were prepared to share these more freely with friendly foreign governments than with provincial administrations. In the present context of federal-provincial relations, however, the federal government appears more sensitive to provincial responsibilities which may have significant implications for federal policies than at least some of the provinces.

In general, the relative success of cooperative federalism in recent years in harmonizing to some tolerable degree the objectives of the federal and provincial governments has depended much more on the attitudes of the officials involved and on the restraints they have placed on their own behaviour than on the development of more institutionalized procedures of intergovernmental collaboration. The existing structures are extraordinarily complex and work as well as they do largely because the individuals involved, including both elected and appointed officials, have come to know and respect each other in their increasingly frequent contacts. Whether or not this somewhat personalized fabric of cooperation could survive the dislocation of a rapid displacement of the present personnel is a matter of conjecture.

2. Political competition and articulation

The preceding chapters of this study have analyzed cooperative federalism exclusively as it relates to interactions between the federal and provincial executives. It would, however, be unrealistic in such an evaluation to ignore completely the political context within which these relations take place, to ignore the fact that the overriding decisions in federal-provincial relations are made by successful politicians who must periodically fight campaigns for re-election and who must continually defend their public conduct both in their respective legislatures and outside. There are two difficulties of a broadly political nature in the contemporary variant of cooperative federalism.

First, federal-provincial relations have dealt increasingly with policy matters of the most fundamental kind, matters which a democratic community has a disposition to settle by the processes of free and open debate and political competition. Yet the success of the governments concerned in reaching tolerable settlements requires a considerable degree of insulation from publicity and from certain varieties of partisan political pressures.

Second, the interdependence of federal and provincial officials in their policy-making and policy-executing roles exercises strong influences towards collaborative behaviour. There are, however, fewer such influences on elected officials in their partisan political capacities.

The situation involving the so-called Fulton-Favreau formula illustrates one of the kinds of political difficulties which cooperative federalism may face. From the time that federal-provincial discussions on an amending procedure were reactivated by the Minister of Justice in 1961, until the publication of the draft formula upon which all the governments had agreed in the summer of 1964, there was little public debate on the issue even among specialists in constitutional matters and it was impossible for those outside government to know, except in a general way, what was going on.[2] Between the time the draft formula was agreed upon and the spring of 1965 the projected amendment was approved by the legislatures of all the provinces except Quebec without causing the incumbent provincial administrations significant political difficulties. By this time, however, considerable opposition to the Fulton-Favreau formula had been aroused—opposition from members of the Progressive Conservative and New Democratic parties in the House of Commons, from the Union Nationale and several influential private groups in Quebec and both from French- and English-speaking specialists in constitutional matters. The federal and Quebec governments thus faced a difficult situation. They had been precluded because of the relative and confidentiality of the discussions preceding the agreement from cultivating public support for the

---

2 Mr. Fulton did, however, submit the draft proposals to a selected group of university law teachers for their comments.

new procedure. The matter at hand was a complex one and the draft formula was the result of a complicated compromise among the governments involved. Yet many of its critics put their arguments in terms of broad and easily understandable considerations quite unrelated to the acceptability of their proposals to the 11 governments. Despite these difficulties, the failure of either or both of the administrations to press the issue to legislative approval would place on them the onus for delaying the enactment of a Canadian amending procedure which had been under discussion for nearly 40 years. Such a failure might also complicate their relations with administrations which had secured the assent of their legislatures. It is likely that similar situations will arise in the future. Fundamental policy discussions will be carried on in confidence between the federal and provincial governments and will culminate in an agreement which becomes the subject of vigorous debate largely precluded until that time. Neither the members of the opposition parties nor the other members of politically influential publics have apparently fully accepted as legitimate the fact that high policy may be made by federal-provincial agreement. Because of this, policies devised by these procedures may be subjected to more severe criticism than if they were made by a single jurisdiction, and criticism somewhat harder for their supporters to answer.

The relationships between federal and provincial political parties and the impact of these relations on the stands on public issues that these parties take are extraordinarily complex and have never been systematically examined.[3] In some cases the electoral success of a federal or provincial party is significantly aided or frustrated by actions of the party of the same name at the other level; in other circumstances there may be little interdependence. Partisan political interactions between members of Parliament and members of the same parties in the provincial legislatures are conditioned by this kind of factor, by financial and other relationships between federal and provincial party organizations, by antagonism and friendships growing out of previous political experience and by other influences. In most cases, however, it would appear that successful federal and provincial parties have resources of funds, organizations and popular support independent of party fortunes at the other level. It seems that usually only very weak parties are effectively subordinated to their electorally more successful federal or provincial counterparts. In circumstances where the federal government and that of a province bear the same party label there is thus no assurance that their relations will be harmonious, and Canadian political history has many contrary examples. On the other hand, where federal and provincial parties in power are of different complexions, there are no overriding partisan political inhibitions imposed on collaboration in policy matters. In general, however, the influences on the federal and provincial administrations to collaborate because of their mutual interdependence in policy matters have little counterpart in the partisan political custom.

---

[3] For one of the few systematic attempts in this direction see Edwin R. Black, "Federal Strains within a Canadian Party", *Dalhousie Review,* Vol. XLV (1965), pp. 307-23.

3. The legitimation of cooperative federalism

If cooperative federalism is in the long run to survive, the politically influential publics in Canada must be persuaded that this is a legitimate way of making crucial public decisions. Such persuasion will be extraordinarily difficult in the face of alternative proposals for reforming our federal institutions, proposals which are on the surface simpler and more conceptually consistent. These difficulties inherent in the complexities of the existing procedures and institutions are compounded by the incompatibility between cooperative federalism and at least three influential systems of ideas about how government in Canada should be carried on.

First, cooperative federalism is difficult to defend in terms of British parliamentary traditions. The underlying assumption of this tradition is that the legislature is sovereign—in the United Kingdom over all matters and in federal countries over all those matters conferred on it by the constitution. This assumption is challenged when the actual locus of decision-making is transferred from the cabinet, which is collectively responsible to the elected chamber, to intergovernmental bodies. Cooperative federalism has been called "government by diplomacy" by one student of the Canadian constitution. Contemporary democratic theory and practice, both where British parliamentary traditions prevail and elsewhere, have found it extraordinarily difficult to deal with situations involving the external relations of governments.

Second, cooperative federalism in its symbolic aspects gives Quebec no special status in the Canadian federal system. Daniel Johnson has said of this system:

> Au lieu d'une véritable constitution, nous avons un régime mouvant, qui est constamment en mutation et qui est le produit des accords formels ou tacites entre Ottawa et la majorité des provinces. *L'autorité suprême du pays . . . c'est une institution qui n'est même pas mentionnée dans l'Acte de l'Amérique britannique du Nord.* C'est le forum des conférences fédérales-provinciales. Et là, le Québec n'a pas plus de droits que Terre-Neuve.[4]

The Honourable Jean-Luc Pepin in the most systematic defence of cooperative federalism that has ever been made[5] has argued that this alternative recognizes both "cette réalité socio-politique du binationalisme" and "un statut particulier" for Quebec in the Canadian federal system. However, in the formal aspects of federal-provincial relations and in the strict adherence to the rule that the various contracting-out options are available to all the provinces, the symbol, if not the substance, of the equality of the province is upheld.

Third, cooperative federalism to be successful requires a degree of secrecy in decision-making which is believed by many to be incompatible with the re-

---

4 Daniel Johnson, *Egalité ou indépendance* (Montréal, 1965), p. 73.
5 Hon. Jean-Luc Pepin, "Le fédéralisme coopératif" in Conférence annuelle de l'Institut canadien des affaires publiques, *Le Canada face à l'avenir* (Montréal, 1964), p. 113-24.

quirements of democracy. Members of the working press have become increasingly restive with the confidential nature of these processes and many have suggested that conferences of prime ministers and premiers be held in public. The necessity for secrecy until the results of federal-provincial negotiations are concluded can be expected to inhibit the legitimation of cooperative federalism.

B. Cooperative Federalism and Constitutional Change

Those who wish changes in the Canadian federal system can be divided into two groups—those who press for such reforms to come through the processes of federal-provincial collaboration and those bent on explicit alterations in the text of the existing constitution. The debate between them is not easily joined. Persons who are convinced that a substantial rewriting of the constitution is necessary often appear to place a high value on clarity and explicitness in our governmental arrangements and on the symbolic significance of a constitution as embodying the fundamental moral and political principles on which the regime is founded. By these tests, cooperative federalism is of course deficient. On the other hand, supporters of a new constitution have not, so far as I am able to discover, made a careful study of the traditions and institutions of Canadian federalism as they have evolved in the past five years, or of the possibilities that some or most of the objectives they seek could be attained through the processes of federal-provincial interaction. But proponents of cooperative federalism have not investigated in any detail the incidence of formal constitutional arrangements on these institutions or the constraints that these arrangements impose on the attainment of particular substantive objectives.

Our evaluation of the relative appropriateness of the two broad alternatives as procedures of constitutional evolution will proceed in terms of answers to three questions.

First, if we assume that changes will require the agreement of the federal government and those of most if not all of the provinces, is it more likely that agreement will be secured for explicit constitutional change or for adaptation through federal collaboration on particular public policy matters?

Second, can the relations between the federal and provincial governments be more appropriately regulated through interactions between federal and provincial executives than through other procedures?

Third, is it appropriate to amend the constitution to provide explicitly for the institutions and procedures of federal-provincial relations?

1. The necessity for federal-provincial agreement

So far as I am able to discover, those who wish the Canadian constitution to be rewritten have never seriously considered whether or not it is likely that politically influential elements in the country could be brought to agreement on this matter. This applies to supporters in Quebec of the associated states solution, to Peter J. T. O'Hearn[6] and to Marcel Faribault and Robert M. Fowler[7] who have presented detailed draft constitutions and to those persons who have called for a new constitution without suggesting what they believe its nature should be. It appears unlikely that the required measure of agreement could be secured in the near future. The political relations between the "two founding races" are in a critical and fluid state. The institutions and procedures of federal-provincial relations are evolving rapidly. I would therefore agree with one scholar who remarked "to try to redraft the Canadian constitution now would be the same as trying to write a peace treaty while a war was still on." It is possible, however, to foresee limited changes in the constitution. One could imagine agreement to drop its obsolete sections and improve its literary qualities. Perhaps progress could be made toward a constitutional bill of rights binding on all governments and not subject to unilateral amendment by any. It may be possible to find agreement on more adequate protection for French-speaking and English-speaking cultural minorities. On the other hand, any attempt to rewrite the constitution to change in a fundamental way the division of legislative powers between Parliament and the provinces would require simultaneous federal-provincial agreement on a very wide range of basic political issues. It seems to me unlikely that such an agreement will emerge in the immediate future.

The processes of cooperative federalism allow politicans and civil servants to search for agreement where it can be found. I argued in the last chapter that the current circumstances of federal-provincial interdependence make necessary effective measures of intergovernmental collaboration in respect to fairly fundamental policy alternatives. On the other hand, a federal-provincial conference, unlike a constitutional convention, deals with specific proposals for action and does not have to strive for agreement on matters of abstract definition or on how to deal with hypothetical situations which may arise in the future. In the crucial area of the direction and control of the Canadian economy Jacques Parizeau has advanced a persuasive argument which is applicable to an even broader range of problems facing the Canadian federal system:

> [can we] conclude . . . that changes in the constitution are likely to help the organization of adequate and co-ordinated economic policies? Personally, I doubt this very much. On the contrary, the constitution as it stands now has helped to narrow the areas of conflict. To attempt, in present circumstances, a full revision or redrafting of the constitution means really that the whole front will be ablaze; any rational solution to urgent problems of economic policies might have to be postponed for a long time. It would seem much more fruitful to find first an empirical equilibrium between the governments and then draft it into a legal text.[8]

---

[6] Peter J. T. O'Hearn, *Peace, Order and Good Government* (Toronto, 1964).

[7] Marcel Faribault and Robert M. Fowler, *Ten to One: The Confederation Wager* (Toronto, 1965).

[8] Jacques Parizeau, "Prospects for Economic Policy in a Federal Canada" in Crépeau and Macpherson (eds.), *The Future of Canadian Federalism*, p. 57.

2. "Executive" federalism and other alternatives for regulating federal-provincial relations

There are two alternatives to cooperative federalism in regulating the relations between the federal and provincial governments. The first is that the judiciary should assume a more active role in delineating the respective powers, privileges and responsibilities of the two levels. This appears to be unrealistic in the light of recent experience in Canada and in other developed federations. Judicial interpretation of the constitution is almost inevitably sporadic and the predilection of the courts is to emphasize the exclusive jurisdiction of central and regional governments rather than the articulation of their activities. Furthermore, in Canada at least, many of the more important problems of federal-provincial relations, particularly as these concern fiscal matters and the direction and control of the economy, do not seem appropriate for judicial determination. The second alternative is to vest in some group or groups other than the courts the tasks of making some of the most important decisions in Canadian federalism. Such a group or groups would require some degree of independence of both levels of government. The Rowell-Sirois Report recommended "the establishment of a permanent and independent Commission to advise the federal government on the payment of National Adjustment Grants to the provinces and to reappraise each five years the criteria according to which such subsidies were paid." This recommendation received little support at the time it was made and has since been regarded as one of the commission's less constructive suggestions. In his recent book proposing a new Canadian constitution Peter J. T. O'Hearn suggests a "Federal Council" which, according to his draft constitution:

> shall consist of Delegates of the Government in Canada. Each Provincial Government shall appoint one Delegate and the Government of Canada shall appoint Delegates not exceeding in number the Provincial Delegates. The Chairman shall be elected from the Delegates of the Government of Canada and the Council shall meet at the Call of the Chairman or any Five Delegates. The Council may make a binding Allocation between the Government of Canada, on the one Hand, and the Governments of the Provinces, on the other Hand, for any Period not exceeding Ten years, of the Powers to tax and borrow, and may determine the limits of Rates or Amounts that shall apply to the Allocation; but to do so a Majority of the Delegates of the Provincial Governments representing a Majority of the Population of Canada, according to the latest general Census, must concur.[9]

It is significant that O'Hearn's proposal would permit such a "binding Allocation" of taxation and borrowing powers to be imposed on any or all of the provinces without their consent provided that the federal government and the requisite number of other provinces agreed. This condition alone would appear to make the proposal unrealistic. In general, the past history and present circumstances of Canadian federalism make it very unlikely that the federal government and the provinces will choose to have their relations

---

[9] *Ibid.*, p. 45.

regulated in fundamental ways either by the courts or by independent executive agencies explicitly charged with these responsibilities; nor, in my opinion would they gain any important advantages by doing so.

3. The constitutional recognition of cooperative federalism

Is it appropriate to redraft the constitution to provide for the institutions and procedures of cooperative federalism? The draft constitution suggested by Marcel Faribault and Robert M. Fowler provides for three federal-provincial agencies—an economic development bank, a fiscal commission and an economic and social council.[10] Under the proposed constitution each of these bodies would be composed of four members appointed by the federal government and two each appointed by Quebec, Ontario, the four western provinces and the Atlantic provinces. The economic and social council would be an information-gathering agency to transmit to all jurisdictions materials on "the general trend of the Canadian economy, its medium and long-term prospects, its productivity, and the rate of growth, as well as on the comparative growth of the several Canadian provinces, the improvement of the standard of living in their several regions and the general betterment of social relations in Canada." The economic development bank was to aid in the development of depressed regions, to remedy serious and unforseen economic disturbances in particular provinces and to "aid in the execution" of important interprovincial projects. The major task assigned to the fiscal commission was to advise the governments concerned on their taxing and spending policies. The "statutes, regulations and by-laws" of the latter two groups were to be determined, according to the draft constitution, by "protocol between the federal government and the provinces by a three-fourth majority of the latter."

Faribault and Fowler nowhere demonstrate that the institutions and procedures they suggest would be preferable to the ones which are now in process of evolution. There is no evidence given, for example, that the proposed social and economic council would proceed more effectively than the present Economic Council of Canada in its rapidly developing pattern of relations with counterpart agencies in the provinces. Would the "fiscal commission" be more adequate in the devising or implementing of rational taxation and spending policies than the institutions which are now developing? Would the proposed federal-provincial bodies work under the direction of the increasingly frequent meetings of premiers and prime ministers? Such matters appear to have been ignored. Serious proposals for reform in federal-provincial relations must of necessity be based on a careful assessment of the adequacy of existing patterns of interaction. There is no evidence that Faribault and Fowler have done this.

It would seem prudent to try to rewrite the Canadian constitution only after the limits of adjustment possible through the procedures and institutions of cooperative federalism have clearly been reached. As we shall see in the last pages of this study there was some evidence early in 1966 that these limits were being approached.

---

10 *Ibid.*, pp. 145-48.

C. Cooperative Federalism: The Limits of Adjustment

In its legal-constitutional, political and administrative dimensions Canadian federalism has since 1867 demonstrated great resources of adaptability. The major procedures of adaptation in the postwar period have become the processes of federal-provincial executive interaction rather than constitutional amendment or changing patterns of judicial review. In the past 10 years through these interactions the dominance of the federal government established during the Second World War has been attenuated by the effective reassertion of provincial vigour and purpose. Is there then the danger that the influence of the federal government in part or all of the country will be so weakened by piecemeal attrition that Canadian federalism in any recognizable form will cease to exist? For the reasons presented in the concluding pages of this study, I believe this danger to be "clear and present."

The first kind of danger to the Canadian federal system in cooperative federalism is that provincial pressures for autonomy will so weaken the federal government that it will be unable to discharge its responsibilities for the integration and development of the Canadian economy, for economic stabilization and growth and for interregional and interpersonal equalization. There are strong forces towards the enhanced power of the provinces. The proportion of total public expenditures made by the provinces and local authorities is likely to continue to increase, barring rapid increases in defence spending. The new and more specific kinds of social and economic policies which now seem to be necessary make less feasible than before certain kinds of federal control over these matters. The provinces are likely to continue to attract able and purposeful people to their public services. In the House of Commons elected in November 1965, the under-representation of certain provinces in the government party and cabinet may work to make the governments of these provinces the most effective outlet for their distinctive sentiments and interests. Despite these influences, there are strong countervailing forces at work to restrain the further weakening of federal power, at least in the governments of the provinces other than Quebec if not the general public in English Canada. Several premiers have expressed their anxiety about this trend very explicitly and the government of Ontario has been particularly sensitive to these considerations. None of the other provinces has shown any desire to take advantage of the contracting-out option and none has been willing to cooperate with Quebec on a permanent basis to weaken federal influence. It appears too that all of these provinces are actively seeking increased federal financial assistance for particular functions, specifically for higher education and health services. It seems likely that the support of other provincial administrations for federal power will increase as the pressures of the Quebec government for autonomy are pressed more aggressively and as the implications of the *statut particulier* alternative become more apparent.

The second kind of danger, and the one I believe more immediate, is that cooperative federalism will result in a situation in which the political and constitutional relationships between the people of Quebec and those of the other provinces will be so tenuous and so fragmentary—and so much mediated through the government of Quebec rather than being carried on within the institutions of the federal government—that a constitutional revolution destroying Canadian federalism will have been effected. The Lesage administration when it came to power and for some time afterward asserted the traditional Quebec position that it was demanding for itself only what under the constitution belonged equally to all the provinces; Mr. Lesage's defence of the Fulton-Favreau formula was largely on the grounds that any procedure for amendment acceptable to Quebec must provide for unanimous provincial consent in respect to changes in the most fundamental aspects of the constitution. The existing constitutional system, however, makes possible a very considerable amount of *de facto* differentiation between the position of Quebec and that of the other provinces. The Lesage government exploited these possibilities in a sophisticated and successful way. In its last months in power the official position of the Lesage administration apparently reversed the traditional position of the equality of all the provinces and embraced the doctrine of the *statut particulier*. The Honorable Paul Gérin-Lajoie at his convocation address to Carleton University in April 1965, gave advance notice to the new position by questioning in somewhat hypothetical terms the traditional viewpoint that in a constitutional sense Quebec was a province "comme les autres."[11] In his speech to the Ste-Foy Chamber of Commerce on December 14, 1965, Premier Lesage committed his government to the *statut particulier* alternative in the most explicit way.[12]

The claims for a special status for Quebec made by the Lesage government in its last year in office were more than a *post hoc* justification of the con-tracting-out arrangements which had already been implemented. These arrangements, so far as Quebec was concerned, confined the federal authorities, with several important exceptions, to matters within federal legislative jurisdiction. The attainment of such an objective did not satisfy the require-ments of the Lesage government for a wider range of provincial autonomy or for an enhanced provincial influence over federal policy-making. In his Labour Day address in 1965, the Premier asserted that as his adminis-tration came to formulate more far-reaching and explicit plans in respect to manpower and employment it would press for modifications of federal activities in these fields, particularly those of the National Employment Service.[13] The new social security policy, whose outlines were announced by the Honourable René Levesque in November 1965, included a system of family

---

[11] Hon. Paul Gérin-Lajoie, "Convocation Address to Carleton University, April, 1965" (Quebec, Department of Education, Information Service, mimeo.). "Up to the present, Quebec has asked nothing for itself which it would be unwilling to recognize for the other provinces. But one may wonder if this is the correct attitude to take!" (p.5) and "What objection or difficulty would there be if Canada were to adopt a constitutional regime which would take account of the existence of two 'nations' or 'societies' within one Canada?" p. 7.

[12] Reprinted in *Le Devoir,* 23 et 24 décembre, 1965.

[13] *Le Devoir,* 3 septembre, 1965.

allowances based on very different principles than the federal scheme[14] and the same kind of considerations would logically have justified an attempt to replace the federal Old Age Security programme with a provincial one. As Quebec plans for regional development became more explicitly formulated it became reasonable to expect more aggressive efforts to bring federal developmental policies through the Department of Industry, ARDA and other agencies into harmony with provincial requirements. The assertion of the "personnalité internationale" of Quebec was leading to increasingly insistent demands that, without federal supervision or control, the province should be able to enter into direct relations with foreign nations in regard to matters within provincial legislative jurisdiction. The objectives of the Lesage government in the projected steel complex, the newly-created public sector of the mining industry, new plans for rationalizing agriculture and so on could be expected to result in new pressures to influence federal policies closely connected with these objectives. In December 1965, Mr. Lesage announced the creation of a committee under the chairmanship of Jacques Parizeau to study and report by the end of 1966 on the activities of certain classes of financial institutions and appropriate provincial legislation which might be enacted to regulate them. Eric Kierans is reported to have informed the federal-provincial conference the same month that Quebec would find contracting-out applied to new federal programmes unacceptable and would demand fiscal equivalents without undertaking any commitments about the service or facility in question.[15] Thus the pressures of the Lesage government in respect to specific fields of policy-making were working steadily towards a situation in which Quebec had a significantly larger scope of *de facto* autonomy than that possessed by the other provinces.

The creation of a special status for Quebec has implications of the most fundamental kind for the workings of the institutions of the federal government. If the present trends continue, Parliament will deal increasingly with matters for which Quebec has assumed exclusive responsibility within that province. Increasingly, important federal agencies which deal with matters of crucial concern elsewhere in Canada will have only a tangential relationship to the people and government of Quebec. Increasingly, federal elections will revolve about matters which have a direct relevance only outside Quebec. Such a situation will likely create new tensions between Quebec and the rest of Canada, and it seems unlikely that English Canada will accede simultaneously to pressures for both a special status for Quebec and a more influential role for French-speaking citizens from Quebec in the institutions of the federal government.

One might argue that here are changes which might be made in the structure and workings of federal institutions to accommodate the situation of a *statut particulier*. Paul Sauriol, editorialist with *Le Devoir*, envisaged a group of reforms in which the normal traditions of parliamentary government

---

14 *Ibid.*, 20 novembre, 1965.
15 *Ibid.*, 14 décembre, 1965.

would prevail concerning matters within the exclusive jurisdiction of the federal authorities, while in "les domaines mixtes" the responsibilities would be assumed either by a reconstituted Senate or some federal-provincial body to which each level would delegate its powers in these affairs.[16] It seems unlikely, however, that such a solution could harmonize the differing conceptions of Quebec and the rest of the country on the appropriate role of the federal government.

The establishment of a *statut particulier* for Quebec within the Canadian constitutional system has important implications for the organizational relations between English- and French-speaking Canadians outside the governmental sphere. The theory and practice of the constitutional *statut particulier* mean that the most important political relations between the two cultural communities are conducted by their respective leaders "at the summit." This pattern of political relations would have to sustain and be sustained by corresponding kinds of interactions among private and quasi-public associations, those primarily concerned with public policy matters. In general terms, a special status for Quebec makes less possible the establishment of effective bicultural organizations on a country-wide basis than does a situation in which all the provinces assume broadly the same responsibilities. During a period when the division of functions between the two levels of government is a matter of controversy, organizations including important elements from the two cultural communities are subjected to severe internal strains when French Canadians from Quebec wish their province to have the exclusive powers to deal with affairs which other Canadians see as appropriate objectives of federal action. As particular aspects of the *statut particulier* are implemented, associations dealing with such vital concerns of public policy as higher education, welfare and health services, the exploitation and conservation of natural resources, municipal government, manpower and collective bargaining and so on can be expected to organize themselves into autonomous of semi-autonomous Quebec and non-Quebec elements. It is possible and even probable that the organizations will carry on some kind of formal relationships but these relations will be almost of necessity of a "fraternal" variety, precisely because their major focuses of attention are on different governments. It is to be expected also that these associations will be almost exclusively unicultural in both form and spirit. English-speaking Canadians from Quebec and French-speaking Canadians outside Quebec will find these associations inadequate vehicles for expressing their particular sentiments and interests.

The situation as it is evolving thus contains these elements.

First, so far as the provinces other than Quebec are concerned, the pressures towards autonomy which began in the late 1950s seem for the time being to have run their course. Among these administrations there is apprehension about the further weakening of federal power.

Second, the province of Quebec continues to press her demands both for a wider range of autonomy and for an enhanced degree of influence in matters

---

16 Editorial, *ibid.,* 17 décembre, 1965.

within the legislative jurisdiction of the federal authorities.

Third, as the *de facto* differentiation between the position of Quebec and that of the other provinces increases, deep incompatibilities are revealed between federalism and the normal workings of federal parliamentary institutions, and between the *statut particulier* situation and the increased influence of French-speaking Canadians in the institutions of the federal government.

Can the continuing procedures of federal-provincial interaction enable the Canadian constitutional system to adapt to the new and contradictory demands now being made upon it? This seems unlikely. The directions in which the system is now being taken involve a constitutional revolution. There is nothing in the Confederation settlement as it was planned in 1864-67 or as it subsequently evolved which provides for a *statut particulier* in the form and dimensions clearly contemplated by the two successive governments of Quebec. It seems improbable that change of such a fundamental nature can be effected through piecemeal federal-provincial negotiation. Because Quebec has now charted its course in such explicit terms it is likely that in the future the federal government and the other provincial governments will evaluate Quebec demands within the framework of broader considerations than they have done in the recent past. The institutions and procedures of cooperative federalism have shown some capacity to deal with questions of ever-increasing generality. Federal-provincial relations in the period after the Second World War were dominated by considerations relating to specific programmes and facilities. More recently progress has been made concerning broader functions of government. The Tax Structure Committee has been charged with questions related to the most fundamental aspects of federal and provincial policies and more particularly with attempting to find agreement on broad expenditure-priorities. There may be continued success in these directions. It seems improbable, however, that federal and provincial executives could by agreement effect a revolution that would change the constitutional ties between Quebec and the rest of Canada to a quasi-diplomatic rather than a federal variety.

In spite of the analysis given above, I believe that it would be imprudent to take a deterministic view of the current crisis in the Canadian federal system.

On the one hand, it is unreasonable to take comfort in the "pendulum theory of federal and provincial powers," which asserts that there are somehow inherent forces at work which will as in the past prevent the attenuation of the powers of one level or the other to the extent that federalism is destroyed. There are of course conceivable circumstances which would lead to the effective reassertion of federal power so far as the government and people of Quebec are concerned. The partial or complete mobilization of the country in response to a deteriorating international situation would bring this about. It is possible to imagine a situation where politically influential groups throughout Canada come to believe that decentralization of power was costing too much in terms of economic stability and growth. Some new federal political leadership might emerge which would successfully commit the country to a bold and popular programme of reform, even in the face of the opposition of the government of Quebec and perhaps the governments of some other provinces. It is impossible to predict the likelihood of these circumstances occurring. It is unreasonable, however, to believe that any or all of them are inevitable.

On the other hand, it seems that Canadian federalism has not yet passed the point of no return. It is possible that the Quebec leadership will press its demands towards the *statut particulier* less aggressively than a reading of recent official pronouncements would lead one to believe. Fortunately, viable political arrangements do not need to conform to standards of logical consistency. It is possible that Canadians may be able to agree on a set of devices which allow each of the contradictory demands on the Canadian constitutional system to be met in part. Perhaps some new distribution of revenues, revenue sources and functional responsibilities can be effected which would provide both for the dominance of the federal government in economic matters and exclusive provincial responsibility, without the existing extent of federal involvement, in matters of provincial concern. Such a development would help to ensure the historic role of the federal government in economic matters and would also mitigate the difficulties inherent in a special status for Quebec within the Canadian federal system. Perhaps too the demands of the government of Quebec concerning particular matters will be discussed in the future within a framework which considers the cumulative impact of these demands on the survival of Canadian federalism. It is this last alternative rather than the piecemeal adjustments of cooperative federalism which gives best hope for the immediate future.

Part Five

Regionalism and Canadian Federalism

23 Regional Interests and Policy in a Federal Structure*

J. E. Hodgetts

Almost overnight, regionalism in Canada has become the current fashion and a subject for much intellectual speculation as well as administrative experimentation. This symposium** is but one of many testimonials to the growing interest in the subject. In 1964, the Committee on Statistics of the Canadian Political Science Association considered the problem. Early in 1965, Queen's University sponsored a conference on areas of economic stress that was the forerunner to a much larger conference on regionalism convened by the Province of Ontario. The Institute of Public Administration of Canada selected regionalism as the theme for its autumn conference. Recent reports of a royal commission in New Brunswick and of a legislative committee in Ontario are implicitly concerned with regionalism in so far as they propose basic remodelling of the local government services in their respective provinces. The Resources Ministers Council is grappling with the concept, as are also the federal departments of Industry and of Agriculture. On the international plane, the St. Lawrence Seaway and the Columbia River development have projected more grandiose conceptions of regionalism. In short, regionalism, with concomitant regional administrative structures, is being advanced as an answer to the new problems of interdependence that cut across traditional political boundary lines, whether they be municipal, provincial, or national.

The title chosen for this symposium suggests that regional interests are, indeed, a reality within the Canadian federal structure and that policy must accommodate itself not only to the familiar strains of dominion-provincial tensions but to the newer cross-currents of regionalism. The detailed implications of regionalism cannot be considered here, but resort to the analytical tools of the new school of systems analysts may help to develop certain general conclusions.

In essence, the systems analyst would picture the Canadian political system as a box surrounded by the environment. "Inputs" from the environment are

* From *Canadian Journal of Economics and Political Science*, Vol. XXXII no. (February, 1966), pp. 3-14. Reprinted by permission of the author and publisher.
** This paper is a revision of a contribution made to a Symposium on "Regional Interests and Policy in a Federal Structure" sponsored jointly by the Association of Canadian Law Teachers and the Canadian Political Science Association, University of British Columbia, June, 1965.

J. E. HODGETTS – Professor of Political Science, University of Toronto.

typically divided into demands and supports. Within the box marked "'Canadian political system" the demand inputs are subjected to a conversion process that produces "outputs" which lead back to the environment; presumably the outputs must satisfy the demands or create new ones if they are to generate support for the system.[1]

Thus systems theory as envisaged by Gabriel Almond, one of its leading proponents, circulates through three phases—input, conversion, output. "The inputs and outputs which involve the political system with other social systems are transactions between the system and its environment; the conversion processes are internal to the political system."[2] Stability of the political system is found when (again according to Almund) "The demands can be handled by the political system; the strains which they impose are bearable without any basic change in structure or culture. The outputs are responsive to the demands in expected or legitimate ways; and the supports are responsive to the outputs again in expected or legitimate ways."[3]

In the light of this analysis regional interests would be treated as demand inputs, policy as an output, and the federal structure, in its widest sense, as the system that makes its transactions with the environment and in which the mysterious alchemy of the conversion process takes place.

What might be termed the classical model of the Canadian federal political system incorporates at least three sets of assumptions which may be stated in terms of the input-output model of the system analysts. The first assumption, on the input side, relates to the way in which the dispersed interests of free and rational individuals are pooled into a reservoir of will power to be channelled into the political system as the driving force for public policy outputs. The prerequisites are free speech, free association, the ballot, and a consensus that accepts the temporary ascendency of majority opinion. The transaction is accomplished preferably by two parties competing in the task of mobilizing nation-wide majorities. Parliament is the lens for bringing these demand inputs to a focus, sifting out the "demand overloads," and converting the remainder into public policy.

The classical model assumes, further, a separation between the agencies that are responsible for reconstituting, in the form of public policy, the scattered wills of the people and the agencies responsible for implementation of policy. That is to say, on the output side of the system, the executors of policy are viewed as separate from and subordinate and instrumental to the substantive policy-formers.

Finally, the addition of a federal framework complicates but does not necessarily disturb the tidiness of the traditional model. The classical conception of federalism assumed that the provinces occupied relatively clearly

---

[1] The clearest, most succinct, and up-to-date description of political systems analysis is in Gabriel A. Almond's "A Development Approach to Political Systems", *World Politics*, Vol. XVII no. 2 (January, 1965) pp. 183-214.

[2] *Ibid.*, p. 189.

[3] *Ibid.*, p. 193.

defined areas of local self-determination separated from an equally clearly defined set of jurisdictions assigned by the British North America Act to the central government. Thus, the democratic processes of policy formation could operate in virtually autonomous compartments whose edges touched but did not interpenetrate enough to cause confusion or require much collaboration.

The facts of Canadian life one hundred years ago may have approximated the conditions postulated by this classical model in which provincial political subsystems worked in relative isolation within a national system having rigidly defined jurisdiction. Today, however, it is clear not only that the circumstances with which public policy must come to grips have altered drastically but also that the assumptions implicit in the classical model have been eroded or warped by the many factors that have contributed to the shift from independence to interdependence of all the units embraced within the Canadian political system. There are now more elements attracted out of the orbit of other systems such as the family, the church, or the economy and, because they are assumed to have political relevance, they must swell the demand inputs of the political system. At the same time, these more numerous and more heterogeneous elements have to be rallied to the support of the system.

These transforming forces necessitate substantial revision of the classical model of the Canadian political system. Advanced students in political science courses are alerted to the necessity for adopting a more sophisticated analysis; practising politicians, on the other hand, are still often reluctant to admit that the conversion processes over which they preside have shifted their power centres, even though the old constitutional forms may have persisted.

Thus, the first assumption of a simplistic chain of demand reaching from the electorate to sovereign policy-making Parliament must be adjusted to make allowance for the growth of a mass electorate, the uneven expansion of individual constituencies, and the consequent growing heterogeneity of the interests and demands forcing themselves on elected representatives. Moreover, there are numerous indications that parties are losing their power to mobilize majorities drawn from all sections, thereby diminishing the integrating and articulating functions required of them by our political system. Parliament, itself, as the point of focus and conversion for the demands on the input side shows signs of the confusion which exists in its supporting party and electoral adjuncts. No matter how it extends the number of sitting days, Parliament as a corporate institution (rather than a mere reflector of party strengths in the nation) finds itself wedded to inefficient procedures, poorly organized, and inadequately staffed with the permanent expert help it needs nowadays to provide the information and knowledge required to grapple with complex public business. In short, the policy-making initiative has long since shifted to the executive.

Deriving from this shift and related to the growing complexity of public affairs, the classical view of a dichotomy between politics and administration —policy-making and execution—has disappeared to be replaced by administrative policy-making and adjudication. And, as the power centres change within the political system, our traditional channels leading from electorate to

Parliament are no longer adequate to transfer the demand inputs to the relevant conversion machinery in the political system. New channels, new methods of aggregating, consolidating, and sifting demands have to be invented. By the same token, additional devices for measuring the effectiveness of the outputs in meeting demands and thereby generating supports for the system are needed. The old "feedback" devices (to borrow yet another term from the systems analysts)—the elected representative and the local party organization—require supplementation. Similarly, the role of the judiciary in ensuring fair play and thereby fortifying the support inputs for the system is pre-empted, in part, by the bureaucracy.

The classical conception of federalism has also undergone drastic revisions now submerged under the vague title "co-operative federalism."[4] On the one hand, the notion of self-determining, self-contained, viable administrative jurisdictions for each of the several provinces and the central government has been undermined by nation-wide transportation and communication links; "provincial" economies have been displaced by economic interdependence and complementarity; the forward thrust of the federal government into monetary and fiscal policies gives a new prominence to the centre and constrains the activities open to the provinces; governments at all levels by intruding into economic life as regulators or operators and by the rapid accretion of their welfare functions have been compelled to deploy their assigned powers to the fullest extent. It is not surprising that these efforts should end up on collision courses—that friction is generated, and that both duplication and jurisdictional no-man's lands should appear. The positive but sporadic and piecemeal efforts to ameliorate these jurisdictional and functional imbalances give rise to the new approach characterized as co-operative federalism. At the moment, however, the term more aptly describes the frame of mind with which governments face new problems and needs rather than a stable set of mechanisms for collaboration.

For two decades following publication of the report of the Rowell-Sirois Commission the conclusion, derived from this convergence of pressures reinforcing the trend toward interdependence, was that the central government would have to play the main role on the Canadian stage. Mobilization of society and the economy for all-out war pushed the provinces temporarily into the background and confirmed the pre-eminent role of the Dominion. During the war and for some time after the Canadian political system performed virtually as a single system. Now the pendulum has swung decisively in the other direction. The nationalistic modernizing revolution in Quebec is only the most dramatic expression of a fresh provincial self-assertiveness that derives in part from a buoyant economy and from mounting expenditures on such programs as education, welfare, health, highways, and resources that

---

[4] The precepts of classical federalism and the forces that have contributed to the growth of so-called "co-operative federalism" are perceptively developed in J. A. Corry, "Constitutional Trends and Federalism" in A. R. M. Lower, F. R. Scott, *et al, Evolving Canadian Federalism* (Durham, N.C., 1958), pp. 92-125.

fall within provincial jurisdiction. But these advances of the affluent society cannot readily or sensibly be undertaken by reverting to the old pattern of a congeries of loosely connected subsystems. Now more than ever before it would seem imperative that we view the Canadian federation as a single political *system*. If co-operative federalism is to become more than a pious platitude of the politicians, the forces of interdependence and the interpenetration of the functions performed at all three levels by the traditional units of government compel us to adopt this new perspective on an old principle.

At first blush it might be assumed that the proliferation of regional structures will inevitably produce further irritants for the Canadian federal structure and that we will be driven even farther away from the ideal model of a single Canadian system. On the other hand, it may well be that the new stress on regionalism is a measure of the growing recognition that one cannot work the Canadian political system as a series of discrete compartments contained by traditional political boundaries. No more can one expect that long-standing departmental portfolios, whether provincial or federal, will provide the right mix of function or of appropriate jurisdictional reach for dealing with the new combination of skills and authority required by regionalism. Nor, finally, can we expect that the conventional channels for mobilizing the interests of the nation will adequately serve the new regional structures and the policy to be developed by them.

These generalized observations require elaboration and clarification. First, the meetings attached to the terms regionalism and regional interest ought to be stated. Regionalism, as used here, should not be confused with sectionalism, for as two American authorities claim: "Sectionalism—as a spirit, as a movement and as a political rallying point—tends to emphasize rivalry, provincialism, isolation, and self-sufficiency."[5] They go on to say that "the new regionalism . . . emphasizes the recognition of diversity of land and culture, the idea of integration and balance: integration of region with the whole nation, and balance of region with region."[6]

This spatial concept of a region supplemented by a homogeneity of culture or other features has enjoyed a paramount place amongst the analytical concepts applied to American politics and government. Thus David Lilienthal can remark that

> The growth and development of our national policies is not the result of conflicts between states; it represents an attempted reconciliation between the interests of the various natural regions . . . .
> Modern regionalism, by contrast, rests squarely upon the supremacy of the *national* interest. It admits that there are problems and resources common to areas larger than any single state—a river basin, for example. It recognizes that certain points of view develop in some portions of the country and are not shared by the nation as a whole. It affirms and insists,

---

[5] Richard Carlton Snider and H. Hubert Wilson (eds.), *Roots of Political Behaviour: Introduction to Government and Politics* (New York, 1949), pp. 452-53.
[6] *Ibid.*, p. 453.

however, that the solution of regional problems and the development of regional resources are matters of concern to the whole country.[7]

Regional Interests and Policy

It would appear, then, that Americans have long become accustomed to thinking of a region as something more than a state but something less than the whole nation. Parenthetically, one may observe that even within the US counterpart of our Canadian Political Science Association the standard regions are enshrined in the subunits of the national Association, i.e., the Pacific Northwest, the Southern, the Western, etc. Political Science Associations.

In Canada, on the other hand, we are far less clear about the existence of regions with identifiable interests separate from the interests historically contained in and expressed through provincial units. In the First Annual Review of the Economic Council, under a Table labelled "Level and Growth of Personal Income per capita by region," we find the "regions" entitled Atlantic (with a footnote to say Newfoundland is excluded), Quebec, Ontario, Prairies, and British Columbia. This nomenclature, which is quite typical, reveals how quickly we exhaust the regional concept when applied across the nation: once the Maritimes and the Prairies have been mentioned we immediately fall back on the standard political, provincial boundaries. As for that region called the Canadian North, experienced observers are the first to proclaim its heterogeneity and the consequent impropriety of viewing it as a single entity. At the federal level positive administrative recognition of this restricted regional concept is to be found only in such agencies as the Atlantic Development Board, the Prairie Farm Rehabilitation Administration and the Northern Affairs Branch in the Department of Northern Affairs and National Resources.

Thus, if we are defining our region in national terms and thinking of it as an identifiable area having sufficiently common interests that they can be articulated and aggregated and urged on the federal government as part of the demand inputs of our political system, we really have nothing to compare with the American situation. The explanation for this difference may lie in the lack of party discipline in the US Congress and the popular nation-wide election of the Chief Executive. The fluidity of party lines in Congress permits bloc voting across party lines to take place without undermining the parties or the completely separate office of the presidency. In Canada, the rigour of party discipline imposed on MP's virtually eliminates the possibility of bloc voting in the name of the Prairies, the Maritimes, or any other region of transprovincial dimensions. We have no "corn belt" or "cotton bloc" voting. Indeed, the only way a regional interest can be assembled is through the political party processes *within* each province, by which means a Social Credit ramp from Alberta or a New Democratic party bloc from Saskatchewan may consolidate a minority voice in the House of Commons—but, once again, it should be noted, we are compelled to equate so-called regional interests with the separate provincial interests.

---

[7] Quoted in *Ibid.*, pp. 463-64, from David E. Lilienthal, *TVA: Democracy on the March* (New York, 1944).

The popular election of the President under a system in which the majority winner takes all of the electoral vote in each state has made it possible to identify regional groupings of states that either hold the balance of power or have a species of veto power in the determination of the presidential winner. In Canada, while we now recognize that a national election tends to turn on the prime minister and the opposition leaders and thus becomes more like a US presidential election, in place of the concentration of support by identifiable blocs of states, the process is splintered into individual constituency contests that prevent us from identifying a genuine regional influence on the final outcome.

If the concept of region viewed from the national perspective in Canada lacks the substance and political influence that may be claimed for it in the United States, at the provincial level it is clearly emerging as a significant working concept. The increasing emphasis placed on region within the provinces derives from two complementary pressures. First, it has long been apparent to students of local government that the traditional political units are proving increasingly unsatisfactory in meeting the costly demands of urbanization, industrialization, and secularization. The problem is that functions have spilled out over the political boundaries, while authority to perform the functions remains legally chained to the traditional units of local administration. And, as functional responsibilities grow in number and expand in scope, the financial, technical, and manpower resources required for adequate performance need to be pooled across political boundaries. Over the last decade or so these deficiencies have become more marked under the impact of rapid social and technological change. The solution, reiterated in one official report after another, is amalgamation to form larger units or, at a minimum, a merger to perform specific functions.

Further support for the stress on region comes from a more recent acknowledgement by the provinces that there are actually elements missing from their existing organizational apparatus; there is a growing awareness that new functional needs and programs cannot be handled either by the long-standing departmental machinery of the province or even by the merging of present units of local government. One can think here, specifically, of the conservation authorities in Ontario or the more ambitious regional development associations in the same province.[8] The increasing respectability of government planning and the urgent demands for conserving and purifying our soil, water, and air all add to the pressures for a regional approach to these problems. The recently created Saskatchewan Water Resources Commission is an excellent

---

[8] The guiding philosophy for the development associations is that: "Local development serves the local citizen best when it takes into account regional development and harmonizes with it. Today more than ever before, the township, the village, the town, city, county and district are economic partners. What each does affects the other. We live in regional economic neighbourhoods and this is not a theory; it is a fact." See brochure of Ontario Department of Economics and Development, Regional Development Division, *Regional Development*.

example of a new agency for investigation, planning, co-ordination, and regulation of the development and use of water and related land resources—a multi-purpose assignment with which no single existing department could cope.[9] And, it should be added, not only are provincial and local authorities responding to these pressures, the federal government, too, is making its contributions through such legislation as the recent Agricultural Rehabilitation and Development Act which has fostered regional projects like the one for the Gaspé and has relied on two other regionally based federal agencies— the Prairie Farm Rehabilitation Administration and the Maritime Marshland Rehabilitation Administration—for its "operational arm."[10] The new Department of Industry, under Part II of its authorizing statute, visualizes yet another range of designated development areas.

The proliferation of new agencies, the amalgamation of old agencies, and the recombining of divisions pulled out of existing agencies would appear to provide ample testimony for the thesis that "regional interests" now constitute a significant element in the demand inputs to which the Canadian political system is clearly responding. This conclusion is nevertheless suspect on two counts. First, as already indicated we must discount the influence of regionalism of the American type that rallies interests and demands other than those that have always been expressed through traditional provincial political units. Second, one can go further by asserting that regionalism, at any level one wishes to take it, does not generate spontaneous demands that thrust themselves on the political system and are instrumental in influencing the policy outputs of the system. The region, in this particular stage of development at any rate, is not so much the creator of policy as the creature of policy.

Rephrasing this contention in terms of systems analysis, it can be argued that regionalism is not part of the demand inputs entering the system, but is a creation of the political system itself. David Easton, one of the founding fathers of the systems approach, has anticipated this possibility by coining the expression "withinput"[11] to apply to the not-uncommon situation where events and conditions within the political system may be as significant as any environmental inputs in shaping the ultimate outputs.

Obviously, there has to be a region if we are to think of a regional interest which, in turn, we visualize as shaping or influencing the control of public policy. What is argued here is that in most instances the region is, so to speak, the natural outcome of the adoption of a particular program or policy. The execution of the policy entails the creation of administrative units that must be set up on a regional basis in order to provide the most appropriate combination of functions and resources. In short, the policy, by defining the function or

---

[9] *Statutes of Saskatchewan*, chap. 32 (1964). The Commission brings together the permanent heads of the three agencies which each carry responsibility for a part of the task, together with three other cabinet appointees; the provincial premier is the minister responsible for the Commission — thereby suggesting its essentially co-ordinative role.
[10] *Statutes of Canada*, 9-10 Eliz. II, chap 30 (1961). See Department of Agriculture, *Annual Report for 1962-63*, p. 56.
[11] *A Framework for Political Analysis* (Englewood Cliffs, 1965), p. 114.

program, explicitly or implicity creates a concept of the region required for the particular purposes envisaged.

One or two illustrations may serve to buttress what may appear to be a perverse attempt to put the cart before the horse. In the case of "the areas of slow economic growth" to which the Department of Industry was authorized to direct its services, it is clear that the regions might properly be called "bureaucratic constructs." The Minister explained, in 1964, how the initial designation of the areas was based on thirty-five national employment service areas "to bring about quick results and meet an emergency situation." He went on to say that his department was "presently engaged with the departments of finance and labour in making a detailed and exhaustive review of criteria for designating areas . . . which will enable us to single out those areas where special efforts will be required over the years if they are to participate more fully in the general prosperity of the country."[12] In this operation we find little evidence of pre-existing regional interests urging their demands on government; rather, we see the areas "designated" initially on the most convenient, available criteria and ultimately on the basis of more sophisticated statistical data processed within the public service itself.

The regional development program in the Province of Ontario affords a less extreme but perhaps more typical example. While stressing the element of partnership between "province, local municipal governments, and public-spirited local groups and individuals," the official pronouncement goes on to state quite frankly: "In initiating and financially supporting regional development through legislation, the Government of Ontario in the 10 Development Associations has officially recognized both the real need of, and the great potential benefits, which stem from this Provincial-Municipal partnership." It would not be unfair to claim that the Government of Ontario, and more precisely the Regional Development Division of the Department of Economics and Development, has, in effect, said to the municipalities: "Look, whether you know it or not, you have certain common regional interests in such matters as promoting tourism, industry, research and conservation and community planning; we, as a Department, can deal with you best if you organize in regional groups; we are prepared to go half way in financing such organizations; and we confidently expect 'regional interests' will soon cluster around the organizations to which we shall be happy to respond in formulating subsequent policies." Again, we may conclude that the political system and not the environment has initiated the input in order to facilitate the conversion process and so trigger a policy output.

In my view this is the normal flow of events as they bear on the alleged forces of regionalism. Parenthetically, it is worth noting that this particular sequence has not been uncommon in the development of pressure group relations with the political system. The government has found it more convenient to respond to an organized pressure rather than attempt to negotiate with individuals or isolated groups. Thus, in 1906 the Department of

---

[12] *Debates,* House of Commons (Canada, 1964), p. 7395.

Agriculture sponsored the meeting of the Canadian National Live Stock Association, and in 1914 helped finance the Sheep Breeders Association. H. H. Hannam, once president of the Canadian Federation of Agriculture, claimed that the Federation was brought into being because the first Bank of Canada Act called upon "organized agriculture" (then non-existent) to nominate members to the Bank's board of directors. And, just as advisory committees have been popular devices for giving official recognition to organized functional groups in the political system, so too, we almost invariably find provisions for setting up advisory adjuncts to the newer regional organizations.[13]

A final example, drawn from the Province of Quebec, illustrates one further aspect of the positive contribution of the political system to regionalism. The significant reorganization of the educational system of that province has apparently followed the path already described; that is, the political system has produced a global educational program and the ministry has designed the administrative apparatus which they think will permit the most effective implementation of the general goals. Decentralization was necessary and areas had to be designed for administrative purposes. One of the marked features of this development has been the extent to which political and permanent officials alike have had to carry the appeal to the regions in order to enlist their interest and participation. Some senior civil servants—and not merely those in educational administration, for much missionary work has had to be undertaken in other fields as well—have been perturbed by their inevitable public identification with a particular policy. This had its parallel in the Province of Saskatchewan two decades ago and perhaps Quebec civil servants, witnessing the recent exodus from that part of the West after a change in government, may fear that history will repeat itself in their province. In any event, reverting once more to systems analysis, we find that this particular experience in Quebec illustrates not only how the political system can generate its own demands but can at the same time take positive action to create its own supports by manipulating the regional environment in the way just described. The reliance on advisory committees, in conjunction with such programs, shows that in the absence of spontaneous regional interests to create demands and provide supports, the government itself has had to create the organizational framework in which such demands and supports might be expected to germinate. These examples of a pervasive and universal development also buttress an earlier contention; our traditional techniques for aggregating demands and supports—the geographic consistency, the political party, and Parliament itself—have had to be supplemented and possibly even by-passed by these more direct and deliberately constructed tools.

It would be tempting to extend this paper to take into account more specific bureaucratic responses to the forces of regionalism. One might, for

---

[13] For example, the appropriate Minister is authorized to appoint advisory committees under the Agricultural Rehabilitation and Development Act and the Department of Industry Act and the Saskatchewan Water Resources Commission Act.

example, describe in detail the particular organizational pattern developed by each federal department and agency to resolve the problem of administering a federal domain where three-quarters of the work force has to be employed outside the headquarters area. On the whole, however, such a detailed story would simply reinforce the main conclusions of this paper, namely, that there are few genuinely spontaneous regional interests in Canada that have an independent impact on policy; and where they do exist our political system, working through disciplined parliamentary parties, only permits them to be aggregated and articulated within conventional provincial boundaries. Thus the growing recognition of regions is basically an artifice of administrators who, working within the political system, play a creative role in constructing regions appropriate to the functions entrusted to them; in some cases, this positive initiatory role may even compel public servants to desert their neutrality in order to generate support from a sometimes indifferent environment which has to be alerted to the task of formulating its own interests around the regional construct. Finally, it may perhaps be argued that, once over the present formative stage, the genuine need for a regional approach to policy-formation and implementation will in itself begin to create self-generating demand and support inputs which will no longer be bureaucratically inspired.

It remains to be seen whether parties can retain their role as aggregators of demands based on new regional interests that are not necessarily tied to the traditional provincial units or whether, along with the proliferation of advisory committees, we will need to design new mechanisms for this purpose. The larger question of Parliament's capacity to convert such regional demands into acceptable policy outputs also constitutes a major challenge to our ingenuity. Meanwhile, at the present intermediate stage of growth, governmental agencies are all energetically throwing themselves into the breach and we are already faced with such a maze of special regions that we may be unable to co-ordinate disparate regional entities. If this development persists we must abandon any hopes we have of gearing our institutions and policies to the conception of a single Canadian political system.

24　Regional Aspects of Federal Economic Policies*

Economic Council of Canada

National policies of particular significance for regional growth and development have taken many forms. The whole complex of measures cannot be considered in any detail here. But this section will provide a basis for appraising some of the regional effects of policies in several key areas: federal development expenditures; tariff policy; transportation policy; and manpower policy.

Regional Distribution of Federal Development Expenditures

The definition, identification and provincial allocation of what we have termed federal development expenditures involve some tricky conceptual problems and, inevitably, a certain degree of arbitrariness.[1] But even with these cautions in mind, this type of approach throws up some useful insights into the problem.

Development or growth-related expenditures should be defined to include all programs that may increase the supply and use of productive resources or improve their productivity. Such a broad definition would in the first instance at least encompass programs for health care, education, labour force mobility, development of natural resources and industry, applied scientific research and technology, transportation, communication and other production-related social capital. For the purposes of this Chapter, social welfare, defence, public debt service, national administrative and routine regulatory expenditures were excluded. Revenue equalization payments, on the other hand, were included. Although their ultimate use cannot be broken down, it can be assumed that they are used to support the largest provincial cost items—education, health and transportation.

For some preliminary insight into their regional impact, growth-related expenditures of the federal government as defined above for the fiscal year 1964-65 (the latest year for which it was possible to make the calculations)

---

[1] The methods of allocation employed are similar to those used in an earlier federal government study for the total budget of fiscal year 1961-62. See Reply of the Minister of Finance to Question No. 741 by Mr. Balcer, made Order for Return, July 22, 1964, House of Commons (Ottawa, November 4, 1964). It should be noted, however, that in the present analysis two-thirds of all expenditure allocated was based upon its provincial location (compared to two-fifths in the previous study). The same reservations on techniques of distribution, the significance of a single year's data and the rapid growth and change in expenditures, that were noted in the earlier study, apply to the estimates here for 1964-65.

---

* From *Fifth Annual Review: The Challenge of Growth and Change*, (Ottawa: Queen's Printer, 1968) pp. 150-160, 177-180. Reprinted by permission of Information Canada.

350

were allocated provincially. In all, these expenditures amounted to $2,566 million or about 35 per cent of the total federal budget.

Table 1 shows a rather striking result of this analysis. There was a strong tendency for per capita federal development expenditures to be highest in provinces with the lowest per capita incomes. Indeed, in Prince Edward Island and Newfoundland these expenditures were the equivalent of more than one-quarter of personal income per capita. Quebec was perhaps the most notable exception to the general pattern in 1964-65, in part because this province had not yet built up to high levels of expenditure under the Hospital Insurance and Trans-Canada Highway programs. Also the expenditures in Saskatchewan were particularly high in 1964-65 as a result of the large outlays for the South Saskatchewan Dam.

Table 1 —   **Per Capita Personal Income and Federal Development Expenditure by Province**

	Personal Income 1964		Federal Development Expenditure, 1964-65	
	$	Rank	$	Rank
Ontario	2,153	1	98	10
British Columbia	2,118	2	114	9
Alberta	1,839	3	128	8
Saskatchewan	1,838	4	185	5
Manitoba	1,801	5	151	6
Quebec	1,626	6	132	7
Nova Scotia	1,384	7	201	4
New Brunswick	1,263	8	212	3
Prince Edward Island	1,236	9	344	1
Newfoundland	1,981	10	310	2
Canada	1,849		133	

NOTE: Per capita personal income is averaged for three years, 1963-65, indicated by a bar over the centre year 1964.

SOURCE: Based on data from Dominion Bureau of Statistics and estimates by Economic Council of Canada.

In the light of these figures, it can certainly be concluded that these federal expenditure programs worked to narrow existing income differences among the regions. If other federal expenditures, especially social welfare programs, were included, these results would be reinforced. But income maintenance alone is likely to be only a palliative. The more important question concerns the contribution of these expenditures to the acceleration of long-term growth rates—that is, to the forces and processes generating income growth based on productivity advances.

As we noted earlier, our present analysis does not enable us to measure the quantitative impact of various programs on the growth of the regions. Instead, we have tried by appropriate classification of the 1964-65 expenditure programs (Chart 1) to detect any conscious, deliberate strategy of improving performance in the low-income regions by increasing utilization of resources or raising output per employed person. Undoubtedly some of the federal programs have done just this—the more recent manpower programs provide a notable example—but our appraisal fails to reveal any clear over-all design for coping with the underlying problems of regional imbalance.

Chart 1 —   **Per Capita Federal Development Expenditure by Region, 1964-65**

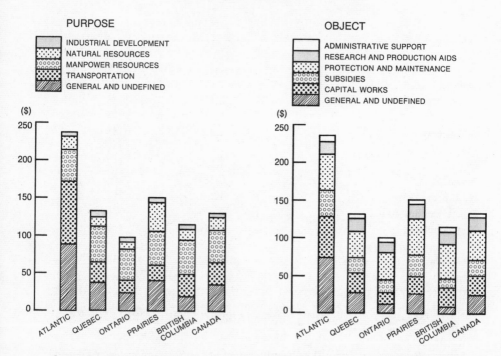

Source: Based on data from *Public Accounts of Canada, 1964-65,* and estimates by Economic Council of Canada.

In all regions except the Atlantic Provinces the largest proportion of federal development expenditures, by purpose, in 1964-65 was devoted to manpower programs. These programs . . . appear to rate quite high in respect of the requirements for accelerated regional growth indicated by our earlier analysis. On the other hand, most of the expenditures in the lowest-income region, the Atlantic Provinces, were on transportation and various residual or undefined programs.

Our appraisal, rough as it is at this stage, suggests that the considerations entering into the wide array of transportation expenditure programs in the Atlantic Provinces have not primarily been those relating to our requirements for accelerating regional growth. At least, it is not apparent that they have been part of any co-ordinated and conscious design in the appropriate directions.

The residual category of programs includes a long list of comparatively small items related to general development, such as the national statistical services, certain scientific and technological research, basic mapping and technical surveys and the national parks service. But it is dominated by the inclusion of federal revenue equalization payments to the provinces. We assume that the payments support growth-related provincial expenditures, especially education, health and transportation, but to what extent these can be claimed to reflect a deliberate design for the acceleration of growth is very much an open question.

The allocation of expenditures by object also fails to reveal any particularly conscious aim to accelerate growth in the low-income regions. The classification suggests that there was some redistribution towards the Atlantic Provinces in the form of capital expenditures that might be consistent with such an aim. But there were also larger expenditures per capita in these provinces on subsidies which, though they may have assisted in income maintenance, have had questionable results for the promotion of economic growth.

Although it is difficult to detect a clear regional development strategy in the 1964-65 expenditure figures, major changes in a number of programs have been implemented in recent years which seem likely to produce a more appropriate regional impact. These include the change in the calculation of revenue equalization payments to lower-income provinces, the institution of fiscal transfers for post-secondary education, the extension of manpower training, changing transportation policies and the growth of applied area development programs. . . .

Corresponding to the issue of regional distribution of federal development expenditures is the obverse issue of the regional impact of the federal tax structure. In the past the federal government has made use of particular tax incentives or concession arrangements in order to assist the longer-run growth of certain industries or designated areas. Where these industries or the defined areas are substantially concentrated in certain regions, such tax incentives and concessions have had important regional effects. Unfortunately these effects have not been closely investigated; indeed, even the Royal

Commission on Taxation paid little direct attention to this question. To what extent such tax incentives and concessions have either been based on considerations directly related to, or have influenced, regional growth and balance in the sense which concerns us in this Chapter therefore cannot be delineated at this time.

National Tariff Policy

Of all the major instruments of national economic development, perhaps none has proved to be a more potent source of interregional tension than the system of protective tariffs and related commercial policy devices. It is a time-honoured and enduring ritual at federal-provincial conferences on fiscal and economic problems for Ontario to remind the country that it provides about 45 per cent of the total direct tax revenues flowing into the national treasury, and for the Atlantic and western provinces to rejoin that, among the various burdens they carry, the tariff provides Ontario with its sheltered market while most of their own producers must sell abroad at competitive world prices. Over the years regional unevenness of the cost of the protective tariff has been regularly used to support arguments for providing an elaborate structure of regional and national transportation subsidies, special assistance to primary producers in agriculture, fisheries and mining, tax concessions of particular regional interest, and revenue equalization payments to the lower-income provinces.

As we have already indicated, the initial purpose and effect of the protective tariff, together with a national transportation system, was to establish an east-west trading relationship, involving a considerable degree of regional economic specialization. The manufacturing and industrial core of the country developed in Ontario and Quebec, with a strong primary resource orientation in the other regions. The expectations of the Atlantic Provinces that they would also perform an important national manufacturing and service function was frustrated both by changing technology and by the westward shift of North American population and activity. How much this broad historical picture of regional patterns might have been altered by a basically different commercial policy cannot be known. But it is relevant for our purposes to look at the regional effects of the tariff in the present day, and to suggest how the problem of regional balance might be affected by freer trade.

In broad terms, we can distinguish two major influences upon the various regions resulting from the imposition of a tariff on imported goods—one from the side of consumption and the other from the side of production.

The broad structure of the tariff and the traditional view of its national and regional impact are generally familiar. One of the main effects of tariffs is that purchasers of goods pay higher prices for certain commodities than they would pay for the same goods at duty-free import prices. The amount involved is what has been called the "cash cost" of the tariff. Earlier studies have suggested that this "cash cost" of the Canadian tariff is substantial. Not only do Canadian consumers pay substantially more for many finished products as a result of the tariff, but most Canadian producers pay more for a wide variety of materials, machinery and components as a result of the tariffs on these items; and these higher costs of production are reflected in the prices of goods produced in Canada. All Canadian consumers and producers share in the cash cost of the tariff to the extent that tariffs affect the price of the goods they buy. But the impediments that tariffs impose to access to some cheaper sources of supply in adjacent areas of the United States tend to result in a somewhat larger cash cost in the Atlantic Region and the western provinces than in Central Canada.

But a far more important effect of tariffs is that they tend to depress the levels of output per employed person in Canada. In particular, tariffs shelter or cause inefficiency in contemporary Canadian industry by encouraging product diversity over a wide range of protected products, limiting efficiencies that could otherwise be gained from scale and specialization. This was one of the major conclusions in Chapter 6 of our *Fourth Annual Review,* in which we indicated that the effects of Canadian and foreign tariffs combined are reflected in higher prices for machinery and other material inputs, and in the basic structural pattern of large net imports of manufactured products.[2] Recent studies have concluded that this "production effect" of the tariff (both Canadian and U.S.) may be very substantial—indeed that the economic costs to Canada may be significantly higher than the "cash cost" of the Canadian tariff—and that these combined economic costs may constitute a very significant element in the large and persistent gap in productivity levels and in the average levels of real standards of living between Canada and the United States. In fact, this element could well be even larger than that arising from the educational disparities between the two countries discussed in the *Second Annual Review.*

In summary, the consumption aspect of the national tariff suggests important relative gains in real income for the Atlantic, Prairie and British Columbia regions if the tariff were reduced or eliminated. There would be little net change in Quebec, and some relative decline in Ontario. But if the production aspects of the tariff are even more important than the consumption aspects, large, new and difficult questions arise about tariffs—questions which cut across many traditional views. For example, is it perhaps the main manufacturing regions of Central Canada, rather than the Atlantic Region or the western provinces, that are now bearing the main economic costs of tariffs? Also, is it possible that substantial tariff reductions, even though they would benefit Canadians in all parts of the country, may have the effect of *widening* rather than *narrowing* regional income disparities—particularly between Ontario and the Atlantic Region? And have the tariff reductions over the past two decades in fact been tending to offset other forces working towards the narrowing of interregional disparities (thus helping

---

2 See also D. J. Daly, B. A. Keys and E. J. Spence, *Scale and Specialization in Canadian Manufacturing,* Staff Study No. 21, Economic Council of Canada, (Ottawa, Queen's Printer, 1968.)

to explain the stubborn persistence of the wide disparities in Canada)? The Council does not have answers to such questions at this time, but these and related questions raise important issues requiring further examination.

National and Regional Transportation

Since Confederation, transportation has played a key role in federal development policy. Recently, the federal government's expenditures on transportation and communications have been running at an annual level of well over half a billion dollars, and it is estimated that they have been equivalent to roughly one-eighth of total railway transportation costs, one-quarter of air transportation costs, and about one-third of water transportation costs. For roads and pipelines the federal outlay is relatively small.

These figures hardly begin to convey the importance of the federal government's role in this field. They embrace such programs as subsidies and subventions, grants, direct construction of physical facilities and the provision of services with or without charge to the industry. But federal transportation policy covers an even wider spectrum including loans, regulation and control of commercial rates and services, and restrictions on entry into certain forms of transportation. In addition, of course, federal Crown agencies such as the Canadian National Railways and Air Canada operate major transportation systems. Both direct expenditures and the regulatory functions have had pronounced regional impacts.

Federal government programs have undoubtedly stimulated the development of various transportation systems beyond the level that could be supported solely by the market. These programs, along with technological improvements in the transportation industry itself, have undoubtedly also stimulated and encouraged the development of resources and certain lines of economic activity in the various regions in many ways, some of which are described below. They have contributed to national economic integration and they have raised the average level of income in all parts of Canada. But from a regional perspective the net effect of this wide range of policies has been to increase the pull towards the more highly industrialized regions of Central Canada. In this sense at least, these policies may have complicated the task of achieving a better regional balance in economic development.

Over the last 20 years, federal response to transportation requirements has been immensely complicated by the swift advance of transport technology and the emergence of competitive forms as well as the rapid changes in the structure of the economy. It has been difficult to find a consistent and coherent focus in federal transportation policy. Many of the specific programs, however, have obviously been framed to provide an economic advantage to one region or the other, and it is this aspect of policy that we are concerned with here. Unfortunately, it is still not possible in many cases to measure these benefits, although techniques now emerging promise some progress in this direction, so that it is not always clear that the intended advantages were actually achieved. What follows is a brief summary of the effects of federal transportation policies in the various regions of Canada.

Atlantic Region—As indicated in Chart 1, the four Atlantic Provinces received the largest per capita share of federal transportation expenditures in 1964-65. National transportation policies seem clearly to have provided the Atlantic Region with more adequate transportation facilities than would have been provided on a purely commercial basis. But this has not enabled the Region effectively to overcome the handicap of distance from the central Canadian market. Even in maritime transport, the improvement of the St. Lawrence Seaway, and particularly the extension of the navigation season, has tended to reduce the Atlantic Region's role. However, this role may be strengthened in the future through new technological developments of many kinds, perhaps including the giant freight liners and containerization.

Several federal transportation policies, beginning with the construction of the Intercolonial Railway, were specifically designed to tie the Atlantic Region in with Central Canada. Two subsequent attempts to enable the Region to export to central Canadian markets—the Maritime Freight Rates Act (which provided an annual federal subsidy of about $15 million) and freight subventions on movement of coal—seem to have produced only marginal benefits. Indeed, the main effect of the latter has been to prolong the life of a declining industry at a high national cost relative to the benefits involved.

There have also been policies designed mainly to improve difficult internal communications in the Atlantic Region. Such policies include the subsidies on the Prince Edward Island and Newfoundland ferries; the subsidies to coastal shipping; the rail rate reductions under MFRA for intraregional rail transportation; and the highway grants made by the Atlantic Development Board, in addition to the federal expenditures in the Atlantic Region for the Trans-Canada Highway. The proposed causeway to Prince Edward Island is of the same nature. Whatever the long-run benefits flowing from some of these policies, their over-all contribution to an improved regional balance could be very much enhanced if they were formulated and implemented within the context of a comprehensive regional planning framework.

Prairie Region—The Prairie Region is perhaps the best example of both the successes and the difficulties of national transportation policies in Canada. The great distances from external markets and sources of supply, the nature of its basic agricultural industry and land settlement, and unduly optimistic expectations all contributed during earlier periods of development to the building up of a very large and ultimately expensive internal transportation system. Both private and public sectors were involved in programs of over-investment in the system.

Federal transportation policies designed specifically to aid the Prairie Region have been confined largely to reducing the transport cost of its exports. The Crow's Nest Pass rates on grain, the feed grain freight subsidies, the establishment of the Port of Churchill, the national oil policy and associated pipeline construction, the St. Lawrence Seaway, all have had this effect. Only the railway "bridge" subsidy (whose effect has been very small) was intended to reduce certain freight costs in both directions although the Port of Churchill and the Seaway also have this potential.

The effect of the Crow's Nest Pass grain rates is clear. Whether or not the rates are remunerative to the railways, they have kept the costs of grain shipments to export markets lower in some years than they would otherwise have been. In 1961, the MacPherson Commission on Transportation concluded that there were years in which the revenues from Crow's Nest Pass grain rates failed to cover all the properly assignable costs of the movement, thus suggesting that there was some income benefit to grain producers. On the other hand, the long-run effect of such rates was probably to slow the pace of adjustment of prairie agriculture. Construction of the Seaway also provided income benefits to grain producers.

Pacific Region—With the exception of certain coastal shipping subsidies, the role of national transportation policy in the Pacific Region in the past has consisted chiefly of measures to link a viable, resource-based Pacific-oriented economy to the Atlantic-oriented central region. This was the principal aim of building the transcontinental railways, developing the transcontinental airlines and constructing the Trans-Canada Highway. Exports from the Pacific Region move largely by sea, and freight charges from other regions are influenced by the availability of the water alternative and U.S. rail competition.

The first change in the eastward orientation of transport policies came when policies were modified to promote the more extensive use of West Coast ports for exports. First the Crow's Nest Pass rates were made applicable to the West Coast. This was followed after the Second World War by the application of feed grain freight assistance to British Columbia, the removal of the mountain rail freight differential and the provision of subsidies for the movement of coal to the Pacific for export.

It seems clear that the national transportation policy will need to focus more on increases in West Coast transportation facilities, particularly in the form of investments in seaport and aviation facilities and north-south and trans-Pacific air routes. The growing importance of Pacific coastal and overseas trade will be as significant for this region as traditional outlets have been for Central Canada.

Central Canada — The original transportation policies were specifically designed to link other regions more closely to Central Canada. In spite of various elements of transportation policy intended to meet special regional needs and to moderate regional disabilities, national transportation policies have undoubtedly continued to support the primacy of Central Canada in terms of economic maturity and per capita income. For instance, government expenditures on water transportation have been largely concentrated on the improvement of the facilities of the main internal waterway in Canada—the Great Lakes-St. Lawrence system—with a consequent increase in the economic role performed by the centres located on this route. Both the rail lines and airline routes have a strong east-west orientation hurdling natural barriers and again enhancing the function of the central region. Employment in the air industry has become increasingly concentrated in Central Canada, particularly in Montreal. Moreover, air transportation, together with vastly improved methods of communication, has enhanced the advantage of the Toronto and Montreal metropolitan areas in supplying an increasing range of managerial and professional services.

The central region's large population, together with its concentration of industrial activity, has provided a basis for economies of scale and specialization in the form of lower transport costs and a greater variety of transport services. Federal policies controlling rail rates in the past were designed, among other things, to reduce differences throughout Canada between a rate charged on a high-density line and a low-density line. To the extent that it left rail rates higher in Central Canada than they otherwise would have been, it has probably brought about some loss of rail traffic to trucks—traffic which perhaps could have moved at lower real cost by rail. The virtual freeing of railway freight rates from government control will introduce greater flexibility of rate adjustment to the advantage of Central Canada, but rates in all regions are likely to be closer to the real costs of moving goods.

Implications for Policy

Clearly, the formulation of federal economic policies with significant regional implications has a long and varied history running through a number of stages and influenced by a wide variety of considerations. But the stark fact remains that the historical mix of market forces and public policy has not resulted in any significant narrowing of regional income disparities. So whatever the considerations were in the past, we are concerned that attention now be focused more intensively on this objective in the future.

Standing back from the varying and detailed facets of policy, one might hazard the view that federal policies have, on balance, probably prevented interregional disparities in per capita income from widening. This judgment is the more credible when one considers the ad hoc or short-run responses of government policy to economic emergencies and the distribution of expenditures among the various regions. On the other hand, it must be said that there is little indication that these have contributed to a stronger basis for self-sustaining growth in the lagging regions of the country.

The unavoidable impression that emerges from our review of federal economic policies is that they have exerted a pervasive but inconsistent impact upon the various regional economies. If federal policies are to contribute effectively to improved regional balance, an essential first step is that the goal of improved regional balance—including both the narrowing of regional disparities and the fuller utilization of available resources in the lagging regions—should be more prominently and consistently taken into account in the formulation and adaptation of federal policies. This is an overriding need. Second, there should be continuing, comprehensive and systematic appraisal of alternative policy measures to improve regional balance. As a basis for such appraisal we believe that it is now possible to develop and use much better information and techniques of analysis than in the past. The absence of a clear commitment to improved regional balance and of comprehensive and systematic assessment of policy alternatives will inevitably mean conflict, waste, frustration and the ultimate failure of policy.

A commitment to a regional development policy necessarily involves the articulation of appropriate guidelines. On the basis of our analysis to date, we suggest these:

—*Improving the utilization of manpower resources.*
   Policies to this end should aim, first, to increase opportunities for higher-income employment by encouraging labour mobility from low- to high-productivity sectors within the region; second, to increase employment opportunities on the basis of the region's resource and locational advantages, especially its potential advantages; and, third, to facilitate the ready movement of productive factors among regions in response to high-earning opportunities.

—*Raising the level of productivity within each region.*
   This should involve raising the level of skill and education of labour and management—human resource development; adoption of advanced technological methods in production; the concentration of economic activity in growth centres; and more efficient use of both labour and capital in the processes of production.

—*Assuring the adequate expansion of growth-related public services.*

—*Stimulating innovation, the application of new technology and the development of new viable lines of economic activity.*

These guidelines suggest that public policy should reinforce the market process of efficient resource allocation and make it work more powerfully and smoothly. Our view is that measures aimed at achieving greater self-generating growth processes in the lagging regions represent a superior method of securing improved regional balance than programs which merely maintain income through transfer payments. Not only do the former policies hold generally greater promise for achieving larger long-term benefits in relation to costs, but they are also more likely to facilitate reconciliation between the goal of improved regional balance and our other basic economic and social goals.

This brings us to two sets of reconciliation problems which confront regional development policies. The first is the possible conflict between maximum national economic growth and improved regional balance. There should be no difficulty if the means adopted to accelerate the rate of growth of income per person in the lagging regions would simultaneously raise the national rate of economic growth. There are good reasons for doubting that such an outcome is probable under all circumstances. For example, a significant shift in resources from higher- to lower-income regions may result in the creation of productive employment opportunities and viable bases for accelerated growth in the lower-income regions at the "cost" of retarding the rate of national economic growth. Thus, in a variety of different ways, there are likely to be "trade-offs" between growth of the national economy and the growth of lagging regions—in much the same fashion as there are "trade-offs" between levels of unemployment and price stability.

The second problem is related to our federal system of shared responsibilities. Particular regions or provinces may set objectives for themselves which are basically incompatible with our defintion of the goal of regional balance. For example, any significant volume of out-migration of population and labour force from a region may be viewed as detrimental to its conception of an appropriate rate of regional economic expansion. In other words, the region may feel that the achievement of full employment of both the existing and potential regional labour supply should override the objective of a more efficient use of resources, perhaps with a consequent built-in bias for maintaining industrial and occupational structures at relatively lower productivity levels than would otherwise have prevailed in the region. To the extent that reconciliation problems exist in this sense—and it must be admitted that the relationship between out-migration and economic growth is a complex one—they will need to be resolved in the context of a wide range of cultural and political, as well as economic and social, considerations.

These are complex issues which require much more explicit recognition and detailed assessment than have been accorded them in the past. In this context, reconciliations will obviously be facilitated by agreement that a process of "levelling up" among regions to higher standards of economic performance, and hence of income, is greatly to be preferred over a process of "levelling down". This should be the crux of federal and provincial policy approaches to regionally balanced development in Canada.

It is also important to recognize the diversity of regions and the necessity for flexible adaptation of national approaches to particular regional circumstances. Certain broad national policies—for example, stabilization policies—provide a necessary though not sufficient condition for achieving the goal of improved regional balance. But strict adherence to the principle of nondiscriminatory application in all national policies can result in inappropriate rigidity in federal support for regional development. What seems to be required is greater attention to the means for meeting some of the differing regional needs. In this context, we believe that the federal government must be prepared to experiment with new innovations in policy approaches and development techniques in the lagging regions. This calls, in turn, for specially designed and much more technically advanced research and policy-planning, together with improved administrative machinery, both at the centre of federal government decision-making and within the regions.

For obvious reasons, the Atlantic Region, more than any other, has been the focus of a wide range of federal government programs and departmental activities. To promote the more efficient achievement of the aims of these programs and activities, to avoid conflict and contradiction among such activities, and to avert confusion and uncertainty in the minds of the regional authorities who have to deal with the various federal departments and agencies, *We recommend that all federal area development programs affecting the four provinces should be co-ordinated within one planning and administrative agency.* Specifically, the framework being erected by the ADB will soon be at hand for guiding in a consistent manner the activities of ARDA, ADA and the Cape Breton Development Corporation. We view the formation of such an agency as an urgent need within the revised framework of departmental responsibilities.

Such an integrated agency would substantially strengthen the administration of federal policies affecting the Atlantic Region. But two further steps must be taken to meet the requirements of effective planning and implementation of policy. The first is the creation of an effective central review and appraisal system to assure co-ordination in programming among all federal departments and agencies. Second, adequate machinery must exist to facilitate joint federal-provincial planning and administration within the area.

The latter suggestion gives rise to the broader issue of federal-provincial co-operation throughout the country. Federal policies exert a pervasive impact in all regions. Yet, under our federal system of government, the responsibilities for growth and development are shared between the central and provincial authorities. It is encouraging that in recent years increased attention has been focused on the need for federal-provincial consultations. Indeed, the constitutional review that was launched earlier this year opens up challenging possibilities for new paths and new approaches for federal-provincial co-operation. Within the terms of reference of that review, scope is provided for airing possible conflicts between national and regional economic goals and for suggesting how they might appropriately be reconciled. Out of this review should emerge the development of more effective, continuing machinery for federal-provincial co-operation on the whole range of issues and policies relating to improved regional balance.

25   A Case for the West*

Harry E. Strom

PART I

Introduction

One of the most critical dilemmas facing Canadians is the existence of inequality and injustice among people of different backgrounds, living in different regions of the country—a condition which has fostered feelings of alienation. The symptoms of this alienation are all around us. The most important in the context of this Conference is the persistent agitation for an independent Quebec.

To a large degree it has been the consciousness of alienation and inequality on the part of Canadians of French origin which has brought these matters to our attention, and has made them subjects of national concern.

Because the underlying causes of alienation and inequality perceived by the French Canadians have to do with such matters as the original terms of Confederation, language rights, governmental jurisdiction and divisions of power, it is only natural that the remedies proposed would involve substantial Constitutional reforms.

Ours is a self-conscious age. We welcome the resurgent spirit and consciousness of our French-speaking citizens, and their understandable desire for a new cultural and economic role in Confederation.

We must recognize the deep feelings of alienation and inequality of treatment that are felt by regional groups in Canada which are neither of French extraction, French-speaking, or resident in the Province of Quebec. These feelings may not be cultural in nature, but could prove to be just as dangerous to Confederation as friction between the English and French cultures.

The causes of these other discontents are of such a nature that they may not be readily remedied by Constitutional reforms, but may require actions on the part of Parliament and provincial legislatures of a substantially different nature.

---

* An Address to the Federal Provincial Constitutional Conference, February, 1969. Reprinted by permission of the author.

HARRY E. STROM – Premier of the Province of Alberta, 1968-1971.

363

PART II

The Need for Full Participation and Equality

It is my hope that ten years hence we will be able to say that Canada's internal political unity is assured because the alienation and unequal treatment of minority and regional groups has ended; that Canadians of French extraction feel at home in Canadian Confederation, and that other minorities and regional groups feel completely at home in Canada.

The Government of Alberta wants to play a constructive part in the elimination of those things that divide us.

Let me suggest approaches that seem to us to have merit. Where minority alienation or inequality exist within a province it is the primary responsibility of the provincial government to recognize these conditions and to treat them. If the problems of alienation and inequality overlap provincial boundaries and require national accommodation or intervention, or accommodation by other provincial governments, then the province concerned should make representation to the Federal Government.

Provincial governments should take their lead from the Federal Government to make Canadians in other provinces feel at home in Confederation. The Federal Government must be regarded as the ultimate guardian of Canadian unity.

Every effort should be made by the provinces to makes those accommodations which emerge from these Constitutional Conferences and which are necessary to end the alienation of feelings of inequality of Canadians in the various regions of Canada.

Let me discuss for a moment the application of these principles, firstly, to the case of French Canada, and secondly, to the case of Western Canada.

It is now evident that many French-speaking Canadians have bad feelings of alienation from the mainstream of Canadian life. Since the majority of French-speaking Canadians are resident in the Province of Quebec, it was only to be expected that the government of that province should have been acutely conscious of this alienation and inequality, and should have resolved to do something about these conditions.

The Government of Quebec was quite right in concluding that the problems of dissatisfaction felt by many French-speaking Canadians within its jurisdiction could not be successfully dealt with through action by the Government of Quebec alone.

If citizens of French origin resident in Quebec are to be made to feel fully at home within Canadian Confederation, then the conditions giving rise to the alienation and inequality in their case require national accommodation to their needs, and in addition, certain accommodations on the part of other provincial governments.

We recognize that in order for French-speaking people in Quebec to feel at home in Confederation, action must be taken not only in Central Canada, but on a national scale.

Where changes in Alberta are required to accommodate the French Canadian case, I want to point out that we can get a positive response from our people if we can say that the Government of Quebec has made certain representations to the Federal Government concerning problems of alienation and inequality experienced by its people, and that the Federal Government has recommended what we in Alberta can do to help alleviate these problems.

With specific reference to steps taken in Alberta to accommodate those of French language and origin, we have to date made provision for French to be the language of instruction in Grades I and II, and the language of instruction fifty percent of the class day in Grades III and up, in those areas where there is a need and an interest. In addition, thousands of our students are taking French in elementary and secondary schools.

The availability of teachers of the French language is always a problem, and we are encouraging the training of additional teachers.

I should point out that only six percent of our population is of French origin. Alberta's cultural heritage is a mosaic of many ethnic groups, all contributing to the richness of our nation. We want to provide opportunity for all groups to develop culturally and economically.

Although we have reservations about some of the recommendations of the Federal Government, it is our hope to make French Canadians feel more at home in Confederation.

The question, Gentlemen, is how can we create conditions which will make Western Canadians feel confident about their role in Confederation?

Are you willing to demonstrate an equal concern, and an equal preparedness to understand and to act upon the problems of alienation and inequality to which Western Canadians are subjected?

For the sake of Canadian unity, it is time certain things were said frankly and without prejudice about the need to cope wtih increasing feelings of alienation in the West, and inequalities in the situation of the West.

In general, Western Canadians can be led to sincerely believe that the Federal Government's judgment is fair and its recommendations deserving of confidence when it calls upon us to respond to the case of Quebec, only when the Federal Government demonstrates an equal sensitivity with respect to the case of the West, and a preparedness to recommend those steps necessary to deal with economic discrimination against the West.

PART III

People of the West

As Premier of Alberta, I can speak officially only for that Province, but I feel fully confident that many of the sentiments which I will express in stating the case for the West as perceived by Albertans, will echo kindred sentiments in the hearts of Canadians living in other Western Provinces and the Northern Territories.

Let me say that it would be a tragic and profound mistake on the part of either the politicians or the press, or the general public of Central Canada, to underestimate or dismiss out of hand the profound dissatisfaction which does exist among many people in Western Canada. There is a real lack of understanding and appreciation of our regional interests and problems and aspirations in other parts of this country. We deeply resent the picture which is often painted of the West in the minds of the people of Central Canada.

Westerners are naturally concerned that minds which hold misconceptions may be reluctant or incapable of appreciating our dissatisfactions and our aspirations.

I repeat, however, that it would be a tragedy if this were to continue.

This is essentially what happened in the case of French Canada. For years and years, spokesmen were saying, "We are not happy in Confederation. We have an orientation which you do not understand, and which you do not try to understand. We have aspirations which cannot be realized under the present system. We are subject to inequities which must be remedied".

But for years and years, the strength and legitimacy of these complaints were either ignored or underestimated.

I can only repeat that it would be a double tragedy if a similar mistake were to be made with respect to the West.

In general, the accommodations which we require include changes in attitude, changes in the orientation of various Federal departments, changes in the operating policies of the Federal Government, and a creation of new policies to cope with the causes of our dissatisfaction.

Allow me now to list some major areas in which Western Canadians feel that their concerns have been ignored, and their aspirations frustrated.

1. Western Resource Industries

The economy of the West is based to a very large degree upon the production of certain raw resources. We are endeavoring to develop secondary industries, but no matter how much secondary industry we acquire, the specific raw resource industries will continue to be the base of the Western economy, and our primary contribution to the economy.

The growth of these industries is beyond the control of regional government, though to some extent within the control of the Federal Government. I refer especially to national transportation policy and to tariff regulations.

This need not be a bad situation if it were not for the fact that when Westerners examine the Federal Government's priorities in industrial development, the order which they see is the following: the manufacturing industries in Eastern and Central Canada, the raw resource industries of Eastern and Central Canada, then, the raw resource industries of Western Canada, and finally, the manufacturing industries of Western Canada.

This order of priorities is not a figment of our imagination.

What Western Canadians legitimately desire, if economic justice is to prevail within Confederation, is that our raw resource industries be given the same priority as the manufacturing industries of Eastern and Central Canada.

We desire this equality of priority to be demonstrated, not simply in conference communiques but in concrete ways.

For example, when the Federal Government sets tariffs we could like it to give full consideration not only to the needs of certain Eastern industries for protection, but equal consideration to the fact that the costs of these tariffs are to a large extent borne by consumers and Western industries, which must compete with high production costs and high transportation costs in an international market.

It is time the Federal Government recognized the harmful effect of the tariff system on the West, and indeed on the economic health of the nation.

Thirteen years ago, Professor J. H. Young estimated for the Gordon Commission that the tariffs were costing the people of Canada one billion dollars a year.

No reliable figures on the current cost of the tariff system are available. But we have no reason to suppose the figure would be any lower.

It is true the cost of the tariff system is borne by all Canadians. But not all Canadians benefit from it.

It was set up, as we all know, for the protection of secondary industry in Central Canada, chiefly in Ontario. Very few Western industries today gain any benefit from it. And most ironically, the tariff system has failed to achieve its very objective of fostering Canadian secondary industry.

A study of Professor J. H. Dales of the University of Toronto showed some time ago that despite tariffs, Canadian economic growth has lagged behind that of the United States since 1870; that the ratio of our secondary manufacturing to theirs is no higher now than it was in *1910*.

And yet, Gentlemen, one of our major industries, agriculture, has been *rising* in productivity compared with the United States, despite very limited tariff protection.

For us, the tariff system symbolizes the economic imbalance of Confederation.

We see the logic of protecting infant industries but some of the "infants" are now eighty years of age and we are tired of paying their pensions.

If the Federal Government is prepared to use its influence to secure entrance to foreign markets for Canadian producers, we want it to work as hard on behalf of the raw resource industries of the West.

The Federal Government used its influence to the benefit of Eastern Canadian manufacturers in securing the recent U.S.-Canada Auto Pact. Will you use your influence to the same extent to help us secure a U.S.-Canada oil pact which will assure the marketability of a larger portion of Alberta's petroleum production in the United States, in the future?

In the field of transportation, we all know that what the expenditures of the National Harbours Board in Eastern ports and the expenditures of the Federal Government on the St. Lawrence Seaway have meant, but we in the West, when we consider this whole matter of transportation policy, are wondering what further efforts will be made, such as a Prince Rupert port, to improve the movement of our products to seaboard and to foreign markets. particularly in a westerly direction.

The things that I have mentioned are matters of real concern to Western Canadians. They disclose the existence of economic inequities which we desire to see removed.

When Quebec complained of inequities in French-English relations, the Government of Canada perceived that some of these inequities were real and appointed a Commission on Bilingualism and Biculturalism to help remedy the situation.

The Alberta dissatisfactions to which I have referred in the preceding paragraphs are not so much cultural as economic, but they too are real, and they too cause Canadians in the West to feel economically discrimintaed against in their own country.

We would therefore ask the Government of Canada to remove these inequities. For example, we would suggest the appointment of a commission on tariffs and freight rates, to examine our problems and to recommend solutions.

Albertans await with interest to see if the problems of Western Canada provoke as positive a response as the problems of Canadians in other regions.

2. The Pacific Community

Canada's foreign policy and trade policy has been traditionally oriented toward the Atlantic community.

This is understandable historically, but as we look to the future, as Western Canadians we are frankly more interested and more excited in looking to the West rather than back to the East. There has developed in recent years, among a substantial portion of our population, an increased interest in Japan with its millions of people and its shortage of resources; and in Asia with its new nations struggling toward development, and a population that is the largest potential market in the world.

Western Canadians therefore ask that shifts occur in the policy of this country to give as much recognition and attention to the Pacific community as it does to the Atlantic community. If it is one of the functions of the Federal Government to represent Canadians abroad, as Canadians resident in Western Canada we ask that our interests be particularly represented in Eastern countries.

We ask the Federal Government to take special steps to bring the Western Provinces into stronger and better relationships with these countries.

The Federal Government is not reluctant to take special steps to allow strengthening of relations between French-speaking nations abroad and the French parts of Canada, even to the point of increasing foreign aid to French Africa.

Let the Canadian Government send joint Canada-Quebec delegations to French educational conferences in Africa if that is what is desired by Canadians in one part of the country, but at the same time, let the Federal

Government send new and stronger joint Canada-Manitoba, Canada-Saskatchewan, Canada-Alberta and Canada-British Columbia trade delegations to the nations of the Pacific community.

At the same time, to facilitate this policy shift, there should also be shifts in the personnel of some of Canada's trade and diplomatic missions, particularly in the Asian countries. Many Western Canadians are tired of going to Asian countries and meeting with well-meaning, but Eastern-Canadian oriented civil servants who can relate the name of every major company doing business in Montreal or Ottawa or Toronto, but who have never heard of some of the international concerns of Winnipeg, Regina, Edmonton, Calgary or Vancouver. These people represent the interests of some Canadians, but they do not represent our interests.

In articulating this desire of Western Canadians for stronger and better trade and diplomatic representations with the countries of the Pacific community, I am well aware that within recent months the Prime Minister himself has spoken admirably on this subject and verbally acknowledged the desirability of what we request. Western Canadians have applauded the Prime Minister's words in this regard. But at the same time we are regrettably aware that the only significant action which has been taken in the field of Canadian-Asian relations, since the present Government came to power, has been a negative one. I refer to the recent tightening of import restrictions on Japanese goods.

Would it be a national tragedy for Canadian consumers to be able to purchase low cost Japanese colour television sets if it meant that some workers in Eastern Canada would have to be retrained for new jobs?

High import duties on Asian manufacturers do more than restrict imports. They reduce the amount of Canadian exchange which Asian countries have to purchase Canadian raw materials. Since the bulk of these raw materials are materials produced in the West, such policies restrict our trade and depress the standard of living of our workers.

3. The North

To many people in Eastern and Central Canada, the idea of northern development is a romantic but rather impractical notion, something which may occur in the distant future, but something which is not of much relevance right now.

But to many Western Canadians, northern development is not something which can be left to the future but something which is already upon us. If the integration of transportation networks, population movement, social services and educational opportunity in the Northwest is to be accomplished smoothly, northern development planning and action on the part of the Federal Government should be much further along than it is at present.

If we compare the development of Alaska in recent years with the development of the Yukon and Northwest Territories, we are disappointed. The painfully slow and often tragic story of northern development in Canada is not the fault of the tiny bands of pioneers who now reside there. The basic blame must be borne by the Federal Government.

Alaska is being developed by a southern people—the Americans. It is appalling that we, a northern people, have not been able to match their efforts, at least in imagination and purpose, if not in magnitude.

The Federal Government of the United States granted Alsaka her status as a state. The Federal Government of Canada has had the responsibility of managing our northern territories for as long a period, and yet to date the prospect of greater autonomy for the Yukon or the Northwest Territories is not even in sight, and the residents live under a suffocating Federal colonialism.

And so, we Western Canadians ask, what about northern development?

If the Federal Government does not intend to act, or cannot act, would the Government contemplate giving the Western Provinces an extension of their jurisdiction? Northern development is an aspiration of Western Canadians. Opportunities for its fulfillment must be provided.

4. The Financing of Western Development

Development embodies our aspirations. National policies and attitudes which retard our development or relegate our concerns to a low priority position are the inequities which we seek to have redressed. A positive response to our developmental needs must involve action and development financing.

We do not ask for handouts or preferential treatment. Rather, we ask that a national fiscal and monetary policy, recognizing the uniqueness of our situation, be developed and pursued along with policies recognizing the uniqueness of other regional areas.

In particular, in the field of capital formation we wish to point again, as we have in the past, to our most urgent need for domestic capital investment in Western potential. We request policies that encourage the diffusion of existing capital rather than its centralization in the few key industrial areas, and which encourage more Canadians to become shareholders.

We wish also to point out that not only domestic capital, but foreign capital will be required for Western economic development.

It is sad, but true, that in the history of Western Canada there has often been a greater willingness on the part of foreign investors to gamble on our potential than there has been on the part of investors in Eastern and Central Canada.

In Alberta's experience, for example, we simply could not find entrepreneurs in the financial centres of Central Canada with sufficient resources or interest in Alberta to gamble on our oil in the early days. If it hadn't been for American capital, much of our petroleum would still be in the ground.

So we ask the Federal Government not to pursue policies that restrict the flow of foreign capital to our regions, but rather to pursue policies which will encourage it.

We ask for a positive economic nationalism, not a negative one.

We ask for an economic climate which seeks to encourage all the foreign capital and technology we can absorb, as long as it respects our sovereignty.

We know the fears of United States domination in the Canadian economy.

Our hope is that our economy become as Canadian as possible, and that every Western Canadian become an investor. But we also believe that when necessary, and it is necessary now, we utilize foreign capital and technology extensively, as long as we acquire a fair return on the development of our resources for our people.

We as Canadians can still retain the economic and political controls required to ensure that foreign investors behave responsibly and in accord with Canadian interests.

In Alberta, much of our petroleum industry is U.S.-owned. Ownership, however, does not involve blanket control, and the difference can be established by wise legislation. No fair-minded and knowledgeable person could demonstrate that American oil companies run Alberta. They operate by our rules, and we both benefit.

We sincerely believe that there is such a thing as a fair partnership in international economic relations. Both sides can benefit, and this is what we mean when we talk about "encouraging foreign investment".

We ask you therefore to recognize our specific needs in the field of capital formation. We have a need for more domestic investment and a need for foreign capital and technology as well.

In the field of monetary policy we ask you to recognize the difference in our state of economic development as compared with that of Eastern and Central Canada. We are just beginning to build our secondary industries. We ask therefore for an end to blanket monetary policies and interest rate regulations that treat the country as though every region were at the same stage in its capital formation and industrial expansion.

When you tighten credit across the board because the economy is heating up, what this means in Ontario is that a factory which is already built must defer its expansion. But what it means in Manitoba, Saskatchewan, Alberta and British Columbia, and in parts of Quebec, is that the factory doesn't get built at all.

The discriminatory nature of blanket monetary policy is one of the primary causes of the slow growth of secondary industry in the West.

In the United States the central bank is organized on a regional basis. Might not the same thing be done in Canada with *real autonomy* for regional branches of the Bank of Canada, which would enable them to take into account the unique economic needs of the areas they serve?

In recognition of the high regard which many Western Canadians have for the capabilities of enlightened private enterprise, we ask for an expanded role for the private sector in the field of social services and social development.

We wish to be able to say to private enterprise, for example, that for every fifty offices, build a day care centre—for every five factories, build a vocational training institute—for every ten thousand dollars of physical resources you extract from an underdeveloped region, create economic opportunities for under-privileged citizens. And if you will do this, we will make it profitable on a limited basis, so long as the total cost to us is less than what it would have been if we tried to do the same thing ourselves, and as long as the standards are those acceptable to our citizens.

What we ask of the Federal Government is policies which will facilitate this kind of private involvement; particularly we ask that the private sector be allowed to write off, for taxation purposes, at least a portion of the expenses incurred in meeting such social obligations.

Finally, in the area of regional development programming, we ask that the regional development department of the Federal Government pay much more attention to developing areas of the West.

Even more important, we ask the Federal Government to invest in high potential as well as depressed areas. We ask for a balance. In the past three years the Federal Government has committed hundreds of millions of dollars for comprehensive economic development programmes in low income areas. How much money has the Government poured into high potential areas? These figures should at least be related, and if they were, the West would receive a much higher proportion of regional development funds from the Federal Government than is presently the case.

Often the terms of reference of development funding programmes, such as the original Area Development Incentives Act, are drawn up in such a way that the incentives are not of the type that would fully stimulate manufacturing developments in Western areas. We seldom experience *meaningful* prior consultations.

In short, therefore, we ask particularly that the Federal Government distinguish between—or at least strike a balance between—welfare economics and development economics on the part of its regional development department.

These are some of the major financial concerns of Alberta. We ask and await a positive response. Without such a positive response it will be increasingly difficult to ask our people to make sacrifices to remedy the financial concerns of others.

In particular, we ask for more flexible guidelines in foreign investment and the increased participation by all Canadians in capital ownership. We ask for specialized rather than blanket monetary policies. We seek regional reserve banks to serve regional economies, tax concessions on limited profit opportunities for the private sector in the field of social development, and equity in regional development policy.

5. *Fair Representation in National Discourse*

In presenting these concerns of Alberta, let me touch on the matter of representation in national discourse.

I have already alluded to the fact that much Federal legislation in areas where the West has vital concerns is formulated without any real consultation with us. Because of the proximity of provincial governments in Central Canada to the national capital, they sometimes appear much more influential than ourselves in securing Federal legislation favourable to their requirements and often equally unfavourable to our requirements.

We would consequently ask that greater consultation take place between the Federal Government and the Governments of Western Canada on those issues in which they are vitally affected.

We need, and desire, more equitable representation on Federal Government boards, commissions, task forces and so on. Even this will not bring us positive returns unless there is also an effort on the part of the Federal Government to consult with us much more freely and much more readily than it has in the past.

The problem of obtaining fair representation for the West in national discourse goes far beyond the acquisition of a fair representation in government circles. Even more important is the need for a fair representation of the needs and concerns of the people of the West among the general public in Central Canada.

We often get the impression that the national media and the representatives of the media in the large centres of Central Canada are not interested in the views of the representatives from the West. There is too little interest, it seems, in reporting the attitudes of our representatives in depth to the people of the nation as a whole, but particularly to the large population centres in Central Canada.

There is not much that governments can do to ensure the presentation of broader viewpoints to the general public. I therefore appeal to journalists, commentators, and the many men of good will in Central Canada to help raise the level of dialogue between our two regions of the country.

6. The Need for Changes in Tax Sharing Agreements and All Financial Arrangements

Many of the points we have discussed point to the need, indeed the absolute necessity, for a new look at tax sharing and financial arrangements between the provinces and the Federal Government. The growing chasm between the tax resources and fiscal responsibilities of the provinces is fast becoming our greatest domestic affliction.

PART IV

Conclusion

In conclusion, my message to the Conference is this:

We will co-operate with the Federal Government to the fullest extent of our ability to bring regional alienation and inequality in Canada to an end, but there must be a corresponding effort on the part of the Federal Government and the provincial governments of Central Canada to recognize and accommodate the concerns of the West.

National accommodation to the concerns of the West will require more than Constitutional changes.

It calls far more for practical changes in the attitudes, emphases and implementation of the operational policies and decisions of the Federal Government.

In any event, when future Constitutional changes or new national policies are proposed, we will examine them very closely to see if they provide opportunities for the realization of the aspirations of Western Canadians.

26 Report on Maritime Union*

John Deutsch et al

Clearly, the developments and changes of the post-war decades, now moving with accelerating speed, are bringing new and far-reaching challenges to
the people of the Maritimes. It is clear, also, that these challenges confront
not simply the peoples and governments of the individual provinces, but, the
region as a whole. Consequently, the course of events in the future, the opportunities which will be available to all the people of the Maritimes will depend,
in considerable measure, on the nature and adequacy of the response from
the region as a whole.

There is no doubt that the three provinces together constitute a region with
a distinct identity and a large number of common characteristics and interests.

> They have shared in the same colonial history and in the Canadian
> nation-building experience. They have, again, despite some obvious
> differences, much the same mixture of people. Their loyalties and ideals
> are similar, characterized as they are by democratic traditions, adherence
> to British institutions, a sense of individuality, and a measured quality
> and pace of life . . . .
>
> In relation to the rest of Canada and to one another, the economies of
> these provinces fluctuate together under varying conditions (e.g. depres-
> sion, war, prosperity, inflation and anti-inflation policies); respond in
> much the same way (e.g. population movements); and have much the
> same characteristics and problems (e.g. a persistent lag below the national
> standards of income, unemployment and underemployment; age dis-
> tribution patterns; high incidence of poverty; difficulties in maintaining
> public services and financial difficulties arising from high-risk industrial
> development programmes.) Naturally enough, the provinces stand on
> much common ground and share much the same approaches in their
> dealing with the federal government.[1]

If there is a large inherent interest for common action by the people of the
region, how is it to be done, for what purposes and by what means? The
possibilities can be grouped conveniently, for purposes of analysis, into three
basic approaches; e.g. extensive informal co-operation, structured formal
co-operation, and some form of union.

---

[1] Guy Henson, *Interprovincial Relations in the Maritime Provinces* (Fredericton, Maritime Union Study, 1970), pp. 8-9.

* From *Maritime Union Study: The Report on Maritime Union Commissioned by The
Governments of Nova Scotia, New Brunswick, and Prince Edward Island.* (Fredericton,
New Brunswick, The Queen's Printer). Reprinted by permission of Fred Drummie,
Executive Director, Maritime Study Group and Information Canada.

Informal Co-operation

Historically, the large inherent common interests of the peoples of the region have expressed themselves in the periodic and persistent movements for Maritime Union[2] and in the development of a large and growing network of informal voluntary co-operation between both private groups and governmental organizations.

> It may be safely said that one may look far and without success to find another such sub-normal group of provinces or states, within a federal state, which have developed so many forms of private and official interprovincial co-operation as have the Maritime or Atlantic provinces.
>
> Here, people have formed voluntary organizations to serve their needs in virtually every sphere of human activity; trade, business and industry; occupations and professions, transportation, education, culture, recreation, health, welfare, labour, fraternal and service; research and development; and religion.[3]

A special survey carried out by the Dalhousie Institute of Public Affairs found there were approximately 181 active interprovincial organizations in the Atlantic and Maritime provinces.[4] Forty-three of these were established since 1960. The reasons for this rapid growth were stated as follows:

> The real reasons, as stated by the respondents during the study, are two (1) in internal regional needs, the advantages to be derived from consolidation of efforts; and in (2) in meeting external needs and pressures, the advantages of joint action in advancing or protecting regional interests.
>
> Other influences, in part related to size and regional advocacy, can also be identified. They include (1) the necessity or desire to bring about an interchange of ideas and information, to maintain standards, and to co-ordinate plans; and (2) the merging of provincial identity with a wider regional sense of community.[5]

In the governmental sphere there has developed, also, a large and growing network of informal and voluntary co-operative arrangements and activities. There are periodic meetings of the Maritime premiers, and of ministers with their opposite numbers, to discuss common problems and to exchange information. There is a much larger inter-change between administrative, professional and technical officials in innumerable regular and *ad hoc* meetings.[6] The vast majority of these intergovernmental consultations and inter-changes are purely voluntary. Generally they are not based on formal

---

[2] J. Murray Beck, *The History of Maritime Union: A Study in Frustration.*
[3] Guy Henson, *Interprovincial Relations in the Maritime Provinces,* pp. 2-3.
[4] Dalhousie Institute of Public Affairs and Richard H. Leach, *Interprovincial Relations in the Maritime Provinces* (Fredericton, Maritime Union Study, 1970), Part 1, p. 5.
[5] Guy Henson, *Interprovincial Relations in the Maritime Provinces,* p. 5.
[6] Dalhousie Institute of Public Affairs and Richard H. Leach, *Interprovincial Relations in the Maritime Provinces.* See Part II "Interprovincial Co-operation in the Maritime Provinces" for a thorough description and assessment of the subject.

arrangements, do not involve commitments and are not supported by specific administrative machinery or resources. In the relatively few cases of more formal and specific undertakings, such as the Maritime electric power pool, very particular objectives are sought.

Undoubtedly, many valuable results flow from this extensive system of informal and voluntary co-operation. It is likely that more could be accomplished by its further developments. However, our analysis of the experience in the Maritime region and elsewhere demonstrates convincingly that there are severe limitations to what can be accomplished by this method. The possibilities in the private sphere have been, and are somewhat more promising than in the governmental sphere, where not very much of real substance can reasonably be expected. This is not because of a peculiar perversity but because of the very fundamental political and social issues involved.

> The evaluation of individual organizations, or of these organizations as a whole, is beyond the scope of the present report. Enough facts have been adduced to indicate the danger of romantic notions about interprovincial co-operation or of an assumption that co-operation offers an easy path to massive and concerted regional effort.[7]

Furthermore:

> In fact, while attempts have been made at interprovincial co-operation within the region, there is no great body of evidence to indicate any really effective effort at political or administrative co-ordination, much less actual unification. . . .
>
> The paradox lies in that, while in matters of a private nature a good deal has taken place, where it comes down to more vital matters of public policy constraints of historical, political and social limits seem to have prevailed.[8]

Formal Co-operation

The limitations and inadequacies of informal and voluntary co-operation could perhaps, be overcome in some useful measure by the introduction of more formal and structured methods. Here reference is made primarily to the inter-governmental sphere. Instead of informal or casual arrangements, steps could be taken to establish intergovernmental committees, consultative bodies, and intergovernmental agencies with specific terms of reference, assigned functions, and formal constitutions. In most cases, such formal bodies would need to be equipped with a secretariat and expert help, with specific resources and facilities. There would be regular reports and accountability to the appropriate political bodies and authorities.

This kind of formal co-operative machinery could be established throughout

---

[7] Dalhousie Institute of Public Affairs and Richard H. Leach, *Interprovincial Relations in the Maritime Provinces,* Part I, p. 28.

[8] R. M. Burns, *Experience of National and International Co-operative Institutions* (Fredericton, Maritime Union Study, 1970), pp. 4 and 10.

the governmental structure. It would be headed-up by a council of premiers which, unlike the present council, would have a secretariat, terms of reference, fairly frequent regular meetings, and a measure of accountability to the legislatures. There would be inter-provincial committees of ministers in each of the important fields of government, again with terms of reference and some particular responsibility to develop common policies and programmes. Where necessary the ministerial committees would be supported by a secretariat. Below the political level there would be formal inter-provincial committees of officials to carry out a variety of functions, i.e. prepare proposals, give advice, and co-ordinate specified administrative activities. Also, there could be established certain inter-governmental agencies to carry out particular functions for all three governments, i.e. research, statistical and economic services, promotional activities for the region, etc.

The establishment of machinery designed to accomplish much more formal co-operation would make possible a larger measure of united action in the interests of the region as a whole. However, there are a number of serious drawbacks to this method. Firstly, it would unquestionably result in a further multiplication of bureaucracy and thus add to governmental overheads which are already disproportionately burdensome in the region.[9] Secondly, much time and energy would have to be devoted to meetings, consultations, and comings and goings of all kinds. The process would be cumbersome and slow. Finally, and most important, there would be no executive power for common action in this whole system of formal co-operation. The entire system would depend on the powers of persuasion. While many useful things could be accomplished in this way in regard to professional, technical and specialized matters, not much of substantial significance could be expected in the realm of basic policy decisions. The political representatives who must make these decisions will continue to be responsible to provincial legislatures and their political lives will continue to be dependent on local political support. Consequently, agreements are likely to be confined to matters of individual provincial interest and local political feasibility. In these circumstances it is very difficult to cope effectively with the interests of the region as a whole, especially where compromises and accommodations inside the region are involved, as they almost always are. These limitations have been clearly demonstrated over and over again in the history of such arrangements, both national and international.[10]

Some Form of Union

The limitations inherent in any form of voluntary inter-governmental co-operation, whether formal or informal, could be overcome in varying degrees by going one step further. This would involve the conclusion of prior agree-

---

[9]See Appendix B "The Growth of the Civil Service" as well as the brief of the Atlantic Provinces Economic Council in *Public Briefs/Soumissions* (Fredericton, Maritime Union Study, 1969), pp. 27-54.

[10] See the discussion in *Interprovincial Relations in the Maritime Provinces* and *Experience of National and International Co-operative Institutions.*

ments by the governments concerned to carry out certain functions in common. The agreements would specify the functions to be performed, would delegate the necessary powers to a common decision-making body and would prescribe the procedures to be followed in achieving the united purpose. In other words, the agreement would establish a union for a particular purpose, or purposes.

In the context of the Maritime region one could conceive of three kinds of union; an administrative union, an economic union, and full political union. . . . . There is considerable scope in the case of the three relatively small Maritime governments for the reduction of costly overheads by the joint administration of many government services. Such joint administration could accomplish significant savings through the elimination of duplication, the attainment of more efficient scale, and the better use of the modern methods and highly skilled manpower. Among the activities and services which could be considered for joint administration would be: the collection of taxes, particularly consumer taxes such as retail sales taxes, gasoline taxes, etc.; motor vehicle licensing and motor vehicle regulations of all kinds; various health services involving large administrative functions; some parts of the management and conservation of similar natural resources; the collection and maintenance of many kinds of records and information; and many routine inspection and regulatory services.

Uniform legislation and regulations would be desirable and no doubt essential in some instances, but not in every case. However, such uniformity would in itself make a very important contribution to the common welfare of the region by reducing the cost and complexity of doing business across the provincial boundaries among three relatively small provinces. Differing legal requirements and regulations administered by different authorities affect many aspects of business and constitute a general, and in many cases a wholly unnecessary drag on commerce.[11]

The joint administration of services would require the development of a prior agreement, or agreements, among the three governments. Such agreement would define the services to be administered and provide for the allocation of costs, the manner in which the joint management would be constituted, and the duties and responsibilities that would be assigned to such management. This intergovernmental agreement, or agreements, would constitute, in effect, an administrative union.

An administrative union would not make possible (nor would it be designed for the purpose) common action on matters of basic policy. It would not make possible general economic planning and common policies for economic development.

> In areas like education and welfare, and in economically sensitive areas of industrial development, all extremely important in any plans for economic and social growth, we face not only different concepts and standards but vested interests which can be difficult to overcome.[12]

---

[11] Atlantic Provinces Transportation Commission brief in *Public Briefs/Soumissions,* pp. 55-60.

[12] R. M. Burns, *Experience of National and International Co-operative Institutions,* p. 45.

In order to comprise the vital matters of economic development and growth it would be necessary to extend the arrangements for union to the full scope of economic union. Such an economic union could be established by a formal agreement between the three governments providing for: (a) a joint planning body to make recommendations to governments on all matters of economic policy and to prepare a basic regional strategy for development and growth; (b) the prior acceptance of the concept of a single regional policy of promotion and development in regard to all important fields, i.e. industrial development, tourist trade, agriculture, etc.; (c) uniformity of legislation and regulation in respect of all important economic matters (company law, labour law, etc.) in order to ensure freedom of movement of labour, capital and enterprise among the three provinces; and (d) joint negotiation with the federal government concerning all matters of regional economic development.

Economic union, if successful, could go a long way in providing the means required for the realization of the basic common interests of the Maritime region. However, there are two very important reservations. Again, as in the case of a large network of arrangements for formal co-operation, there is the substantial danger that another heavy layer of bureaucracy would be built on top of the already large overhead of three separate governments. More important, the successful working of economic union would be entirely dependent upon vital political decisions which have to be taken by three independent governments, each of which must look to local political support. In these circumstances it is not possible to count on the likelihood that the necessary critical decisions to achieve the common regional interest can be accomplished. The history of economic unions in various parts of the world does not give one any confidence. They have never accomplished much for long unless they had before them the ultimate goal of full political union.

Obviously, full political union would provide the most effective machinery for the fullest possible attainment of the common objectives of the region. By this means the large common interest of all the people of the region could be worked for without the complexities, delays, frustrations, and costly overheads inevitably associated with other forms of co-operative effort. On the other hand, it is a very far-reaching step which involves the creation of a single provincial government for the region and the complete abrogation of the existing governments of the individual provinces. Clearly the process would require a great deal of work and much difficult negotiation. To accomplish full political union it would be necessary: (1) to prepare and agree upon a constitution for the new single provincial government; (2) to negotiate new financial and constitutional arrangements with the federal government; (3) to transfer the liabilities and assets of the existing provincial governments to the new government; (4) to unite the existing administrative bodies and agencies into a single provincial administration; (5) to unify a large number of separate statutes and regulations into a single body of provincial law; and (6) to develop a new set of municipal arrangements for the single province.

Aside from these extensive and challenging tasks there are the more fundamental matters concerning the loyalties, historical associations, and democratic values that attach to the close relationships that have prevailed for so long with each of the governments of these old provinces. It remains to assess all these considerations and to weigh them in the light of the challenges which the future will bring to the people of the Maritime region.

CONCLUSIONS

It is both trite and very important to emphasize that the course of action to be taken to achieve the common interests of the region in future, must be decided by the people of the Maritimes themselves. We are fully aware that all that can be done here is to present information and to draw attention to considerations that should be kept in mind. We turn now to the considerations which we think are particularly relevant in the light of the special studies and surveys which were carried out for this study.

Political organizations and administrative machinery are means to an end, and are not ends in themselves. Consequently, the people of the Maritimes will wish, first of all, to weigh the issues that are involved in the ends they seek and the role they wish to play in the Canadian nation. The central question is, to put it very starkly, does a significant majority of the people of the Maritimes attach importance to achieving a more rapid rate of economic development in order to raise average living standards and to provide more adequate employment and career opportunities in the region; or is a higher priority assigned to the maintenance of local attachments, local diversities, local autonomies, small scale relationships, and the existing structure and pace of life? Neither one of these courses is inherently more virtuous in itself than the other; it is a matter of choice and emphasis. Naturally, there will be a desire on the part of many to have "both worlds". Unfortunately this will be even less possible of attainment in the future than it has in the past because of the new challenges which now confront the people of the region.

Quite clearly the maintenance of the existing attachments, qualities and structures, can be accomplished most conveniently by the retention of the present political arrangements, i.e. the three separate provincial governments. The historical and traditional loyalties to the individual provincial entities are strong; the attachments to local diversities and interests are more intense than elsewhere in the country. There is a reluctance in many quarters to accommodate change.

> . . . The people of the three Maritime provinces have had a long experience of living within the influence of the political institutions they know and, presumably, these have to some substantial degree reflected their wants and their desires. 'The devil you know' is an aptly applied expression in assessing many human reactions and when we combine with this the resistance to change inherent in a basically politically and socially conservative community, it is more understandable that there has been no eager rush to embrace the apparent benefits of political union, or even those of extensive administrative co-ordination. The local political sense is seemingly highly developed in most parts of the

Maritimes, and there is an understandable reluctance to dilute what power remains by a broader base, even if it might be more efficient and economical.[13]

The resistance to change in existing political structures is reinforced by the established relationships and interests that are associated with governments; these tend to be particularly intimate and strong. It can be expected that various influential groups, the holders of franchises and concessions, the bureaucratic apparatus, and many who have vested interests in the existing arrangements, would be apprehensive of changes that might bring uncertainties and new approaches. There is no question that in the Maritimes many of these factors weigh heavily in the direction of the status quo.

If it is considered that the weight of these influences is decisive, there is no doubt that ways would be found whereby the region could adjust to the changing circumstances of the future on the basis of the existing political arrangements. The likelihood is that the future would be like the past. Our study of the problems and the evidence of experience have convinced us that the three individual governments of the region, even if supported by greater efforts to achieve voluntary co-operation, will not be able to overcome in a substantial way the disabilities that have operated for many years. However, under these conditions, the people of the Maritimes could maintain their provincial loyalties and traditional way of life within the framework of the larger Canada, where there is freedom of movement of people, goods, and capital. Within this framework there are also federal equalization payments, federal contributions to social services, and subsidies for income support and economic development.

In these circumstances the adjustment to inadequate opportunities for employment and worthwhile careers would be accomplished by the out-migration of population to the rest of Canada, and by higher rates of unemployment and under-employment than elsewhere in the country. The consequences in poverty, low incomes, and inequality would be relieved by transfer payments and subsidies to the extent determined from time to time by the federal authorities. This has been the regime of the past, and clearly it is not an impossible course for the future. It is immediately attractive because it involves the least disturbance of established ways in the short-run, while the risks and costs in the long-run can easily be set aside as phantoms in the murky future.

Another possibility would be to turn over the task of regional planning, and of establishing long range regional goals, to the federal authorities. If the federal government is determined to achieve a substantial reduction in regional disparities, it would be driven to such course because, otherwise, the costs would be prohibitive.

In order to carry out the present policies for regional economic expansion, the federal authorities make agreements with the individual provincial governments. A number of such agreements have been made with each of the

---

[13] R. M. Burns, *Experience of National and International Co-operative Institutions,* p. 5.

Maritime governments, pertaining to individual provinces or to parts of each province. These agreements cannot, and do not, deal in any co-ordinated way with the larger and more basic problems of the region as a whole. Consequently, what can be accomplished is inherently limited, and the costs are inevitably higher than they need to be. In order to overcome these serious shortcomings, the federal authorities are attempting to promote more effective planning on a regional basis. For this purpose a federally appointed advisory body has been established. The results obtained from these efforts will depend upon federal initiatives, and upon the degree of success that can be achieved in co-ordinating the programmes of three individual provincial governments, which, as history has shown, can be affected strongly by competitive aims and purposes.

The abrogation of responsibility for regional planning and long range regional policy to the federal government, is a possible course for the future. The advantage of this course would be that it would not require any formal changes in political organization; the three individual provincial governments would continue as they are, and the various concerns and interests associated with them would remain, apparently, undisturbed. Admittedly, if federally in-spired regional policy is to have any success, some measure of meaingful co-ordination between the three governments would have to be achieved, which could restrain somewhat the existing independent courses of action; but, the individual provincial governments would be there to protect particular local concerns, values, and interests against encroachment from either centralizing influences or sub-ordination to the larger common welfare. There are two important disadvantages in this possible course for the future.

Firstly, the initiative for regional planning and regional policies would rest primarily with the distant central authorities in Ottawa. They would deter-mine in large measure the role of the region in the Canadian hegemony. The possibilities for a meaningful measure of regional self-determination and self-realization would be severely limited, as it has been in the past. The second main disadvantages lies in the fact that there would be a vital dependence on the persistence and consistency of the federal authorities both to devise and carry out regional policies, and to bear the costs for a sustained period of years. Should the population of the rest of the country continue to grow more rapidly than that of the Maritimes, the degree of dependence and the risks would become progressively larger, not smaller.

If the Maritime provinces are not prepared to accept the conditions and the risks inherent in a chronically dependent region in the Canadian federation, they will have to find a more realistic way of influencing their own future. The new challenges which confront the region . . . call for early and consistent decisions. In our view, an effective and positive response (as con-trasted with a passive response) to these challenges is not possible on the basis of individual governments in this small region. . . . Such a positive response, if that is what is desired, could be achieved only by means of an adequate and meaningful method of regional co-operation.

The form of co-operation chosen would have to be capable of carrying out three very important tasks in a meaningful way; i.e. (1) regional economic planning and the implementation of regional programmes; (2) negotiation of regional requirements and interest with the federal authorities and the other provinces; (3) the reduction of unnecessary overhead costs and the achievement of administrative efficiency. . . . We have come to the conclusion that the usual ways of intergovernmental co-operation and limited agreement are not likely to be adequate to achieve the vital tasks listed above. The means and ends are simply not commensurate with each other in the circumstances of the Maritime region. Unless political institutions are established which have the capacity to make decisions in the common interest, the required tasks are not likely to be accomplished.

> Each province is, itself, diversified. Each in some ways competes with the others, although there are joint interests in competitive areas such as tourism, industrial attraction and fisheries. While the provinces may stand to gain more from concerted advancement of their joint interests, the impulse to narrow competitive gain can overthrow, at any given moment, the joint approach to larger benefits of regional development. . . .
>
> . . . Provinical governments are elected to represent the interests of citizens and taxpayers. In each province the legal, moral, and political responsibility of premiers, ministers, members of the legislature, and public administrators, is to the electorate of the province. . . .
>
> . . . Co-operative arrangements among provincial governments have not led, and cannot lead, to total or comprehensive administrative unity in vital areas, and particularly in development planning and industrial development. . . .
>
> . . . In the absence of effective unified planning, can the most effective economic development plans be made and carried out in the region? Can maximum federal and other funds be obtained for development purposes? And can the obtainable funds for all sources be used to best advantage? The answers must be negative.[14]

We agree with the observations by Dr. Luther Gulick, and Dr. Richard Leach, on the fundamental political problems involved in these questions.

> Political leaders inherently become leaders of the population within the jurisdiction which is laid out as the basis of their election. They are not working for people that lie beyond. They seek solutions within their town, their suburb, or their city, and they look with great skepticism upon the demand that they join hands with others in finding a solution until the situation gets so bad that the community as a whole rises up and says, 'Look, there isn't any solution on the basis of these small bits and pieces. The solution must be broader in character. . . .'[15]
>
> Moreover, the very nature of the Canadian Parliamentary system serves to push politicians in one province apart from those in another. Elections occur at different times and in response to different issues,

---

14 Guy Henson in *Interprovincial Relations in the Maritime Provinces*, pp. 9, 16 and 17.
15 Luther Gulick, *The "Little" Economics: Problems in U.S. Area Development* (New York, Committee for Economic Development, 1959), p. 22.

which forces the politician's mind's eye to be turned inward most of the time, and very often a legislator lacks the opportunity to extend his view extra-provincially, which arises naturally in the course of administrative work.[16]

It is frequently argued that there is an advantage in having three individual provincial governments in respect of relations with Ottawa, because the three together can present an effective united front to promote common regional interests. Our study of the history of these relations confirms the conclusions reached by Professor Burns, that far less has been accomplished than might have been expected.

> Even in such an obvious area of mutual interest as the economic and financial relationship with the government of Canada, we find little evidence of anything but rare and sporadic attempts at presenting a united front. While undoubtedly there are political and economic questions of local concern which place a practical limitation on a fully united position in all matters, one would have expected that over the years it could have been possible for the Maritime provinces to have developed a much more effective presentation of a regional case under joint sponsorship than under divided and sometimes competitive interests.
>   . . . there does seem to have developed a sort of competition for federal favours, which when combined with a political base, has made any cohesive approach to federal aid more difficult to achieve.[17]

Co-operation by the three governments in joint approaches has tended to be most effective in regard to the negative aspects of common regional interests. They have achieved a measure of success in eliciting various subsidies for income support and the bolstering of declining activities. However, experience has shown that these transfers, while comforting in the short-run, have made little or no positive or constructive contribution to the solution of the basic problems of the region.

If the people of the Maritimes decide that they wish to reverse the trends of the past, and develop conditions which would bring more adequate opportunities in the region on the basis of self-determined objectives, it will be necessary to establish immediately a method of co-operation which would envisage the attainment of full political union as a definite goal. We have come to this conclusion after a careful consideration of the advantages and disadvantages of the various possible courses of action that might be pursued to cope with the new challenges that confront the region.

Three critical requirements would have to be fulfilled in order to implement the recommended course of action. Firstly, strong leadership in favour of this course would have to be forthcoming in the region in both political and private quarters; secondly, active co-operation and material support would have to be forthcoming from the federal authorities; and thirdly, suitable machinery

---

[16] Dalhousie Institute of Public Affairs and Richard H. Leach, *Interprovincial Relations in the Maritime Provinces*, Part II, p. 97.
[17] R. M. Burns, *Experience of National and International Co-operative Institutions*, pp. 10 and 24.

would have to be established to devise and carry out common regional policies and to negotiate the agreements necessary for the progressive attainment of political union.

Whether or not strong leadership is forthcoming would depend on the real wishes of the people of the region. If there are substantial bodies of opinion in favour of a strong positive response to the new challenges, the necessary leadership is likely to be forthcoming. If the response is weak, scattered, or indifferent, the choice is willy-nilly for the status quo, and effective leadership in the opposite direction is sure to come. In that event, the other new initiatives which have been suggested would be irrelevant and of no avail.

Strong regional leadership, and active co-operation and support from the federal authorities, would be equally essential. The federal authorities would have to be willing to work with representative regional bodies (appointed on the basis of responsible regional decisions) to devise and carry out regional economic policies and programmes. The federal authorities would also have to be prepared to commit the necessary financial support out of the federal regional expansion programmes and fiscal transfers in accordance with the agreed regional plans and policies. The support would have to be on a scale and on a basis of priorities which are acceptable to the representative regional bodies, as well as to the federal authorities.

In order to develop the new form of co-operation which looks to political union as a definite aim, suitable new machinery and procedures would have to be established as soon as possible. This machinery would have to be devised so as to carry out effectively the following tasks:

(1) Regional economic planning
(2) Regional negotiations with the federal authorities
(3) Establishment of common administrative services
(4) Development of uniform legislation
(5) Co-ordination of existing provincial policies
(6) Preparation of a constitution for a single provincial government for the Maritime region.
(7) Implementation of successive steps leading to political union.

In our view the machinery required to carry out these tasks would consist of the following essential elements: —

The Council of Maritime Premiers
The Maritime Provinces Commission
The Joint Legislative Assembly.

The Council of Maritime Premiers

The Council of Maritime Premiers would consist of the three premiers of the Maritime provinces. Unlike the present practice, the Council would meet regularly and relatively frequently, at least four times a year. The duties of the Council would be to consider recommendations from the Maritime Provinces Commission, to approve joint submissions and negotiate with the federal authorities on behalf of the region, to co-ordinate policies of the three provincial governments, and to secure agreements between the three governments for common action. The Council should have authority to appoint sub-committees of ministers from the three provinces to study and report on specific matters. The Council would have a small permanent secretariat of one or two officers to organize and expedite its work.

The Maritime Provinces Commission

The Maritime Provinces Commission would consist of five full-time members appointed by the Council of Premiers—two from a list of nominees proposed by the Government of Nova Scotia, two from a list of nominees proposed by the Government of New Brunswick, and one from a list of nominees proposed by the Government of Prince Edward Island—plus a Chairman appointed by the Council of Premiers. Needless to say, all these persons should have outstanding qualifications. The terms of appointment would be for a period of five years, with provision for renewal. Decisions in the Commission would be taken by majority vote, the Chairman having an additional casting vote in case of a tie.

The duties of the Maritime Provinces Commission would be to prepare for submission to the Council of Premiers a long-term plan of regional development; to recommend to the Council of Premiers common regional policies; to prepare proposals for the joint administration of specific public services; to prepare proposals for the unification of public services; to recommend to the Joint Legislative Assembly proposals for uniform legislation; to prepare for the Joint Legislative Assembly proposals for a constitution of a single Maritime Province; to prepare for the Council of Premiers and the Joint Legislative Assembly, proposals, timetables and procedures for the progressive implementation of political union; to recommend to the Council of Premiers and to the Joint Legislative Assembly, budgets and the allocation of costs for joint services and projects; and to prepare annual reports to the Joint Legislative Assembly on progress toward regional co-operation and unification.

The Commission would be given the resources and authority to engage a relatively small but highly qualified staff to assist with its work, and to employ special consultants as needed, either from the existing government services or from outside.

The Joint Legislative Assembly

The Joint Legislative Assembly would consist of all the members of the three provincial legislatures meeting in joint session. The Joint Assembly would meet once a year for a few weeks to receive and discuss reports from the Council of Premiers, and from the Maritime Provinces Commission. The Joint Assembly would consider proposals from the Maritime Provinces Commission for uniform legislation, for budgets for joint services and projects, for the constitution of a united Maritime province, and for the procedures and timetables for the progressive implementation of political union. The Joint

Assembly would also have the duty of determining the method by which the final step of ratification of union would be accomplished, i.e. whether by referendum, constitutional convention, or by some procedure in the Joint Assembly itself.

The three speakers of the three existing provincial legislatures would alternately act as speakers of the Joint Assembly. The Joint Assembly would elect a steering committee annually, say five members, to organize and arrange its work. The Joint Assembly would have authority to appoint special committees from among its members to study and report on particular matters and proposals.

As can be seen, these recommendations envisage the adoption of a program of formal co-operation and joint action which moves progressively to full political union, which should be accepted as a definite objective from the outset. The intervening steps would in themselves constitute important progress in advancing common regional interests, and in solving urgent regional problems. For example, the Maritime Provinces Commission might give early consideration to the implementation of the recommendation made by the Association of Atlantic Universities that a single University Grants Committee be established for all the Maritime universities to deal with their financial needs and future development.[18] The experience gained during the early stages of these co-operative efforts should be of material help in resolving particular issues that must be dealt with before full political union can be implemented.

At the end of, say, five years it would be desirable to make a realistic assessment of the results achieved, and of the progress made toward full political union. If the outcome of this assessment is not encouraging and it appears that political union cannot be accomplished within, say, a further five years, the entire program should be reconsidered. Unless political union remains a definite objective and a definite possibility, there is the distinct danger that a third or fourth layer of government overhead would be laid on top of the already high overhead costs in the region. Furthermore, unless full political union can be accomplished within a reasonable time, it is unlikely that co-operative efforts will continue to be effective and constructive for very long. It will be necessary to try to avoid the "worst of all worlds" which would results from the mere piling up of bureaucracies, costs, complications, and uncertainties on top of already serious disabilities.

There are, of course, a number of "nitty-gritty" matters that would have to be dealt with as political union is approached. For example, there is the matter of a capital for the united province. It is our conviction that this should not constitute an insurmountable difficulty. With modern methods of communication and transportation, we see no need for concentrating all government services and departments in a single capital. We would envisage an appropriate rearrangement of departments and services among the existing three provincial

---

[18] Association of Atlantic Universities, *Higher Education in the Atlantic Provinces for the 1970's*, p. 93.

capitals, so that there would not be any significant disturbance to the economic and employment base of any of the three cities concerned. A seat would have to be chosen for meetings of the new legislature, but this need not involve large numbers of people or vast new structures. It probably would be wise to select a new central and convenient location for this purpose.

There are such other important matters as the status of the French language, and of educational and cultural rights in the new province, the name of the new province, the design of its new flag, etc. We have envisaged that these very pertinent and politically delicate questions could be dealt with most appropriately and democratically by the new co-operative machinery which we have recommended. It is recognized that some of these could be serious stumbling blocks if narrow attitudes prevail. However, it is important that these not be elevated into huge issues at the outset. An effort should be made to allow joint consultative and co-operative machinery to be established which, if successful, is more likely to find satisfactory and acceptable solutions.

Our recommendations arise from the conclusions we have reached on the basis of many special studies, the lessons of experience, and the logic of the circumstances. We are aware that in human affairs where matters of inequality, opportunity, and intangible values are involved, rationality and logic do not necessarily prevail. The means of communication are equally available for the propagation of logic, fear, or prejudice. However, our studies of surveys of public attitudes indicate that there are substantial bodies of opinion in each of the provinces which would respond favourably to proposals for Maritime Union if leadership were forthcoming. We have sought to present information and specific proposals which would be helpful to those who must make the decisions.

27 Geo-Politics and the Canadian Union*

John Conway

The position of the Prime Minister of Canada vis-à-vis the provincial premiers has changed radically since 1867. At the Federal-Provincial Conference in Ottawa in February 1969, it was apparent that Prime Minister Trudeau had no primacy conceded to him as of right. In fact it was doubtful whether he was

* From Ontario Advisory Committee on Confederation, *Background Papers and Reports,* Vol. 2 (Toronto, Queen's Printer and Publisher), pp. 28-49. Reprinted by permission of the author and Information Canada.

JOHN CONWAY – Assistant Professor, Division of Humanities, York University.

considered *primus inter pares* by any except those heads of provinces who still regard themselves as premiers rather than prime ministers. To the disinterested observer Trudeau appeared to have only that authority which he could establish by reason of his own powers of intellect and personality. Did Trudeau still consider himself the "new boy", as he had described himself at the Commonwealth Conference? Did he recognize that his office is no longer what it was and decide to act accordingly? Whatever the reason, the tone he set was different from that set by Lester Pearson at the 1968 conference. Pearson had tried to be the leader. He had told the conference that a new creative act of statesmanship on a national level was essential, implying that the British North America Act had outlived its usefulness. What was at stake, he said, was the very survival of Canada as a unified political society.[1]

At the conference in 1969, Trudeau became a negotiator, dealing with the delegates on a less abstract level. The idea of a nation with something distinctive to contribute to the world in the way of political institutions was lost sight of, if in fact it ever came up. Instead the emphasis was shifted by the provinces to money and regional development, and by Ottawa to the rights of individuals. Trudeau spoke not of abandoning the British North America Act in favour of a new "act of accommodation" (to use Pearson's phrase), but of revising the Constitution. It should be modernized, he said, to conform with contemporary realities. His greatest concern, however, was to safeguard the interests and the rights of the citizen, and to ensure that they had precedence over the rights of governments.[2] This admirable concern for individual

---

[1] Opening statement by the Prime Minister of Canada, the Right Honourable Lester Pearson, Constitutional Conference, Ottawa, February 5, 1968.

We all know that French Canada today feels a deep dissatisfaction with its place in Confederation. The reasons for that are complex and of varying significance. I have said in the past and I repeat now that I believe most of those reasons to be entirely justified. But this is not the occasion either to try to analyze why there is discontent in French Canada or to weigh judiciously everything that has contributed to produce that result. What is far more important is to admit that this dissatisfaction is a fact and to recognize that, if it is allowed to continue without remedy, it could lead to separation and to the end of Confederation. Equally important is to recognize that it lies within our power to prevent this, to remove the causes of discontent, to lay the groundwork for a new great act of accommodation which will ensure the hopes and aspirations of all Canadians. It is nothing less than this that we must commit ourselves at this Conference. . . . Let me be explicit: what is at stake in my opinion is no less than Canada's survival as a nation.

[2] Opening statement by the Prime Minister of Canada, the Right Honourable Pierre Elliott Trudeau, Constitutional Conference, Ottawa, February 10, 1969.

Nous voulons reviser notre constitution. Nous voulons la moderniser, la rendre plus conforme au réalités contemporaines. Mais notre véritable détermination, notre motivation profonde, c'est d'abord et avant tout de servir le citoyen, de sauvegarder ses intérêts, d'assurer la protection de ses droits et la réalisation de ses aspirations. Voilà notre préoccupation première, et qui nous est commune à tous. D'autant plus que tous ensemble nous représentons et servons les mêmes Canadiens. Les souverainetés peuvent bien être partagées entre divers paliers de gouvernement, mais le citoyen, lui, reste unique et indivisible. . . . Nous décidons de placer les droits fondamentaux du citoyen avant les droits des gouvernements. Voilà tout.

rights is characteristic of Trudeau and his thinking (it is reflected in his proposed revisions of the Criminal Code). Nonetheless, one had hoped for something rather less atomistic in his view of Canada and Canadians. He made no reference to the past and, as far as I could make out, he had no vision of the future. In short Trudeau did not present us with any idea of how he expected Canada to develop over the next twenty or thirty or fifty years, nor did he attempt to define what the country might become.

The provinces were even less concerned with the concept of Canada as a nation, rather than as a collection of individuals and sectional interests. The opening statement by Saskatchewan's Premier Ross Thatcher made this perfectly clear. Thatcher said that in his view the constitutional problem was of secondary importance. The main problem, the one that really mattered, was financial.[3] Specifically, the allocation of taxing powers which was appropriate in the nineteenth century was not adequate to the needs of the provinces today. Walter Weir, speaking for Manitoba, agreed. It was not inadequacies of the Constitution that disrupted the unity of Canada, but lack of fiscal equity.[4] The Premier of Alberta introduced a new and significant theme—that of regionalism. Increasingly over the past five years the problem of national unity has become much wider and deeper than the simple reconciliation of English and French. There are kinds of separatism in Canada other than that of Quebec. Harry Strom made this very clear. He told the conference that there was deep dissatisfaction among the people of western Canada about eastern unawareness of, or unconcern with, western problems and western aspirations. He accused central Canada of being either reluctant to admit or incapable of realizing what the West was, what it wanted, and what it hoped to be. Then he turned to a theme which is as old as the western provinces themselves but which gathers strength and seriousness as those provinces grow in wealth, population, and power: the issue of the tariff. The tariff was

[3] Opening statement by the Honourable D. G. Steuart, Deputy Premier of the Province of Saskatchewan, Constitutional Conference, Ottawa, February 10, 1969.

. . . we come to this Conference somewhat in a spirit of impatience. We continue to believe that there are problems facing our people which have a far higher priority than constitutional reform, of the kind presently proposed by the Federal Government. We consider that the basic objectives of this Conference should be to settle the financial aspects of Confederation. The taxing powers that were appropriate for an earlier era no longer match the relative constitutional responsibilities of the different levels of government. We insist that financial difficulties facing all governments are today the major challenge to the continued existence of our Country — not the Constitutions. Westerners are not impressed by the recent financial policies of Ottawa. To us they represent confrontation, shock treatment, further upward tax revisions, and interference in provincial tax fields.

[4] Opening statement by the Honourable Walter Weir, Premier of the Province of Manitoba, Constitutional Conference, Ottawa, February 10, 1969.

. . . what is being eroded, and which (sic) must be protected now, while we await a new Constitution, is the ability of the Provinces to meet their constitutional requirements with the present tax base. The economic foundation of our Nation is threatened. The Federal Government has been aborting the present Constitution. The one matter, more than any other, which affects the unity of the Nation is the lack of fiscal equity, which is the basis of equality of opportunity.

designed to protect the manufacturing interests of the East, without concern for economic ventures in the West. Consequently, benefits have accrued to few western industries. Moreover, said Strom, the tariff has been harmful to the economic progress even of the East, for it has encouraged a slackness in method and management that has put the country well behind the United States in the growth of the GNP and in the development of secondary manufacturing.[5]

If the western provinces approached the question of regionalism from a position of economic strength, the Atlantic provinces approached it from a position of economic weakness. Premier G. I. Smith of Nova Scotia told the conference that regional disparities constituted a problem which was fully as urgent as the matter of language rights and culture. He assured the delegates that he neither advocated support for economically unviable industries, nor

---

[5] Opening statement by the Honourable Harry E. Strom, Premier of the Province of Alberta, Constitutional Conference, Ottawa, February 10, 1969.

Let me say that it would be a tragic and profound mistake on the part of either the politicians or the press, or the general public of Central Canada to underestimate or dismiss out of hand the profound dissatisfaction which does exist among many people in Western Canada. There is a real lack of understanding and appreciation of our interests and problems and aspirations in other parts of this Country. We deeply resent the picture which is often painted of the West in the minds of the people of Central Canada.

Westerners are naturally concerned that minds which hold misconceptions may be reluctant or incapable of appreciating our dissatisfactions and our aspirations. What Western Canadians legitimately desire, if economic justice is to prevail within Confederation, is that our raw resource industries be given the same priority as the manufacturing industries of Eastern and Central Canada.

We desire this equality of priority to be demonstrated, not simply in conference communiqués but in concrete ways. For example, when the Federal Government sets tariffs we would like to give full consideration not only to the needs of certain Eastern industries for protection, but equal consideration to the fact that the costs of these tariffs are to a large extent borne by consumers and Western industries, which must compete with high production costs and high transportation costs in an international market.

It is time the Federal Government recognized the harmful effect of the tariff system on the West, and indeed on the economic health of the nation.

Thirteen years ago Professor J. H. Young estimated for the Gordon Commission that the tariffs were costing the people of Canada one billion dollars a year.

No reliable figures on the current cost of the tariff system are available. But we have no reason to suppose the figure would be any lower.

It is true that the cost of the tariff system is borne by all Canadians. But not all Canadians benefit from it.

It was set up, as we all know, for the protection of secondary industry in Central Canada, chiefly in Ontario. Very few Western industries gained any benefit from it. And most ironically, the tariff system has failed to achieve its very objective of fostering Canadian secondary industry.

A study by Professor J. H. Dales of the University of Toronto showed some time ago that despite tariffs, Canadian economic growth has lagged behind that of the United States since 1870; that the ratio of our Gross National Product to theirs has fallen; that the ratio of our secondary manufacturing to theirs is no higher than it was in 1910.

. . . when future Constitutional changes or new national policies are proposed, we will examine them very closely to see if they provide expanded opportunities for the realization of the aspirations of Western Canadians.

expected economic equality among the various regions of Canada. Some provinces are naturally richer than others. But the economic growth of the country as a whole is bound to be impeded if large sections of it remain permanently less productive than the others.[6] Louis Robichaud was no less emphatic on this score. "Somewhere," he said, "words must be found that reconcile all Canadians to a sense of common responsibility for all . . . wherever they may live."[7] It is interesting to contrast the regionalism of the West with the regionalism of the Atlantic provinces. Western regionalism tends towards autonomy verging on a kind of separatism. The regionalism of the Atlantic provinces

---

[6] Opening statement by the Honourable G. I. Smith, Premier of the Province of Nova Scotia, Constitutional Conference, Ottawa, February 10, 1969.

Regional disparity is another matter which we believe should receive as urgent attention (as the matter of language rights and culture). We do not believe that it will ever be possible to achieve absolute equality of development as between the regions of Canada or that we should try to do this. And we do not advocate any action which will slow down the development of those regions which are growing more rapidly, and continuing, as they do, to contribute to the nation as a whole.

Let me say, too, that we do not seek subsidization for unproductive economic development. What we are seeking is assistance in developing a viable economy of greater growth.

We believe that it is possible, desirable and necessary to reduce very greatly the disparities of development so clearly apparent as between regions. We also believe this can be done without slowing down the rate of economic growth in other regions.

Further, we believe it is clearly in the national interest to do this. We believe Canada can best develop her full potential if all regions are making their maximum contribution to the general growth. And this growth as a nation is bound to be impeded if large portions of the Country fall and stay substantially behind the rest of the Country.

The unity of Canada is threatened by regional disparity just as it is threatened by linguistic or cultural differences.

[7] Opening statement by the Honourable Louis Robichaud, Premier of the Province of New Brunswick, Constitutional Conference, Ottawa, February, 1969.

Let us reflect for a moment on the special problem of regional disparities which played so important a part in the debate last February and which remain of vital interest to the Country as well as to all of the other Atlantic provinces.

I am very much aware of how difficult it is to convert this concept of regional disparity into constitutional terminology as such. I do not argue now, nor did I suggest earlier, that the constitutional régime of the future must somehow stipulate specifically that all regions shall be equal in their revenues or economic strength, governmental and individual. . . . But somehow this belief must pervade and reconstruction of the framework of Canadian society. Somewhere words must be found that reconcile all Canadians to a sense of common responsibility for all with minimum standards for all, wherever they may live.

Nature and accident have given advantages of resources and market location, of technology and opportunity, to some parts of our Country over others. Perhaps it is impossible to envisage the total balancing of these geographic, resource and technological inequalities. But not to recognize them, not to have a fundamental national policy about them, is to perpetuate inequality as an implied national pattern, yielding to nature and accident what should be overcome by effort and inventiveness. Without prejudging therefore what the Constitution will say, it is clear that New Brunswick must envisage national policies that deal vigorously with regional resource, capital or technical deprivation.

of necessity relies upon a strong central power in Ottawa. This stand was forcefully and intelligently expressed by the Premier of Prince Edward Island, Alex Campbell, to my mind one of the most impressive and promising delegates at the conference. Premier Campbell said that the federal government must have the means to deal effectively with the problem of regional disparities. At the same time he was not prepared to grant all power to Ottawa. There is a difference, he maintained, between a strong central government and a strong centralized government. In any event the balance between federal and provincial powers must be preserved. To illustrate his viewpoint, Campbell cited James Wilson, one of the Fathers of the American Constitution:

> Wilson, in summarizing the constitutional dilemma which faced the United States in 1787, remarked that: "Each state endeavoured to cut a slice from the common loaf to add to its own morsel until at length the Confederation became frittered down to the impotent condition in which it now stands . . . what danger is there that the whole will unnecessarily sacrifice a part? But reverse the case and leave the whole at the mercy of each part and will not the general interest be continually sacrificed to local interests?"[8]

This quotation was apt and perceptive. That the idea of the primacy of the federal authority had been seriously eroded was clear throughout the conference. In fact it had been clear at the 1968 conference. The province of

---

[8] Opening statement by the Honourable Alex B. Campbell, Premier of the Province of Prince Edward Island, Constitutional Conference, Ottawa, February, 1969.

. . . I would like to reaffirm our position on the need for a strong central government. At the Confederation of Tomorrow Conference I said, "Strength in this context means financial strength to provide a sufficiently large economic field within which to exercise political and economic influence towards national ends." I would add at this time that the Federal Government must have the means to deal effectively with the problem of regional disparities. Though we regard a strong "central" government as necessary, we do not necessarily support a strongly centralized government. The centralization of government operations has proven totally ineffective in correcting the regional imbalances which have developed over the years. I expect to deal with these questions at greater length during this Conference. However, before leaving the subject of a strong central government, I would like to sum up Prince Edward Island's position by quoting one of the Fathers of the American Constitution, James Wilson. Wilson, in summarizing the constitutional dilemma which faced the United States in 1787, remarked that: "Each state endeavoured to cut a slice from the common loaf to add to its own morsel until at length the Confederation became frittered down to the impotent condition in which it now stands . . . what danger is there that the whole will unnecessarily sacrifice a part? But reverse the case and leave the whole at the mercy of each part and will not the general interest be continually sacrificed to local interest?"

[9] Opening statement of the Honourable W. A. C. Bennett, Premier of the Province of British Columbia, Constitutional Conference, Ottawa, February 5, 1968.

The National Government's proposal to entrench certain areas of legislative capacity by their confinement within the formal words of constitutional enactment is not only a restriction of the principle of legislative supremacy, which has so far been the underlying philosophy of our parliamentary system, it is, as well, a drastic re-arrangement and reduction of legislative competence at the expense of provincial jurisdiction within Canada.

British Columbia[9] and the province of Ontario[10] each had asserted the primacy of the provincial jurisdiction in its own areas of competence, and its opposition to any effort on the part of the federal authority to encroach on that jurisdiction for the benefit of the general interest.

The reasons for this erosion of the federal authority are fairly clear. In 1867 the Atlantic provinces had substantial status arising from their respective histories. Nova Scotia had close ties with both England (Halifax was the base for a British naval squadron) and New England, and had developed a lively provincial culture. New Brunswick was the home of a large segment of the United Empire Loyalists; in fact, the region had been developed specifically to accommodate them. Charlottetown in Prince Edward Island was the locus for the conference which discussed the possibility of Confederation. Together the Atlantic provinces acted as the midwife at the birth of Confederation, and for decades they gave the nation many of its most important federal politicians (including three prime ministers). At the same time, the economic power of British North America was centred in Montreal and Toronto, and the initiative for federation came from Canada West and Canada East. The British North America Act was drawn up in the context of these historical facts. This setting, together with the disastrous example provided by the American Civil War, gave primacy (both in law and in fact) to the government in Ottawa. (Professor Alexander Brady makes this clear in his paper, *Federal-Provincial Conferences*, presented in June 1967.) In Sir John A. Macdonald's view, the functions of the provincial governments were limited strictly to matters of local concern, and the members of the dominion Parliament were the only representatives in Ottawa. He rejected any ideas of formal intergovernmental relationships between province and dominion.[11]

---

[10] Propositions of the Government of Ontario submitted to the Continuing Committee of Officials on the Constitution as of December, 1968.

The theory of federalism requires each order of government to act independently within its jurisdictions. Such independence is seriously impaired when one order of government must approach the other for financial aid to discharge its basic responsibilities, for its decisions are subject to review and to pressure for change by its pressing needs for funds. The net result is a blurring of the federal system's distribution of powers and a decrease in efficiency of government and in public satisfaction.

[11] Federal-Provincial Conferences, Preliminary Draft of a Paper by Alexander Brady, June, 1967.

Joseph Pope tells us that Sir John A. Macdonald believed "that the functions of the Provincial Governments are strictly limited to matters of local concern, and that the only constitutional representatives of a province in its relations with the Dominion are the members of the Parliament of Canada from that Province." Pope's interpretation of his leader's view was not wild fancy. It is confirmed by Macdonald's own remark in a letter to the Lieutenant Governor of Nova Scotia in 1886 that "the representatives of Nova Scotia as to all questions respecting the relations between the Dominion and the Province sit in the Dominion parliament and are the exponents of the wishes of the people with regard to such relations." In brief Macdonald repudiated any idea of a formal system of inter-governmental relations, although in hard fact he was compelled to deal with individual governments on financial and other matters.

For reasons which are not difficult to understand, this primacy continued until very recently. At the initiative of Ottawa, the Canadian Pacific Railway was completed and British Columbia thereby entered into Confederation. At the initiative of Ottawa, the prairie provinces, the Yukon, and the Northwest Territories were created. At the initiative of Ottawa, a great influx of immigrants from Great Britain and Europe was effected between 1896 and 1912. During the Laurier administration the country was linked together a second time by another transcontinental railway.

Much has been made of the importance of communications in bringing Canada together, but very little has been said about one particular kind of communications: that between men of common origin. As a unifying factor in the development of Canada, it has been extremely significant. To an important degree, leaders in the new provinces came from Ontario and the Maritimes. Until 1939 Vancouver, for example, was controlled financially and in the professions almost entirely by such men. Men who were born and educated in Ontario or the Atlantic provinces, then went to Winnipeg, Regina, Calgary, or Vancouver as doctors, lawyers, clergymen, merchants, bankers, school teachers, and university professors, thought of the West as an extension of the East. It was in their consciousness that Canada existed as a developing and unified young nation. Another notion of unity was provided by the immigrants from Great Britain at the turn of the century, at the height of British and European imperialism. For them, Canada was a unified colony, part of the Empire which welded into a higher unity all its constituent parts. These first generation immigrants to the West from Ontario and the Maritimes and from Great Britain are no longer effective forces in the country and soon will disappear altogether.

Given this background, it was natural that the primacy of Ottawa should be perpetuated by the centralizing needs of the two World Wars and the Great Depression. It is only in the past fifteen years that the position of Ottawa has—without intentional planning—been seriously modified. With the disappearance from the Canadian consciousness of the idea of both colony and nation, and with the gradual dispersion of the needs of the 1930's and 1940's, socio-economic and geo-political forces have operated freely to relocate power and authority.

Let me list a few symptoms of this change. French Canada can no longer be handled by the Prime Minister's Quebec lieutenant, as it could be as recently as the era of Mackenzie King and Lapointe. Ontario is the financial and industrial centre of Canada. The historical authority of the Atlantic provinces has vanished; they are Canada's poverty area, looking—as was apparent at the conference—not to Ottawa for assistance (except as broker) but to the rich provinces.

At the conference the prime ministers (rightly so called) of Ontario, Quebec, and British Columbia conducted themselves as representatives of semi-independent principalities. Why should they not? They represented great power and great riches, actual and potential, with none of the ambiguity that attaches to the federal government in the present state of our Constitution.

The same is true, with some variations, of the representatives of Alberta, Saskatchewan, and Manitoba. Prime Minister Trudeau directed the conference with intelligence and skill. But we need only compare his attitude on this occasion with the attitude of the President of the United States towards state governors to see how changed our policy has become over the past decade. The presidency is the symbol of national unity. The prime ministership is not. In the past such a symbol was provided—rather dimly but effectively enough, considering our stage of development—by the British monarch, particularly if his representative in Canada was a member of the royal family. Today, however, we have no charismatic office in our governmental structure.

This is not to say that the decentralization of authority from Ottawa to the provinces is to be deprecated. Perhaps we have evolved a new and better system—certainly one corresponding more to the facts—than that devised in 1867. I do believe, however, that our Constitution should reflect the real situation.

The main fact is that we have no paramount central authority accepted unquestioningly as such from the Atlantic to the Pacific. That is the precise opposite of what was intended by the Fathers of Confederation. It is one of the ironies of modern history that the intentions of both the Fathers of the American Republic and the Fathers of the Canadian Confederation should have been so completely frustrated. Under the American Constitution the authority of the central power was intended to be minimal. In fact today that central authority is imperial and neo-caesarist. Under the British North America Act the central authority was intended to be powerful so as to avoid the dangers to which states' rights seem to have exposed the Union. In fact today the central authority is uncertain and on the defensive, while the provinces—at least the rich and powerful ones—assert their rights with complete self-confidence. At the conference in 1968 Prime Minister Pearson was almost apologetic in his assertion of federal authority. He assured the provincial delegates that he would be open and receptive to the wishes and the proposals of every province, adding that he would have to draw the line somewhere.[12] Trudeau, then Minister of Justice, assured the conference that he had no intention whatsoever of taking any power *away* from the provinces. Quite the contrary, he was prepared to *surrender* some power to the people of Canada.[13] Premier Robichaud thought that

---

[12] Opening statement by the Prime Minister of Canada, the Right Honourable Lester Pearson, Constitutional Conference, Ottawa, February 5, 1968.

In our initial discussions this week the representatives of the Federal Government will, of course, be receptive to the wishes and open-minded to the proposals of every Province. But I would be less than candid if I failed to point out that there are certain Federal positions which must be maintained.

[13] Statement by the Honourable Pierre Elliott Trudeau, Minister of Justice and Attorney General of Canada, on a Constitutional Charter of Human Rights. Constitutional Conference, Ottawa, February 6, 1968.

I wish to make it clear that in proposing this measure there is no suggestion that the federal government is seeking any power at the expense of the provinces. We are stating that we are willing to *surrender* some of our power to the people of Canada, and

. . . it is time for an honest examination as to whether the forms and symbols of 1867 are appropriate to the life, and times, and mood of 1968. We can all surely agree that the B.N.A. Act as a piece of prose, and as an exercise in symbolism, is deficient to the point of calculated boredom. (Perhaps it is a revelation of the Canadian character!)[14]

The Prime Minister of Quebec, Daniel Johnson, told the meeting flatly that the federal and provincial governments were equal. Relations between the two orders of government must be on a level of cooperation, not subordination.[15]

These reservations about the Constitution and this reluctance to recognize any paramount federal authority were repeated at the conference of 1969. The Premier of Nova Scotia spoke as an equal when he told Trudeau that there had been a lack of meaningful discussion between his government and the federal government. His language was not as precise as that of Daniel Johnson the previous year, but it was perfectly clear that he too believed that relations between the two orders of government must be on a level of coperation.[16] Walter Weir, perhaps without realizing the full implication of what he was saying (and this makes it only the more striking), questioned the authority of the federal civil service. It would be improper, he said, for civil servants to make decisions or even to direct research in the constitutional review. This is to be reserved to the political leaders of the country.[17] By "political leaders" it was apparent that he did not mean simply Prime Minister Trudeau and the

---

we are suggesting that the provincial governments surrender some of *their* power to the people in the respective provinces.

[14] Opening statement by the Honourable Louis Robichaud, Premier of the Province of New Brunswick, Constitutional Conference, Ottawa, February 5, 1968.

[15] Opening address by the Honourable Daniel Johnson, Prime Minister of Quebec, to the Constitutional Conference, Ottawa, February 5, 1968.

According to the principle of autonomy, member-states of a federation are given legislative and fiscal powers by the constitution itself and not by the federal state. Relations between the two orders of government must be on a level of co-operation, not subordination.

[16] Opening statement by the Honourable G. I. Smith, Premier of the Province of Nova Scotia, Constitutional Conference, Ottawa, February 10, 1969.

There is no point in dwelling on old grievances or refighting old battles, but, Mr. Prime Minister, I do wish to bring to your attention that at times in the past there has been a lack of meaningful consultation, and it should not carry on into the future if we hope to develop the degree of co-operation which is necessary to the harmonious workings of a federal union.

[17] Opening statement by the Honourable Walter Weir, Premier of the Province of Manitoba, Constitutional Conference, Ottawa, February 19, 1969.

The Manitoba Government . . . proposes . . . that a new Continuing Committee of Cabinet Ministers from each of the jurisdictions be created to direct the course of constitutional investigation on which we are engaged. This committee, representative as it should be of the elected governments in the Provinces and in Ottawa, will be in a better position to undertake the continuing process of examination and assessment.

Obviously a staff of highly qualified civil servants must continue to undertake research and generally to service the work of the constitutional review. But it is improper for them to make decisions in this area or indeed to direct the research which must be the concern of the political leaders of the Country.

members of his Cabinet. Alberta wished to see the decentralization of the Bank of Canada with real autonomy for the branches, so that they could devote themselves to the economic needs of their particular areas.[18] Most interesting, British Columbia wished to federalize the Supreme Court of Canada, feeling that British Columbia members of the Court should take part in deciding cases in which the province was involved.[19] Speaking for Quebec, Jean-Jacques Bertrand said simply, ". . . we need a completely new constitution, tailored to the ideas and needs of today."[20] In the *Working Paper on Foreign Relations* Quebec rejected the notion that under the present Constitution only the Government of Canada has power to make treaties in international law, and said further that even if this were true, it should be changed. The Paper also reminded the conference that thirty years ago the Government of Ontario had argued before the Privy Council the right of the province to advise the Crown in matters where its legislative powers apply.[21] Quebec was not alone in questioning the sole competence of the federal government in the area of foreign affairs. Without going to the Cartesian extremes of the Quebec *Working Paper,* Harry Strom indicated that Alberta was as much concerned about foreign affairs as Quebec when provincial interests were

---

[18] Opening statement by the Honourable Harry E. Strom, Premier of the Province of Alberta, Constitutional Conference, Ottawa, February 10, 1969.

The discriminatory nature of blanket monetary policy is one of the primary causes of the slow growth of secondary industry in the West.

In the United States the central bank is organized on a regional basis. Might not the same thing be done in Canada with real autonomy for regional branches of the Bank of Canada, which would enable them to take into account the unique economic needs of the areas they serve?

[19] Opening statement by the Honourable W. A. C. Bennett, Premier of the Province of British Columbia, Constitutional Conference, Ottawa, February 10, 1969.

When the constitutional validity of a statute of a particular Province is in issue, British Columbia considers it desirable that those Judges appointed from that Province or from the region of which that Province is a part sit on the hearing of the case.

[20] Opening statement by the Honourable Jean-Jacques Bertrand, Prime Minister of the Province of Quebec, Constitutional Conference, Ottawa, February 10, 1969.

. . . we need a completely new constitution, tailored to ideas and needs of today.

[21] Constitutional Conference Continuing Committee of Officials Working Paper on Foreign Relations. Notes prepared by the Quebec Delegation, Quebec, February 5, 1969.

The Canadian Government has sought to show that under Canada's present constitution only the Government of Canada has the power to make treaties at international law. We do not accept this conclusion. . . . We wish however to state that even if this were true under the present constitution, it should be otherwise in the new constitution. . . . We would do well to remember that Quebec is not the first province to seek a measure of international capacity. More than thirty years ago, before the Judicial Committee of the Privy Council, the Attorney General for Ontario put his case this way:

"There are no grounds whatever for saying that the parties to advise His Majesty in matters relating to the jurisdiction of the Provinces have in some way come to be the Dominion Ministers. The Province has the right to advise the Crown in matters where its legislative powers apply. Ontario has a right to enter into an agreement with another part of the British Empire or with a foreign State."

involved.[22] Many more examples of the absence of a defined and accepted central authority can be found in the documents of both conferences.

Two further considerations should be introduced into this discussion. First, our political problems and troubles in Canada exist within, and are necessarily affected by, the wider context of world events in the final decades of the twentieth century. These are, and from all indications will continue to be, revolutionary years. One of the most prominent features of this revolution is the crisis in the legitimacy of authority. The authority of the church—since the middle ages the ultimate source of political and social stability—is being challenged. So is the authority of the university and of the state. In Canada, the revolution has its most vocal and colourful expression in the Province of Quebec, where federal authority is being questioned and rejected. But as I mentioned earlier, the problem is not confined to Quebec. In British Columbia, for example, the tendency is simply to ignore central authority whenever possible.

Second, Canada is a country of modest importance in relation to the rest of the world. We have so far displayed little creativity in philosophy, in literature, or in the arts that is sufficiently distinctive to attract a discriminating international audience, although the age of affluence and a habit of mutual congratulation sometimes obscure this fact. That we have been totally barren in the area of political theory is evident from the intellectual sterility of the British North America Act and from our surprising refusal to do away with it. For a brief time at the end of the Second World War we invented and gave meaning to the concept of the middle power. But that time soon passed, and our foreign policy became what it had always been, a policy of accommodation rather than of initiatives. This is well illustrated by the apparent intention of the present Prime Minister of Canada to withdraw from NATO without offering the western world any alternative political idea except the pious platitudes which were perfected by Mackenzie King and left by him as a

---

[22] Opening statement by the Honourable Harry E. Strom, Premier of the Province of Alberta, Constitutional Conference, Ottawa, February 10, 1969.

The Federal Government is not reluctant to take special steps to allow strengthening of relations between French-speaking nations abroad and the French parts of Canada, even to the point of increasing foreign aid to French Africa.

Let the Canadian Government send joint Canada-Quebec delegations to French educational conferences in Africa if that is what is desired by Canadians in one part of the country, but at the same time, let the Federal Government send new and stronger joint Canada-Manitoba, Canada-Saskatchewan, Canada-Alberta and Canada-British Columbia trade delegations to the nations of the Pacific community.

At the same time, to facilitate this policy shift, there should also be shifts in the personnel of some of Canada's trade and diplomatic missions, particularly in the Asian countries. Many Western Canadians are tired of going to Asian countries and meeting with well-meaning, but Eastern-Canadian-oriented civil servants who can relate the name of every major company doing business in Montreal or Ottawa or Toronto, but who have never heard of some of the international concerns of Winnipeg, Regina, Edmonton, Calgary or Vancouver. These people represent the interests of some Canadians, but they do not represent our interests.

legacy to his Party and his country. Provincial governments have been affected by this. After the disappearance of the British Empire, which had radiated some of its glory on Ottawa, it was only a matter of time until the constituent parts of Canada came to regard the central government in the manner it is regarded internationally.

It was clear at the conference that no single idea unifies this country. Even at the 1968 conference, where Prime Minister Pearson had done his best to remind his audience that man does not live by bread alone, the references to Canada were no more than platitudinous and money-conscious. Ross Thatcher of Saskatchewan commented:

> At the outset of this conference may I say without equivocation that Saskatchewan favours a *strong central government.* In our opinion the federal administration must have adequate *financial* and *monetary* resources to cope with *economic recession,* to ensure *stable economic growth,* to combat either *inflation or deflation.*[23]

That a central government might have some meaning other than that of a central bank did not occur to the Premier of Saskatchewan. However, Mr. Thatcher's less than Aristotelian view of politics should have come as no surprise. Two or three months earlier at Prime Minister Robarts' Confederation of Tomorrow Conference, the Attorney General of British Columbia, representing W. A. C. Bennett, announced that his province had a "pork chop" attitude to the problems that were about to be discussed. He added that Canadians were a practical people. If they found themselves to be impractical, he said, they went elsewhere. This left at least one member of his audience wondering who had been the most impractical — Harry Johnson, John Kenneth Galbraith, or Lord Beaverbrook. The contributions of the other delegates, although usually phrased with more elegance, were rarely on a much higher level of abstraction.

So it was at the conference in 1969. To be sure there was one brief aspiration expressed by Prime Minister Trudeau in his opening address:

> Si nous voulons que ce pays soit un pays et non pas un agglomerat de territoires à administrer, nous devons pour lui donner une âme, reconnaître une fois pour toutes les principes et les idéaux qui sont communs et qui nous inspirent.[24]

But these sentiments evoked no response from the provincial representatives, nor were they further elaborated by the Prime Minister. The appearance of a central authority conducting the sessions did not conceal the fact that in reality five different types of social and political regions were meeting there and asserting their individual needs.

---

[23] Opening statement by the Honourable W. Ross Thatcher, Premier of the Province of Saskatchewan, Constitutional Conference, February 5, 1968.

[24] Opening statement by the Prime Minister of Canada, the Right Honourable Pierre Elliott Trudeau, Constitutional Conference, February 10, 1969 (unrevised copy).

There was British Columbia, which has never had any kind of traditional society except the surface Anglicisms once provided by retired British army and navy officers and retired British businessmen from India, China, and Southeast Asia—British Columbian types that no longer exist. British Columbia came into effective existence when the Canadian Pacific Railway reached Vancouver in 1886. A strong and lively capitalism from the beginning exploited the forests, the fisheries, and the mines there. Its expansiveness was halted by the two wars and the depression but resumed with the postwar technological revolution. Consequently, the most aggressive kind of capitalism is appropriate and at home in the province, and has been given full encouragement by the Social Credit government under W. A. C. Bennett, British Columbia has no past; it looks only to the future. Bennett's plans for a millenium of growth and prosperity for his province are more Californian than they are Ontarian, and indeed the social climate of the province resembles that of California more than that of the rest of Canada.

The prairie provinces form an area of agricultural capitalism, a distinctive combination of the rural anti-urbanism on which John Diefenbaker drew so strongly for support and the prosperity brought about by foreign wheat sales. At the conference the prairie provinces expressed a real distrust of the East. The remarks in this connection have been cited already, in the opening statement of the province of Saskatchewan. Premier Strom, speaking for Alberta, said:

> We often get the impression that the national media and the representatives of the media in the large centres of Central Canada are not interested in the views of the representatives from the West. There is too little interest, it seems, in reporting the attitudes of our representatives in depth to the people of the nation as a whole, but particularly to the large population centres in Central Canada.[25]

This feeling of lack of essential unity with Central Canada was expressed by Manitoba's Minister of Finance in an address on February 17, 1969.

> We are ready always to move towards unity. Our people would expect no less. The Conference on the Constitution sharpens the issues now. Many thousands of our people have heard the debate at first hand. They expect the federal partner—their federal partner—to meet the real needs of this country. If this is finally made clear to the federal authorities, then we can hope that before too much longer, Ottawa will move with us away from conflict toward compromise. The lesson taught by our history leaves no other choice.[26]

This offhand assumption of disunity between Manitoba and Ottawa is startling.

---

25 Opening statement by the Honourable Harry E. Strom, Premier of the Province of Alberta, Constitutional Conference, Ottawa, February 10, 1969.
26 *The Threat to Canadian Unity — The Forgotten Lesson of Rowell-Sirois,* Address by the Honourable Gurney Evans, Minister of Finance for the Province of Manitoba, to the East Kildonan Kiwanis Club, February 17, 1969.

Ontario has two faces. It is the modern, highly urbanized industrial state, the industrial and financial centre of Canada, powerful and conscious of its power, believing that in the end where Ontario leads the rest of English-speaking Canada will follow (there is good reason today to question that belief). It is also Upper Canada, with all that the term implies. In contrast to British Columbia, Ontario does have a past and a tradition. It has families that have been rich and educated and rooted in the same place for generations. It has, with one or two Maritime exceptions, the oldest and most prestigious schools and universities outside the Province of Quebec. Ontario thus has much of the kind of confidence New York enjoys, as well as much of that found in New England. It is at the forefront in industry and finance; and at the same time it is aware that it and Quebec were the founding provinces of Confederation, and that it antedates Confederation.

The uniqueness of the Province of Quebec needs no emphasis. While other parts of Canada may have feelings of kinship with the United States or Great Britain, for Quebec there is nothing but Canada. In this sense Quebec is more purely Canadian than any of the other areas or provinces. This is why, despite the dazzling success of Expo '67, French Canadians did not see much to celebrate in the centennial year. "Were it repeated ad infinitum," said Daniel Johnson at the 1968 Conference, "no one — at least among my fellow Quebecers who have been here for over 300 years — could be made to believe that Canada began in 1867."[27] Quebec used to be a traditional Catholic society, religious and rural in its inherited ethos. It is now arriving in the twentieth century suddenly and with increasing acceleration. It is no longer rural in its outlook. It is questionable how religious it remains, particularly among the rising generation. Quebec has transferred to its distinctiveness as a *patrie* much of the commitment and intensity formerly devoted to religion. It has a stronger sense of self than any other part of Canada. On the first day of the conference the Quebec flag fluttered on the limousine of Prime Minister Bertrand as it drew up to the West Block. Not even Prime Minister Bennett's limousine carried such an insignia.

The Atlantic provinces, like Ontario, have a past and a tradition; but unlike Ontario, they are poor. At the Confederation of Tomorrow Conference in 1967 Alex Campbell remarked that whereas the citizens of the rich provinces were asking themselves whether they could afford colour television and a second car, his constituents were wondering whether they could afford to bring the plumbing indoors. It must be remembered that the Atlantic provinces have not undergone that economic rationalization and development of resources which we characterize by the term "modernization". This is partly due to their poverty; and it is partly due to the fact that, given that in Canada loyalties are regional (and nowhere more than in the Maritimes), they have not taken the obvious step of uniting and thus forming a common front which would have infinitely more strength than each has individually. It made some

---

[27] Opening statement by the Honourable Daniel Johnson, Prime Minister of the Province of Quebec, Constitutional Conference, Ottawa, February 5, 1968.

sense in 1867 that Prince Edward Island should be a province, although even then Maritime union was being discussed. It makes no sense today when its Premier speaks for a constituency no larger than the population of Kitchener, Ontario.

The Yukon and the Northwest Territories were not represented at the conference. This meant that the conference could not take cognizance of the problems of many Indian and all Eskimo Canadians. Nor could the conference discuss investments of foreign capital in the natural resources of the Northwest Territories. Strom was very much aware of this. He compared the development of Alaska with that of the Yukon and the Northwest Territories.

> Alaska is being developed by a southern people—the Americans. It is appalling that we, a northern people, have not been able to match their efforts, at least in imagination and purpose, if not in magnitude.[28]

He referred to the "suffocating Federal colonialism" under which the residents of the Yukon and the Northwest Territories live, and asked that if the federal government did not intend to act or could not act, would it give jurisdiction over these parts of Canada to the western provinces. Alaska had been made a state and was flourishing? Why should the Canadian north be left to the uninspired administration of eastern civil servants?[29]

---

[28] Opening statement by the Honourable Harry E. Strom, Premier of the Province of Alberta, Constitutional Conference, Ottawa, February 10, 1969.

. . . to many Western Canadians, northern development is not something which can be left to the future but something which is already upon us. If the integration of transportation networks, population movement, social services and educational opportunity in the Northwest is to be accomplished smoothly, northern development planning and action on the part of the Federal Government should be much further along than it is at present.

If we compare the development of Alaska in recent years with the development of the Yukon and the Northwest Territories, we are disappointed. The painfully slow and often tragic story of northern development in Canada is not the fault of the tiny bands of pioneers who now reside there. The basic fault must be borne by the Federal Government.

Alaska is being developed by a southern people — the Americans. It is appalling that we, a northern people, have not been able to match their efforts, at least in imagination and purpose, if not in magnitude.

The Federal Government of the United States granted Alaska her status as a state. The Federal Government of Canada has had the responsibility of managing our northern territories for as long a period, and yet to date the prospect of greater autonomy for the Yukon or the Northwest Territories is not even in sight, and the residents live under a suffocating Federal colonialism.

And so, we Western Canadians ask, what about northern development?

If the Federal Government does not intend to act, or cannot act, would the Government contemplate giving the Western Provinces an extension of their jurisdiction? Northern development is an aspiration of Western Canadians. Opportunities for its development must be provided.

[29] *Ibid.*

Strom's remarks made clear that the haphazard political geography of Canada must be changed. Subsequently, Bennett's plan for reorganization, although expressed with his customary hyperbole, was one of the few creative ideas to come out of the sessions. (I believe it has been endorsed by Prime Minister Robarts.) It had been stated earlier in the *Proposals of the Province of British Columbia on the Constitution of Canada, December, 1968.*

> . . . . I believe the time has come to recognize that in the interests of economic realities the boundaries of some of the Provinces will have to be altered and the separate existence of some other Provinces will have to be abolished so as to provide five viable and effective political units consonant and in conformity with the five economic regions of Canada. Imagine the increased efficiency and resultant substantial savings to the Canadian taxpayer that would result.
>
> In keeping with the principle units conforming with the economic regions of Canada, British Columbia calls for the Federal Government to extend by legislation the boundaries of each of the applicable Provinces northward to the northern limits of continental Canada. Furthermore, the topographical characteristics support communication links and trade patterns running north and south rather than east and west.[30]

Bennett's theories could be implemented in several ways. The Yukon and the Northwest Territories could be made provinces thus releasing them from the dead hand of bureaucratic administration. But they would be relatively powerless. Another possibility would be to sound out a prairie union among Alberta, Saskatchewan, and Manitoba, and add to such a union the Northwest Territories. This seems to be what Bennett had in mind when he spoke of "five viable and effective political units consonant and in conformity with the five economic regions of Canada". But such a prairie and northwest province would surely be too vast and would in many ways constitute a separate country unto itself. Moreover, the regional loyalties of the prairie provinces would seem to be already too well established as to make this scheme dubious, if not unworkable.

The best plan perhaps would be to extend the boundaries of British Columbia to include the Yukon and the boundaries of Alberta, Saskatchewan, and Manitoba to the limits of continental Canada. The Atlantic provinces should form one political, and therefore one economic, unit. All of this cannot be done with a stroke of the pen. But then neither was the Confederation of 1867. There is nothing sacrosanct about the original boundaries, which have in fact been modified from time to time as need has required. On the contrary there is every reason to make them accord with the regional loyalties and economic interests that dominate Canadian political life. Our task is not to act upon the assumption of a national loyalty which exists only to a slight degree. Rather, it is to elicit clear articulation of the varying regional attitudes, which have been blurred over for so long. We want to find out why the

---

[30] Proposals of the Province of British Columbia on the Constitution of Canada, December, 1968. Submitted by the Honourable W. A. C. Bennett, Premier and Minister of Finance of British Columbia.

regions feel as they do, rather than pretend that such feelings do not exist, or are of marginal importance, or are negative and uncreative. By rearranging our political boundaries along the lines I have suggested, or in some other logical fashion, by accepting the fact of regionalism as the basis for Canadian federation, we may be taking the first important step on the road to a new Constitution suited to the realities of our times. At the 1969 conference there was scarcely a word or a concept from any delegate to suggest that Canada was anything more than the sum of its parts. If its parts are redefined more realistically, we may well find that a concept of the meaning of the whole will emerge. Jean-Jacques Bertrand came closest to expressing this when he said in his opening statement:

> . . . constitutional reform offers the only permanent solution for the deep crisis afflicting Canada. We need fresh agreement on basic issues; we must state very clearly the ground rules for relations between governments; we must reconsider the constitutional structure of our country, the form it is to take, the ends it is to pursue, so that our political institutions may not only meet the needs of the hour but those that will arise in days to come.[31]

Canada presents a problem and a case study of the greatest interest for the political scientist, because in Canada the centralizing trend of the modern state is reversed. Richard Goodwin, writing in January in *The New Yorker* on the present American discontents, singled out centralization and consequent big government as the most troubling development in our times for the average American citizen. It has made the citizen feel that he has no control over the forces that affect his life, that the casting of a ballot is meaningless because it could not in any event put an end to the bigness and the impersonality that overwhelm him.

Canada has been exempt from what appears elsewhere to be an irresistible trend. Two reasons for this exception are clear enough. Education under the British North America Act is reserved to the provinces. This means that the provinces, not Ottawa, preside over the educational and technological revolution which may well be the most important phenomenon of our time. To put it another way, intellectual energy can be channelled towards decentralized rather than centralized power. The clearest example of this is to be found in the Province of Quebec, where provincial agencies have been established which require for their proper functioning almost the whole of Quebec's intellectual output. The same is true of Ontario, although since Ontario tends to think of itself as English-speaking Canada this is often overlooked or at least undefined. Until 1939 the federal civil services had a near monopoly of Canadian administrative talent. That monopoly does not exist today. Talent seeks the place where the power resides that can properly utilize and reward it.

The second reason for the trend towards decentralization in Canada is that, because of the accidents of history. Canada confronts international

---

[31] Opening statement by the Honourable Jean-Jacques Bertrand, Prime Minister of the Province of Quebec, Constitutional Conference, Ottawa, February 10, 1969.

problems indirectly and at second hand. The Department of External Affairs will not bring to an end the war in Southeast Asia. It is unlikely that it will even contribute meaningfully to the termination of that war. Canada can do little to halt the arms race. We would be deluding ourselves were we to believe that we could effectively mediate between the U.S.S.R. and the United States or the U.S.S.R. and China. Canadian foreign policy, as I have already pointed out, is a policy of accommodation not a policy of initiatives. This being the case, there is no need for a centralized authority at Ottawa strong enough to confront the major powers of the world. Washington does that for us whether we like it or not, just as Whitehall did until 1939. Moreover, we do not have internal problems — such as race in the United States or in South Africa — of such seriousness and intensity as to require centralized authority for decision-making.

The fact of the matter is that there is a serious disparity between what Ottawa and the British North America Act say we are and what we really are. This is the clearest message to emerge from the conference. Canada is not a nation, but acts as though she were. As Alexander Brady has pointed out in *Democracy in the Dominions,* Canada is "an aggregation of sectional communities."[32] An American political sociologist elaborated on this statement in 1963.

> Canada is not a nation in the full sense of a socially unified people possessing a consciousness of nationality and a sense of patriotism although the Canadian state has the instruments of national sovereignty, it has neither the embedded symbols of legitimacy nor the deep loyalties to the political community which Americans and Britishers take for granted. . . . Canada has remained in the British Commonwealth, and, while this pseudo-legitimacy has reinforced a sense of national unity, it has prevented the development of a truly national solidarity.[33]

Now this may be all to the good. I am rather inclined to think that it is. We have seen to what extremes nineteenth-century nationalism can go. But our situation must be expressed positively, not simply felt negatively as was so apparent at the conference. What we need — and I think what the world needs now — is a poliitcal theory of regionalism. Then we must have a constitution based on that theory.

Canadians are a fortunate people. Our history and our geography have so far protected us against the dangers of twentieth-century super-government. We are unburdened by huge defence budgets and we have a minimum of international commitments. But this does not entitle us to play the role of Pangloss and say that all is well in this best of all possible worlds. Nor does it entitle us to play the role of the flower child of the western world, as the *Times Literary Supplement* accused us of doing several months ago. We have within our society the germ of a political theory that is more suited to the

---

[32] Alexander Brady, *Democracy in the Dominions* (Toronto, University of Toronto Press, 1947), p. 83.
[33] Robert R. Alford, *Party and Society* (Chicago, Rand McNally & Company, 1963), pp. 254-55.

twentieth century than is the romanticism of Rousseau, the legalistic contract of Locke, the narrow pain-pleasure theories of the utilitarians, or the millenial expectations of Marxist thought. But if we are a fortunate people, in addition we are in some respects a very curious people. We recoil from any potentiality for greatness that we might possess. This perhaps is due to the fact that until 1939 we lived in the shadow of a British greatness, which we revered and had no desire to challenge, and now we live in the shadow of an American greatness, about which we feel many ambiguities. This uncertainty about ourselves is evident in the unconsciously self-deprecatory tone of our newspaper columnists, so apparent to the Canadian who has lived abroad for some years. It is apparent in the massive insecurity exhibited at the recent Montreal symposium devoted to the emigration to Canada of foreign intellectuals. (Apparently it occurred to none of the participants in the symposium that foreign intellectuals might want to come to Canada because our country has perhaps the freest political order and potentially one of the most humanly rewarding social orders in the world today.) It is this hesitation to recognize what we have achieved and to institutionalize that achievement that we must overcome.

More than that, we have a political and social responsibility to our own people. We are presented with moral problems not envisioned in 1867 and therefore not provided for by the British North America Act. If there is any meaning to Canadian citizenship, by what right are the residents of British Columbia infinitely richer and exposed to infinitely greater economic opportunities than the residents of Newfoundland and Prince Edward Island? Newfoundland was not, of course, part of Canada until 1949, and in 1867 the economic disparities between Canada West and the Atlantic provinces were not particularly striking. British Columbia and the prairie provinces did not exist. What we have to do is devise a federal structure in which there is some real sense of participation on the part of all regions in disposing of that economic power which is chiefly concentrated in two or three of them. At the same time we must avoid the harmful centralizing tendencies of the modern, rational, bureaucratic state. To achieve this we must not oppose a Quebec against a vague Canadianism which the rest of us are assumed with little justification to share. We must accept our regionalisms (of which Quebec is only one) as a product of history, and we must seek to understand them. They should be the basis for that division of sovereignty which is the essence of a federal union. However, we cannot arrive at a division of powers which will function if we do not take into account the fact that the various regionalisms are based on different historical experiences, in many cases on different and complex traditions. This is why a purely rational formula for revenue equalizations in any particular year will not endure for long and cannot be the basis of a new and lasting union. If Canada has any distinctive role in the world, and therefore any reason for existing beyond the enjoyment of material affluence, it is to discover and articulate the political philosophy which will bring about that union. The task is urgent. The 1969 conference showed little more than signs of gradual deterioration and disintegration. Time is running out.

Part Six

Quebec and
Canadian Federalism

28 Quebec and Canadian Federalism*

Alexander Brady

Canada's federation is distinct from the other two major federations in the English-speaking world in resting upon an alliance of two peoples and two cultures. Other differences exist, but this is fundamental. Since 1867 the dualism of culture has been slowly woven into the political fabric of the nation, although outside Quebec its implications are still not always appreciated or wholly accepted. With the appearance in 1956 of the *Report of the Royal Commission of Inquiry on Constitutional Problems*,[1] English-speaking Canadians have little excuse for misunderstanding the position of their French-speaking compatriots. The Commission was appointed by provincial statute in January, 1953, under the chairmanship of Judge Thomas Tremblay. Its bulky report is never likely to be widely read. It is prolix and sometimes repetitious to the point of tedium; its analysis would have been more telling had it been tidier and more compressed. Yet, despite such flaws, it is a landmark in the literature of federalism: it describes and explains more fully than any other public document the position and anxieties of Quebec in the federal state, and defends the concept of a strict federalism as the essential basis for the success of Canada's national experiment. For the Tremblay Commissioners the issue of Quebec in the federation and the issue of the French in the nation are one and the same. In harmony with their theme they submit numerous recommendations. We cannot, however, assess these or do justice to their premises, without first reviewing briefly the historical position of Quebec in Canadian federalism.

At Confederation the political thinking of leaders in British North America swung between two positions, both empirical. Some of the Fathers had originally feared that the federal principle, especially as exemplified in the neighbouring republic, implied a dispersal of power that would drain the strength, increase the cost, and jeopardize the survival of a new state in North America. Sir John A. Macdonald's first preference, like that of Sir Charles Tupper, was a legislative rather than a federal union. Yet he and his associates quickly yielded to the logic of the fact that the existing colonies enjoyed local

---

[1] Four vols. (Quebec, 1956). Hereafter called the *Tremblay Report*.

* From *The Canadian Journal of Economics and Political Science*, Vol. XXV no. 3 (August, 1959), pp. 259-70. Reprinted by permission of the author and the Canadian Political Science Association.

ALEXANDER BRADY – Professor Emeritus, Department of Political Economy, University of Toronto.

autonomy and were unwilling to surrender it.[2] The two Canadas, moreover, possessed a single legislature, but had been compelled by the differences in their cultures to conduct their affairs almost as in a federation. This was the main circumstance which changed Macdonald's mind on the nature of the new state: the French as a minority feared that in legislative union "their institutions and their laws might be assailed, and their ancestral associations, on which they prided themselves, attacked and prejudiced."[3] The French were emphatic in contending for genuine federalism, and those among them who opposed the projected confederation did so because it appeared to offer a provincial autonomy that was shadowy and insufficient. The presence of dual cultures and diverse social values among the people of the St. Lawrence Valley was thus basic in shaping the decision of the Fathers for a federal state.

Since 1867 Quebec has remained consistently attached to a strict federalism as a protector of its own culture and the cultural dualism of Canada. It has been the chief citadel of resistance to centralizing conceptions and homogenizing tendencies. Its position has sometimes been backed by Ontario, which usually however acts independently for reasons of its own. In the first three decades after Confederation Ontario might seem to have been even more emphatic in assailing the centralizing pretensions of Ottawa. Under Oliver Mowat (1872-96) it checkmated the manoeuvres of Sir John A. Macdonald, who never wholly subdued his original bias for a legislative union and persistently endeavoured to restrict the role of the provincial legislatures and to exalt that of the national Parliament. But, in Mowat's successive legal contests and triumphs before the Privy Council, Quebec was Ontario's vigilant and reliable ally. Its jurists and politicians were equally keen to elaborate the powers of the provinces under section 92. In Judge T. J. J. Loranger among others it had a constitutional expert who in the eighties presented with distinguished clarity the provincial case. "If the federal pretensions prevail," wrote Loranger in 1883, "and if the principle of the provinces' inferiority and dependence of their legislatures with regard to the federal authority is recognized, in less than half a century their absorption will be accomplished and the federal system will give way to the legislative union so rightly feared in our province."[4]

In politics, two Quebec figures in the first half-century of federation especially advanced the provincial cause: Honoré Mercier and Wilfrid Laurier. Both reflected the inflamed feelings of French Canadian nationalism in the eighties provoked by the sorry events of the Riel Rebellion and its aftermath. Both, and especially Laurier, also responded to the more stable emotions about provincial rights which in greater or lesser degree have inspired all French leaders since 1867. Mercier's principal achievement was his convening an interprovincial conference in 1887 to examine the relations of the

---

[2] See, e.g., *Parliamentary Debates on the Subject of the Confederation of the British North American Provinces* (Quebec, 1865, reprinted Ottawa, 1951), p. 29.
[3] *Ibid.*
[4] Quoted in *Tremblay Report,* Vol. 1, p. 67.

provinces with the federal government. Under the chairmanship of Oliver Mowat five provincial premiers there adopted resolutions that challenged and rejected the centralist policies of Macdonald. Although their request, including a surrender by the federal government of its power to disallow provincial acts, were not acceptable to Ottawa, the case for provincial autonomy received an important impetus from its formal affirmation.

Laurier's leadership of the national Liberals (1887-1919) secured, by quiet persuasion at the highest levels in Ottawa, a sympathy for Quebec's position and for provincial autonomy in general. "The only means of maintaining Confederation," he declared in 1889, "is to recognize that, within its sphere assigned to it by the constitution, each province is as independent of control by the federal Parliament as the latter is from control by the provincial legislatures." This dictum is important, not for its novelty, but for the fact that it influenced Laurier's tactics and policies throughout his career. It was evident in his stand on the Manitoba school question before his electoral triumph in 1896, and in office he never lost a French Canadian's anxiety for the autonomy of the provinces. Admittedly he was aided by the stream of events. In successive decisions from that of *Hodge* v. *The Queen* in 1883, the Privy Council consolidated and fortified the power of the provincial legislatures, while the growth in population and industry of Quebec and Ontario enhanced the prestige of their governments and goaded them to seek in the courts that larger legislative competence essential for developing their natural resources. In employing the power of disallowance Laurier and his colleagues sought to pursue a fresh course. They did not consider the power obsolete (although privately Laurier told Blake that it was alien to the federal idea), but generally avoided its use as a corrective of the alleged errors and injustices committed by provincial legislatures, and confined it to cases where the legislation affected federal or imperial interests. No other view, they were convinced, could secure provincial autonomy and local democracy. Laurier's governments between 1896-1911 admittedly disallowed thirty provincial statutes, but of these twenty issued solely from the legislature of British Columbia and affected both Canadian and imperial interests by dealing adversely with the employment and status of Asiatics. Since 1896 only one Quebec act has been disallowed compared with five in the preceding twenty-nine years and only two Ontario acts compared with eight in the earlier period.[5]

Soon after the passing of the Laurier régime, there appeared fresh threats to provincial autonomy, which were mainly related, as they still are, to the issues of finance. On a small scale before the First World War and on a larger scale after it, national governments began to make grants to the provinces on conditions which implied a federal control over their use. This new procedure came from a quickened and wider sense of national interest in the policy-makers at Ottawa, coupled with a desire to circumvent the

---

[5] See G. V. La Forest, *Disallowance and Reservation of Provincial Legislation* (Ottawa, Queen's Printer, 1955), Appendix A.

restrictions imposed on them by the constitution. They were persuaded that, without loss of provincial autonomy, the provinces and the national government might create an *ad hoc* partnership for certain desirable ends with funds jointly contributed. Grants, such as those provided in 1919 to encourage technical education, trespassed on the legislative field of the provinces, but the provincial governments could not resist the temptation to accept virtual supplements to provincial revenue.

From the outset leaders in Quebec viewed this form of federal largesse with disquiet or positive disfavour. Ernest Lapointe, a prominent French Canadian spokesman in the Liberal Opposition at the close of the First World War, attacked conditional grants. In his view they intruded on provincial jurisdiction and were unfair to non-concurring provinces, whose citizens were taxed to benefit those in other provinces.[6] Indirectly but forcibly, a federal government thus exerted coercion in fields where its action was either constitutionally ambiguous or invalid. It practised generosity at the price of provincial autonomy, and employed its own relative affluence to entice and bribe impecunious provinces, whittle away their independence, and generally impair their freedom to manoeuvre. In Quebec this argument has ever since rendered doughty service in the polemic of federal-provincial relations.

The inter-war ministries of Mackenzie King, wherein Ernest Lapointe sat as an influential member, were on the whole unsympathetic to conditional grants, although the social and political compulsions of the time involved them in this policy in some degree. In July, 1924, a special committee of the Commons advocated that the federal and provincial governments should share the costs of old age pensions for needy persons over seventy. The Liberals were reluctant to reject a proposal that might win popularity. King himself was deeply interested in policies of social welfare and alert to their importance in political strategy. Hence in 1927 his Government sponsored a scheme whereby it would pay half the cost to every province which agreed to provide old age pensions. The provinces, beginning with British Columbia, made such agreements, and finally in 1936 New Brunswick and Quebec participated, although the Quebec government still viewed old age pensions as an undesirable federal intrusion into the provincial field. It could not, however, continue to ignore the unpalatable facts that if it remained outside the scheme its people would be helping to pay for pensions they were not free to enjoy.

Despite the precedent of old age pensions, the inter-war administrations of Mackenzie King, influenced by their French Canadian supporters, never displayed enthusiasm for conditional grants. Quebec resented them as the vehicle of a vigorous federal policy. Its leaders had no wish to see the national government in a position to exert pressure on the provinces. Such grants placed it in this position because they implied centralized authority in making decisions by lawmakers and officials in Ottawa, the majority of whom were English Canadians.[7]

---

[6] *House of Commons Debates* (1919), p. 3794.

[7] For Mackenzie King's concern for the position of the provinces in this matter see *Ibid.*, 1931, pp. 1959ff.

Since 1939 profound changes in Canadian society and ways of thought have involved a heavier subsidization of the provinces. National enactments have multiplied conditional grants until today there are half a hundred different kinds. Some, such as those relating to the reclamation of land and to fisheries, mainly concern specific provinces and regions. Others, such as those in public health and old age assistance, appeal to all the provinces, and enlist the active support of all, including Quebec. This accentuated trend in federal action is traceable to social forces linked with industrialism and nationalism, accelerated by war and the preparation for war. The appetite of a growing industrial people for public services within provincial jurisdiction has sharpened, especially for highways, welfare and health services, and education. Federal governments, of course, might have left the provinces alone to cope with these services as best they could, but they have been persistently pressed by public opinion to feed them with federal funds. In some cases the pressure has been strongest from people in the relatively poor and less favoured areas, but it commonly comes from certain organized interests in all the provinces and especially from the more industrialized regions. The more rapid the pace of urbanization, the more varied and insistent are the demands on the national treasury. On their part federal politicians are loath to miss an opportunity of winning votes by spending money, and now find it easy to justify expenditure on the grounds of a compelling national interest. Since their primary concern is to placate the electors, they must listen to the numerous pressure groups, which often are indifferent to the political and legal facts of federalism and rationalize their own interests in terms of a national interest. Thus the Liberal party, ascendant in Ottawa for the first dozen years after the Second World War, became fired by a stronger nationalism, and rapidly retreated from its former scruples about encroaching on provincial jurisdiction. In successive enactments after 1940 it sponsored abundant grants, conditional and unconditional.

The Tremblay Commission, in surveying this panorama of post-war change, admit with evident sorrow that "a vast network has been spread which binds the provinces to the central government and which, to a certain extent, provides them with the financial means of discharging their legislative functions, but always at the discretion and on the terms of the wealthy and powerful donor."[8] In all this the French Canadians as the chief defenders of traditional federalism face a difficult dilemma. Either they must patiently resign themselves to a course of events that threatens to erode the older federalism or pursue more resolutely than hitherto the policy of survival by withdrawal. Some fear that they have no choice, and that the decision is made for them by the speed and inexorable strides of an industrialism which transforms their society, exposes them to a stream of influences from outside, and assimilates them in character to English-speaking Canadians. Since 1939 Quebec, with rich mineral resources, abundant water power, and a high birth rate, has shared substantially in the country's material expansion. Its industrial production has multiplied five-fold, and light industries such as textiles

---

[8] *Tremblay Report,* Vol. II, p. 214.

have yielded ground to heavy industries such as mining and metallurgy. Industrialism in the province was born long before, but the Second World War accelerated its growth. The drift from farm to factory was quickened. The old rural framework of life, in which for generations the relatively isolated culture of the French Canadians was sustained, is crumbling now that only a fifth of the people live in strictly rural areas. As urban dwellers and industrial workers they undergo much the same experience as labour else-where in Canada, respond to the prevalent appetite for social security, and are likely to be no less eager for the services that the federal treasury can ensure. With the progress of industrialism a variety of interests in French Canadian society, notably organized labour, establish a rapport with like interests in Ontario and other provinces, and become less diffident in dealing with a government in Ottawa. Quebec may still resemble a cultural island within the nation, but an island now with numerous bridges that diminish its isolation.

The Union Nationale party led by Maurice Duplessis has held office in Quebec since 1944, and in the face of these forces has vehemently defended the province's autonomy. It has freely exploited the sentiments of French Canadian nationalism aroused by the depression of the thirties and the sub-sequent tensions of the Second World War. Yet it is difficult to determine precisely how much the longevity of M. Duplessis' régime is due to his display of autonomist convictions. Other obvious factors contribute: his smoothly working political machine, his rare art in winning support by dexterous use of patronage, and his gains from an electoral distribution of seats that bears little relation to the rapid urbanizing of the population. Despite his strong position, he has found it expedient to accept many conditional grants from Ottawa; others he has brusquely rejected. His criterion for acceptance or rejection is the extent of the threat to the traditional autonomy of the prov-ince. Thus he entered into agreements to obtain substantial grants from the federal treasury for health services, including hospital construction, general public health, and the control of tuberculosis and cancer. Although he also accepted the conditions prescribed in 1952 for joint provincial and federal old age assistance for the needy, he rejected the federal subsidies to aid in building the Trans-Canada Highway through Quebec. Even more emphati-cally he rejected the subsidizing of Quebec universities from federal funds because it touched, not merely traditional provincial jurisdiction, but the sensitive nerves of culture. For him this was an appropriate battle ground. "What counted in Judas' betrayal of Christ," he declared, "was not the sum of thirty pieces of silver but the fact that Judas had betrayed his Master." Acquiescence in such federal action would merely stimulate Ottawa to indulge further in an interference all the more unwarranted in being needless, since the provincial government itself could adequately sustain the colleges of the province, especially if the federal authority left it appropriate fields for direct taxation. This point raises the controversial and basic question of the taxing power, which has occasioned the most prolonged and wordy debates between Ottawa and Quebec.

The modern issue of taxation originated as a by-product of the First World War, when the national government in 1916 resorted to direct taxes on war profits and in the next year on general income. After the war the income tax survived as an important instrument in federal policy, and provoked in Quebec strong protests. "Ottawa," asserted Premier Taschereau in 1920, "has unceremoniously arrogated to itself our own sources of revenue." But the federal income tax was there to stay, and the facts of the depression in the thirties helped to secure its permanence. The depression, however, had contrasting and conflicting effects within the federation. In English-speaking Canada, especially in the west, the current of opinion now ran more strong than before towards a heavy reliance on Ottawa. The taxing power of the federal government was accepted as an inevitable adjunct to its responsibility. In Quebec, by contrast, the current of opinion ran turbulently in the opposite direction. The harsh tensions of the depression merely exacerbated French Canadian nationalism, raised more urgently the persistent theme of cultural survival, and made the régime of M. Duplessis after 1936 more uncompromising than any previous government in clinging to every element of provincial autonomy. In the economic and social facts of the time Quebec sensed a new and greater menace to the position that it was obligated by long tradition to defend. The Sirois Commission (appointed in August, 1937) was naturally viewed by M. Duplessis as objectionable because it was appointed without prior consultation with the provinces and unilaterally investigated matters that were crucially important to them. His government made explicit to the Commission its opposition to any abridgement of provincial rights, or any significant change in the federal pact unless accepted by all the provinces.

At that time, however, Quebec's position was not isolated. Four other provincial governments also argued before the Sirois Commission against any drastic change, fiscal or otherwise, in the existing distribution of federal power. Only the four then most needy provinces, Manitoba, Saskatchewan, Nova Scotia, and Prince Edward Island, were ready to barter their right to tax for provincial aid. All four proclaimed fidelity to federalism, but, in their precarious financial plight, a secure revenue had more appeal than fiscal liberty. The conference of January, 1941, convened by Ottawa to get agreement for implementing the principal recommendations of the *Sirois Report,* adjourned in failure on the second day because Ontario, British Columbia, and Alberta rejected a revision of the federal system on the terms recommended, and the national Government could consider no others. From September, 1939, to August, 1944, Quebec was ruled by the Liberals under Adélard Godbout, who cautiously did not commit himself. "We are here," he remarked, "to study; we will listen and we are ready to co-operate."

After the Second World War the issue of federal taxation appeared to Quebec in a more ominous light. To meet the urgent necessities of war the federal Government had secured (in 1942) the agreement of all the provinces to vacate in its favour the right to levy personal income and corporation taxes and to accept compensation in annual grants. Here was a means that with provincial consent and without a constitutional amendment might at any time augment the fiscal initiative of Ottawa, and for many reasons Ottawa was anxious that it should endure into the peace. Public sentiments at the time incessantly pressed the federal Government to do and prepare for countless things. Fears of a post-war depression and haunting memories of unemployment in the thirties were in the air. Conceptions of an economy managed through fiscal controls seeped into the thinking of federal ministers and public servants. The ideas of Maynard Keynes took root in the Department of Finance, and to lend them scope it seemed essential to have federal control over the major and most remunerative taxes. Hence at the Dominion-Provincial Conference on Reconstruction (1945-6) Ottawa submitted to the provinces far-ranging proposals, buttressed by a series of supplementary studies, which among other things would have left to it an exclusive access to personal income and corporation taxes and succession duties, while in return Ottawa provided per capita provincial grants.

Quebec, like some other provinces, viewed these plans of Ottawa as a serious menace to federalism. If they were fully implemented, the major initiative in social policy would irretrievably shift to the national capital, and provincial independence in finance and manoeuvrability in policy would drastically diminish. In the words of the Quebec brief the proposals would "exclude the provinces from the most important fields of direct taxation and to that extent deprive them of the exercise of the powers assigned to them by the constitution." Ontario's plea was similar. It denied, moreover, that centralization could provide protection against depression, although it would certainly violate federal principles. Yet neither Quebec nor Ontario outdid in vigorous and eloquent protest the Premier of Nova Scotia, who declared that if the proposals were accepted, "provincial autonomy will be gone. Provincial independence will vanish. Provincial dignity will disappear. The provincial governments will become mere annuitants of Ottawa."

The Conference of 1945-6 dissolved in acrimony and without accomplishment. The wartime agreements, however, ran their course to 1947. In the interval certain fundamental facts in the situation worked inexorably in favour of Ottawa, especially the inequality of the provinces in economic and financial strength and hence their divergence in interpreting the nature of the federal bond. The financially weak or less favoured naturally saw advantages in retaining payments from Ottawa. On principle they were not really averse to rental agreements provided that they got good terms, although for purposes of bargaining they might appear appropriately coy. Their outlook on the federation fundamentally differed from that of Quebec, because they were not preoccupied with the feeling of having to defend through federalism a distinct culture. Consequently they were disposed to take a short-run view of federal matters. The necessities of the day dominated, for under pressure from their electorates they thought primarily of services to which they were committed and must become committed, and of how to secure the revenue necessary to finance them. Even the strong and affluent among the English-speaking provinces do not act very differently, but their strength commonly permits them to take longer views.

This circumstance in the situation makes plain why Ottawa, after failing to obtain agreement for a general scheme, could successfully resort to the tactic of individual agreements on the basis of new formulae. By the beginning of 1948 seven provinces and in 1949 Newfoundland had signed such agreements. Quebec and Ontario then alone remained outside, but in 1952 Ottawa, armed with different formulae, was able to win Ontario and isolate Quebec. The history of these years illustrates how expediency dominates in Canadian federalism. With the rapidly changing society an elaborate process of individual and constant bargaining between the federal and provincial governments is the accepted norm, and the provinces rarely present a united front. On such a basis the federation will continue to operate, for it serves best the shortrun interests of Ottawa and all the provinces except Quebec.

The Tremblay Commission, aided by the numerous briefs of organized interests in the province, assess Quebec's place in the federation in the light of history and philosophy. Much of their detailed report, with its wealth of facts, surveys the past and analyses the present in order to underline the special identity of the French community in Canada's evolution, its relation to the federal structure after 1867, and the threats to its survival and the survival of federalism that result from the forces of the twentieth century, especially industrialism, depression, and war.

The historical section of the report is invaluable, and, despite a bias on some matters, is likely to be acceptable to scholars outside Quebec. Agreement on facts, however, does not imply agreement on their interpretation. The historical struggle of the French Canadian for cultural survival gives him a special point of view, which the Tremblay Commission express in terms of an appropriate philosophy. This philosophy is a form of Catholic pluralism, emphasizing the necessary freedom for cultural groups to operate and survive, combined with the assumptions of a liberal nationalism. Federal policy, it is argued, should be determined, less by the material conditions and appetites of the society, than by the wholesome impulses towards the freedom of cultural groups and the freedom of the individual to develop his personality in a group. The goals of the Canadian nation should be association not assimilation, diversity not uniformity, the vitality of all the distinct groups in the state and not their standardization. These concepts of liberal Catholic philosophers, such as Jacques Maritain, are readily translated into the traditional French Canadian attachment to a strict federalism, stressing the full autonomy of the province with its aggregate of usages and traditions. This pluralist philosophy might have found an uncongenial environment in the Quebec of the nineteenth century under its dominant ultramontanism. But in the 1950's it seems to fit comfortably into the French Canadian heritage.

What kind of offspring in practical recommendations does this marriage of history and philosophy produce? The Tremblay Commission are explicit about what it should produce. They formulate many recommendations, some of which differ greatly in content and purpose from those of the Sirois Commission twenty years ago. They primarily seek to stop the erosion of federalism, threatened by the centralizing pressures of Ottawa especially in finance. They launch what they hope are destructive assaults against the "new federalism" and its apologists, English and French, and single out for criticism the views of a French Canadian advocate, Maurice Lamontagne, author of *Le Fédéralisme canadien*.[9] "To believe and to try to have it believed," they wrote, "that there is respect, in Canada, for the autonomy of the provinces, because they are allowed to exist as mere administrative units to which the central authority will distribute living allowances, is mere self-deception and an attempt to deceive others. It confronts true federalism with mere administrative decentralization which is to be found in any state but which does not truly allow autonomy of the regional and local communities."[10]

The Tremblay Commission think of a genuine federal state as one wherein financial and political powers are so apportioned between the federal and unit governments that their self-operating and self-governing functions are unfettered by interferences from one another. "There can be no federalism," they write, "without autonomy of the state's constituent parts, and no sovereignty of the various governments without fiscal and financial autonomy."[11] Such a federal structure must ensure the identity of the whole and the identity of the parts. It implies, not isolation, but close co-operation among the several governments. This general concept of federalism is one to which many modern political theorists would readily subscribe. The inevitable question, however, is, what division of power has most logic in a given situation? Even among genuine liberal pluralists it is far from easy to secure agreement on this thorny issue in view of the speed of economic and social change. The modern industrial economy never stands still, and every major innovation affects profoundly the federal jurisdiction.

The Tremblay Commission naturally enough use a criterion calculated to ensure for a province an authority sufficiently broad to protect its culture. They are confident that the constitution drafted by the Fathers provided this authority, and that in the past the Judicial Committee and the Supreme Court of Canada jealously upheld it. The real threat to the federation in the present generation comes from the centralizing actions of an Ottawa forgetful that federalism implies two orders of government and not one. The national authority has employed various expedients, such as conditional grants, to encroach on provincial jurisdiction. It has freely invoked ancillary powers in the B.N.A. Act, and has used the financial incapacity of the provinces as an excuse for doing countless things, while its own inroads in the field of direct taxation accentuate their incapacity. The Commission are particularly critical of the national government for exercising powers, as in some forms of education, allegedly ancillary to those in section 91. Ottawa may properly legislate for the Indians, the penitentiaries, the armed forces, agriculture, immigration, and radio, but assumes that each of these subjects has an educational aspect that justifies its intervention in the field of education associated with the

---

9 (Québec, Les Presses de l'Université Laval, 1954).
10 *Tremblay Report,* Vol. II, p. 276.
11 *Ibid.,* Vol. III, p. 294.

subject. Judge Tremblay and his colleagues comment caustically on the manner in which the Massey Commission, by what they deem a series of specious arguments, establish a right of the federal government to intervene in certain fields of education and then transfer this right into a duty in the name of the public welfare and spiritual values. They think that the extravagant use of ancillary powers seriously threatens the survival of the federation, and quote with approval Justice Duff's view that the "division of legislative authority is the principle of the British North America Act, and if the doctrine of necessarily incidental powers is to be extended to all cases in which inconvenience arises from such a division, that is the end of the federal character of the Union."[12]

On this premise the Tremblay Commission consider that for the future federal power should be employed, not to displace the provinces, but to establish the conditions, including a sufficient and independent revenue, that would allow them to play the special role assigned to them under the constitution. The provinces need fiscal powers commensurate with their legislative powers, and can secure them only by a logical division of the field of direct taxation between them and the national government. Yet, even with a careful division of the taxing power, some provinces would likely remain unable to obtain revenue sufficient to finance services comparable with those of their wealthier or more industrialized neighbours, and for this situation the Commissioners think that the appropriate remedy is a "financial equalization organism."[13] Instead of leaving solely to Ottawa the major task of combatting economic depressions, the provinces should for this purpose be brought into a close co-operative relation with Ottawa and be organized to participate in the anti-cyclic policy according to their capacity and the requirements of their constitutional role.[14] In a period of depression they, like the federal government, should be able to sell bonds to the Bank of Canada. The Commission emphasize the value of a permanent committee of the federal-provincial conferences to secure continuity of co-operation in the interval between conferences, and in addition a permanent council of the provinces, confined exclusively to them, somewhat on the lines of the Council of State Governments in the United States. One body that they have in mind now already exists in the Federal-Provincial Continuing Committee on Fiscal and Economic Matters.

Such briefly is the main case of the Tremblay Commission for a revitalized federalism. It is both radical and controversial. Its chief argument and proposals are derived from briefs submitted to the Commission, and unquestionably represent important bodies of opinion in the province of Quebec, although not all that province's opinion is necessarily well represented. A convinced federalist elsewhere in Canada could accept the main thesis of the Tremblay Commission that decentralization is desirable to invigorate local autonomy in all the provinces. But the patent fact is that in English-speaking Canada, in

---

12 *Ibid.*, Vol. II, p. 236.
13 *Ibid.*, Vol. III, p. 297.
14 *Ibid.*, Vol. III, p. 299.

the post-war years especially, the current of nationalism has run powerfully in the opposite direction and has been stimulated by the evident insecurities of the national state in the contemporary world. The dangers to Canada's survival as a political entity have among English-speaking Canadians weakened the federal spirit. Moreover there is a growing sense that many problems of social life can best be settled nationally and that social progress demands national standards. Hence the pressure of special interests for action from Ottawa has increased rather than diminished. With its larger and more flexible source of income Ottawa can most effectively achieve what these special interests want. Federal politicians, moreover, with the indispensable help of the national treasury, never cease to angle for votes by promising many things and doing many things. The very nature of democracy is contributory to this end. Here are nationalizing forces, which at present are not easy to control in order to guarantee the complete integrity of the federal system.

Yet federalism in Canada has not suffered a final eclipse. It is not on the road to dissolution. Many of the provinces constitute immense territories with abundant resources, and already have grown into populous and prosperous communities which are destined to become more populous and more self-confident. They will increasingly require all the legislative and administrative powers that they now possess to achieve effective regional planning and development. Consequently their political leaders will be anxious to erect defences against the continued seepage of power and initiative to Ottawa. Much of the distinctiveness in Canada's nationality in the future must derive from the recognition of its cultural dualism, and the more this fact is appreciated the more sensitive will be the concern for federalism. In the meantime Quebec's devotion to the federal idea has served a national purpose; it has helped to lessen the danger of excessive centralization in Ottawa and the equal danger of a rigid framework advantageous to Ottawa. Rigid arrangements acceptable today may be intolerable tomorrow. Flexibility is prime condition for a healthy federalism, and paradoxically Quebec by its unbending position has been its guarantor.

29　What Does Quebec Want?—1967*

Daniel Johnson

Introduction

Our delegation is delighted to have this opportunity to set forth, before the representatives of the various governments gathered here, Québec's objectives regarding the constitution she desires for the Canada of tomorrow.

Nor can she fail to acknowledge the great merit redounding to her sister province for having undertaken, at a most appropriate moment, to convene this conference whose historic import we fully appreciate, and which historians will record as a decisive step in our country's development.

We have prepared this document especially for our English-speaking fellow-countrymen and we should like them to study it with the same equanimity as we sought to attain in preparing it. For we are here to open a dialogue and we take it for granted that this conference is only the first of many. For us, it represents the initial stage in an exchange of views, an exchange for which the pressing need is now apparent and whose scope will be unprecedented.

The many difficulties along our road cannot serve as an excuse for refusing the challenge confronting us. And, at the present juncture, we do not believe we are really in any position to do anything but accept it.

Statement of the Issue

If we are to determine as fittingly as possible what the "Confederation of Tomorrow" should be, we must first examine Canada as it is today.

An Imperilled Confederation

We are now living in a divided country searching for identity and racked by inner tensions.

Why is this so? Why, when a few short years ago most people did not have the slightest premonition of such a crisis, why are some of us now suddenly obliged to accept as a working hypothesis the hitherto unthinkable possibility of Canada's dissolution? What has taken place which can account for the astonishment in some circles, the dismay in others at such a development?

What has happened is that Québec, mainstay of French Canada, questioning the validity of the country's political structure, seeks a reallocation of powers

* From Government of Quebec. *Preliminary Statement by Mr. Daniel Johnson, Former Prime Minister: Confederation of Tomorrow Conference,* (Toronto, November, 1967). Reprinted by permission.

DANIEL JOHNSON — Former Prime Minister of the Province of Quebec.

between the two orders of government and concrete recognition for French Canada of rights equal to those always enjoyed by English-speaking Canada Such aspirations, expressed more forcefully and consistently than ever before, first surprised English-speaking Canada and then produced opposition to what seemed a threat to the established order. In fact, we have reached the point where quite a few French-speaking Canadians believe that persistent misunderstanding makes any statement of their aspirations to English-speaking citizens a waste of time. A considerable number among the latter, we realize, are satisfied with the present political system and hold that no concession should be made to the vague demands of what they believe to be a vociferous and extremist minority. Thus the two groups which a century ago established Canadian Confederation are becoming more firmly entrenched in their "two solitudes". More seriously still, these two solitudes are increasingly out of touch with each other's reality; in the end, lack of co-operation between them can destroy Canada.

Québec's representatives at this conference are in an excellent position to assess the present state of mind among French-speaking Canadians living in Québec and to foresee where it may lead if our country's two main cultural groups do not soon reach an understanding to rebuild Canada on new foundations.

A Century-old Experience

French Canadians assume that the 1867 confederative act was designed to let them develop in accordance with their own culture.

One hundred years ago, the Fathers of Confederation entrusted to the provinces both those spheres of activity which, at the time, seemed properly to depend on local initiative and those which seemed essential to protect language, religion and culture.

Today, after a century's experience, French Canadians have become aware of three things. First of all, whenever members of their community living in provinces other than Québec have sought to obtain rights equal to those enjoyed by English-speaking Canadians, the 1867 constitution has proved impotent. Of course neither English Canada's nor the French-Canadian nation's rights are expressly acknowledged in the constitution. Yet we might have expected French Canadians living outside Québec to have been treated with more understanding and greater broad-mindedness. Unfortunately this did not happen and numerical superiority was often used to withhold from French-language minorities basic community rights essential to their survival and development. They were even stripped of rights they already had. Eventually, French Canadians were, to all intents and purposes, reduced to feeling truly at home only within Québec's borders, even though, despite everything, some French-speaking groups continue to survive in all provinces, especially in certain areas of Ontario, the Atlantic Provinces and Manitoba.

The second thing French Canadians have noticed is that there has always been a clear tendency for the federal government to take over, partly or wholly, responsibilities assigned to the provinces in the 1867 constitution.

In Québecers' eyes, the constitutional or political justifications with which the central government has sought to explain its encroachments have often smacked of sophistry. Certainly no one would say that during the last twenty-five or thirty years the federal government has acted against its will. All it needed as an excuse for action was inaction by some provinces. Provincial governments wanting to act on their own behalf then had to follow suit or lose major financial advantages. The story of joint programmes is a good case in point.

And thirdly, French-speaking Canadians realize that the 1867 division of responsibilities between governments no longer permits the French-Canadian nation to develop as effectively as it desires. During these last hundred years, the economic, social and administrative roles assigned to the public sector have grown enormously. State activities have become vastly more complex, and are sure to become more so as time goes on. Citizens are now directly affected by government action on a host of matters for which local and private initiative were formerly responsible. French-speaking Canadians feel that several such new realms of government intervention are, like education in 1867, vital instruments for their collective self-expression. They now want to keep control over these fields because, in the long run, not merely their full development as a people but their very survival will depend on it.

An Inevitable Crisis

Quebecers have always known that if their enterprises are to attain success in Canada, they must exert themselves more than other Canadians, who have the dual advantage of numerical superiority and favouring Canadian economic and political institutions. But in addition, they now find their road to full self-achievement encumbered with fresh obstacles, including some which, under present conditions, seem more difficult to overcome than those they have met in the past. In general, during the last decade, not a minority but a majority of Quebecers have become aware that their situation is likely to grow worse if they do not act promptly to remedy it.

In sociological terms, Quebecers have witnessed the disintegration of the way of life which traditionally protected them. They had survived in good part because they lived in isolation, locked in upon themselves, clinging to the past in a typically rural environment where the state's presence was marginal. Almost overnight, they found themselves in an industrial society requiring massive intervention by the state, open to the whole of North America and exposed to the influence of foreign, especially American, culture, backed by such powerful means of communication as speedy transport, highways, cinema, radio and television.

In demographic terms, they have become aware that, even though they form some thirty per cent of Canada's population, they constitute a tiny group in comparison with the North American English-speaking community.

On the economic level, they have come to understand that the industrial society in which they were henceforth to live had not been created by them, but by others not sharing their cultural values. And also that, in a world where economic might confers enough *de facto* advantages to make *de jure* claims unnecessary, they were—not always through their own fault—seriously lacking in means for effective action.

In political matters, as we have already said, they have realized that Canada's structure itself worked to their disadvantage and that the 1867 constitution was far from giving them the protection they had traditionally anticipated.

Taking all this into account, it is incontrovertibly evident that our nation no longer has a choice. If it passively accepts the present situation, it will inevitably take the road to slow but sure assimilation into the great North-American mass.

Hence, it has become vital that it do everything in its power to correct the present situation.

As French-speaking Canadians, we have the unshakeable conviction that we form a viable community sharing one of the greatest cultures in the western world, speaking an international language and endowed with vast human potentialities. That is why, despite all difficulties, we are resolved to preserve our identity. But there is more than this. The very act of asserting ourselves as a nation will certainly help greatly in giving Canada the identity she needs to distinguish herself from her powerful neighbour to the south. Moreover, we are convinced that, in future, nations like ours will have a role to play out of all proportion to their demographic strength. In short, we are willing to gamble on our possibilities as a people and want to act accordingly. Several obstacles we now face as a nation can be overcome by our own efforts and by Québec Government action. But there are other aspects of this problem for which we alone cannot find a solution. We know that it can be solved if English Canada makes a serious effort. Up to a point, this community will have to alter its traditional approach to relations between our two linguistic groups. It will also have to abstain from opposition to substantial change in the country's political structure and in the present division of powers between the Canadian and Québec governments.

What we in Québec have become accustomed to call the Canadian constitutional problem is thus not wholly juridical in nature. We are dealing with a basically political and social problem, one of whose causes stems from the present constitution.

An Impotent Constitution

A country's constitution is its fundamental law. To some extent, it lays down the rules of the game. In doubtful cases, appeal should be had to it, and it should be interpreted by appropriate tribunals. Governments under its sway must conform to it. Therefore, it is essential that a constitution properly reflect sociological reality in the country to which it applies and truly derive from the aims and aspirations of the human communities making up that country.

Does the 1867 British North America Act, even as interpreted and amended since its passage, meet these requirements, which are certainly not unreasonable for so obviously important a document as a constitution? To ask the question is already to suggest the answer, which is a forthright negative. The 1867 constitution no longer in any sense conforms to present Canadian reality. We shall not undertake here any juridical analysis or study in semantics. We shall merely point out specific characteristics of today's Canada and her problems, then try to see how closely the present constitution does reflect these characteristics and whether it can contribute to solving new problems as they arise. The conclusions will be self-evident.

1) In Canada there exists a French-Canadian nation of which the mainstay is Québec. It can likewise be said that there exists an English-speaking nation, although its cohesion and self-awareness may, for understandable reasons, be less apparent than they are among French Canadians. Each of these two nations must have its fundamental right to full development recognized by the other, in law and in fact, if we want Canada to be able to operate as a political entity and advance as an economic entity. The most serious Canadian problem today is precisely that of the relation which should obtain between these two communities. Here the present constitution offers no guidance, since it wholly ignores this essential aspect of Canadian reality. Our constitution does not recognize the existence in our country of sociological groups called "nations", "nationalities" or "societies". Even though it refers to some individual religious rights and regulates the use of the English and French languages in a few federal and Québec public bodies it provides no specific rights for the communities which speak these languages.

2) Canada now comprises ten provinces, no one like any other in people, size, climate, problems or resources. Logically, it would not seem desirable to formulate policies conceived as though all the country's provinces had been cast in the same mold. Yet except for a few provisions of secondary importance—accidental or transitory—our constitution in principle now keeps all provinces on the same footing. It provides no opportunity for special federal-provincial arrangements adapted to conditions in a given province. In practice, these special arrangements can be effected but, whatever the intention may be, they cannot help appearing exceptional or temporary. In short, our constitution makes some allowance for special situations existing when a given province entered confederation; but, divorced from day-to-day reality, it does not allow for continuance and even intensification of differences between provinces once they became members of confederation.

3) Because of changes in the technical and social order, Canada today is faced with a whole series of problems which the Fathers of Confederation, however vivid their imagination, could not conceivably have foreseen. Consider, for instance, town-planning policy, regional development, economic stability, telecommunications, atomic energy, the space age, manpower policies, educational television and many other contemporary developments. Our constitution is silent on these matters. Therefore, when a new problem arises in Canada, we are more and more likely to base each government's responsibilities for it, not on constitutional principles, but on considerations of the moment which, in turn, derive from a variety of factors such as relative capacity to act, financial resources or merely the political power

wielded by a given area of government. Hence, even though there is a written document called the British North America Act from which we may expect some light to be cast on such traditional fields as education and municipal institutions, the allocation of new tasks among governments has not been guided by this document but by decisions mainly based on exigencies of the day. In some instances, the old constitution has been amended to furnish grounds for action that was predetermined in any case. In others, the method used was to imagine the opinions Fathers of Confederation would have held. Whether or not the provinces have participated in reaching such decisions, it is still true that our present constitution, perhaps admirable during the age of steam trains, no longer suits Canada's needs in this era of interplanetary rockets.

4) In addition, the modern world has stimulated more frequent and continuing relations between nations, groups and regions. This is as true at the Canadian as at the international level. Within Canada, developments in recent years have led governments to have increasing recourse to federal-provincial or interprovincial conferences to settle problems as they arose. Such meetings have become a necessity. It is hard to imagine how Canada could function efficiently today were not the representatives of the various governments to gather at more or less regular intervals to discuss among themselves policies to be followed. For the moment we do not intend to say how we believe these conferences should be prepared and managed; the fact remains that so essential a means for co-ordination and consultation is not even mentioned in the country's present constitution. Hence, intergovernmental meetings in Canada result far more from political, financial or administrative accidents than from rational and formal machinery for reciprocal consultation. In theory, nothing prevents their being eliminated at any time, even if such a turn of events is at present unlikely. It is also significant that a good many of these conferences are now made necessary by the ill-defined division of powers between the country's governments. So we are faced with a constitution which, over the years, has become vacuous whenever there is need to allocate public responsibilities whose very existence could not be foreseen in 1867, a constitution, moreover, including no clear provision or procedure for implementing the intergovernmental coordination often made necessary by its own omissions.

5) In international affairs, the situation created by the present constitution is equally confused. Practice established during the past half century, and not any constitutional text, gives the federal government responsibility for what we call foreign policy. Yet nowhere is this defined. Nor does the constitution say anything about the bonds of every kind which, more tightly and in increasing number, link modern nations in fields almost all of which it reserves to the provinces. As a result, efforts to resolve any differences which may arise today between governmental sectors over relations they may or may not have with foreign countries or organizations are based on more or less acrobatic interpretations of the constitution or of constitutional practice.

6) Nothing in our constitution clearly provides for settling such disagree-

ments, whether they relate to international relations, culture, manpower or the administration of justice. In several essential matters, there is not even provision in the constitution for amending it. Until now, every attempt to reach an acceptable amending formula has been based on an inaccurate interpretation of Canadian society.

To our minds, these few examples constitute sufficiently obvious evidence of the rift between our constitution and the reality to which it supposedly applies. If to this be added the fact that no clear-cut rule, still valid today, governs the sharing of tax resources among Canadian governments, the only straightforward conclusion to be drawn, in our view, is that our country's fundamental law not only has a superannuated look, but is in fact a compilation of various unrelated customs, conventions and juridical documents and no longer fits the needs of modern government for the aspirations of the French-Canadian nation.

Alarming Empiricism

Some people have claimed that the present constitution has been flexible enough to adjust to the changing conditions which marked the last few generations and that it did not prevent us from finding workable solutions to several federal-provincial problems in recent years. We feel that such arguments are invalid on two counts.

First, the constitution has never been instrumental in settling federal-provincial disagreements. When we did work out temporary or permanent compromises, especially for Québec, they came as a result of intergovernmental discussions which at times had every aspect of open warfare. Indeed, it was lack of an explicit constitution, complicated by basic political factors, that led to these clashes, costing both sides much wasted energy and creating misunderstandings which have yet to be cleared. Surely, in a country such as ours, there must be a better way of reaching an effective and lasting solution to difficulties attending allocation of responsibilities and distribution of the resources needed to carry them out. At any rate, we in Québec are probably most directly concerned and we do not see why negotiations between governments in Canada should always take place in such an atmosphere of conflict.

Second, the French-Canadian nation considers the present constitution no longer capable of providing the guarantees that should properly be expected from it. It is no secret that, even if our constitution is always subject to interpretation whenever new problems spring up, both the interpretation and resulting practical arrangements usually favour the government sector whose political position is stronger; at times, this may be the federal government, at others, the provincial governments. Nothing in Canada today indicates which way the scale will tip in future. In a country with a single society, such a situation would at worst create administrative complications or regional uneasiness; in ours, it spells a lasting threat to the French-Canadian community and, with time, creates unbearable conditions. French Canada is quite prepared to take up the awesome cultural challenge it faces on the North-

American continent, but cannot be reconciled to the prospect of fruitless struggles in its own country caused by its permanently unsettled situation.

Levelling criticism at a constitution because it is inexplicit or behind the times does not necessarily mean that the critic wants an inflexible replacement. We would readily agree that, however well drafted, a constitution cannot possibly contain answers to all problems.

True, constitutional problems seldom seem to take priority; but when they do, particularly in a federal system, political rather than legal implications become the issue. It seems to us that we are indeed going through one of those rare phases when, owing to their direct repercussion on the citizen's daily life, questions related to our country's constitution—therefore our political institutions—take precedence. We must tackle them at the earliest opportunity, lest conditions grow worse, and so that we may concentrate our efforts on the solution of other urgent problems.

The Canadian Duality

The two languages widely spoken in our land, English and French, are both international languages. Those who speak French live mostly in one part of Canada, Québec, where they constitute the great majority of the population.

Being the first Europeans to settle in this country, they are convinced that they form a nation in the sociological sense of the word. They have their own government, public and private economic, financial and administrative and cultural institutions. In short, they have a civilization of their own.

Because she also happens to be the home of an English-speaking society with a culture of its own, Canada is thus a binational country. Indeed, it is one or other of these two nations or cultural communities which has been joined by those of various origins whose arrival has enriched Canada since the beginning of the century.

In its relationship with the rest of the country, Québec, as the mainstay and homeland of French Canada, is confronted by two kinds of problems which are not easily differentiated because in practice they often overlap.

When we consider for instance highway construction, some financial arrangements between governments, sales tax collection, measures designed to reduce water pollution, there are a host of questions where all provinces, Québec included, meet on common ground.

But when we come to socio-cultural problems, Québec's position is altogether different from that of the other provinces. We have in mind not only education, culture and language, but also social security, health, municipal institutions, certain credit establishments, regional development, adult training, manpower policies, cultural exchanges with other countries or, to put it briefly, everything that may be used as an instrument for French-Canada's assertion and promotion of her economic, social and political institutions.

A New Covenant

What then must be done to pave the way for the Canada of tomorrow is to lay the foundation of a covenant without which we shall continue to live in confusion, victims of contradictions arising daily between our anachronistic constitution and Canadian reality.

The last half of this statement contains certain proposals in this respect for purposes of discussion.

The Canada of Tomorrow

If Canada of Tomorrow is to endure, it must rest on a new constitution that, as now, must group within the country a certain number of territories, which may be called provinces or states. More important however, it must also permit association by two societies co-operating within common institutions as well as respect for the basic collective rights and legitimate aspirations of each.

In the following paragraphs, rather than submit the draft of a new constitution in legal form, we shall elaborate briefly on issues which we feel should be the object of constitutional provisions. In each instance, we shall formulate opinions on which we would heartily welcome open discussion; we would like to know what English-speaking Canadians think of them, for what really matters—and such is the immediate purpose of our meeting— is that we get our heads together in order to examine the broad elements of the problem, without embarking on discussion of details. Besides, the Government of Québec will have to weigh the implications of positions taken by the Estates General of French Canada and study the report prepared by our Parliamentary Committee on the Constitution. Naturally, we are also awaiting the report of the Royal Commission on Bilingualism and Biculturalism.

We feel that the new constitution should be aimed at four goals:

(1) defining clearly the principles that are to guide Canadian political life;

(2) working out a new distribution of powers and resources to promote development of the French-Canadian nation and free evolution of English-speaking Canada;

(3) institutionalizing or establishing certain machinery for intergovernmental consultation, co-ordination and action;

(4) modifying the operation of some Canadian organizations and institutions, modernizing others and creating new ones so that, as a whole, they may reflect Canada's binational identity.

Fundamental Principles

A constitution is much more than a legal document; it is a guide and a source of inspiration. Objectives shared by all citizens must be embodied in the fundamental principles on which it rests as well as the ties which bind together nations, communities, groups and individuals of different language, history and culture.

With these considerations in mind, we believe that the constitution should begin by proclaiming Canada's absolute sovereignty.

The constitution should also acknowledge the existence in Canada of two nations, bound together by history, each enjoying equal collective rights. The new constitution must clearly spell out the principle that English and French are the country's two official languages.

The constitution must include a charter of human rights applying to the central government's constitutional jurisdictions. As for us, the Québec Government intends to insert in Québec's constitution a charter of human rights covering matters under provincial control.

Finally, a provision must sanction the principle of economic interdependence, mutual support and co-operation between states or provinces with every regard for the country's binational character.

As for Québec's internal constitution, it must naturally fall under its own exclusive jurisdiction.

Distribution of Powers

The division of powers between central government and member-states remains the keystone of any federal constitution. To make headway, we submit certain proposals.

We believe that, as is the case in most federations, provinces or member-states of Canada must retain all powers not expressly granted to the central government. In this way, we should have a better idea where the latter's jurisdiction begins or ends, and friction caused by encroachment from the centre would be greatly reduced.

Needless to say, we want to have reserve and disallowance powers eliminated from federal prerogatives and the Parliament of Canada divested of its declaratory power. Perhaps these provisions had some justification in earlier days, but we think that today, in matters within their jurisdiction, the provinces must be given complete internal sovereignty.

Other Québec positions have already been made known. Thus, in the brief submitted in September 1966 to the fourth meeting of the federal-provincial Tax Structure Committee, we stated: "As the mainstay of a nation, it wants free rein to make its own decisions affecting the growth of its citizens as human beings (i.e., education, social security and health in all respects), their economic development (i.e., the forging of any economic and financial tool deemed necessary), their cultural fulfilment (which takes in not only arts and literature, but the French language as well), and the presence abroad of the Québec community (i.e., relations with certain countries and international organizations)."

Further in the brief, we stated that, while awaiting a new constitution, we would first have to proceed with a re-arrangement of functions, which might even be initiated within the framework of our present constitution: "By this process, the Québec Government would gradually become solely responsible within its territory for all public expenditures on every form of education, old age security, family allowances, health, employment and training of the labour force, regional development and, in particular, municipal aid programmes, research, fine arts, culture, as well as any other social or cultural service within our jurisdiction under the present constitution. Existing federal programmes in these fields would be taken over by Québec, which would maintain their portability where applicable."

It is not our place to tell the other provinces how powers in the Confederation of Tomorrow should be divided between them and the federal government. We merely wish to make a few comments which may be pertinent.

We have just outlined the Québec Government's general objective. To reach it, Québec will necessarily have to obtain a new constitutional distribution of tasks giving her broader powers than she now exercises. We feel these broader powers are vital to Québec, but this does not mean that we in any way object to the other provinces seeking exactly the same powers if they so desire.

If in fact they are willing to assume the same tasks as Québec, it is quite conceivable to envisage a new constitution which would confirm much greater decentralization of powers to all provinces than now exists.

Naturally, we realize that other provinces may be prepared to entrust the central government with some powers which Québec believes she must herself exercise. In our view, such an arrangement is not incompatible with federalism and solutions of this kind should be used without hesitation whenever sociological conditions in the country make them necessary. In this case, all provinces would at the outset, be granted identical constitutional powers, provided that constitutional provision would make possible administrative or legislative delegation to the federal government. This way, the provinces themselves would decide the actual extent of their responsibilities under the new system.

Not wanting to prejudge their attitude on this matter, we thought it might be helpful to open the dialogue by stating some of our own positions, for later comparison with theirs.

Intergovernmental Co-operation

If it is important to establish clearly the responsibilities of each area of government, it is equally essential to indicate here the methods of co-operation which should exist between each. The modern world no longer tolerates impassable barriers between governments, any more than it permits attributing any particular problem to a single cause. Québec is fully aware of this fact; she feels she must increase her jurisdictional range in the Canada of Tomorrow, not in order to isolate herself, but rather to be in a better position to bring her own contribution to collective wealth through interdependence. Each government must be concerned with the impact of its actions on other governments.

Thus, even though the federal government has jurisdiction over currency, it must always reckon with the fact that monetary policy has concrete repercussions on other governments' action. Similarly, nobody will deny the provinces' exclusive responsibility for municipal affairs, but does this mean that their activities in this field have no effect on decisions required of the federal government in others? Not at all. And certainly the influence which provinces exert on one another is often apparent, even if each merely acts within the limits of its own jurisdiction.

As far as we are concerned, we prefer to establish a clear division between governmental responsibilities, then provide machinery for intergovernmental co-operation.

Above all, it is our feeling that we should institutionalize federal-provincial and interprovincial conferences. Of course, the constitution could not fix the frequency or agendas of such meetings. That would be unrealistic. It would probably be sufficient to stipulate the right of any government to take the initiative for convening such conferences.

Similarly, we should provide for the existence of well defined machinery for intergovernmental consultation and co-operation on economic policy. Here again, it would not be necessary to enter into details, but merely to express juridically the practical consequences of our incontestable economic interdependence. Economic policies in Canada cannot and must not depend exclusively on one government, in this instance federal. The provinces have and will continue to have a major interest in this field. There can be no question of excluding them from formulating and implementing various economic policies, particularly fiscal policies, if only because of the size of their own budgets and their influence on the economy. In any case, Québec cannot agree to stay out of the economic policy field, for that would be tantamount to allowing another government to decide the course of her whole economy.

Fiscal matters, and more specifically fiscal arrangements are not on the agenda of this conference, in accordance with the wishes of the Ontario Government which convened it. It is obvious that in the context of a new constitution to exclusive jurisdictions must correspond exclusive or paramount fiscal powers.

Further, in order to ensure the right of each citizen to comparable services, wherever he may live in Canada, the mechanisms of fiscal arrangements should be improved and, if necessary, institutionalized.

It is also our impression that we would have everything to gain by setting up a permanent interprovincial secretariat which, among other functions, would help keep provincial governments better informed on one another's legislation, administrative reforms, problems as well as the solutions adopted, policies and other matters. In addition, such a secretariat would permit more thorough preparation for interprovincial meetings of cabinet ministers and civil servants.

Canadian Institutions

Whatever their immediate functions, it seems essential to us that federal institutions in the Canada of Tomorrow take clear count, in their structure and aims, of the country's binational character. We want to express a few thoughts on the subject, in spite of the fact that this meeting is not a federal-provincial conference.

Steps should first be taken, by required means, to ensure genuine, effective and proportionate participation in the federal public service by French-speaking Canadians. There have been recent improvements in this respect, but this movement should be stepped up; above all, definite mechanisms should be provided to translate it rapidly into fact. In addition, it is vital that French become a current working language within all administrative services directly or indirectly dependent on the federal government, both in Ottawa and in areas with a French-language population. The same should be done in the Armed Forces.

We also think the federal capital should reflect the linguistic duality of the population. Equality of the two official languages should be confirmed in all capital area government services, be they federal, provincial or municipal. To this end, the purely federal "National Capital Commission" should become a tripartite "Federal Capital Commission" in which the three governments most directly concerned, those of Canada, Ontario and Québec, would have equal prerogatives, each delegating to it the powers needed to administer an appropriate territorial area and assuming a proportionate share of its operating costs.

We further think it advisable to create a genuine constitutional tribunal whose composition would reflect the federal character of our institutions and the Canadian cultural duality.

We believe, also, that it would be advantageous to investigate the possibility of transforming the current Senate into a true federal House having a bicultural character.

Finally, we believe that establishment of a permanent federal-provincial commission on linguistic rights would do a good deal to ensure the recognition, in practice, by all governments concerned, of the equal rights of our two communities in this respect. Citizens and corporate bodies who felt their linguistic rights had been prejudiced would be entitled to lodge grievances or complaints with the commission. This advisory institution should in no way limit the competence of the constitutional tribunal with respect to language rights.

Of course, there are many things we might add concerning changes we think necessary in other Canadian institutions, such as the Canadian Broadcasting Corporation, the National Film Board, etc.

The Language Question and French-Canadian Minorities

In concluding, it is important to draw very special attention to one of the major Canadian problems of the day: the status of French in Canada. We have already touched several times on this question, which we consider basic.

The Québec Government is committed to making French a true national language in Québec, while respecting the linguistic rights of the minority. We are currently studying various means of promoting generalized use of French throughout our territory, so that French-Canadian Quebecers in their home province may live and work in their mother tongue, just as English-speaking Canadians live and work in their own language in the other provinces.

But this will not solve the whole problem. Essentially, what French Canadians want is to be themselves and develop normally like any other people; in Québec and in other parts of Canada. More particularly, they want to create in Québec an environment conducive to their own growth. They also want it to be possible for members of their community settled in other provinces to develop as English-speaking Canadians can do in Québec.

In a country like ours, we must begin by ensuring public education at all levels in Canada's two official languages wherever the English or French-speaking group is sufficiently large. Obviously, this does not rule out the necessity of providing the French or English-speaking groups with means of acquiring good command of the majority language in their environment. As for other government services such as departments, courts, administrative bodies, we believe the best way to avoid problems and render justice to the greatest number of people concerned is to deal with the question on a regional basis, without regard to provincial boundaries.

We expect to continue the dialogue initiated here at subsequent meetings.

30   What Does Quebec Want?—1970*

Robert Bourassa

This is the first time since its election to office that the new Government of Québec is broaching the constitutional question at a federal-provincial meeting. Even if this meeting is, in fact, a working session on very specific matters, we felt it was not out of order in this statement to indicate the attitude our government intends to adopt regarding constitutional revision.

I CONSTITUTIONAL REVISION

Discussions concerning constitutional revision have now been held for nearly three years. Since the "Confederation of Tomorrow" Conference held at Toronto in November 1967, and the first Conference in February, 1968, meetings and committees have multiplied. By now considerable work has been done, but if we consider the magnitude of the task to be done we must admit that concrete results still remain rather modest.

* From Government of Quebec, *Statement by Mr. Robert Bourassa, Prime Minister and Minister of Finance: Constitutional Conference, Ottawa, September 14 and 15, 1970.* Reprinted by permission of the Honourable Robert Bourassa.

ROBERT BOURASSA – Prime Minister of the Province of Quebec.

Special attention has been paid to problems concerning official languages. A new review has been undertaken of the overall fiscal and economic relations between the two orders of government; from it we can hope for the birth of a new economic federalism, better adapted to the realities of our times, and more likely to lead to a better allocation of wealth among the members of the federation.

At the conference of finance ministers in Winnipeg, last June, I maintained that improved fiscal and economic relations between the governments were a prerequisite to constitutional reform since it would make it possible for us to create that atmosphere of relaxation and understanding which is essential for the success of our discussions on constitutional structures.

The improvement in the present mechanisms ensuring economic coordination and wealth redistribution is part and parcel of the process of constitutional reform. In fashioning effective means of fighting regional inequalities, we shall give federalism a positive meaning. The same applies to the means which will allow us to influence economic conditions. This is why our government wishes to attach major importance to the immediate establishment of a true economic federalism. In this connection we have, among other things, suggested the idea of a stabilization fund which would complement the action of the present mechanisms ensuring economic coordination and regionalization of federal fiscal policies.

I stress the importance we attach to improving the present machinery, especially in the economic and fiscal areas. Yet, such an improvement would not be enough if it did not lead to a reform in depth of our constitutional structures.

II OBJECTIVES

Constitutional revision is forcing us to discover and invent new ways and means of doing things, capable of meeting the dual requirement of our federal system: respect for the two founding communities and balance of powers when dealing with the great pursuits of tomorrow.

Québec's identity

We want an invigorating federalism, one that decentralizes, one that places confidence in the governments that it joins together. We believe that between secession's easy-sounding truths and the pure and simple abandonment of our responsibilities to another government, the federative formula is the best one. To be sure, this is conditional on a strict respect for the special characteristics of our culture and the aspirations of the Québec community. This requires, therefore, a flexible federalism, which will express our true freedom as Quebecers within the structures of a dynamic participation in the great plans involving Canada as a whole. We consider that such an option is to be preferred to the constraints which might well be the consequence of a political sovereignty severed from the realities of our times.

Our choice is made. But at the same time, it forces us to prove our case that it is the best suited to ensure the most favorable conditions of existence for the citizens we have the honour to serve. Not only the economic but also the social and cultural conditions of their existence.

I have confidence that the new federalism which will arise from our discussions will stimulate the flowering of our individual as well as our collective freedoms. Freedom of association, of participation, of voluntary delegation of powers, indeed, but also freedom to withdraw, not to commit ourselves when we deem that any given jurisdiction can be exercised in a better way, with more efficiency and greater coherence, by this or that order of government.

Should anyone insist upon putting a tag on the attitude our government will take for as long as it retains the mandate of managing Québec affairs, I would say that it will be a sober one, a firm one and one free of bias. We do not want to become the prisoners of slogans and miracle formulas, shortcuts which are sometimes alluring but which prevent a fair appraisal of concrete situations.

Our only guide will be the highest interest of the citizens who expect from us something other than endless palavers and perpetual studies. With a view to maintain and develop our identity, whenever the calm examination of a particular problem reveals that citizens will best be served by such or such an order of government, here will be our stand, a stand we shall defend without electioneering concern and without ulterior motives.

I can already appraise all the efforts that we will have to make towards reassessing the situation during the coming months. For it is obvious that the present structures of the Canadian federation are ill-suited to our requirements.

We will therefore have to conscript our energies in record time in order to arrive quickly at concrete solutions. We are given another chance to change some of the particularly antiquated and inoperative aspects of the type of federalism we now have. But our Québec fellow-citizens will not tolerate any longer either the excessive slowness of the revision procedure of our constitution, or the lingering chaos which stems from it.

Our government will adhere less to the symbolic value of words than to the substance of problems and their rational definition. We shall not claim additional powers for the simple pleasure of winning a battle or extort a concession from the central government, for this would be engaging in a political childishness poorly consistent with the interests it is our mandate to protect.

However, we expect from those with whom we deal enough political mautrity to appreciate what the stakes are in this federal challenge we put before our fellow-citizens on the occasion of the April 29 [1970] election. A challenge whose one of the elements is the necessity to have the participation of the Québec government in the process of decisions of the central government which have a significant impact on the economic, social and cultural development of Québec.

It is from this general point of view that the present Québec Government is approaching the task of constitutional revision. Against an illusory sovereignty, it proposes instead a full freedom of action within federal structures respectful of the distinctive character of Québec, its particular cultural traits but also its great need of catching up in the economic area.

The new federal contract, therefore, must satisfy these pressing requirements.

Indeed, this is the best way to attain one of the fundamental goals of the Canada of tomorrow: the preservation and development of the bicultural character of the Canadian federation.

When we talk about biculturalism, we are forced to acknowledge that, without Québec, there would be no French fact in Canada. For it is in Québec that we find the roots of this reality. Consequently, if we want Canada to maintain this bicultural character, we must make sure that Québec is in a position to ensure that conditions will favor the flowering of French fact. It will succeed in this by a maximum use of the jurisdiction it already has as well as by the exercise of certain powers which will increase the effectiveness and radiance of its linguistic and cultural personality.

In addition, it is also undeniable that all Quebecers want to organize their participation in social life and the improvement of their environment first of all within the framework of institutions conceived by them and in which they participate fully. Quebecers are holding on firmly to the possibility of expressing themselves collectively through public structures, hence a government, they control fully; they will never agree to give this up.

The constitutional policy of our government will therefore hold to the premise that Quebecers require and want, on the one hand, to manage their own government in order to be allowed to develop their own cultural entity, where the whole of Québec is involved, and on the other hand, to participate, where the whole of Canada is involved, in a prosperous bicultural federation, capable of managing its own affairs and ensuring a minimum of equality between its citizens and regions while making a contribution to the progress of the international community.

Some basic attitudes will guide the people of Québec in the years to come just as they have already begun to influence the people of today. They will insist on attaining greater participation in decisions likely to affect them. Much more than in the past, they will also be concerned with the quality of their environment and of their social life. Finally, they will attach greater and greater importance to everything connected with the equality of the country's citizens and regions. In my opinion, it will be to the extent that the Canadian federative formula will permit them to answer the questions of participation, of the quality of the human condition, and of equality, that Quebecers will be able, while affirming their own identity, to contribute to the life and growth of the country as a whole.

Yet, achieving each of these objectives which everybody is willing to accept without questioning them, I am sure, will have a powerful impact on the constitutional framework and the division of responsibilities between the two orders of government. I shall here limit myself to the major aspects.

Economic policy

In the economic field, the action of the central government, often very tech-nical in nature, and sometimes carried out in circumstances where decisions have to be taken rapidly, has specific effects which can be very diverse on the economic structure of one part of the country.

It must be stressed here how direct the influence of certain decisions concerning monetary policy, fiscal policy, or trade policy, including customs duties, can be on the economic activity of our regions. The interest of the federation as a whole requires us to search at once for flexible ways and means to participate in the formulation of policies regarding these matters. Already, information and basic data are more readily available than they were in the past. But it must be clearly understood that for our part, we shall have to continue our efforts of research and analysis in order to have complete files at our disposal. This should not be interpreted as an attempt to make it difficult to reach decisions. On the contrary, only when we shall clearly know those aspects of economic reality which deeply influence our development, even if they constitute fields outside our administrative competence, shall we be in a position to contribute to consultation effectively.

No one should be astonished if we insist more and more, on the basis of definite facts and concrete propositions, upon a better coordination of federal decisions. In this way, sterile discussions and useless suspicions will be avoided once policies have been announced.

Social Policy

The qualitative aspects of the physical environment and social life will also influence the division of tasks between governments. How shall we define their action in planning human resources, in solving urban problems, in adding to the value and worth of leisure, so that provinces can play in these areas the predominant rôle which is theirs. This is especially important in Québec where the social environment should mirror the cultural dimension which represent the fundamental distinctive trait of our federation.

Changes occuring in the Québec environment will depend in a large measure on the social policies we shall apply. We know the latter are necessarily made up of interrelated and varied initiatives whose complexities are bound to inten-sify, whether they involve income support programs, social services, manpower training and employment, health services, including health insurance, youth, and housing. This obvious interrelation is not presently adhered to; two gov-ernment sectors are active in these areas of jurisdiction, and there is no guarantee, in spite of all efforts to achieve coordination, that what one is doing will not impede what the other is doing.

It will be enough, as an example, to make specific reference to health and social services, as well as income security.

No one would dare deny that policies in matters of health services and social services come primarily under the jurisdiction of the provinces. Never-theless, in actual fact, the federal government has always set priorities and fixed available resources through the means of rigid financial programs. Whether such restrictive financing procedures such as conditional grants are involved (hospital insurance, health insurance, the Canada Assistance Plan), or more flexible mechanisms such as the setting up of assistance funds (health resources fund, demonstration projects fund) they have none the less the same fundamental drawbacks.

As for income security, we deem it essential that the provinces be given a predominant position in the formation of programs if they are indeed to be cohesive and take into account manpower policies and regional characteristics of the economy. Indeed, an income security policy could not be drawn up without regard to the objectives of social and manpower services.

If we claim for Québec priority in responsibility for working out policies in matters of health, social services, income security and manpower, we nevertheless acknowledge the essential rôle played by the federal government in providing acceptable living standard for all Canadians. This is why, in the field of income security, we would be willing to study a formula whereby the financial participation of the federal government would be determined for each province on the basis of social indicators reflecting adequately regional inequalities. Such a participation could, for instance, take the form of supplementary payments to equalization and of benefits paid under programs which the government of Canada would continue to administer. Other formulas for the federal financial participation could also be studied. All we wish, is to make sure that all possible avenues are explored.

The administration of income security programs is too closely linked to empirical methods, in our opinion, to be the criteria for determining the jurisdiction of one order of government in one field of activity or another. Such administration could be entrusted to the federal government, or to provincial governments, according to whether the programs defined by each of the provinces are of a type better suited to a centralized administration or, on the contrary, require a decentralized management, or again whether they differ too widely from those current in other provinces as to their objectives and methods. The important thing is that in the case of programs administered by the federal government, they be compatible with income securiy policies laid down by the provinces and that a satisfactory link be established with the services.

We believe that revising the Canadian constitution should make it possible to use an entirely new approach in the field of social policies. Just as the magnitude and origin of social inequalities differ, so should the stategy used in the fight against these same inequalities vary from one province to another. From these objectives and this strategy will emerge the priorities, the content and the methods most appropriate to the programs.

Equality

An equitable distribution of collective wealth between citizens and regions of Canada has always been one of the implicit objectives of our federation.

We must admit, however, that we are a long way from having reached that objective. It can even be said that in 1867 there was greater economic equality between the four founding provinces than is the case now. It is therefore necessary to take a resolute stand so that the economic growth of the country may achieve a better balance. This implies that the search for equality, or if one prefers, the lessening of inequalities, will be one of the clearly mentioned objectives in the new Canadian constitution, and that powers will be distributed between governments in such a manner that this objective can be achieved.

Cultural life

I am also thinking about certain important sectors of our national life in which methods of close participation between the central government and the members of the federation will have to be defined. They involve communications, immigration and external relations.

Québec wishes to play a part in the formulation of public policies in these areas because they directly affect the existence and the future of its society.

Where communications media are concerned, satellites, television, radio, whether by air waves or cables, it would be illogical for our government to remain aloof from activities involving these powerful instruments of information, teaching and popular education. Thus, we are willing to consider any formula of effective participation in the working out and definition of government communications policies. This is required not only because of our specific cultural needs, but because of the very nature of federalism whose primary function is to feature the prevailing traits of the communities that it associates. In this respect, we believe we are in a position to make a highly valuable contribution, simply due to the fact that our government, at its own level, is perforce the interpreter closest to Québec's socio-cultural realities.

As for immigration, the federal government would gain by making sure it has the participation of the members of the federation, in a better position to know about their requirements concerning manpower and the type of immigrants they wish to accept. Québec will have concrete propositions concerning this.

There is also no doubt that Quebecers will wish, among other objectives, to keep an open window on the outside world and benefit from a coming together of the nations. In many cases, the Canadian contribution entails matters concerning which the members of our federation, because of their present or future constitutional powers, are or will be the only ones having the know-how and technical skills. This is why it will be necessary to adjust our means of operation through which the Canadian and Québec contribution to international progress becomes the result of the common efforts of our governments.

III QUESTIONS UNDER STUDY

The new Québec government believes it is fitting it should give its opinion concerning the progress achieved in revising the constitution since it was undertaken nearly three years ago.

1. The working document of officials

Québec representatives on the Continuing Committee of Officials on the Constitution tabled, more than two years ago, a working document which was subsequently made public and has been used as a general frame of reference concerning Québec's position in constitutional matters. Even if this working document was never designed to represent the official position of Québec, it has received a certain amount of publicity and it is necessary to define more accurately the position of the new Québec government with regard to it.

A few remarks on certain specific aspects of this working document are called for. In its opening pages, propositions are found concerning the monarchy, parliamentary government, the official name of the federation, the existence of the two nations and the right to self-determination, which have provoked a flow of comments and proved highly controversial. The present Québec Government would like all its partners to make a thorough study of each of these propositions, but it wants to emphasize that it is not interested in starting a quarrel around words or symbols. What does interest us is the substance of the constitution and the possibility of arriving at a better distribution of powers and resources. To be sure, we wish that on these different matters there may develop in Canada a consensus which would agree with that prevailing in Québec; that would be a remarkable achievement towards a new definition of the Canadian identity. But we do not believe this should be a prerequisite to a study in depth of all aspects of the constitution; at any rate, we can come back to this when discussion on essential points has made greater progress.

As for the distribution of powers suggested in the working document, it must first of all be emphasized that even though it is very detailed, it remains incomplete; for instance, such important matters as the criminal code, unemployment insurance, fisheries and interprovincial trade are not dealt with. In addition, not enough attention, it seems, has been paid to certain problems concerning the future such as the quality of the environment, research and communications. In that respect, it will be necessary, therefore, to complement the propositions already made. This necessary updating process is now underway and in certain cases more explicit proposals will soon be drawn up.

I should now like to explain the stand of our government concerning discussions already held at the level of the Prime Ministers or ministerial committees. In doing so, I have no wish to criticize or endorse the arguments used by our predecessors: I simply want to set the record straight on a few points dealt with at prior conferences and meetings.

2. Spending power

The federal proposals regarding the spending power were examined at the working sessions of June 1969 and at the third Constitutional Conference.

First of all, they propose to subject the federal power to make conditional grants to the prior consent of a certain number of provinces. Québec continues to believe that ideally, this federal spending power in fields under the exclusive competence of the provinces simply should not exist and that the federal government would do well to simply give it up. Nevertheless, Québec would be ready to accept the federal proposals provided that the form of compensation for non-participating provinces be improved in such a way that these provinces are not really affected in exercising their constitutional right of non-participation.

3. The Taxing Powers

The principle that both orders of government have access to all taxation fields seems to us clearly admitted. This is a major improvement compared to the present situation. Certain exceptions, such as customs duties reserved to the federal parliament and property taxes reserved to the provinces also seem to us to be rightfully established. Broadly speaking, we might say that the only major point of discussion concerns succession duties: whereas Québec argues that it is practically impossible for a federal act on succession duties to respect at the same time both civil and common law institutions, the federal government maintains that it is technically possible. Québec would be ready to revise its stand on the matter if, before the end of the constitutional discussions, the federal government were to succeed in amending its present law on succession duties in such a way as to make it conform to the spirit of our civil law.

We must not forget, however, that it remains to translate these principles into reality. Taxation questions soon become very technical, with their own, often forbidding, language. Constitutional principles will not slove the whole question. Access to several revenue sources will not automatically settle the fiscal problem as a whole. Indeed, fiscal decisions have their effect on economic development. It is not enough to have the power to tax if the economic circumstances of the moment are such that it is preferable not to do so. Access to all taxation fields does not solve the thorny question of the relative place of each order of government within the whole tax base. For, we can only achieve a workable equilibrium if, within the framework of general principle, we can ensure the necessary flexibility so that each order of government may find in the exercise of its fiscal powers the receipts it needs and this, without disturbing the overall economic growth or the sectional equilibrium of the economy.

4. Regional inequalities

Nobody doubts that the fight against regional inequalities is urgent; it is one of the objectives of federalism and I have already made reference to it. On this subject, the work of constitutional revision seems fairly advanced. We are in agreement with the trends that have started to emerge. As I have said previously, it is clear that this question should be given special mention in the text of the country's constitution. It remains to be determined if such mention should be part of the preamble of the constitution or be a separate article in it. Since these questions are presently being examined by our government officials, we can revert to them later.

5. Income security and social services

At the third Constitutional Conference the question of social policy was brought up or, more specifically, the question of income security and social services. This was the first public discussion of a complicated question on which it was known that initial positions would be highly divergent. It is therefore not surprising that agreement could not be reached on every aspect of this problem. As far as our government is concerned, it, at present, sees no serious reason to change the position held until now by Québec. Moreover, we expect to give effect to the resolution of the last Constitutional Conference urging that the ministers responsible for problems concerning manpower should meet in order to examine in depth the allocation of tasks in this field.

As I said elsewhere in this statement, social policy is for us a matter of capital importance to which we give priority.

6. The official languages

The new Québec Government has had occasion to make known its position on the non-constitutional aspects of this question at the meeting of the Ministerial Committee on the Official Languages held in May 1970. I shall recall here that our government attaches great importance to the use of French as the working language in Québec, to its official use in federal public agencies and to its use as the language of instruction for French minorities in the other provinces.

7. Fundamental rights

The present Québec Government is favorable to the adoption of a constitutional charter of human rights which would be binding on both the federal government and the provinces. In our opinion, such a charter would not prevent the adoption of supplementary charters at the federal or provincial level particularly on such matters as rights to equality or economic rights where administrative action is often necessary. As has already been agreed, the adoption of such a charter should in no way alter the distribution of constitutional powers between governments.

8. The Judiciary

Québec has proposed to the Ministerial Committee on the Judiciary that the court of last resort be so constituted as to give every guarantee of impartial arbitration between governments, that jurisdiction of last resort in provincial matters should remain at the provincial court level, and that the judges of these courts be appointed by each province. Our government believes that these proposals should continue to be discussed with a view to their eventual inclusion in the text of the new constitution. At the same time, it wishes to reiterate the importance it attaches to the creation of a court of last resort in constitutional matters. Although the practical difficulty of establishing what constitutes a constitutional matter has been stressed, Québec believes that such a court is an essential element in maintaining the new constitutional equilibrium.

IV IMPENDING WORK

The discussion on the constitution ought to be carried on speedily. Above all, it should be brought to a prompt conclusion.

We should be looking for a constitutional framework better suited to solve our present problems and more in harmony with our individual and collective aspirations. In order to attain it, we shall have to enter a phase of intensive discussions, where will emerge consensus and solutions. I am therefore most happy that the present working session is tackling, for the first time, two new subjects of major importance: management of the environment and financial institutions.

With regard to impending work, I would like to make three suggestions.

(1) Firstly, I believe we must continue in depth discussions concerning the distribution of powers which is, in fact, a fundamental question. In this connection, it would be appropriate to give particular attention to the implications deriving from the necessary respect for the distinctive character of Québec and from the demands for participation, for the creation of a social environment suited to our aspirations and for the fight against inequality— questions I have dealt with in the second part of this statement.

(2) Within the range of discussions pertaining to a new distribution of legislative competences, I further suggest that we examine most attentively the possibility of including in the revised consitution a clause to allow delegation of legislative powers between the two orders of government. The delegation of legislative powers offers several advantages. It introduces an element of flexibility in a distribution of powers which are often too rigid. It allows for correction of any judicial interpretation which does not respect the spirit of the constitution. It makes possible the elaboration of programs on a regional basis. In addition, the delegation of powers is in conformity with the flexibility of federalism, since it sets up varying degrees of centralization or decentralization in the relations of the central government with the members of the federation. This provision, moreover, exists in other federal constitutions.

(3) Finally, it seems to me that it would be essential to give greater attention to the problem of intergovernmental relations. This is a pressing problem, particularly in the fiscal and economic fields. I already suggested at Winnipeg that instructions be given to the Continuing Committee of Officials on Economic and Fiscal Matters to analyse the present machinery of inter-governmental cooperation in the light of studies so far conducted on the

subject. This suggestion met with the approval of most of the delegations. Thus, here again, it would be easy to speed up discussions.

CONCLUSION

The new government of Québec intends to make a dynamic contribution to constitutional revision, and this in the respect for its present constitutional powers and through its will to share in the policies of Canada as a whole. At one and the same time, it will make a double contribution by the enrichment of the Québec personality, which it seeks faithfully to mirror, and by the effectiveness of its initiatives at the Canadian level.

Finally, our government sees in constitutional revision an unparalleled opportunity and, taking into account the circumstances which prevail in Québec, perhaps the last opportunity to build a country that will match the aspirations of Canadians.

A country where citizens and governments will, in complete good faith and without reservations, work together in the pursuit of the aims which I took the liberty to outline briefly in the present statement and which seem to me to correspond to the highest interests of Québec and of Canada. (translated from french)

31   Grid of the Distribution of Powers*

Government of Quebec

*Reprinted by permission of the Government of Quebec. This paper has been prepared from Quebec's Working Paper dealing with the proposed Constitutional revision submitted to the Secretariat of the Constitutional Conference on July 17, 1968 and subsequently made public. The diagram that follows is a presentation of Quebec's proposal.

PROPOSAL FOR THE DIVISION OF POWERS BETWEEN FEDERAL AND PROVINCIAL GOVERNMENTS OF CANADA

Quebec's Provisional Proposals

SUBJECT	EXCLUSIVE FEDERAL JURISDICTION	EXCLUSIVE PROVINCIAL JURISDICTION	JOINT JURISDICTION	COMPULSORY CONSULTATION INTER-PROV. AND/OR FED.-PROV.	PRIORITY OR DECIDING JURISDICTION	JURISDICTION LIMITATIONS	REMAINING POWERS
Establishment of new Canadian Constitution			Issued in Canada without recourse to London				
Fundamental Principles of the Constitution			Unanimity				
Internal Federal Constitution	Exclusive Federal Jurisdiction					Canadian Constitutional Charter of Fundamental Rights and Principles	
Internal Provincial Constitution		Exclusive Provincial Jurisdiction				As above	
Private Civil Rights (general)		Exclusive Provincial Jurisdiction				Charter of Fundamental Rights	
Private Rights Commercial (general)	See also Nos. 29 and 30	General Provincial					
Public Administrative Rights (general)	Exclusive Federal for its public and para-public institutions	Exclusive Provincial for its public and para-public institutions					
Public Criminal Rights (general)	To be determined	To be determined				Charter of Fundamental Rights	

SUBJECT	EXCLUSIVE FEDERAL JURISDICTION	EXCLUSIVE PROVINCIAL JURISDICTION	JOINT JURISDICTION	COMPULSORY CONSULTATION INTER-PROV. AND/OR FED.-PROV.	PRIORITY OR DECIDING JURISDICTION	JURISDICTION LIMITATIONS	REMAINING POWERS
Municipal Rights (general)		Exclusive Provincial					
Working Rights (general)	Special Federal in Federal undertakings	General Provincial					
Administration of Justice	Federal in implementing its own laws and regulations	General Provincial in implementing both Fed. and Prov. laws				Charter of Fundamental Rights	
Judiciary system	Special Judiciary system to implement Fed. laws and regulations	Judiciary system to implement Prov. and Fed. laws				Charter of Fundamental Rights	
Constitutional Court			Joint	Compulsory consultation		Constitutional Court set by Constitution itself	
Fiscal	Tariffs	Tax and succession rights	Joint	Compulsory consultation			
Defence and armed forces	General Federal						
Internal security		General Provincial	Joint in certain cases (war, insurrection)	Compulsory consultation		Charter of Fundamental Rights	
Foreign Policy	General Federal						

SUBJECT	EXCLUSIVE FEDERAL JURISDICTION	EXCLUSIVE PROVINCIAL JURISDICTION	JOINT JURISDICTION	COMPULSORY CONSULTATION INTER-PROV. AND/OR FED.-PROV.	PRIORITY OR DECIDING JURISDICTION	JURISDICTION LIMITATIONS	REMAINING POWERS
International relations	General Federal	General Provincial in provincial jurisdictional areas		Compulsory consultation			
Banking system	Federal						
International trade	Federal						
Weights and Measures	Federal						
Monopoly and restrictive trade policies regulations in private enterprise	Federal						
Bills of Exchange & Promissory Notes	Federal						
Certificates of invention, trade marks & Patent Rights	Federal						
Canadian citizenship	Federal						
Post Office	Federal						

SUBJECT	EXCLUSIVE FEDERAL JURISDICTION	EXCLUSIVE PROVINCIAL JURISDICTION	JOINT JURISDICTION	COMPULSORY CONSULTATION INTER-PROV. AND/OR FED.-PROV.	PRIORITY OR DECIDING JURISDICTION	JURISDICTION LIMITATIONS	REMAINING POWERS
Transport	Federal on water and air international and inter-provincial; national and inter-provincial railways	Highways					
Federal Public Functions	Federal						
Establishment of Provincial Societies	Federal in Federal concerns	Provincial in Provincial concerns					
Establishment of Private Societies	Special Federal in areas that come under specific Federal powers	General Provincial					
Agriculture			Joint	Compulsory consultation		Federal or Provincial according to subject area	
Immigration		See No. 42	Joint				
Statistics			Joint				
Census			Joint				
Bankruptcy			Joint				
Radio broadcasting and theatre			Joint				

SUBJECT	EXCLUSIVE FEDERAL JURISDICTION	EXCLUSIVE PROVINCIAL JURISDICTION	JOINT JURISDICTION	COMPULSORY CONSULTATION INTER-PROV. AND/OR FED.-PROV.	PRIORITY OR DECIDING JURISDICTION	JURISDICTION LIMITATIONS	REMAINING POWERS
Marketing of agricultural products, food and drugs			Joint				
Education		Provincial Exclusive					
Social Security		Exclusive Provincial					
Marriage & Divorce		Exclusive Provincial					
Import Markets and control of financial institutions other than banks		Exclusive Provincial					
Integration of immigrants		Exclusive Provincial					
Industry and labor in Provincial territory	Special Federal when relating to Federal areas	General Provincial					
Prisoner rehabilitation		Exclusive Provincial					
Exploration, conservation and development of resources		Exclusive Provincial					

SUBJECT	EXCLUSIVE FEDERAL JURISDICTION	EXCLUSIVE PROVINCIAL JURISDICTION	JOINT JURISDICTION	COMPULSORY CONSULTATION INTER-PROV. AND/OR FED.-PROV.	PRIORITY OR DECIDING JURISDICTION	JURISDICTION LIMITATIONS	REMAINING POWERS
Territorial management		General Provincial		Compulsory consultation in the case of important Federal investment			
Municipal urban organization and urban and housing development		Exclusive Provincial					
Recreation, leisure and sports		Exclusive Provincial					
Spending power	Federal limited to Federal matters and power to grant unconditional subventions to Prov. for economic relief if qualifying criteria is made						
Regional disparities			Joint	Compulsory consultation			
Public Property	Special Federal limited to Federal property (limited expropriation powers)	General Provincial (unlimited expropriation powers except Federal property)					
Fundamental Rights	Exclusive Federal for certain fundamental rights	Exclusive Provincial for certain fundamental rights	Joint for certain fundamental rights	Compulsory consultation			

SUBJECT	EXCLUSIVE FEDERAL JURISDICTION	EXCLUSIVE PROVINCIAL JURISDICTION	JOINT JURISDICTION	COMPULSORY CONSULTATION INTER-PROV. AND/OR FED.-PROV.	PRIORITY OR DECIDING JURISDICTION	JURISDICTION LIMITATIONS	REMAINING POWERS
Economic policies			Joint	Compulsory consultation	Federal		
Science & Technology			Joint	Compulsory consultation			
Communication		Provincial General	Joint in certain areas (radio-communication)	Compulsory consultation	Federal or Provincial in certain subject areas		
Native population		Exclusive Federal					
Emergency powers	Exclusive Federal					Fundamental principles of the constitution, charter of fundamental rights and eventual control of constitutional court	
Remaining Powers (General)		Exclusive Provincial					
Formulas of amendment to the constitution			Several possible formulas. Unanimity in subjects considered, unanimous fundamentally, and a more flexible formula for other subjects				

32 Foreign Relations and Quebec

Howard A. Leeson

By now it is quite evident to most Canadians that the "Quiet Revolution" in Quebec is placing tremendous strains on our federal system, strains from which it may not survive. In many areas of jurisdictions it has become politically necessary for the government in Ottawa to recognize the special needs of the "nation of Quebec." Of many areas still in dispute one is the place of the provinces in external relations, and more specifically, treaty-making and subsequent implementation through legislation. To the supporters of greater autonomy for Quebec it is a crucial area of sovereignty. To the ardent centralist, or the status quo federalist, it is an area of jurisdiction that must remain exclusively in the hands of the federal government. Debate on the issue has been carried on by the federal and provincial governments, academics, and journalists. No apparent agreement has been reached. The purpose of this essay is to examine all of the important legal and political arguments and present as complete an overview as possible.

Part I — BACKGROUND

Clause 132 of the British North America Act, explicitly stated how Canada's international obligations would be fulfilled.

> The Parliament and Government of Canada shall have all powers necessary or proper of performing the obligations of Canada or any province thereof, as part of the British Empire, towards foreign countries, arising under treaties between the Empire and such foreign countries.[1]

It is obvious that the federal parliament and government of Canada were given sweeping powers to legislate regardless of the division of powers in the B.N.A. Act if the legislation was necessary to implement a treaty between the Empire and a foreign country. As Viscount Dunedin wrote in his decision on the *Radio Case* in 1932, "The only class of treaty which would bind Canada was thought of as a treaty by Great Britain and that was provided for by Section 132."[2] No one could have conceived in 1867 that early in the twentieth century Canada would have an international identity of her own.

---

[1] Great Britain, *British Statutes*, 30 Victoria, c. 3 (1867), "The British North America Act", quoted in R. MacGregor Dawson, *Democratic Government in Canada*, 6th Edition (Toronto, University of Toronto Press, 1970), p. 163.

[2] (1932) 2 D. L. R. at 83 (P. C.) quoted in Vincent C. MacDonald, "Canada's Power to Perform Treaty Obligations," *The Canadian Bar Review*, Vol. XI (November, 1933), p. 587.

HOWARD A. LEESON — Graduate Student, University of Alberta.

Section 132 served Canada quite well in the period 1867-1923. As part of the Empire all treaties signed were covered by the B.N.A. Act leaving no room for controversy. From the beginning the federal government pressed for greater Canadian involvement in treaties relating specifically to Canada and gradually her international responsibilities increased. At first Canada won the right to appoint a joint plenipotentiary who, with the British Ambassador, actually helped in treaty negotiations. By the beginning of the twentieth century British participation in the area of trade negotiations had been reduced to the nominal role of signing a treaty actually negotiated by Canadians. The commercial treaties with France in 1907 and 1909 are excellent examples of this technique.[3]

During the period 1918-1923 Canada was able to persuade the British government that treaties with specific reference to Canada should be negotiated and signed by the Canadian government in the name of His Majesty. Although not formalized until 1926, this method was adopted in 1923, when a Canadian Cabinet Minister negotiated and signed the Halibut Fishery Treaty with the United States without words of local limitation and excluding the British government completely.[4]

After 1923 several treaties were negotiated, signed, and ratified by the Canadian government in the name of His Majesty. It appeared that a smooth transition had taken place with the treaty-making power passing from the Imperial government to the federal government of Canada. In 1932 the first serious challenge to this assumption took place.

In 1932 the provinces challenged the constitutionality of legislation passed by the federal government to implement two international conventions. Ultimately the Judicial Committee of the Privy Council was called upon for a ruling. The first agreement was an aerial navigation convention signed in Paris in 1919, the second, The International Radiotelegraph Convention and Annexed General Regulations, signed in 1927. In the case of the former the Privy Council decided that it qualified as an Empire treaty according to section 132 of the B.N.A. Act and that any legislation arising from it must be *intra vires*.[5]

The *Radio Case* was somewhat different. It was argued by the provincial counsel that the Radiotelegraph convention was obviously not an Empire treaty and that parts of the legislation implementing it fell under provincial jurisdiction. Therefore the federal legislation passed to implement the treaty must be *ultra vires*.[6] As stated earlier the Privy Council replied that in 1867 it was not contemplated that Canada would one day not be part of the British Empire

---

[3] G. P. de T. Glazebrook, *A History of Canadian External Relations* (Toronto, McClelland and Stewart Ltd., 1966), pp. 120-45.

[4] Vincent C. MacDonald, "Canada's Power to Perform Treaty Obligations," *The Canadian Bar Review*, Vol. XI (November, 1933), pp. 590-91.

[5] (1932) ID. L. R. 58, A. C. 54 quoted in Vincent C. MacDonald, "Canada's Power to Perform Treaty Obligations", . . . *The Canadian Bar Review*, Vol. XI (November, 1933), p. 664.

[6] MacDonald, *The Canadian Bar Review*, Vol. XI, p. 664.

and hence there was no section in the B.N.A. Act dealing with this problem. Their Lordships concluded that

> It is not therefore expected that such a matter should be dealt with in explicit words in either Section 91 or Section 92. . . . Being therefore not mentioned explicitly in either Section 91 or Section 92 such legislation [implementing the Radiotelegraph convention] falls within the general words at the opening of Section 91.[7]

What the Privy Council had done was declare Section 132 dead and breathe life into the emasculated general clause of Section 91 to give the federal government the treaty power.[8] Both parties to the case were critical of the decision. Federal supporters felt that the Privy Council should not have so decisively declared Section 132 inoperative. They felt this could lead to future problems. They were right. In 1937 a decision of equal weight, but opposite tenor, brought about the present stalemate.

The famous *Labour Conventions Case,* decided in 1937, was sparked by the passage of legislation in the federal parliament to implement three conventions relating to the International Labour Organization Treaty, which had been ratified by the executive in 1935.[9] The subjects of the legislation dealt with the eight hour day, minimum wages, and weekly rest.

The province of Ontario attacked the federal legislation implementing these conventions, arguing that it was clearly a subject of provincial jurisdiction.[10] The Supreme Court of Canada divided evenly on the issue and an appeal was made by the Federal government to the Privy Council. The Privy Council upheld the position of the province of Ontario and declared the federal legislation *ultra vires.* Their argument was as follows:

> For the purposes of Sections 91 and 92, i.e. the distribution of legislative power between the Dominion and the Provinces, there is no such thing as treaty legislation as such. . . . It follows from what has been said that no further legislative competence is obtained by the Dominion from its acession to international status. . . . It must not be thought that the result of this decision is that Canada is incompetent to legislate in performance of treaty obligation. In totality of legislative powers, Dominion and Provincial together, she is fully equipped. . . . While the ship of state now sails on larger ventures and into foreign waters she still retains the water-tight compartments which are an essential part of her original structure.[11]

---

[7] *Ibid.,* p. 666.

[8] *Ibid.,* pp. 667-68.

[9] These conventions had been signed in 1919, 1928 and 1921 respectively.

[10] J. Y. Morin, "International Law — Treaty-Making Power — Constitutional Law — Position of the Government of Quebec", *The Canadian Bar Review,* Vol. LXV (March, 1967), p. 164.

[11] *Attorney-General for Canada* v. *Attorney-General for Ontario* (1937) A. C. 351-54 quoted in W. R. Lederman, "Legislative Power to Implement Treaty Obligations in Canada", *The Political Process in Canada,* J. H. Aitchison (ed.) (Toronto, University of Toronto Press, 1963), pp. 174-75.

This was a dramatic reversal of the position taken by Viscount Dunedin in 1932. Lord Atkin totally rejected the idea that the residual powers of Section 91 included the right of the federal government to implement a treaty through legislation if that area of legislative authority fell to the provinces. In doing so Lord Atkin chose to pass over the sweeping terminology of Viscount Dunedin in which he had referred to the powers of Section 91.[12]

Mildly stated, Canada was left in an ambiguous position. It appeared that the federal government might sign treaties but in some cases would have to ask the provinces to pass the legislation required to implement them, a difficult task when there were nine provinces to deal with. After 1937 the federal government chose to avoid treaties on constitutionally sensitive areas.

After the Second World War the types of treaties became more numerous, especially with the advent of the United Nations. As early as 1946 Professor H. F. Angus pointed out that Canada would have difficulty signing some of the declarations of the United Nations.[13] He was quite correct in his assessment.

In an article written for the *Canadian Journal of Economics and Political Science* James Eayrs cites some of the situations that arose.[14] In 1947 when Canada was asked to vote in favour of a resolution calling for member countries to familiarize their children with the United Nations charter and other important aspects of the organization, she was unable to do so because education was a provincial responsibility and the federal government would not have been able to pass legislation to implement the treaty in Canada. Similarly a year later, the Canadian delegation was unable to vote for a declaration of human rights.[15] Other examples were the Declaration of Women's Rights of 1953, and the Human Rights Declarations of 1954 and 1957.[16]

The impression should not be left that Canada was immobilized in international relations. Though there were many problems associated with the cumbersome procedures required by the necessity of provincial consultation, they were not insurmountable and the issues spotlighted were seldom of international necessity. The whole issue took a more serious turn however, when Quebec, in the full flush of cultural awakening, decided to exercise international privileges which Ottawa would not accept as valid.

During the period 1959-1965 there had been considerable agitation within Quebec for more cultural contacts with France. One of the first manifestations

---

[12] W. R. Lederman, "Legislative Power to Implement Treaty Obligations in Canada", *The Political Process in Canada,* J. H. Aitchison (ed.) (Toronto, University of Toronto Press, 1963), pp. 174-75.

[13] H. F. Angus, "The Canadian Constitution and the United Nations Charter", *Canadian Journal of Economics and Political Science,* Vol. XII no. 2 (May 1946), pp. 127-35.

[14] J. Eayrs, "Canadian Federalism and the U.N.", *Canadian Journal of Economics and Political Science,* Vol. XVI (May, 1950), p. 172.

[15] *Ibid.,* pp. 179-81.

[16] F. H. Soward, "External Affairs and Canadian Federalism", in *Evolving Canadian Federalism,* A. R. M. Lower, F. R. Scott, *et al.* (Durham, N. C., Duke University Press, 1958), pp. 147-49.

of this was the establishment of a programme of exchanges and cooperation between the Ministry of Youth for the Province of Quebec, and the Association pour L'Organisation des Stages en France, concluded in December, 1963.[17] In 1964 the government of Quebec indicated interest in concluding an agreement with France to implement educational exchanges. The agreement was signed on February 27, 1965.[18] During the negotiations Ottawa had not been represented but apparently had been following their progress. To preserve the federal claim to exclusive jurisdiction in International agreements, Ottawa passed a note to the French Ambassador in Ottawa on the same day the agreement was signed in Quebec. The note stated that the federal government approved of the treaty.

The government of Quebec took a different view of the entente. Writing in Le Devoir, April 14 and 15, 1965,[19] Paul Gerin Lajoie clearly indicated that Quebec intended to pursue some type of independent international policy.

En realité cet événement a surtout demontré la determination du Quebec de prendre, dans le monde contemporaine, la place qui lui revient et d'assurer, à l'exterieure autant qu'à l'interieure, tous les moyens nécessaires pour realizer les aspirations de la societé qu'il représente.[20]

The issue appeared to simmer through the remainder of the year until on November 17, 1965 Ottawa signed an accordie cadre with France which was designed to facilitate arrangements between the provincial government and the French Government.[21] There was no official comment from the Quebec government but on November 24, 1965 they signed an additional cultural agreement with France, apparently taking immediate advantage of the new accorde cadre.[22]

No major confrontation between Quebec and Ottawa took place again until 1968 when Quebec, but not Canada, was invited to the Conference of African and Malgasy Education Ministers, February 5-10, and the subsequent Paris meeting, April 22-26, 1968. The international status of the Quebec delegation was never publicly defined but it appeared that they were treated as any of the other delegates. The federal government decided to break diplomatic relations with Gabon because of this supposed slight to Canada. Communication between Quebec and Ottawa on the Gabon affair was ineffectual despite personal letters between Prime Minister Pearson and Premier Johnson.[23]

A short time later another incident in Africa took place. In Nigeria, at an education conference in February, 1969, the Canadian and Quebec delegations

---

17 Paul Martin, Federalism and International Relations (Ottawa, Queen's Printer, 1968), p. 26.
18 L. Sabourin, "Politique Etrangere et Etat du Québec," International Journal, Vol. XXX (Summer 1965), pp. 352-53.
19 Le Devoir, April 14, 15, p. 5.
20 Ibid.
21 Martin, p. 28.
22 Ibid.
23 Mitchell Sharp, Federalism and International Conferences on Education (Ottawa, Queen's Printer, 1968), pp. 32-38.

came separately, sat together, but under different flags, and paid their own expenses, an altogether childish and absurd demonstration.[24] Since the presentation of the Quebec White Paper on foreign relations, in 1969, it appears that both sides are adopting a calmer approach. This then is the background of major events leading to the differing positions taken regarding the role of the provinces in foreign affairs. It is now time to look at the remarkably different interpreations that have arisen from them.

Part II — LEGAL ARGUMENTS

The federal government supports its position by presenting arguments in four areas, international law, comparison with other federal states, domestic constitutional law, and finally an argument of national necessity. International law provides little support for either the federal or provincial position in this dispute. The only definitive statement on the issue was prepared by the International Law Commission. Article 5, section 2, of the draft articles prepared by the International Law Commission reads: "States members of a federal union may possess a capacity to conclude treaties if such a capacity is admitted by the federal constitution and within the limits there laid down."[25] It is obvious the Commission did not wish to pass any binding rules in this area and in fact even this section was deleted in the final draft, apparently after intensive lobbying by the Canadian delegation.[26]

Federal supporters contend that international experience is moving away from the type of thinking embodied in the original draft of section 2 above. Writing in *The Canadian Bar Review*,[27] Gerald L. Morris calls the original section 2: "A polite bow to the constitutional forms of the U.N. members."[28] He also contends that the only two examples of constituent states of a federal union with representation in the U.N., Byelorussia and the Ukraine, were special concessions to the U.S.S.R. necessitated by the post-war situation and are not likely to repeat themselves.[29] Jean-Pierre Goyer, Parliamentary Assistant to the Minister of External Affairs, in a speech to the House of Commons, argued that the international system would not be prepared to accept the proliferation of international entities that would accompany an action such as the right of provinces to engaged in treaty-making, or representation at the United Nations.[30]

---

[24] Edward McWhinney, "Canadian Federalism: Foreign Affairs and Treaty Power", *Ontario Advisory Committee on Confederation, Background Papers and Reports* (Toronto, Queen's Printer, 1970), p. 128.

[25] Gerald L. Morris, "The Treaty-Making Power: A Canadian Dilemma", *The Canadian Bar Review*, Vol. XLV (September, 1967) p. 497.

[26] McWhinney, *Ontario Advisory Committee on Confederation: Background Papers and Reports*, Vol. II, p. 117.

[27] Morris, *The Canadian Bar Review*, Vol. XLV, pp. 498-500.

[28] *Ibid.*

[29] *Ibid.*, pp. 493-94.

[30] Jean-Pierre Goyer, "Foreign Policy and the Provinces", *External Affairs* (November 1969), p. 389.

In examining other federal states in the world the Dominion government supporters conclude that no other federation allows the type of international freedom that is desired by Quebec. Countries with some flexibility in this respect are the United States, U.S.S.R., the Federal Republic of West Germany, and Switzerland. In the United States the constitution requires that Congress and the President must authorize any international compacts desired by the states, giving the central government effective control. In West Germany and the Soviet Union the constituent states may conclude treaties with foreign countries but they are subject to the control or direction of the central government.[31]

Article 9 of the Swiss constitution gives the Cantons the right to conclude treaties with other states as long as they are not: "Prejudicial to the Confederation."[32] This power has been used twice since the Second World War. The most common practice is to have the central government conclude any necessary agreements. Federal supporters argue that although Article 9 is there the trend is toward central control of external contacts and its only significance lies in the fact that it illustrates the trend proposed by Mr. Morris.[33]

The next step is to look at the Canadian constitution and attempt to determine which government is actually charged with the responsibility for treaty-making, and to what extent the federal government can pass legislation to implement them. Section 132 of the B. N. A. Act and the important judicial decisions pertaining to the subject have already been presented. It only remains to look at the federal interpretation of them.

The federal government sees the movement of responsibility for Canada's external relations during the period 1867-1923, as one from the Imperial government to the Dominion government of Canada. The Imperial Conference of 1926 confirmed Canada's right to operate as an independent international entity. The agent which had been active in securing and utilizing these rights was the federal government, not the provincial governments.[34]

Federal supporters further argue that the *Radio Case* of 1932 confirmed their position. As stated earlier Viscount Dunedin concluded that Section 132 was no longer operative and therefore treaty matters now fell under the general powers in Section 91.[35] The federal government, in *Federalism and International Relations*, concedes that the right to pass legislation to implement treaties was curtailed somewhat by Lord Atkin's decision in the *Labour Conventions Case* of 1937, but they point out that Chief Justice Duff of the Supreme Court of Canada explicitly upheld the right of the Dominion government to conclude treaties and rejected the notion that the provinces had this power. Federal supporters point out that the Privy Council did not strike down this opinion. With this as a basis they contend there can be no doubt

---

31 Martin, pp. 12-13.
32 Morris, *The Canadian Bar Review,* Vol. XLV, p. 495.
33 *Ibid.*
34 Martin, p. 13.
35 Lederman, *The Political Process in Canada,* p. 173.

that the federal government has at least the exclusive right to negotiate and conclude treaties for all of Canada and implement them in their area of jurisdiction.[36]

The final federal argument is one of national necessity. They maintain that it is absolutely necessary for Canada to speak with one voice in international affairs.[37] More than one voice would fragment Canadian foreign policy, rendering it incoherent in some areas. They contend that all aspects of external relations are in some way inter-related. No one area such as education can be treated without affecting other areas. Finally if Canada were to present a fragmented voice to the world community it would leave he country vulnerable to possible subversion by other countries.[38]

Given the present bifurcation of the power to implement treaties through legislation the federal government's solution is essentially one of greater consultation and co-operation. The federal government would strive to accommodate all the legitimate needs of the provinces with both the English and French world communities. However, in the final analysis the right to negotiate and conclude treaties with foreign countries must be a federal responsibility.[39]

To a great extent the provincial position, with Quebec in the vanguard, is a refutation of the federal position. For purposes of clarity this section will deal first with the refutations of federal arguments and then present those further arguments not mentioned in the federal stand, most of which are found in the Quebec government's *Working Paper on Foreign Relations,* issued at the Constitutional Conference of February 5, 1969.[40]

While the Quebec government has not itself attempted to bolster its case by comparison to other federal states, several academics, sympathetic to the provincial cause, have done so. In his analysis of this problem J. Y. Morin devote an entire section of his previously cited article to the comparative case. The federal states of West Germany and Switzerland are given particular attention. The conclusions he draws were quite different from those of Gerald L. Morris whose views were discussed above in support of the federal case.[41] Professor Morin thinks Switzerland is an excellent example of a country that has allowed the treaty-making power to be shared between the central and constituent state governments. Article 9 of the Swiss constitution reads as follows:

> Exceptionally, the Cantons retain the right to conclude treaties with foreign states in respect of matters of public economy, frontier relations, and police; nevertheless, such treaties must not contain anything prejudicial to the Confederation or other Cantons.[42]

---

[36] Martin, p. 14.
[37] Goyer, *External Affairs,* p. 389.
[38] *Ibid.,* pp. 390-91.
[39] Martin, pp. 29-42.
[40] Government of Quebec, *Working Paper on Foreign Relations, Constitutional Conference,* February 5, 1969.
[41] Mr. Morris wrote in reply to Mr. Morin.
[42] Morin, *The Canadian Bar Review,* Vol. LXV, p. 167.

He concedes that the Cantons have not made much use of the article since the Second World War, but the important thing appears to be that the article is there, has been used, and the Swiss confederation has not foundered on it.[43]

The constitution of the German Federal Republic also allows the states to conclude treaties to the extent of their power to legislate. Professor Morin cites several of the treaties signed by the states of West Germany.[44] It is interesting to note that the Germans adopted their formula after comparing the systems of other federal states, including Canada and the United States, and rejected the more centralized procedure of a country like the United States.

The Quebec brief of 1969 and an article by Edward McWhinney[45] give an excellent summary of the criticisms of the constitutional position of the federal government. As already noted above the key support for the federal arguments lies in the opinion of Chief Justice Duff, head of the Supreme Court of Canada in 1937. His opinion in the *Labour Conventions Case* was that only the federal government was competent to conclude treaties. The federal government pointed out that Lord Atkin never challenged this opinion and therefore it must be valid. The Quebec government argues that this assumption is incorrect. They point out that the Privy Council explicitly stated that it did not consider the issue relevant to that of legislative competence and thus refrained from giving an opinion on it.[46] The exact words were: "Their Lordships mention these points for the purpose of making it clear that they express no opinion on them."[47] Since the Privy Council expressed no opinion, and the opinion of Chief Justice Duff was just that, an opinion and not a decision of the Supreme Court, Quebec supporters declare it is not at all clear that only Ottawa can conclude treaties.

In further refutation of the federal government stand Edward McWhinney presents the other side of the evenly split Supreme Court decision of 1937, which the federal government is strangely silent on. Justice Rinfret argued strongly that the federal government should not hold the sole right to conclude treaties if it could not implement them.[48]

> It does appear that it would be against the intendment of the British North American Act that the King or the Governor-General should enter into an international agreement dealing with matters exclusively assigned to the jurisdiction of the provinces solely upon the advice of the federal ministers who . . . are prohibited by the constitution from assuming jurisdiction over these matters.[48]

---

[43] *Ibid.*, p. 168.
[44] *Ibid.*, pp. 168-69.
[45] McWhinney, *Ontario Advisory Committee on Confederation, Background Papers and Reports*, II, p. 115.
[46] Quebec Brief, p. 15.
[47] *Attorney-General For Canada* v. *Attorney-General For Ontario* (1937) A. C. 348, 349 quoted in Government of Quebec, *Working Paper on Foreign Relations* (February 5, 1969).
[48] McWhinney, *Ontario Advisory Committee on Confederation, Background Papers and Reports*, II, p. 122.
[49] *Ibid.*, p. 122.

The provincial argument is that Section 132 is inoperative, no clear decision has been rendered in favour of a federal treaty-making power, and the whole issue is yet to be clarified. A clear decision was rendered on the legislative implementation issue. That was in favour of the provinces, and it still stands.

The Quebec brief goes on to argue that there are case decisions which support a provincial right to conclude treaties. They contend that *The Liquidators of the Maritime Bank of Canada* v. *The Receiver-General of New Brunswick*, 1892, and *Bonanza Creek Gold Mining Co.* v. *The King*, 1916,[50] imply that not only the legislative but the executive powers are distributed by the B.N.A. Act. The latter case states:

> The British North America Act has made a distribution between the Dominion and Provinces which extends not only to the legislative but to the executive authority. . . . The effect of . . . the British North America Act is that . . . the distribution under the new grant of executive authority in substance follows the distribution under the new grant of legislative powers.[51]

The conclusion of provincial supporters is that since the provinces have exclusive legislative competence in some areas the Lieutenant-Governor must necessarily have executive authority in the area. The logical extension is that the provincial governments, with both legislative and executive competence must have the authority to deal internationally, since the federal government lacks legislative authority in some areas.[52]

The federal argument that it is necessary for Canada to speak with one voice in international relations is disposed of by pointing out that this has never been the case.

> Le débat en cours ne concerne pas les attributions déjà reconnues aux provinces de participer a toutes sortes d'activités internationales. Car, en fait, les provinces ont dupuis longtemps aquis possibilité de participer a des echanges internationaux de toutes sortes.[53]

Spokesmen for Quebec reject the idea that the province is seeking a free hand in international affairs, which conceivably could cause difficulty for Canada's foreign policy.

> Plusieurs voudraient que le Quebec jouissent des mêmes avantages qu'ont l'Ukraine et la Biélorussie. Théoriquement, la chose et peut-être possible, mais en admittent même qu'Ottawa en vienne à accepter l'idée du statut particulier, on voit mal comment les autres pays federaux accepteraient de donner leur assentiment a une telle practique internationale qui s'averait une précedent dangereux.[54]

---

50 Quebec Brief, p. 18.
51 *Ibid.*
52 *Ibid.*, p. 19.
53 Sabourin, *International Journal*, Vol. XX, p. 351.
54 *Ibid.*, p. 359.

Quebec maintains it does not want to play the role of an independent country. They only wish to open up those contacts they feel necessary with the French speaking world. As a counter to the federal offers of cooperation, the Quebec government offered its own alternative which reiterates its stand that the provinces have the right to conclude treaties but softens this stand by proposing rather extensive consultation techniques.[55] In effect each side is quite willing to consult the other, after its own final authority has been recognized.

SUMMATION OF LEGAL ARGUMENTS

To a great extent many of the arguments used by both sides are simply window dressing. Certainly the International Law Commission would be anxious to avoid any clash with the internal constitution of any state with regard to treaties. Therefore it is not surprising to find they have left the issue to be settled by the individual governments within the context of their own constituions.

Comparison with other federal states is also of limited value, except insofar as it could affect the conditions of a new constitution or amendments to the existing one. However, it is a potent argument for those supporting the provincial position that the West Germans adopted the looser formula more similar to the Canadian position than that of the United States which is more centralist. The fact that both the constitution of West Germany and the constitution of Switzerland allow for treaties by the constituent states of the federation also supports the provincial stand, but the federal supporters are quite right in stating that it appears at present that the trend is toward more central control of treaties in Switzerland. In the final analysis the comparative arguments do not add much support to either side.

The legal issue must then come down squarely on the legal interpretations of the B.N.A. Act. All but a minor number of writers are agreed that Section 132 is inoperable. The dispute is then left to the major decisions by the Privy Council and the Supreme Court. Both the federal and provincial governments are guilty of strained interpretations of these decisions. It is difficult to accept the federal assumption that silence by the Privy Council on Chief Justice Duff's opinion that only the federal government could conclude treaties meant acceptance. The Privy Council clearly stated that it was giving no opinion on the subject, which presumably meant just that. *The Labour Conventions Case* is no proof of exclusive federal competence to conclude treaties. Nor can the cases cited by the Quebec government, *Maritime Bank,* and *Bonanza Creek,* be accepted as proof of the executive competence of the Lieutenant-Governor to conclude treaties. One must agree with Mr. Gerald Morris that his powers relate to domestic, local issues and never were intended to support provincial treaty-making rights.

The conclusion must be there is no conclusion, until there is a clear legal

---

[55] Quebec Brief.

decision favouring one side or the other. The federal government has been concluding treaties and presumably will continue to do so. A provincial government could attempt to do so and force a legal decision but despite all the legal positioning it is doubtful either side will force a court decision. The political realities of the situation make this course too risky. It is to these political considerations we now must turn.

Part III

While the arguments have been essentially legal in nature, the issue is quite obviously political. The awakening nationalism in Quebec has quite naturally led it to search out its heritage in France and to establish new contacts with the French speaking world. To have these contacts controlled and reviewed by another government would make a mockery of the quest. If Quebec were allowed to pursue the type of international role it desires the important questions are, to what degree is it different from the traditional role of the provinces, and what would be its impact on our federal system?

Even the most superficial examination of provincial contacts with foreign countries shows that the role sought by Quebec is not essentially different from what has already existed. As an example, Quebec established an Agent-General in Great Britain in 1874, in Paris in 1882 and in Belgium in 1911.[56] None of these were considered to be Canadian offices. They were recognized as offices of the Province of Quebec. Ontario and New Brunswick had already established offices in London in 1868.[57]

A great many international contacts have been made by the provinces in their areas of legislative competence. Ontario and the West Indies, including Bermuda, have contacts dating back to 1941. In that year the Ontario Minister of Education and the Director of Education for Bermuda signed an agreement which made possible the training of Bermudan teachers in Ontario. Since then over 300 teachers from Bermuda have benefited under the agreement. At the time it was not thought necessary to have a treaty, or even to inform the federal government. Other projects of a similar nature have been carried out in the West Indies.[58]. And yet when Quebec decided to initiate a similar type of programme with France the federal government suddenly decided its control of international relations was threatened.

There are many other examples of provincial contacts with other nations. Ontario is a member in several international organizations involving the Great Lakes area, separate from the Canadian participation. Manitoba has reached accords with Minnesota on mutual water, without the need of a

---

[56] Jacques Brossard, Andre Patry, and Elizabeth Weiser, *Les Pouvoirs Extérieurs Du Québec* (Montréal, Les Presses de L'Universite de Montréal, 1967), pp. 67-68.
[57] *Ibid.*
[58] Ronald G. Atkey, "Provincial Transnational Activity: Approach to a Current Issue", *Ontario Advisory Committee on Confederation, Background Papers and Reports* (Toronto, Queen's Printer, 1970), Vol. II, pp. 156-57.

federal treaty or surveillance.[59] Six Canadian provinces are represented in Washington and enjoy many of the privileges of consuls, though they are not envoys of the federal government.[60] Beyond these semi-official contacts the provinces are constantly sending delegations throughout the world in search of economic advantages. Trade delegations from the wealthier Canadian provinces are generally found at functions like World Fairs.

These are only a small sample of the numerous examples that show that the federal government does not now have, or ever had in the past, complete control of all international contacts. It has maintained exclusive jurisdiction over some areas, specifically relating to national defense, but not all areas. To attempt now to gather all international contacts under the aegis of the federal government would be a departure from tradition and not adherence to it.

To a great extent the argument over a bifurcated treaty-making power is a red herring. Very few international agreements are carried out by treaty. The vast bulk are covered by simple agreements. The United States makes an excellent example of this. To circumvent their cumbersome treaty ratification process the President of the United States generally finalizes most international agreements by executive agreement. Treaties are reserved for those issues of great importance. Quebec's contacts with the francophone community could also be carried out by simple agreements between the governments involved and by-pass the treaty process entirely. Other countries would be fully aware they were dealing with a province and not the Dominion government.

CONCLUSIONS

Given the range and extent of provincial contacts with foreign countries the federal reaction to Quebec's expanded international role has been somewhat hysterical and certainly inconsistent, especially regarding the Gabon affair. It is correct that the federal government was snubbed by Gabon, probably because of a Gaullist whim or mood, but the reaction of Ottawa was almost irrational. Given the provincial responsibility for education, and the nationalist sentiment in Quebec the best federal reaction would have been silence. The course pursued by Ottawa gave the appearance, perhaps correctly, that it was determined to restrain Quebec, the implication being that Quebec must be involved in some dark plots with foreign countries. In so doing the federal government opted for confrontation politics at the exact time that patience and compromise were needed.

The government of Quebec was not entirely blameless. They surely must have recognized that they were being used to further de Gaulle's international ambitions. But to imply that the government of Quebec was playing the role of a sovereign nation is totally incorrect.

---

[59] *Ibid.*, pp. 158-59.
[60] Brossard, pp. 68-69.

As previously stated the issue is political, not legal. The key to the situation lies in federal recognition that Quebec is not a province just like the others, but has special interests to pursue in areas such as education and culture. Imaginative policies which help Quebec to pursue these special interests while remaining within confederation should be the overriding goal of the government. Unfortunately the opposite is the case. At every turn the federal government has sought to ensure that it will have ultimate control over Quebec's foreign contacts, as if that province cannot quite be trusted.

There are several things the federal government could do to ease the situation. They should immediately adopt a policy of welcoming Quebec's cultural and educational ties with the francophone community making clear that arguments which have no implications for defense or foreign policy are the business of that province alone. Dual representation for international education conferences to which Canada is to send only one delegation is another suggestion. Depending on the type of conference and its location the Quebec government could nominate up to one half of the delegation.

More boldly, the federal government could cede the initiative to Quebec in the area of cultural contacts with the francophone community. Such a policy has many attractive possibilities and may be only common sense. If Quebec were to implement programs or exchanges with the francophone community that are considered to be beneficial to French Canadian culture or education in Quebec, it is reasonable to expect that French Canadians resident in other parts of Canada could also benefit from these contacts. It makes little sense for the federal government to negotiate separate agreements when it could simply accept and adapt programs already worked out by the Quebec government.

One should not attempt to minimize the difficulties inherent in the above suggestion. Petty jealousy on the part of the federal or other provincial governments might block such a move. More legitimately the government of New Brunswick might feel that its large Acadian population could be better represented by establishing its own contacts. Many other difficulties might arise in attempting to secure cooperation. However the overriding consideration must be to make attempts to move away from the sterile position of the status quo.

All of the foregoing suggestions recommend one thing: special status for Quebec in the area of foreign affairs. In this author's opinion English Canadians must come to the realization that Quebec is special and not just another province like the others. Quebec is special because it encompasses a different culture, a culture which they legitimately do not wish to see destroyed. To acknowledge special status for Quebec is to acknowledge the obvious. The course the federal government has pursued in the dispute over treaty-making and external relations is one dedicated to the proposition that Quebec is no different than the other nine provinces in Canada. This course is not only unrealistic, but dangerous. The end result can only be to strengthen the forces of separation in Quebec and perhaps ultimately cause the breakup of confederation.

SELECTED BIBLIOGRAPHY

PART ONE

Birch, A. H., *Federalism, Finance and Social Legislation in Canada, Australia and the United States* (Oxford, Clarendon Press, 1955).

Bowie, R. R., and Friedrich, C. J. (eds.), *Studies in Federalism* (Boston, Little, Brown and Company, 1954).

Center for the Study of Democratic Institutions, *Two Faces of Federalism: An Outline of an Argument about Pluralism, Unity, and Law* (Santa Barbara, California, 1961).

Davis, Rufus, "The Federal Principle Reconsidered", *Australian Journal of Politics and History,* I (November, 1955), pp. 59-86; II (May, 1956), pp. 223-45.

Dicey, A. V., *The Law of the Constitution,* 16th ed., (London, Macmillan and Co. Ltd., 1959).

Duchacek, Ivo D., *Comparative Federalism: The Territorial Dimension of Politics* (New York, Holt, Rinehart and Winston, Inc., 1970).

Earle, Valerie, (ed.), *Federalism: Infinite Variety in Theory and Practice* (Itasca, Illinois, F. E. Peacock Publishers, Inc., 1968).

Franck, Thomas M., (ed.), *et al., Why Federations Fail: An Inquiry into the Requisites for Successful Federalism* (New York, New York University Press, 1968).

Friedrich, C. J.,"New Dimensions of Federalism", *Proceedings of the American Society of International Law* (1962-1963), pp. 238-40.

Friedrich, C. J., *Trends of Federalism in Theory and Practice* (New York, Frederick A. Praeger, Publishers, 1968).

Lijphart, Arend, "Cultural Diversity and Theories of Political Integration", *Canadian Journal of Political Science,* IV (March, 1971), pp. 1-14.

Livingston, W. S., (ed.), *Federalism in the Commonwealth: A Bibliographical Commentary* (London, Cassel, 1963).

Livingston, W. S., *Federalism and Constitutional Change* (Oxford, Clarendon Press, 1956).

Macmahon, A. W., (ed.), *Federalism, Mature and Emergent,* (Garden City, New York, Doubleday, 1955).

McWhinney, E., *Comparative Federalism: States' Rights and National Power* (Toronto, University of Toronto Press, 1962).

May, R. J., "Decision-Making and Stability in Federal Systems", *Canadian Journal of Political Science,* III (March, 1970), pp. 73-87.

May, R. J., *Federalism and Fiscal Adjustment* (Oxford, Oxford University Press, 1969).

Mill, J. S., *Considerations on Representative Government* (Chicago, Henry Regnery Company, 1962). See Chapter XVII.

Morin, J.-Y., *Le Fédéralisme: Théorie et Critique* (Montréal, Les Presses de l' Université de Montréal, 1963).

Paradis, Jerome B., "Language Rights in Multicultural States: A Comparative Study", *Canadian Bar Review*, XLVIII (December, 1970), pp. 651-97.

Riker, W., *Federalism: Origin, Operation, Significance* (Boston, Little, Brown and Company, 1964).

Rockefeller, N. A., *The Future of Federalism* (New York, Atheneum, 1963).

Sawer, G. F., *Modern Federalism* (London, C. A. Watts & Co. Ltd., 1969).

Sharma, B. M., *Federalism in Theory and Practice*, 2 Vols, (Chandausi, India, Bhargava and Sons, 1951).

Watts, R. L., *New Federations; Experiments in the Commonwealth* (Oxford, Clarendon Press, 1966).

Wheare, K. C., *Federal Government*, 4th ed. (New York, Oxford University Press, 1963).

PART TWO

Aitchison, J. H., (ed.), *The Political Process in Canada* (Toronto, University of Toronto Press, 1963).

Angus, H. F., "The Working of Confederation: A Western View", *Canadian Journal of Economics and Political Science*, III (August, 1937), pp. 345-53.

Beck, J. M., "Canadian Federalism in Ferment", in Leach, R. H. (ed.), *Contemporary Canada* (Durham, N. C., Duke University Press, 1968).

Beck, J. M., *The Shaping of Canadian Federalism: Central Authority or Provincial Rights?* (Toronto, Copp Clark, 1971).

Black, E. R., "Federal Strains Within a Canadian Party", *The Dalhousie Review*, XLV (1965), pp. 307-23.

Brunet, Michel, "M. Maurice Lamontagne et sa conception du fédéralisme canadien", *Revue d'Histoire de l'Amérique Française*, VIII (September, 1954), pp. 262-78.

Burns, R. M., *The Evolving Structure of Canadian Government* (Winnipeg, The University of Manitoba Press, 1966).

Cairns, Alan C., "The Electoral System and the Party System in Canada", *Canadian Journal of Political Science*, I (March, 1968), pp. 55-80.

Careless, J. M. S., "Nationalism, Pluralism and Canadian History", *Culture*, XXX (March, 1969), pp. 19-26.

Cheffins, R. L., *The Constitutional Process in Canada* (Toronto, McGraw-Hill Company of Canada, 1969).

Clarkson, Stephen, "A Programme for Binational Development", in Russell, Peter (ed.), *Nationalism in Canada* (Toronto, McGraw-Hill Company of Canada, 1966).

Cole, Taylor, "Commonwealth Federations Old and New: Canada and Nigeria", in Hamilton, W. B., Robinson, K., and Goodwin, C. D. W. (eds.) *A Decade of the Commonwealth 1955-1964* (Durham, N. C., Duke University Press, 1966).

Creighton, D. G., "Confederation: The Use and Abuse of History", *Journal of Canadian Studies,* I (May, 1966), pp. 3-11.

Crépeau, P. A. and MacPherson, C. B., *The Future of Canadian Federalism* (Toronto, University of Toronto Press, 1965).

Dubuc, Alfred, "The Decline of Confederation and the New Nationalism", in Russell, Peter (ed.), *Nationalism in Canada* (Toronto, McGraw-Hill Company of Canada, 1966).

Engelmann, F. C. and Schwartz, M. A., *Political Parties and the Canadian Social Structure* (Scarborough, Ontario, Prentice-Hall of Canada Ltd., 1967), *passim*.

Falardeau, J.-C., *Quelques épines du fédéralisme canadien* (Toronto, Canadian Institute of International Affairs, 1945), pp. 15-23.

Forsey, Eugene, "Our Present Discontent", in Ontario Advisory Commission on the Constitution, *Background Papers and Reports,* Vol. II (Toronto, Queen's Printer, 1970).

Forsey, Eugene, "Present Problems of Confederation", *Journal of Canadian Studies,* I (August, 1966), pp. 13-23.

Hawkins, Gordon (ed.), *Concepts of Federalism,* 34th Couchiching Conference (Toronto, Canadian Institute on Public Affairs, 1965).

Hoffman, David and Ward, Norman, *Bilingualism and Biculturalism in the Canadian House of Commons,* Vol. 3 of the Documents of the Royal Commission on Bilingualism and Biculturalism (Ottawa, Queen's Printer, 1970).

Hurley, James Ross, "Federalism, Co-ordinate Status and the Canadian Situation", *Queen's Quarterly,* LXXIII (Summer, 1966), pp. 157-66.

Johnstone, John C., *Young Peoples' Images of Canadian Society* (Ottawa, Queen's Printer, 1969).

Levitt, Kari, *Silent Surrender: The Multinational Corporation in Canada* (Toronto, Macmillan Company of Canada Limited, 1970).

Maheux, A., *Problems of Canadian Unity* (Quebec, Editions Bois-Francs, 1944).

Mallory, J. R., *Social Credit and the Federal Power in Canada* (Toronto, University of Toronto Press, 1954), *passim*.

Meisel, John, "The Stalled Omnibus: Canadian Parties in the 1960's", *Social Research,* XXX (Autumn, 1963), pp. 367-90.

Noel, S. J. R., "Consociational Democracy and Canadian Federalism", *Canadian Journal of Political Science,* IV (March, 1971), pp. 15-18.

Ormsby, William, *The Emergence of the Federal Concept in Canada, 1839-1845* (Toronto, University of Toronto Press, 1969).

Paltiel, K. Z., "Federalism and Party Finance: A Preliminary Sounding", in Committee on Election Expenses, *Studies in Canadian Party Finance* (Ottawa, Queen's Printer, 1966), pp. 1-21.

Perry, J. Harvey, "The National Capital Problem", in Ontario Advisory Commission on the Constitution, *Background Papers and Reports,* Vol. II (Toronto, Queen's Printer, 1970).

Porter, John, *The Vertical Mosaic* (Toronto, University of Toronto Press, 1965), *passim*.

Rogers, N, "Federal Influences on the Cabinet", *Canadian Bar Review,* II (1933), pp. 103-21.

Rogers, N., "The Political Principles of Federalism", *Canadian Journal of Economics and Political Science,* I (August, 1935), pp. 337-47.

Rowat, D. C., "The Problems of Governing Federal Capitals", *Canadian Journal of Political Science,* I (September, 1968), pp. 345-56.

Rowat, D. C., "Recent Developments in Canadian Federalism", *Canadian Journal of Economics and Political Science,* XVIII (February, 1952), pp. 1-16.

Ryerson, Stanley B., *Unequal Union* (Toronto, Progress Books, 1968).

Sabourin, Louis (ed.), *Le système politique du Canada: institutions fédérales et québecoises* (Ottawa, Editions de l'Université d'Ottawa, 1969).

Scarrow, H. A., "Federal-Provincial Voting Patterns in Canada", *Canadian Journal of Economics and Political Science,* XXVI (May, 1960), pp. 289-98.

Schwartz, Mildred A., *Public Opinion and Canadian Identity* (Berkeley, University of California Press, 1967).

Scott, F. R., "The Development of Canadian Federalism", *Papers and Proceedings of the Canadian Political Science Association,* III (1931), pp. 231-47.

Scott, F. R., "Social Planning and Canadian Federalism", in Oliver, M. (ed.), *Social Purpose for Canada* (Toronto, University of Toronto Press).

Smiley, D. V., *The Canadian Political Nationality* (Toronto, Methuen, 1967).

Smiley, D. V., *Constitutional Adaptation and Canadian Federalism Since 1945.* Vol. 4 of the Documents of the Royal Commission on Bilingualism and Biculturalism (Ottawa, Queen's Printer, 1970).

Smiley, D. V., "Federalism, Nationalism and the Scope of Public Activity in Canada", in Russell, Peter (ed.), *Nationalism in Canada* (Toronto, McGraw-Hill Company of Canada, 1966).

Smiley, D. V., "Two Themes of Canadian Federalism", *Canadian Journal of Economics and Political Science,* XXXI (February, 1965), pp. 80-97.

Smith, Denis, "Prairie Revolt, Federalism and the Party System", in Thorburn, Hugh G. (ed.), *Party Politics in Canada,* 2nd ed. (Scarborough, Prentice-Hall of Canada Ltd., 1967).

Trudeau, P. E., "The Practice and Theory of Federalism", in Oliver, Michael (ed.), *Social Purpose for Canada* (Toronto, University of Toronto Press, 1961), and in Trudeau, P. E., *Federalism and the French Canadians* (Toronto, Macmillan of Canada, 1968).

PART THREE

General

Arès, Richard, *La Confédération: Pacte ou Loi?* (Montréal, Editions de l'Action Nationale, 1949).

Atkey, Ronald G., "Provincial Transnational Activity: An Approach to a Current Issue in Canadian Federalism", in Ontario Advisory Commission on the Constitution, *Background Papers and Reports,* Vol. II (Toronto, Queen's Printer, 1970).

Borden, R. L., *Canadian Constitutional Studies: The Marfleet Lectures* (Toronto, University of Toronto, 1922).

Brady, Alexander, "The Distribution of Legislative Power: Some Facts and Issues", in Ontario Advisory Commission on the Constitution, *Background Papers and Reports,* Vol. II (Toronto, Queen's Printer, 1970).

Canada, *Memorandum on Dominion Power of Disallowances of Provincial Legislation* (Ottawa, King's Printer, 1938).

Forsey, Eugene, "Disallowance of Provincial Acts, Reservation of Provincial Bills and Refusal of Assent by Lieutenant-Governors Since 1867", *Canadian Journal of Economics and Political Science,* IV (February, 1938), pp. 47-59.

Forsey, Eugene, "Disallowance of Provincial Acts, Reservation of Provincial Bills, and Refusal of Assent by Lieutenant-Governors, 1937-47", *Canadian Journal of Economics and Political Science,* XIV (February, 1948), pp. 94-97.

Gibson, Dale, "Interjurisdictional Immunity in Canadian Federalism", *Canadian Bar Review,* XLVII (March, 1969), pp. 40-61.

Hendry, M. L., *Memorandum on the Office of Lieutenant-Governor of a Province: Its Constitutional Character and Functions* (Ottawa, Queen's Printer, 1955).

Keith, A. B., "The Principles of the Canadian Constitution", *Journal of Comparative Legislation and International Law,* XXII, Series 3 (1940), pp. 216-17.

Kennedy, W. P. M., *The Constitution of Canada, An Introduction to its Development and Law,* 2nd. ed. (London, Oxford University Press, 1938).

Kennedy, W. P. M., *et al.,* "A Symposium on Canadian Constitutional Problems", *Canadian Bar Review,* XV (June, 1937), pp. 393-507.

La Forest, G. V., *Disallowance and Reservation of Provincial Legislation* (Ottawa, Queen's Printer, 1955).

Le Dain, G. E., "Reflections on the Canadian Constitution After the First Century", *Canadian Bar Review,* XLV, No. 3 (September, 1967), pp. 402-408.

McNairn, Colin H., "Transportation, Communication and the Constitution: The Scope of Federal Jurisdiction", *Canadian Bar Review,* XLVII (September, 1969), pp. 355-94.

McWhinney, Edward, *Judicial Review,* 4th ed. (Toronto, University of Toronto Press, 1969).

Mallory, J. R., "Compact Theory of Confederation", *Dalhousie Review,* XXI (October, 1941), pp. 342-51.

Mallory, J. R., "Disallowance and the National Interest: The Alberta Social Credit Legislation of 1937", *Canadian Journal of Economics and Political Science,* XIV (August, 1948), pp. 342-57.

Mallory, J. R., "The Lieutenant-Governor's Discretionary Powers: The Reservation of Bill 56", *Canadian Journal of Economics and Political Science,* XXVII (November, 1961), pp. 518-22.

O'Hearn, P. J. T., *Peace, Order and Good Government: A New Constitution for Canada* (Toronto, Macmillan, 1964).

Rogers, N., "The Compact Theory of Confederation", *Canadian Bar Review,* IX (June, 1931), pp. 395-417.

Saywell, J. T., *The Office of Lieutenant-Governor: A Study in Canadian Government and Politics* (Toronto, University of Toronto Press, 1957).

Stanley, G. F. G., "Act or Pact? Another Look at Confederation", in Cook, R., Brown, C., and Berger, C. (eds.), *Confederation* (Toronto, University of Toronto Press, 1967).

Varcoe, F. P., *The Distribution of Legislative Power in Canada* (Toronto, Carswell, 1954).

Civil Liberties

Brett, Peter, "Reflections on the Canadian Bill of Rights", *Alberta Law Review,* VII (1968-69), pp. 294-308.

Canada, *A Survey of the Contemporary Indians of Canada, I,* Hawthorn, H. B. (ed.), Department of Indian Affairs and Northern Development (Ottawa, Queen's Printer, 1967).

Cohen, Maxwell, "Human Rights: Programme or Catchall, A Canadian Rational", *Canadian Bar Review,* XLVI (December, 1968), pp. 554-64.

Green, L. C., "Canada's Indians — Federal Policy, International and Constitutional Law", *Ottawa Law Review,* IV (Summer, 1970), pp. 101-31.

Hucker, John and McDonald, Bruce C., "Securing Human Rights in Canada", *McGill Law Journal,* XV (June, 1969), pp. 220-43.

Kernaghan, Kenneth, "Civil Liberties and a Constitutional Bill of Rights", in Vaughan, Frederick, Kyba, Patrick, and Dwivedi, O. P. (eds.), *Contemporary Issues in Canadian Politics* (Scarborough, Prentice-Hall of Canada, Ltd., 1970).

Lederman, W. R., "Concerning a Bill of Rights for Canada and Ontario", in Ontario Advisory Commission on the Constitution, *Background Papers and Reports,* Vol. NII (Toronto, Queen's Printer, 1970).

Lederman, W. R., "The Nature and Problems of a Bill of Rights", *Canadian Bar Review,* XXXVII (March, 1959), pp. 4-15.

Lysyk, "The Unique Constitutional Position of the Canadian Indian", *The Canadian Bar Review,* XLV, No. 3 September, 1967), pp. 513-53.

MacGuigan, R., "Civil Liberties in the Canadian Federation", *University of New Brunswick Law Journal,* XVI (May, 1966), pp. 1-15.

Russell, Peter H., "A Democratic Approach to Civil Liberties", in Vaughan, Frederick, Kyba, Patrick, and Dwivedi, O. P. (eds.), *Contemporary Issues in Canadian Politics* (Scarborough, Prentice-Hall of Canada, Ltd., 1970).

Schmeiser, D. A., *Civil Liberties in Canada* (London, Oxford University Press, 1964).

Scott, F. R., *Civil Liberties and Canadian Federalism* (Toronto, University of Toronto Press, 1959).
Scott, F. R., "The Privy Council and Minority Rights", *Queen's Quarterly,* XXXVII (October, 1930), pp. 668-78.
Tarnopolsky, Walter S., *The Canadian Bill of Rights* (Toronto, Carswell, 1966).
Trudeau, P. E. (Minister of Justice), *A Canadian Charter of Human Rights* (Ottawa, Queen's Printer, 1968).

Confederation

Canada, *Parliamentary Debates on the Subject of the Confederation of the British North American Provinces,* 8th Provincial Parliament of Canada, 3rd Session (Quebec, Hunter and Rose, 1865).
Creighton, D. G., *British North America at Confederation* (Ottawa, Queen's Printer, 1939).
Creighton, D. G., *The Road to Confederation: The Emergence of Canada: 1863-1867* (Toronto, Macmillan, 1964).
Mayo, H. B., "Newfoundland's Entry into the Dominion", *Canadian Journal of Economics and Political Science,* XV (November, 1949), pp. 505-22.
Morton, W. L., "Geographical Circumstances of Confederation", *Canadian Geographical Journal,* LXX (March, 1965), pp. 74-87.
Pope, Joseph (ed.), *Confederation Documents: A Series of Hitherto Unpublished Documents Bearing on the British North America Act* (Toronto, Carswell, 1895).
Trotter, R. G., "Some American Influences Upon the Canadian Federation Movement", *Canadian Historical Review,* V (September, 1924), pp. 213-28.
Waite, P. B. (ed.), *The Confederation Debates* (Toronto, McClelland and Stewart, 1963).
Waite, P. B., *The Life and Times of Confederation, 1864-1867,* 2nd ed. (Toronto, University of Toronto Press, 1962).

Constitutional Amendment

Alexander, E. R., "A Constitutional Straight Jacket for Canada", *Canadian Bar Review,* XLIII (March, 1965), pp. 262-313.
Angers, F.-A., "La formule Fulton-Favreau et la théorie du pacte", *Action Nationale,* LV (septembre, 1965), pp. 31-42.
Angers, F.-A., "Le livre blanc sur l'amendement de la constitution", *Action Nationale,* LIV (avril, 1965), pp. 824-30.
Canada, *Constitutional Conference of Federal and Provincial Governments, Proceedings . . . January 10-12, 1950* (Ottawa, King's Printer, 1950); *Second session, September 25-28, 1950* (Ottawa, King's Printer, 1950).
Canada, *Method of Amending the British North America Act: Report and Minutes of Evidence before the Special Committee of the House of Commons* (Ottawa, King's Printer, 1935).
Favreau, G. (Minister of Justice), *The Amendment of the Constitution of Canada* (Ottawa, Queen's Printer, 1965).

Gérin-Lajoie, Paul, *Constitutional Amendment in Canada* (Toronto, University of Toronto Press, 1950).

Goldenberg, H. C. and Underhill, F. H., "The Problems of Constitutional Amendment in Canada", *Papers and Proceedings of the Canadian Political Science Association,* VI (1934), pp. 238-50.

Laskin, Bora, "Amendment of the Constitution: Applying the Fulton-Favreau Formula", *McGill Law Journal,* XI (1965), pp. 2-18.

Lederman, W. R. *et al,* "Constitutional Amendment in Canada", *McGill Law Journal,* XII (1966-67), pp. 337-612.

Constitutional Review

Atkey, Ronald G., "The Provincial Interest in Broadcasting under the Canadian Constitution", in Ontario Advisory Commission on the Constitution, *Background Papers and Reports,* Vol. II (Toronto, Queen's Printer, 1970).

Benson, Edgar, *The Taxing Powers and the Constitution of Canada* (Ottawa, Queen's Printer, 1969).

Canada, *Constitutional Conference, Ottawa, First Meeting, February, 1968* (Ottawa, Queen's Printer, 1968).

Canada, *Constitutional Conference, Ottawa, Second Meeting, February, 1969* (Ottawa, Queen's Printer, 1969).

Canada, *Constitutional Conference, Ottawa, Third Meeting, December, 1969* (Ottawa, Queen's Printer, 1970).

Cohen, Maxwell, "The Canadian Federal Dilemma", *McGill Law Journal,* XIV, No. 3 (1968), pp. 357-70.

The Confederation of Tomorrow Conference Proceedings, Toronto, November 27-30, 1967 (Toronto, Queen's Printer, 1968).

Forsey, Eugene, "The Senate", in Ontario Advisory Commission on the Constitution, *Background Papers and Reports,* Vol. II (Toronto, Queen's Printer, 1970).

McWhinney, Edward, "The Nature of a Bicultural Constitutionalism", in Ontario Advisory Commission on the Constitution, *Background Papers and Reports,* Vol. II (Toronto, Queen's Printer, 1970).

Magone, C. R., "What is Wrong with the British North America Act", in Ontario Advisory Commission on the Constitution, *Background Papers and Reports,* Vol. II (Toronto, Queen's Printer, 1970).

Russell, Peter H., "Constitutional Reform of the Canadian Judiciary", *The Alberta Law Review,* VII (1968-69), pp. 103-29.

Smiley, D. V., "The Case Against the Canadian Charter of Human Rights", *Canadian Journal of Political Science,* II (September, 1969), pp. 277-91.

Smiley, D. V., and Burns, R. M., "Canadian Federalism and the Spending Power: Is Constitutional Restriction Necessary?" *Canadian Tax Journal,* XVII (November-December, 1969), pp. 467-82.

Trudeau, Pierre Elliott, *The Constitution and the People of Canada* (Ottawa, Queen's Printer, 1969).

Trudeau, Pierre Elliott, *Income Security and Social Services* (Ottawa, Queen's Printer, 1969).

Trudeau, Pierre Elliott, *Federal-Provincial Grants and the Spending Power of Parliament* (Ottawa, Queen's Printer, 1969).

Watts, R. L., "Second Chambers in Federal Political Systems", in Ontario Advisory Commission on the Constitution, *Background Papers and Reports,* Vol. II (Toronto, Queen's Printer, 1970).

The Courts and the Constitution

Brossard, Jacques, *La Cour Suprême et la Constitution: Le forum constitutionnel au Canada* (Montréal, Les Presses de l'Université de Montréal, 1968).

Browne, G. P., *The Judicial Committee and the British North America Act* (Toronto, University of Toronto Press, 1967).

Cohen, Maxwell, "The Judicial Process and National Policy — A Problem for Canadian Federalism", *McGill Law Journal,* XVI (June, 1970), pp. 297-311.

Freund, Paul A., "A Supreme Court in a Federation: Some Lessons from Legal History", *Columbia Law Reform,* LIII (May, 1953), pp. 597-619.

Freund, Paul A., "Umpiring the Federal System", in MacMahon, A. W. (ed.), *Federalism: Mature and Emergent* (Garden City, New York, Doubleday, 1955).

Gibson, Dale, "Constitutional Law . . . Federalising the Judiciary", *Canadian Bar Review,* XLV (December, 1966), pp. 674-78.

Gray, V. E., "The O'Connor Report on the British North America Act, 1867", *Canadian Bar Review,* XVII (May, 1939), pp. 309-37.

Johnson, C. O., "Did Judah P. Benjamin Plant the 'States Rights' Doctrine in the Interpretation of the B. N. A. Act?" *Canadian Bar Review,* XLV, No. 3 (September, 1967), pp. 454-77.

Laskin, Bora, *Canadian Constitutional Law: Cases, Text and Notes on Distribution of Legislative Power,* 2nd ed. (Toronto, Carswell, 1960).

Laskin, Bora, "Peace, Order and Good Government Re-examined", *Canadian Bar Review,* XXV (December, 1947), pp. 1054-87.

Laskin, Bora, "The Supreme Court of Canada: A Final Court of Appeal of and for Canadians", *Canadian Bar Review,* XIX (December, 1951), pp. 1038-79.

Lederman, W. R., "The Concurrent Operation of Federal and Provincial Laws in Canada", *McGill Law Journal,* IX (1962-1963), pp. 185-99.

Lederman, W. R. (ed.), *The Courts and the Canadian Constitution* (Toronto, McClelland and Stewart, 1964).

Lederman, W. R., "Thoughts on Reform of the Supreme Court of Canada", in Ontario Advisory Commission on the Constitution, *Background Papers and Reports,* Vol. II (Toronto, Queen's Printer, 1970).

MacDonald, V. C., *Legislative Power and the Supreme Court in the Fifties* (Toronto, University of Toronto Press, 1961).

MacDonald, V, C., "Privy Council and the Canadian Constitution", *Canadian Bar Review,* XIX (December, 1951), pp. 1021-37.

McWhinney, E., "Federal Supreme Courts and Constitutional Review", *Canadian Bar Review,* XLV (September, 1967), pp. 578-607.

McWhinney, E., *Judicial Review in the English Speaking World,* 3rd ed. (Toronto, University of Toronto Press, 1960).

Mallory, J. R., "The Courts and the Sovereignty of the Canadian Parliament", *Canadian Journal of Economics and Political Science,* X (May, 1944), pp. 165-78.

Olmsted, R. A., *Canadian Constitutional Decisions of the Judicial Committee, 1864-1954* (Ottawa, Queen's Printer, 1954).

Palmer, E. E., "Federalism and Uniformity of Laws: The Canadian Experience" *Law and Contemporary Problems,* XXX (Spring, 1965), pp. 250-69.

Rogers, N., "Constitutional Impasse", *Queen's Quarterly,* XLI (November, 1934), pp. 475-86.

Russell, P. H. (ed.), *Leading Constitutional Decisions: Cases on the B.N.A. Act* (Toronto, McClelland and Stewart, 1965).

Russell, P. H., *The Supreme Court of Canada as a Bilingual and Bicultural Institution,* Vol. 1 of the Documents of the Royal Commission on Bilingualism and Biculturalism (Ottawa, Queen's Printer, 1969).

Russell, P. H., "The Supreme Court's Interpretation of the Constitution Since 1949", in Fox, P. (ed.), *Politics: Canada,* 2nd ed. (Toronto, McGraw-Hill Company of Canada, 1966).

Scott, F. R., "Centralization and Decentralization in Canadian Federalism", *Canadian Bar Review,* XXIX (December, 1951), pp. 1095-1125.

Scott, F. R., "The Consequences of the Privy Council Decisions", *Canadian Bar Review,* XV (June, 1937), pp. 485-94.

Senate of Canada, *Report to the Honourable the Speaker Relating to the Enactment of the British North America Act, 1867,* (O'Conner Report) (Ottawa, King's Printer, 1939).

Smith, Alexander, *The Commerce Power in Canada and the United States* (Toronto, Butterworth and Co., 1963).

Strayer, B. L., *Judicial Review of Legislation in Canada* (Toronto, University of Toronto Press, 1968).

Treaty-Making and Foreign Affairs

Delisle, R. J., "Treaty-Making Power in Canada", in Ontario Advisory Commission on the Constitution, *Background Papers and Reports,* Vol. I (Toronto, Queen's Printer, 1967).

Eayrs, J., "Canadian Federalism and the United Nations", *Canadian Journal of Economics and Political Science,* XVI (May, 1950), pp. 172-83.

Fitzgerald, G. F., "Educational and Cultural Agreements and Ententes: France, Canada, and Quebec . . . Birth of a New Treaty-Making Technique for a Federal State?" *American Journal of International Law,* LX (July, 1966), pp. 529-37.

Goyer, Jean-Pierre, "Foreign Policy and the Provinces", *External Affairs* (November, 1969), pp. 387-94.

Hendry, J. M., *Treaties and Federal Constitutions* (Washington, Public Affairs Press, 1955).

Laskin, Mr. Justice Bora, "The Provinces and International Agreements", in Ontario Advisory Commission on the Constitution, *Background Papers and Reports*, Vol. I (Toronto, Queen's Printer, 1967).

Lederman, W. R., "Legislative Power to Implement Treaty Obligations in Canada", in Aitcheson, J. H. (ed.), *The Political Process in Canada* (Toronto, University of Toronto Press, 1963).

MacDonald, V. C., "Canada's Power to Perform Treaty Obligations", *Canadian Bar Review*, XI (November, 1933), pp. 581-99; (December, 1933), pp. 664-80.

McWhinney, Edward, "Canadian Federalism: Foreign Affairs and Treaty Power: The Impact of Quebec's 'Quiet Revolution' ". in Ontario Advisory Commission on the Constitution, *Background Papers and Reports*, Vol. II (Toronto, Queen's Printer, 1970).

McWhinney, Edward, "The Constitutional Competence Within Federal Systems as to International Agreements", in Ontario Advisory Commission on the Constitution, *Background Papers and Reports*, Vol. I (Toronto, Queen's Printer, 1967).

Martin, Paul, (Secretary of State for External Affairs), *Federalism and International Relations* (Ottawa, Queen's Printer, 1968).

Morin, J.-Y., "Treaty-Making Power — The Position of the Government of Quebec", *Canadian Bar Review*, XLV (March, 1967), pp. 160-73.

Morris, G. L., "The Treaty-Making Power: A Canadian Dilemma", *Canadian Bar Review*, XLV (September, 1967), pp. 478-512.

Sabourin, L., "Biculturalism and Canadian Foreign Policy", in Gordon, J. King (ed.), *Canada's Role as a Middle Power* (Toronto, The Canadian Institute of International Affairs, 1966).

Sharp, Mitchell (Secretary of State for External Affairs), *Federalism and International Conferences on Education* (Ottawa, Queen's Printer, 1968).

Soward, F. H., "External Affairs and Canadian Federalism", in Lower, A. R. M., Scott, F. R., *et al., Evolving Canadian Federalism* (Durham, N. C., Duke University Press, 1958).

PART FOUR

General

Aitchison, J. H., "Interprovincial Co-operation in Canada", in Aitchison, J. H. (ed.), *The Political Process in Canada* (Toronto, University of Toronto Press, 1963).

Blackburn, G. A., "A Bilingual and Bicultural Public Service", *Canadian Public Administration,* XII (Spring, 1969), pp. 36-44.

Bowland, James G., "Geographical Decentralization in the Canadian Federal Public Service", *Canadian Public Administration,* X (September, 1967), pp. 323-65.

Caplan, Neil, "Offshore Mineral Rights: Anatomy of a Federal-Provincial Conflict", *Journal of Canadian Studies,* V (February, 1970), pp. 50-61.

Caplan, Neil, "Some Factors Affecting the Resolution of a Federal-Provincial Conflict", *Canadian Journal of Political Science,* II (June, 1969), pp. 173-86.

Cole, Taylor, *The Canadian Bureaucracy and Federalism, 1947-1965* (Denver, University of Denver, 1966).

Corry, J. A., *Difficulties of Divided Jurisdiction* (Ottawa, King's Printer, 1939).

Doern, G. Bruce, "The Role of Royal Commissions in the General Policy Process and in Federal-Provincial Relations", *Canadian Public Administration,* X (December, 1967), pp. 417-33.

Fenton, A., "Resources Ministers' Council: A Model for Government Co-operation", *Canadian Business,* XXXVI (April, 1963), pp. 40-47.

Gouin, L. M. and Claxton, Brooke, *Legislative Expedients and Devices Adopted by the Dominion and the Provinces* (Ottawa, King's Printer, 1939).

Innis, H. A., "Decentralization and Democracy", *Canadian Journal of Economics and Political Science,* IX (August, 1943), pp. 317-30.

Kristjanson, B. H., "Some Thoughts on Planning at the Federal Level", *Canadian Public Administration,* VIII (June, 1965), pp. 143-51.

Leach, R. H., "Interprovincial Co-operation: Neglected Aspect of Canadian Federalism", *Canadian Public Administration,* II (June, 1959), pp. 83-99.

Lederman, W. R., "Some Forms and Limitations of Co-operative Federalism", *Canadian Bar Review,* XLV (September, 1967), pp. 409-36.

Lindenfield, R., "Hospital Insurance in Canada: An Example in Federal-Provincial Relations", *Social Service Review,* XXXIII (June, 1959), pp. 148-60.

Sharp, Mitchell, *Federalism and International Conferences on Education* (Ottawa, Queen's Printer, 1969).

Smiley, Donald V., "Canadian Federalism and the Resolution of the Federal-Provincial Conflict", in Vaughan, Frederick, Kyba, Patrick, and Dwivedi, O.P. (ed.), *Contemporary Issues in Canadian Politics* (Scarborough, Prentice-Hall of Canada, Ltd., 1970).

Taylor, K. W., "Co-ordination in Administration", in *Proceedings of the Ninth Annual Conference, 1957* (Toronto: Institute of Public Administration of Canada, 1957), pp. 253-73.

Fiscal Relations

Angers, F.-A., "Conséquences des nouveaux arrangements fiscaux proposés par le gouvernement Diefenbaker", *Canadian Public Administration,* V (mars, 1962), pp. 1-8.

Angers, F.-A., "La dernière conférence fédérale-provinciale" *Action Nationale,* LVI (novembre, 1966), pp. 251-55.

Bladden, V. W., "The Economics of Federalism", *Canadian Journal of Economics and Political Science,* I (August, 1935), pp. 348-51.

Brady, Alexander, "Report of the Royal Commission on Dominion-Provincial Relations", *Canadian Historical Review,* No. 3 (September, 1940), pp. 245-53.

Breton, A., "Theory of Government Grants", *Canadian Journal of Economics and Political Science,* XXXI (May, 1965), pp. 178-79; Weldon, J. C. "Reply with Rejoinder", *Canadian Journal of Economics and Political Science,* XXXII (May, 1966), pp. 230-42.

Bryden, M. H., *Occupancy of Tax Fields in Canada,* Canadian Tax Paper No. 42 (Toronto, Canadian Tax Foundation, 1965).

Burns, R. M., "Choices for Canadian Federalism", *Canadian Tax Journal,* XIII (November-December, 1965), pp. 512-18.

Burns, R. M. *et al.,* "Federal-Provincial Implications", *Report of Proceedings at the Nineteenth Tax Conference on the Report of the Royal Commission on Taxation* (Toronto, Canadian Tax Foundation, 1967), pp. 385-407.

Canada, *Dominion Government and Canadian Municipalities Informal Conference.* (Ottawa: Queen's Printer, 1958).

Canada, *Dominion-Provincial Conference; 1935, Record of Proceedings, Ottawa, December 9-13, 1935.* (Ottawa: King's Printer, 1936).

Canada, *Dominion-Provincial Conference on Reconstruction, 1945; Dominion and Provincial Submissions and Plenary Conference Discussions* (Ottawa, King's Printer, 1946).

Canada, *Dominion-Provincial Conference; January 14-15, 1941* (Ottawa, King's Printer, 1941).

Canada, *Dominion-Provincial Conference, 1957* (Ottawa, Queen's Printer, 1958).

Canada, *Dominion-Provincial Conference, 1960* (Ottawa, Queen's Printer, 1960).

Canada, *Federal-Provincial Conditional Grant and Shared-Cost Programs, 1962* (Ottawa, Queen's Printer, 1962).

Canada, *Federal-Provincial Tax Structure Committee, Ottawa, September 14-15, 1966* (Ottawa, Queen's Printer, 1966).

Canada, *Proceedings of the Conference of Federal and Provincial Governments, December 4-7, 1950* (Ottawa, King's Printer, 1951).

Canada, *Proceedings of the Federal-Provincial Conference, 1955* (Ottawa, Queen's Printer, 1955).

Canada, *Report of Proceedings of the Federal-Provincial Conference, 1963* (Ottawa, Queen's Printer, 1964).

Canada, *Report of the Royal Commission on Dominion-Provincial Relations* (Rowell-Sirois Report) (Ottawa, King's Printer, 1940).

Canada, *Report of the Royal Commission on Taxation,* 6 vols. (Ottawa, Queen's Printer, 1966), *passim.*

Canada, *Statements, Notes on Proceedings, Communiqué of the Federal-Provincial Conference, October 14-15, 1964* (Ottawa, Privy Council Office, 1964), (mimeographed).

Curtis, C. A., "Municipal Finance and Provincial-Federal Relations", *Canadian Journal of Economics and Political Science,* XVII (August, 1951), pp. 297-306.

Dupré, J. Stefan, "Contracting Out: A Funny Thing Happened on the Way to the Centennial", in *Report of the Proceedings of the Eighteenth Annual Tax Conference, 1964* (Toronto, Canadian Tax Foundation, 1965), pp. 208-18.

Eggleston, Wilfred and Kraft, C. T., *Dominion-Provincial Subsidies and Grants* (Ottawa, King's Printer, 1939), (mimeographed).

Gettys, Luella, *The Administration of Canadian Conditional Grants* (Chicago Public Administration Service, 1938).

Goldenberg, H. C., "Social and Economic Problems in Canadian Federalism", *Canadian Bar Review,* XII (September, 1934), pp. 422-30.

Graham, John F., Johnson, A. W. and Andrews, J. M., *Inter-Government Fiscal Relationships,* Canadian Tax Paper No. 40 (Toronto, Canadian Tax Foundation, 1964).

Hanson, E. J., *Fiscal Needs of the Canadian Provinces,* Canadian Tax Paper No. 23 (Toronto, Canadian Tax Foundation, 1961).

Hood, W. C., "Economic Policy in Our Federal State", *Canadian Tax Journal,* XII (November-December, 1964), pp. 389-97.

Institute of Intergovernmental Relations, *Report: Intergovernmental Liaison on Fiscal and Economic Matters* (Ottawa, Queen's Printer, 1969).

Intergovernmental Policy Co-ordination and Finance (Toronto, Queen's Printer, 1970).

Johnson, J. A., "Provincial-Municipal Intergovernmental Fiscal Relations", *Canadian Public Administration,* XII (Summer, 1969), pp. 166-80.

La Forest, G. V., *The Allocation of Taxing Power Under the Canadian Constitution,* Canadian Tax Paper No. 46 (Toronto, Canadian Tax Foundation).

Lynn, J. M., *Studies of the Royal Commission on Taxation, No. 23, Federal-Provincial Fiscal Relations* (Ottawa, Queen's Printer, 1967).

MacKintosh, W. A., *The Economic Background of Dominion-Provincial Relations* (Ottawa, King's Printer, 1939). Reprinted (Toronto, McClelland and Stewart, 1964), J. H. Dales (ed.).

McLarty, R. A., "Organizing for a Federal-Provincial Fiscal Policy", *Canadian Tax Journal,* XV (July-August, 1967), pp. 413-20.

McQueen, R., "Economic Aspects of Federalism: A Prairie View", *Canadian Journal of Economics and Political Science,* I (August, 1935), pp. 352-67.

Maxwell, J. A., *Federal Subsidies to the Provincial Governments in Canada* (Cambridge, Harvard University Press, 1937).

Moore, A. Milton, Perry, J. Harvey and Beach, Donald I., *The Financing of Canadian Federation, the First Hundred Years,* Canadian Tax Paper No. 43 (Toronto, Canadian Tax Foundation, 1966).

Musgrave, R. A., *Theoretical Aspects of Fiscal Federalism, Part II: The Fiscal Theory of Political Federalism,* Conference on Public Finances, (April 10-11, 1959) (New York, National Bureau of Economic Research, 1959).

Perry, J. H., "What Price Provincial Autonomy?" *Canadian Journal of Economics and Political Science,* XXI (November, 1955), pp. 432-46.

Ratchford, B., "Constitutional Basis of Public Expenditure in Canada", *Canadian Tax Journal,* VIII (1960), No. 5, pp. 330-36. No. 6, pp. 423-29.

Richardson, J. H., *Economic and Financial Aspects of Social Security* (Toronto, University of Toronto Press, 1960).

Salyzyn, Vladimir, "Federal-Provincial Tax Sharing Schemes", *Canadian Public Administration,* X (June, 1967), pp. 161-66.

Scott, F. R., "The Constitutional Background of Taxation Agreements", *McGill Law Journal,* II (Autumn, 1955), pp. 1-10.

Smiley, D. V., *Conditional Grants and Canadian Federalism: A Study in Constitutional Adaption,* Canadian Tax Paper No. 32 (Toronto, Canadian Tax Foundation, 1963).

PART FIVE

Anderson, Owen, *The Unfinished Revolt* (Toronto, McClelland and Stewart Limited, 1971).

Atlantic Provinces Economic Council, *Atlantic Canada Today* (Fredericton, Maritime Union Study, 1970).

Beck, J. M., *The Government of Nova Scotia* (Toronto, University of Toronto Press, 1957).

Beck, J. M., *The History of Maritime Union: A Study in Frustration* (Fredericton, Maritime Union Study, 1970).

Brewis, T. N., *Regional Economic Policies in Canada* (Toronto, Macmillan Company of Canada Limited, 1969).

Brewis, T. N. and Paquet, G., "Regional Development in Canada: an Exploratory Essay", *Canadian Public Administration,* XI (Summer, 1968), pp. 123-62.

Brossard, Jacques, Immarigeon, Henriette, La Forest, G. V., and Patenaude, Luce, *Le territoire Québecois* (Montréal, Les Presses de l'Université de Montréal. 1970).

Burns, R. M., *Experience of National and International Co-operative Institutions* (Fredericton, Maritime Union Study, 1970).

Cameron, David M., "Regional Integration in the Maritime Provinces", *Canadian Journal of Political Science,* IV (March, 1971), pp. 24-25.

Cameron, John R., and Graham, John F., *Provincial-Municipal Relations in the Maritime Provinces* (Fredericton, Maritime Union Study, 1970).

Canada, *Report of the Royal Commission on Financial Arrangements Between the Dominion and the Maritime Provinces* (White Commission) (Ottawa, King's Printer, 1935).

Canada, *Report of the Royal Commission on Maritime Claims* (Duncan Commission) (Ottawa, King's Printer, 1927).

The Dalhousie Institute of Public Affairs, and Leach, Richard H. *Inter-Provincial Relations in the Maritime Provinces* (Fredericton, Maritime Union Study, 1970).

Dehem, Roger, *et al.,* "Concepts of Regional Planning", *Canadian Public Administration,* IX (June, 1966), pp. 152-200.

Donnelly, M. S., *The Government of Manitoba* (Toronto, University of Toronto Press, 1963).

Fergusson, C. C., "Maritime Union", *Queen's Quarterly,* LXXVII (Summer, 1970), pp. 167-79.

Findlay, Peter C., *Maritime Union: Implications for the French Language and Culture* (Fredericton, Maritime Union Study, 1970).

Fox, Paul W., "Regionalism and Confederation", in Ontario Advisory Commission on the Constitution, *Background Papers and Reports,* Vol. II (Toronto, Queen's Printer, 1970).

Hebal, J. J., "Approaches to Regional and Metropolitan Governments in the United States and Canada", *Canadian Public Administration,* X (June, 1967), pp. 197-208.

Hedlin, Ralph O., "Economics of One Prairie Province", *Canadian Public Administration,* XIII (Winter, 1970), pp. 354-59

Howland, R. D., *Some Regional Aspects of Canada's Economic Development* (Ottawa, Queen's Printer, 1957).

Krueger, Ralph R., "The Provincial-Municipal Government Revolution in New Brunswick", *Canadian Public Administration,* XIII (Spring, 1970), pp. 51-59.

Krueger, R., Sargent, F., de Vos, A., and Pearson, N. (eds.), *Regional and Resource Planning in Canada* (Toronto, Holt, Rinehart and Winston, 1963).

Lynn, James H., *Public Finances in the Maritime Provinces* (Fredericton, Maritime Union Study, 1970).

MacKinnon, Frank, *The Government of Prince Edward Island* (Toronto, University of Toronto Press, 1951).

Mallory, J. R., *Social Credit and the Federal Power in Canada* (Toronto, University of Toronto Press, 1954).

Market Facts of Canada Limited, *The Maritimes and Maritime Union: An Opinion Study* (Fredericton, Maritime Union Study, 1970).

M. D. T. Associates, *Medicare, Public Health Services and Maritime Union* (Fredericton, Maritime Union Study, 1970).

M. D. T. Associates, *Welfare Services and Maritime Union* (Fredericton, Maritime Union Study, 1970).

Murphy, Arthur, O'Sullivan, J. F., and Sheffield, E. F., *Region-Wide Policies for Higher Education* (Fredericton, Maritime Union Study, 1970).

Nova Scotia, *Report of the Royal Commission, Provincial Economic Inquiry* (Jones Report), 2 vols. (Halifax, King's Printer, 1934).

Ontario's Proposals for Fiscal Policy Co-ordination in Canada (Toronto, Queen's Printer, 1970).

Plumptre, A. F. W., "Regionalism and the Public Service", *Canadian Public Administration, VIII* (December, 1965), pp. 548-57.

Public Briefs, (Fredericton, Maritime Union Study, 1970).

Schindeler, Fred, *Responsible Government in Ontario* (Toronto, University of Toronto Press, 1969).

Shoyama, T. K., "Some Financial and Economic Implications of One Prairie Province", *Canadian Public Administration, XII* (Winter, 1970), pp. 344-53.

Smith, W. Y., and Wilson, Thomas, *Maritime Union and Economic Planning* (Fredericton, Maritime Union Study, 1970).

Strayer, B. L., "The Constitutional Processes for Prairie Union", *Canadian Public Administration, XIII* (Winter, 1970), pp. 339-43.

Thorburn, Hugh G., *Politics in New Brunswick* (Toronto, University of Toronto Press, 1961).

Wade, Mason (ed.), *Regionalism in the Canadian Community, 1867-1967* (Toronto, University of Toronto Press, 1969).

Ward, Norman, and Spafford, Duff (eds.), *Politics in Saskatchewan* (Toronto, Longmans, 1968).

Whalen, H., "Public Policy and Regional Development: The Experience of the Atlantic Provinces", in Rotstein, A. (ed.), *The Prospect of Change: Proposals for Canada's Future* (Toronto, McGraw-Hill Company of Canada, 1965).

Winter, J. R., *Federal-Provincial Fiscal Relations and Maritime Union* (Fredericton, Maritime Union Study, 1970).

Yeomans, D. R., "Decentralization of Authority [satellite system]", *Canadian Public Administration, XII* (Spring, 1969), pp. 9-25.

PART SIX

Allard, M., *The Last Chance, The Canadian Constitution and French Canadians* (Québec, Editions Ferland, 1964).

Angers, F.-A., "Les états associés, formule d'indépendance", *L'Action Nationale, LIV* (juin, 1965), pp. 959-76.

Arès, R., "Le Statut particulier, minimum vital pour le Québec", *L'Action Nationale, LIV* (juin, 1965), pp. 979-98.

Boily, Robert, *Québec 1940-1969. Bibliographie: le systeme politique québecois et son environment* (Montréal, Les Presses de l'Université de Montréal, 1971).

Bonenfant, J. C. and Falardeau, J.-C., "Cultural and Political Implications of French-Canadian Nationalism", *Canadian Historical Association Report* (Ottawa, 1946), pp. 56-73.

Brossard, Jacques, *L'Immigration: Les droits et pouvoirs du Canada et du Québec* (Montréal, Les Presses de L'Université de Montréal, 1967).

Brunet, M., "Continentalism and Quebec Nationalism: a Double Challenge to Canada", *Queen's Quarterly,* LXXVI (Autumn, 1969), pp. 511-27.

Brunet, M., *La présence anglaise et les Canadiens; études sur l'histoire et la pensée des deux Canadas* (Montréal, Beauchemin, 1958).

Canada, *Report of the Royal Commission on Bilingualism and Biculturalism,* Vol. I *The Official Languages* (Ottawa, Queen's Printer, 1967).

Cohen, Maxwell, "Canada and Quebec in North America: a Pattern for Fulfillment", *Queen's Quarterly,* LXXV (Autumn, 1968), pp. 389-400.

Comeau, Paul-André, "Acculturation ou assimilation: technique d'analyse et tentative de mesure chez les Franco-ontariens", *Canadian Journal of Political Science,* II (juin, 1969), pp. 158-72.

Cook, Ramsay, *Canada and the French-Canadian Question* (Toronto, The Macmillan Company of Canada, Limited, 1966).

Cook, Ramsay, "The Canadian Dilemma", *International Journal,* XX (Winter, 1964-65), pp. 1-19.

Cook, Ramsay, *French-Canadian Nationalism: an Anthology* (Toronto, The Macmillan Company of Canada, Limited, 1969).

Corbett, E. M., *Quebec Confronts Canada* (Baltimore, Johns Hopkins Press, 1967).

Croisat, Maurice, "Planification et Fédéralisme", *Canadian Public Administration,* XI (Fall, 1968), pp. 309-21.

Cultural and Educational Sub-committee, "French-Language Public Secondary Schools in Ontario", in Ontario Advisory Commission on the Constitution, *Background Papers and Reports,* Vol. II (Toronto, Queen's Printer, 1970).

Dawson, R. McG., *The Conscription Crisis of 1944* (Toronto, University of Toronto Press, 1961).

Dufour, André, "Le Statut Particulier," *Canadian Bar Review,* XLV (September, 1967), pp. 437-53.

Faribault, M. and Fowler, R. M., *Ten to One: The Confederation Wager* (Toronto, McClelland and Stewart, 1965).

Forsey, Eugene, "The B. N. A. Act and Biculturalism", *Queen's Quarterly,* LXXI (Summer, 1964), pp. 141-49.

Forsey, Eugene, "Canada: Two Nations or One?" *Canadian Journal of Economics and Political Science,* XVIII (November, 1962), pp. 485-501.

Forsey, Eugene, "Professor Morin's Modest Proposal", *Canadian Forum,* XLIV (September, 1964), pp. 121-25.

Guindon, H., "Social Unrest, Social Class and Quebec's Bureaucratic Revolution", *Queen's Quarterly,* LXXI (Summer, 1964), pp. 150-62.

Genest, J., "Les corrupteurs du fédéralisme", *L'Action Nationale,* LVIII (janvier, 1969), pp. 413-21.

Government of Quebec, *Working Paper on Foreign Relations* (Quebec, 1969).

Jones, R., *Community in Crisis* (Toronto, McClelland and Stewart, 1967).

Keyfitz, N. "Canadians and Canadiens", *Queen's Quarterly,* LXX (Summer 1963), pp. 163-82.

Kwavnick, D., "French Canadians and the Civil Service of Canada", *Canadian Public Administration,* XI (Spring, 1968), pp. 97-112.

Kwavnick, D., "The Roots of French-Canadian Discontent", *Canadian Journal of Economics and Political Science,* XXXI (November, 1965), pp. 509-23.

Lajoie, A., *Les structures administratives régionales: déconcentration et décentralisation au Québec* (Montréal, Les Presses de l'Université de Montréal, 1968).

Lamontagne, Maurice, *Le fédéralisme canadien: évaluation et problèmes* (Québec, Les Presses de l'Université Laval, 1954).

LaTouche, Daniel, "Anti-séparatisme et messianisme au Québec depuis 1960", *Canadian Journal of Political Science,* III (December, 1970), pp. 559-78.

Le Conseil de la Vie Française en Amérique, *Nothing More; Nothing Less* (Toronto, Holt, Rinehart and Winston, 1967).

Lesage, J., *Un Québec fort dans une nouvelle confédération* (Quebec: Queen's Printer, 1965).

Lower, A. R. M., "Two Ways of Life: The Primary, Anithesis of Canadian History", in Cook, Ramsay, Brown, C. and Berger, C. (eds.), *Approaches to Canadian History* (Toronto, University of Toronto Press, 1967)

Manning, H. T., *The Revolt of French Canada* (Toronto, University of Toronto Press, 1962).

Marier, Roger, "Les objectifs sociaux du Québec", *Canadian Public Administration,* XII (Summer, 1969), pp. 181-97.

Morin, J.-Y., "The Need for a New Canadian Federation", *Canadian Forum,* XLIV, No. 521 (June, 1964), pp. 64-66.

Morin, J.-Y., "The Treaty-Making Power of Quebec", in Vaughan, Frederick, Kyba, Patrick, and Dwivedi, O. P. (eds.), *Contemporary Issues in Canadian Politics* (Scarborough, Prentice-Hall of Canada, Ltd., 1970).

Oliver, M., "Confederation and Quebec", *Canadian Forum,* XLIII (November, 1963), pp. 179-83.

Oliver, M., "Quebec and Canadian Democracy", *Canadian Journal of Economics and Political Science,* XXIII, No. 4 (November, 1957), pp. 504-15.

Pépin, Gilles, *Les tribunaux administratifs et la Constitution: Etude des articles 96 à 101 de l'A. A. N. B.* (Montréal, Les Presses de l'Université de Montréal, 1969).

"Le Québec Contemporain: Eléments bibliographiques", *Canadian Journal of Political Science,* I (March, 1968), pp. 107-18.

Quebec, *Royal Commission of Inquiry on Constitutional Problems* (Trembly Report) (Quebec, Queen's Printer, 1956).

Quinn, H. F., *The Union Nationale: A Study in Quebec Nationalism* (Toronto, University of Toronto Press, 1963).

Rioux, Marcel, *Quebec in Question,* translated by James Boake (Toronto, James Lewis and Samuel).

Rioux, Marcel and Martin, Yves (eds.), *French Canadian Society:* I (Toronto, McClelland and Stewart, 1964).

Ryan, Claude, "L'égalité est-elle possible?" *Journal of Canadian Studies,* I (August, 1966), pp. 3-13.

Ryan, Claude, "The Possible Contents of Special Status for Quebec", in Vaughan, Frederick, Kyba, Patrick, and Dwivedi, O. P. (eds.), *Contemporary Issues in Canadian Politics* (Scarborough, Prentice-Hall of Canada, Ltd., 1970).

Scott, F. R. and Oliver, M. (eds.), *Quebec States Her Case* (Toronto, The Macmillan Company of Canada, Limited, 1964).

Sloan, T., *Quebec: The Not-So-Quiet Revolution* (Toronto, Ryerson Press, 1968).

Trudeau, P. E., *Federalism and the French Canadians* (Toronto, The Macmillan Company of Canada, Limited, 1968).

Trudeau, P. E. (ed.), *La grève de l'amiante* (Montréal, Editions Cité Libre, 1956).

Vaillières, Pierre, *The White Niggers of America* (Toronto, McClelland and Stewart, 1971).

Wade, Mason (ed.), *Canadian Dualism: Studies of French-English Relations* (Toronto, University of Toronto Press, 1960).

Wade, Mason, *The French-Canadians, 1760-1967,* rev. ed. 2 vols (Toronto, The Macmillan Company of Canada, Limited, 1968).

Wilson, Frank, "French-Canadian Separatism", *Western Political Quarterly,* XX (March, 1967), pp. 116-31.